THE ETERNAL WORD

God Speaking To Us

WILLEM J. OUWENEEL

AN EVANGELICAL INTRODUCTION TO
REFORMATIONAL THEOLOGY
VOL I/1

PART I: SCRIPTURE:
THE REVEALED SOURCE FOR THEOLOGY

AN EVANGELICAL INTRODUCTION TO REFORMATIONAL THEOLOGY

Part I: Scripture: The Revealed Source For Theology
I/1 *The Eternal Word*: God Speaking To Us
I/2 *The Eternal Torah*: Living Under God

Part II: God: The Personal Source Behind Theology
II/1 *The Eternal God*: God Revealing Himself To Us
II/2 *The Eternal Christ*: God With Us
II/3 *The Eternal Spirit*: God Living In Us

Part III: Redemption: The Christ-Centered Heart of Theology
III/1 *The Eternal Purpose*: Living In Christ
III/2 *Eternal Righteousness*: Living Before God
III/3 *Eternal Salvation*: Christ Dying For Us
III/4 *Eternal Life*: Christ Living In Us

Part IV: Consummation: The Lived Shape of Theology
IV/1 *The Eternal People*: God in Relation To Israel
IV/2 *The Eternal Covenant*: Living With God
IV/3 *The Eternal Kingdom*: Living Under Christ

Part V: Method: The Comprehensive Foundation of Theology
V/1 *Eternal Truth*: The Prolegomena of Theology

THE ETERNAL WORD

God Speaking To Us

WILLEM J. OUWENEEL

PAIDEIA
PRESS

PAIDEIA
PRESS

The Eternal Word: God Speaking To Us

This English edition is a publication of Paideia Press (P.O. Box 500, Jordan Station, Ontario, Canada L0R 1S0). Copyright © 2021 by Paideia Press. All rights reserved. Except for brief quotations in critical publications or reviews, no part of this book may be reproduced in any manner without prior written permission from Paideia Press at the address above.

Unless otherwise indicated, Scripture quotations are from the ESV® Bible (The Holy Bible, English Standard Version®). Copyright © 2001 by Crossway, a publishing ministry of Good News Publishers. Used by permission. All rights reserved.

Scripture quotations or references marked as NKJV are taken from the New King James Version®. Copyright © 1982 by Thomas Nelson, Inc. Used by permission. All rights reserved.

Scripture quotations or references marked as NIV are taken from the Holy Bible, New International Version®, NIV®. Copyright © 1973, 1978, 1984, 2011 by Biblica, Inc.™ Used by permission of Zondervan. All rights reserved worldwide. www.zondervan.com. The "NIV" and "New International Version" are trademarks registered in the United States Patent and Trademark Office by Biblica, Inc.™

Book Design by: Steven R. Martins

ISBN 978-0-88815-294-7

Cataloguing-in-Publication data:

Printed in the United States of America

*The sum of your **word** is truth,
and every one of your righteous rules endures **forever**.*
                                                    Psalm 119:160

*[T]he **word** of our God will stand **forever**.*
                                                    Isaiah 40:8

*Heaven and earth will pass away,
but my **words will not pass away**.*
                                                    Matthew 24:35

*[Y]ou have been born again,
not of perishable seed
but of imperishable,
through the living and abiding word of God;
for . . . the **word** of the Lord remains **forever**.*
                                                    1 Peter 1:23, 25

The Word of God is the one permanent factor in human history.
                                        Mendel Hirsch, *Die Haftoroth* (1896)

Table of Contents

Series Preface		i
Author's Preface		v
Abbreviations		vii
Chapter 1	Divine Revelation and Human Knowledge	1
Chapter 2	A Twofold Revelation	63
Chapter 3	General Revelation (1)	119
Chapter 4	General Revelation (2)	185
Chapter 5	The Inscripturation of the Eternal Word	245
Chapter 6	The Canon of Scripture	303
Chapter 7	Inspiration: Starting Points and Models	379
Chapter 8	Inspiration: A New Approach	437
Chapter 9	The Fundamentalist View of Scripture	503
Chapter 10	The Credibilist View of Scripture	561
Chapter 11	The Modernist View of the Old Testament	611
Chapter 12	The Modernist View of the New Testament	671
Bibliography		733
Scripture Index		795
Subject Index		813

Table of Contents Expanded

Series Preface		i
Author's Preface		v
Abbreviations		vii
1 Divine Revelation and Human Knowledge		1
1.1 The Idea of Revelation		2
1.1.1 Importance for Theological Prolegomena		2
1.1.2 The Knowledge of God		5
1.2 Revelation First		8
1.2.1 Three Approaches		8
1.2.2 Revelation as Problem		11
1.3 Biblical Terminology		14
1.3.1 Sources of Manifestations		14
1.3.2 Ways of Revelation		16
1.3.3 The Mysteries		18
1.4 Modal Approaches		20
1.4.1 Introduction		20
1.4.2 The Two Lowest Modalities		22
1.4.3 The Physical Modality		24
1.5 Four Higher Aspects		26
1.5.1 The Perceptive Modality		26
1.5.2 The Formative-Historical Modality		28
1.5.3 The Lingual Modality		31

		1.5.4 The Social Modality	33
	1.6	Does Divine Revelation Exist?	34
		1.6.1 Supra-Rational Belief	34
		1.6.2 Prior Belief	36
		1.6.3 Theological Research Needed	37
		1.6.4 No Retreat into Irrationalism	38
	1.7	The Hermeneutical Circle	41
		1.7.1 The Supremacy of Reason	41
		1.7.2 Proving our Prejudices?	43
		1.7.3 *Petitio Principii?*	44
	1.8	Forms of Hermeneutics	46
		1.8.1 (Non-)Congenial Hermeneutics	46
		1.8.2 Falsified Theories	48
		1.8.3 Two Circles	49
	1.9	The *Testimonium Spiritus Sancti internum* and *externum*	52
		1.9.1 The Heart's "Facts"	52
		1.9.2 The Two Testimonies	53
		1.9.3 Criticism	55
	1.10	The Subject–Object Gap	56
		1.10.1 Coherence	56
		1.10.2 Scripture and Spirit	58
		1.10.3 A Final Comment	60
2	A Twofold Revelation		63
	2.1	Different Divine Revelations: An Introduction	64
		2.1.1 Speech, Words, Voice	64
		2.1.2 General and Special Revelation	66

2.2	Objections	68
	2.2.1 The Enumeration of Heyns	68
	2.2.2 Traces in Other Religions?	70
	2.2.3 John 1:9	73
2.3	Revelation and the Fall	76
	2.3.1 Various Opinions	76
	2.3.2 No Connection with the Fall	78
2.4	General Revelation	79
	2.4.1 Nine Characteristics	79
	2.4.2 Theism and the Zodiac	83
2.5	General *Versus* Special Revelation	86
	2.5.1 Overlap	86
	2.5.2 On the Boundary	88
	2.5.3 Practical Significance	91
2.6	The Underlying Dualism Exposed	93
	2.6.1 The Church and State Dualism	93
	2.6.2 The General/Special Revelation Dualism	94
2.7	Coherence and Unity	96
	2.7.1 Work-Revelation Is Also Word-Revelation	96
	2.7.2 Word-Revelation Is Also Work-Revelation	98
	2.7.3 Summary	100
2.8	Three Views: Karl Barth	102
	2.8.1 Rejection of General Revelation	102
	2.8.2 Refutation	104
2.9	Three Views: Emil Brunner	107

	2.9.1	The Rule for This Moment	107
	2.9.2	The True Antithesis	108
2.10	Three Views: Paul Althaus		111
	2.10.1	*Contra* Natural Theology	111
	2.10.2	Althaus' Own Natural Theology	112
	2.10.3	Millard J. Erickson's Summary	115

3 General Revelation (1) — 119

3.1	Revelation and Creation Order	120
3.1.1	The Problem	120
3.1.2	Creation As a Mechanism?	121
3.1.3	Creation and Preservation	123
3.2	Revelation on the Law-Side	124
3.2.1	Law-Order and Torah	124
3.2.2	Manifestation of God's Will	126
3.2.3	God's Commanding "Word"	128
3.3	Revelation on the Subject-Side	129
3.3.1	Three Domains	129
3.3.2	The Covenant Aspect	132
3.4	Creation and Law (1)	134
3.4.1	Creational Word and Sustaining Word	134
3.4.2	The Law as Boundary	136
3.5	Creation and Law (2)	138
3.5.1	Was the Law Created?	138
3.5.2	Law and Lawfulness	140
3.5.3	Summary: The Law as "Side" and "Boundary"	141

3.6	Objectionable Approaches	143
	3.6.1 Six Errors	143
	3.6.2 Rationality and Rationalism	146
	3.6.3 Again, God and the Law	147
3.7	Natural and Supernatural	149
	3.7.1 Two Orders?	149
	3.7.2 Miracles	152
3.8	The Meaning of the Law-Order	154
	3.8.1 Natural Laws and Norms	154
	3.8.2 The Responsive Structure	155
	3.8.3 Law and Time	157
3.9	The Law as Idea	160
	3.9.1 The Natural Modalities	160
	3.9.2 The Spiritive Modalities	163
3.10	The Law-Order and the Fall	165
	3.10.1 Did the Fall Affect God's Laws?	165
	3.10.2 Common Grace	167
	3.10.3 Sin and Nature	169
3.11	The Law-Order and Christ	171
	3.11.1 Created and Uncreated Law	171
	3.11.2 The Law's Two Natures	172
3.12	The Torah and Its Relationships	175
	3.12.1 Torah and Logos/Chokmah	175
	3.12.2 One Law/Wisdom for All Things	177
3.13	Torah and *Agapē*	179
	3.13.1 Love, Essence of the Torah	179
	3.13.2 Torah and Covenant	181

4	General Revelation (2)	185
4.1	Natural Theology and Romans 1	186
	4.1.1 Natural and Supernatural Theology	186
	4.1.2 Romans 1:20–21	189
	4.1.3 Awareness of God	192
4.2	Natural Knowledge of God	194
	4.2.1 Confusion of Revelation and Theology	194
	4.2.2 Various Views	195
	4.2.3 A Liberal Approach	197
4.3	Creation "in Christ"	199
	4.3.1 Various Views	199
	4.3.2 The View of Barth	200
	4.3.3 Comments	203
4.4.	Creation and Re-Creation	205
	4.4.1 One World, One Kingdom	205
	4.4.2 The View of G. Spykman	208
4.5	Two Alternatives	209
	4.5.1 *Creatio Continua*	209
	4.5.2 *Creatio Nova*	211
	4.5.3 Again: Structure and Direction	213
	4.5.4 The Twofold Revelation	216
4.6	God and History	218
	4.6.1 God of the Nations	218
	4.6.2 God the Universal Judge	220
4.7	Making History Autonomous	222
	4.7.1 Modernism and History	222

	4.7.2 Rigidity	224
	4.7.3 Conservatism and Progressivism	226
4.8	Law-Order and Science	228
	4.8.1 "Theological Ethics"	228
	4.8.2 The Law-Order and the Special Sciences	230
	4.8.3 Difference between Theology and Natural Science	232
4.9	Law-Order and Positivizing	235
	4.9.1 The Positivizing Task	235
	4.9.2 Difficulties of Positivizing	237
4.10	Biblicism	238
	4.10.1 Appeal to Bible Verses	238
	4.10.2 Principles and Positivizations	240
	4.10.3 Motivation and Judgment	242

5 The Inscripturation of the Eternal Word — 245

5.1	Revelation and Inscripturation	246
	5.1.1 The Word and Its Registration	246
	5.1.2 Any Further Revelation?	248
	5.1.3 Prophecy	250
5.2	Discussion Around the Bible	251
	5.2.1 Three Reports	251
	5.2.2 Discussion Among the Reformed Churches Liberated	254
	5.2.3 Discussion Necessary	256
5.3	Inscripturation and Incarnation	258
	5.3.1 The Eternal Word in Temporal Form	258

	5.3.2	Parallelism of Scripture and Christ	260
	5.3.3	Incarnation and Inscripturation: A Parallel?	263
5.4	Forms of God's Word	265
	5.4.1	Various Suggestions	265
	5.4.2	My Own Proposal	267
	5.4.3	Scripture and Humanity: Parallels	269
5.5	Revelation: Propositional or Personal?	271
	5.5.1	Two Approaches	271
	5.5.2	A False Dilemma	272
	5.5.3	Revelation and Relationship	274
5.6	Coherent Structural Wholes	276
	5.6.1	The Underlying Theory	276
	5.6.2	Scripture As a Coherent Structural Whole	278
5.7	The Three Foundational Idionomies	279
	5.7.1	The Physical Idionomy	279
	5.7.2	The Historical-Formative Idionomy	280
	5.7.3	The Lingual Idionomy	281
5.8	The Pistical Idionomy	284
	5.8.1	Pistical *Versus* Religious 284	
	5.8.2	Modal Aspects of the Pistical Idionomy	286
5.9	The Word and the Words	289
	5.9.1	The Bible: God's Word or Expression of God's Word?	289
	5.9.2	No Separation Between Word and Words	290

5.9.3 "Word" As Concept and Idea		292
5.10 The Modal Ideas		296
5.10.1 The Natural Modalities		296
5.10.2 The Mental Modalities		299
6 The Canon of Scripture		**303**
6.1 Origin of the Canon		304
6.1.1 Stating the Problem		304
6.1.2 A Starting Point		306
6.1.3 Bible Quotations from Non-Biblical Sources		308
6.2 Earliest Canon Suggestions		310
6.2.1 The Old Testament	310	
6.2.2 The New Testament	313	
6.2.3 Additional Notes	316	
6.3 Character of the Canon		317
6.3.1 Active and Passive Canon		317
6.3.2 Spurious Sources		319
6.4 The Process of Canonization		321
6.4.1 Historical and Supra-Historical		321
6.4.2 The Old Testament		322
6.4.3 The New Testament		324
6.5 Ordering		326
6.5.1 Two Canons		326
6.5.2 The Old Testament Canon in the New Testament		327
6.6 Criteria of Canonicity		329
6.6.1 The Canon Determines the Canon		329
6.6.2 A Supra-Rational Criterion		332

  6.6.3 Again, the Hermeneutical Circle 334
6.7 The Question of the *Notae Canonicitatis* 336
  6.7.1 Divine Providence and Church Responsibility 336
  6.7.2 The Deuterocanonical Books 339
  6.7.3 Formal Recognitions 341
6.8 The Lingual Criterion 342
  6.8.1 What Is It? 342
  6.8.2 The Old Testament 344
  6.8.3 The New Testament 346
6.9 The Historical-Formative Criterion 349
  6.9.1 Authority 349
  6.9.2 Four Other *Affectiones* 350
  6.9.3 Prophecy and Authority 354
  6.9.4 Misunderstanding the Bible's Authority 357
6.10 The Lesser Criteria 359
  6.10.1 The Physical-Biotic Criterion 359
  6.10.2 The Logical-Analytical Criterion 360
  6.10.3 The Social Criterion 361
  6.10.4 Economic, Aesthetic, Juridical, Ethical, and Pistical Criteria 363
6.11 Post-Apostolic Books? 364
  6.11.1 Forgeries or Not 364
  6.11.2 Arguments for Apostolicity 366

	6.11.3 Second Peter and Revelation	367
	6.11.4 Summary	369
6.12	Additional Matters	370
	6.12.1 The Vague Boundary between Scripture and Tradition	370
	6.12.2 Degrees of Canonicity?	372
	6.12.3 Loss of the Criterion of Coherence	375
7 Inspiration: Starting Points and Models		379
7.1	Introduction	380
	7.1.1 The Divine and the Human Aspects	380
	7.1.2 Scripture on Inspiration	381
7.2	The Gospels	383
	7.2.1 God's "Speaking"	383
	7.2.2 The Readers' "Reading"	385
7.3	Second Timothy 3	387
	7.3.1 Introduction	387
	7.3.2 *Theopneustos*	388
	7.3.3 Knowing *Versus* Doing	390
7.4	First Peter 1	393
	7.4.1 The Spirit of Christ	393
	7.4.2 Four Lessons	393
7.5	Second Peter 1	395
	7.5.1 Three Lessons	395
	7.5.2 Finer Details	397
	7.5.3 Summary	398

7.6	First Corinthians 2	400
	7.6.1 First Series Leading to Enlightenment	400
	7.6.2 Second Series Leading to Enlightenment	402
	7.6.3 Comparison	404
7.7	Theories of Inspiration (1)	406
	7.7.1 Introduction	406
	7.7.2 *Spatial:* the Dualistic Theory	408
7.8	*Kinematic:* the Mechanical Theory	410
	7.8.1 Introduction	410
	7.8.2 Prudence	412
	7.8.3 Background	414
	7.8.4 Development	416
7.9	Theories of Inspiration (2)	417
	7.9.1 *Energetic:* the Dynamic Theory	417
	7.9.2 *Biotic:* the Organic Theory	420
	7.9.3 *Perceptive:* the Scope Theory	423
7.10	Theories of Inspiration (3)	425
	7.10.1 *Sensitive:* the Sensitivistic Theory	425
	7.10.2 *Logical:* the Intuition Theory	426
	7.10.3 *Historical-Formative:* the Actualistic Theory	427
7.11	Theories of Inspiration (4)	430
	7.11.1 *Lingual:* the Dialogical Theory	430
	7.11.2 *Aesthetic:* The Musical Instruments Theory	433
	7.11.3 *Ethical:* the Marriage Theory	435

8	Inspiration: A New Approach	437
8.1	The Immanent-Transcendent Problem	438
	8.1.1 Ott's Three Options	438
	8.1.2 Three Erroneous Views	440
	8.1.3 No New Dualism	441
8.2	The Enlightenment-Inspiration Problem	442
	8.2.1 Objective and Subjective	442
	8.2.2 Being and Becoming	444
	8.2.3 No Deism	446
8.3	The Humanity of Scripture	447
	8.3.1 God's Word and Human Word	447
	8.3.2 Historical and Supra-Historical	449
	8.3.3 Humans Employed by God	451
8.4	Human Aspects	453
	8.4.1 Five Aspects	453
	8.4.2 Five More Aspects	456
	8.4.3 Human Limitations	458
8.5	Verbal Inspiration: Faith and Theory	460
	8.5.1 An Ancient Belief	460
	8.5.2 A-Contextual Atomism	463
	8.5.3 God and Scripture	466
8.6	Old Testament Quotations in the New Testament	469
	8.6.1 Midrash and Typology	469
	8.6.2 Passages Not Quoted Word for Word	470
	8.6.3 Quotation According to Application	473

8.7	Textual-Critical Aspects	475
	8.7.1 The Old Testament	475
	8.7.2 The New Testament	476
	8.7.3 The Ending of Mark's Gospel	478
8.8	The Authority of Scripture	480
	8.8.1 Urging *Versus* Forcing	480
	8.8.2 The Example of Jesus	483
	8.8.3 The Example of Paul	484
8.9	Authority *Versus* Inerrancy	486
	8.9.1 The Peculiar Nature of Inspiration	486
	8.9.2 Contradictions	488
	8.9.3 What Biblical Authority Is Not	490
8.10	The Unity of the Bible	493
	8.10.1 Comparing Scripture with Scripture	493
	8.10.2 The Center of Scripture	496
	8.10.3 The Unity of the Old and New Testaments	498
9	**The Fundamentalist View of Scripture**	**503**
9.1	Historical Background of Fundamentalism	504
	9.1.1 Early History	504
	9.1.2 Later History	506
9.2	An Attempted Description	508
	9.2.1 Extreme and Moderate	508
	9.2.2 New Terminology	510
	9.2.3 Significance	511

9.3	The Inerrantist View of Scripture	512
	9.3.1 What Is an Error?	512
	9.3.2 The Chicago Statements	514
	9.3.3 The View of J. I. Packer	515
9.4	Scientistic Dualisms within Inerrantism	517
	9.4.1 Epistemological Dualism	517
	9.4.2 Anthropological Dualism	519
	9.4.3 Ontological Dualism	522
9.5	Scientism and "the Facts"	524
	9.5.1 Facts and Glasses	524
	9.5.2 The Second Chicago Statement	526
	9.5.3 A Debate	528
9.6	The Correspondence Theory in the Bible?	530
	9.6.1 Taught by the Bible?	530
	9.6.2 Ordinary Experience	532
	9.6.3 Praxis and Theory	533
9.7	Other Philosophical Theories in the Bible?	535
	9.7.1 Prejudices of the Opponents	535
	9.7.2 "Factual Evidence"	537
	9.7.3 The Biases of Inerrantism	538
9.8	Fundamentalism and Biblicism	540
	9.8.1 Some Natural Modalities	540
	9.8.2 Some Normative Modalities	543
	9.8.3 Absolutizing Positivizations	545
9.9	Biblioscientism	548
	9.9.1 In the Natural Sciences	548
	9.9.2 In Historical Science	550
	9.9.3 In Theology	551

9.10 Fundamentalism and Modernism	552
9.10.1 Scientism	552
9.10.2 Scholasticism	554
9.10.3 Dehistoricization	556
9.11 Other Similarities	557
9.11.1 Elimination of Scripture	557
9.11.2 Separating Scope and Periphery	559
10 The Credibilist View of Scripture	561
10.1 The Central Problem	562
10.1.1 Contra Errantism	562
10.1.2 Contra Inerrantism	564
10.1.3 The Heart of the Matter	565
10.2 "Trustworthy" Is Not "Inerrant"	567
10.2.1 The Faith Level	567
10.2.2 The Theoretical Level	568
10.2.3 Infallibility and Inerrancy	570
10.3 Unverifiability	571
10.3.1 Three Shortcomings	571
10.3.2 The Missing *Autographa*	573
10.3.3 Inerrant Copies and Translations	574
10.4 Unfalsifiablity	576
10.4.1 Errors That Do Not Threaten Inerrancy	576
10.4.2 Observational Descriptions of Nature	578
10.4.3 Other Cases of Possible Errors	580

	10.4.4 Variant Selections of Material in Parallel Accounts	581
10.5	Conclusions	584
	10.5.1 What I Am *Not* Saying	584
	10.5.2 The Falsifiability Criterion	585
10.6	"Errors Are Allowed"	586
	10.6.1 Irregularities	586
	10.6.2 Restrictiveness	588
	10.6.3 Refutation	590
10.7	Views of Inerrancy	592
	10.7.1 Inaccuracy *Versus* Deceit	592
	10.7.2 Qualified Inerrancy	593
	10.7.3 Inerrantist Protests	594
10.8	Faith Is Oblivious to Any (In-)Errancy Problem	596
	10.8.1 The Theoreticalization of Ordinary Life	596
	10.8.2 The Idea of Truth	598
10.9	Inerrantist Response	599
	10.9.1 Rationalism *Versus* Existentialism	599
	10.9.2 Conquering the Contrasts	601
	10.9.3 Against Scientism	602
10.10	The Scope of Scripture	604
	10.10.1 Concentration *Versus* Reduction	604
	10.10.2 Again, the Center–Periphery Dualism	606
	10.10.3 Nature and History	607
11	The Modernist View of the Old Testament	611

11.1 What Is Biblical Criticism?	612
11.1.1 Misunderstandings	612
11.1.2 Two Types of Criticism	614
11.1.3 Underlying Bias	615
11.2 Unavoidable Questions	618
11.2.1 Genesis and Deuteronomy	618
11.2.2 Other Problems	621
11.2.3 Criticism Alien to the Bible	623
11.3 Other Literary Questions	626
11.3.1 Deutero-Isaiah	626
11.3.2 The Dating of Daniel	627
11.4 Development of Biblical Criticism	629
11.4.1 Earliest Development	629
11.4.2 The Pentateuch Documentary Hypothesis	631
11.4.3 Philosophical Foundation	633
11.5 A Case Study: Julius Wellhausen	634
11.5.1 Wellhausen and His Forerunners	634
11.5.2 The Alleged Evolution of Israel's Religion	636
11.5.3 Reading into the Text	640
11.6 The Unity of Genesis	643
11.6.1 *Toledot*	643
11.6.2 Other Aspects	644
11.7 Naturalism and Other Postulates	646
11.7.1 Biases	646
11.7.2 Survey	649

- 11.7.3 Theological Post-Postmodernism — 651
- 11.8 Historicism — 654
  - 11.8.1 The Enlightenment Influence — 654
  - 11.8.2 Form Criticism — 655
  - 11.8.3 Friedrich Schleiermacher — 657
- 11.9 Old Testament Scholarship and Archeology — 658
  - 11.9.1 Worlds Apart — 658
  - 11.9.2 Some Examples — 660
- 11.10 Kenneth A. Kitchen — 662
  - 11.10.1 General Criticism — 662
  - 11.10.2 The Times of Moses — 663
  - 11.10.3 The Times of the Patriarchs — 665
- 11.11 Newer Viewpoints — 666
  - 11.11.1 Dever and Others — 666
  - 11.11.2 The Debate Continues — 668

12 The Modernist View of the New Testament — 671
- 12.1 New Testament Criticism — 672
  - 12.1.1 Striking Parallels in the Gospels and Epistles — 672
  - 12.1.2 The Critics' Biases — 674
- 12.2 The Historical Jesus — 676
  - 12.2.1 Jesus an Ordinary Man — 676
  - 12.2.2 Religious Parallels — 678
- 12.3 Founders of Form Criticism — 679
  - 12.3.1 The Form-Critical Method — 679
  - 12.3.2 Mythical Influences — 681

12.3.3	Literary "Forms"	683
12.4	Consequences	684
12.4.1	Kerygma and Mythology	684
12.4.2	The Second Quest for Jesus	686
12.5	The Third Quest	687
12.5.1	A New Search for the Historical Jesus	687
12.5.2	The Jesus Seminar	690
12.5.3	Conclusions	692
12.6	Misunderstandings	693
12.6.1	Jesus the Jew	693
12.6.2	First Misunderstanding	695
12.6.3	Second Misunderstanding	697
12.7	Biblical-Critical Methodology: Objections	698
12.7.1	Western Presumption	698
12.7.2	No Objective Evidence	699
12.7.3	Ignorance about the Philosophy of Science	702
12.7.4	A Disintegrating Approach	703
12.7.5	Circular Arguments	704
12.8	Other Epistemological Considerations	706
12.8.1	Speculationism	706
12.8.2	Methodological Criteria	707
12.8.3	Four Approaches	709
12.9	The Authenticity of the Gospels	710
12.9.1	Gospel Harmonies	710
12.9.2	An Example of a "Contradiction"	712
12.9.3	Son of God, Son of Man	715

12.10	Theological Compositions		716
	12.10.1 The Gospels		716
	12.10.2	The Early Letters	717
	12.10.3	Preacher and Preached One	719
12.11	A Tetralogy		720
	12.11.1	One or Four Portraits of Jesus?	720
	12.11.2	The Canonical Gospels	722
	12.11.3	John and the Holy Spirit	724
12.12	Four Pillars		726
	12.12.1 The Life of Jesus		726
	12.12.2 The Teaching of Jesus		728
	12.12.3 Examples and Closing		730

Bibliography	733
Scripture Index	795
Subject Index	813

Series Preface

BY MEANS OF THIS PREFACE, the editor and publisher of this series wish to help the reader both understand and process the content of these volumes.

The capacities and erudition of Dr. Willem J. Ouweneel need no demonstration or defense from us. His voluminous work and prodigious writing stand as a testimony to his love for the Lord Jesus Christ, God's Word, and God's people.

But these volumes present ideas that will surprise some, anger others, and possibly confuse still others. Both the editor and publisher disagree with some of Dr. Ouweneel's assertions and conclusions, but this is not the place for offering our counter-arguments. That requires an altogether different venue. Nevertheless, discerning readers will legitimately wonder why this editor and publisher invested effort and resources in putting these volumes into print.

At least three reasons justify that investment. Each of them is very sensitive.

The first reason is: *self-examination*. Some of our readers may conclude that, in presenting his exegetical, doctrinal, and historical case, Dr. Ouweneel is "coloring outside the lines" of what they have come to believe. He challenges deeply and firmly held convictions and beliefs, like those associated with Israel, with the law of God, with election and reprobation, with infant baptism, with covenant theology, and with justification. At each point, his challenges call us readers to self-examination, regarding our love for Scripture, for the God of Scripture, and for the Truth revealed and incarnated personally in Jesus Christ. One of Ouweneel's challenges is for us believers in Jesus Christ who are Reformed and Presbyterian church members to recognize that there are millions, even billions, of Jesus-believers who disagree with us *and are nevertheless genuine Christians*. And they ought to be acknowledged as such.

The second reason is: *repentance*. Coming, as they do, from one who lives and teaches outside the orbit of many of our readers, Dr. Ouweneel's observations about the state of our (numerous) churches and of our (interminable) doctrinal squabbles ought to embarrass us Reformed and Presbyterian church members. Our incessant polemicizing, our cantankerous stridency, and our offenses against the unity of Christ's church seriously compromise the gospel's witness to the watching world. Brothers and sisters, we must repent of these, for the sake of the gospel, for the sake of the church's witness, and for the sake of our children.

The third reason is: *ecumenicity*. This reason may indeed strike you as strange, but one of the salutary outcomes of reading Dr. Ouweneel's arguments can be this: *not* that you surrender your commitments and convictions that are being challenged, but instead that you come to *respect* and *love* those Jesus-believers who don't share them with you. These Christians are those whose spiritual pilgrimage and gospel-guided history have not brought them to the same place on the road, but who nonetheless are walking the same road as we.

You may well be asking: How, then, is this different from advocating doctrinal relativism? If these distinctive features of Reformed confession and theology are biblical, then why is Dr. Ouweneel being given a microphone for proclaiming his criticisms and rejections of these distinctive emphases of Reformed teaching? The short answer is this: So that from

Series Preface

this brother in Christ, this close cousin in the faith, this fellow pilgrim-soldier, we may learn how to lock arms with other Jesus-believers as we face unbelief in our day, even if we can't hold hands. So that we may learn what it means to be Jesus-believers *first*, Reformed or Presbyterian confessors *second*, and only then, *thirdly, theological advocates*.

So we leave you with this challenge: Why do you believe what you believe? What is your biblical warrant? Dr. Ouweneel presents fairly the various positions prevalent within Christianity. The reader will learn why others believe what they believe, and why they don't emphasize certain teachings in the same way that we do.

These books, then, are *not* for the faint of faith. But they *are* for those wanting to grow up and mature into the unity of faith in our Lord Jesus Christ (John 17: 20-23; Eph. 4:13).

Nelson D. Kloosterman, editor
John Hultink, publisher

Author's Preface

THIS IS THE FIRST VOLUME in a series on the "unseen, eternal" things of God (cf. 2 Cor. 4:18). This volume is in fact basic for the entire series, since it deals with divine revelation, more specifically with the Bible as the divinely inspired, authoritative and reliable Word of God. This volume deals with subjects such as general and special revelation (and the historical background of this distinction), the so-called inscripturation of the Word of God (its being put in written form, called the Bible), the canonization of Scripture (the historical fixing of the canon, that list of books that are viewed as belonging to the Bible), and the divine inspiration of Scripture (i.e., its God-breathed character).

Three main current attitudes toward the Bible are dealt with: fundamentalism, modernism, and credibilism. It is argued that fundamentalism and modernism (in the form of Old and New Testament criticism) exhibit not only essential differences but also some remarkable similarities. The latter include in particular their shared underlying rationalism and scientism. Their main difference is the underlying supernaturalism and anti-supernaturalism (in short: naturalism), respectively.

This volume is a re-working and expansion of Volume XI of my *Evangelisch-Dogmatische Reeks* (*Evangelical Dogmatic Series,* published in Dutch by Medema (located in Vaassen and later Heerenveen, the Netherlands, consisting of twelve volumes in total).[1]

Bible quotations in this book are usually from the English Standard Version.

I thank Dr. Nelson D. Kloosterman again very warmly for his expert editorial work on the manuscript of this book. And I am again deeply thankful to my publisher, John Hultink, for his constant encouragement in this entire project.

Willem J. Ouweneel
Summer 2018

---

1. In the present volume these are referred to as Ouweneel (2007; 2008; 2010a; 2010b; 2011a; 2012).

Abbreviations

Bible Versions

AMP	Amplified Bible
AMPC	Amplified Bible, Classic Edition
ASV	American Standard Version
CEB	Common English Bible
CEV	Contemporary English Version
CJB	Complete Jewish Bible
DARBY	Darby Translation
DLNT	Disciples' Literal New Translation
DRA	Douay-Rheims 1899 American Edition
ERV	Easy-to-Read Version
ESV	English Standard Version
EXB	Expanded Bible
GNT	Good News Translation
GNV	1599 Geneva Bible
GW	God's Word Translation
HCSB	Holman Christian Standard Bible
ICB	International Children's Bible
ISV	International Standard Version
JUB	Jubilee Bible 2000
KJ21	21st Century King James Version

KJV   King James Version
LEB   Lexham English Bible
MEV   Modern English Version
MOUNCE   Mounce Reverse-Interlinear New Testament
MSG   The Message
NABRE   New American Bible (Revised Edition)
NASB   New American Standard Bible
NCV   New Century Version
NET   New English Translation
NIV   New International Version
NLV   New Life Version
NKJV   New King James Version
NOG   Names of God Bible
OJB   Orthodox Jewish Bible
PHILLIPS J. B. Phillips New Testament
RSV   Revised Standard Version
TLB   Living Bible
TLV   Tree of Life Version
TPT   The Passion Translation
VOICE   The Voice
WE   Worldwide English (New Testament)
WEB   World English Bible
YLT   Young's Literal Translation

Other Sources

BabT   Epstein, I., ed. 1961. *The Babylonian Talmud*. London: Soncino Press.
BT   Kelly, W., ed. 1856–1920. *Bible Treasury: A Monthly Review of Prophetic and Practical Subjects*. Available at

Abbreviations

	https://bibletruthpublishers.com/bible-treasury/lpvl22465.
CD	Barth, K. 1956. *Church Dogmatics*. Trans. by T. H. L. Parker et al. Vols. 1/1–4/1. Louisville, KY: Westminster John Knox.
CNT	Commentaar op het Nieuwe Testament
COT	Commentaar op het Oude Testament
CR	*Corpus Reformatorum*. 1st series and 2nd series. 87 vols. Brunswick: Schwetschke, 1834–1900.
CW	Darby, J. N. n.d. *The Collected Writings of J. N. Darby*. Kingston-on-Thames: Stow Hill Bible and Tract Depot.
DD 2	Kuyper, A. n.d. *Dictaten Dogmatiek*. Vol. 2: *Locus de Sacra Scriptura, Creatione, Creaturis*. Kampen: J.H. Kok.
DD 3	Kuyper, A. n.d. *Dictaten Dogmatiek*. Vol. 3: *Locus de Providentia, Peccato, Foedere, Christo*. Kampen: J.H. Kok.
EBC	Expositor's Bible Commentary
EDR	Ouweneel, W. J. 2007–2013, 2018. *Evangelische Dogmatische Reeks*. 12 vols. Vaassen/Heerenveen: Medema.
EGT	Nicoll, W.R. ed. 1979. *The Expositor's Greek Testament*. 5 vols. Grand Rapids, MI: Eerdmans.
KV	Korte Verklaring der Heilige Schrift
NC	Dooyeweerd, H. 1984. *A New Critique of Theoretical Thought*. Vol. 1: *The Necessary Presuppositions of Philosophy* (1953). Vol. 2: *The General Theory of the Modal Spheres* (1955). Vol. 3: *The Structures of Individuality of Temporal Reality* (1957). Jordan Station: Paideia

	Press.
NICNT	New International Commentary on the New Testament
NICOT	New International Commentary on the Old Testament
NIGTC	New International Greek Testament Commentary
NIVAC	NIV Application Commentary
PNTC	Pillar New Testament Commentary
RC	Dennison, J. T., Jr., ed. 2008–2014. *Reformed Confessions of the 16th and 17th Centuries in English Translation.* 4 vols. Grand Rapids, MI: Reformation Heritage Books.
RD	Bavinck, H. 2002–2008. *Reformed Dogmatics.* Edited by J. Bolt. Translated by J. Vriend. 4 vols. Grand Rapids, MI: Baker Academic.
RGG	Galling, K. ed. 1986. *Die Religion in Geschichte und Gegenwart.* 6 vols. Tübingen: Mohr (Siebeck).
ST	Chafer, L. S. 1983. *Systematic Theology.* 15th ed. 8 vols. Dallas, TX: Dallas Seminary Press.
TDNT	Kittel, G. et al., eds. 1964–1976. *Theological Dictionary of the New Testament.* Translated by G. W. Bromiley. 10 vols. Grand Rapids, MI: Eerdmans.
TNTC	Tyndale New Testament Commentaries
WA	Luther, M. 1883–2009. *Luthers Werke. Weimarer Ausgabe.* Weimar: Böhlau Verlag.
WBC	Word Biblical Commentary

Chapter 1
Divine Revelation and Human Knowledge

The secret things belong to the LORD *our God,
but the things that are* **revealed** *belong to us
and to our children forever,
that we may do all the words of this law.*

                              Deuteronomy 29:29

For the LORD *God does nothing
without* **revealing** *his secret to his servants
the prophets.*

                                        Amos 3:7

Summary: *God is the revealing God, which means that he reveals primarily* **himself***. Humanity is on the receiving side; without the receiver, divine revelation would not occur. God's revelation addresses each and every human in their deepest essence, not just their feelings and reason, but their heart.*

More than ever, revelation has become a problem today: how can we know that it exists, underlying as it does all our theology? How does the Bible speak of it? What are the various ways whereby God reveals himself? We attempt to approximate the notion of revelation through some modal aspects of cosmic reality (arithmetic, spatial, physical, perceptive, formative-historical, lingual, and social).

The belief in divine revelation is not necessarily *irrational*, but it is certainly – not only supra-theoretical but – supra-rational. Such a belief, or the corresponding unbelief, precedes and underlies all pre-theoretical and theoretical thought. Yet, this belief, or unbelief, must as such definitely become the object of theological investigation. This situation implies the so-called "hermeneutical circle," from which no thinker can escape. It must not be confused with the fallacy known as begging the question (Lat. petitio principii), or circular argument.

Finally, this chapter deals with the relationship between the *external* testimony of the Holy Spirit, viz., in the Bible (Lat. testimonium Spiritus Sancti externum) *and the internal testimony of the Holy Spirit, viz., in the human heart* (Lat. testimonium Spiritus Sancti internum). *This matter is viewed against the background of what is traditionally called the subject–object difference.*

1.1 The Idea of Revelation

1.1.1 Importance for Theological Prolegomena

IN SYSTEMATIC THEOLOGY, I distinguish between its *external* prolegomena of theology, which are of a philosophical nature,[1] and its *internal* prolegomena, which are of a strictly theological nature. The latter involve first and foremost the matter of divine revelation. Everything that systematic theology says after the prolegomena is viewed as being rooted somehow in divine revelation. This is because here is where we claim to find the foundation for our knowledge of divine things. Therefore, the notions of revelation in general, and biblical revelation in particular, are of essential importance in every Christian theology,[2] and, incidentally, also in a Jewish or an

---

1. See the future volume in this series dealing with the scientific-philosophical aspects of theology.

2. See Gunton (1995); Fackre (1997); Wolterstorff (1995); Lewis and Demarest (1996, 1:Part 1); Saucy (2001, chapters 2–4); Jensen (2002); Lamont (2004, chapter 7); Morrison (2006); see also the five models of revelation proposed

Islamic theology. What actually *is* revelation? If it exists, how can we know this for sure? How can we know where to find it? How can we be sure that we are truly dealing, at whatever point in reality, with divine revelation? Does the entire Bible equal divine revelation, or must we rather say that we find divine revelation *in* the Bible? Do we find it equally in the Old and New Testaments? Do we find it also in the so-called deuterocanonical books? Or in the Talmud, or the Qur'an? Or in the post-apostolic, early Christian writings?

In the Belgic Confession, Article 2, Reformed Christians confess that God reveals himself in creation, but that he "makes Himself more clearly and fully known to us by His holy and divine Word, that is to say, as far as is necessary for us to know in this life, to His glory and our salvation."[3] Article 3 continues,

> We confess that this Word of God was not sent nor delivered by the will of man, but that "men spake from God, being moved by the Holy Spirit," as the apostle Peter says [2 Pet. 1:21]; and that afterwards God, from a special care which He has for us and our salvation, commanded His servants, the prophets and apostles, to commit His revealed word to writing; and He Himself wrote with His own finger the two tables of the Law. Therefore, we call such writings holy and divine Scriptures.[4]

Is this confession correct? Does it correspond with what the Bible testifies about itself? Must we take this self-testimony seriously? These are a few of those elementary questions that this volume seeks to answer. Throughout the centuries, Jews and Christians have believed that God can be known, and *is* known, because he has revealed himself in Holy Scripture. He has revealed himself insofar — for his deepest being is unfathomable and inscrutable — as is needed for humans to be able to enter into a relationship with him, to worship him, to

---

by Dulles (1985), which are still debated, as well as Goldingay (1994).
3. *RC* 2:425.
4. *RC* 2:426.

travel through life in fellowship with him, and to enter eternal bliss with him.

Throughout the centuries, Jews and Christians have also believed that God has revealed, and reveals, himself — at least as far as his "eternal power and divine nature" are concerned (Rom.1:20) — through creation and history. Not only in creation but also in history, in the sense of God's upholding the created world (Heb. 1:3), preserving it through successive epochs until the end of the ages. However, it is our conviction that God's revelation in creation and history can be really understood only in the light of the written Word of God, that is, Holy Scripture (the Bible). Ultimately, no revelation of God can be really and genuinely known apart from the written Word of God. Also God's revelation in the person of Jesus Christ is known to us through the written Word of God; other than this Word there are scarcely any reliable sources that speak of him.

From at least the time of medieval theology, this close connection between revelation and Scripture is a common element in the Christian tradition.[5] Thus, Thomas Aquinas wrote, "For our faith rests on the revelation made to the apostles and prophets who wrote the canonical books, not on a revelation, if such there be, made to any other teachers" (Lat. *Innititur enim fides nostra revelationi apostolis et prophetis factae qui canonicos libros scripserunt, non autem revelationi, si qua fuit, aliis doctoribus facta*), i.e., teachers of other religions, such as post-biblical rabbis or Islamic teachers. For our purpose at this juncture, I would mention the tenth, eleventh, and twelfth theses of Carl F. H. Henry about the notion of revelation (freely rendered):

(10) God's revelation is rational communication passed on in the form of understandable ideas and meaningful words, that is, in conceptual-verbal form. In other words, it has been communicated in the ordinary, human language of the Holy Scripture.

---

5. Cf. Pannenberg (1991, 218–19).

(11) The Bible is the reservoir and channel of divine truth. I add here that it is not the *only* reservoir and channel, for also in creation and history, something of God's truth becomes manifest, as we will see. To go a step further, basically, *all truth is God's truth.*[6] There is nothing that deserves the name "truth" apart from God; as says Jeremiah 10:10 says: "The LORD God is the Truth" (JUB; Heb. YHWH *Elohim emet*).

(12) The Holy Spirit oversees the communication of divine revelation, first by inspiring the prophetic-apostolic writings, and second, by illuminating and interpreting the scripturally given Word of God, so that the readers thereof indeed understand it (see §§7.6 and 8.2 on the difference and connection between inspiration and illumination; there, we will also deal with the question whether Scripture or the reader is illuminated).[7]

In the course of our investigation, various elements in these statements will be implicitly dealt with, such as: is everything in Scripture so rational and conceptual? What exactly is the relationship between the Bible and truth? What is the precise role of the Holy Spirit in divine revelation? What are the differences between revelation, illumination, and inspiration?

1.1.2 The Knowledge of God

It is not entirely self-evident that knowledge of God presupposes divine revelation, at least revelation as an *external* source of knowledge, whether divine revelation in nature or in Holy Scripture or in the person of Jesus Christ. There have been movements within Christianity that viewed divine revelation also, or even primarily, as an *internal* source of knowledge. Usually these movements can be divided into two groups: on the one hand, those who viewed *reason*, on the other hand, those who viewed *feeling* (or inner experience) as a primary

---

6. Holmes (1977, book title).
7. Henry (1976, 12–15; cf. 1979a, 248–487; 1979b, 7–493).

source of knowledge of God. In the high Middle Ages, we find these three views:[8]

(a) *Peter Abelard* is *the* representative of those who believe that, in principle, all divine truths can be entirely derived by reason.[9] Humans could have had knowledge of these truths through reason even if God had never granted any external revelation concerning them. Few theologians would wish to defend such a view today, but at least Abelard has made a strong contribution to the rational analysis, and subsequent confirmation, of the great truths of faith, and thus to apologetics. He sincerely believed that not only can the existence of God be rationally demonstrated, but also that it is rationally certain that, if God exists, he is necessarily a Triune God. He believed the same about the two natures of Christ, the atoning death of Christ, resurrection, and so on. That we possess divine revelation in Holy Scripture about these matters is good, but for the rationally thinking person, strictly speaking this would have been unnecessary.[10]

(b) *Thomas Aquinas* partially agreed with Abelard; thus, he also believed that the *that* of God (i.e., his existence) can indeed be determined with the help of reason. He tried to show this through his five proofs of God (which he called the *quinque viae*, "five ways," leading to God); we speak here of natural theology (see extensively, §4.1). However, for the *what* of God (the Trinity, and all other great truths of Christianity), we depend on (external) revelation by God, says Thomas (for supernatural theology). Here lies the basis for Thomas' duality of nature–grace (or nature–supernature), which became a real dual*ism* that has infused all subsequent Western thinking. Apart from this, also in Thomas' thought, human reason (which he feels was not seriously affected by the Fall) is of eminent importance. It is particularly through ordinary reason that religious communication on the part of Christians

---

8. See extensively, Brown (1969).
9. See Marenbon (1997); Brower and Guilfoy (2004).
10. See especially Abelard, *Tractatus de unitate et trinitate divina* (1121).

remains possible with Jews and "Gentiles"[11] (here, Muslims).

(c) *Eckhart von Hochheim*, better known as *Meister* (= Master) *Eckhart*, agreed in many respects with the rationalism of Abelard and Thomas, yet is known particularly as the father of modern mysticism. He followed the thought of Plotinus and Pseudo-Dionysius, representatives of Neo-Platonism. Accordingly, inner seeing (experiencing) is more important than thinking. We encounter here typically Neo-Platonic notions like the emanation of persons from the Godhead and the immanence of God in creatures, through which union with the Godhead is possible. Eckhart identified within the human soul an uncreated element, which he referred to as intelligence. Through this, an ontic connection between God and humans is an *a priori* reality; ultimately, the righteous will be transformed into God. We are not concerned here with further details of his teaching, but only with this mystical dimension.

In such approaches, we always encounter kernels of truth. What practical significance would an objective external revelation of God have if humans did not possess reason (or also feeling, experience, the will, the heart) through which this external revelation can be inwardly, subjectively embraced? In the words of philosopher and theologian Andree Troost: "Revelation is an act of God in which he addresses humans, speaks to them, so that the God who reveals himself is, in (dis)obedience of faith, always *answered* with *concrete human believing*, no matter with what contents this is filled."[12]

We will return to discuss this extensively: there is no objective revelation of the Spirit in nature and Scripture without this same Spirit inwardly illuminating humans (their reason, their feelings, their wills, their hearts) — unless humans resist this work of the Spirit. True knowledge of God arises from this synthesis of the objective external revelation and the subjec-

---

11. For the latter, see his *Summa contra Gentiles* (completed 1264).
12. Troost (2004, 255).

tive apprehension and realization thereof in the human heart. A genuine revelation of God would exist even if no human being took this revelation to heart, but this would be a very abstract way of speaking about divine revelation. Equally extreme would be the opposite view: revelation arises only in this interaction between the external communication of God and the inner apprehension thereof within a human being.

Yet, it is true: if revelation is viewed as genuine *communication*, there must be not only an (objective) "sender" but also a (subjective) "receiver." This receiver is that person who, by virtue of the capacities given by God (reason, will, feeling), inwardly receives what is communicated. God's revelation acquires its inner meaning only if, and when, humans effectively receive, embrace, and apprehend it, and begin living and acting according to it.

1.2 Revelation First

1.2.1 Three Approaches

Historically speaking, the warrant for beginning our exposition of the internal prolegomena with the notion of revelation is less self-evident than it might seem. In fact, this is a rather modern approach. Traditionally, two approaches are far better known, as has been pointed out by Hendrikus Berkhof.[13]

(a) The *Roman Catholic* approach: *the church first*. Traditionally, the theology of the Roman Catholic Church places *ecclesiology* (the doctrine of the church) as internal prolegomena at the beginning of systematic theology. This is because the church (read: the Roman Catholic Church) is viewed as the primary receiver, custodian, and interpreter of divine revelation. Thus, only through the church can a person come into contact with this revelation, and therefore only through the church (and its sacraments) can a person enter into a relationship with God.

This approach was developed especially in opposition to

---

13. Berkhof (1986, 43).

the Reformational approach (see [b]), that is, during the time of the Counter Reformation (sixteenth century). Over against the four attributes or properties (Lat. *proprietates*) that early Protestant theology ascribed to the Bible (see [b]), Rome developed its doctrine of the four attributes (Lat. *proprietates*) of the church. These are its unity (Lat. *unitas*, especially institutional-organizational), its holiness (Lat. *sanctitas*), its catholicity or universality (Lat. *catholicitas*, in the sense of the Roman Catholic Church),[14] and its apostolicity (Lat. *apostolicitas*, rooted in the apostolic teaching and succession).

This approach was rather rationalistic-apologetic, so that many Roman Catholic theologians gradually became less satisfied with it (to name just one point: the attributes of unity, holiness, catholicity, and apostolicity characterize *all* Christians, not just one denomination out of many, no matter how old and venerated this denomination may be). Especially after the First World War, many of them preferred the third pathway identified below.

(b) The *early Protestant* approach: *the Bible first*. At the beginning of their systematic theology, in an equally rationalistic-apologetic manner, early Lutheran and Reformed theologians developed as internal prolegomena a doctrine of Scripture in opposition to the claims of the Roman Catholic Church. They developed their doctrine of the four attributes (Lat. *proprietates*) or properties (Lat. *affectiones*) of Scripture. These are the authority (Lat. *auctoritas*) of Scripture as above the authority of any ecclesiastical institution; its necessity (Lat. *necessitas*), since without Scripture, we know essentially nothing about divine things; its perspicuity or clarity (Lat. *perspicuitas*); and its sufficiency (Lat. *sufficientia*), which means that no other divine source is needed (also called the perfection of Scripture [Lat. *perfectio*], meaning that Scripture is complete with respect to our needs; for a further explanation §6.9). Several centuries later, the course on dogmatics developed by

---

14. See Ouweneel (2010a, 40, 453–54, 484–85).

Abraham Kuyper was arranged entirely around these four characteristics of the Bible.[15]

In the twentieth century, many Protestant theologians became as dissatisfied with their approach as Roman Catholic theologians had become with theirs, particularly after the rise of historical criticism (see chapters 11–12). They too began preferring the third way identified below. I am omitting discussion here of a possible fourth approach, found among certain types of fundamentalism, especially in extreme Pentecostal and Charismatic circles, which consists of outright subjectivism. This approach views what is considered to be the voice of the Spirit in the present moment as more authoritative than Holy Scripture.[16] In such circles, "God speaks through me" may become more important than "God speaks through the Bible" (cf. §1.9, where we will consider the relationship between Word and Spirit more closely).[17]

(c) In opposition to the two traditional approaches, there is the *contemporary* approach, in which the internal prolegomena usually involves a discussion of the notion of revelation.[18] For many Roman Catholic theologians, the church has lost its once-evident status as the unassailable keeper and interpreter of divine revelation. Similarly, for many Protestant theologians, the Bible has lost its traditional position as being equivalent to the written Word of God. Both movements sought a more encompassing concept, one that goes back further than both the church and the Bible, and have found it in the notion of revelation.

This is an understandable development, because both

---

15. Kuyper (*DD* 2).
16. Potgieter (1990, 10).
17. Some hyper-Calvinists run the same risk if they place the pious experience (Dutch: *bevinding*) of the soul above God's objective promises in his Word.
18. See Barth (*CD* I/1); Heyns (1988, chapter 1); Pannenberg (1991, §4); Berkhof (1986, chapters 7–18); Van Genderen and Velema (2008, chapter 2); Erickson (1998, Part II); not Berkhof (1949); Spykman (1992); see also Waldenfels (1996, 2000) for an extensive bibliography regarding the concept of the history of revelation.

the church and the Bible presuppose, and arise from, divine revelation. In the end, both a church-centered theology and a Bible-centered theology derive their authority from God's revelation. Yet, this third approach has its own problems, as we will see.

1.2.2 Revelation as Problem

Otto Weber saw a disquieting sign in assigning this position of primacy to the concept of revelation. He argued that the *concept* of revelation became more important in direct proportion to the way in which the *matter* denoted by it became more doubtful: as "God" (according to the common picture of him) became the increasingly problematic object of a human discovery, the concept of revelation became something like a fading memory of the *deity* of God, as theology's final fortress, laboriously defended against strong forces within its own domain as well. In short, the *concept* of revelation, and the way it is emphasized today, has become an indication that theology no longer lives by the *reality* of revelation.[19]

As I see it, there is truth in Weber's concern. Revelation has become a theological *problem*, whereas before this, it had been a self-evident matter. Roman Catholic theologians emphasized the priority of the church precisely because the latter was viewed as the bearer and keeper of divine revelation, and Reformational theologians did the same with the Bible. Revelation as such was not in dispute. This is no longer the case. *What was it* that the Roman Catholic Church, or the Bible, respectively, was considered to be bearing and keeping?

We must not blame the Enlightenment all too easily for the fact that the reply to this question is no longer self-evident. On the contrary, for a truly scholarly theology, *nothing* must be taken as *a priori* self-evident. Whereas the heart's faith (which is pre-theoretical, and even supra-rational, i.e., it transcends reason) may *a priori* accept the church, or the Bible, respectively, as the bearer and keeper of divine reve-

---

19. Weber (1981, 172).

lation, theology has the duty of critically scrutinizing every claim of self-evidence, that is, turn it into a logical-theoretical problem for analysis.[20] Therefore, we cannot be mistaken if we, too, begin our bibliology (doctrine of the Bible) with a discussion of the idea of divine revelation. On the contrary, this is required not only (externally) because of the critical objections of our time, but also (internally) because of the inner necessity of theoretical theological thought itself.

This challenge must not be underestimated, for it is permeated with difficulties. Hendrikus Berkhof pointed out that, on the one hand, revelation is a marginal notion in the Bible, simply because it was considered to be self-evident.[21] On the other hand, many modern investigators insist that the offensive aspect of the idea of revelation is equally self-evident. We will have to navigate between these two claims of self-evidence. We will have to supply a theological warrant for our faith in divine revelation without falling into the snare of either

(a) (uncritical) fundamentalism and biblicism (for which positions no problems exist at all; one need only blindly accept its theses; cf. §§4.10 and 9.8); or

(b) a scholastic[22] supranaturalism or rationalistic-scientistic apologeticism (which positions claim that the problem of revelation can be solved purely rationally; cf. §§3.6.2 and 10.9); or

(c) modern immanentism, positivism, materialism, agnosticism, or postmodernism (which positions claim that this very rationality makes it impossible for [post]modern people

---

20. From Gk. *proballō*: that which is "thrown" before someone, as an obstacle that must be overcome.
21. Berkhof (1986, 43); cf. Westermann (1982, 25–27) on the Old Testament, and Schulte (1949) on the New Testament.
22. Here and throughout the book, the term "scholastic" refers not to "schoolish distinction lechery and sophisticated divisions," but to a "conscious combining" of "biblical thoughts with non-Christian philosophy," as Troost put it (2004, 361 note 9).

to continue to accept the notion of revelation; cf. chapters 11–12).

A striking example of someone who fell into the third snare was H. Kuitert.[23] In his popular dogmatics, he eliminated the idea of divine revelation in the most superficial way. He argued that it made no sense to use this notion at all, first, because other religions also claim to be rooted in some revelation (I would respond: so what?), and second, because we cannot use this notion in an exclusive way in our dialogue with other religions since this would make a dialogue *a priori* impossible (but all dialogue starts with conflicting views, I would say). If Christians call the Christian teachings in the Bible "God's revelation," Kuitert wished to see in this nothing more than an evaluative judgment about their own faith tradition. Therefore, Kuitert did not build his dogmatics on divine revelation but on the subjective feelings and deliberations of modern humans. So today people can produce systematic theologies that are based no longer on God having spoken, but only on believing people having spoken.

In our investigation, we will see that the subjective element in our feelings and deliberations plays a greater role than orthodox theologians in earlier times would have accepted. However, *faith* can be called faith precisely because it is convinced of a reality that surpasses these subjective feelings and deliberations, that is, a reality that cannot be reduced to these feelings and deliberations. The point is not, as Kuitert insisted, how we can speak of these things in a wise and modest way to adherents or other religions and thought systems; at best, this matter is a later concern. The point is rather whether the acceptance of this reality can be founded on objective arguments that are not tainted with our own emotions and reflections.

---

23. Kuitert (1993, 16–17; cf. 1988, 18, 30; see also 1999).

1.3 Biblical Terminology

1.3.1 Sources of Manifestations

First, let us briefly consider how the notion of revelation is dealt with in *the* source of Christian tradition and theology: the Bible. The claim that God reveals himself to people is expressed in Scripture through a variety of terms. God speaks to people, instructs them, announces to them, appears to them, makes himself known, and so on. God is not immediately accessible to humanity. At first, he is hidden: "[Y]ou are a God who hides himself, O God of Israel, the Savior" (Isa. 45:15). God "who alone has immortality, who dwells in unapproachable light, whom no one has ever seen or can see" (1 Tim. 6:16).[24] Humans can learn to know God if he, on the basis of a decision of his own free will, manifests himself to them, steps out of his hiddenness toward people.[25] It is not humans who reveal God to others, but God who reveals himself to humans.

In the Old Testament, God uses various means to accomplish this, such as:

A. *With an emphasis on seeing:*
1. Appearances (e.g., Gen. 12:7), sometimes in quite an impressive way: "[T]he glory of the LORD appeared" (Exod. 16:10; Lev. 9:23; Num. 14:10; 16:19, 42; 20:6).
2. "Seers" (those who receive visions from God; Heb. *ro'ēh*, e.g., 1 Sam. 9:9–11).
3. Visions are mentioned from Genesis 15:1 to Habakkuk 2:2–3.

B. *With an emphasis on hearing:*
4. An audible voice of an invisible being speaking (Num. 7:89; 12:8; 1 Sam. 3:4–10).

C. *Both seeing and hearing:*
5. Dreams of people (e.g., Gen. 28:12–17).

---

24. Cf. Berkhof (1986, 54–56).
25. Cf. *TDNT* 3:556–92.

6. Prophets (from Gen. 20:7 to Mal. 4:5).
7. Angels (Gen. 19:1), especially the Angel of the LORD (e.g., Gen. 16:10-11; 22:15-18).

D. *In other ways:*
8. Signs to people (e.g., Gen. 24:12-15; Judg. 6:17).
9. Trance in certain people, leading to "prophetic" statements (Num. 11:25-26).
10. Urim and Thummim[26] (e.g., Ezra 2:63; cf. 1 Sam. 23:9-11).

In these forms, true revelation occurred along with false (imaginary or deliberately imitated) revelation. Therefore, criteria are supplied indicating how one can distinguish between the two. For instance, if a prophet announces an unconditional miraculous sign, and this word is not fulfilled, then he is a false prophet (Deut. 18:21-22). But if a prophet announces an unconditional miraculous sign, and this word is indeed fulfilled, then, if he leads the people to follow idols, he is still a false prophet (13:1-5). Thus, one must watch whether their predictions come true, but also consider their message: if it is in agreement with preceding revelations, then it is valid. A true prophet(ess) speaks in agreement with the Word of God *and* makes predictions that come true. And subjectively, he or she lives a godly life, and the effects of his or her words on the hearers are beneficial (cf. 1 Cor. 14:3).

Revelation was given not only to people who themselves remained passive. It was also possible to actively submit one's questions to the Lord. This was done by the high priest using the Urim and Thummim, or by consulting a prophet (e.g., 1 Sam. 9-10; 1 Kings 14), or after asking, by receiving the reply in a dream (cf. 1 Sam. 28:6). This form of revelation made it all the more important for Israel not to consult false sources of revelation, such as mediums and necromancers (Lev. 19:31; 20:6; cf. Deut. 18:10-11; Isa. 8:19). Therefore, Wolfhart Pan-

---

26. Lit. lights and perfections, which is equivalent to "revelation and truth"; see Exod. 28:30; Lev. 8:8; Deut. 33:8; Ezra 2:63; Neh. 7:65.

nenberg believed that in Israel, too, the origin of the notion of revelation seemed to lie in the arena of manticism.[27] This is rather speculative, but, indeed, there is a certain phenomenological correspondence between biblical ways of revelation and certain forms of mantics. However, the Bible makes a sharp distinction between the origins of the revelations involved.[28] The source is either of the following three:

(a) One's own mind (cf. for dreams Eccl. 5:2, 6; Isa. 29:8).
(b) God (cf. for dreams Num. 12:6; Joel 2:28).
(c) The world of the spirits, that is, the world of the:

* spirits of the dead (Heb. *obot*) and soothsaying spirits (Heb. *yiddeconim*) (Lev. 19:31; 20:6; 1 Sam. 28:7; Isa. 8:19; 19:3);
* demons, devils, goat idols, satyrs (Heb. *secirim*) (Lev. 17:7; 2 Chron. 11:15);
* evil spirits, demons, devils (Heb. *shēdim*) (Deut. 32:17; Ps 106:37).

1.3.2 Ways of Revelation

Through the means mentioned, God has revealed himself in his various attributes (holy, righteous, loving, gracious, merciful, etc.), as the Creator and Sustainer of the world, as the covenant God of his people Israel, as the Lord of history who both exalts peoples and nations and brings them low, as the Redeemer God extending his hand in grace to fallen humanity (cf. Acts 17:26-27). The aim of revelation is that humans would enter into a *relationship* with him, would know him, commune with him, love him, serve him, and worship him. This in its turn serves a still higher goal: the honor and glorification of God.

It is remarkable that the Old Testament does not contain

---

27. Pannenberg (1991, 199); he gave an extensive analysis of biblical forms of revelation (217–34), leading to a greater emphasis on the relationships between revelation and history (244–51); cf. his further defense of this view (251–81); also see Pannenberg (1968).
28. Cf. Ouweneel (2004, 299–323; cf. 2018e, §11.9).

a key term for "revealing" or "revelation." It approaches the matter through forms of rather different Hebrew verbs, such as *gl-h* (piel, e.g., "to reveal"), *r-'-h* (niphal, "to make oneself seen, show oneself"), *y-d-ᶜ* (niphal, "to make oneself known"), *y-r-h* (hiphil, "to show, to teach"), *d-b-r* ("to speak"), *'-m-r* ("to say"), and others.[29]

In the New Testament, various word groups are used to communicate the notion of revelation. However, of these, only the first (see [a] below) is rendered in the Vulgate as *revelatio/revelare*, "to reveal," literally, "to remove a veil" (Latin *velum*), "to disclose," "to manifest." The first two of the following word groups are the most important ones.[30]

(a) The Greek words *apokalyptō*, literally "to take away a covering or shell or veil (reveal)," and *apokalypsis* (cf. English "apocalypse"), the act of taking away a covering. There is an important eschatological meaning of these terms: the "revelation" of Jesus Christ from heaven (2 Thess. 1:7), that is, his second coming.[31] In addition, *apokalypsis* refers in particular to the divine revelation of hidden things or mysteries (see §1.3.3), by God, by Christ, by the Holy Spirit, whether general truths or specific clues (Isa. 56:1 LXX; Matt. 11:25, 27; 16:17; Luke 2:32; 10:21–22; Rom. 16:25; 1 Cor. 2:10; 3:13; 14:6, 26, 30; 2 Cor. 12:1, 7; Gal. 1:12, 16; 2:2; Eph. 3:3, 5; Phil. 3:15; 1 Pet. 1:12; Rev. 1:1).

(b) The Greek words *phaneroō*, literally, "to (actively) make appear" (to loom from the dark, to make visible, to manifest) and "to (passively) become visible, appear, manifest itself," and *phanerōsis*, "appearance, manifestation" (only in 1 Cor. 12:7; 2 Cor. 4:2; in the Vulgate, usually rendered as *manifestare* and *manifestatio*). The verb is used both for things that, and for persons who, appear (see especially Mark 16:12, 14; John 1:31; 2:11; 3:21; 9:3; 17:6; 21:1, 14; Rom. 1:19; 3:21; 16:26; 1

---

29. Berkhof (1986, 102); the Heb. word *torah* is derived from *y-r-h*.
30. Cf. Schulte (1949).
31. Cf. Isa. 40:5, "the glory of the LORD shall be revealed [from Heb. *g-l-h*]," which ultimately refers to the coming of Messiah.

Cor. 4:5; 2 Cor. 2:14; 3:3; Col. 1:26; 4:4; 1 Tim. 3:16; 2 Tim. 1:10; Titus 1:3; Heb. 9:8, 26; 1 Pet. 1:20; 1 John 1:2; 3:5, 8; 4:9; Rev. 15:4). Also compare the related forms of the Greek words *emphanizō* (John 14:21–22), *epiphainō* (Titus 2:11; 3:4), and *epiphaneia* (2 Thess. 2:8; 1 Tim. 6:14; 2 Tim. 1:9–10; 4:1, 8; Titus 2:13). *Epiphainō* refers exclusively to the first, and *epiphaneia* exclusively to the second coming of Christ.

Of lesser significance are the following two terms:

(c) The Greek verb *dēloō*, from *dēlos*, "manifest, clear, plain, evident" (cf. *dēlos poiein*, "to make manifest" in the sense of "to betray," Matt. 26:73; *dēlos estin*, "it is plain," 1 Cor. 15:27; Gal. 3:11). The verb means "to announce, make known, bring to light, make plain" (1 Cor. 1:11; 3:13; Col. 1:8; Heb. 9:8; 12:27; 1 Pet. 1:11; 2 Pet. 1:14). The word has the meaning of future divine revelation only in 1 Corinthians 3:13 (Lat. *manifestum esse*, "to become manifest"), and the meaning of revelation through the Holy Spirit (in the former prophets and in Scripture) in 1 Peter 1:11; Hebrews 9:8 (*significare*); 12:27 (*declarare*). In these meanings, the verb is closely related to *apokalyptō*.

(d) The Greek verb *gnōrizō*, "to make known" or "to observe/know" (Vulgate: usually *notum facere*). The verb refers to making known *to* God by humans (Phil. 4:6), and further to revelation *by* God to humans (Luke 2:15; John 15:15; 17:26; Acts 2:28; Rom. 9:22–23; 16:26; Eph. 1:9; 3:3, 5, 10; Col. 1:27). Divine truths are "made known" by the apostles (1 Cor. 12:3; 15:1; 2 Cor. 8:1; Gal. 1:11; Eph. 6:19; 2 Pet. 1:16).

1.3.3 The Mysteries

As a counterpart of these various terms for revealing (§1.3.2), we find the Greek term *mystērion* as a reference to what *is being* revealed.[32] The word was probably derived from Greek *myeō*, "to initiate into the mysteries." In the New Testament, this verb is found only in Philippians 4:12, "[I]n everything and in all things I have been *initiated* [others: I am instructed, I have learned], both to be full and to be hungry, both to

---

32. Cf. Weber (1981, 173–74); see *TDNT* 4:802–828.

abound and to be in want" (YLT; cf. DARBY); many others, ". . . I have learned the secret." Paul argues, possibly ironically, that he has been initiated into the mysteries of being both full and hungry, and so on, through his practical experiences in the school of Christ.

The ancient Greek versions of the Old Testament and early Christian literature use the term to refer to God's secret or mysterious thoughts, counsels, and decrees, which must be *revealed* to those for whom they are intended;[33] and because they surpass human reason, they must be *explained* as well. These mysteries involve:

(1) the kingdom of God (Matt. 13:11) (the secret things about the kingdom, especially its present hidden character[34]);
(2) the headship of Christ, particularly regarding the consummation of the ages (Eph. 1:9-10);
(3) the secret aspects of God's counsel regarding Israel (Rom. 11:25);
(4) the secret aspects of God's counsel regarding the Gentile nations (Col. 1:26-27);
(5) Christ in relationship with the church (Eph. 3:3-4, 9-11; 5:32; Col. 1:27; 2:2; 4:3);
(6) the full Christian truth (Rom. 16:25-26);
(7) the secret aspects of the gospel (Eph. 6:19);
(8) the secret aspects of godliness (i.e., Christ; 1 Tim. 3:16); and
(9) the hidden wisdom of God (1 Cor. 2:7);
(10) the transformation of living believers at Christ's second coming (15:51).

Other passages are of a more general nature (1 Cor. 2:1; 4:1; 13:2; 14:2; 1 Tim. 3:9; Rev. 10:7; cf. 1:20; negatively: 17:5, 7; 2 Thess. 2:7). In many of these passages, the notion of

---

33. Danker (2000, s.v. *mystērion*).

34. See Ouweneel (2018j, §3.2).

"revealing" or "manifesting" is implicitly explained.

In a certain sense, what is a mystery is no longer a mystery after it has been revealed. In the Bible, the mysteries in view are almost always mysteries that until now *have been* revealed by God (remarkable exception: Rev. 10:4-7). Yet, they remain hidden to unbelievers, that is, those who have not yet apprehended this revelation, or have no understanding of it (cf. 1 Cor. 2:14, "natural" people do not understand anything of the things of God, even though these have been revealed). They also remain hidden to those who have heard them but do not possess the spiritual maturity to understand them (cf. vv. 6-7, the "secret and hidden wisdom of God," imparted among "the [spiritually] mature"; "spiritual humans" understand all things of God, the "carnal" ones do not, 1 Cor. 2:14-3:3).

Unlike for Paul Tillich, it does not seem sensible to continue calling the things that are known but not perceived "mysterious," because this term has connotations ("cryptic," "secretive," even "creepy") that, strictly speaking, are not present in the Greek term *mystērion*.[35] The *mystērion* in the biblical sense does not involve numinous things, exalted mysterious realities, but very straightforward things of God.

1.4 Modal Approaches

1.4.1 Introduction

As I have explained elsewhere,[36] we can speak of a notion like the transcendent revelation of God only with the help of concepts that belong to our experienced, empirical reality. In such cases, these concepts function as border concepts or border *ideas* because they refer to matters that surpass the boundaries of our experienced, empirical reality.[37] "Ideas" involve terms familiar to our experience—adopted from everyday life—that refer to transcendent matters. We have no

---

35. Contra Tillich (1968, 1:108–111).
36. Ouweneel (1995, §4.2.2; 2008, 24–35, 66–68, 148–49; 2014).
37. See especially Strauss (1973; also 1988, 146–51; 2009, §5.12); Troost (1983, 24–25).

other way of proceeding because we simply have no other terms at our disposal. The fact that God has no difficulty with this approach is evident from the fact that the Bible is full of such terms from everyday life, which are used to construct ideas in order to give us an impression or approximation of transcendent realities. This always involves matters that we can know only in logically objectifiable terms but matters that themselves surpass logical objectification. Such matters can only be *approximated* by a logically objectifiable act, which leads to the formation of an idea. By means of such ideas we *approximate* the transcendent reality—certainly in a rational way but without constraining it within our rational grasp.

In the notion of divine revelation, we are dealing with this kind of idea. When we speak of *revelation* in a strictly immanent-logical (or experiential-logical) way—which consists of removing a *velum* ("veil, covering, shell, curtain")—we are dealing with a *physical concept* because this concept involves immanent-physical properties as constitutive conceptual characteristics. These are matters that function within the boundaries of what Dutch Christian philosopher Herman Dooyeweerd has described as the physical modality or modal aspect of empirical reality (see §1.4.3).[38] In simpler terms: *re-velation* refers to a literal (physical) taking away of a literal (physical) covering. However, this physical term can also be used as an idea to refer to a supra-physical matter (i.e., transcending the physical), such as when we speak of the revelation of, or by, God. Here, revelation is not a strictly physical concept but rather a physical idea (mental representation of a thing that as such is strictly transcendent). This idea is certainly logical-rational—we can logically analyze it—but at the same time it is only a representation, an image, an approxima-

---

38. See extensively, Dooyeweerd (*NC*); some introductions to this work are provided by Kalsbeek (1970); Van Woudenberg (2004); Troost (2005); and Ouweneel (2010a, 45–48; 2014). Reformational philosophy distinguishes many such modalities, ranging from the arithmetic and the spatial aspects to the moral and the pistical aspects.

tion of something that itself transcends the logical. Of things that transcend rational concepts we can still form a (rational!) image, an idea. The image *refers* to that supra-rational reality, but it is not identical with it. Thus, we form for ourselves an image, an idea, of the notion of divine revelation, but we cannot encompass, or enclose it within our immanent-rational concepts.[39]

All these things will become clearer when we look at several examples. We will consider various modal aspects with the intention of using the concomitant immanent terms as ideas, in order to get a deeper insight in the transcendent revelation of God. I wish to emphasize here that *each* idea to be mentioned is like a window to the *entire* revelation of God in its transcendent fullness and unity, not only some aspect of this revelation.[40] At the present moment, by way of introduction, I choose only seven modalities; several other ones will be discussed when we deal with the notion of the Word of God (§§5.7–5.8).

1.4.2 The Two Lowest Modalities

(1) *Arithmetic aspects*. God is both the Subject of his revelation (the One from whom revelation issues by the decision of his will) and the Object of it (revelation is *about* him). In the tremendous plurality that characterizes revelation, it always concerns the One. Ultimately, in its kernel, the entire revelation of God is self-revelation, even where it involves God's counsel with regard to humanity. In this self-revelation, the entire Trinity is always involved: the Father (Matt. 16:17) reveals, the Son (11:27) reveals, and the Spirit (1 Cor. 2:10-14) reveals. In other words, God's revelation is a revelation concerning himself (the Father), namely, "in Christ" (the Son), and "through the Holy Spirit." This Trinitarian aspect

---

39. Theologians usually speak here of "metaphors"; however, this is a literary term, whereas we need logical terminology here. Expressed in a Dooyeweerdian way: concepts and ideas are logically qualified, metaphors are lingually qualified; cf. Strauss (1988, 130–38).

40. Strauss (1991, 128).

of revelation cannot be approximated in a conceptual-arithmetic way; if it were different, any speaking of a Tri-Unity (3 = 1) would be nonsense. Rather, we can speak of the Trinity, and thus of the intrinsic unity of divine revelation, only as an (supra-arithmetic) idea.[41]

Just as there is one God, there is also one coherent revelation, even though the latter radiates into a multiplicity of aspects, authors, books, words, and acts. As we will see extensively, general and special revelation do not constitute a dualism but a unity, in which Scripture is the guiding center.

(2) *Spatial aspects*. As I see it, Daniel Strauss has rightly argued that, in the part–whole relationship, we are dealing with a spatial matter (which I cannot elaborate here).[42] With regard to revelation, the part–whole relationship, if applied as an idea, can cast light on the way God has revealed himself. God is infinitely more than what is known about him through revelation; revelation is a partial event. At the same time, however, it is not a part of God but *God* who, according to his being, has been made known through his revelation. This matter of the part–whole relationship can be approximated only in the form of an idea. This means that the divine revelation is *pure*; what we know through it about God is true not only at the moment of revelation. It is not just what God was pleased to present to us at a certain time in a certain way; rather, revelation involves what God really *is*.[43] At the same time, divine revelation is not *adequate* (encompassing), for the infinite God is too great to be entirely revealed within the finiteness of the human experiential horizon.

Moreover, even with regard to the cosmos, revelation is always a *partial* event; in other words, God never reveals everything about everything. Therefore, when Reformer John Calvin speaks of the element of *accommodation* (which here

---

41. Ouweneel (2008, chapter 2).
42. Strauss (1991), 63–64; (2009), §3.3.2.
43. See Ouweneel (2013, §3.3.3); also see volume II/I in this series.

means a certain adaptation to the human level of understanding) in divine revelation,[44] this involves the fact that God's self-revelation is not exhaustive, all encompassing, *not* that it would be impure (an "acting-as-if").[45]

1.4.3 The Physical Modality

(3) *Physical aspects.* Revelation entails an uncovering, an unveiling, like removing a veil that forms a covering of God with regard to humanity. However, in another respect, revelation entails covering up, concealing, putting on a physical covering, as a necessary means through which physical people can get to know God. Even as the "revealed God" (Lat. *Deus revelatus*), God in a certain sense remains the "hidden God" (Lat. *Deus absconditus*), as German Reformer Martin Luther put it.[46] Thus, God has revealed himself most exaltedly in his Son, who *became flesh* (John 1:14; cf. 1 Tim. 3:16; Heb. 2:14; 1 John 4:2–3; 2 John 1:7), as well as in Scripture, in which the eternal Word became "solidified" in human language (adapted to human understanding), in a physical form. In both cases, God reveals himself, and at the same time, he conceals himself behind the covering of human flesh and of human language in a human book, respectively. It does not make God less or different. On the one hand, the Son *is* (the Word of) God, Scripture *is* the Word of God. *As* God, God becomes known to humans through revelation. On the other hand, God's revelation always occurs within the human experiential horizon and with means that are proper to the created cosmos. This always entails a certain measure of concealment: the revelation of God in Christ, or in the Bible, is at the same time *covering* through human flesh and human language, respectively.

Mysticism claims that God can reveal himself in an *immediate* way. This not only basically implies erasing the ontic

---

44. Cf. Calvin, *Institutes* 1.10.2; 1.11; 1.13.1; cf. Troost (2005, 257).
45. Cf. Berkhof (1986, 50–53).
46. Cf. Ebeling (1979, 256).

boundary between Creator and creature, but in addition this would necessarily mean the death of humans (Exod. 19:21; 33:20; Judg. 13:22).[47] The Word shares in cosmic creatureliness in a *mediate* way, which means that it always needs a "revelational carrier," as Gerhard Ebeling called it.[48] This is what Karl Barth called the "world-orientedness" of revelation.[49] Even in cases of seemingly immediate revelation, such as God's speaking face to face with Moses (Exod. 33:11; Num. 7:89; 12:8; Deut. 34:10), this speaking is necessarily covered or concealed in the form of a human voice in order to be audible to Moses (cf. 1 Sam. 3:4-9, where Samuel confuses the LORD's voice with a human voice). As Hendrikus Berkhof put it,

> Even if God, for example, would reveal himself in a mysterious voice, a blinding flash, or an experience of rapturous ecstasy, these would still be phenomena that are part of our earthly reality. They are thus thinkable apart from an encounter with God, and in themselves do not prove anything. Simultaneously they mediate and veil revelation.[50]

Let me add two notes here. First, I wish to make clear that we can certainly speak of this physical covering (flesh, book, voice) in a *conceptual*-physical way. At the same time, this veiling of God is part of the divine act of revealing, which can be approximated only in the form of an *idea*.

Second, we must not confuse God's hiddenness as intended here with other forms of divine hiddenness.

(a) There is an *ontic* hiddenness, which lies enclosed in the proper nature of the Creator, the creature, and revelation. This is what was intended in the previous argument (cf. 1 Tim. 6:16).

(b) The latter is very different from a *hamartiological* hiddenness, caused by the Fall and removed by redemption (or

---

47. Cf. Weber (1981, 199).
48. Ger. *Offenbarungsträger*; Ebeling (1979, 250).
49. Ger. *Welthaftigkeit*; Barth (*CD* I/1:165–74).
50. Berkhof (1986, 51).

among God's people: temporary sins, lifted by repentance and confession); see, for instance, Psalm 27:9 ("Hide not your face from me. Turn not your servant away in anger"; cf. 30:7) and Isaiah 1:15 ("When you spread out your hands, I will hide my eyes from you; even though you make many prayers, I will not listen; your hands are full of blood"; cf. 45:15; 54:8; 59:2; 64:7).

(c) Further, there is a *redemptive-historical* hiddenness in the God-is-dead theology: God who supposedly withdraws himself because of human emancipation (the "eclipse of God").[51]

(d) Sometimes, the righteous experience a hiddenness of God that to them is a trial; see, for instance, Psalm 88:13-14, "I, O LORD, cry to you; in the morning my prayer comes before you. O LORD, why do you cast my soul away? Why do you hide your face from me?" (cf. 55:1, "Give ear to my prayer, O God, and hide not yourself from my plea for mercy!").

(e) God "hiding" his face can also be a synonym of forgiving (this is the opposite of Ps. 27:9; see [b]): "Hide your face from my sins, and blot out all my iniquities" (Ps. 51:9).

(f) I may add here God's *seeming* hiddenness, as is claimed by the wicked; see, for instance, Psalm 10:11, the wicked "says in his heart, 'God has forgotten, he has hidden his face, he will never see it [i.e., my sin]."

1.5 Four Higher Aspects

1.5.1 The Perceptive Modality[52]

Romans 1:20 contains two words that have been derived from the Greek verb *horaō*, "to see": *ta aorata autou*, "things about God that people cannot see" (ERV), and *kathoratai*, "have been clearly perceived." In other words, what cannot be "seen" of God is yet "clearly seen" (KJV), namely, through his revelation.

---

51. Cf. Berkhof (1986, 54–56); see extensively, Ouweneel (1994); the expression "eclipse of God" is from Jewish scholar Martin Buber (2015).

52. Elsewhere I have explained why I think that Dooyeweerd's "psychical" modality in fact contains two modalities: the perceptive and the sensitive modality (Ouweneel [1986]).

Divine Revelation and Human Knowledge

And what can be "clearly seen" of God, if we understand this in the form of a perceptive idea, is *entirely* seen, even today. Whoever has seen the Son, *has* seen the Father (John 14:9). Even though there is the future *apokalypsis*, the appearance of Jesus Christ, this does not justify the claim that divine revelation today is not yet complete.[53] It was complete the very moment the last words of the Bible had been written (perhaps these were the words of John 21:25, if we can trust the current dating of the New Testament books).

Today, Christ is "hidden" with God (cf. Col. 3:3), invisible to human eyes on earth, so that his coming will be a "re-appearance," so to speak. But it will not be a "re-incarnation," a renewed incarnation, for today he is with God in bodily form (cf. Col. 2:9; Luke 24:39-43), and he will return in his glorified body (Phil. 3:20-21). He will come as the "Son of Man" (e.g., Matt. 16:27-28; 24:27, 30, 37, 39; 25:31; 27:64), that is, as a Man (spirit, soul, body). Therefore, his re-appearance cannot be placed on the same level as his incarnation. The event of his "manifestation in the flesh" (cf. 1 Tim.3:16) is unique and completed.[54] It took hundreds of years, and perhaps more than a thousand years, for the Bible to be written — it took a few moments for the Logos to acquire a material (bodily) form in Mary's womb.

At this second coming, Jesus will manifest himself to the physical eyes of his people, and also to the eyes of the entire world (Rev. 1:7), just as he manifests himself today through Scripture to the enlightened eyes of a receptive heart in the power of the Holy Spirit (cf. Eph. 1:17-18), that is, in a subjective sense. However, this does not in the least change the fact that, in an objective sense, God *has* revealed himself once and for all in Jesus Christ, just as he *has* revealed himself once and for all in the Scriptures (even though their writing took centuries). Only in a very specific sense is there a continual revelation of God in history and culture, as centered in Christ,

---

53. Cf. Brunner (1949, 20).

54. See Ouweneel (2007, chapter 9).

moving along from the incarnation to the consummation (cf. §§3.1 and 4.4).

1.5.2 The Formative-Historical Modality

God's revelation goes back to several *attributes* of God, among which is the power of his will: God is *capable* of revealing himself. Power is the meaning kernel of the formative-historical modality in the Dooyeweerdian sense; with regard to God we can speak of power only in the form of a transcendent idea. Parallel to this, we notice that revelation goes back to a decision of God's *will*: he *desires*, he is *prepared*, and *decides*, to reveal himself. This decision is entirely voluntary:[55] God is neither forced nor urged to reveal himself, as is expressed in the traditional Latin term *aseitas* (being *a se*: being "God-as-such," "God-in-himself," existing by himself).[56] He could have been satisfied with the eternal and perfect fellowship within the Trinity; but this communication inward (Lat. *communicatio ad intra*) among the persons of the Trinity becomes the ground for his communication outward (Lat. *communicatio ad extra*) toward human beings, his highest creatures.[57] Thus, revelation goes back to an *act* of God: he was not only powerful and willing to reveal himself, but he *has* revealed himself. Moreover, on the basis of his own sovereign power, he himself determined the contents, locations, times, and modes of his revelation.

In his being, God is independent of his self-revelation because (a) the latter is not some necessary, compulsory *emanation* of (i.e., something issued from) him, (b) God does not exist *by virtue of* his self-revelation, and (c) he existed from all eternity before the voluntary, self-chosen time (insofar as one can speak of time in eternity) of the beginning of his

---

55. Contra Kuyper (n.d.-1, 20, 22), who claims to know specifically that God "must" have a *Verbum* ("Word"), and that having a *Verbum* implies that God "must" declare this *Verbum*.
56. See Ouweneel (2013, §4.3.1).
57. Ibid., §3.3.3.

self-revelation. Compare here expressions such as "before the foundation of the world" (Eph. 1:4; cf. John 17:24; 1 Pet. 1:20) and "before the times of the ages" (2 Tim. 1:9 JUB; Titus 1:2; cf. Rom. 16:25).

God's self-revelation presupposes beings *to whom* this revelation can come. These are necessarily creatures (everything other than God is a creature), namely, human beings, who also have their potentialities (from Lat. *potentia*, "power"; the latter word itself comes from Latin *potere*, "to be able," derived from *potis*, "powerful"). Human beings have been provided with the capacities to accept and understand this revelation, even though this is possible only through the *power* of the Holy Spirit. Objective revelation becomes the subjective possession of the believing person through the illumination of the Spirit (cf. John 16:14; 1 Cor. 2:12-14). Thus, there is a distinction between revelation and illumination: revelation is the objective disclosure of the truth, whereas illumination means that the believer is subjectively enabled to accept and understand this truth (cf. §7.6).

The fact that we can only approximate divine revelation through immanent border-concepts or ideas, not through concepts, is directly linked with the fact that revelation as such, in its unity and beauty, is both a supra-historical event (i.e., transcending history) and one that manifests itself in the plurality and diversity *within* immanent-historical reality. The eternal Word (Lat. *Verbum aeternum*) was prior—a word that must not be understood in any immanent-physical or immanent-historical sense but in a transcendent sense—and secondarily within historical time, this Word became the revealed Word (Lat. *Verbum revelatum*). God's eternal Word preceded the human words with which it pleased God's Word to clothe itself.

Therefore, what Otto Weber wrote is only half true: "As a word of decision, the Word of God is unconditionally temporal; . . . ."[58] Hendrikus Berkhof committed the same error in

---

58. Weber (1981,180; cf. 185).

claiming that revelation is not a "heavenly event," but occurs on earth and in phenomenal forms that are given with earthly life.[59] To me, it seems more correct to say that, according to its *immanent* aspect, revelation is an earthly event, but according to its *transcendent* aspect, it is also a heavenly event. Later, however, Berkhof seemed to distinguish more clearly.[60] Here, he called revelation "supra-earthly," and rightly argued that neither must the supra-earthly be absolutized at the expense of the earthly phenomenal forms of revelation, nor must revelation be reduced to the purely earthly and temporary, which could be interpreted only *a posteriori* by certain witnesses as revelation of God.

In summary, revelation is both a transcendent (supratemporal) and an immanent (temporal-historical) event. As to the latter: revelation is a historical event, first in the sense that the transcendent revelation expresses itself in its entire immanent-functional diversity *within* history. Second, it is a historical event in the sense that revelation itself, in this diversity, has a history. That is, it passes through a number of historical-developmental phases. God reveals himself in successive dispensations[61] in a different, and often richer (additional), and sometimes also new manner, than in previous dispensations (see, e.g., Exod. 6:2; Rom. 16:25-26; 1 Cor. 2:6-10; Eph. 3:4-6; Heb. 1:1-2; 1 Pet. 1:10-12). This is linked with the fact that revelation is a *pluriform* event, which means that God reveals himself in different dispensations and to different people or groups of people in different ways: differently before the lawgiving on Mount Sinai than after it, differently before Calvary's cross than after it, differently to Noah than to Abraham, differently to Israel different to the nations, differently to the church than to Israel, and so on.

---

59. Berkhof (1986, 51).
60. Ibid., 52.
61. See Ouweneel (2011a, chapter 14).

1.5.3 The Lingual Modality

If it is true that God's revelation becomes the spiritual possession of the accepting and believing person, it is equally true that God's self-revelation is and remains his own possession. It never becomes an autonomous quantity, which could be severed from God and with which humans could deal as it pleases them. In this sense it never becomes the possession of humans. This is directly linked with the lingual[62] character of God's revelation (speaking of it in the form of an idea), namely, as Word. That is, God addresses the word to people, and expects from them a counter-word (response).[63] Humans listen to, and respond to, God's Word, but this Word remains *God's* Word, the word of his mouth (Ps. 33:6; Isa. 45:23; 55:11; Ezek. 3:17; 33:7; Matt. 4:4 [Deut. 8:3]).[64] Therefore, strictly speaking, humans cannot speak God's Word to themselves; they are, and remain, only hearers (receivers) of God's revelation. They receive the Word, but not in such a way that the gift could ever be severed from the Giver. The Word keeps addressing them on behalf of God, as God's own enduring Word.

We might presume here a connection with the claim by Karl Barth that God's revelation is not a *datum* ("something given") but a *dandum* ("something to be given").[65] Yet, there is a difference. According to Barth, we do not have the Word of God in Scripture, but Scripture is only God's Word as "event" (Ger. *Ereignis*). That is, each time it must *become* God's Word for humans in a concrete situation (§7.10.3). The "is" in the statement, "Scripture is God's Word," is a "being in becoming" (Ger. *Sein im Werden*); it is only there if and when God is active toward people.[66] I see this differently. In Scripture,

---

62. Notice that I do not use the term "linguistic"; lingual has to do with language (Lat. *lingua*), whereas linguistics is the science of language.
63. Cf. German, *Wort – Antwort*; Dutch, *woord – antwoord.*
64. Cf. Weber (1981, 180).
65. Cf. Muis (1989, 85, 90).
66. Barth (*CD* I/1:88–99; I/2:404–405).

we are dealing with objective revelation; thus, this written revelation is there in its entirety; God speaks, apart from the question whether someone is listening. But at the same time, we do not have this revelation at our disposal; it rather has people at its disposal. That is, people never possess it independently of God and of the working of his Spirit. In a subjective sense, people recognize and receive it as God's Word if and when they (actively) open their hearts to it, or if they are (passively) touched by it (see further in §1.9).

Emil Brunner, too, seemed to wrestle with the matter.[67] He wrote that the Word of God (also) exists "in the form of revealed human words." In my view, this is not sufficiently precise. It is not the human words that have been revealed but God's Word has been revealed in the form of these human words. This is not splitting hairs—I see the distinction as essential.[68] I do appreciate, however, that Brunner emphasizes in the same passage that God's Word is not behind the human words, as if these words merely attempt to give expression to it, but rather God's Word coincides with them. God's Word and the human words in which it is contained coincide completely.

Of course, such a statement leads to a certain tension, namely, between saying that God's Word has been revealed in human words and the saying that God's Word coincides with these human words. This tension need not give rise to any concern, as long as we realize that the human words of Scripture coincide with God's Word *in its immanent plurality and diversity,* and that the eternal Word coincides with the human words of Scripture *in their transcendent concentration, integration, unity, and fullness.* I would not know how to express the matter more clearly than in this Dooyeweerdian terminology (see further in chapters 5-7).

---

67. Brunner (1949, 22–23).
68. Tillich (1968, 1:122–26).

1.5.4 The Social Modality

Revelation is not a kind of social encounter between God and humans in the sense that both parties would deliver their own contribution to it, as it happens in an encounter between people on equal footing (*synergy*). On the contrary, revelation is an absolutely sovereign act on behalf of God, upon which humans can and did exert no influence. However, through the working of God's Spirit, people can enter into it by accepting it in faith, responding to it, obeying it; the Word gives life, makes people spiritually alive (John 1:4, 13; 6:63; James 1:18; 1 Pet. 1:23). As I said, revelation would be revelation even if no people responded to it.[69] Thus, revelation does not presuppose social partnership, even though it does constitute those who answer to it as partners (cf. 1 Cor. 3:9, "God's fellow workers").[70]

At the same time, it is true that revelation is not non-committal; it is an urgent, *authoritative* event. Divine revelation never leaves people to do as they please, but demands of them acceptance and commitment. This also means that God's self-revelation never involves exclusively himself: it also involves the social relationships (viewed as an idea) into which he wishes to enter with people. Humans are not involved in the *act* of revelation as such, but they definitely are involved in its *contents*,[71] and in the expected *response* to it.

Thus, it is understandable that, according to Otto Weber, in mysticism there can be no question of revelation because the mystic finds the divine only in the depths of his own Ego. The only objection could be that Weber seems to overlook the fact that in mysticism we sometimes also might be dealing with occult (paranormal, that is, not subjective but objective) revelation: also a spirit can speak to a person (cf. 1 Sam. 28:8; 1 Kings 22:21; Job 4:15-17; 20:3; Hos. 4:12; Acts 23:9; please note,

---

69. Van Genderen (2008, 36–37); contra Berkhof (1986, 65).
70. Weber (1981, 194–95).
71. Cf. Ebeling (1979, 253), although I think he goes too far in viewing revelation exclusively in an infralapsarian way.

in all these passages this is not a bad spirit).

The social aspect of revelation comes to expression not only vertically in the social relationship into which God wishes to enter with humans, but also horizontally: since God's covenant with Noah (Gen. 9), divine revelation is also a community-creating event. God's revelation aims at binding people not only to himself but also to each other. God's revelation on Mount Sinai did not simply come to individual Israelites; rather, it constituted them a *covenant* people.[72] God's revelation through Jesus and the apostles formed, and forms, Jewish and Gentile Jesus-believers into a community, the church of God, the body of Christ. The apostle Paul prays that God may give believers "a spirit of wisdom and revelation in the knowledge of him; having the eyes of your [plural] heart enlightened, that ye [plural] may know what is the hope of his calling" (Eph. 1:17–18 ASV), and part of this calling is that the believers have been "called in one body" (Col. 3:15).

1.6   Does Divine Revelation Exist?

1.6.1   Supra-Rational Belief

The central question for the internal prolegomena of systematic theology is this: Does the kind of revelation as described above really exist, and how can we know that it exists? This is a question relevant not only in the field of theology but also in that of the philosophy of religion. As an answer to the question, the following reasoning seems to me the most appropriate.

First thesis: *Belief in the divine revelation is a supra-rational, supra-theoretical insight of the regenerated heart.*[73]

(a) Of fundamental importance in the view presented here is the insight that each systematic-theological investigation of Scripture is religiously determined, that is, is governed by a religious ground-motive, which primarily drives a person's

---

72. See Ouweneel (2018b, especially chapter 7).

73. For important background information on these paragraphs, see Ouweneel (2013; 2014; 2015).

Divine Revelation and Human Knowledge

transcendent Ego (the "heart"), and hence the immanent functions of the human mind. Such a ground-motive also contains, or excludes, an idea concerning Scripture being revelation of God. Such an idea is a transcendent insight of faith, which surpasses all immanent-logical understanding.

Please note that I make a sharp distinction between "religious" in the transcendent sense, and "religious" in the immanent sense.[74] Some human words and actions are religious in the latter sense, such as praying, reading the Bible, preaching, evangelization, pastoral work, whereas other words and actions are not, such as bicycling, buying groceries, washing the dishes, eating, painting. However, *all* human words and acts are religious in the transcendent sense, that is, they occur before the face of God (Lat. *coram Deo*), are inspired by the Spirit or by the flesh, are determined by the (faith condition of the) religious, transcendent heart; there are no such things as "neutral" bicycling, buying, washing, eating, and painting.[75] The apostle Paul clearly expresses this: "[W]hether you eat or drink, or whatever you do, do all to the glory of God" (1 Cor. 10:31). "[W]hatever you do, in word or deed, do everything in the name of the Lord Jesus, giving thanks to God the Father through him" (Col. 3:17).

From now on, when I use the word "religious," I mean religious in the transcendent sense (Dooyeweerd often used for this the term "central-religious"); when I mean religious in the immanent sense, I will use the term "pistical" (derived from the Gk. noun *pistis*, "faith, belief"). "Religious" in the transcendent sense refers to what drives people at the deepest level in all their actions; hence the term "ground-motive." A ground-motive (from the Lat. verb *movere*, "to move") is what drives not only people's (immanent) thoughts, feelings, words, and actions but first and foremost their (transcendent)

---

74. The Dutch language distinguishes here between "religieus" and "godsdienstig."

75. Regarding the neutrality concept, in connection with two-kingdom theology, see extensively, Ouweneel (2017).

hearts (hence "ground-").

(b) The supra-rational, supra-theoretical truth of God, embodied in divine revelation, is communicated to the believer's heart through the power of the Holy Spirit. It is active in this heart as a religious ground-motive. Thus, God's revelation can neither be acquired nor comprehended by human reason alone, even though it certainly does not exclude reasons (see the third and fourth theses in §§1.6.3–1.6.4).

(c) Divine revelation itself must be carefully distinguished from the *a posteriori* logical-rational-analytical *immanent* theories that are produced by theological investigation with regard to such notions as "revelation," "God's Word," the "truth of God," and so on. Such theories may approximate the truth and meaning of revelation, but because of the latter's transcendent character, revelation always surpasses all human theories; it can never be enclosed within them. It even surpasses all pre-theoretical thought.

1.6.2 Prior Belief

Second thesis: *Belief in divine revelation precedes and determines every systematic-theological theory, not the other way around.*

(a) The conviction that Scripture is or is not a revelation of God can never be the pure *result* of systematic-theological investigation, as both fundamentalism (it *is* God's revelation) and modernism (it is *not* God's revelation) have often claimed. On the contrary, it is the other way around: such a conviction is necessarily the *religious presupposition* of each systematic theology.

(b) All notions such as "revelation," "God's Word," the "truth of God," and so on, can and must be subjected to theoretical-theological reflection, and it is to be hoped that they will yield useful, albeit fallible, theological theories. However, the supra-rational, supra-theoretical truth of God is not at all affected by such fallible theories.

(c) Two other distinctions must be made. First, a distinction between people's beliefs and their formulations thereof. The formulations of people's faith in divine revelation, no matter how strongly they are rooted in their respective confessional traditions, as well as their theological theories concerning divine revelation, are never beyond criticism, much less infallible. However, their supra-rational, supra-theoretical ground-motive *is* beyond all criticism. In the publications mentioned above, I have argued why it could not be otherwise. People's ultimate religious, transcendent conviction concerning divine revelation (for or against it) precedes all their discussions about it, and determines it, not the other way around.

(d) The second distinction is between people's religious (transcendent) ground-motive and their (pre-theoretical and immanent) pistical beliefs. Their beliefs about divine revelation are always fallible—and sometimes incorrect—concretizations of their ultimate religious conviction, and as such are open to criticism. However, the ultimate religious conviction as such is not open to criticism, and *cannot* be open to it, precisely because it precedes all people's criticisms, and determines and underlies them. If people would try to criticize a person's ultimate religious conviction concerning divine revelation, their criticism would be entirely determined by their own ultimate religious conviction concerning divine revelation. Even if a person would wish to combat the idea of an ultimate religious conviction as such, it is my ultimate religious conviction that such combating would be governed by that person's own ultimate religious conviction. We cannot get the notion of divine revelation (or the rejection of it) within our (pre-theoretical or theological) grasp because such a notion itself has all our beliefs and theories in its grasp.[76]

1.6.3 Theological Research Needed

Third thesis: *Even though belief in divine revelation determines*

---

76. See again Ouweneel (2013; 2014; 2015), in each of which I emphasize the essential difference between, on the one hand, a religious ground-motive and, on the other hand, each confession or theology.

people's systematic theology, this revelation as well belief therein can and must become the object of systematic-theological investigation.

Systematic theology definitely has the task to investigate and analyze *a posteriori* the conviction that the Bible is or is not divine revelation. The same is true for God's revelation in nature (Belgic Confession, Art. 2) and his revelation in the person of Jesus Christ. However, theology can carry out this task properly only if it acknowledges *a priori* that its investigation cannot reach any further than the analysis of the immanent, empirical form that the eternal Word has assumed, that is, nature or Scripture or Christ. The eternal (transcendent) Word itself, or God's revelation itself, cannot be enclosed in theoretical or even pre- or supra-theoretical human words.

This is true even though, indeed, the eternal Word has been inscripturated (put in written form) in the immanent, empirical form of the Bible, and has been incarnated in the person of Christ (chapter 5). This immanent, empirical form can and must be thoroughly investigated by theologians, and, as much as possible, explicated with theological concepts. However, the transcendent matter *of which* nature or Scripture or the Man Christ is the immanent form can at best be approximated in the form of ideas.

1.6.4 No Retreat into Irrationalism

Fourth thesis: *The view represented here concerning belief in divine revelation is no retreat (flight) into irrationalism.*

(a) Irrationalism means that irrational (more correctly, non-rational) elements of human nature, such as the will and feeling, are at least as important as, if not more important than, reason. However, the non-rational must never be confused with the supra-rational. The non-rational involves *immanent* factors besides, and other than, reasons, such as volition, emotion, and the like. The supra-rational is of a *transcendent*, religious nature: it involves what surpasses reason, but also the will, feeling, and so on. Thus, the non- and irrational concerns the immanent functions of the human mode of existence; the supra-rational concerns the human transcendent heart.

Between these two, no separation must, and can, be made at all. This is because the immanent functions *are* nothing but the transcendent heart itself, viewed in its empirical diversity; and the transcendent heart *is* nothing but the immanent functions themselves, viewed in their unity and fullness.[77] Thus, at the foundation of my reasoning so far, there is an anthropological view of the relationship between, on the one hand, functions such as thinking, feeling, and believing, and, on the other hand, the transcendent heart. I am convinced that in such an anthropological approach the age-old dilemma of choosing reason or feeling is basically overcome.[78] This occurs as soon as we realize that both are nothing but immanent-modal functions of the religious, transcendent heart, each of which has its own place, and none of which can be deduced from another one. Where this is grasped, a view that emphasizes the *supra*-rational can never be dismissed as a form of *ir*rationalism.

(b) The fact that rational arguments are adduced for our belief in divine revelation shows as well that the view presented here concerning this belief is no retreat into irrationalism or mysticism. I am convinced that many good logical-rational arguments can be adduced for the belief that divine revelation exists, and that the Bible is the written record of it, and not, for instance, the book of Mormon, the Talmud, the Qur'an, or the Vedas.[79] Even if each ultimate religious conviction concerning divine revelation is necessarily *supra*-rational (not *ir*rational, *non*-rational, or even less, *anti*-rational), this does not exclude my having good *rational* arguments for my standpoint concerning divine revelation.

---

77. In addition to the publications mentioned, see Ouweneel (2008, chapters 6–8).
78. Cf. Ouweneel (2018l, chapter 6).
79. Cf. Ouweneel (1995, §5.2.2).

I am fully aware that such rational arguments are entirely governed by my ultimate transcendent, religious conviction concerning divine revelation (see §1.6.1). However, first, this is true for *any* conviction concerning divine revelation, also those of, for instance, liberals or atheists. Second, this transcendent, religious conviction does not stop me from believing (1) that it is more reasonable to believe concerning Scripture what it testifies about itself, namely, that it is the Word of God, than not to believe so, and thus to reject this self-testimony of Scripture; and (2) that it is more reasonable, in investigating Scripture, to be led by the contents of Scripture itself than to be led by non-biblical elements of thought, like scholastic or humanistic elements. It is more reasonable to study Scripture, including its claim to be divine revelation, from its own center than from perspectives that are foreign to its essence.

In systematic theology, both belief in divine revelation and the rejection of such belief function within a respective paradigm that involves a certain view of reality (ontology or cosmology) and of knowledge (epistemology). Such a paradigm itself is necessarily always governed by a God-oriented or an apostate ground-motive. Apparently, we can never escape a certain ultimate commitment,[80] that basic attitude of the heart, which is either governed by Scripture's own self-understanding in the power of the Holy Spirit, or opposes this self-understanding in the imagined power of one's own sinful flesh. Given the standpoint chosen here, it seems that a person cannot escape the following conclusion: on the one hand, the claim that divine revelation exists is ultimately determined by the heart that is in the grip of this divine revelation. On the other hand, the claim that divine revelation does not exist is ultimately determined by the heart that is in the grip of an apostate, hostile attitude toward this divine revelation.

---

80. Cf. the "religious naturalist" Henry N. Wieman (1963).

1.7 The Hermeneutical Circle[81]

1.7.1 The Supremacy of Reason

At the end of the previous section, we touched upon a central problem in the philosophy of science. This problem is that, apparently, we cannot escape the circle of our theoretical and pre-theoretical presuppositions, our paradigms and worldviews. We must pay a little more attention to this point from the perspective of one of the main theological disciplines, that is, hermeneutics. Not only in theology but also in literary science and philosophy, hermeneutics is what we may call the science of interpretation. In theological hermeneutics, theologians have often referred to the so-called "hermeneutical circle," which is closely related to the circle just described,[82] but originally meant something different, namely this: we cannot avoid explaining the elements of a text (here, the text of the Bible) from its entirety, and at the same time explaining this entirety from its elements. It was the German philosopher Martin Heidegger who turned this strictly *literary* problem into a *philosophical* problem: we cannot avoid interpreting the world from our presuppositions, and at the same time choosing our presuppositions on the basis of our understanding of the world.[83]

For a long time, theology has suffered under rationalism, that is, the absolutizing of reason, of logical-analytical thought. This is one of the great plagues of our Western intellectual tradition. Irrationalism is an equally great plague, but is of a more recent date. Many theologians, both orthodox and liberal, have believed, *and* believe, that they would be able to design a systematic theology that could entirely encompass Scripture, that is, could logical-rationally get all of Scripture within its grasp. In such a systematic theology, each conclusion is logically derived from the biblical data. Because of the

---

81. Regarding this, see Ouweneel (1987a, 59–67; 1987b, 29–35; 2018l, chapter 3).
82. Cf. Berkouwer (1975, 119–20, and references).
83. Heidegger (1962).

authority of reason, each logical conclusion *from* biblical data would necessarily have the same truth content, and thus the same authority, as those biblical data themselves. Compare the Westminster Confession (I.6): "The whole counsel of God concerning all things necessary for His own glory, man's salvation, faith and life, is either expressly set down in Scripture, or *by good and necessary consequence may be deduced from Scripture*" (italics added). This was the view of many Protestant theologians affected by scholasticism, beginning with Theodore Beza,[84] and still seems to be view of many.

Who or what determines whether a deduction was carried out "by good and necessary consequence"? The laws of logic? But notice the following syllogism:

Major premise: God is the Father of his earthly children.
Minor premise: A father is a male who, through sexual intercourse with a woman, has begotten one or more children.
Conclusion: God is a male who, through sexual intercourse with a woman, has begotten one or more children.

Why do theologians reject this conclusion? The logic of the syllogism is impeccable. One escape might be that the term "Father" in the major premise is only a metaphor. But is this correct? I think not; the answer has little to do with metaphorical language but much more with the distinction between concepts and ideas. In the major premise, we are dealing with the *idea* of a Father, in the minor premise we are dealing with the *concept* of a father. What may be true for the concept of a father (masculinity, intercourse) may not be true for the idea of a father. I have discussed this problem elsewhere.[85]

This kind of theology suffers from the traditional rationalistic overestimation of science as a pure enterprise of neutral,

---

84. See extensively, Kickel (1967).
85. Ouweneel (2013, §§1.5.3 and 5.1.2).

unprejudiced, objective reason. History shows how (systematic) theology, whether orthodox or liberal, has been trapped repeatedly in such a rationalistic-humanistic view of science. Such a theology is not salvaged by moving to the other extreme, that of *ir*rationalism, but only by grasping that both reason and feeling, or the rational and the irrational, are nothing but immanent functions of the transcendent heart, as we saw. The heart always precedes reason, just as our religious, transcendent faith precedes our immanent-religious beliefs, and these precede our theoretical acts such as hermeneutics.

1.7.2 Proving Our Prejudices?

When we have grasped the things we just considered, we do not have to be ashamed of basing our entire systematic-theological work upon the existential insight concerning the Bible as the inspired Word of God. The believer has this insight neither rationally, nor irrationally, nor a-rationally, but supra-rationally. Therefore, it is entirely acceptable that Johannes C. Sikkel began his introduction to hermeneutics as follows: "The interpretation of Holy Scripture must begin with the believing acknowledgement that Holy Scripture is the Word of God."[86] (The question in what sense Scripture, as given within the immanent experiential horizon, can be called the basically transcendent Word of God, is discussed in chapter 5 below.) This *a priori* insight concerning the Bible can never be obtained as the *result* of any theoretical (philosophical or theological) activity, no matter how orthodox. Nobody will ever be brought by merely scientific arguments to the recognition that the Bible is the inspired Word of God.

Frederik W. Grosheide pointed[87] to the example of the Johann C. K. von Hofmann, who believed that his scientific research would *prove* that Scripture is what he believes it to be.[88] Even in the twentieth century, such a positivistic op-

---

86. Sikkel (1906, 7).
87. Grosheide (1929, 20).
88. Von Hofmann (1869, 1:53).

timism could still be encountered here and there, not only among various fundamentalists but also among mainstream theologians. An example: Werner G. Kümmel claimed that Karl Lachmann had supplied an irrefutable argument[89] for the priority of Mark's Gospel in relation to Matthew's and Luke's Gospels.[90] Others have rightly refuted such a claim of irrefutability.[91] (To put it a bit bluntly: there *are* no irrefutable arguments — including this one.)

In such examples we encounter the "hermeneutical circle," here in the form of a circular argument. It gives the impression that, *starting* from the heart's *a priori* conviction that the Bible is, or is not, God's Word, one could theoretically *prove a posteriori* that the Bible is, or is not, God's Word. This is impossible. As Karl Barth put it, "[T]o prove that [viz., the primacy of the Bible as the Word of God] we should obviously have to put ourselves in a place above proclamation and the Bible, ..."[92] This is what American philosopher Hilary Putnam nicely described as a "God's eye point of view."[93] In other words, we are not dealing here with a theoretical-scientific (immanent) *result*, but with a supra-theoretical, *a priori* (transcendent) *faith insight*. Such an insight can only be the fruit of the Holy Spirit. It is brought about not primarily within the intellect, but in the regenerate heart, and from there it pervades the logical as well as the other functions. The recognition that the Bible is the Word of God is a matter of believing confession, which issues from the regenerate heart, which itself is governed by God's Word, through the power of the Holy Spirit.

1.7.3 *Petitio Principii?*

The things just considered do not constitute a primarily rational-scientific, that is, hermeneutical or systematic-scientific

---

89. Lachmann (1835).
90. Kümmel (1972, 148).
91. E.g., Du Plessis (1988, 295).
92. Barth (*CD* I/1:259).
93. Putnam (1981); cf. Sankey (2004).

insight (immanent), but rather a supra-rational, religious insight of the heart (transcendent). Similarly, biology, psychology, linguistics, economics, and every other discipline are ultimately based upon an (explicit or implicit) ground-conviction, concerning God, Christ, the Bible, creation, humanity, reason, the soul, and so on, no matter how little this usually seems to be realized. In this regard, there is no basic difference between theology and the other disciplines.[94] The only distinct aspect of theology is that the faith conviction concerning Scripture is not only its religious *starting point* but also that the systematic-theological *analysis* of this faith conviction forms one of its subjects.

Wolfgang Trillhaas described the problem of the hermeneutical circle as an apparent *petitio principii* ("begging the question," or circular reasoning), and referred to the objection of some who saw in it a threat to the scientific character of dogmatics for the following reason: "[T]hrough a *petitio principii*," dogmatics "presupposes not only reason but also faith, and in this way excludes such people who think and work rationally and methodically who do not have faith from the cooperation and the understanding of the matter, and thus acts arbitrarily and unscientifically."

Trillhaas considered this objection to be partly justified. However, he argued that, in fact, faith is nothing but a specific attitude toward its object, which we, for instance, encounter in art as well.[95] In this way, he wished to salvage the scientific character of dogmatics.[96] I would rather say that, if this presupposition of faith is in conflict with the scientific character of dogmatics, there can be no science at all. This is because *all* science, not only theology or art, is founded upon some faith, which is not an attitude in any immanent sense (*beliefs*) but *faith* in the transcendent, religious sense of the word. The theologian who does not have "the" (biblical) faith is simply

---

94. Kuitert (1988, 79, 93); Spykman (1992, 121); Ouweneel (2014; 2015).

95. Trillhaas (1972, 49–50).

96. See also ibid., 50–53.

a person who performs their theological work on the basis of a different, namely, apostate, faith. *What* must be called biblical, and *what* apostate, is a matter of theological debate; but faith itself precedes all debate.

1.8 Forms of Hermeneutics

1.8.1 (Non-)Congenial Hermeneutics

In my view, we can basically distinguish two kinds of systematic-theological hermeneutics. The one hermeneutic is non-congenial: it finds its religious starting point in a scholastic or humanistic idea of autonomous reason, and thus exalts itself beyond God and Scripture, no matter how great its (pretended) reverence for the Bible may be. It is a hermeneutic that believes it is possible to determine in how far the Bible may be called a reliable, divine Word revelation of God. Whether, in this way, it arrives at a positive or a negative result, does not matter right now — my point is that in both cases we are dealing with the same starting point.

The other hermeneutic is congenial: it finds its religious starting point in Scripture itself, which is *a priori* believingly accepted as the Word of God. It does not do so on the basis of the results of some orthodox theology but on the basis of the *preaching* of the Word, the Spirit-led appeal of this Word to a person's heart and conscience.[97] Such preaching may be influenced *a posteriori* (positively or negatively) by theological notions, but primarily it is a basic *a priori* of systematic theology. There is no neutral, unprejudiced, objective hermeneutic, and this is true for *each* scholarly enterprise. There is only a hermeneutic, or systematic theology, that is *obedient* or *disobedient* to the Word.

In addition, there is no infallible hermeneutic either. Orthodox and liberal theologians differ in their pre-theoretical, pre-rational starting points. But at the same time, they have one feature in common: they produce only fallible results. This has not always been clearly grasped. In various classi-

---

97. Cf. Ouweneel (1995, §1.2.3).

cal hermeneutical introductions, I found little or no understanding of the relative value of human (systematic-)theological theories, a phenomenon that seems to betray continued loyalty to ancient rationalism.[98] It was only in the systematic theology of American dogmatician Lewis Sperry Chafer that I found a hint of recognition: "Among all the major divisions of Bibliology, hermeneutics, or the science of interpretation, holds a unique place, being, as it is, wholly the work of men. Its results, therefore, at best, are characterized by imperfections due to human limitations."[99]

If this is not recognized, the idea may easily arise that theological arguments themselves could prove that the Bible is or is not God's Word. Or even worse, the idea might arise that hermeneutical analyses of the belief that the Bible is God's Word, or theories concerning the contents, meaning, and bearing of this belief, would have virtually the same status as biblical statements themselves. No matter how orthodox, theories concerning these and other beliefs are invariably rooted in theoretical and pre-theoretical presuppositions, which ultimately rest in a religious ground-motive. Fallible scientific and scholarly theories, no matter how orthodox, can never be placed on the same level as the perfect ground-motive *behind* these theories. It is painful to see how inattentive theologians seem to be regarding this kind of faith presuppositions behind their theories. Thus, Winfried Corduan spoke exclusively—and critically—of the humanistic presuppositions that influence liberal hermeneutics, but he did not devote a word to the worldviews and philosophical and theological presuppositions undergirding orthodox hermeneutics.[100] Apparently, this was because he was not aware of them, or refused to acknowledge them.

Let me illustrate the distinction between people's theories and their pre-theoretical faith with one example. People's

---

98. See Sikkel (1906); Grosheide (1929); Greijdanus (1946); Bleeker (1948).
99. Chafer (*ST* 1:115).
100. Corduan (1984).

(pre-scientific) *belief*, and their (pre-scientific) confession, that the Bible is the infallible, inspired Word of God, is rooted in this infallible, inspired Word of God itself. However, each systematic-theological *theory* concerning this infallibility and this inspiration is itself neither infallible, nor inspired, but a fallible piece of human work. Of course, in people's analysis of Scripture's infallibility and inspiration, they may try to stay as close to Scripture as possible, to speak in the vein of the Bible as much as possible. However, this speaking in the vein of Scripture depends on people's understanding of the Bible. Here we encounter the hermeneutical circle in its original, literary meaning: people interpret each Bible verse from the entirety of the Bible, and they explain this entirety from their understanding of the distinct verses.

1.8.2 Falsified Theories

Elsewhere, I have argued extensively that theological theories cannot be taken directly from the Bible because nothing in the Bible is theoretical.[101] This is precisely the reason why many theologians do not like to speak of theological "theories." They claim that they are merely repeating in their own words what the Bible says. However, they do not realize that the Bible itself does not contain any theory, or even any pre-theoretical doctrine, concerning its own infallibility and inspiration; *theologians themselves create such a theory*. As Karl Popper said of natural-scientific theories, all such theological theories are always *free* creations of the human mind, the results of an almost poetical intuition.[102] Theories are *created*. Of course, a good theory is one that supplies as plausible a warrant as possible for the teaching of Scripture concerning its infallibility and inspiration, and—to say it in a Popperian way—has so far superbly resisted various attempts to falsification. However, this does not change the fact that the *formulation* of each theory is entirely the work of the theologian. And this formulation

---

101. Ouweneel (2013, chapters 6–14).
102. Popper (2002b, 192).

can, under further analysis, turn out to be a rather weak approximation, if not a complete failure.

Take as an example the doctrine of mechanical inspiration, which in its time was spread almost universally among both Roman Catholics and Protestants, and possessed a status of unassailability. At least in its most consistent form, it viewed the Bible writers like a kind of dictaphone or other voice recorder (see §7.3.3). As widely spread as the theory was at the time, it is just as widely unpopular today. We can quietly view it as a *refuted* theological theory. In other words, among orthodox Christians, it is viewed today as an *incorrect* (viz., scientistic) immanent-theoretical formulation of a *correct* transcendent, supra-theoretical faith concerning the inspiration of the Bible.

The doctrine of the Bible's organic inspiration seems to be much better because it has grasped much more clearly the organic involvement of the Bible writers in the writing of the text. However, this theory, too, in certain formulations, can easily suffer from certain wrong presuppositions (see §7.4.1). Its deficiencies come to light, for example, in the way the relationship between the human and the divine elements in the Bible is sometimes understood. This relationship is sometimes incorrectly viewed within the scholastic framework of the nature–grace dualism (or nature–supernature dualism). The Bible is not a (dualistic) composite of natural and supernatural elements, just as humans are not (dualistic) composites of bodies and souls,[103] and just as Christ is not a (dualistic) composite of two separate natures, which could almost be viewed as two distinct persons.[104]

1.8.3 Two Circles

With regard to the hermeneutical circle, at first glance, it may seem as if committing the fallacy of *petitio principii* ("begging the question") is inevitable, consisting of the following steps:

---

103. See Ouweneel (2008, chapters 6–8; 2018l, chapter 6).
104. See Ouweneel (2008, chapters 3 and 9).

(a) The (Enlightenment) *starting point* of liberal hermeneutics is that the Bible is not the Word of God but only the word of humans, no matter how Spirit-enlightened these writers may have been.

(b) Biblical statements that speak of the Bible's own character as Word of God are viewed from this perspective: whatever their claims may be, such statements are words of humans. In the formulation of H. Kuitert: all speaking about Above comes from below, as well as the speaking that claims to come from Above.[105]

(c) From this doctrinal starting point and these rationalistic-scientific arguments, the assumed *conclusion* is *that* the Bible cannot be the Word of God.

In a perfectly analogous way, we encounter this *petitio principii* in orthodox hermeneutics:

(a) The *starting point* of orthodox hermeneutics is that the Bible is the infallible, inspired Word of God, albeit clothed in the word of humans.

(b) Biblical statements that speak of the Bible's own character as Word of God are viewed from this perspective: they have been formulated by humans but they come from God.

(c) From this doctrinal starting point—and with often equally rationalistic-scientific arguments—the assumed *conclusion* is *that* the Bible is the infallible, inspired Word of God.

Thus, the view that the Bible is, or is not, the Word of God seems to be both the beginning and the end of the investigation. We can compare this with the circular argument that Frederik W. Grosheide identified:

> For we already assumed that the New Testament as part of God's special revelation has its own character, and to this end we used data that are presented by the New Testament itself. It is impossible, however, to avoid such a way of acting. The fact that the New Testament possesses its own character is a matter

---

105. Kuitert (2005).

of faith, and that faith is placed in the hearts by the Holy Spirit in connection with people's reading of the New Testament. After all, Holy Scripture has its authority in itself because it is from God. This must be believed; it cannot be proven. Here is a closed circle, outside of which one cannot adopt a position without surrendering one's position. Scientifically, one can only attempt to clarify the matter and make it more acceptable.[106]

Indeed, we are dealing with a hermeneutical circle here from which we cannot escape. However, this is not necessarily a circular argument because the two "circles" are definitely not identical. In the words of Heinrich Ott,

> The fact *that* we at all ascribe authority to the Bible thus has a double foundation: 1. the fact that God has revealed himself, 2. the fact that he has revealed himself *once for all and for all people*... On the other hand, of course, it is only when we hear this biblical message that we understand that the two presuppositions are true. Thus, there is a circle here; however, not a defective circular argument, which is not able to prove anything, but a so-called 'hermeneutical circle,' in which two concepts or thoughts mutually explain each other.[107]

As I said, we would be dealing with a genuine circular argument if we were to claim that the (supra-theoretical faith) insight that the Bible is the Word of God could ever be the *fruit* of scientific research. Such an idea is just as rationalistic-scientistic as the idea of others that scientific arguments could ever prove that the Bible is *not* God's Word. There is no such a thing as neutral, objective data that could ever provide such proofs, whether for the one or for the other view. All so-called "proofs" necessarily function only within the framework of people's presupposed worldviews and paradigms.

---

106. Grosheide (1929, 19).
107. Ott (1972, 45).

1.9 The *Testimonium Spiritus Sancti internum* and *externum*

1.9.1 The Heart's "Facts"

Because orthodox systematic theologians view their presuppositions as superior, they cannot afford to produce less impressive scholarly results than their humanistic colleagues. *Starting* from the perfect *supra-rational* religious ground-motive of orthodox systematic theology, it is, as we saw, definitely possible to supply *rational* arguments to support the conviction that the Bible is God's Word. The faith choice of the heart precedes reason logically but not chronologically. That is, in the religious sphere, the heart's faith choice is a supra-rational, transcendent matter, but at the same time, within immanent-empirical reality, it is a meaningful, *intelligent*, choice of common sense. It is a commitment whose warrant can be supplied through *intellectual* arguments that show why it is more sensible to believe the Bible's self-testimony than to reject it.

Over against traditional Christian approaches, the liberal theologian can never appeal to the solid, objective facts of modern science because such facts do not exist, and the notion of "modern" (read: highly authoritative) science is fictional. Conversely, over against humanistic approaches to the Bible, the orthodox theologian can never appeal to the solid, objective facts of the Bible because these do not exist either. Facts always necessarily function within the framework of paradigms. During the nineteenth and twentieth centuries, belief in such neutral facts was represented by positivism and neo-positivism, but unfortunately, it gradually came to permeate Christian thought as well. Thus, Gustav Aulén told us that the guiding star for systematic theology, as in all scholarly investigation, is the same: objectivity, factuality.[108]

Another example was Norman Geisler, who placed humanistic philosophies concerning the (in)fallibility of Scrip-

---

108. Aulén (1960, 18).

ture over against the "factual evidence" (!) of the Bible in this regard.[109] This is nothing but a form of Christian positivism, which is just as untenable as secular positivism. Unfortunately, the former is still quite strong, whereas by now the latter is more or less extinct, except among certain natural scientists, especially theoretical physicists.

Facts are always embedded within the religious conviction with which they are approached. It is not "the facts" that prove the Bible to be God's Word, but the facts *become* real "facts" only when the *heart* has come in the grip of this Word through the Holy Spirit. Therefore, in the end, the systematic theologian will have to fall back upon his *faith*—faith in the transcendent, religious sense of the word. Such faith is not a kind of last retreat against the attacks of reason, as some would have it. On the contrary, both biblical faith and apostate faith are the only sources from which reason can be nourished.[110]

1.9.2 The Two Testimonies

Otto Weber directly related the matter of the hermeneutical circle to that of what is called "the internal testimony of the Holy Spirit" (Lat. *testimonium Spiritus Sancti internum*), which occurs within the believer's heart.[111] The belief that the Bible is Word of God cannot be objectively proven, or disproven, through rational arguments. If, therefore, Fritz Buri claimed that, for both Lutheran and Reformed Christians, the internal testimony of the Holy Spirit within the believer is the factual proof for the inspiration of Scripture, and thus for the truth of soteriology,[112] he cannot have meant this in the theoretical, or even pre-theoretical-logical (immanent) sense, but only in the supra-logical, religious (transcendent) sense.

When we say that the belief that Scripture is Word of God

---

109. Geisler (1979a, 333).

110. Ouweneel (1995, §5.1.3).

111. Weber (1981, 240–48); cf. Ouweneel (2018e, especially chapter 8).

112. Buri (1956, 282–83).

cannot be proven in an objective-rational way, we mean to say that we do not possess a criterion that can be made evident for everyone. Our arguments that supply the warrant for our belief that in the Bible we hear God's Word are *a posteriori* arguments. That is, only after a person, through the Spirit, has accepted Scripture as Word of God, can that person can interpret this experience with Scripture in a pre-theoretical, rational way, and subsequently in a theological way, but never other than by his *a priori*, transcendent faith. We can never get outside the circle; we cannot take some objective standpoint somewhere outside, much less beyond, Scripture in order to determine its status. We can only *testify* of a Spiritual experience that we have had with Scripture, and even the content of this testimony is determined by our *a priori*, transcendent faith.

As we have seen, there is no reason to be concerned about such a circle. On the contrary, the Christian believes that every true belief and testimony concerning Scripture is the work of the Holy Spirit. This means that the Spirit is active both in the Word that comes to believers and in the response that their hearts give to it. The latter is what John Calvin has called the "internal" or "hidden testimony of the Holy Spirit" (Lat. *testimonium Spiritus Sancti internum* or *arcanum*).[113] The origin of this doctrine must likely be found with Martin Luther.[114] The biblical starting point for this doctrine is Romans 8:16, "The Spirit himself bears witness with our spirit that we are children of God"; this is the internal testimony of the Holy Spirit in the hearts of the believers (also cf. 9:1, "my conscience bears me witness in the Holy Spirit"). Remarkably enough, Otto Weber called this doctrine the only new element that Protestant theology has contributed to the doctrine of the authority of Scripture.[115]

---

113. Calvin, *Institutes* 1.7, especially 1.7.4; cf. Dee (1918, 114–16); Krusche (1953); Berkouwer (1967, 41–82).

114. WA 30.2:688.

115. Weber (1981, 242).

The essential question with respect to this *testimonium Spiritus Sancti internum* is whether it is independent of the "obviousness" of Scripture—what could be called the "external testimony of the Holy Spirit" (Lat. *testimonium Spiritus Sancti externum*). It is mysticism and spiritualism that have answered this question in the affirmative.[116] According to Otto Weber, Calvin moved along the edge of this attractive view but—in Weber's view fortunately—he ultimately resisted this temptation.[117] From the *testimonium Spiritus Sancti internum*, he moved back to Scripture. That is, only when a person hears the testimony of the Holy Spirit does one know that God is speaking personally in Scripture; but only in Scripture does one learn what God's personal speaking entails. The subjective evidence *concerning* Scripture and the objective testimony *of* Scripture are basically identical.[118] This is an entirely new description of the reason why we can never escape the hermeneutical circle. There can be no criterion of some internal testimony of the Spirit that is independent of, and stands over against, some obviously evident Scripture.

1.9.3 Criticism

Of course, it would be easy enough to criticize such a view of the hermeneutical circle, and of the identity between Scriptural evidence and Scriptural testimony. Heinrich Alsted appealed to the internal testimony of the Spirit, and David Friedrich Strauss commented negatively about this. I quote here Karl Barth's comments—in his own peculiar style—on this criticism by Strauss:

> D. F. Strauss was right to criticize this rule [i.e., Alsted's appeal]: "Who can now attest the divinity of this [Scriptural] witness? Either itself again, which is nobody: or a something, perhaps a feeling or thought in the human spirit—this is the Achilles' heel of the Protestant system . . . . Indeed [Barth continues], who

---

116. Cf. Althaus (1967, 211); Heyns (1976, 127).

117. Weber (1981, 242).

118. Althaus (1967, 212).

does attest the divinity of this witness? What Strauss failed to see is that there is no Protestant "system," but that the Protestant Church and Protestant doctrine had necessarily and gladly to leave his question unanswered, because there at its weakest point, where it can only acknowledge and confess, it has all its indestructible strength.[119]

Let me try to express in my own terminology what I understand Barth to be saying. Ultimately, on the (transcendent, supra-rational) level of faith, the testimony concerning Scripture surpasses the entire (immanent-rational) dilemma between the *testimonium internum* and the *testimonium externum*. This is not a matter of theological weakness but of imperishable strength—the combined supernatural strength of the Holy Spirit and of Holy Scripture. In our heart of hearts, we know through the power of the Holy Spirit that Scripture is God's own Word. But we also know it through Holy Scripture itself, just as it is through Scripture that we know about the Holy Spirit. There is an intricate interplay here of Scripture and Spirit, which we now must investigate a little more closely.

1.10 The Subject–Object Gap

1.10.1 Coherence

Otto Weber presumed—rightly so, I think—the presence of the ancient subject–object gap in this entire discussion (see previous section).[120] That is, the danger here is that the objective testimony of Scripture is placed in opposition to the subjective testimony of the Spirit in the human heart. Such a gap does not need to exist if we realize that so-called subjects and so-called objects are always, all of them, subjected or submitted (Lat. *subiectus*) to the same law of God.[121] Thus, it is not only all (logical, lingual, social, economic, aesthetic, moral, etc.) *objects* in the human mind that are subject to the

---

119. Barth (*CD* I/2:537).
120. Weber (1981, 243–35); cf. Ouweneel (1995, §6.1.1).
121. See Ouweneel (1995, §6.3.2; 2013, §§14.5.3–14.5.4).

(logical, lingual, social, economic, aesthetic, moral, etc.) laws of God, but also humans as (logical, lingual, social, economic, aesthetic, moral, etc.) *subjects* are subject to these laws, including their very hearts. Thus, there is a (transcendent) relationship between God's Word and the human heart, which includes, among other things, the Law of Love (cf. Rom. 5:5). That is, through the Holy Spirit, in their hearts believers submit to this Law as it addresses them from Scripture, and this is worked out by the Spirit in all their (logical, lingual, social, economic, aesthetic, moral, etc.) functions.

According to the concomitant immanent (logical, lingual, social, economic, aesthetic, moral, etc.) laws of God's creation order, Scripture fits with human nature. That is, it is not an objective datum in itself; rather it is proper to its ontic structure to address humans, to anticipate human response and submission. It is *one single* work of God to (externally, objectively) testify *to* humans — through Scripture, by means of his Spirit — and to (internally, subjectively) testify *in* humans by means of this same Spirit. The external-objective testimony and the internal-objective testimony cannot be separated, much less be placed in opposition to each other (dualism); they are subject to the same immanent divine (logical, lingual, social, economic, aesthetic, moral, etc.) laws and the same transcendent divine Law of Love.

This view has some important implications.

(a) It supplies us with one of the answers to the bibliology of dialectical theology,[122] namely, this: it is impossible to hold the (Barthian) view that Scripture can be Word of God only *insofar as* it is confirmed by the *testimonium Spiritus Sancti internum* (see §7.10.3). If we would claim such a thing, we would create rivalry between the testimony of the Spirit and the testimony of Scripture. This is impossible for those who view these testimonies as essentially one.

(b) Along the same lines, this view supplies us with an

---

122. Cf. Ouweneel (1995, §§5.2.3, 4.2.4, and 4.3).

answer to the bibliology of fundamentalist theology, with its overestimation of human reason, as if reason could derive from the *testimonium Spiritus Sancti externum* of Holy Scripture in a logical-analytical manner the evidence for the claim that the Bible is the Word of God. In other words, those who hear this testimony of the Spirit in Scripture are not led to accept some theological theory concerning the origin of the Bible, but rather to submit to God's Word and obey it.

(c) This view also contradicts mystical theology, which, as we saw, severs the *testimonium Spiritus Sancti internum* from Scripture. Moreover, mysticism appeals to believers to concentrate upon their own spiritual state, as if the latter could give them the confirmation of what is truly Word of God. However, faith assurance does not rest upon our private experiences, to which supposedly also belongs the *testimonium Spiritus Sancti internum* if severed from Scripture. On the contrary, this assurance rests upon the one, both external and internal, testimony of the Spirit through Scripture, in a direct coherence of the two. That is, just as the external testimony of Scripture is nothing without the internal testimony of the Spirit, the internal testimony of the Spirit is nothing without the external testimony of Scripture. The two are not available separately.

1.10.2 Scripture and Spirit

We must notice here again that this work of the Spirit through Scripture and in the believer's heart is a transcendent, and therefore supra-rational, event. As a consequence, we cannot enclose it within a theological theory. In theological discussion this has often been overlooked, as, for instance, in the debate caused by Hermann Rahtmann in 1621, under the influence of Pietism.[123] Rahtmann defended the thesis that Scripture offers only an external communication of God's Word but does not by itself bring about the enlightenment that leads to conversion. He claimed that the latter was exclu-

---

123. See Weber (1981, 284–85) for references.

sively the work of the Holy Spirit, which is *new* (additional) in regard to the testifying work of Scripture. The Bible is an axe, which becomes active only if and when it is governed by an arm. However, Rahtmann's opponents defended the thesis that the Word of God (Lat. *verbum Dei*) is active not only when in it read, preached, or heard (Lat. *in usu*) but also before, and apart from, it use (Lat. *ante et extra usum*).

Karl Barth pointed out that both parties were guilty of exaggeration.[124] Thus, for instance, Andreas Quenstedt viewed Scripture and preaching as means (Lat. *media*) in which the highest power and efficacy (Lat. *summa vis et efficacia*) would be continually present, merely by themselves. David Hollaz even spoke of a "hyperphysical [i.e., supernatural] power" (Lat. *vis hyperphysica*) in Scripture.[125] Such views dangerously border on seeing Scripture as an object that works magically (a danger of which Quenstedt apparently was aware). This danger, as well as others, is a necessary consequence of conceptualizing, and theorizing about, the transcendent, supra-rational relationship between Scripture and the Spirit.

In the longstanding argument between Lutheran theology (the Spirit works through the Word [Lat. *per verbum*]) and Reformed theology (the Spirit works with the Word [Lat. *cum verbo*]; cf. the Canons of Dort 1.12; 3/4.13), we encounter the same danger. The former theory can easily lead to a magical Word automatism, and the latter to de-Spiritualizing the Word and to the idea of an autonomous activity of the Spirit.[126] The danger lies not in the faith intention behind such views — each of which, of course, contains a kernel of truth — but in the presumption of theoretical thought. B. Wentsel rightly stated that, on the one hand, it is incorrect to depict Scripture as a book that in itself is dead and must be resuscitated repeatedly by the Spirit, and on the other hand, to claim that the Spirit is identical with Scripture, or lies enclosed in the letters, as a

---

124. Barth (*CD* I/1:110).
125. Cf. Karner (1957, 115–16).
126. Berkhof (1986, 59).

kind of incarnation of the Spirit.[127] The former may lead to a denial of inspiration, while the latter may lead to bibliolatry.

We cannot possibly go any further than careful, practical faith statements, such as:

(a) Scripture is God's Word, independent of subjective experience, and surpassing the latter.

(b) Scripture always has divine power, also over against all unbelief, just as the sun produces heat behind the clouds, and seeds retain their power also in infertile soil (the metaphor comes from Hollaz).

(c) This power is the power of the Holy Spirit, which is subjectively effectuated where there is faith.

To ask whether Scripture has power in itself, or whether this power is that of the Holy Spirit, apart from Scripture, is simply to pose a false dilemma.

1.10.3 A Final Comment

Let me conclude this chapter with an interesting quotation from Walter Kreck, who turned against the views of Quenstedt, Hollaz, and others, although his argument is somewhat disfigured by Barthian exaggeration.

> Here [i.e., in the view just mentioned] the Word of God becomes an actuality that lies within the Bible word, the revelation becomes revealedness. The incarnated Word becomes letters [cf. Rom. 7:6; 2 Cor. 3:6]. All securities that people have tried to adduce — such as the reference to the Holy Spirit — could not prevent that the living torrent of revelation was captured within a reservoir because the serving letter became the master. Instead of playing the role of John the Baptist and pointing to Christ, Scripture itself became object of faith. In wishing to find the authority of God's Word in the written letter, people robbed it of its very sovereignty. This is a deeply tragic event because in this way, in the midst of orthodoxy, people against their will paved the way for rationalism. This is because — not beginning with

---

127. Wentsel (1981, 195–96).

the Enlightenment and its concomitant historical criticism, but already through this doctrine of inspiration—natural theology [see §4.1) was smuggled into the church, like a Trojan horse. For it is *theologia naturalis* ["natural theology"] if one turned the revelation into revealedness, and the gospel into a sum of doctrinal truths. In this way, orthodoxy itself became a destroyer of biblical authority. Because it dissolved the counterpart of revelation that it wished to safeguard with its doctrine of inspiration through the undialectical identification of God's Word and Scripture, by turning this Word into an accessible entity. Thus, as historical awareness increased, it provoked a biblical criticism that, for its part, put the matter to the test and carried the identity of God's Word and Scripture being asserted here to its absurd consequences.[128]

There are unpleasant Barthian overtones here, which elsewhere in the present volume will be dealt with extensively. Apart from them, Kreck correctly—implicitly or explicitly—identified the dangers of (a) a doctrine of mechanical, docetic inspiration (see §7.8), (b) a deistic, natural-theological view of Scripture (see §4.1), and (c) the rationalism of early-Protestant orthodoxy. Rationalism did not begin with Enlightenment theology but had already dominated scholastic theology, both that of medieval Roman Catholic and that of early Protestant theologians. The Enlightenment brought a lot of changes, but in one point it did not change at all, namely, in the rationalistic methodology of theology. On the contrary, Enlightenment theology was *evoked* by Protestant scholastic rationalism, albeit against the latter's will. All these points will be dealt with in the remainder of this book.[129] There, we will see that the theology that presents itself as the fiercest combatant of Enlightenment theology (see chapters 11-12), namely, fundamentalist theology (see chapter 9), is essential-

---

128. Kreck (1970, 248).
129. Cf. Brunner (1949, 226–27; Beker and Hasselaar (1978, 44–50; Heron (1980, 7), who similarly points out the rationalism of both early Protestant and Enlightenment theology.

ly based upon the same starting point, namely, rationalistic methodology. As the French say, *Les extrèmes se touchent* ("the extremes meet each other").

Chapter 2
A Twofold Revelation

[God] **reveals** *deep and hidden things;*
he knows what is in the darkness,
and the light dwells with him.
Daniel 2:22

The heavens declare the glory of God,
  and the sky above proclaims his handiwork.
Day to day pours out speech,
  and night to night ***reveals*** *knowledge...*
The Torah of the L<small>ORD</small> *is perfect,*
  reviving the soul;
the testimony of the L<small>ORD</small> *is sure,*
  making wise the simple.
Psalm 19:1-2, 7-8

Summary: *For ages, theologians have distinguished between "general" and "special revelation" (or the "work-" and the "word-revelation") of God. As a practical confession of faith this is all right. However, scholastic theology has turned this distinction into a dualism, according to the pattern of the nature–grace dualism. One* of the consequences was that the two revelations were thought to be a pre- and a post-Fall phenomenon, respectively, which I reject. Equally mistaken, in my view, is the Barthian rejection of a general revelation altogether (one of the causes of this rejection being the confusion of general revelation and the idea of "natural theology").

In opposition to these views, I defend the notion of general revelation, and argue for the essential unity of general and special revelation. Over against the horizontal dualism of these two revelations as invented by scholasticism (which corresponds with, e.g., the church–state/society dualism), I place the vertical dualism or antithesis (God–Satan, Spirit–flesh). I emphasize that the **work-revelation** is also **word-revelation**, and the vice versa; in other words, the separation of the two is mistaken. Misunderstandings concerning the two revelations are illustrated by means of three German theologians: Karl Barth, Emil Brunner, and Paul Althaus. They differed on several important points, but all three kept presupposing the underlying scholastic nature–grace dualism.

2.1 Different Divine Revelations: An Introduction

2.1.1 Speech, Words, Voice

FROM ANCIENT TIMES, THEOLOGY DISTINGUISHED between two kinds of revelation. The first kind, so-called "general revelation" (also called "work-revelation," God's revelation in his creational works) is the subject of chapters 3 and 4. The second kind, so-called "special revelation" (also called "word-revelation," God's revelation in the written words of Scripture) is the subject of the remainder of this book.

By faith we know and confess that God has created the world, and that this Creator-God reveals himself in his created works: "The heavens declare the glory of God, and the sky above proclaims his handiwork. Day to day pours out speech, and night to night reveals knowledge" (Ps. 19:1–2). "The voice of the LORD is over the waters; the God of glory thunders, the LORD, over many waters" (29:3). God "did not leave himself without witness, for he did good by giving you rains from heaven and fruitful seasons, satisfying your hearts with food and gladness" (Acts 14:17). "[H]is invisible attributes, namely, his eternal power and divine nature, have been clearly perceived, ever since the creation of the world, in the things that have been made" (Rom. 1:20).

Incidentally, the reasoning in Psalm 19 is not obvious right away. Verses 3-4a say, "There is no speech, nor are there words, whose voice is not heard. Their voice goes out through all the earth, and their words to the end of the world." The *crux* here is verse 3, which has been interpreted in various ways.

(a) The Septuagint (as well as, e.g., Campegius Vitringa [d. 1722] and Ferdinand Hitzig [d. 1875]) render this verse: "There is no speech, nor are there words, whose voice is not heard (or, is not audible)" (ESV). This could be read to mean: whatever speech may go out from the celestial bodies and the sky, there are always people who effectively understand this speech.

(b) The version of Martin Luther, John Calvin, and other Protestants echoes the former: "There is no speech nor language, where their voice is not heard" (KJV, WEB). If we read the text this way, it may refer to the universality of the message going out from the universe (vv. 1-2): it comes to each language and every nation in the world.

(c) Another rendering is this: "There is no speech, and there are no words, yet their voice is heard" (DARBY). That is, the message of the celestial bodies and the sky does not involve (human) words, yet it is clear and understandable.

(d) Heinrich Ewald rendered verse 3 as follows: "Without a sound or word, silent in the skies, their message reaches out to all the world" (cf. TLB).

(e) Karl Barth made the verse independent and contrary, so that in fact verses 1-2 are contradicted: the heavens declare, the sky proclaims, the day pours forth speech, the night preaches, but actually there are no speech, no words, no voice.

The commentaries choose very differently; for instance,

Millard J. Erickson prefers (a), Willem A. Van Gemeren prefers (b), and Frederik W. Grosheide preferred (c).

2.1.2 General and Special Revelation

As indicated by the Bible passages mentioned, we know about this self-revelation of God *in his works* through his self-revelation *in Scripture*, that is, in the inscripturated Word of God. In other words, on the basis of God's *word-revelation* we recognize the cosmos as God's *work-revelation*. People might think that this work-revelation of God would speak for itself. But in reality, we truly recognize it as divine *revelation* only in light of the word-revelation.

We find the distinction between the two types of revelations in, for instance, the Belgic Confession, Article 2:

> We know [God] by two means: First, by the creation, preservation, and government of the universe; which is before our eyes as a most elegant book, wherein all creatures, great and small, are as so many characters leading us to "see clearly the invisible things of God, even his everlasting power and divinity," as the apostle Paul says (Rom. 1:20). All which things are sufficient to convince men and leave them without excuse. Second, He makes Himself more clearly and fully known to us by His holy and divine Word, that is to say, as far as is necessary for us to know in this life, to His glory and our salvation.[1]

The Westminster Confession (I.1) also says that ". . . the light of nature and the works of creation and providence do so far manifest the goodness, wisdom, and power of God, as to leave men inexcusable (Rom. 2:14–15; 1:19–20; Ps. 19:1–3; Rom. 1:32; 2:1), . . ." though the word-revelation is needed to lead people to salvation.

Please note that these are confessions, not theological statements; that is, we hear the *church* confessing here, not the academy. Moreover, such confessions are pre-theoretical, or even supra-theoretical. At the same time, it is true that theo-

---

1. *RC* 2:425.

logical *science* has the task of supplying the *theoretical warrant* for the logical distinctions in this *pre-theoretical* confession. Ever since the Apologists,[2] theology has distinguished between these two kinds of revelation. Let us have a closer look at the differences between them, first through the following distinction, which will be elaborated in the following sections:

(a) God's *general* or *universal revelation* (Lat. *revelatio universalis*) is addressed to humans, and to humanity as a whole. It is also called *natural* or *mediate revelation* because it is viewed as occurring by itself, in a natural way, as well as in a mediated way, that is, by means of nature, without any spoken or written word of God. Therefore, we find traces of the knowledge of this revelation in all religions. We see how this revelation comes to expression in nature, not only in external nature but also in the internal nature of humans and the history of humanity, which also includes culture (as being "disclosed nature"; see §3.3.1). Therefore, this revelation is also called *creational revelation*, a term that refers to God's self-revelation not only in the actual *work* of creation but also in the *work* of providence. Thus, we also use the term *work-revelation*.

(b) God's *special* or *particular revelation* (Latin *revelatio particularis*) is addressed to individual persons (Adam, Noah, the patriarchs), subsequently to Israel, and afterward to Christianity in particular, but beyond this, through Holy Scripture, to all nations that are prepared to listen. Please note that, in this respect, this revelation is just as universal as general revelation. It is also called *supernatural* or *immediate revelation* because it occurs in a special, direct way through the supernatural miracle of divine inspiration (chapters 7–8) and inscripturation (chapter 5). It is immediate because God does not speak indirectly here, as he does in nature, but directly ("thus says the LORD"), sometimes even with an audible voice (Num. 7:89; 12:8; 1 Sam. 3:4–10). Even where God does

---

2. Justin Martyr, *Apology* II.8, 10, 13; Tertullian, *Apologeticus pro Christianis* II.18; Irenaeus, *Adversus Haereses* II.6, 9, 28; III.25; IV.6; see more extensively Bavinck (*RD* 1:302–303).

not speak with direct speech, Bible writers claim to pass on the words of God (e.g., Rev. 17:17; 19:9). Therefore, we find this revelation brought to expression in Scripture, called the "Word of God" (cf. Matt. 15:6; John 10:35; Eph. 6:17; Heb. 4:12; 1 Pet. 1:23; 1 John 2:14), so that we can speak here of *word-revelation*.

2.2 Objections

2.2.1 The Enumeration by Heyns

This traditional distinction of two kinds of revelation has not gone uncriticized, both with regard to the relationship between these two kinds of revelation and concerning the notion of a universal revelation in general. The latter criticism dates especially from the twentieth century.[3] J. A. Heyns summarized some of the objections to the idea of general revelation as follows (rendered in my own words).[4]

(a) *All* revelation is a *special* act of God, so that the juxtaposition of *natural* and *special* revelation must be rejected; that is, all revelation is special revelation. Initial reply: the reverse would be equally true; i.e., if nature entails the entire created cosmos, then any special message of God—especially Holy Scripture—belongs to natural revelation in the widest sense of the term because Scripture is a creational work, too.

(b) The absolutely sufficient and unique redemptive revelation in Jesus Christ is affected and threatened by the idea of general revelation, which ostensibly would be independent of Jesus Christ. Initial reply: such an objection evaporates if general revelation is *not* severed from Jesus Christ (see below for my arguments).

(c) The goal of revelation, namely, the encounter with, and creating a relationship between, the creature—*in concreto*: humanity—and God, cannot occur on the basis of general revelation alone; thus, general revelation cannot have a real revela-

---

3. Cf. Bavinck (*RD* 1:chapters 10–12); Berkouwer (1955); Vander Stelt (1978).
4. Heyns (1988, 7).

tional character. Initial reply: this is a *non sequitur*: something that is insufficient revelation can still be revelation.

(d) The distinction between two kinds of revelation easily suggests a *separation* (cleft) between (supposed) general and special revelation, which could seriously threaten the unity of the divine revelation. Initial reply: this is correct; however, there is a way to speak of this twofold revelation without allowing such a cleft. Not every duality is necessarily a dualism.

(e) The term "revelation" (divine self-disclosure) is too strong a description of the way God is known in and through creation. Initial reply: see (c) above.

Unfortunately, without any further specification, Heyns tells us that not all these objections can be accepted as legitimate but that, nonetheless, the distinction between general and special revelation is not entirely valid. I would like to make the following observations (see this and the next section).

Objections (a) and (e) are related. Klaas Schilder in the Netherlands tried to meet these two objections by suggesting that God is *manifest* (Gk. *phaneros*) in nature and history but *manifests* himself (as an act) through a Word that is added to this nature, namely, Scripture (*phanerōsis*).[5] Jacob Kamphuis, tried to refute this view, though not with a theological argument but with a primarily confessional argument, referring to Belgic Confession, Article 2.[6] Later, Kamphuis referred to Romans 1:19 ("God manifested it to them," ASV), which would show that God is not only manifest in creation but manifested himself in it. However, this cannot be a decisive argument against Schilder if we accept a distinction between a manifesting that is given *eo ipso* with creation (i.e., with God's creational word) and a manifesting as an additional act, that is, God's direct speaking (i.e., Word) through creation to humanity. Moreover, the latter point, namely, that both nature

---

5. Schilder (1936, 12).
6. Kamphuis (1982, 16).

and Scripture involve "word of God," seems to be a strong argument for the view that, also in nature or the cosmos, we are dealing with divine revelation (see §§2.7.1 and 2.7.2, and extensively, chapter 3).

2.2.2 Traces in Other Religions?

Objections (b) and (c) mentioned by Heyns (see previous section) especially reflect the view of Karl Barth, and will be dealt with in §2.8, while (d) will be dealt with first (§§2.5 and 2.6). However, before we enter into these objections, we must pay special attention to one point in our description of natural revelation. This is the claim that we find traces of such natural revelation in all religions. This point has been a matter of much debate.[7] Almost by definition, all religions live by the conviction that the Absolute can be known through revelation,[8] which is the same as saying that all religions believe in the knowability of Higher Things. All humanly developed religions are an amalgamation of the original divine revelation and human apostate elements.[9] That is, all apostate religions contain a residue of the original (general) revelation of God, albeit in a heavily corrupted form as a consequence of sin and demonic blinding (cf. 2 Cor. 4:4, "the god of this world has blinded the minds of the unbelievers").

The truth is not unknown to the pagans; they really did receive it to some extent, especially through tradition, which goes back to Noah and his sons (Gen. 6–9). However, they "hold" this truth in unrighteousness (Rom. 1:18 KJV); the participle "holding" is Greek *katechontōn*; this difficult verb has been rendered in quite different ways: "suppress" the truth (NIV, NASB); "hinder," "silence" it, "detain," "hide" it, "withhold," "prevent (it) from being known," and so on. All these renderings have in common that the Gentiles at least know the truth (cf. v. 21, "although they knew God") but subse-

---

7. Cf. Buri (1956, 229–31, 234–37, 242–45, 249–54).
8. Berkhof (1986, 45).
9. See Wentsel (1982, 53–58, 87–90) and cf. §4.1.

A Twofold Revelation

quently do bad things with it, which amount to not giving heed to this truth.

Through regeneration and the illumination of the Spirit, the truth that is present in creation can be known in principle. In practice, this is possible only if this truth is referred to its true point of concentration, namely, Jesus Christ (cf. John 14:6). Only then can this truth be basically understood in its uncorrupted unity and fullness.[10] Outside Israel, we know in the Old Testament positive examples of Gentiles who knew (certain aspects of) the truth, such as:

(a) Melchizedek, king of Salem (Gen. 14:18-20; cf. Ps. 110:4; Heb. 5:6, 10; 6:20; 7:1-22).

(b) Job and his friends: Eliphaz the Temanite, Bildad the Shuhite, Zophar the Naamathite, Elihu the Buzite (Job 2:11; 32:2); at least Job knew the name YHWH (1:21); the others also knew the name *El Shaddai* (8:3, 5; 11:7; 15:25; 22:3, 17, 23-26; 32:8).

(c) Jethro, Moses' father-in-law (Exod. 18; Jethro uses the name YHWH in v. 10, but maybe he learned this name from Moses).

(d) The Gentile tribe of the Kenites, such as Heber and his wife Jael (Judg. 4:11, 17; see also Gen. 15:19; 1 Sam. 30:29; cf. also point [g]).

(e) Hiram, the king of Tyre (1 Kings 5, especially v. 7, "Blessed be the LORD this day, who has given to David a wise son to be over this great people").

(f) Naaman, the Syrian commander, who came to know the Lord through his healing (2 Kings 5).

(g) Jehonadab (or Jonadab) the son of Rechab (2 Kings 10:15; cf. especially his descendants, the Rechabites in Jer. 35; in 1 Chron. 2:55, the Rechabites are connected with the Kenites; see point [d]).

(h) Ebed-melech, the Ethiopian eunuch (Jer. 38:7-12).

---

10. Ouweneel (1995, chapter 6).

(i) King Nebuchadnezzar made several confessions of faith (no matter their value) (Dan. 2:47; 3:28-29; 4:34-35).

(j) The same holds for king Darius the Mede (Dan. 5:31; 6:26-27).

(k) The same holds for king Cyrus the Persian (Ezra 1:1-4).

The first two examples are the most impressive because Melchizedek as well as Job and his friends did not have any knowledge of God through Israel. It seems to have been the same with the prophet Balaam (Num. 23-24), but this was a negative example. Unfortunately, Balaam and other Old Testament persons who knew the truth but suppressed it are in the majority. The light has shone in the *world* and gave light to *each* human (cf. §2.2.3) but the world did not "know" it (Gk. *egnō*, NIV: "recognize" it). In its darkness, it did not "comprehend" it (Gk. *katelaben*, "perceive, grasp"; for a very different rendering see ESV: "overcome" [others, "defeat, extinguish, suppress, overpower"] it) (John 1:5, 9-10).[11]

By nature, Christians, Muslims, Hindus, and so on, are all equally sinners. The difference is that true Christians are those who, by the grace of God and through the work of his Spirit, were allowed to open their hearts to the *uncorrupted center* of God's creational revelation, namely, Holy Scripture (see §2.7.2 for the exact meaning of this). In contrast to this, the other Gentile religions know only a part of the *periphery* of God's creational revelation, and do so in a heavily *corrupted* form.

Indeed, we recognize that all apostate religions contain something — only a corrupted residue — of God's *protevangelion* (as we might call it). However, this recognition hardly justifies the exaggerated interest that many Christians have developed since World War II for other world religions. This development often claims a basic equality, or even just a certain resemblance, between other world religions and Christi-

---

11. Cf. Calvin, *Institutes* 1.3 and 1.6.

anity.[12] Karl Rahner viewed the adherent of a non-Christian religion in certain respects as an "anonymous Christian."[13] Ben Wentsel pleaded for a balanced evaluation of non-Christian religions, with an open eye for the elements of truth in paganism, even though these are present in a concealed, distorted, darkened form;[14] as he put it, "The longing for God and the resistance against him are often interwoven."

Though speaking of an exaggerated interest, I do wish to emphasize that the post-war interest in other religions has also had a positive outcome. It provided a missiological correction with regard to past iconoclasm on the part of missionaries who lacked (sufficient) respect for other religions and their adherents. After the Second World War, missionaries were called upon everywhere to change this attitude of superiority. Persuasion made more room for conversation, monologue for dialogue. These corrections were necessary, but some people went to the other extreme. Respect and dialogue do not imply that all religions are equivalent when it comes to knowing and serving God.

2.2.3 John 1:9

Here I want to focus on the remarkable word order in John 1:9, which states literally: the true light "lightens every person coming into the world" (Gk. *phōtizei panta anthrōpon erchomenon eis ton kosmon*). This word order has drawn the attention of many expositors because it seems as if the apostle wished to say that the divine Light gives light to every person *who is* (or, *when*) coming into the world. According to some, this would mean: in their mother's womb, or at the time of birth.[15] There are remarkable rabbinical parallels, such as: "You give light . . . to all who come into the world,"[16] and the Talmudic

---

12. See Hick (2004); Hick and Knitter (2005); cf. Berkhof (1986, 50); Van Genderen (2008, 49–52).
13. Rahner (1966, 5:115–32).
14. Wentsel (1982, 62).
15. See extensively, Ouweneel (2018f, §13.2.3).
16. Lev. Rabbah 31.6.

statement that the child is illuminated by the Torah in their mother's womb.[17] Such statement would make general revelation more general than anything else: all humans would receive some divine revelation before they even beheld creation.

This coupling of the Greek participle *erchomenon* with the Greek noun *anthrōpon* goes back to Chrysostom, Euthymius, and the Vulgate (Lat. *quae inluminat omnem hominem venientem in mundum*); compare the KJV: ". . . which lighteth every man that cometh into the world." Theologian and philosopher Frank de Graaff believed that the text refers to the illumination of all humans in their mothers' wombs, and wished to derive from this the notion of the pre-existence of the human soul[18] — an idea that is foreign to the Jewish-Christian tradition, and instead goes back to Plato and certain pagan schools.

In my view, expositors such as Marcus Dods and Leon Morris rightly stated that the entire sense of John 1:1-14 goes against such an interpretation.[19] The apostle John attaches a special meaning to the description "coming into the world," which is reserved exclusively for Christ (6:14; 11:27; 16:28). Moreover, in a passage that culminates in the incarnation (v. 14) we would expect a statement about Christ's coming into the world rather than about any arbitrary person's coming into the world. Incidentally, even if the Greek participle *erchomenon* is connected with *anthrōpon*, we must not necessarily think here of a person's birth, nor of his time in his mother's womb, as if the enlightenment necessarily would have occurred *there*. In John's Gospel, "coming into the world" means taking one's place in the midst of the people (3:19; 9:39; 12:46-47; 16:28). However, certainly because of the parallel with "in the world" in verse 10, we must think here of the Light coming into the world, that is, Christ.

---

17. Niddah 30b.
18. De Graaff (1987, 134–35).
19. Dods (1979, 687); Morris (1971, 93–94).

Apart from the interpretations that I have just rejected, the statement of John 1:9 is certainly remarkable. Whether it occurs before or, as I prefer, after a person's birth, the Logos that came into the world "gives light to everyone" (ESV). Marcus Dods mentioned that this is the verse on which Quakers based their doctrine that God supplies every human with sufficient saving light;[20] the early Quaker Robert Barclay wrote, "This place doth so clearly favour us that by some it is called 'the Quakers' text,' for it doth evidently demonstrate our assertion."[21] This seems to me rather exaggerated because many expositors, including non-Quakers, do believe that in our cosmos there is sufficient saving light for every human.[22]

It is also fascinating that our verse, John 1:9, was adduced by the Greek church fathers as an argument for their thesis that the divine Logos had led the pagan philosophers (especially Socrates and Plato, also Aristotle) in their philosophical investigations.[23]

According to John 1:9, every human receives a certain amount of light from God, even if this would be nothing more than God's general revelation in his creational works. Romans 1:20 says that this testimony of God in creation is sufficient to leave every human without an excuse. The verse does not say that each person is effectually brought *into* the light (cf. John 3:19–20). In the narrower sense, however, the verse could mean that "every human who receives light," that is, "comes to knowledge of God," receives this light "through Christ alone."[24] However, I would rather take the verse literally: *every* human is given light, understanding this in the wider sense: every human (objectively) receives so much light as to be left without excuse; whether one (subjectively) admits

---

20. Dods (1979, 686).
21. Barclay (1827, Fifth/Sixth Proposition, §xxi).
22. See Ouweneel (2018f, §13.2.3).
23. E.g., Justin Martyr, *Dialogue with Trypho* 2; Clement of Alexandria, passim.
24. So Bouma (1927, 32).

this light into their heart is another matter.

John 1:9 does not necessarily mean, as has been presumed, that the pagan who does not know the gospel but does live after the coming of Christ, receives more light than the pagan who lived before this coming. The reason is that both have at their disposal the same light (a) of creation (Rom. 1:19-21), as well as (b) of their consciences (2:5-16). Not to mention (c) the Noahic tradition of divine judgment and grace, which after the Flood, no matter in what corrupted form, must have been passed on to all the nations by Noah's sons and their descendants.[25]

2.3 Revelation and the Fall

2.3.1 Various Opinions

Another one of the theological points of discussion that Heyns (§2.2.1) brought up only implicitly[26] concerns whether the distinction between general and special revelation is founded upon, or presupposes, the Fall. This has been debated many times.[27] It has often been asserted that the former revelation dates from before the Fall, whereas the latter revelation became necessary only after the Fall. Heyns believed the latter to be the case, and stood with this view in a well-established tradition. Abraham Kuyper referred to special revelation after the Fall as an "auxiliary Revelation," that is, an addition to general revelation that had become necessary through the Fall. He called it abnormal since it presupposes guilt and estrangement, and thus the necessity of forgiveness and atonement.[28]

My second witness is G. C. Berkouwer, who followed Kuyper's line: "In this distress of concealment, God reveals himself *anew* in a historical act of mercy, in the revelation of the enmity which he posits, and which is consequently an act

---

25. See Ouweneel (2000b, 37–53).
26. Heyns (1988, 7, 52).
27. Cf. Berkouwer (1955, 308–311, and references).
28. Kuyper (1898, 361).

of reconciliation."²⁹ And a little later:

> If, in this connection, we speak of *the* divine revelation, then we do this from the viewpoint of the blinding of the world and its falling away from God. In view of this guilt and "lostness," the church speaks of the new, special revelation of God. Most profoundly, the distinction between general and special revelation does not concern subtle speculation, but a confession of *separation* and *guilt*.³⁰

We must note here that neither Kuyper nor Berkouwer intends to separate general and special revelation. General revelation cannot, as Roman Catholic theology suggests, be a separate source of knowledge, on the basis of which reason, even apart from faith, could come to a certain, though incomplete, natural knowledge of God. However, by making special revelation to depend on the Fall, Berkouwer is forced to maintain the ancient theological duality of general and special revelation.

In this context, Jacob Kamphuis rejected every distinction between work- and word-revelation that is based upon the Fall.³¹ I agree with this rejection but not with the arguments that he adduced for it. Kamphuis pointed out that, also in Paradise, God revealed himself *both* in the works of his hands, visible to the newly created humans, *and* in his word, which was given to the first humans in order to make known to them God's commandments (Gen. 1:28; 2:16–17). Personally, I would rather say that the work-revelation, too, is in fact *word-revelation* because in it we "hear" God's creational and providential *word* (see the next chapter). The heavens "declare" and the sky "proclaims" (Ps. 19:1). The Son upholds all things through the *word* of his power (Heb. 1:3). Therefore, even before the Fall, God addressed the first humans *through his word* such that the distinction between, on the one hand,

---

29. Berkouwer (1955, 310).
30. Ibid., 310–311.
31. Kamphuis (1982, 15).

his creational and providential word and, on the other hand, his commanding word is only secondary.

2.3.2 No Connection with the Fall

My main objection to the argument of Kamphuis (see previous section) is that it seems far more obvious to assign God's words to Adam in Genesis 1–2 not to God's special revelation but to God's general revelation.[32] In fact, such a view emphasizes all the more clearly the incorrectness of a strict distinction, if not separation, between the word- and the work-revelation: the word-revelation is also work-revelation, and the work-revelation is also word-revelation, as we will see below. That is, God's words belong to his works, and conversely, in his work-revelation we hear his (creational and providential) word. Again, I basically agree with the conclusion of Kamphuis, but for different reasons.

Indeed, there is no such thing as some general (or work) revelation before the Fall, and some special (or word) revelation after the Fall, as I will further explain below. Already now, we may discern that such a distinction between the two kinds of revelation must be erroneous because it suggests that special revelation is not only an addition to, but also a *replacement* of general revelation. This can never be the case because, on the one hand, also after the Fall general revelation fully retains its character of *revelation*, through which people can arrive at a certain true knowledge of God if they are not too corrupted by evil (or rather, if the Holy Spirit intervenes).

On the other hand, strictly speaking, special revelation is not more accessible to natural humans than general revelation. Although is it *revelation*, the corruption of humanity through sin has closed people's eyes entirely to it (cf. Rom. 1:21, "although they knew God . . ., they became futile in their thinking"; Eph. 4:18, "darkened in their understanding, alienated from the life of God because of the ignorance that is in them, due to their hardness of heart"). People need the regen-

---

32. Cf. Troost (1978, 113).

eration and the illumination by the Holy Spirit to recognize *both* kinds of revelation as revelation, and to imbibe its contents, to grasp it, and to accept it as God's message to them.

Therefore, special revelation must never be set against general revelation because this would yield a scholastic or humanistic dualism. What we call special revelation is nothing but a further, post-Fall, development within the one and only revelation of God. God's revelation in Genesis 3 is a new phase after his revelation in Genesis 2, just as his revelations in, for instance, Genesis 9 or 12 are new phases in regard to his revelation in Genesis 3. Of course, I do not deny the catastrophic rupture that the Fall has brought about in human history.[33] I merely deny that this rupture has caused a dualism in the revelation of God. This will be elaborated in the next chapter.

2.4 General Revelation

2.4.1 Nine Characteristics

Our defense of speaking about twofold revelation can be made a lot more concrete by describing in some detail what this involves. Thus, precisely by clearly outlining special revelation, we can come to a sharper picture of what is involved in general revelation.[34] I will mention nine points, based principally on Psalm 19 and Romans 1-2 (see the elaboration of them in the following chapters of this book); in each case, I will identify certain schools or groups of people that deny the truth mentioned, thus indicating that, apparently, general revelation is not evident to all Christian or non-Christian thinkers.

(a) The *existence* of God: the first thing that the cosmos shows is God's mere "being there": "[W]hoever would draw near to God must believe that he exists [Gk. *estin*, "he is"] and that he rewards those who seek him" (Heb. 11:6). The Bible does not supply us with proofs for this existence of God — it simply takes this existence for granted. He is there right from

---

33. Cf. Ouweneel (2018l, chapters 8–10).
34. Cf. Demarest (1982, 227–62); Lewis and Demarest (1996, 1:72–75).

the start: "In the beginning, God created the heavens and the earth" (Gen. 1:1).

This is denied by atheists and doubted by agnostics.

(b) The *simplicity* of God, as expressed in the Belgic Confession (Art. 1): "We all believe in the heart and confess with the mouth that there is one only simple and spiritual Being, which we call God."[35] Here the word "simple" is not synonymous with "uncomplicated, plain, basic," or even "dull, feeble-minded," but with "uncompounded, single." This does not refer to the unity of the three divine persons but to God's being one, as Israel confesses every day in the *Shema: Shema, Yisrael,* YHWH *Eloheynu* YHWH *echad,* "Hear, Israel, the LORD our God, the LORD is one" (KJV: "The LORD our God is one LORD"; NABRE: "The LORD is our God, the LORD alone"; LEB: "Yahweh our God, Yahweh is unique"). There is only one like him, he is one of a kind. "You shall have no other gods before me" (Exod. 20:3). This is what God revealed on Mount Sinai; but it had already been embedded in his general revelation in nature. This is the argument that the apostle Paul used on the Areopagus: the obvious unity of the human race points to one divine origin (Acts 17:26).

This is denied by many polytheists, though we observe that some polytheists accept, in addition to many lower gods, the existence of one supreme god.[36] This provides a smooth transition to those monotheists—including Jews and Christians—who, in addition to the one God, accept the existence of "divine beings" ("sons" of God, celestial beings, angels; cf. Job 1:6; 2:1; 38:7; also see Gen. 6:4).

(c) God is the *source of life and blessing*: it belongs to the common experiences and convictions of very different cultures that the single or supreme deity is a source of life and blessing for humanity (Acts 17:25, 28), the God who gives to humanity "rains from heaven and fruitful seasons" (14:17;

---

35. *RC* 2:475.
36. So, e.g., Celsus, as we know him from Origen, *Contra Celsum*.

here, too, Paul addressed pagans, among whom he could appeal to generally current insights). With King Belshazzar, Daniel could declare that the king's breath was in God's hand (Dan. 5:23). This awareness seems to be deeply anchored within natural humans; Friedrich Schleiermacher spoke in this connection of humanity's feeling of absolute dependence (Ger. *schlechthinnige Abhängigkeit*).[37]

This is denied by deists, who believe that God created the universe but after this work of creation is no longer concerned with it.

(d) Pagans may quarrel about the degree to which God is transcendent or immanent (cf. pantheism, which equates the divine and the cosmic), but nobody denies that God engages in a certain measure of *activity* within the human world (cf. again Dan. 5:21-23; Acts 14:17; 17:24-28). Thus, the eternal God (Deut. 33:27; Isa. 40:28 CEV; Rom. 16:26; cf. Ps. 90:2 NET; 93:2 NOG) is the God of *history*. In the decline of decadent cultures and nations, pagans have always seen the avenging hand of the deity or the gods (cf. point [h]). The apostle Paul appealed to a universal awareness when he warned about "a day on which he [i.e., God] will judge the world in righteousness" (Acts 17:31).

This too is denied by deists, as well as by all kinds of liberal theologians, who do not believe in such a future judgment of God.

(e) God is necessarily *autonomous*; how else could he have existed before he had called into existence any creature? Compare again Acts 17:25, where Paul says that God is not "served by human hands, as though he needed anything, since he himself gives to all mankind life and breath and everything." Therefore, it is part of God's nature that he is unlimited in *power*; Romans 1:20 says that pagans have "clearly perceived" God's "eternal power" "in the things that have been made." The notion of such power is expressed in theological terms

---

37. Schleiermacher (1928).

such as omnipotence and sovereignty.

By making God too dependent on humans, open theism[38] is in danger of diminishing the truth concerning God's autonomy and omnipotence.

(f) God is *invisible*, that is, he cannot (normally) be perceived with created eyes; Romans 1:20 therefore speaks (literally) of "his invisible things" (Gk. *ta aorata autou*; cf. KJV); God is the "invisible" God (Col. 1:15; 1 Tim. 1:17; Heb. 11:27; cf. Exod. 33:20; 1 Tim. 6:16).

Nonetheless, pagans have attempted repeatedly to depict the single or supreme deity, or more broadly to incorporate him into the empirical reality, e.g., by worshiping him "in" his creatures (cf. Rom. 1:23). This is one reason why God forbade his people to make any kind of images or representations of God, and to venerate these (Exod. 20:4-6).

(g) Similarly, the *order*, *regularity*, and *rationality* of the cosmos point to the rationality of God himself (regarding the *logos* in the cosmos, and the corresponding *logos* of God, see §3.6.2; cf. Rom. 1:20 OJB, God's "invisible characteristics ... are *perceived intellectually* [Gk. *nooumena kathoratai*] in the things which have been created").

Some schools, like some animists, have denied this rationality of God, and have equated the divine with the capricious, the incalculable.[39]

(h) In general, partly due to their innate conscience, pagans did not wish to deny that the single or supreme deity is *righteous*, and thus is the norm of all righteousness (cf. Rom. 1:32, "they know God's righteous decree"; 2:14-15, "when Gentiles ... by nature do what the law requires, they are a law to themselves. ... They show that the work of the law is written on their hearts, while their conscience also bears witness"). In addition to general revelation in nature, that is, *outside* humans, one might call this divine revelation *within*

---

38. See Ouweneel (2018d, §1.3.2 and chapter 4).
39. Cf. extensively, Jaki (1974; 1978).

human nature: the innate normative awareness points to a Norm-giver, who at the same time is Judge over normative as well as anti-normative behavior. German philosopher Immanuel Kant made the *Sollen* ("thou shalt") and *Pflicht* (the human sense of duty) the cornerstone of his entire ethics.[40]

This did not keep pagans from an often extremely dissolute way of life, though (cf. Rom. 1:24–32; Eph. 4:17–19; 1 Pet. 4:3–4). The awareness of righteousness is counterbalanced by lives in unrighteousness because of the sinful nature that is in them.

(i) It has always been obvious to pagans that the single or supreme deity was worthy of their *worship* (cf. Acts 17:23). Each religion knows its own form of worship (cultic customs).

Again, this did not keep pagans from withholding this worship from the deity because of their sinful nature (cf. Rom. 1:21, "although they knew God, they did not honor him as God or give thanks to him"). That is, the *outward* rites and ceremonies may be maintained, whereas the hearts are far removed from God (cf., even among Israel, Mal. 1:8, "'When you offer blind animals in sacrifice, is that not evil? And when you offer those that are lame or sick, is that not evil? Present that to your governor; will he accept you or show you favor?' says the LORD of hosts").

2.4.2 Theism and the Zodiac

The entire enumeration we have just provided involves nothing else than the sole deity (or, for many pagans, the supreme deity in addition to and beyond many other gods) and his attributes.[41] We are dealing here with what is called *(mono)theism*: the belief in the one God (*contra* polytheism), the personal God (*contra* animism), who is benevolent toward humans and is worshiped by humans, who transcends the world, which is his own creation (*contra* pantheism), and who at the same time is continually concerned with it (*contra* deism).

---

40. Kant (1997).
41. See extensively, Ouweneel (2018b).

These attributes are very important. But it is also important to emphasize what they do *not* involve. In them, we hear nothing about the predicament of humanity, and about redemption and reconciliation, God's means of restoration. Nor do we hear about God's great projects: God's covenant, God's kingdom, and God's church.[42] Indeed, the Bible speaks of a covenant in which the celestial bodies are involved (Jer. 33:25), but this hardly compares with the covenants that God made with people. The Noahic covenant does encompass the entire creation, and the rainbow is the sign of that covenant (Gen. 9:1-17), but this could never be recognized as a sign apart from special revelation. As far as the kingdom is concerned, there is God's general rule over all the things he created (cf. Exod. 15:18; Ps. 93:1; 96:10; 99:1). But again, the true nature of this can hardly be grasped apart from special revelation. In the case of the church project, the need for special revelation is even stronger (cf. Eph. 3:4-5; Col. 1:24-27).

Incidentally, the question arises here whether it is true that the story of redemption can be read in the signs of the Zodiac, as has been asserted.[43] Not only are the claims that have been made in this respect highly speculative, but we can also adduce against them some basic objections. Genesis 1:14-18 speak of the "greater light" (the sun) and the "lesser light" (the moon) and the stars as "signs," but signs with agricultural, not redemptive-historical, significance. This is particularly true for the sun and the moon, by which months and seasons are determined, and in this way also fertile and non-fertile seasons. However, some stars are significant, too, namely, those that are visible in some seasons and not in others; I mention only the significance of the star Sirius in the constellation Canis Maior (Greater Dog) (the so-called heliacal rising of Sirius marked the flooding of the Nile in ancient Egypt). The

---

42. See, respectively, Ouweneel (2018b; 2018j; 2010a; 2010b).
43. See especially Seiss (1972); Bullinger (1984); and many popular publications based on them.

A Twofold Revelation

wish to perceive in certain constellations the biblical story of redemption has more to do with pious imagination than with thorough historical and religious-scientific arguments.

There is more paganism than Christian gospel in the Zodiac.[44] Astrology sees an age-old connection between Core, the "wheat virgin," and the star Spica (= "ear [of wheat]"), the main star in the Zodiac sign *Virgo* ("Virgin"). It seems that the *Notre Dame* ("Our Lady," the Madonna), the cathedral of Paris (France), was constructed such that it is oriented toward this constellation. One of its windows shows that, in former ages, the goddess of fertility was worshiped here. *Virgo* represented in Babylon the "Celestial Virgin," Ishtar, the main goddess. It may be that such interpretations of the Zodiac go back to the earliest revelation of God, as given to Noah and his sons, and that knowledge of this revelation was distorted in an idolatrous way by pagans.

The opposite process was Christianizing these pagan ideas. Thus, here and there on the French countryside, the Madonna is still venerated as the "Ear Mother" or "Wheat Mother," just as many ancient pagan religions presented their main goddess as the goddess with the ear of wheat. On the right Bernward door of the cathedral of Hildesheim (Germany), the Madonna is depicted with the ear—a totally unbiblical image.[45] The reason is clear: this Madonna is the Christianized representation of the Babylonian goddess Ishtar and the Egyptian goddess Isis.

What was the principal process here: Christianizing a pagan fertility goddess with an ear of wheat, *or* is this goddess herself nothing but the paganized representation of the woman of Genesis 3:15, the memory of which was transmitted by Noah and his descendants? Even if the latter is the case, this is still far removed from reading the Christian gospel into the Zodiac.

---

44. See Ouweneel (1998, 139, 309), and references there.
45. https://core.ac.uk/download/pdf/10695304.pdf p. 268 shows a picture with the Madonna holding a scepter in the form of an ear of wheat (as explained on p. 56).

2.5 General Versus Special Revelation

2.5.1 Overlap

A summary of special generation is basically identical with a summary of the contents of Holy Scripture, and of course, this is not our task right now. However, it makes sense to try to determine the boundary between general and special revelation a little more precisely, that is, to investigate what belongs to each kind of revelation. All things mentioned in §2.4 are also part of special revelation, whereas, conversely, many things that belong to special revelation definitely do not belong to general revelation. Here, we remember the claim of Peter Abelard (§1.1.2) that, in principle, the doctrine of the Trinity could be derived exclusively by means of logical arguments, that is, without any knowledge of Scripture. Is this correct?

I think there is a modicum of truth in this view. For instance, quite apart from the biblical revelation, we take it for granted that there is a certain connection between Creator and creature, and that, if humans know love, the Creator himself must be a God of love. We could not possibly imagine that things would be different. However, what does it mean that God is love (1 John 4:8, 16)? Did he *become* love only when he had created beings whom he could begin to love? Did he, at that moment, turn himself into a God of love? And how could he at all create loving creatures if he himself had not been love beforehand? No, it could not be otherwise: from eternity, God has been a God of love. If he created beings "after his likeness," this also included the fact that, if God is love, these beings could give and receive love as well.

However, there is a new problem here: how meaningful is it to speak of a God of love in past eternity when there was yet no person to whom God could show his love? Was this love only his *self*-love? Would the Bible speak with such joy and gratitude about God's love if the eternal basis for this was primarily *self*-love? The only conceivable reply seems to be that it makes sense to speak about a God of love in past eternity only if God is several persons, *each of whom* loves the *other* (cf. John 17:24c, the Father loved the Son before the foundation of the world). Apart from whether their number should be exactly three, these considerations do lead to the kernel of the doctrine of the Trinity. In this sense, one might venture the claim that the doctrine of the Trinity also belongs to general revelation because a God of love is inconceivable without him being a plurality of persons loving each other. At the same time, we may wonder, of course, if we would have ever come to this line of reasoning without knowledge of the Trinity from special revelation. The argument mentioned has some apologetic force, for instance in witnessing to Jews and Muslims, who also believe in a God of love. But we should not overestimate its force.

Another example, of many, is the doctrine of the resurrection. We know about it from the Old Testament, and much more from the New Testament, and wonder if we would have ever known of it if we had not possessed special revelation. At the same time, we notice that many religions and cultures have a certain awareness of resurrection, that is, of new life from death, or new life through and beyond death. Particularly in the alternation of the seasons in the more temperate zones of the world, many nations have experienced the continual transition from life to death (autumn) as well as from death to life (spring): "Look at the fig tree, and all the trees. As soon as they come out in leaf, you see for yourselves and know that the summer is already near. So also, when you see these things taking place, you know that the kingdom of God is near" (Luke 21:29-31). The awareness of this alternation is rather strong in the Jewish festivals: the Jewish religious year begins in the month of spring, the month Abib (Exod. 12:2; 13:4; 23:15; 34:18; Lev. 23:5; Deut. 16:1),[46] that is, the month

---

46. Cf. Ezek. 3:15 about the Babylonian *Tel-abib* ("hill of the maturing ears"), which gave its name to the Israeli city of Tel Aviv.

of the "maturing ears"[47] (the month of the "resurrection" of buried seeds, as people experienced it; cf. John 12:24; 1 Cor. 15:36).[48] The three pilgrim festivals of Israel (cf. Deut. 16:16) were harvest festivals (cf. Exod. 23:16; 34:22): the Passover (the festival of the barley harvest), the Feast of Weeks (the festival of the wheat harvest), and the Feast of Booths (the harvest festival of the olives and the grapes).

Other metaphors from daily life that were viewed as hints of death and resurrection were sunrise and sunset, and people's falling asleep and waking up. Compare "falling asleep" in the sense of dying (Matt. 27:52; John 11:11; 1 Cor. 15:6, 18, 20 etc.), and "awakening" in the sense of a (literal or figurative) becoming alive (Isa. 26:19; Dan. 12:2; Eph. 5:14). Thus, in many ways, people experienced the "dying" and "reviving" of nature. Those pagans who did not burn their dead ones but buried them—often even with tomb gifts—expected them to become alive again one day. Here again, one might argue that the awareness of the resurrection does not belong to special revelation but rather to general revelation.

2.5.2 On the Boundary

Given the considerations in the previous section, we see how we are moving here along the interface between general and special revelation. We are dealing here with a boundary that can hardly be sharply drawn because—knowing general revelation too well—we can no longer ascertain what, on the basis exclusively of general revelation, we could have known of God and divine things. However, a rule of thumb might be that everything that pagans have come to believe (in whatever distorted form), and that is also accepted by Christians on the basis of Scripture, in a certain sense may be assigned to general revelation. We have seen that this contains much

---

47. Cf. Exod. 9:31, "the barley was *abib*," that is, "in the ear."
48. Also the ancient Roman year began with the month of spring, March (therefore, February has only 28 days; this is what was left of the 365 days; "September" until "December" literally means the "seventh" until the "tenth" month).

more than God's "eternal power and divinity" (Rom. 1:20 WEB): without special revelation, the pagan is supposed to be aware of a God who is not only Creator but also Law-Giver; not only Law-Giver but also Judge. Pagans were even familiar with the meaning of a vicarious sacrifice in order to turn away the vengeance of the deity, though usually in a primitive and distorted form.[49]

In this way we find that not everything in special revelation is entirely new to the pagan; but what the pagan does know is one-sided and distorted knowledge. Such "knowledge" is basically rather the "ignorance that is in them" because their hearts have not been led by it to a relationship with the true God (Eph. 4:18). Special revelation puts all this alleged knowledge in its right form and in the right perspective. With special revelation there is no more "groping" in darkness (Acts 17:27 NKJV) but there is a having found, a knowing. Here is no more futility of the mind, no more darkening of understanding (Eph. 4:17–18) but believers now have the eyes of their hearts enlightened (1:18). And in particular: whatever humans by nature know through general revelation is, as we saw, suppressed by them in their wickedness (Rom. 1:18 CJB). But when, by the power of God's Spirit, special revelation enters their hearts and they live in its grip, they will be set free by the truth (John 8:32).

This does not mean that people without (the knowledge of) special revelation are necessarily lost.[50] I have dealt extensively with this matter of exclusivism *versus* inclusivism in another volume,[51] defending the thesis that salvation is universally available, also for those who never get a chance to hear the gospel. This means that, in principle, they can be saved if they respond in faith to the revelation that they do have, even if this is no more than general revelation. The apostle Paul

---

49. Cf. Ouweneel (2018f, §§9.3–9.4).
50. Contra Lewis and Demarest (1996, 95).
51. See Ouweneel (2018f, §13.3); for the various views, see extensively, Okholm and Phillips (1995); Fackre et al. (1995).

says explicitly that God "will render to each one according to his works: to those who by patience in well-doing seek for glory and honor and immortality, he will give eternal life.... There will be ... glory and honor and peace for everyone who does good, the Jew first and also the Greek. For God shows no partiality" (Rom. 2:6-11; also see vv. 12-16). However, in light of the New Testament's entire teaching we must make the following comments.

(a) The salvation of any person is found in Christ alone and in his sacrifice, even if a person has never heard of him: "[T]here is salvation in no one else, for there is no other name under heaven given among men [and women] by which we must be saved" (Acts 4:12). "[T]here is [only] one mediator between God and men, the man Christ Jesus" (1 Tim. 2:5).

(b) The salvation of any person is accomplished by the Holy Spirit. Rebirth is "(out) of the Spirit" (John 3:5), the renewal of a person is "of the Holy Spirit" (Titus 3:5; cf. Rom. 7:6). "It is the Spirit who gives life" (John 6:63; cf. Eph. 2:5; Col. 2:13).

(c) The salvation of any person is conditional upon personal humbling, repentance, and confession of sins: all such persons "should repent and turn to God, performing deeds in keeping with their repentance" (Acts 26:20). "If we confess our sins, he is faithful and just to forgive us our sins and to cleanse us from all unrighteousness" (1 John 1:9).

In principle, the crucified Christ draws *all* people to himself (John 12:32). "Therefore, as one trespass led to condemnation for all men, so one act of righteousness leads to justification and life *for all men*" (Rom. 5:18). "God our Savior ... desires *all people* to be saved and to come to the knowledge of the truth" (1 Tim. 2:3-4). "For the grace of God has appeared, bringing salvation *for all people*" (Titus 2:11). "The Lord is ... patient toward you, not wishing that any should perish, but that *all* should reach repentance" (2 Pet. 3:9). Please note that these passages do *not* teach that all people are indeed effectually saved. But they do teach that God has brought about a salvation that is intended for all people. Whether they repent and accept this salvation in faith is another matter.

2.5.3 Practical Significance

It is of great practical significance to try to map out the boundaries of general revelation because this revelation offers a universal foundation for interpersonal and intercultural communication.[52]

(a) *Shared stewardship.* If God is the Creator of the world and the Source of all life, blessing, fertility, and so on, this implies the shared responsibility of all humanity to be good stewards of this created reality: to be good to fellow humans, but also to plants and animals, to protect life that is vulnerable, not to pollute air and water unnecessarily, not to waste the natural resources of humanity, to create optimal conditions under which individuals and nations can flourish.

(b) *Shared rationality.* Thomas Aquinas emphasized that Christians, Jews, and Muslims can enter into dialogue with each other on the basis of the capacity for reason that the Creator has granted to all of them. As a consequence, people of very different backgrounds are able to understand each other to some extent. In the vertical dimension, human understanding has been darkened by sin (Eph. 4:18) but when it comes to the horizontal structure of the human mind, all humanity acknowledges in principle the same arithmetic and spatial, kinematic and energetic, biotic, perceptive and sensitive, logical and historical, lingual and social, economic and aesthetic, juridical and ethical, and even pistical laws. On the basis of these laws, people of very different religious and cultural backgrounds can, for instance, do science together, but also make political treaties, or have political, ideological, and cultural conversations.

---

52. See extensively, Lewis and Demarest (1996, 82–90). Cf. also what I have said elsewhere about God's common grace (Ouweneel [2008, 244; 2018d, §§1.8 and 2.4.2]).

(c) *Shared morality.* As the apostle Paul says, "[W]hen Gentiles, who do not have the law, by nature do what the law requires, they are a law to themselves, even though they do not have the law. They show that the work of the law is written on their hearts, while their conscience also bears witness, and their conflicting thoughts accuse or even excuse them" (Rom. 2:14-15). The Ten Commandments, especially the last six of them, referring to the relationship with the neighbor, entail a certain universal code that is proper to all eternity.[53] To all people, one can appeal to a common sense of justice, a universal awareness of righteousness, as expressed, for instance, in Psalm 15:2-5: the righteous one (Heb. *tsaddiq*) is the one "who walks blamelessly and does what is right and speaks truth in his heart; who does not slander with his tongue and does no evil to his neighbor, nor takes up a reproach against his friend; in whose eyes a vile person is despised, but who honors those who fear the LORD; who swears to his own hurt and does not change; who does not put out his money at interest and does not take a bribe against the innocent" (see also Isa. 33:14-15). Because of this common sense of justice, all more or less civilized countries have an impartial judicial system and a moral education, taught both at home and in schools, based on similar moral principles.

(d) *Shared responsibility toward God.* Our shared responsibility toward creation (point a) and our shared rationality and morality (points b and c) imply a foundation for apologetics and for missionary activity. The gospel never appears out of the blue; it always necessarily ties in with what people know—in whatever elementary way—about creation, about justice, about morality, about God. Those wishing to practice effective apologetics and effective missiology will not pursue these activities apart from what people already know, or think they know, but will place themselves alongside their listeners

---

53. See, e.g., the striking similarities between the Ten Commandments and the Code of the Babylonian king Hammurabi (about 1700 BC?); see Driver and Miles (2007).

on the shared foundation of God's general revelation. This is the attitude that the apostle Paul took in his preaching in Acts 14 and 17, and also in Romans 1-2. Everything that we proclaim to people concerning God's *special* revelation is rooted in what people know, or could have known, on the basis of God's *general* revelation. In other words, no proper bibliology (doctrine of Scripture) can do without a proper assessment of the place and nature of this general revelation.

2.6 The Underlying Dualism Exposed

2.6.1 The Church and State Dualism

It is very important that we now endeavor to obtain deeper insight in the exact relationship between God's word- and work-revelation, as they have been called. In my opinion, this can be done in a responsible way only if we realize that a discussion of this matter always presupposes, implicitly or explicitly, a certain cosmological view of the created reality. No matter how Scriptural a certain theological view of God's work-revelation may seem to be—for instance, because of all the Bible verses that are quoted in it—unfortunately it may still be rooted in a (partly) pagan cosmology. Especially when theology is insufficiently aware of its cosmological ground-questions, as has so often been the case, it can easily fall into the snare of a view of creation colored by pagan cosmology.

By far the most important of such pagan influences that burden theological investigation of divine revelation sprouts from the scholastic dualism of nature and grace (or supernature).[54] Historian T. Holland implicitly indicated that this scholastic dualism, especially in the form of the separation between the church and the supposedly neutral state, arose first not in the thirteenth century but in the eleventh century.[55] In this century, the papacy became steadily stronger, and in the so-called investiture battle got into a heavy conflict with

---

54. Cf. Troost (1978); Ouweneel (2008, 128-31).
55. Holland (2009, see the Preface).

the Holy Roman emperor. This conflict came to an end only when bishop Ivo of Chartres introduced the distinction between secular and spiritual rule. In pre-Napoleonic times, a prince-bishop, such as the one of the Swiss city of Basel, the German cities of Köln or Münster, the Austrian city of Salzburg, or the Dutch city of Utrecht, was a secular prince over his diocese as well as the spiritual leader of the (Roman Catholic) church in his territory. In 1122, a compromise was reached, which was called the Concordat of Worms: henceforth, new bishops would receive their spiritual office from the pope, and any secular tasks from the emperor.

This has been a decision of enormous historical significance. To a certain extent, the familiar separation between church and state was born here, which was formally codified in the constitutions of Western countries only in recent centuries. In this way, the scholastic dualism of nature (including the state) and supernature (including the church) received its solid cultural-historical foundation, which it still possesses, for instance, in North American two-kingdom theology. Elsewhere, I have endeavored to thoroughly combat and refute this devastating theology.[56]

2.6.2 The General/Special Revelation Dualism

In scholastic dualism, general revelation belongs to the "lower level" of nature, the domain of God's mediate acting, and special revelation belongs to the "upper level" of grace, the domain of God's immediate acting. Not only in Roman Catholic but also in Protestant theology, this scholastic dualism obtained a strong foothold almost from the beginning. Theologians have often been conscious of this dualism, and often tried to eliminate it. This was done, for instance, either by enclosing nature eschatologically in grace (Karl Barth; see §2.8), or, conversely, by enclosing grace in nature by dismissing special revelation as a form of supernaturalism and metaphysics (thus many liberal theologians).

---

56. Ouweneel (2017).

Usually, such futile attempts did and do presuppose the nature-grace dualism itself. It is so profoundly embedded in our Western culture that thinkers cannot dispense with it. They cannot transcend it because (a) it is in their Western DNA, and (b) they are unaware of a viable Christian alternative. To a large extent, since the Middle Ages the history of theology and of theoretical thinking in general is the story of repeated swings between the poles of nature and grace (supernature), often rigidly bound together in a dialectical synthesis. At certain times the pole of the natural, at other times the pole of the supernatural was emphasized, and the reactions that inevitably followed were dismissed as irrelevant.

A more balanced view, more in the spirit of Scripture, involves much more than some vague talking about a harmony between nature and grace (supernature), or about a harmony in the testimony of Scripture concerning the word- and work-revelation, as we find, for instance, with G. C. Berkouwer.[57] Andree Troost[58] pointed to the insecure way in which Berkouwer spoke about the matter by saying sometimes that word- and work-revelation are not,[59] and at other times that they are, independent.[60] In itself, it is correct, as Berkouwer pointed out, that we should not embark upon a theological quest for a unity in God's revelational acting such that we "go beyond faith in making a comprehensible rational synthesis."[61] However, this does not mean that any synthesis concerning God's revelation is impossible. In fact, *as long as this synthesis is not viewed on the rational level,* or as reaching out "beyond faith" (in whatever sense of this description), a synthesis would be possible. What is theologically distinguished as word- and work-revelation should find its unity not "beyond faith" but *in* faith in the ultimate religious sense of the

---

57. Berkouwer (1955, 316).
58. Troost (1978, 107; cf. also 121).
59. Berkouwer (1955, 306–308).
60. Ibid., 313.
61. Ibid., 308.

term. It is our *transcendent* faith that surpasses reason as one of the immanent functions of the transcendent believing heart and that, in this way, transcends also all theological problems.

2.7 Coherence and Unity

2.7.1 Work-Revelation Is Also Word-Revelation

In the present discussion, we would make a lot more progress if we began emphasizing the inner coherence and unity of the whole of God's revelation, namely, in their common origin and bearing. The work- and the word-revelation are basically one single revelation for the following primary reasons (see this and the next section).[62]

(1) The entire creation, which is also God's *work*, is nothing other than the embodiment of God's *Word*: God creates through his word. Recall the phrase used ten times in Genesis 1, "And God said." "By the word of the LORD the heavens were made" (Ps. 33:6; cf. v. 9); all things were made through the Word (John 1:1–3); God calls into existence the things that do not (yet) exist (Rom. 4:17b). That is, within time, the eternal Word of God received shape in God's creation in all its various aspects; this took place "in" Christ, who in person is the Word (*Logos*) of God and the Root of creation.

Two notes are pertinent here. First, the term "embodiment" is not ideal because it might be taken in the sense of emanation (an issuing from God's being), or a pantheistic deification of God's works. Perhaps the word "manifestation" would be more prudent. However, I am calling to mind the Greek term *morphōsis*, "(outer) form," "formulation," "embodiment," namely "of knowledge and truth," "embodied" in the law (Rom. 2:20).[63]

Second, Christ is the Root of creation, not in the sense of Romans 15:12 and Revelation 5:5; 22:16 ("root of Jesse/David"), where "root" is actually "sprout" (AMPC), "descendant" (GNT). Rather, Christ is the Root in the sense of Colossians

---

62. Cf. Troost (1978, 122–26; 2004, 272–73, 325–26).
63. Cf. Danker (2000, s.v. *morphōsis*): Ger. *Verkörperung*, "embodiment."

A *Twofold Revelation*

1:16-17: all things have been created "in him," "through him and for him"; all creation is rooted in him. In this regard, Andree Troost wrote important things about the conspicuous *absence*, in the Belgic Confession, Article 2, of this notion of the creation occurring "in Christ."[64] He said in strong language (in a heading): "Confess this article of faith in the church, but combat it as theology."[65]

Ultimately, work-revelation, which is so carefully distinguished from word-revelation, is in fact itself *word-revelation*, namely, revelation in the form of God's creational word in Christ. He spoke, and it came to be (Ps. 33:9), and God still speaks *through* this word (Ps. 19:1). In creation, we hear the "wordless" Word of God (vv. 3-4). God the Son "upholds" this world by the continual *word* op his power (Heb. 1:3) as a continually commanding Master (Job 38:11-12, 34 "said . . . commanded . . . lift up your voice"; Ps. 104:7 "rebuke"). In this sense, God's creational word is always *actual* (Lat. *actus*, "act, action"); that is, God's (creational and providential) words and his (creational and providential) acts coincide. God's word is act, and his act is word. This corresponds with the fact that Hebrew *davar* means both "word" and "thing, matter," sometimes with the meaning "act."[66] The Greek *logos*, "word," can also sometimes mean "thing, matter" in the sense of "act" (e.g., Acts 8:21; 15:6). The distinction between word and work fails because the sharp distinction between word and work cannot be biblically maintained.

Therefore, Andree Troost wrote with reference to Gerhard von Rad,

> God's words are working words, creating words, words with effect in history. God calls into existence [Rom. 4:17], he sends forth his breath [Ps. 104:30 CJB], and it becomes spring, and con-

---

64. Troost (2004, 225–26 [with reference to Van Kooten (2002)], 272–73, 325–26, 330–34; cf. 437–39).
65. Ibid., 273.
66. See Van Gemeren (1996, 1:912–15).

versely: his acts are eloquent ["well-speaking," from Lat. *loquor*, "to speak"]. So eloquently that they are sometimes understood by pagans. Also outside Israel, people often feared the threats or the acts of that mighty God of Israel [e.g., Exod. 15:14–16; Judg. 7:14; 1 Sam. 4:6–8; Ps. 99:1].

Also from Genesis 1 we know that God spoke to Adam. There was the personal encounter and the address. Therefore, there is not a single reason to characterize the so-called twofold revelation of God as work- and word-revelation. To faith, the inner unity of what God spoke in creating, what he keeps speaking in upholding, and what he said to Adam in addressing him, is *a priori* the one, reliable Truth of God, which addresses humans in their total humanity.[67]

2.7.2 Word-Revelation Is Also Work-Revelation

(2) Just as the creation is not only work-revelation but also word-revelation, conversely, Scripture is not only word-revelation but also work-revelation. It is a work of God, just as much as nature and the cosmos are his works. Indeed, in Scripture we are dealing with the *un*created, eternal Word of God, which, however, within the immanent-empirical creational reality, has received shape in human writing, in human language, in a human book. As such, the Word of God, in the form of Scripture, has participated in creation, that is, in the works of God in Christ. Of course, among all these works, Scripture does assume an exceptional position. In the words of Andree Troost: within the unity of God's creational revelation, Scripture constitutes the "radiating and guiding *center*" of this revelation.[68]

The eternal Word, as being "with the Father" (cf. John 1:1–2; 1 John 1:1–2), is not revelation, at least not to humanity. The Word *became* revelation[69] the moment it entered into, or took

---

67. Troost (1978, 122–23).
68. Troost (1978, 121); Dutch: *stralend en richtingwijzend centrum*.
69. Other than in appearances of the pre-incarnate Christ, e.g., as the Angel of the LORD; see Ouweneel (2008, chapter 5; 2018b).

A Twofold Revelation

part (participated), in creational reality. It did so, on the one hand, in the incarnation of the Word in Christ, and on the other hand, in the inscripturation of the Word in Scripture (for this parallel, see §5.3). As far as this immanent creational form of the Word is concerned, it is nothing but part of general or creational revelation. Word- and work-revelation are one, just as God's Word and God's work are one.

Thus, word-revelation itself is actually *creational* revelation in the sense that God's eternal, transcendent Word comes to humanity in an inscripturated, immanent form, in the temporal shape of a divine work of creation. In no way may we drive some scholastic-dualistic wedge, or any other kind of wedge, between word- and work-revelation. This is the very reason why, as I have argued elsewhere,[70] there can be no room for a fundamental separation between theology (the supposed science of the word-revelation) and the other disciplines (the supposed sciences of the work-revelation).[71] Theology, too, focuses on God's *creational* revelation, of which Scripture forms the center. The *entire* revelation of God is theology's study field, though viewed from its own specific modal viewpoint: theology studies reality from the viewpoint of the pistical (or faith) modality. Thus, again, the *entire* revelation of God, including Scripture, is the study field of the other disciplines, though always viewed from their own respective specific modal viewpoints: the physical aspect in physics, the biotic aspect in biology, the lingual aspect in linguistics, the social aspect in sociology, the moral aspect in ethics, and so forth.[72]

Thus, *all* disciplines (special sciences) are focused upon the *entire* revelation of God, including Scripture, in such a way, however, that each discipline has its own modal viewpoint. Theology does not simply study the Bible, but the content of the Bible viewed according to its pistical aspect. The-

---

70. Ouweneel (1995, §3.2).

71. This is a vital point in the argument of Ouweneel (2017).

72. See extensively, Ouweneel (1995), and the next volume in this series.

ology is also interested in the rest of God's created reality, but always as viewed according to its pistical aspect. In other words, in principle theology is interested in *all* pistical phenomena, within and beyond Scripture. So, too, the biologist, the historian, the economist, the art historian, or the ethicist can be interested in the Bible, namely, in the biotic, historical, economic, aesthetic, and moral aspects, respectively, of its content. At the same time, we must always maintain the exceptional position of Scripture in the whole of God's revelation. "[I]n your light do we see light" (Ps. 36:9). In the light of Scripture we receive light over all the rest of God's creational revelation. The Bible is the spotlight, in whose light alone the entire the creational revelation can be genuinely understood. Only in *its* light is everything in God's word-/work-revelation genuinely recognized as *revelation*.

2.7.3 Summary

By way of summary, we may conclude that various traditional views concerning the twofold divine revelation are rather unsatisfactory.

(a) Strictly speaking, the terms word-revelation and work-revelation are rather unclear. In all its parts and aspects, word-revelation is necessarily work-revelation, and the reverse is equally true.

(b) The distinction between God's creational and God's scriptural revelation is not satisfactory, either, because it overlooks the fact that Scripture, as the immanent, temporal form of the transcendent, eternal Word, fully participates in creational reality. Thus, scriptural revelation is creational revelation, although in this case we cannot claim the opposite: God's revelation in nature is not scriptural in the sense that it has the character of written Word of God. I say this in spite of the elegant, but entirely metaphorical, statement of the Belgic Confession, Article 2: God's creation, preservation, and government of the universe "is before our eyes as a most elegant book, wherein all creatures, great and small, are as so many characters leading us to 'see clearly the invisible things of God, ...'"[73]

(c) In the rest of this book, I will keep using the undoubtedly handy and well-established terms "general" and "special revelation." This is not necessarily a problem as long as we maintain that the so-called "special" revelation does not constitute a "special" act of God, distinct from and "added" to his previous, more "general" revelation, allegedly because this would have become necessary after the Fall. From the very first, God addressed humanity on the basis of a relationship of fellowship, also before the Fall. Here, it does not make any fundamental difference that God's words to pre-Fall humanity were not, and his words to post-Fall humanity were, scripturally recorded.

(d) The traditional distinction between the book of Scripture and the book of Nature is not entirely satisfactory. If the word "nature" is taken here in a narrower sense, it would wrongly exclude culture and history as modes of God's revelation. If the word "nature" is taken in the wider sense of "creational reality," it is no longer distinct from Scripture since, as we saw, the latter belongs to God's creational works as well. As a (practical) *confession*, like the Belgic Confession—that is, not as a theological *theory* about the precise relationship between the two—the distinction is acceptable as long as the "book of Nature" is understood as encompassing the entire immanent, empirical creational reality outside Scripture. Incidentally, the Belgic Confession, Article 2, does not necessarily create a contrast between the two revelational categories (nature and Scripture) but speaks of the creation and preservation of the entire world from a redemptive-historical point of view.

---

73. *RC* 2:425.

2.8 Three Views: Karl Barth

2.8.1 Rejection of the General Revelation

G. C. Berkouwer extensively discussed the views of Karl Barth concerning divine revelation,[74] and spoke of an offensive campaign by Barth against natural theology. This theology believes it to be possible to acquire knowledge about God through the consideration of the cosmos merely on the basis of natural reason (Lat. *ratio naturalis*), which is not necessarily illuminated by God's Spirit. In the description of Millard J. Erickson: "The core of natural theology is the idea that it is possible, without a prior commitment of faith to the beliefs of Christianity . . . to come to a genuine knowledge of God on the basis of reason alone."[75]

This theology will be dealt with more extensively in §4.1; the question that must be discussed here is Barth's more general view of revelation.[76] In his opinion, the only way to eliminate natural theology is simply to reject the entire idea of general revelation. In a certain sense, he even rejected special (i.e., Scriptural] revelation because the only revelation that he acknowledged was God's one and unique revelation in Jesus Christ.[77] It is more a matter for Christology to investigate how Barth viewed this revelation of *God* in the *Man* Jesus as a revelation of concealment and self-estrangement. Of great importance for us at this moment, in our study of the Christian doctrine of revelation, are the consequences of Barth's Christomonistic view of revelation for his view of the traditional distinction between general and special revelation.

Karl Barth was not the first to deny natural revelation. This denial began with Albrecht Ritschl and his school, as an explicit attempt to get away from any form of metaphysics in the field of theology. The greatest merit of such thinkers in

---

74. Berkouwer (1955, 21–57).
75. Erickson (1998, 181).
76. Cf. Heyns (1988, 14–15).
77. Cf. Berkhof (1986, 51): the appearance, humiliation, and exaltation of Jesus involve the "actual revelation" of God's heart.

A Twofold Revelation

this regard has been that they have helped to refute the notion of natural theology.[78] However, in doing so they threw away the baby of general revelation along with the bathwater of natural theology. It is, as Erickson correctly summarized in a heading, "General Revelation, But Without Natural Theology."[79]

As I said, Barth in fact also rejected special (scriptural) revelation, namely, in its character as revelation. In his view, the Old Testament is not revelation; it merely points forward to the expected revelation, that is, Jesus Christ, who is the center and focal point of God's revelation. Emil Brunner, who originally was congenial with Barth's views, did not go this far.[80] On the one hand, he called the Old Testament an "anticipatory and preliminary" revelation, and at the same time the "forerunner" of the revelation in Jesus Christ. In agreement with Barth, however, Brunner, too, maintained that neither Scripture nor Jesus Christ *is* revelation. In his opinion, the receiving subject belongs to the full reality of revelation as well; without this subject, the revelational forms do not "become" revelation, they are not "performed."[81] This tension between "being" and "becoming" will be dealt with more extensively in §§8.1–8.2.

To return to Barth, in his opinion even the New Testament is not revelation (despite the fact that new things are told to us in the New Testament that had not yet been revealed by Christ; see, e.g., Eph. 3:4–12). In Barth's view, the New Testament merely refers back to the revelation of God that occurred in Jesus Christ. Even what happened with Jesus, or was done to him, his words and acts, his virgin birth, the empty tomb, is not revelation. These events are merely signs that point to the actual revelation as it became manifest in the incarnated

---

78. Cf. Buri (1956, 227, 237–42), who explains why he opposes the idea of divine revelation in Christ alone.
79. Erickson (1998, 194).
80. Brunner (1949, 16–17).
81. Ibid., 23.

Logos, whose human name is Jesus. Everything in Scripture, just like everything in the cosmos, must and can be read only in the light of God's one, exclusive revelation in Christ. And if we do not find revelation of God in the Bible, we will surely find even less revelation of God in nature. Every notion of general or creational revelation is pushed aside by Barth as "revelational universalism," that is, the wish to see revelation everywhere within reality. There is no knowledge of God through Scripture or nature apart from his revelation in Jesus Christ.

2.8.2 Refutation

Herman Dooyeweerd saw in Barth's view nothing but a new form of the medieval scholastic nature–grace dualism.[82] Through the *separation* (not just distinction) by William of Ockham between nature (the natural life of humans) and grace (i.e., the supernatural Christian life), this dualism permeated Luther's view of the relationship between law and gospel.[83] The law is viewed as constraining sinful nature, which is seen as standing in opposition to evangelical grace. Here the scriptural creation motif disappears behind the motif of Fall and redemption. According to this view, nature with its law-ordinances has no relationship at all with evangelical grace. Thus, this nature is not being restored by God's redemption but will ultimately be destroyed.

Martin Luther did not advocate world flight. On the contrary, according to him, it is God's will that the Christian submit to the ordinances of this sinful world and serve God in one's profession.[84] However, Luther did not see any intrinsic connection between the Christian religion and the Christian's daily life, nor between the Creator God, who places us under the natural ordinances, and the Redeemer God, who sets us

---

82. Dooyeweerd (1963, 134–42); cf. Heyns (1977, 89–90).
83. Cf. Ouweneel (1995, §3.1.1; 2017, 184–86); Luther considered himself a member of Ockham's school; see quotations in Oberman (1992, 120).
84. For Luther, *Beruf* (profession) was *Berufung* (calling).

free from the law. When it came to the secular government, the judicial system, the social structures, humans have no other light than that of blind natural reason. In these views, Luther remained a medieval scholastic.

In Barth's denial of any intrinsic connection between nature and grace Herman Dooyeweerd and J. A. Heyns saw the aftereffect of Luther's antithesis between law and gospel. After Luther, there were only two options available to Lutheran theology: emphasize either the pole of law and nature, or the pole of gospel and grace. In the former case, the priority is granted to the autonomous world, science, and society. Those who choose this pathway make Christian faith in fact subservient to secularization, in which a constantly increasing part of reality is severed from God and his Word. In the latter case, the priority is given to church, faith, and preaching. This implies a bifurcation of life, which may even lead to a flight from society. In the nineteenth century, theologians such as Friedrich Schleiermacher, Albrecht Ritschl, and Ernst Troeltsch were responsible for a strong emphasis on the former pole. In a reactionary way, Karl Barth went to the other extreme, placing all emphasis on the latter pole, without liberating himself from the underlying dualism as such, the dualism of law and nature *versus* gospel and grace.

In this dualism, the "vertical" antithesis between God and Satan, or between Spirit and flesh, is completely confused with another (supposed) antithesis perpendicular to it, the horizontal antithesis between, on the one hand, nature, world, science, and society, and, on the other hand, grace, church, faith, and preaching. It is the typical confusion between structure and direction, which I have discussed extensively elsewhere.[85] The genuine antithesis within cosmic reality, the one between God and Satan, between the Spirit and the flesh (cf. Rom. 8:1-17; Gal. 5:16-26; 1 Pet. 4:1-6; 1 John 4:1-6), involves the second pole, that is, the direction (orientation) of

---

85. Ouweneel (2008, 73–74, 95–97, 246–50; 2014; 2015; 2017, 66–69).

the human heart. Perpendicular to it we have the structure of the created world with its many distinct societal relationships. In no way may we drive a wedge between, for instance, the church and the world (here in the sense of society), or between religious (church) life and natural (everyday) life.

Dialectical theology (Karl Barth, and at first also Emil Brunner, Friedrich Gogarten, and others) strongly rejected the idea of an antithesis between Spirit and flesh within the secular domain. Therefore, it also combated every idea of a Christian philosophy and science, a Christian societal order, Christian art, Christian politics, and the like. It is quite ironic that Barth saw in such a Christian culture an unbearable expression of a synthetic model, which views the relationship between nature and grace as one of a continually ascending line, just as in the Roman Catholic view. Apparently, Barth did not see that he himself was trapped in the traditional nature–grace dualism.

It is surely true that Barth wished to be a fierce opponent of modern humanistic thought, and placed God's Word far beyond all humanistic hubris, and this must be appreciated in his thinking. However, he did not see that, by severing nature from grace, he had in fact surrendered nature to the power of that same humanism. Barth differed from traditional Lutheran theology in that he viewed nature no longer in an Aristotelian-scholastic way. However, in agreement with late scholasticism (William of Ockham) and Martin Luther, Barth denied every connection between Christian faith and natural life. Because he believed that sin has corrupted nature in such a drastic way, he believed that all knowledge and knowability of the creation ordinances[86] was altogether lost. Therefore, Barth rejected every idea of creation ordinances that would provide guidance in the everyday (personal and collective) life of Christians.

J. A. Heyns rightly concluded, "[A] reduced concept of

---

86. See Geesink (1925).

revelation—from general to special, and the latter concentrated in Jesus Christ—leads to the isolation of theology and to the secularization of the sciences."[87] Of course, this did not begin with Barth but with the scholasticism of the high Middle Ages. However, unfortunately, Barth continued this line with great strength, and gave it a leading position in the twentieth century.

2.9 Three Views: Emil Brunner

2.9.1 The Rule for This Moment

Emil Brunner, though originally congenial to Barth's thinking, later chose a different path.[88] He did view himself as standing on a common foundation with Barth in the sense that both emphasized the revelation of God in Jesus Christ (which is correct as long as this is not defended at the expense of God's revelation in nature and Scripture). Both also combated—again, rightly—the idea that the church possesses two sources of knowledge: revelation *and* reason, revelation *and* nature, revelation *and* history. However, Brunner blamed Barth for having drawn two erroneous conclusions from this common foundation: (a) Barth denied any remnant of the original image of God in human beings that might have survived the Fall, and (b) Barth denied every form of divine revelation in nature, in human conscience, and in history. On the basis of Romans 1 (God's revelation in creation) and Romans 2 (God speaking to humans through their consciences), Brunner claimed that there are undeniably *two* revelations: not just one in Jesus Christ, but also one in creation. The only question remaining concerns the relationship between these two revelations of God.

Brunner categorically rejected Barth's assertion that the acceptance of natural revelation would necessarily entail natural theology in the Roman Catholic sense. When it came to resistance to natural *theology*, Brunner wished to stand along-

---

87. Heyns (1977, 157); cf. also Wentsel (1982, 59–60).
88. Brunner (1937; 1946; 1949; cf. Berkouwer (1955, 37–47).

side Barth against Rome; but this did not prevent him, unlike Barth, from defending the notion of natural *revelation*. Brunner viewed creation ordinances as the expression of God's common grace (Lat. *gratia communis*) but subsequently depreciated these ordinances by dealing with them within the framework of a dialectical antithesis between creation ordinances and the divine Law of Love as the commandment for the (present) moment (Ger. *Gebot der Stunde*). In agreement with Luther's view of the law, Brunner viewed creation ordinances as severe and loveless because of their universal character. As such, they supposedly ruled sinful human nature with a firm hand. This rigid law must be breached by the evangelical Law of Love, which does not acknowledge any universal rule (i.e., a rule that rigidly holds under all circumstances) but only the commandment for the (present) moment.[89] For example, as a creation ordinance, marriage may be indissoluble, but as a law it does not express God's *factual will*. That will is manifested only in the Law of Love, which can break through this rigid universal ordinance as the commandment for this moment.[90]

Regardless of the differences between Barth and Brunner concerning divine revelation — I have mentioned only a few — Brunner's thinking was undeniably governed by precisely the same nature–grace motif, as expressed in his antithesis between creation ordinances and the commandment for the (present) moment. Although with Brunner this comes to light less sharply than with Barth, I see the main problem in the fact that Brunner did not properly discern the *religious antithesis* either.[91] This point deserves some more attention.

2.9.2 The True Antithesis

To begin with: if we wished to distinguish a certain *duality* at all, it would not be the scholastic horizontal *dualism* (separa-

---

89. See especially Brunner (1937).
90. Cf. Kalsbeek (1970, 222).
91. Cf. Spykman (1992, 65–66).

tion and antithesis) between nature and grace, or, directly related with this, between the creation order and the redemptive order. Rather, it would be the vertical *duality* (not dualism) of the transcendent, religious human heart and immanent-modal-functional cosmic reality. This can never be taken to be a du*alism* because the heart is nothing but the focal point *of the functions themselves*, and the functions are nothing but the refraction *of the heart itself*.[92] The two cannot be separated, much less opposed to each other. Religiously and transcendently, the creation is centered in the human heart as the *personal* root unity of the entire cosmos. *Superpersonally*, the reborn heart, in the power of the Holy Spirit, participates in the spiritual community in Christ, the last Adam (1 Cor. 15:45), just as the apostate heart participates in the equally spiritual community of the first (apostate) Adam.

Here, the true antithesis is to be found. In the personal sense, it is the antithesis between the apostate and reborn heart (the heart turned away from God and the one re-oriented toward God, respectively), and in the superpersonal sense, between the first Adam and the last Adam. This is something fundamentally different from the supposed antithesis—which at best ought to be a distinction—between creation and re-creation, or between the created world and the redeemed world. Again, the true antithesis, that is, between God and Satan, or between the Spirit and the flesh, involves what Dutch philosopher Dirk H. Th. Vollenhoven called "direction" (directedness, vertical orientation), that is, it concerns the heart's religious orientation: for or against the God of the Bible, for or against Christ.

This antithesis should never be confused with a supposed antithesis perpendicular to it: an artificial and wrongly imagined *structural* antithesis *within* the created reality. The former, *biblical* antithesis, the one between the Spirit and the flesh, runs right through the natural (the cosmos) as well as

---

92. See extensively Ouweneel (1986; 2008, chapters 6–8; 2014).

through the supernatural (the heart), that is, right through the two regiments (realms, kingdoms) as Luther distinguished them. The battle between the Spirit and the flesh is felt both *within* the church and *within* the world (i.e., society), both *within* the sacred and *within* the secular domain, both *within* the realm of people's (temporal-immanent) *beliefs* (to be carefully distinguished from people's transcendent *faith*) and *within* the realm of people's rational thinking.[93]

Our conclusion must be that nature and grace are not at all different realms.[94] The apostate creation and the redeemed creation are the *same* creation: the former is the creation, before its restoration, *directed* toward Satan and sin in an apostate way; the latter is the creation restored through regeneration (re-creation) and renewal by the Spirit toward, re-directed toward, God and his Word.[95] There is no room here for any dualism between law and gospel: the redemptive word (see chapter 3) is enclosed within the eternal Torah, and the redeemed creation is submitted to this same eternal Torah.[96] Every scholastic dualism of this type drives a wedge between God's creational and redemptive *work*, whose unity and center are given in the person of Christ, who is both God's creational and God's redemptive *Word*. In my view, over against Brunner's distinction between the severe and rigid creation ordinances and the Law of Love, we posit the biblical unity of both God's word and work in both creation and redemption. Nothing in this life or in this world could be viewed as *not* standing under the rule of God, as expressed in the one and only creational and redemptive Word, that is, Christ. In the next two chapters, I will discuss this more extensively.

---

93. Again, see extensively, Ouweneel (2017).
94. See extensively, Ouweneel (2018l).
95. Regarding the relationship between creation and re-creation, see extensively, Ouweneel (2012, §14.1).
96. Regarding this notion, see extensively, Ouweneel (2018a).

2.10 Three Views: Paul Althaus

2.10.1 *Contra* Natural Theology

Paul Althaus[97] agreed with Emil Brunner — *contra* Karl Barth — that God's revelation in Jesus Christ is *not* God's first and only self-testimony to humanity but stands in a close relationship with the continuing revelation of God.[98] It is remarkable that Althaus concluded from the outset that earlier theology had rightly spoken of a twofold revelation: general and special revelation. He therefore condemned recent attempts to abolish the notion of general revelation, and to limit revelation to Jesus Christ. On the basis of Romans 1-2, and in opposition to Barth and Brunner, he pleaded for such a general or primordial revelation (Ger. *Uroffenbarung*).[99]

In Romans 2:14-15, the apostle Paul says,

> [W]hen Gentiles, who do not have the law, by nature do what the law requires, they are a law to themselves, even though they do not have the law. They show that the work of the law is written on their hearts, while their conscience also bears witness, and their conflicting thoughts accuse or even excuse them.

Barth explained this in such a way that excluded any notion of general revelation. Althaus called this exegesis by Barth an "act of pure desperation,"[100] and concluded that we must distinguish between God's redemptive revelation in Jesus Christ and his original self-testimony or primordial or ground-revelation.[101]

For Althaus, the decisive theological reason to teach a primordial revelation is the recourse in the gospel to this general revelation because the guilt of humanity involved the rejection of this primordial revelation.[102] He then continued with

---

97. See in particular Althaus (1952); cf. Berkouwer (1955, 47–57), who referred to the first (1947) edition of Althaus (1952); I will quote from the third edition.
98. Althaus (1952, 37).
99. Ibid., 38–39.
100. Ibid., 40.
101. Ibid., 41.
102. Ibid., 42; cf. 42–50.

the description of the battle surrounding primordial revelation.[103] Originally, neither Roman Catholics nor Protestants doubted the idea of a twofold revelation. However, under the pressure of Kantian epistemology, Wilhelm Herrmann, Barth's teacher at Marburg, began to narrow revelation in a Christological way.[104] In this way, nature and history were "de-deified" (Ger. *entgöttet*), or at least these no longer have meaning for arguing our certainties concerning God; these certainties reside not in nature and history but in Jesus Christ alone. The history of religion school opposed this view,[105] but in the twentieth century, a new Christomonistic view of revelation arose with the work of Karl Heim,[106] and especially with Barth.[107]

2.10.2 Althaus' Own Natural Theology

Perfectly correctly, Althaus blamed Barth for confusing this primordial revelation and rational (if not rationalistic) natural theology.[108] These two must be severed completely, for the latter is the "worst heresy" and the "source of all theological apostasy."[109] This strong language becomes all the more amazing when we discover that the sequel of Althaus's argument consists of simply another variety of this accursed natural theology. As he himself explained, "God's self-testimony [in the primordial revelation] takes place in a decisive way not through theoretical persuasion but in *immediate perception*, in *living experience* in the reality of our lives . . .; in the 'immediate self-awareness,' as Schleiermacher said, pre-theoretically, in a living having-been-seized."[110]

---

103. Ibid., 51–61.
104. Ibid., 54.
105. Ibid., 54–56.
106. See his main work: Heim (1931–52).
107. Althaus (1952, 56–57).
108. Ibid., 57–58.
109. Ibid., 58.
110. Ibid., 62–63.

In this human experience of reality around them, humans become aware of God.[111] This does not mean that through causal-rational thinking, we conclude that God exists ("everything that I observe points to God"). No, we are dealing here with an "immediate experience."[112] In my view, G. C. Berkouwer rightly concluded that this is more than just the recognition of the objective knowability of God through the works of his hands.[113] Althaus definitely claimed a true natural knowledge of God. Whatever differences he may have seen with regard to the natural theology of the Roman Catholic Church, at least there is this similarity that, for Althaus too, this natural knowledge of God involves the *that* of God, not the *who*: his existence, not his being. Therefore, he claimed that, on the basis of this knowledge, we know ourselves to be in the hands of the Power of Destiny (Ger. *Schicksalsmacht*), which we recognize "as *a* force"; we are "in the hands of a [!] *Lord* over us."[114] However, such *a* force, or *a* Lord, resembles much more the *prima causa* or the "unmoved mover" of Aristotelianism, and Roman Catholic theology based upon it, than the God whom we encounter in Psalm 19 and Romans 1. In this respect, there ultimately does not seem to be any essential difference between Roman Catholic natural theology and the view of Althaus.

The fact that this is really Althaus' intention is evident from the remainder of his argument: God's self-testimony in human existence and history.[115] According to Althaus, the experience of God in history in its certainty and validity is not based upon, nor bound to, the gospel, that is, faith in Christ. In his view, this experience is truly and basically pre-Christian, that is, possible and real before any encoun-

---

111. Ibid., 63.
112. Ibid., 64.
113. Berkouwer (1955, 49).
114. Althaus (1952, 65–66).
115. Ibid., 66–71 and 71–76, respectively.

ter with God in Jesus Christ.[116] There is a kind of universal, non-Christian faith in God, and according to Althaus, theology must seriously appreciate this faith as a true relationship with the Lord of history.[117] Moreover, God reveals himself in theoretical thought, in the human mind in general, and in nature.[118] Indeed, it is not the God of the gospel about whom we learn from nature,[119] but this does not change the fact that it is God's self-testimony that we encounter here. We find him in the order, harmony, and efficiency of nature.[120] Therefore, humans cannot be excused with regard to Christ because Althaus saw a direct continuity between natural knowledge of God and God's revelation in Christ.[121]

I really do not know what is preferable: Barth's fierce rejection of any form of creational revelation, or Althaus' introduction of simply another form of natural theology, namely, a general revelation of a pre-Christian nature, entirely independent of Christ and Scripture. It is this very independence that is objectionable: there is no salvation through general revelation, that is, apart from the person and the atoning work of Christ, as we know him from Holy Scripture, and apart from the power and guidance of the Holy Spirit, whom we know from Scripture as well.

In fact, the common denominator of Barth and Althaus seems to be that both — deliberately or involuntarily — continued to presuppose the ancient scholastic dualism of nature and grace, here in the form of general revelation as distinct from, and even opposed to, some kind of special revelation. Althaus fully maintained this medieval dualism, though in a new formulation; Barth simply rejected one of the two components. Is there a different way? I believe there is. This dif-

---

116. Ibid., 72.
117. Ibid., 73.
118. Ibid., 76–79, 79–82, and 82–90, respectively.
119. Ibid., 83.
120. Ibid., 87–90.
121. Cf. Thielicke (1977, 25–27).

ferent way cannot be anything else than the rejection of the nature-grace dualism *itself*. This will be explained in the following two chapters.

2.10.3 Millard J. Erickson's Summary

Let me now provide a preliminary summary of my treatment of general revelation. I do so in the words of Millard J. Erickson, which I will paraphrase.[122]

(1) *Shared basis*. The significance of general revelation lies, first, in the fact that there is some common ground on which believers and unbelievers can meet each other. All people have a certain awareness of God, no matter how weak and vague, no matter how much suppressed or buried it may be within people. Often, it can be very meaningful to trace these elements of knowledge, and to link one's message to them. In this way, it may be easier for the interlocutor to understand certain elements of the gospel. Jesus and Paul gave the example to the present-day evangelist: they linked their message to the insights and ideas of their listeners; think of Nicodemus (John 3:1-21), the Samaritan woman (4:1-30), the Lycaonians (Acts 14:8-19), and the Athenians (17:16-34).

(2) *Shared truth*. Emphasizing general revelation brings to light that there definitely is truth apart from special revelation. "[Y]our word is truth" (John 17:17) — but not all truth is to be found in Scripture. British-American philosopher Arthur F. Holmes said, "All truth is God's truth,"[123] that is, truth contained not only in special but also in general revelation. Everything that is true is basically related to the being-ness of the cosmos, in which God manifests himself. First, there was general revelation, and only later — in a certain sense as a supplement (as well as a culmination) — came special revelation. However, for us, the reverse is also true *a posteriori*: general revelation, which is studied by all academic disciplines (including theology), is a supplement to special revelation. What

---

122. Erickson (1998, 198–99).
123. Holmes (1977, book title).

is true in all the disciplines is by definition *God's* truth: truth revealed in general revelation concerning the cosmos, nature, the human mind, human society.

(3) *No excuse.* General revelation is of great significance for all those people in history, and also at present worldwide, who never heard or hear the gospel. Because people can intelligently perceive something of God's majesty in God's creation, they are without excuse, says Romans 1:20. They even *know* God, says verse 21, although, generally speaking, they do not do anything sensible with this knowledge. They know (something of) the truth of God but they suppress this truth in unrighteousness (v. 18 NKJV, NIV). Thus, all people are responsible to God as their Creator and Judge. The fact that people can know something about God from creation is not a discouragement for gospel preaching but rather an incentive: the gospel provides the essential completion of the knowledge of God already obtained.

(4) *The religions.* Due to the phenomenon of general revelation, we understand why there are so many religions on earth: every non-Abrahamic religion is, in its own specific (humanly deficient) way a response to this general revelation. (Judaism is based upon the Old Testament but lacks the inspired exegesis of it by the New Testament; Islam is the apostate response to the [limited and deficient] knowledge of Muhammad regarding the Old and the New Testaments.) Thus, pagan religions are not just human imaginations; they *always* contain elements of truth, which they did not invent themselves; these elements were adopted from God's general revelation. Pagan religions are not lies — at least not *just* lies — but distorted truths (which is not the same). For instance, God takes the pagan gods seriously (Exod. 12:12; Num. 21:29; Judg. 11:24; Ps. 82:1; Isa. 46:1; Jer. 51:44), although (a) they are not really gods but apostate angels, and (b) they have been wrapped within a mass of pagan fabrications.[124]

---

124. See extensively, Ouweneel (2018m).

(5) *Connection*. Special revelation does not stand by itself but is closely linked to general revelation; as I said, essentially they form one single revelation. Therefore, special revelation must not be viewed by itself as if it had nothing to do with general revelation. They complete and strengthen each other. If a person has never contemplated with wonder the starry sky or the depths of the human mind, how will they learn anything from God's special revelation? Let me finish this chapter by quoting two philosophers. Ancient Greek philosopher Plato in his *Theaetetus* put the following words in Socrates' mouth: "... this experience is very much a philosopher's, that of wondering. For nothing else is the beginning (principle) of philosophy than this, and, seemingly, whoever's genealogy it was, that Iris was the offspring of Thaumas [= wonder], it's not a bad one."[125] In my words, what person will begin seeing the wonders of Scripture who has not learned to *begin* wondering about the world around them? The other quotation is from Immanuel Kant: "Two things fill the mind with ever new and increasing admiration and awe, the more often and steadily we reflect upon them: the starry heavens above me and the moral law within me."[126]

---

125. Plato (1986, lines 155c-d).
126. Kant (1997, 133 [5:161]).

Chapter 3
General Revelation (1)

[W]hat can be known about God is plain to them,
because God has shown it to them.
For his invisible attributes,
  namely, his eternal power and divine nature,
have been clearly perceived,
  ever since the creation of the world,
  in the things that have been made.
So they are without excuse.

Romans 1:19–20

Summary: *The problem of the relationship between general and special revelation is as complicated as that between creation and (redeemed) re-creation. Former attempts to describe creation as a mechanism must be criticized; it affects God's continual (providential, sustaining) activity within creation. God reveals himself on the law-side of creation (law-order, God's commanding "Word") as well as on its subject-side: in nature, history, culture, technology, etc.*

Much attention is given to the concept of the "law" that applies to creation, and which in fact is God's continual commanding within cosmic reality. God's law has been described as a boundary between

Creator and creation: between what is above and what is under the law. Viewed as God's own Word, the law is uncreated; viewed as a "side" of all creation, it is part of creation. Regarding this matter, many errors can be pointed out in the history of thought. The same holds when it comes to the (often scholastic-dualist) view of the natural and the supernatural, or to the view of miracles, or of natural laws and norms, or of law and time, or of the law and the Fall, or of the law and Christ.

As an idea, the notion of the law can be approximated with the help of the theory of the modal aspects of reality. God's law is viewed in relation to God's Word, God's Torah, God's Wisdom, God's Love, and God's covenant.

3.1 Revelation and Creation Order

3.1.1 The Problem

GORDON J. SPYKMAN SAW AS ONE of the most basic issues for any study concerning the prolegomena of Reformational dogmatics a clear understanding of the relationship between creation and redemption. In the terminology of classic theology, this involves the relationship between general and special revelation. In spite of sin, there is a basic continuity that applies to our lives in the world with regard to the structures of creation, also after the Fall. Traditional theology ascribes this to common grace, which might be described more accurately as preserving or upholding grace. At the same time, our lives display a radical *dis*continuity as far as the direction of our lives is concerned. Older theologies ascribed the renewal of this direction to special grace. The gospel is the redemptive re-proclamation of God's enduring Word: "Heaven and earth will pass away, but my words will not pass away" (Mark 13:31). It is a second, redemptively republished edition of God's creational word, now in lingual form.[1]

In this way, Spykman described in a few words the problem that will occupy us now: general revelation in its relationship with special revelation, and the concomitant relationship

---

1. Spykman (1988, 143).

between creation and re-creation, between the old (pre-Fall) world and the new (post-redemption) world. The new world is not a replacement of the old world, nor is it simply a restoration of the old world, but it is an *elevation* of the old world.[2]

Before we discuss divine revelation as we find it in Holy Scripture—in short, scriptural or special revelation (chapters 5 and further)—we must first consider God's revelation in the cosmos, in short, creational or general revelation. In the previous chapter, I indicated that the use of these terms might seem to support the notion of a revelational dualism, and thus create confusion. Yet, I will keep using them for lack of better terms, and in agreement with common usage. We do remember, though, that Scripture is part of the cosmos, too, and that there can be no question of a dualism of any kind.

3.1.2 Creation As a Mechanism?

On the basis of the Bible, the Christian knows the cosmic order—the law-order that God has instituted for the entire cosmic reality—as a *creation order*. That is, an orderly system, which must be explained from the creational power and will of God. Within this order, we distinguish numerous creation ordinances within empirical reality. Even pre-theoretically, faith can appeal here immediately to Bible passages such as: all things are rooted in God's sovereign creational *will* (Rev. 4:11).

God's will involves his demand of obedience. All creatures obey God's *word*, in the sense of natural laws (Job 37:5; 38:34; Ps. 33:6, 9; 104:7; 119:89; 148:8). The celestial bodies obey God's ordinances, appointment, decrees, commandments, in brief: God's order (Job 38:33; Ps. 119:91; 148:6; Isa. 45:12; Jer. 31:35; 33:25). Nature on earth also obeys his voice, his commands, his word (Ps. 104:6-7; 147:15, 18). Concerning day and night, God made a *covenant*, which is the same as saying that, due to God's covenantal faithfulness, day and night follow a

---

2. For an extensive discussion of this, see Ouweneel (2012, §14.1.1; 2017), chapter 9.

fixed rhythm (Jer. 33:20, 25; cf. Ps. 89:2-3, 5, 37).

These ordinances must never be understood in any deistic sense, that is, as a set of fixed laws that God instituted once, at the time of creation, which since then apply and function in an autonomous way, independent of the Creator. Creation is not a kind of enormous machine, which works by itself; on the contrary, creation stands under the continual *command* of God.

Viewing creation as a machine or mechanism has led to much debate. According to natural philosopher Robin G. Collingwood, the Western view of nature during the seventeenth and eighteenth centuries was rather mechanistic.[3] He argued, however, that though this does not necessarily assume a deistic thought system, it was a consequence of the Christian view of God. Viewing creation as a machine does not necessarily imply the absence of God in the deistic sense, but rather the presence of God as the great Mechanic. According to Dutch philosopher Reijer Hooykaas, a genuine mechanism is always a product of design, and the Christian founders of modern mechanistic views emphasized that the picture of a machine or mechanism necessarily implied a Maker somewhere out there.[4] Yet, as Hooykaas rightly emphasized, the machine model is inadequate. Once a machine has been made, to a large extent it has become independent of its maker. God, however, never abandons his work, else the "world machine" would break down. He is not only its Creator but also its Preserver (Sustainer, Upholder).

Philosopher Dick Stafleu argued that, in the strict sense of the term, the mechanistic view must be rejected without further ado because it involves an absolutization of the kinematic modality of cosmic reality (in the Dooyeweerdian sense), and thus diminishes other modalities of reality.[5] However, he

---

3. Collingwood (1945, 103).
4. Hooykaas (1972, 13–16).
5. Stafleu (1987, 242–44).

also argued that seventeenth- and eighteenth-century natural science was not at all that mechanistic, as is often supposed; the views of well-known Christian natural scientists such as astronomer Johannes Kepler and physicist Isaac Newton were not mechanistic in the strict sense of the word.

3.1.3 Creation and Preservation

Over against the idea of creation as a machine or mechanism in any mechanistic, or even deistic sense, Scripture indeed places great emphasis on what is called the work of *preservation* (or *upholding*). This is the continual sustenance of creation by God's providence, so that everything that occurs in reality and in history is connected to God's direct acting.[6] In the more general sense, Scripture claims that God not only created all things in, through, and for Christ, but also that all things *hold together* in Christ (Gk. *ta panta en autōi synestēken*; Col. 1:16-17; cf. Sirach 42:15 GNT, "The words of the Lord brought his works into being, and the whole creation obeys his commands").

Nowhere is the role of God's word in the work of preservation expressed more poignantly than in Hebrews 1:2-3,

> ... in these last days he [i.e., God] has spoken to us by his Son,[7] whom he appointed the heir of all things, through whom also he created the world. He is the radiance of the glory of God and the exact imprint of his nature, and he upholds [sustains, Gk. *pherōn*] the universe by the word of his power [Gk. *tōi rhēmati tēs dynameōs autou*[8]].

God *created* the world through the Son, and it is the Son who *upholds* the world by his powerful *word*, as it were, by

---

6. Therefore, I would rather not say that God's work of preservation occurs through the independent functioning of forces inherent to the cosmos, as Smit argued (1980, 181). Fortunately, Kobus Smit himself rightly pointed to the danger of substantialism (1984).
7. Gk. *en huiōi*, more precisely, "in Son," that is, in the person of the Son (AMP, DARBY).
8. An apparent Hebraism; the sense is: "by his powerful word" (cf., e.g., Ps. 87:1, "mounts of holiness" [JUB] = "holy mountains").

constantly commanding all things.

There are many other references to God's work of preservation: God "gives to all mankind life and breath and everything" (Acts 17:25), and, "In him we live and move and have our being" (v. 28, quoting from the poet Aratus). In Daniel 5:23, the prophet speaks to the king about "the God in whose hand is your breath." In addition, we find in the Bible numerous statements about God's direct acting in nature: he sends the rain and the snow, the storm and the ice (Job 37:2-14; 38:22-38; Ps. 104:13), he feeds and leads the plants and the animals (Job 39:1-33; Ps. 104:10-11, 14, 16, 27-30), and makes the springs gush forth in the valleys (Ps. 104:10). He governs the celestial bodies (Job 38:31-33; Ps. 104:19-23).

Sometimes, there are direct references to God's *word* in this work of upholding, as in Hebrews 1:3. Thus, we find that God speaks in and through the thunderstorm (Ps. 29:3-9), at God's "rebuke" the waters flee (Ps. 104:7), God commands the day and the night (Job 38:12; cf. Matt. 5:45 about sunrise), and he lifts up his "voice to the clouds" (Job 38:34). This is all God's immediate acting and speaking in nature. Not only this: all these acts of God are described as his *wonders* (or miracles; Job 5:9; 9:10; 37:14, 16; Ps. 139:14; cf. Exod. 7:3; 11:10; see §3.7.2). The scholastic distinction between natural and supernatural miracles—or, for instance, natural and supernatural *charismata* (1 Cor. 12:7-11)[9]—is entirely foreign to Scripture (see §3.7.1). In everything we see God's miraculous acting. This is all perfectly natural for him, no matter how miraculous these acts may appear to us.

3.2 Revelation on the Law-Side

3.2.1 Law-Order and Torah

As we have seen, Scripture speaks both of God's creation ordinances *for* nature and of God's acting *in* nature, and these are both aspects of the same matter. The biblical speaking of ordinances upon which creational reality is founded points

---

9. Ouweneel (2018e, §12.2.1).

General Revelation (1)

to the fixed regularity that obtains in the cosmos. We have to do here with God's *law*. The law in the biblical sense is much more than the "law of Moses" (e.g., Luke 2:22) or the "law of Christ" (Gal. 6:2) in its limited ethical-pistical sense. In the widest sense, God's law involves the entire *law-order* that God has instituted for all his creatures. Celestial bodies and other inanimate things, as well as plants, animals, and humans, are all subject to God's law in the widest sense. When we speak of a *creation order*, we recognize this as a *law-order*; that is, from the beginning God has subjected his creation to laws (natural laws, norms, principles).

We will see that this law is God's *Word*, in the very same way the law of Moses and the law of Christ are God's Word. Notice how Jesus alternately uses the terms "commandments" and "word" (John 14:15, 21, 23–24), and notice how the entire Old Testament, even outside the Pentateuch, is sometimes called "law" (Rom. 3:10–19). God's Word is law, and his law is his Word. Therefore, the Christian believes that in the cosmic law-order we are dealing with *divine revelation*: God speaks through this law-order. We can even say that, in this law-order or creation order, God reveals *himself*, or perhaps something *of* himself. When we speak of God's general revelation in nature, this revelation comes to light in the *law-order* of nature because the law is *the word of God's own will* for created reality. As Gordon Spykman put it so eloquently:

> The heaven declare God's glory [Ps. 19:1] by revealing how his Word holds for the movement of heavenly bodies. Similarly, the magnetic [sic] force of gravity declares God's glory by revealing how God's Word holds for falling objects. Again, the scientific notion of capillary action declares God's glory by revealing how God's Word holds for the life of trees.[10]

This matter of God's self-revelation in the law-order deserves our close attention. When we think of the cosmic order as a law-order, which as revelation points to the Cre-

---
10. Spykman (1992, 80–81).

ator-Law-Giver, it may strike us that Hebrew term *torah*, usually rendered as "law," can sometimes mean "revelation." The word, probably derived from the root *y-r-h*, "to teach," originally means "instruction, teaching," and hence sometimes also "revelation, manifestation."[11] Some examples: "Their pleasure and passion is remaining true to the Word [*torah*] of 'I Am,' meditating day and night in his true revelation [*torah*] of light" (Ps. 1:2 TPT; cf. 94:12, where many translations render the word as "teaching" or "instruction"). "Zion's the source of the revelation [*torah*]. God's Message comes from Jerusalem" (Isa. 2:3 MSG). "Because they said no to the revelation [*torah*] of God-of-the-Angel-Armies . . ." (5:24 MSG).[12] In other passages, *torah* also has the broad meaning of revelation of God's will (Isa. 1:10; 42:4, 21; 51:4, 7); this is particularly true where the text speaks of God's revelation to all nations (2:2-4; 42:3-7; 51:4-9).

3.2.2 Manifestation of God's Will

Actually, all divine revelation is always manifestation of God's *will*, whether his creational will or his redemptive will, just as the Sinaitic law, too, is revelation of God's will. Here, we encounter again the connection between the notions of "law" and "creation." In Psalm 19, we are dealing with the one single revelation of God: whether it is God's law-order in the works of nature (vv. 1-7), or the positivized[13] law of God for human life (vv. 8-15), we are dealing with one divine law, that is, one divine revelation.

We see this quite beautifully in Psalm 119. This Psalm forms an acrostic, in which verse 89-96 constitute the *lamed* stanza (i.e., each verse begins with the Hebrew letter *lamed*). This stanza begins with speaking specifically of the cosmic

---

11. Cf. *TDNT* 4:1036-91, where Ps. 1:2 and 94:12 are also mentioned.
12. In these two verses, the Afrikaans translation of 1983 renders *torah* as "revelation," too.
13. The term "to positivize"—to formally codify in laws—has been adopted from the science of jurisprudence.

General Revelation (1)

law-order: "Forever, O LORD, your word is firmly fixed in the heavens. Your faithfulness endures to all generations; you have established the earth, and it stands fast. By your appointment they stand this day, for all things are your servants" (vv. 89-91). But in the same breath, the stanza continues with speaking of the normative law of Sinai, especially the Ten Commandments: "If your law had not been my delight, I would have perished in my affliction. I will never forget your precepts, for by them you have given me life" (vv. 92-93). Basically, the cosmic law and the Sinaitic law constitute one word, one law, one revelation of God.

We find the same in Psalm 147:15-19,

He sends out his command to the earth;
his word runs swiftly.
He gives snow like wool;
he scatters frost like ashes.
He hurls down his crystals of ice like crumbs;
who can stand before his cold?
He sends out his word, and melts them;
he makes his wind blow and the waters flow.
He declares his word to Jacob,
his statutes and rules to Israel.

In verses 15-18, the text refers to the cosmic law, and in one breath the poet moves on to the Sinaitic law. Similarly, we see how, in Proverbs 3:1, the father presents to the son his *torah* ("teaching") as well as the road of "wisdom" (Heb. *chokmah*, i.e., the wisdom of walking in God's commandments), and then suddenly begins to speak of that "other" *torah* or *chokmah*: "The LORD by wisdom founded the earth; by understanding he established the heavens; by his knowledge the deeps broke open, and the clouds drop down the dew" (vv. 19-20). In reality, this is one and the same law (or wisdom, or revelation): God's law (or wisdom, or revelation) both for his works in nature and for human life. The wisdom with which God rules the world, and the wisdom of humans who walk in

God's commandments, are intimately related.

3.2.3 God's Commanding "Word"

In Psalm 119:89 ("Forever, O LORD, your *word* is firmly fixed in the heavens") and 147:15, 18–19 ("He sends out his command to the earth; his *word* runs swiftly. . . . He sends out his *word*, and melts them [i.e., crystals of ice]. . . He declares his *word* to Jacob, his statutes and rules to Israel"), we encounter another term essential to our discussion: "word" (Heb. *davar*). In nature, God melts the ice through his "word," and to his people, God declares his "word," that is, his *Torah*. God reveals himself in his word; this word is always the word of his *will* (his "will-word"). The law is God's word, just as his revelation is his word. Creation has been brought about by, and thus is a manifestation of, God's creational word. God reveals himself by *speaking*. In Genesis 1, God reveals himself, not by becoming visible, but by becoming audible, so to speak, namely, through his tenfold creational word ("And God said . . .").

God revealed himself at Mount Sinai by speaking, and thus made known his will to his people (Exod. 20:1). At Sinai, his transcendent, eternal Word was refracted into ten immanent commandments, which, interestingly enough, are actually called the Ten Words (Exod. 34:28; Deut. 4:13; 10:4; NLV: "Ten Great Laws"; VOICE: "Ten Directives"; YLT: "Ten Matters"). These are ten revelational statements of God, which together constitute God's first positivized covenantal will for Israel. (*How* the passage must be divided into ten parts has been a matter of debate; the Septuagint and the Talmud, Jews and Christians, Catholics, Lutherans, and Calvinists differ on the proper numbering of the commandments.[14])

In these Ten Words, too, we clearly have to do, not just with "law of God" but, with "(self-)revelation of God." First, this is evident from the opening words, which rabbinical tradition considers to be the first of the Ten Words.[15] In them,

---
14. Cf. https://en.wikipedia.org/wiki/Ten_Commandments.
15. Talmud: Makkoth 24a.

God presents or reveals himself by declaring who he is: "I am the LORD your God, who brought you out of the land of Egypt, out of the house of slavery" (Exod. 20:2).

Second, the self-revealing character of God's Torah is evident from the nature of the law, namely, as calling humanity to a holiness that first became manifest in God himself: "I am the LORD your God. Consecrate yourselves therefore, and be holy, for I am holy" (Lev. 11:44; cf. v. 45; 19:2; 20:7-8; cf. 1 Pet. 1:16). This means (a): Act as I *want* you to act, and (b): Become as I *am*. The same is true of the "law of Christ": it is God's will that believers *fulfill* this law (Gal. 6:2); but it is equally God's will that they be conformed to the image of his Son (Rom. 8:29). The two matters amount to the same thing: *obey* Christ, *be* like Christ.

As we will see, God's revelation has a tremendous scope. He reveals himself[16]

(a) in nature in his *creational* and his *providential* word (Rom. 1:19-20; Col. 1:17; Heb. 1:3);

(b) in his *redemptive* word (the gospel; Rom. 3:21-22; 1 Cor. 1:18; 1 Tim. 1:15; 2 Tim. 1:9-10; James 1:21);

(c) in the *incarnated* Word (Jesus Christ; Matt. 16:17; John 2:11; 1 Tim. 3:16; Heb. 9:26; 1 Pet. 1:20; 1 John 3:5, 8);

(d) in the *inscripturated* Word (Holy Scripture; 1 Cor. 2:10-13; Eph. 3:5; 2 Tim. 3:16; 2 Pet. 1:20-21);

(e) in the *preached* Word (Col. 4:4; 1 Thess. 2:13) (see §5.4.1).

3.3 Revelation on the Subject-Side

3.3.1 Three Domains

We can distinguish two sides within cosmic reality: the law-side (see §3.2) and the factual or subject-side. The law-side involves the laws (natural laws, norms, principles) that apply to the facts (inanimate things, plants, animals, humans, events, states of affairs). The factual or subject-side involves the subjects, literally that which is "subject" (subjected) to

---

16. Cf. Heyns (1988, 146–47).

God's laws. God reveals himself in (on, through) the law-side of created reality: it is he who instituted the laws, and these laws also tell us something about himself. But my point right now is that God also reveals himself in (on, through) the subject-side. This comes to light both in nature and in history and culture in the general sense.[17]

(a) In each wondrous work of *nature* we are dealing with God's creational revelation. We behold his majesty in the greatness of the celestial bodies (Ps. 19:1-7) and his faithfulness in the regularity of their orbits (Ps. 89:1-5, 28-29, 36-37; Jer. 33:20, 25). We hear him in the voice of the thunder (Ps. 29), and we experience his powers in the mountains and forests, in the flora and fauna (Job 37-38; Ps. 104, 147).

(b) As far as *history* is concerned, philosopher Jan D. Dengerink argued that the "occurrence of reality," as he called it, is often fixed (constant); however, it is not static or rigid but dynamic.[18] Both the subject-side and the law-side come to further disclosure in this dynamic of reality: on the subject-side, in that things (inanimate things, plants, animals, humans, events, states of affairs) develop, and on the law-side, in that certain laws that earlier had been latent come to disclosure as things or states of affairs originate that did not exist before. Think, for instance, of God's creational laws that had existed from the beginning but which make certain high-tech masterpieces possible only within the last two centuries. In this sense, Dengerink wished to speak of a constantly continuing *dis*closure of what had been *en*closed in God's creational and re-creational word from the beginning.

In history, we are dealing with human actions, with all their mistakes, insecurities, and unpredictabilities. However, history also entails *God's* actions, and as such it is revelation of God, demonstrating to us who and what God is. I emphasize that *God's revelation in history* must be carefully distinguished

---

17. Cf. Berkhof (1986, 65-71).
18. Dengerink (1986, 226).

from the *history of God's revelation*. The latter is also important, but my point right now is that the entirety of human history is redemptive history, that is, revelation of God's continuing redemptive acting. No matter how difficult it may be to *interpret* history, nevertheless from its beginning to its end it is revelation of God in the sense that the God who is "visible" to the believer who perceives God's "hand" in history (cf. Exod. 9:3; Deut. 2:15; Josh. 4:24; 2 Chron. 30:12; Job 12:9; Prov. 21:1; Eccl. 2:24; 9:1; Isa. 41:20) is working his way to the consummation of history in Christ. I will return to this important subject of creation and re-creation in §4.4.

(c) In a special sense, God reveals himself also in *cultural products*: whether it is Handel's *Messiah*, or Da Vinci's *Mona Lisa*, or the Rolls Royce Phantom, or the Alhambra (Granada, Spain),[19] we admire in them God's creational power, reflected in the creative power of humans as those who have been made in God's image. We are dealing here with cultural creations, performed by humans through their God-given ability of discovering and disclosing the creational laws.[20] God reveals himself, on the one hand, in the laws that he instituted for humans (law-side), and on the other hand, in the humans whom he placed in subjection to his laws, as well as in what humans create (subject-side). Culture is nothing more or less than the creative disclosure of nature by humans, according to God's order, and in this way culture can be described as a continual disclosure of the divine revelation in nature.

If we carefully formulate it, even in culture we may distinguish a continual revelation. The disclosure of nature involves the discovery of new aspects of nature, in which new aspects of God's eternal power and divine nature (Rom. 1:20) also come to light. On the law-side of cosmic reality, all the

---

19. Cf. the "aesthetic revelational concept" of Ebeling (1979, 247), although he did not adequately discuss it within the broader framework of what revelation is as such, and of the relationship between general and special revelation (cf. his "religious revelational concept," 248).
20. Smit (1980, 177).

subjective potentialities for human culture were supplied by God right from the beginning, no matter how many centuries it may have passed before they were disclosed. We do realize here, though, that the law-side is revealed both in normative and in anti-normative cultural behavior. God's law is revealed also in torture chambers and in cluster bombs, but then in an anti-normative realization of its intrinsic potentialities. These things may be in accordance with God's physical laws, but they are in conflict with God's moral law. However, they can be in conflict with the latter only because this law *exists* and *applies*, and thus makes the sinful reality possible, and manifests itself within it.[21]

3.3.2 The Covenant Aspect

To us, it may seem self-evident to view natural phenomena as subject to God's *law*, but actually this is a rather recent insight. The idea of "natural laws" arose with the (more or less Christian) founders of the modern natural sciences: astronomer Johannes Kepler, physicist Galileo Galilei, philosopher René Descartes, and physicist Isaac Newton.[22] In the Middle Ages, the concept of law as we know it hardly existed. Only after the Reformation, people began, for instance, to view the laws of the state as rooted in fundamental ideas such as justice, freedom, or human rights, which in turn are rooted in the creation order. The Reformers, especially John Calvin, saw that a one-sided emphasis on God's omnipotence might lead to the erroneous idea that God acts in an arbitrary way. Therefore, they also emphasized God's faithfulness to his covenant regarding his people as well as his faithfulness to the laws that he instituted for creation, which includes the natural laws. Philosopher Dick Stafleu referred to Calvin, according to whom not only the natural laws but all laws, even (*contra*, e.g., René Descartes) the laws of logic, apply only as long as they are upheld by the Creator. This is because of his

---

21. Troost (1983, 191–92).
22. Stafleu (1987, 238–40, 256).

covenant, in which Jesus Christ is the mediator.[23]

Thus, to the cluster of related terms (revelation, law, word, will) we may now add the important term "covenant."[24] I already referred to Jeremiah 33:20 and 25, where God's "covenant with the day" and "with the night" and his "ordinances of heaven and earth" (KJV) are referred to. In Psalm 78:10 ("They did not keep God's *covenant* and[25] refused to walk in His *law*," NKJV), the poetic parallelism points to a clear connection between "covenant" and "law." So elsewhere: "[T]hey have transgressed my covenant and rebelled against my law" (Hos. 8:1). "You have caused many to stumble at the law. You have corrupted the covenant of Levi" (Mal. 2:8; also cf. Deut. 31:9). In Psalm 89 a parallel is drawn between God's faithfulness to the celestial bodies and his covenantal faithfulness to the house of David (vv. 2, 4, 5, 8, 28–29, 36–37).

This emphasis upon God's covenantal faithfulness inspired the founders of the modern natural sciences to search for these natural laws. The Reformers rejected the Platonic and Aristotelian view according to which "ideas" or "forms" must be logically-rationally transparent and self-evident. The Roman Catholics Galileo Galilei and René Descartes still held this view, but the Lutheran Johannes Kepler stated that natural laws are neither logical, nor intuitively self-evident. As philosophers formulate it: the natural laws are not necessary but contingent. If people wish to know them, they ought not to consult their intellect or their intuition but their senses—that is, they ought to do empirical research. In this way, the Reformational view concerning God's faithfulness to his creation enabled the new natural sciences to discover the laws, not *a priori* through logical-rational thought ("imagine how these laws rationally speaking ought to be") but *a posteriori* through observation and experiment, in which rational thought cooperates with empirical investigation. For instance, Aristotle

---

23. Ibid.
24. Cf. Ouweneel (2018b, especially §2.2.1).
25. The "but" in the ESV and other translations is quite confusing here.

thought it was logically self-evident that a heavy object fall faster than a light object, but in 1585, Dutch scientist Simon Stevin showed through experiments that they fall at the same speed.[26]

According to nominalism, every generalization—whereby one reasons from the concrete case to a general rule derived from it (inductive reasoning)—is unfounded, except as a practical means to an ordering of our experiences arising from an economy of thought. However, Johannes Kepler, philosopher Blaise Pascal, physicist Robert Boyle, and Isaac Newton found the basis for such generalization, which underlies all humanly formulated natural laws, in God's covenantal faithfulness in sustaining his creation. These close connections between, on the one hand, God's word or law or covenant in nature and, on the other hand, God's word or law or covenant in his relationship with humanity can help us already now, in this early stage of our investigation, to beware of every sharp distinction, let alone separation, between natural (general, creational) revelation and supernatural (special, redemptive) revelation. I will return this in the next chapter (§4.4).

3.4 Creation and Law (1)

3.4.1 Creational Word and Sustaining Word

In the previous sections we have seen how important God's "word" is in the work of sustaining (upholding) his creation. In every respect, God's work revelation is also *word* revelation, and—this is important to grasp—God's word and God's law are one. All creatures must obey his word, that is, his law. The upholding of creation through God's commanding *word* is a *law-order*, to which the entire created reality is subject. The *torah* is *Weisung*, the preferred German rendering of *torah* by Austrian-Israeli philosopher Martin Buber.[27] This neologism

---

26. Galileo is often credited for this discovery through his experiment using the famous tower of Pisa, but this occurred several years later (between 1589 and 1592).
27. See Buber (1954).

comes from the verb *weisen*, "to point out" or "to point to," but also hints at the etymologically related terms "wise" and "wit," which originally meant "to see."[28] The *torah* is what makes people "see," "know," that is, what makes people "wise" (see §3.12 for the connection between *torah* and *chokmah*, "wisdom").

The *torah* is God's manual for humanity but also for the rest of creation. Therefore, the law-order cannot be autonomous (independent of God), as deists believe. In the Bible, it is one thing to say that nature has been placed under God's *law instituted once and for all*, and to say that everything in nature obeys God's continually spoken *word* (commandments). This word was not just spoken once for all at the beginning of creation but every organism lives and moves continually through God's word, as if the commands are repeated continually anew. God's Word is not only *creational word* but also *sustaining* or *providential word*.[29] God (the Son) upholds everything not just by his power but by the *word* of his power (i.e., his powerful word; Heb. 1:3; cf. the quotation from Ps. 147 in §3.2.2). The power with which God sustains the world consists of his continually spoken word. In everything that occurs in nature, God's hand is continually present, that is, God is continually present in all things with his (commanding) word.

Actually, Scripture does not sharply distinguish between the creational and the sustaining word, and in this way implicitly indicates that they are basically one word. Thus, the Bible sometimes uses the word "creating" where it is clearly the sustenance of the world that is intended:[30] "When you send forth your Spirit, they [i.e., God's creatures] are created" (Ps. 104:30). "I form light and create darkness; I make well-being

---

28. Cf. the Indo-European root *vid-*, Lat. *videre*, "to see"; cf. Gk. *oida* (originally ϝoida), "I know," which actually is a perfect tense: "I have seen."

29. Cf. Heyns (1988, 146–47); Spykman (1985, 16) called this word "law-word."

30. Cf. Paas (1998, 90).

and create calamity; I am the Lord, who does all these things" (Isa. 45:7). "[T]he Lord has created a new thing on the earth: a woman encircles a man" (Jer. 31:22).[31] "[H]e who forms the mountains and creates the wind..." (Amos 4:13). Therefore, it hardly makes sense for James Leo Garrett to claim that God's work in history is not related to general revelation but to God's providence.[32] Not only does this imply separating the creational and the sustaining word, but it also suggests that God's acting in nature, the way he sustains the world, would not be a means whereby God's reveals himself.[33] Thus, God's laws for nature (related to general revelation) and God's acts in nature as well as in history would be separated.

3.4.2 The Law as Boundary

In the Christian confession concerning the law-order, it must be clear beforehand that God is the Origin and Upholder of the cosmic law-order, and at the same time surpasses it. John Calvin expressed this in his remarkable formula: God is beyond the laws, but is not lawless (Lat. *Deus legibus solutus est, sed non exlex*).[34] Herman Dooyeweerd formulated this biblical truth as follows, "In Christ the heart bows under the lex (in its central religious [transcendent] unity and its temporal diversity, which originates in the Creator's holy will), as the *universal boundary (which cannot be transgressed)* between the *Being* of God and the *meaning* of His creation."[35] In short: the law is the *boundary* between Creator and creature.

---

31. There are many explanations of this difficult verse (cf. http://biblehub.com/jeremiah/31-22.htm); my focus right now is simply on the Lord's "creating."
32. Garrett (1990, 45).
33. Erickson (1998, 179n1).
34. Vollenhoven (1933, appendix, n 480) gives the following references: *De aeterna praedestinatione* 1552 (CR 36, col. 361) and *Commentarius in Mosis libros* 5.1563 (CR 52, col. 49 and 131); also see 481–82, and n 2: the *solutus* does not mean "that God, in his relationship to his creature, would not faithfully keep his laws but rather that God—other than his creatures—is not himself under the law."
35. Dooyeweerd (*NC* 1:99; see also 1:108).

General Revelation (1)

In opposition to certain theological objections to this idea of the law as boundary, Dooyeweerd stated:

> As sovereign Origin, God is not *subjected* to the law. On the contrary, this *subjectedness* is the very characteristic of all that which has been created, the existence of which is limited and determined by the law. Christ Jesus also, with respect to His human nature, was *under* the law, but not with respect to His Divine nature. But if every creature is *under* the law, then the limit which the latter sets for the creature's existence can never be transgressed.[36]

Dirk H. Th. Vollenhoven replied to certain objections to the term "boundary" with this explanation:

> For the boundary between God and cosmos cannot of course be spatial, because the spatial itself belongs to what was created, and a spatial boundary can separate something in the cosmos only from something else in the same cosmos, namely, such that the latter lies *outside* the former. However, if someone would believe that God is *outside* the cosmos, he would not do justice to the confession of God's immanence [it is different with God's transcendence; WJO].
>
> Yet, the term "boundary" can certainly be used. . . . For all that is above the law for the cosmos is sovereign over the cosmos, and this honor belongs to the God of Scripture alone. And all that belongs to the cosmos is under God's law, is subject to this law, in other words, is "subject to God".[37]

Vollenhoven implicitly referred to the very important distinction between concept and idea, which we have discussed elsewhere[38] and mentioned in chapter 1; I am assuming that the reader is familiar with it. When we speak of a boundary in the strictly spatial sense, we are dealing with a spatial concept

---

36. Ibid., 99n1.
37. Vollenhoven (1933, 24–25).
38. See extensively, Ouweneel (1995, §4.2.2; 2008, 24–35, 66–68, 148–49; 2014).

in the sense that this concept includes immanent-spatial features as constitutive conceptual characteristics, that is, data that function within the *boundaries* (!) of the spatial modality. However, this spatial term can also be used as an idea in order to *refer* to data that surpass the *boundaries* of the spatial modality (notice how the term "boundary" is used here!), such as when we speak of the law as a boundary. This notion is not a strictly spatial concept but an idea (also called "boundary-concept," in which the term "boundary" is again used as an idea).

At any rate, we should not conclude from the term "boundary" that God is present only beyond the boundary, and not within the cosmos, which is within the boundary, that is, subject to the law. In the words of Andree Troost: "What we, for instance, tend to call 'natural laws' is God's own law-giving presence in nature."[39] God is beyond the law as well as beyond the cosmos, but at the same time he is within the cosmos — but not under the law.

3.5 Creation and Law (2)

3.5.1 Was the Law Created?

If the law is revelation, if the law is God's law-*word*, this is important for whether God's law is part of the cosmos, whether it was created with the rest of the cosmos. On this point, the two brothers-in-law, Dutch philosophers Herman Dooyeweerd and Dirk H. Th. Vollenhoven, did not see eye to eye. Dooyeweerd called the law only a certain *side* of the cosmos *itself* (the law-side), whereas Vollenhoven distinguished between law and cosmos.[40] He spoke of a triad: God - law - cosmos, and believed that the cosmos can be adopted into an ontology, whereas this is not possible with the law.

This triad returned in the "three-factor theology" or

---

39. Troost (2004, 323n4).
40. Vollenhoven (1950, 25–26); see Tol and Bril (1992, 55, 83, 113, 155, 172–73, 184, 190–91); cf. Stellingwerff (1992, 208–10); for the early Vollenhoven, see Kok (1992, 283–90).

"three-factor worldview," as Gordon Spykman called it, namely, God, God's Word, and the cosmos.[41] I wonder, however, whether it is correct and appropriate to call God a "factor" alongside his Word and the cosmos. This formulation at least suggests that all three have their own place within one single ontic order.

According to Vollenhoven, the law is apparently what God has instituted *for* the cosmos, and thus it is distinct from the cosmos as such. Conversely, Dooyeweerd would probably have replied that God has instituted the law for the subjects (the things subject to the law) and that law and subjects each constitute a "side" of the same cosmos: law-side and subject-side. It is difficult to enter more deeply into this dispute because little can be found on the matter in Vollenhoven's writings.[42] However, we can widen the discussion by asking what Dooyeweerd's distinction between law- and subject-side implies for the question whether the law belongs to the cosmos, and thus was created, or not.

This question is linked with another, related question, namely, that of the temporality (and thus, immanence) or supratemporality (and thus, transcendence) of the law.[43] The publication of some texts by Vollenhoven[44] has supplied us with some more access to Vollenhoven's ideas on the matter.[45] We will return to the question whether the law is part of creation in §3.11 below.

Vollenhoven distinguishes three kinds of law.[46]

(a) the central Law of Love *above* the cosmos, which addresses humans alone;

---

41. Spykman (1992, 59–63, 76–77, 92).
42. See Steen (1983, 284–85); Ouweneel (1986, 353); cf. Bril (1986, 256, 275–77).
43. See §§3.6–3.8 and 4.1–4.3; Steen (1983, 48, 233–35); cf. Ouweneel (1986, 346–58).
44. Tol and Bril (1992).
45. See also Tol in ibid., 17, 19, 33–34, 48, 71.
46. Ibid., 55–56, 113–14, 138, 156, 178–79; cf. Stellingwerff (1992, 209–10).

(b) the structural laws *in* the cosmos (which, however, are not a "part" or "side" of the cosmos itself);

(c) the positive law (that is, the law as it is positivized by humans).

The first of the three has to do with creational direction, and the other two with creational structure.[47] In my opinion, from this distinction Vollenhoven could already have concluded himself that the law in meaning (a) is God's *un*created will-word, which subsequently, within immanent reality, refracts into a multiplicity of laws and ordinances (meanings [b] and [c]). I do not see any problem in calling them a "side" of reality as such, which thus belongs to creation. God's transcendent law-word is the *uncreated* law, the law as a "side" of creation is the *created* law (see further in §3.5.3).

3.5.2 Law and Lawfulness

The law as a boundary involves a separation between him who subjects created things to the law (God) and these created things that are subjected to the law (the creature). Each creature demonstrates subjection to God's law by functioning in an orderly or lawful way, that is, by behaving according to the law-order that God has instituted. Each creature possesses the measure of the law in its own nature, and thus behaves according to this measure, lawfully.[48]

There is indeed a close connection between the law-order *for* creatures and the lawfulness or orderliness *of* creatures. As J. A. Heyns put it, "[O]rder is the result of God's ordering [of things] through the law."[49] The (particularly Kantian) term *transcendental*, which must be carefully distinguished from

---

47. For this distinction by Vollenhoven himself, see Ouweneel (2008, 73–74, 95–97, 246–50; 2014; 2015; 2017, 66–69 and passim).
48. Expressive terms for "lawfulness" are the Dutch/Afrikaans *wetmatigheid* and the German *Gesetzmässigkeit*: answering to the measure (*maat* and *Mass*) of the law (*wet* and *Gesetz*); cf. Strauss (1979, 257–58); Strauss and Visagie (1984, 62).
49. Heyns (1988, 110).

"transcendent," refers to the law that sets a *limit* (boundary) to things; in other words, the law-order is the *transcendental condition* of created reality. The law-order determines and delineates reality.

Conversely, the term refers *empirically* to all factual (orderly, lawful) matters that are subject to the law. Or, as philosopher Hendrik Hart would say, the *world order* stands in juxtaposition with the *ordered world*, or empirical reality. In other words: the *universalia* (general laws, principles, norms, concept, universals) stand in opposition to the *particularia* (the concrete things, plants, animals, humans, states of affairs, particulars). Thus, the biotic *order* (the whole of all biotic laws) stands in opposition to the biotic *world*, consisting of biotic *subjects* (living organisms) and biotic *objects* (inanimate things that function within the biotic life of organisms). The social, economic, and juridical *order* (the whole of all social, economic, and juridical laws) stands in opposition to the social, economic, and juridical *world*, consisting of social, economic, and juridical *subjects* (always humans) and social, economic, and juridical *objects* (inanimate things, plants, and animals that function within the social, economic, and juridical life of humans), and so on.

To put it in another way: the (law-)order applies universally; it is one order for all created things. The empirical world exists individually, that is, as a totality of distinct things, plants, animals, and humans. It also exists subjectively, that is, as subject (subjected) to this order. The world order would not make sense without things subjected to it; the ordered world would not make sense without the world order to which it is subject.

3.5.3 Summary: The Law As "Side" and "Boundary"

Herman Dooyeweerd's distinction between the law-side and the subject-side of all created things is rooted in the correlation between law-order and lawfulness (orderliness) as just described. The transcendental aspect (related to the conditions that make the existence of things possible) belongs to the law-side, and the empirical aspect (related to the concrete, observable things) belongs to the subject-side.

There is an ambiguity in this spatial idea of two "sides" because it seems to conflict with that other spatial idea: the law as "boundary" between God and the creature. This might be taken to point to an inherent weakness in the idea of the boundary as such. This idea seems to suggest that the law is not part of creation, that is, the law is not a creature for it is the God-given law *for* the creatures. However, according to the "side" idea the law is a side *of* the created things *themselves*, and thus belongs to the created world (the law could be called its "upper side" in order to emphasize that all created things are "sub-"ject to it).

In my view, this seeming conflict can be solved through a comparison with the "revelation" and "word" ideas discussed earlier. The law in its transcendent meaning of God's law-word does not belong to creation, just as the eternal Word (Lat. *Verbum aeternum*) does not belong to it. God's word is not a creation of his, but is his own creational word *for* creation. This word creates but was not created, no more than the One who speaks this word was created. This is one side of the story.

The other side is this: the law in its immanent meaning participates (takes part) in creational reality, just as the eternal Word (Lat. *Verbum aeternum*) did in the person of Christ (at the time of incarnation) and in the form of Scripture (at the time of inscripturation). As such, I see no difficulty calling law indeed a "side" of created reality; it is "part" of creation as far as both the immanent world and the transcendent human heart are concerned (see further in §§3.9.1 (b), 3.11, and 3.12). Many problems in this domain will be solved as soon as we discover that related terms such as "word," "revelation," and "law" have both a transcendent and an immanent dimension.

3.6 Objectionable Approaches

3.6.1 Six Errors

It is quite understandable that many theologians and philosophers have stumbled over the complicated relationship between God, the law, and the cosmos.[50] Here are a few approaches that I believe must be rejected:[51]

(a) *God is under the law.* This is the view that places God inside the law-boundary as if he, in some way, would be subjected to his own law-order. Thus, the philosopher Gottfried W. Leibniz tried to defend God in his theodicy by asserting that there are situations in the world that even God would not be able to change; so don't blame him for them.[52] And in his view of justice, philosopher of law Hugo Grotius (or, De Groot) argued that, in the field of morality, we are dealing with eternal and unchangeable natural laws to which even God is necessarily subject.[53] God commands the good because it is good. He would not be able to change the eternal fact that the good is simply good, asserted Grotius. However, this claim affects God's sovereign creational will. The good is good because God commands it, and, I would add, God commands it because *God* is good. This addition is important because any voluntarist view of God, which denies that he has a nature, must be avoided.[54]

(b) *God is lawless.* Other thinkers fell in the opposite error, and claimed that God being above the law is tyrannical arbitrariness (philosopher William of Ockham).[55] They fail(ed) to see that even acting in an arbitrary way presupposes a

---

50. See Dengerink (1986, 138–42, 175, 178, actually his entire chapter 4), Kalsbeek (1970, 66–71), and Troost (2005, 54–70).
51. Cf. Heyns (1988, 118): "[E]ach philosophical or other viewpoint that denies, absolutizes, subjectifies, or relativizes the cosmic law-order will have to be rejected on biblical grounds."
52. *Essais de théodicée*, 1710.
53. *De iure belli ac pacis*, 1625.
54. Cf. Plantinga (1980); Wolterstorff (1981).
55. Regarding Ockham and this doctrine, see Ockham (1983).

norm to which this acting is subject, and by which the measure of supposed arbitrariness can be determined. Even the nihilism of philosopher Friedrich Nietzsche and philosopher Jean-Paul Sartre, who have propagated lawlessness, and consequently fell into arbitrariness, was possible only because the world is *not* lawless and normless, and they intuitively thought from the perspective of *this* reality.[56] Ultimately, we cannot say anything sensible about God's arbitrary or non-arbitrary acting because all our thinking remains on this side of the law-boundary. We cannot cross the threshold, and as a consequence, we can think meaningfully only about what is on this side of the law-boundary.

(c) *Erasing the law-boundary.* Equally objectionable as the attempt to place God inside the law-boundary, as if he were subject to his own law-order, is the view that erases the law-boundary between God and the creature. This is done by *pantheism*, which equates God with the cosmos (the divine and the cosmic are identical). One could think here of the motto of Dutch philosopher Baruch Spinoza: "God, or [that is,] Nature" (Lat. *Deus sive Natura*),[57] or of the revival of pantheism in the modern New Age movement; but also of the horizontalizing of faith: God comes to us in the form of "the" poor and oppressed.[58] A very different example is the teaching of Thomas Aquinas concerning the analogy of being (Lat. *analogia entis*), in which God and humanity are viewed as participating in the same being as the first thing known (Lat. *primum notum*), which in its own way also involves an erasure of the law-boundary between God and the creature.[59]

(d) *The law-boundary understood as separation.* In Reformational philosophy, the philosophical idea of the law as boundary is directed especially against all kinds and forms of pantheism (see [c]). *Deism* is the opposite danger because

---

56. Van Riessen (1980, 143; cf. 161).
57. In his *Ethica* of 1677.
58. Regarding this point, cf. Troost (1992b, 130).
59. Smit (1980, 185); cf. Spykman (1992, 65, 225–26, 288).

it created a definitive separation between God and his creature. In this way, the creature is severed from its divine beginning (Gk. *archē*; cf. "beginning" in Rev. 3:14), the sciences are completely secularized, and God is enclosed in his so-called transcendence. Therefore, Andree Troost recommended that we define the idea of the law as boundary more accurately as *boundary-and-connection*.[60] The boundary between two countries is not only a separation but also a connection between the two. The notion of connection can also underscore the fact that the law is always correlated to what is subject to it and to that to which it applies.

(e) *The law reckoned to what is the subject*. Related errors involve confusing the law-side and the subject-side . The law is incorrectly placed on the subject-side of reality, particularly in the human reason (e.g., in nominalism), or in history in its totality (historicism), or in the distinct phenomena (phenomenology), or in a totality of relationships. However, the law must not be localized in the facts, whatever they are, as if only the subject-side of reality would objectively exist. Thus, the subject is placed here above the law, instead of people recognizing the law as boundary between Creator and creator, that is, above the subject.

(f) *The law absolutized*. In the Bible, the law is not absolute but relational; the law expresses a relationship between God (the Law-Giver) and the creature (that which stands under the law).[61] The law may never be absolutized, as is done by (conceptual) realism ("the universals are more real than the particulars"). This view recognizes the law but deifies it to a certain extent. In this way, the Law-Giver is denied.[62] We see this, for instance, in Plato's idealism, which does the reverse of what nominalism does: the law is severed from God

---

60. Troost (1992b, 126–27); cf. Dooyeweerd (1960, 113–14).
61. I formulate it this way, though I am aware of the understandable objection by Dengerink (1986, 129) that speaking of a "relationship" supposes two entities as *relata*, which each have their own "place" in the relational whole.
62. Van Riessen (1980, 144).

and made independent by exalting it beyond humanity to the world of ideas, a metaphysical realm of norms and values, or to a logical world order (Gk. *logos*). Here the boundary between Law-Giver and law is erased by viewing the deity as the Supreme Idea in the world of ideas.

3.6.2 Rationality and Rationalism

Also within the Christian through tradition, there has been a strong tendency to emphasize the rationality of the cosmos (or of God's general revelation), as in the case of the physicist (and priest) Stanley L. Jaki. He argued that this rationality of faith implies that, in some way, empirical phenomena are logically coherent. Human rationality is viewed as a (weak) reflection of God's absolute rationality. But God's rationality is also reflected in the cosmos and in the way the cosmos functions, so that human rationality and cosmic rationality overlap. The Christian character of this idea of rationality must certainly not be exaggerated, for we clearly recognize in it the Greek idea of the *logos*. This was first launched by the Greek philosopher Heraclitus, and later especially by the Stoics (Zeno of Citium). At an early stage, the Greeks associated the notion of the *logos* with the idea of order and coherence. From this, even the idea of cosmic reason was developed (Stoics; Alexandrian-Jewish philosopher Philo; Alexandrian philosopher Plotinus), that is, the idea of the order and coherence (rationality) of the cosmos. The parallel between human and cosmic rationality was originally a Greek idea.

At a later stage, this idea was adopted in Christian thought, where it no doubt had its most fruitful elaboration,[63] though with a rationalist overemphasis upon the rationality of the cosmic order. It was overlooked that, in addition to a world order that is logical, it possesses just as much a physical, a biotic, a perceptive, a sensitive, a historical-formative, a lingual, a social, an economic, an aesthetic, a juridical, a moral,

---

63. The extent to which the logos idea in John 1:1–14 underwent the influence of the Greek logos philosophy is a fascinating subject; cf. *TDNT* 4:77–91.

General Revelation (1)

and a pistical character. All these aspects of the world order are perfectly equivalent to the rational; it is one of the great merits of Christian philosophy to have discovered this.[64] Human rationality corresponds with cosmic rationality, but it is equally true that, for instance, human physicality and morality correspond with cosmic physicality and morality (please remember that all things in the cosmos, latently or actively, function as moral objects in human lives). No priority may be assigned to the logical world order at the expense of the other aspects mentioned.

This logical order focuses only on humans, one-sidedly viewed here as logical subjects (whereas they are just as much historical-formative, lingual, social, economic, aesthetic, juridical, moral, and pistical subjects), together with all non-human things (inanimate things, plants, animals, events, states of affairs), one-sidedly viewed according to their logical object-function, that is, according to their logical objectifiability. In addition to this, however, these things also have perceptive, sensitive, historical-formative, lingual, social, economic, aesthetic, juridical, moral, and pistical object-functions (i.e., they function as objects in the perceptive, sensitive, historical-formative, lingual, social, economic, aesthetic, juridical, moral, and pistical lives of humans). In other words, they can be observed, felt, shaped, named, marketed, taxed, or appreciated by humans, or they are objects of their sense of justice, their affections, and their beliefs.[65]

3.6.3 Again, God and the Law

God is not identical with the law, nor is the law identical with God (although the law is indeed the word of God's own mouth). Only when we speak of the divine law in its transcendent fullness and unity, *as the Word of God in Christ*, can we speak of the eternity and divinity of the law. I say this with

---

64. In addition to many others, cf. Troost (2005); Strauss (2009); Ouweneel (2014).
65. Hart (1981, 189–91).

great prudence in order to avoid any new misunderstandings. This is because we must realize that, in its immanent diversity — in the multiplicity of the numerous laws and norms of empirical cosmic reality — the law (the norm, the principle) is never eternal or divine, not even the law-side of the transcendent human heart. It is *human*; therefore, there can be nothing divine about it.

To use a plain example: the laws of gravity are God-given, yet in themselves they are neither eternal, nor divine. They are natural laws, belonging to the law-side of nature, and are facets of creation, not of the Creator. At the same time, these laws belong to the immanent-temporal refraction of the law according to its transcendent-eternal character, and ultimately this law in its transcendent-religious sense is the word of God's own mouth (cf. Deut. 8:3; Matt. 4:4). Thus, we find both the transcendent and the immanent dimensions in the law of God, just as we found them in the revelation of God, in the Word of God, and similar ideas.

Rationalism emphasizes universal laws, but also exhibits the tendency to place the law in the human subject, that is, to reduce it to, or consider it as a product of, human reason. *Irrationalism* exhibits the opposite tendency: the unique event functions as a kind of law, and is absolutized beyond the stability and universality of the actual law.[66] In these cases, the subject and the law are absolutized with regard to God, and this cannot be made up for by subsequently calling this law internal, natural, or metaphysical.

By way of example we can think here of the discussions concerning "natural rights" in the scholastic and humanistic philosophy of law, as in the case of Hugo Grotius men-

---

66. Van Riessen (1980, 145–46). Strauss (1983, 50–51; 1991, 130–31) argued that nominalism is rationalistic because it recognizes universals (general concepts/ideas) within human reason, as well as irrationalistic because it does not recognize the ontic laws extrinsic to humans, and absolutizes what is uniquely individual.

tioned above.[67] There is no nature-in-itself, no law-in-itself, no creature-in-itself, no substance (in Kantian German: *Ding an sich*) that would or could ever be autonomous with respect to God. Reality must never be narrowed down to either its subject-side or its law-side. The subject must always be viewed in strict correlation with the law-side, that is, as placed under God's law. Otherwise, it is torn asunder because its law-side is severed from it, made independent, placed over against the subject-side.[68]

3.7 Natural and Supernatural

3.7.1 Two Orders?

We now return to the distinction mentioned earlier between God's *natural* acting, that is, according to his own natural laws, and his *supernatural* acting, that is, when he ostensibly breaks through the natural laws that he has instituted. I believe that, no matter how convenient it may be in the *practical* language of faith, such a distinction cannot stand up to theological scrutiny. The origin of this distinction lies in the absolutization of natural laws, particularly in the modern restriction of nature within its closed worldview. Here, miracles are understood either as divinely caused deviations from his own laws (theological fundamentalism; see chapter 9), or as contraventions of God's own law, and therefore impossible (theological liberalism; see chapters 11–12). Both erroneous views presuppose the same nature–supernature dualism, which goes back to the scholastic nature–grace dualism.

The law is never absolute. Our term "natural law" is nothing but our description of the way God usually commands — preserves, sustains, upholds — his creation from moment to moment (§3.8). And the so-called "supernatural" miracles are nothing but what are *for us* God's unusual acts. In both cases we are dealing with God's sovereign acting in the cosmos. It would be unwise to overemphasize this notion of the un-

---

67. Berkouwer (1955, 191–214).
68. Troost (1978, 111); earlier he had described his view more briefly (1972, 172); cf. also Mekkes (1961) and Smit (1980).

usual. Much of what seems to us uncommon, or even supernatural, is possibly uncommon only because of our limited knowledge of the law-order.[69] Instead of speaking of aberrations from the law-order, we must, on the one hand, acknowledge our extremely limited insight in the law-order, and, on the other hand, strongly emphasize the *fixity* and *constancy* of the law. Without this latter, the law would not be law. The degree to which what is subject to the law may be unfixed and inconstant is directly proportional to the degree of the law's fixity and constancy. The degree to which what is subject to the law in uniquely individual is directly proportional to the degree of the law's universality.

The traditional ontological dualism between the natural and the supernatural within theology and philosophy is a variety of scholastic dualism, such that God or the divine is placed in the sphere of the supernatural.[70] The operation of the latter sphere within the natural sphere is viewed either as indirect, mediate, normal, or as direct, immediate, miraculous. In the former case, the supernatural works *through* the natural, in the latter case it works *despite* the natural. The latter is the well-known posture of the supernatural being "against nature" (Lat. *contra naturam*) within scholasticism. J. A. Heyns came dangerously close to this by distinguishing between two "orders":

> God has, if we may put it this way, two orders: a wonder-order and a law-order. His immediate and direct way of acting is wondrous, but his mediate and indirect acting is law-wise. Therefore, we can say that the wonder [miracle] is first, and that

---

69. E.g., if paranormal phenomena exist, they need not be supernatural at all; they may simply be hitherto unexplained in terms of natural laws.

70. Regarding the nature–supernature dualism, see Berkouwer (1952, 205–221) and Vander Stelt (1978, 272–78, 305, 314–15); see also Ouweneel (1987a, 70–72) and Berkouwer (1967, 24–27), and his references to Kuyper and Bavinck, who already expressed criticisms of the nature–supernature dualism. It is bizarre that Loonstra (1999, 18) so easily describes "Reformed scholasticism" as "the academic elaboration of what was the goal of the Reformation."

the law is rooted in the wonder. All this means that, according to its deepest essence, creation is a wonder, and that God uses that law-order by involving it in the totality of his wondrous acts.[71]

In contrast to Heyns, I see no room at all for distinguishing between two orders, for God's acts according to the law are equally called "wonders" (see §§3.1.3 and 3.7.2). Heyns' distinction between God's mediate-indirect and immediate-direct acting is a residue of scholastic thinking. In opposition to this scholastic-rationalistic explanation of the relationship between Creator and creature, we must emphasize that this relationship can never be understood or defined in a theoretical-analytical way; it can only be approximated described in the form of ideas. This has nothing to do with mysticism or irrationalism, but rather with the true biblical revelation concerning God, concerning religion, and concerning the human heart.[72] We cannot grasp this relationship in a logical-rational way, that is, we cannot contain it within concepts (from Lat. *concipere*, "to take hold of, to get a grip on"). Rather, it demands obedient submission and openly confessed acknowledgement.

Philosopher John Vander Stelt also argued that God cannot possibly be identified with some supernatural sphere. Rather, God is the Creator of *all* spheres, and as such he totally transcends all spheres.[73] Moreover, he argued that the visible world is never purely natural, as opposed to the supernatural, as if the natural world would be (semi-)autonomous. We have seen that as created reality, the visible world is *continually* oriented toward the Creator and dependent upon his *continually* spoken word of power. The rigid scholastic dualism of nature and grace (the supernatural) divides created reality into two parts: the natural world, for which God once

---

71. Heyns (1988, 111).
72. Cf. Ouweneel (1986, chapter 5) and (2008, §6.4).
73. See note 71.

long ago instituted natural laws and with which he need not bother any longer (ultimately such a view always degenerates into a form of deism), and the supernatural world, to which belong the angels, heaven, human souls, invisible things, and also the Creator himself.

3.7.2 Miracles

It is important to realize that criticism of the scholastic nature-supernature dualism does not imply a denial of biblical miracles. The only thing I deny is that these miracles must necessarily be interpreted according to this scholastic dualism. The Bible sometimes speaks of miracles ("wonders") that in our view are purely natural, for instance, concerning the weather: "Hear this, O Job; / stop and consider the *wondrous* works of God [or, God's *miracles*, EXB]. / Do you know how God lays his command upon them / and causes the lightning of his cloud to shine?[74] Do you know the balancings [or, hoverings] of the clouds, / the *wondrous* works of him who is perfect in knowledge?" (Job 37:14-16; cf. 5:9; 9:10). Or concerning the development of a child in their mother's womb: "[Y]ou formed my inward parts; / you knitted me together in my mother's womb. / I praise you, for I am fearfully and *wonderfully* made. / *Wonderful* are your works" (Ps. 139:13-14). Again, "wonderful" is here the same as "miraculous" (cf. GW and NOG; also see Exod. 7:3; 11:10, "wonders" is "miracles").

The Bible does not seem to acknowledge any distinction between natural and supernatural miracles. To state this simply: *everything is a wonder that makes us wonder*. If one wishes to maintain belief in biblical miracles—as I do—it is wise to abandon the natural-supernatural dualism for the very reason that on the basis of this dualism, which in the Enlightenment was secularized, biblical miracles have often been *denied*. The reason is that some people—consistent with their frame of thought—asserted that the idea of supernatural miracles is actually unbiblical since such miraculous events disobey nat-

---

74. Did Elihu see the "whirlwind" (storm) of Job 38:1 approaching?

General Revelation (1)

ural laws instituted by God, and thus God himself.

Indeed, the central question here is *whether* there are any miracles that are against nature (Lat. *contra naturam*), i.e., against natural laws. Does not such a claim presuppose a perfect knowledge of natural laws, which is itself a tremendous overestimation of the natural sciences, and presuppose the idea of a closed worldview (i.e., a worldview in which there is no place for an intervening God)? Is it not much better to say with Augustine that miracles are not in conflict with nature but only with the knowledge that we so far have obtained concerning nature?[75] Sixteen centuries later, science has made incredible progress—but Augustine's statement is still true.

Moreover, what do we mean by the term "nature" other than either the nature of created things themselves, a nature that is delineated by God's law, or God's own nature, a nature that is not delineated by any law but is what it is because God is what he is? Miracles that we view as supernatural, or *un*natural, or even *anti*-natural, may perhaps harmonize with God's nature because they always involve God's acts, and even God's being.

Some questions may further clarify this. Was it unnatural for Jesus Christ, the Son of God, through whom God created the world, to walk on water, to multiply five loaves and two fishes, or to change water into wine? Were these miracles not rather perfectly natural for him who is God and Man in one person, the Sustainer of all things? If people wish to use the expression supernatural, let them realize that the supernatural is perfectly natural for God, whereas, conversely, God's perfectly natural acts, such as the thunderstorm and the "balancing" (or "hovering") clouds (Job 37:14-16) and the formation of a child in their mother's womb (Ps. 139:14-17), are *miraculous* ("wondrous") works and acts in the eyes of humans.

---

75. "Not against nature but against what the nature known [to us right now] is" (Lat. *Non contra naturam, sed contra quam est nota natura*), De Civitate Dei XXI.8; cf. Diemer (1943).

3.8 The Meaning of the Law-Order

3.8.1 Natural Laws and Norms

The "meaning"[76] of the law-order, and thus of God's revelation as it comes to light in this law-order, is God's demand that is expressed in it toward his creatures. It is the demand to exist for his glory and honor, to serve him, and with respect to humans, to love him above all: "So, whether you eat or drink, or whatever you do, do all to the glory of God" (1 Cor. 10:31). "[W]hatever you do, in word or deed, do everything in the name of the Lord Jesus, giving thanks to God the Father through him" (Col. 3:17). "We love [or, Let us love, DRA] because he first loved us" (1 John 4:19).

At the same time, this Law of Love exhibits *within* the immanent-cosmic law-order an important difference with the natural laws. The Law of Love applies to humans only, whereas natural laws apply partly or entirely to all creatures; partly, because, for instance, the logical laws of thought do not apply to animals, nor perceptive and sensitive laws to plants, nor biotic laws to inanimate things. All natural laws are *descriptive*: if A, then always B. But norms are *prescriptive*: if A, then B *ought to* follow. Natural laws cannot be trespassed (someone slipping from a tower cannot decide not to fall), whereas humans, as free and responsible creatures, have the intrinsic possibility to disobey normative laws. Natural laws tell us how something *is* (e.g., "iron expands when heated"), norms tell us how something *ought* to be (e.g., "if you wish to act in a logical, historical, social, economic, [etc.] way, then you ought to act according to those and those logical, historical, social, economic, [etc.] norms — but you can also choose to ignore them, and then you will act in an illogical, ahistorical, asocial, uneconomic,[77] [etc.] way").

---

76. A truly Dooyeweerdian term: creation not only "has" meaning (as something that on second thought could be attached to it) but "is" (represents) meaning (is meaningful) because it is God's creation; cf. Kalsbeek (1970, 71–80); Troost (1985/87; 2005, 75–76).

77. Notice, there are no such words as "unphysical," "unbiotic," or "unpsy-

General Revelation (1)

Jan D. Dengerink rejected this distinction by Herman Dooyeweerd between natural and normative laws.[78] He claimed that it was rooted in the Baden variety of Neo-Kantianism,[79] and believed that also in natural laws we are dealing with normativity for humanity.[80] He even asserted that to some extent animals can also function as subjects in (i.e., as functioning under the laws of) the normative modalities (from the logical to the pistical),[81] but then, of course, without any question of normativity in their case. I am not convinced by Dengerink's ideas. First, sins on the arithmetic level (computational errors, miscalculations) are not qualified by the arithmetic modality as such but rather by the logical modality. Second, what we call social behavior, or the propensity for gathering (hinting at the economic), or affection among animals (hinting at the ethical), can be entirely reduced to the instinctive. Thus, such behavior is not qualified by the social, the economic, or the ethical modality, respectively, but by the psychical modalities.

3.8.2 The Responsive Structure

When referring to God's law for created reality, Dengerink often spoke of God's *creational* word,[82] whereas others distinguish between God's creational word and God's sustaining word.[83] Cosmic reality, and therefore also humanity, said Dengerink, exist by, and on behalf of, this creational word. Within God's creation, humans are the only creatures that can and do speak a "counter-word" (i.e., respond) to this word in the full

---

chical" (not to be confused with non-physical, non-biotic, non-psychical; non-biotic means that the biotic laws do not apply, "unbiotic" would mean that certain biotic things would not obey certain biotic laws, which is impossible).

78. Dengerink (1986, 222–23).
79. Ibid., 222–40.
80. Ibid., 176, 231.
81. Ibid., 249.
82. Ibid., 121, 129–32, 188, 193, 253, 335, 338.
83. J. A. Heyns; see notes 15 and 28.

sense of the term (see §1.5.3, including note 62). This law-relationship with God does not stand under any natural law but under the normative law. In the empirical world, humans are the only creatures that have been placed under *norms*.[84] Regarding this creational word, they have response-ability, which they can never escape as long as they are under the creational word, that is, eternally.[85]

Several philosophers—Andree Troost, Jan Dengerink, Henk Geertsema—have tried to express this truth by stating that humans are the only creatures characterized by a "responsive (or, answering) structure."[86] Dengerink linked this with the human act-structure, which I have called the "spiritive structure."[87] The answer ("counter-word") of humans is a response to the invitation of God's creational word in its continual actuality, and at the same time is made possible, as well as carried, by this very same creational word.

Over against the power that goes forth from God's creational word—a word that appeals to human response-ability—he places his covenantal faithfulness.[88] God not only *binds* creation, including humans, to his law but he *binds* himself to his creation (including humanity) in his law, without himself being *bound* to his own law (cf. §3.4.2). In this sense, the law is a revelation of his *faithfulness* to his own creation, and, as we saw, it is even called a *covenant* (Jer. 33:20, 25; cf. Ps. 89:2-3). Because of this unbreakable covenant, humans can

---

84. In the non-empirical, yet created world, angels, too, have been placed under norms: "Bless the LORD, O you his angels, you mighty ones who do his word, obeying the voice of his word!" (Ps. 103:20). "Are they [i.e., angels] not all ministering spirits sent out to serve for the sake of those who are to inherit salvation?" (Heb. 1:14; cf. Ezek. 28:13–15, about a rebellious cherub).

85. Cf. Troost (1969, 21; 1976, 24–54, especially 26–28).

86. Troost (1976, 30); Dengerink (1986, 124, 175, 181, 211, 251, 335, 338–39, 353); Geertsema (2005).

87. Dengerink (1986, 338–39); Ouweneel (1986, 217–60; 2008, 95–98; 2014).

88. Notice how Heb. *chesed* is "faithfulness," either on God's side (covenantal loyalty to his own promises) or on the human side (covenantal loyalty exhibited in obeying God's commandments).

General Revelation (1)

safely trust the lawfulness of reality. For us, this confidence is not only self-evident but also absolutely indispensable for being able to live on this earth. If we, consciously or unconsciously, could not trust natural laws (the law of gravity or inertia, the numerical laws, the physiological laws of the body, etc.), the laws of thought and communication, through which human relationships are possible, and so on, our existence in this world would be completely impossible.

It is important not only to believe in a God who performs miracles, and who sometimes acts within reality in a way that is totally different from what we had thought to be possible or likely, based on our knowledge of the law-order or the natural laws. It is equally important to believe in a God who exhibits his covenantal faithfulness in the fixity and constant regularity of the cosmic law-order.

3.8.3 Law and Time

Another important subject is the relationship between law and time. The views of Herman Dooyeweerd in this regard played an essential role in his thinking but also provoked much discussion, not only among philosophers but also among theologians. This concerned in particular his notion of the supratemporality of the human heart. Elsewhere, I have tried to explain this view and to clear up some misunderstandings, for instance, by replacing the term "supratemporal" with "plenitemporal" (referring to the "fullness" of time) in order to avoid any thought of a dualism.[89] Because of the persisting misunderstandings, I have since developed the habit of replacing the term "temporal" with "immanent," and "supratemporal" (or "plenitemporal") with "transcendent." Of course, in this way the danger, or the accusation, of a dualism is not entirely circumvented; in principle, all the misunderstandings around Dooyeweerd's view concerning the temporal and the supra- or plenitemporal might arise again when we speak of the relationship between the immanent

---

89. Ouweneel (1986, chapters 5–6).

and the transcendent.

Dooyeweerd explained his idea of the temporality of the modal order and the supratemporality of the human heart with the help of the prism metaphor. This involves the idea of—as he called it—the temporal refraction (like the refraction of the one ray of light through a prism into many rays of different colors) within empirical reality, and the supra- (or pleni-)temporal concentration of the law-order (as the concentrations of rays in a focal point) within the human heart, and ultimately in the root of the cosmos: the first Adam and the last Adam, respectively.[90] On the one hand, the heart is the supratemporal (or plenitemporal, transcendent) fullness and unity *of all modal functions themselves*; on the other hand, the functions constitute the temporal (immanent) refraction *of the heart itself*. There is no room here for any form of dualism in the sense of a separation and antithesis between the heart and the functions.

Another well-known metaphor is that of the one root and the many ramifications: the transcendent heart is the root, the immanent-modal functions are the ramifications. The branches are the offshoot of the root *itself*; the root is the concentration point of the branches *themselves*. Here, too, there is no room for any dualism between root and branches; the idea alone would be absurd. The root is the root *of* the branches, the branches are the branches *of* the root.

Now the question arises concerning the relationship in which the law stands to the heart and the functions. The eternal, uncreated God has subjected the transcendent (supra- or plenitemporal), created human heart to his transcendent-religious Law of Love. This is the one law, in its transcendent, integral meaning-fullness and -totality, which, within immanent reality, branches off into many different ordinances, laws, norms, and principles. Just as the plenitemporal heart

---

90. See extensively, Dooyeweerd (*NC* 2:99–107 in particular), and many articles in the journal *Philosophia Reformata*; see references in Ouweneel (1986).

General Revelation (1)

expresses itself in the many temporal functions, the one plenitemporal Law of Love expresses itself through the heart in the temporal, created law spheres[91] in a tremendous variety of ordinances, laws, norms, and principles. Thus, in one's transcendent, religious heart, a person is subject to the transcendent, religious Law of Love; in one's immanent functions, a person is subject to the great diversity of immanent laws of God's creation order: numerical laws, spatial (geometric) laws, kinematic, physical, biotic, perceptive, and sensitive laws, logical, historical, lingual, social, economic, aesthetic, juridical, moral, and pistical norms. In addition to this, there are structural laws: laws that delineate the structure of a certain class of entities (if something is to be called a dog, a factory, or a painting, this entity ought to satisfy certain structural laws, which make dogs to be dogs, factories to be factories, and paintings to be paintings).

We can think here of the same metaphors mentioned earlier: (a) The immanent-temporal laws constitute the refraction of the transcendent-eternal Law of Love, and the Law of Love is the plenitemporal point of convergence and integration (focal point) of all temporal law spheres, of all modal laws and norms, and all entity-defining structural laws that the Creator has instituted for immanent-temporal life. (b) The religious Law of Love is the transcendent-plenitemporal root, the many distinct laws form the immanent-temporal branches.

Dooyeweerd did not claim that the actual concentration point of the cosmos would lie in the transcendent human heart;[92] in his opinion, it lies in the last Adam: Jesus Christ (1 Cor. 15:45). This is conceivable because Dooyeweerd was in search of a concentration point that ultimately transcends the

---

91. Every modal aspect of cosmic reality corresponds with a certain law sphere, with the totality of laws belonging to that aspect: to the physical (biotic, logical, lingual, economic, [etc.]) modality belong the physical (biotic, logical, lingual, economic, [etc.]) laws and norms; see extensively, Ouweneel (2014).
92. *Contra* Frame (1987, 92).

totality of created reality, whereas the transcendent human heart is just as much created as all immanent things in the cosmos. Therefore, *within* the law in its transcendent sense, we must clearly distinguish (*not* create a dualistic division!): on the one hand, there is the law in its uncreated, eternal, divine sense: the law is the eternal Word of God's own mouth, as we saw. On the other hand, there is the law in the sense of the law-side of the human heart, which, as law, is entirely correlated to the heart on the subject-side of created reality, and as such belongs to created reality just as much as the heart itself (cf. §§3.2 and 3.3). In short: there is the uncreated transcendent and the created transcendent.

Compare this now with Jesus Christ himself. The law is the law *for* the creatures, but it is the law *of* Christ (1 Cor. 9:21; Gal. 6:2); it is the (creational) word of him who himself *is* the Word (John 1:1-3, 14). According to his human nature, Christ took part in his own creation (cf. John 1:14; Col. 1:15; Heb. 2:14), and thus placed himself under the law of God (Gal. 4:4), both under the transcendent Law of Love ("your law is within my heart," Ps. 40:8) and under its immanent refraction into the many ordinances, laws, norms and principles of human life. However, according to his divine nature, the last Adam is at the same time himself the Son through whom God has created the world (John 1:1-3; Col. 1:16-17; Heb. 1:1-2), the Son who himself subjected all creation to his law-word, who has *spoken*, yes, who is himself the eternal Logos, the eternal Torah (see further in §§3.11 and 3.12).

3.9 The Law As Idea

3.9.1 The Natural Modalities

As we have seen, we can speak of the transcendent meaning of the law — as God's uncreated revelational and creational word, on the one hand, and as the created law-side of the human heart, on the other hand — only in the form of border-concepts or *ideas*.[93] The reality of this law transcends

---

93. Regarding the nature of ideas, see Ouweneel (1995, §4.2.2; 2014); regard-

General Revelation (1)

the boundaries of created reality, whereas we can nonetheless speak of it in immanent-modal terms, which we are then using as an idea rather than a concept. Let me illustrate this by means of the Reformational-philosophical doctrine of the modal aspects of reality.[94]

(a) *Arithmetic:* The law of God in its transcendent sense is one, single, and unique, whereas, at the same time, a diversity of immanent ordinances, laws, norms and principles come to light in this law. Both unity and diversity characterize God's law. Psalm 119 speaks of the one law or word (many times) but also of the distinct testimonies, precepts, commandments, statutes, and rules.

(b) *Spatial:* In the "supra"-temporality and the "trans"-cendency of God's law we are clearly dealing with a spatial (geometric) idea (not concept), just as in the fact that the law is the boundary for and also a side of creation. We also speak of the law in the form of a spatial idea when we point to its scope, its universal applicability: "For your steadfast love is great above the heavens; your faithfulness reaches to the clouds" (Ps. 108:4).

(c) *Kinematic:* We encounter kinematic ideas in the trans-"cendency" of God's law, that is, its "surpassing, surmounting, rising above" cosmic reality (cf. Lat. *scandere*, "to climb"; *sur*, "beyond"; Vulgar Latin, *passare*, "to step, walk"). We also meet such ideas in the fact that the law exhibits certain motor skills (cf. Latin *movere*, "to move") in its refraction (from the transcendent to the immanent) and convergence (from the immanent to the transcendent). (The opposite of moving is staying: *immanent* comes from Latin *manere*, "to remain.") The Bible speaks, for instance, of the "surpassing

---

ing the manner of speaking about the law as an idea, see Dengerink (1986, 129–32; cf. 223–40). N.B. In the term "law" we are dealing with a use of a juridical concept as an idea.

94. See Dooyeweerd (*NC*); some introductions are Kalsbeek (1970); Van Eikema Hommes (1982); Van Woudenberg (2004); Troost (2005); Strauss (2009); Ouweneel (2014).

power" of God (2 Cor. 4:7), the "surpassing grace" of God (9:14), the "surpassing greatness" of God's revelations (12:7), the "love of Christ" that "surpasses knowledge" (Eph. 3:19), and the peace of God that "surpasses all understanding" (Phil. 4:7).

(d) *Energetic:* God's law is dynamic (Gk. *dynamis*, "power"), has power, is in force for the entire created reality, which exists only by the force of the law. Another energetic metaphor is light; God's law is the light in which his creation can delight: "Your word [i.e., law] is a lamp to my feet and a light to my path" (Ps. 119:105; cf. v. 130, "The unfolding of your word gives light"). This word is also a fire and a hammer: "Is not my word like fire, declares the LORD, and like a hammer that breaks the rock in pieces?" (Jer. 23:29).

(e) *Biotic:* God's law as the word of the living God is the continual source of life for creation: "[T]he word of God is living and active" (Heb. 4:12); ". . . the living and abiding word of God" (1 Pet. 1:23). Keeping God's Word means "life" (Deut. 30:14-20): ". . . For it is no empty word for you, but your very life, and by this word you shall live long in the land that you are going over the Jordan to possess" (32:47).

(f) *Perceptive:* In all aspects of cosmic reality, God's law has become concretely tangible, visible, audible, touchable, palpable. The law-word is the word that God's mouth has spoken (cf. Deut. 8:3; Isa. 1:20; 34:16; 40:5; 58:14; Micah 4:4), and it is heard (in the sense of obeyed[95]) by all creatures, even if there is nothing audible to be heard (cf. Ps. 19:3-4; cf. §2.1.1).

(g) *Sensitive:* God's law is the manifestation of God's great concern and affection toward his people, which moves their hearts: "The law of the LORD is perfect, / reviving the soul; / . . . the precepts of the LORD are right, / rejoicing the heart" (Ps. 19:7-8). Notice the word "delight" in Psalm 119:16, "I will delight in your statutes; / I will not forget your word." "Lead me in the path of your commandments, / for I delight in it"

---

95. Cf. Dutch *horen – ge-hoor-zamen*; Ger. *horchen – gehorchen*.

(v. 35). "I find my delight in your commandments, / which I love" (v. 47; cf. vv. 14, 24, 70, 77, 92, 143, 174).

3.9.2 The Spiritive[96] Modalities

(h) *Logical:* God's law is logically coherent, the manifestation of God's absolute rationality, which is reflected in the order and coherence (rationality) of the cosmos and its way of functioning, and also in the rationality of humans, through which the latter can acquire insight into the cosmos *and* into the law itself.[97] On the one hand, human reason is a reflection of God's reason since humans were created in God's image. On the other hand, God's reason transcends human reason: "For my thoughts are not your thoughts, ... / For as the heavens are higher than the earth, / so are my ways higher than your ways / and my thoughts than your thoughts" (Isa. 55:8–9).

(i) *Historical-formative:* God's law is all-dominating and irresistible because it is the manifestation of God's omnipotence (lit., "all-power") and creational will. The law gives to all things their own specific shapes, exactly such as God has chosen and chooses. The creational as well as providential word of the Son is the "word of his *power*" (Heb. 1:3). "[Y]ou created all things, and by your *will* they existed and were created" (Rev. 4:11).

(j) *Lingual:* God's law is law-*word*, Word of God, utterance of God, manifestation of God, testimony of his eternal power and divine nature (Rom. 1:20), of his glory, testimony concerning the work of his hands (Ps. 19:1–4). God's creation is upheld not just by God's power but by the *word* of his power (Heb. 1:3). All things obey God's word: at God's "rebuke" the waters flee (Ps. 104:7), God "commands" the morning (to appear) (Job 38:12; cf. Matt. 5:45), and he lifts up his "voice to the clouds" (Job 38:34).

(k) *Social:* God's law is the guarantee that within creation everything is related to everything. All things are preserved

---

96. Regarding this term, see Ouweneel (1986, 217–60; 2008, 95–98; 2014).
97. See Strauss (1983, 53–55); Strauss and Visagie (1984, 54–58).

in the coherence of a great creational community because all things (including plants, animals, humans) have been placed under one and the same law. In this way, all things are oriented not just to the law but also toward each other. The same law that rules the skies rules our daily lives (Ps. 119:89-94; cf. 89:2-3, 35-37; Prov. 3:19-27).

(l) *Economic:* God's law is perfectly balanced, effective, efficient, and purpose-oriented: "[S]o shall my word be that goes out from my mouth; / it shall not return to me empty, / but it shall accomplish that which I purpose, / and shall succeed in the thing for which I sent it" (Isa. 55:11). "For the word of God is living and active, sharper than any two-edged sword, piercing to the division of soul and of spirit, of joints and of marrow, and discerning the thoughts and intentions of the heart" (Heb. 4:12).

(m) *Aesthetic:* God's law is perfect in its order, peace, and harmony, just as God himself, whom the law expresses and manifests, is the God of peace, an enemy of disorder (1 Cor. 15:32). "More to be desired are they [i.e., God's commandments] than gold, / even much fine gold; / sweeter also than honey / and drippings of the honeycomb" (Ps. 19:10). "The law of your mouth is better to me / than thousands of gold and silver pieces" (Ps. 119:72).

> Agree with God, and be at peace;
>   thereby good will come to you.
> Receive instruction [Heb. *torah*] from his mouth,
>   and lay up his words in your heart. / If you return to the
>   Almighty you will be built up;
> . . . the Almighty will be your gold
>   and your precious silver.
> For then you will delight yourself in the Almighty
>   and lift up your face to God" (Job 22:21-26).

(n) *Juridical:* God's law gives to all things in cosmic reality their own right and fitting place: "I know, O Lord, that your rules are righteous" (Ps. 119:75; cf. vv. 62, 106, 128, 137, 144,

160, 164, 172). "You have appointed your testimonies in righteousness / and in all faithfulness. / ... Your righteousness is righteous forever, / and your law is true" (vv. 138, 142). "Law" and "justice" are parallel notions (Isa. 42:4; 51:5; Hab. 1:4).

(o) *Ethical:* God's law is in the supreme sense an expression of God's love, a manifestation of his own perfect affection, with which he carries the world in his arms. This law shows God's love for his creation (Ps. 119:64), and appeals to humans to love him (Deut. 6:5; 11:1, 13; 13:3; 30:6; 1 John 5:3) as well as their neighbors (Lev. 19:18; Rom. 13:10; Gal. 5:14; James 2:8; 1 John 4:7, 11-12, 20-21), and even love the law itself (Ps. 119:47-48, 97, 113, 119, 127, 140, 159, 163, 165, 167).

(p) *Pistical:* God's law is the manifestation of God's covenantal faithfulness toward his creation, as we have seen. His law is reliable and trustworthy, so that we may know that we live in a reliable and trustworthy reality. God is faithful, therefore his law-word is faithful: "The LORD's laws are faithful" (cf. Ps. 19:7b CEB; cf. 89:1-2, 5, 8, 14, 24, 33, 37, 49; 119:90, 138).

3.10   The Law-Order and the Fall

3.10.1 Did the Fall Affect God's Laws?

After what I said about the creational character of the law-order, I must now briefly point to the significance of Adam's fall into sin in this context. Of course, this matter is also linked with many theological and philosophical problems, particularly the relationship between creation and re-creation.[98] I must limit myself here to those points that are important for the proper understanding of the "general revelation (also see §4.4 for a more complete treatment of the relationship between creation and re-creation).

At the Fall, creational reality was not corrupted by sin on the law-side but only on the factual or subject-side. In oth-

---

98. See Ouweneel (2012, §14.1; 2017, chapter 9).

er words, the Fall did not affect or alter the law-order. How could it be otherwise? How could sin corrupt God's own creational word, and thus God himself? Only what is subject to, that is, functions as a subject under, the law-order was affected. For a proper understanding of God's revelation in the cosmic law-order, this matter is quite significant. This is because, if sin had also affected the law-order, this would mean that, as Herman Dooyeweerd has argued,[99] the Fall "has *destroyed the nature of creation*. This would mean that sin would play an *autonomous* role over against God as the Creator of all things. And he who maintains this ultimately robs God of his *sovereignty*, and ascribes to Satan the same power as to the Origin of all things."

Along the same lines, Dirk H. Th. Vollenhoven said:

> [T]he norm [stands] as holy [Rom. 7:12] over against what is subject to it, which, except in the human nature of the Mediator [1 John 5:3], since the Fall is always, at least partly, not holy but sinful. Hence, Scripture can speak of the "curse of the law" [Gal. 3:13] over what is subject to it and trespasses it, so that the cosmos ("world"), according to its [i.e., Scripture's] religious dialectics, alternately means "the artwork of God" [cf. Rom. 1:20], or "what lies in the power of evil" [cf. 1 John 5:19], or "what is saved" [cf. John 3:16].[100]

After the Fall, we are still allowed to use the term *creation ordinances* to describe the natural laws and norms to which created reality is subject. They are the laws and norms that God had originally instituted at the time of creation. In this regard, please note two errors.

(a) It is an error to believe that the Fall changed certain natural laws. For instance, some have asserted that the second law of thermodynamics (the law of entropy) would have been put in place only *after* the Fall.[101] Basically, this would amount

---

99. Dooyeweerd (1963, 58; cf. also *NC* 1:63; 2:32–34, 363).
100. Quoted in Stellingwerff (1992, 209).
101. See, e.g., www.articletrader.com/self-improvement/spirituality/

General Revelation (1)

to claiming a total transformation of cosmic reality after the Fall—which would entail an entirely new type of nature, a new creation. However, what changed after the Fall was not God's laws but the functioning of creation *under* those laws (see below).

(b) Frank de Graaff was mistaken to blame John Calvin for speaking of creation ordinances, and to attribute this speaking to Calvin's humanist education.[102] The notion of creation ordinances is thoroughly biblical, as we have seen. What is humanistic is the tendency to make these ordinances autonomous with respect to God, and thus to advance secularization. Of course, with Calvin this was not the case at all.

3.10.2 Common Grace

In the way God has sustained the cosmic law-order, even after the Fall, his grace toward fallen humanity is brought to light. Theologians sometimes speak here of *common grace* (Lat. *gratia communis*, more precisely: *sustaining* or *restraining grace*).[103] This must be distinguished from *special* (more precisely: *saving*) *grace*, as it is revealed in the gospel. This distinction is problematic, too, and infected with the scholastic nature–grace dualism. However, it is undeniable that by his grace God makes his sun rise over the evil and over the good, and sends rain on the just and on the unjust (Matt. 5:45; cf. Acts 14:17), and through this grace, after the Fall, God did not abandon creation and human society to the power of evil.

What changed after the Fall was not the law-order but the direction of the human heart, since the heart had turned away from God and his law. Therefore, Reformational philosophers, especially Dirk H. Th. Vollenhoven,[104] made the theologically very important distinction between *(creational) structure* and

---

a-christian-view-of-entropy.html.
102. De Graaff (n.d., 204).
103. Smit (1980, 182); cf. Berkouwer (1955, 183–87); see extensively, Douma (2017).
104. See Tol and Bril (1992, 62–63,156,158,189–91.

the (*biblical* or *apostate*) *direction* (directedness, orientation) of creation.[105] The Fall did not affect the structures and the structural laws (the laws that cause certain structures to be those specific structures) but rather the direction (directedness) of creation. J. A. Heyns spoke here (in my view, less felicitously) of the essential or substantial sense of creation (read: structure) and its historical sense (read: direction).[106] In the former sense, he called creation "normal," in the latter sense he called it "abnormal since it [i.e., creation] is permeated by sin." In my view, the term "substantial" is far too scholastically tainted to be useful any longer.[107] But it *was* an element of progress that Heyns associated the "substantial" with the law.[108]

The distinction between structure and direction leads to the insight that the radical antithesis between good and evil is not on the law-side but on the subject-side of reality. Over against the biblical orientation toward God we find the apostate orientation, through which, on the subject-side, apostate statements, actions, and even apostate social relationships arise. God-oriented and idol-oriented people stand under the same law-order of God but they live out of different directions of their respective hearts. Both groups speak, act, form social relationships, and always the same norms and principles of God's revealed law-will are involved here. However, the God-oriented person has chosen the obedience to these norms as his life principle—*principle*, for, also with him, the practical realization is often still sinful—whereas the idol-directed person lives in disobedience as a parasite toward God's law.

The term "parasite" involves the following. Even when we are confronted with, for instance, illogical, ahistorical, asocial, uneconomic, unaesthetic, unrighteous, immoral, or disbelieving behavior, we can still indirectly recognize from

---

105. See extensively, Ouweneel (2008, 95–97, 246–50; 2014; 2017, 66–69).
106. Heyns (1988, 109).
107. See Ouweneel (1986, 294–312); cf. Smit (1980, 182–84).
108. Heyns (1988, 110).

General Revelation (1)

it God's law for logical, historical, social, economic, aesthetic, righteous, moral, or believing life. This is possible because the distinction of illogical, ahistorical, asocial (etc.) behavior implies the—conscious or unconscious—application of logical, historical, social (etc.) norms that God has instituted for human life. Thus, sin, too, always presupposes God's law because disobedience points to the norms that are not obeyed. Even in norm-disobedient behavior, the appeal of the norms remains clearly recognizable.

3.10.3 Sin and Nature

The consequences of sin come to light in natural phenomena as well. To be sure, the natural laws did not change. Yet, everywhere in nature we can observe how the subject and its functioning under the law have changed. To this belongs human functioning under the law as well. The natural phenomena themselves have changed, just as humanity, which should have controlled them, has changed through the Fall. As a consequence, humans must experience that they can no longer control the natural phenomena. This is of great importance for their attitude toward nature, and toward God who entrusted nature to them in their capacity as stewards.

Vollenhoven made the following interesting remark concerning "the mutual difference between normative and non-normative laws": "This difference does not correspond with that between higher [normative] and lower [non-normative] modalities because, also in the psychical and biotic domain, healthy stands over against sick as complying, or not complying, with the norm, and also with physical things it is the case that they obey the Mediator."[109] Sickness is a purely natural process, with natural causes, a natural course, and a natural ending. Yet, it does not answer to the norm that God has instituted for organic life, as is clear from the way the Bible describes nature the way God had intended it. That is, concerning the coming Messianic kingdom it is said,

---

109. Quoted in Stellingwerff (1992, 210).

> The wolf shall dwell with the lamb,
> > and the leopard shall lie down with the young goat,
> and the calf and the lion and the fattened calf together;
> > and a little child shall lead them.
> The cow and the bear shall graze;
> > their young shall lie down together;
> > and the lion shall eat straw like the ox.
> The nursing child shall play over the hole of the cobra,
> > and the weaned child shall put his hand on the adder's den
>
> (Isa. 11:6–8; cf. 65:25).

"[N]o inhabitant will say, 'I am sick'" (33:24). "Instead of the thorn shall come up the cypress; / instead of the brier shall come up the myrtle" (55:13). Even if we must take this as figurative language, it hints at God's ideal of nature.

For the purely natural-scientific study of creational reality, any non-ideal functioning of nature makes no difference. The reason is that natural science endeavors to unfold the cosmic law-order, and the laws have not been changed by the Fall.

Both natural laws and norms for human life are *heteronomous*. They have not been posited, invented, or designed by the human reason (or the human will, or human feeling, or human drives, etc.), but instituted by God. Because God as Law-Giver is one, the law, in its transcendent-religious sense, is also ultimately one, no matter how many different (immanent, differentiated) law spheres we may distinguish within this law-order. Therefore, if we recognize that the transcendent-religious meaning of the law, in which all immanent law spheres converge, is summarized in Christ's great Law of Love (Matt. 22:36–40; John 13:34; 15:12, 17; cf. Rom. 13:10; Gal. 5:13–14; 6:2; James 2:8; 1 John 2:7–11; 3:11, 23; 2 John 1:5; cf. Lev. 19:18), we must not sever the natural laws from this meaning-fulness. The Law of Love has not been given *directly* to non-human creatures; that is, the latter do not, as subjects, stand under the Law of Love. However, in his creational plan, God has oriented all creatures toward humanity; no wonder:

the entire empirical reality was created for humanity (cf. Gen. 1:26-28; Ps. 8). Thus, those non-human creatures also stand *indirectly* under the Law of Love, that is (in Dooyeweerdian terminology), through their object functions.[110]

In the creation order, nothing has any meaning in itself but all things have meaning within the coherence of all law spheres, and in their fullness, unity, and identity in the transcendent human heart, and hence in Christ as the "Beginning" (Gk. *archē*), Root, Creator, and Re-Creator (Redeemer) of the new humanity.[111] This brings back to a point mentioned earlier: the relationship between the law and Christ.

3.11 The Law-Order and Christ

3.11.1 Created and Uncreated Law

The most exalted revelation of God is found in Christ. Therefore, it is no wonder that the highest things that can be said of the law, and of God's revelation in it, are associated with the person of Christ. Creation is the manifestation of God's Word. Within time and space, this eternal Word receives a God-given form in the pre-incarnate Christ, who is himself the Word (*Logos*) that was with God, and that was God (John 1:1-3, 14). This is the same as saying that Christ is the Root from which creation has sprouted: all things have been created "in" (through, by means of) Christ, and hold together "in" him (Col. 1:16-17).

Here we encounter the transcendent-religious *depth* in the biblical theme of the law: from the cosmic law-order we arrive at the God-Man Jesus Christ. This is a dimension of faith that could never be the *result* of an empirical-theoretical study of the law-order. On the contrary, it *underlies* all such studies. In science, no matter which one, God's law can play a role only according to its immanent-empirical and -logical aspects. Its transcendent, supra-logical aspects can be known through revelation alone—law aspects that nonetheless must subse-

---

110. See extensively, Ouweneel (2014).
111. Ouweneel (1986, 338-45).

quently be disclosed by philosophy, and, among the various disciplines, particularly by theology.

Theologically, we here encounter an apparently sensitive subject, which involved a difference of opinion between Herman Dooyeweerd and Dirk H. Th. Vollenhoven concerning the relationship between the law and the cosmos (see §3.5.1). This is the place to sharpen our conclusions concerning this debate somewhat further.

On the one hand, the law, in its immanent divergence, belongs to created reality; law-side and subject-side together constitute the cosmos. On the other hand, the law in its transcendent fullness and unity is that which has been instituted *for* all creatures. In the latter sense we cannot say that the law was created, for the law is God's own word *for* creation. There is a certain tension here, which is sensed in J. A. Heyns' presentation as well. He says on the one hand, "To creation . . . God gave his law-order,"[112] as if creation and law-order must be distinguished. On the other hand, he says a little later, in a somewhat contradictory way, "Thus, the law also belongs to creation." I can agree with both statements but only if the law in the former sense is understood as God's own *uncreated* word, and in the latter sense as being a "side" of created subjects: the law in its immanent divergence. Even in the *transcendent* human heart, the Law of Love is the correlate (on the law-side) of this heart (on the subject-side), and as such is part of creation.

In brief: in its immanent meaning, the law always belongs to creation. In its transcendent meaning, it may refer to God's own uncreated word, but it can also be part of creation, namely, of that domain in creation that is transcendent: the human heart.

3.11.2 The Law's Two Natures

As God's *own word*, the law in its ultimate, transcendent sense

---

112. Heyns (1988, 110); cf. Strauss (1977, 34; 1988, 629–31), who shares this view.

General Revelation (1)

cannot possibly be creaturely. To be sure, the law may never be deified by making it autonomous with respect to the Creator. However, the transcendent law *is* divine in the same sense God's word, acts, and power are divine (cf. Rom. 1:20; 2 Pet. 1:3), namely, as belonging to him and going forth from him. Therefore, it is understandable that Andree Troost spoke of the "two natures" of the law, that is, its divine nature and its creaturely nature.[113] The ultimate Law, as God's eternal Word, is divine, infinite and supra-creaturely; the law as a "side" of the cosmos, both immanent and transcendent (as far as the human heart is concerned), is finite and creaturely.

Troost saw here a limited parallel with the two natures of Christ,[114] but I would like to extend the parallel a little further. Notice how closely in Scripture the law is intrinsically associated with Christ in person. In Christ, God is the Law-Giver for created reality, but it goes deeper than this. As God the Son, Christ is not only the Law-Giver; as the God-Man, he *is* the meaning (cf. Gk. *telos*, Rom. 10:4) of the Law at a deeper faith level, namely, at that level in Scripture where there is an inner coherence between the Torah of the Old and the Logos of the New Testament. Christ is "the power of God and the wisdom of God" (1 Cor. 1:24; Gk. *theou dynamis kai theou sophia*).

According to John 1:3, creation exists through (or, by virtue of) the Logos. This Logos must not be viewed here in the ancient sense of intellectual reason, which in ancient thought always refers to human reason, viewed as being reflected in the cosmic logos or rationality.[115] Rather, it must be viewed as the Expression of God's inner being. The Greek term *logos* comes from the verb *legō*, "to speak," and thus "speaks" of (bringsized in words) what God in himself is. The Dutch word is *rede*, which can have the meaning of reason but also the meaning of speech.

---

113. Troost (1992a, 28–29; extensively, 1992b, 119–21, 125–26, 129–30).

114. Troost (1992a, 28; 1992b, 121, 125).

115. Jaki (1974; 1978).

In §3.2 we saw that God's law has "word" character, which is the same as "Torah" character (*torah* is literally "instruction, teaching"). God's law is speech, his Torah is Logos (word).[116] God *speaks* (in order to create, to sustain, to redeem, to instruct); God expresses himself in his Word, and this Word is Christ. Therefore, Christ *is* the eternal Logos, for in him God has perfectly expressed himself, and has revealed who and what he is in himself. Christ *is* the Revelation of God in word and work. From eternity, the Son was, as it were, the (pre-incarnate) embodiment of the Word of God's mouth (cf. §3.9.1), even before this Word had become flesh (John 1:1-3, 14).

However, because of the correlation of word and law, Christ *is* in the same sense the eternal Torah because, for creatures, the Word of God is necessarily always commandment of God. What we call the Ten Commandments are in Hebrew literally the "Ten Words" (Exod. 34:28; Deut. 4:13; 10:4; Heb. *asēret haddevarim*; in rabbinical Heb. *asēret haddibrot*). Similarly, we see how, in John 14:21, Jesus' commandments are parallel with his word (*logos*) in verses 23-24, and how John 12:49-50 (God's *commandment* is eternal life) is parallel with 1 John 1:1-2; 5:20 (Jesus Christ himself is eternal life).[117]

In Christ, the Logos, all God's appeals (commandments) to creation are revealed. We have seen that, in its transcendent fullness, the law is one, but in its immanent refraction it diffuses into many different ordinances. Thus, in the concrete diffusion within immanent reality, the one, eternal *logos* diffuses into many different immanent *logoi* (statements of God; cf. *logos* and *logoi* in John 14:23-24). We can hear the one Word in the many different words that are addressed to us by God or Christ. Similarly, the one, eternal, transcendent Torah is revealed at Mount Sinai, within immanent reality, in

---

116. See the connection between Gk. *nomos* and *logos* in the pseudepigraphal *Preaching of Peter*; cf. the *Epistle of Diognetus* 11:2-3, 7-8; 12:9; quoted in Danker (2000, s.v. *logos*).

117. This point is not grasped in *TDNT* 4:134, where a contrast is construed between *logos* and *nomos* in John 1:1-18.

General Revelation (1)

ten words (the Ten Commandments), precepts for *immanent* human life on earth, which find their converging integration in the *transcendent*, even *eternal* Torah, the eternal Logos (for the connection between the Torah and the words of God, see also Exod. 20:1; 24:3-4; 34:1, 27-28; 35:4; Num. 15:31; 27:14, 21; Deut. 1:26, 43; 4:2, 10; 5:5, 22; 6:6; 9:10, 23; 10:2; 12:28; 28:14, 58; 29:29; 31:12, 24; 32:46-47; Heb. *davar* often has the sense here of "commandment").

Thus, in its emphatic, eternal form, the law far surpasses its Sinaitic (immanent, positivized) form, and coincides with the eternal Logos (cf. the "law of Christ," Gal. 6:2; see also 1 Cor. 9:21, Gk. *ennomos Christou*, "legitimately subject to Christ" [DARBY], i.e., being under the law of Christ). He is the meaning and fullness of the law. He neither did nor does abolish the Sinaitic law but fulfills (Gk. *pleroō*) it (Matt. 5:17), that is, returns it to its eternal *fullness* (*plērōma*) as intended by God, a fullness that surpasses all Sinaitic commandments. Jesus Christ is the *telos* of the law (Rom. 10:4), its meaning and purpose, its contents and destination, and at the same time the end of the limited Sinaitic system, which finds in him its higher fulfillment.[118]

3.12 The Torah and Its Relationships

3.12.1 Torah and Logos/Chokmah

When John 1 begins with saying that the Logos was "with" God (Gk. *pros ton theon*, lit., "over against God," face to face, in an intimate relationship, close fellowship with God[119]), this clearly seems to refer to Proverbs 8:30-31, where eternal wisdom (Heb. *chokmah*) is called a "master workman" (one Heb. word, *amon*),[120] "daily his [i.e., God's; or, filled with] delight, rejoicing before him always, rejoicing in his inhabited world and delighting in the children of man."

This translation of *amon* goes back to the Septuagint (Gk.

---

118. Cf. Ouweneel (2001, 87–91); Stern (1992, 395–96).
119. Morris (1971, 75–76, including n14).
120. Cf. *TDNT* 4:135.

harmozousa, if taken in the sense of "arranging, construing") and the Vulgate (Lat. *cuncta componens*). Thus, the word is thought to be related with *amman* in Song 7:1 ("master, workman, craftsman, artist"). If this rendering is correct, God is the great Architect (Designer) of the universe, and the Son is the executive Builder. In him (i.e., by virtue of his person), through him (i.e., as the means through which God created), and for him (i.e., with him as the world's end goal), all things were created (Col. 1:16; cf. §4.3). This corresponds to a Jewish tradition according to which the Torah is called the building instrument or the blueprint of the Holy One, through which he created the universe.[121]

A very different interpretation is that *amon* is related with *omen*, which means "foster father" or "nursing father" (Num. 11:12; 2 Kings 10:1, 5; Esther 2:7; Isa. 49:23; cf. the feminine form in Ruth 4:16; 2 Sam. 4:4). In this case, *amon* is a small child, a nursling, depending on the care and nourishment of parent(s). If this is the correct approach, Proverbs 8 sketches the lovely picture of the child that delights and feels at ease in the presence of his father. (For the former rendering, see ASV, ESV, NKJV; for the latter rendering, see KJV, DARBY, EXB.)

In Proverbs 8, Wisdom is God's creational wisdom, the Torah that applies to created reality. Here we see God's wisdom in the works of his *hands* (cf., e.g., Job 34:19; Ps. 8:6; 28:5; 102:25), in John 1:1-3 Christ is, as it were, the Word that goes out from God's *mouth* (cf. Deut. 8:3; Isa. 1:20; 34:16; 40:5; 58:14; Micah 4:4). All things were created through God's eternal Wisdom, God's eternal Word. Thus, *Chokmah* is the wisdom that is manifested in God's creation order. The message in Proverbs 8 is that the very same wisdom that God employed in creating the universe must be employed by humans in their practical lives. We found the same in Proverbs 3, which deals with the practical wisdom that is rooted in the fear of the LORD, and that brings blessing upon the ways of the righteous

---

121. Gen. Rabbah on Gen. 1:1, "Through the firstborn, God created the heaven and the earth, and the firstborn is none other than the Torah."

(§3.9.2). In the midst of this statement, the verses 19–20, which are parallel with this wisdom for practical life, speak of the wisdom through which God created the world.

Here and elsewhere (see 1 Kings 3:9, 11–12; Job 28:28; compare also 1 Cor. 2:6 with Heb. 5:14), wisdom is the ability to distinguish practically between good and evil. This simply amounts to obeying God's commandments, God's Torah (Prov. 3:1; 4:2; 6:20, 23; 7:2). The connection between wisdom and law-keeping is seen in Proverbs 2:1–2; 4:4–5; 10:8 and elsewhere: God's Wisdom is manifested in his Torah, while the wisdom of the "son" in Proverbs is manifested in *keeping* the Torah.[122]

3.12.2 One Law/Wisdom for All Things

One and the same wisdom of God (Heb. *chokmah*) applies to celestial bodies, inanimate things, plants and animals on the one hand, and to the moral (but also the logical, historical-formative, lingual, social, economic, aesthetic, juridical and pistical) lives of humans on the other hand. This is exactly the same as saying that one law (Heb. *torah*) of God applies to both the cosmos and humanity. All natural laws and all normative laws go back to the one Torah of God. The Torah—in this wide sense of the word—did not begin to exist at Mount Sinai but existed before the foundation of the world, for it is the *eternal* Wisdom/Word/Law of God.[123]

Sirach 24 expresses this in a beautiful way. Here, a similar description of God's eternal Wisdom is given; Wisdom explains how a place was assigned to her among the people of Israel in the form of the covenantal book of Sinai (cf. Exod. 24:4, 7): "I came forth from the *mouth* of [GNT: I am the *word* spoken by] the Most High. . . . Then the Creator of all things

---

122. Regarding the personification of the Eternal Wisdom in rabbinical tradition, see extensively, Strack/Billerbeck (1924, 353–55).

123. We should not be misled here by the Gk. *ektisen me* ("created me") in the Septuagint rendering of Prov. 8:22 (cf. CEB, GNT, RSV); God's wisdom is necessarily as eternal as he is himself. Therefore, Heb. *qanani* is better rendered as "possessed me" ([N]KJV, ESV).

gave me a commandment, and the one who created me assigned a place for my tent. And he said, 'Make your dwelling in Jacob, and in Israel receive your inheritance.' ... All this is the book of the covenant of the Most High God, the law which Moses commanded us as an inheritance for the congregations of Jacob" (vv. 3, 8, 23 RSV). The Torah is presented here as having existed before the foundation of the world, that is, from eternity. It is said that all things were created through the wisdom of the Torah, that through it the entire human life is sustained, and that it received a place within creational reality in its Sinaitic form.

I also refer here to the Book of Wisdom:

> [W]isdom, the fashioner of all things, taught me [says Solomon]. For in her there is a spirit that is intelligent, holy, unique, manifold, subtle, mobile, clear, unpolluted, distinct, invulnerable, loving the good, keen, irresistible, beneficent, humane, steadfast, sure, free from anxiety, all-powerful, overseeing all, and penetrating through all spirits that are intelligent and pure and most subtle. For wisdom is more mobile than any motion; because of her pureness she pervades and penetrates all things. For she is a breath of the power of God, and a pure emanation of the glory of the Almighty; therefore nothing defiled gains entrance into her (vv. 22-25 RSV).

Similar things could be said of the Word, the Torah ,and the Logos of God. The beauty of such descriptions is that the Torah is not a dry "legal thing" (from Latin *lex*) in our common juridical sense, enacted by God, but the embodiment of his eternal wisdom, of his love for, and his delight in, his creation. The Torah/Chokmah is even the object of God's deepest affection; as such it is personified into a person whom God can love with all his heart. This personification is not just a literary aid but points to a genuine person: Jesus Christ, the Son of God.[124] The Wisdom of God is the eternal Torah, the Logos

---

124. I strongly plead for this identification despite the objections of various exegetes; see, e.g., Ridderbos (1960, 184); an important defender of this

General Revelation (1)

who was with (Gk. *pros*, in fellowship with) God, the Son who was in the bosom of the Father (John 1:18 KJV).

A Jewish tradition says that the eternal Torah was lying in God's bosom before the creation of the world, while God was sitting on the throne of glory.[125] Another such tradition describes that God called her his daughter[126] (please note that both *torah* and *chokmah* are feminine nouns[127]); that God created the world through his firstborn, that is, the Torah;[128] that the words of the Torah are life for the world;[129] that the Torah is light for the world;[130] and that the Torah is full of truth.[131] In a remarkably parallel way, Christ is the eternal Logos (John 1:1-4), the firstborn Son of the Father (Heb. 1:6; cf. Rom. 8:29), even the *only* Son (John 1:14; 3:16, 18; 1 John 4:9), the life of the world (John 6:33, 51), the light of humanity (1:4-9; 8:12; 9:5), the fullness of grace and truth (1:14).

3.13 Torah and *Agapē*

3.13.1 Love, Essence of the Torah

The fact that Christ is the Logos is parallel with the fact that he is the Angel (Heb. *mal'ach*, messenger, representative, who expresses God's being) of YHWH.[132] Christ is the Logos incarnate (John 1:14),[133] Torah incarnate (cf. Ps. 40:8; Matt. 5:17;

---

identification was Windisch (1914).

125. Talmud: Aboth RN 31 (8b); Midrash Ps. on Ps. 90:2 (§12).
126. Lev. Rabbah 20.10 on Lev. 16:1.
127. For the ancient Christian idea that the Virgin Mary would be the incarnation of Sophia (Chokmah—all these words are feminine), see Ouweneel (1998, 59–65, 69–71).
128. See note 119 above.
129. Sifre Dt 306 op 32:2; cf. Prov. 8:35; Deut. 32:47.
130. 4 Ezra 14:20v.
131. Midr. Ps. op 25:10 (§11) (cf. Strack/Billerbeck [1924, 353–58]; *TDNT* 4:135).
132. Ouweneel (2007, 239–46); see the next volume in the present series.
133. It is incomprehensible that Dengerink (1986, 120) states that the Logos is the Triune God; in the New Testament, the personified Logos is always the Son (John 1:1, 14; Cf. v. 18; cf. also 1 John 1:1; Rev. 19:13).

Rom. 10:4; 1 Cor. 9:21; Gal. 6:2), Wisdom incarnate (1 Cor. 1:24, 30; Col. 2:2-3), Love incarnate (1 John 4:8, 16; 5:20: Christ is God, God is love).

The latter statement introduces a new element, alongside Word, Law, and Wisdom. Divine Love (Gk. *agapē*) is the meaning—sum, fulfillment, fullness, end goal—of the law (Matt. 22:34-40; Rom. 13:8-10; Gal. 5:13-14; James 2:8.). The law in its ultimate sense is the transcendent convergence and integration of all immanent law spheres, of all modal and entity laws that the Creator has instituted for all immanent functioning. Love, again in its ultimate, transcendent sense (i.e., as distinct from immanent forms of it, such as matrimonial and parental love, altruism, patriotism, etc.), is the sum, the deepest essence of the Law, and thus—as Herman Dooyeweerd expressed it—the "meaning-totality," the transcendent-religious root-unity of the entire temporal "meaning-diversity."[134]

This is the very reason why the contents of the "new commandment" in John's writings (John 13:34; 1 John 2:3, 7-8; 2 John 1:5) is simply described as love and nothing else. In the New Testament, we find several references to God's commandments for the Christian (John 14:15, 21; 15:10; 1 John 2:3-4; 3:22, 24; 5:2-3; 2 John 1:6; see also 1 Cor. 7:19; 14:37; 1 Tim. 6:14; 2 Pet. 3:2), but these are nowhere enumerated, or even spelled out. This is not necessary because they are nothing but specifications or ramifications of the *one* new commandment of Love. In this one commandment, the entire essence of the eternal Torah is revealed because God himself is love (1 John 4:8, 16). Also see James 1:25 and 2:8-12, where the Law of Love is called the "law of liberty" and the "royal [Gk. *basilikon*] law" (one could say, the "law of God's kingdom [*basileia*]"), summarized as: "You shall love your neighbor as yourself." This is the essence of Augustine's well-known maxim: "love, and do as you like" (Lat. *dilige et quod vis fac*),[135] for in

---

134. Dooyeweerd (*NC* 2:144, 149; 3:71).
135. Homilies on 1 John VII.8.

General Revelation (1)

keeping the Law of Love in principle all the commandments are being obeyed.[136]

Saying that Christ is not only the eternal Torah but also the eternal Logos, the eternal Wisdom and eternal Love, is the same as saying that God's being (wisdom, power, love, light; cf. 1 John 1:5; 4:8, 16) is expressed in the Law, that is, the eternal Torah. Therefore, we can say that Christ, as the image of God (2 Cor. 4:4; Col. 1:15), as "the radiance of the glory of God and the exact imprint of his nature" (Heb. 1:3), *is* the eternal Torah, the Logos, who perfectly goes forth from God because he *is* God. In Jesus Christ, the love of God has received perfect form, both in his person and in his work. And in believers, the love of God also receives form if they keep his commandments, that is, his precepts of love. This is possible only if God's love dwells in them (1 John 2:5, 15; 3:17; 4:7-8, 12, 16; 5:3; cf. Rom. 5:5).

3.13.2 Torah and Covenant

In a particularly beautiful manner, the unity and identity of Christ and the eternal Torah, that is, eternal Love, is expressed in the new covenant.[137] In Jeremiah 31:33, God says of the remnant of Israel during the Messianic kingdom: "I will put my law [*torah*] within them, and I will write it on their hearts" (cf. Heb. 8:10; 10:16). Of course (I would almost say), this is not the law in its limited, immanent, positivized, Sinaitic form. In the new covenant, the Torah will be known in its fulfillment, its fullest, deepest, eternal meaning, as it has been revealed in Christ. Here, there is no essential difference any longer between

(a) the idea that the eternal *Word* is written on human hearts (Deut. 6:6; 11:18; 30:14; Job 22:22; Ps. 119:11; Prov. 4:4; Luke 8:15; Rom. 10:8; cf. Col. 3:15-16, the word [*logos*] of Christ

---

136. Cf. Troost (1976, 19; cf. also 20 on the distinction between Love in the transcendent, supramodal sense and love in the immanent-modal sense; 37, 41, 44).

137. Cf. Ouweneel (2018j, §6.1).

dwells in human hearts);

(b) the idea that the eternal *Law* is written on human hearts (in addition to the verses already mentioned, see 2 Kings 10:31; Ps. 37:31; 119:34; Isa. 51:7; Rom. 2:15);

(c) the idea that the eternal *Wisdom* is written on human hearts (cf. Ps. 51:6; 90:12; Prov. 2:10; 14:33);

(d) the fact that God's eternal *love* is poured into human hearts (cf. Rom. 5:5; 13:8-10, 14);

(e) the fact that *Christ* comes to dwell in human hearts through faith (Eph. 3:17).

Therefore, when the apostle Paul, in his interpretation of the new covenant (2 Cor. 3), applies these facts to Christian believers, he can, without any problem, replace the expression "the law" with "Christ": "[Y]ou show that you are a letter from[138] *Christ* delivered by us [i.e., as ministers of the new covenant, v. 6], written not with ink but with the Spirit of the living God, not on tablets of stone [like the Ten Commandments] but on tablets of human hearts" (v. 3). Here, the Torah in its fullest and deepest (transcendent) sense, as intended in Jeremiah 31:31-34, is shown to be identical with Christ, as intended by Paul, written in the hearts of believers. Please notice here the collective aspect: believers are not individual "letters," but *together* they are "*a* letter of Christ." Compare Colossians 3:9-11: the new person is "Christ all and in all," that is, in all believers together. Christians have not become new persons, although in itself this would be correct to say, but the New Testament never speaks this way. It rather says that we have put on the one "new person" (Col. 3:10; cf. Eph. 2:15; 4:24), that is, the one Christ as displayed in all believers together.

In the law we dealing not simply with an important theological or philosophical concept. No, essentially we have here a supra-theoretical idea, which refers to the deepest things that can ultimately be said about God and his revelation in his

---

138. Or, "about" (PHILLIPS); Gk. *epistolē Christou*, lit., "letter of Christ."

world order, the supreme riches that faith knows. It is vital to remind ourselves constantly of this. This will contribute to the ideal that theology, and Christian-theoretical thought in the wider sense, will always remain embedded in the much wider framework of our supra-theoretical, even supra-rational, transcendent-religious faith, in personal fellowship with, and submission to, the eternal Torah, that is, the eternal Logos, that is, the eternal Wisdom of God: Jesus Christ.

Chapter 4
General Revelation (2)

. . . a living God,
who made the heaven and the earth and the
    sea
and all that is in them.
In past generations he allowed all the nations
to walk in their own ways.
Yet he did not leave himself without witness,
for he did good by giving you
rains from heaven and fruitful seasons,
satisfying your hearts with food and gladness.
Acts 14:15–17

And he made from one man every nation of
    mankind
to live on all the face of the earth,
having determined allotted periods
and the boundaries of their dwelling place,
that they should seek God,
and perhaps feel their way toward him and
    find him.
Yet he is actually not far from each one of us,

> *for "In him we live and move and have our being";*
> *as even some of your own poets have said,*
> *"For we are indeed his offspring."*
>
> Acts 17:26-28

Summary: *Under the influence of scholasticism, many theologians have thought that belief in natural divine revelation implies the validity of natural theology, which could supposedly prove the existence of God purely by rational arguments. Anthropological, hamartiological, and other arguments are adduced to refute this idea. There is a natural awareness of God, but this is corrupted by sin.*

*Another matter where scholastic dualism still plays a role is that of creation and re-creation "in Christ," in which the cosmological aspect is played off against the redemptive aspect. It is argued that it is **this** creation that is renewed, and that this one creation finds its equivalent in the **one** creational revelation of God, of which Scripture is the center. God's general revelation is observed not only in nature but also in history and culture. A biblical view of God's revelation is compared with the modernist approach, in which history is autonomous. Both conservatism and progressivism are analyzed in this context.*

Another example of scholastic dualism is a notion like "theological ethics," which is confused with Christian ethics, a discipline distinct from Christian theology. Finally, the connection as well as the contrast between timeless creation ordinances and their time-bound positivizations are discussed, against the background of the biblicistic appeal to Bible passages.

4.1 Natural Theology and Romans 1

4.1.1 Natural and Supernatural Theology

THE TRADITIONAL VIEW CONCERNING the relationship between general (natural) and special (supernatural) *revelation* cannot be separated from another matter: the erroneous scholastic distinction between natural and supernatural *theology*.[1] Traditionally, natural theology is viewed as the study of natural or general revelation, and supernatural theology as the study of supernatural or special revelation. Since the high Middle Ages, natural theology has been viewed as a theology that can presumably be demonstrated to every reasonable person. That is, it appeals to human nature (read: autonomous reason), and does not necessarily presuppose (supernatural) faith.[2] For instance, this theology believes it can demonstrate the existence of God — the *that* of God, though not the *what* of God — through purely rational arguments.

The theology and philosophy of Thomas Aquinas, called Thomism, claimed that human reason was not entirely corrupted by the Fall. Consequently, it possesses a relative autonomy in the domain of nature, so that reason is able through its own light to derive natural truths from cosmic reality, such as God's existence. According to the same view — *contra*, e.g., Peter Abelard — reason is *not* able to derive *super*natural truths, such as the nature of God, the Trinity, the incarnation, the resurrection, redemption, the last judgment. At best, reason is capable of undergirding these truths apologetically, and of refuting arguments against them. Thus, natural theology is supposed to be subordinate to supernatural theology. It is only a set of "preambles of faith" or "of grace" (Lat. *praeambula fidei* or *gratiae*). In the domain of grace, reason is not entirely put aside but is entirely dependent on Scripture and faith. This faith is a "superadded gift" (Lat. *donum superadditum*) of God, therefore supernatural, and is needed to investigate the supernatural realm of grace. As Thomas Aquinas put it in his famous saying: "[Supernatural] grace does not abolish [obliterate] nature, but perfects [completes] it" (Lat. *gratia non tollit naturam, sed perficit*).[3]

As we have seen, such a distinction between nature and

---

1. See Ouweneel (1995, §3.2).
2. See extensively, Berkouwer (1955, 61–83).
3. *Summa Theologiae* 1, qu. 1, a. 8, resp. 2.

grace, or between natural and supernatural theology, is no longer tenable[4] (even though natural theology in certain forms is still defended[5]). From the viewpoint of its *structure*, human reason is not autonomous at all but depends on the spiritual (apostate *or* biblical) state of the heart, from where all immanent modalities of human functioning proceed, including the logical-rational function of thought. As far as the *direction* is concerned, human reason in the "natural person" (Gk. *psychikos anthrōpos*, 1 Cor. 2:14) is totally perverted as a consequence of the corruption of his heart (cf. Gen. 6:5; 8:21; Prov. 6:14; Jer. 17:9; Matt. 15:18-19; Eph. 4:17). If reason is darkened by sin, it is not capable of demonstrating God's existence from the created reality through purely rational arguments, independent of biblical faith. What is darkened is not the logical laws themselves but the natural person's heart is—the heart that, in a dark way, makes use of these logical laws.

The nature-grace dualism surfaces in all kinds of places in traditional Roman Catholic and Protestant theology.[6] Where the latter has made room for natural theology, it often envisions a parallel *supernatural* theology. However, as Andree Troost put it, both natural and supernatural theology are *un*natural;[7] natural theology is "primarily a logicistically derailed *(un)belief*."[8] The notion of a supernatural or sacred theology[9] involves an unbiblical overestimation of theology,

4. Cf. Pannenberg (1991, 95–107) on the views of Friedrich Schleiermacher and Albrecht Ritschl (d.1889), and Karl Barth.

5. See J. Greco in Zagzebski (1993, 168–98); Hauerwas (2001); Swinburne (2005); the prestigious Gifford Lectures, since 1887 held at Scottish universities, are devoted to the study of natural theology.

6. See Weber (1981, 199–200) and references, on traces of natural theology with Martin Luther, the older Philip Melanchthon, and John Calvin. Abraham Kuyper fully accepted the notions of natural theology (1898, 300–303) and of revealed theology (1898, 369).

7. Troost (1977, 180; 1982, 183; 2004, 30n17).

8. Troost (2004, 41; see 41–44).

9. See, e.g., Bavinck's work (1883) entitled: *De wetenschap der heilige godgeleerdheid* (*The Science of Sacred Theology*), and Kuyper's work (1894): *Encyclopaedie der heilige godgeleerdheid* (*Encyclopedia of Sacred Theology*).

General Revelation (2)

and arise from the same erroneous background as the notion of natural theology, namely, the nature–grace dualism, and the quasi-identification of theology and Scripture. Thus, both kinds of theology are mistaken.[10] God is holy, and his Word is holy (cf. Jer. 23:9). But theology, as a fallible human labor, which is produced by both Spirit-filled and carnal persons, is just as holy, or non-holy, as economics or chemistry.[11]

This notion of a sacred (holy) or supernatural theology is closely related to ideas concerning the (supposed) study object of theology.[12] Even if it were correct to say that its study object is *Holy* Scripture, and that it wishes to be led by the *Holy* Spirit, theology itself would be no more sacred than psychology or legal research that are practiced by serious Christians. However, the idea that the Bible is the study object of theology is also a scholastic notion.[13] Against this background, theology is viewed as the science of the higher domain of grace (to which Scripture is thought to belong). The other disciplines, including philosophy, are assigned to the lower domain of nature, to which natural (autonomous) reason is thought to belong.

4.1.2 Romans 1:20–21

Please note that natural or general revelation is revelation that, according to Scripture, undeniably exists (see chapters 2 and 3 of this book). Also note that, according to a deep-rooted (radical) Christian view of reality, natural theology *cannot* exist. Every debate about this matter necessarily involves a discussion of Romans 1:20-21, which teaches that God's

> invisible attributes, namely, his eternal power and divine nature, have been clearly perceived, ever since the creation of the

---

10. Dooyeweerd (1960, 146). It is all the more remarkable that Gijsbert van den Brink in Van den Brink et al. (1997, 42) locates "the danger of natural theology in the emphasis on the creation ordinances."
11. Cf. Van Zyl (1991, 30).
12. See Ouweneel (1995, §2.3.4; 2015).
13. Cf. Strauss (1988, 137–38).

world, in the things that have been made. So they are without excuse. For although they knew God, they did not honor him as God or give thanks to him, but they became futile in their thinking, and their foolish hearts were darkened.

Perhaps we should view the expression "eternal power and divinity" (Gk. *aïdios autou dynamis kai theiotēs*) as a hendiadys, implying that we render it as follows: God's "eternal divine power."[14] In the cosmos, the majesty of the Eternal One becomes visible.

Other well-known Bible passages that are adduced as proof texts for natural revelation, and often for natural theology, are Romans 2:14-16 (the internal testimony of the conscience); Acts 14:15-17 (God "did not leave himself without witness" or "[self-]testimony"); and 17:26-28 (". . . that they should seek God, and perhaps feel their way toward him and find him. Yet he is actually not far from each one of us").[15] In short: every Bible passage invoked for accepting the notion of general revelation is also invoked as though it were obvious proof for natural theology, whereas the two things are not identical at all.[16]

Romans 1:20-21 does *not* teach that, with the help of natural reason, people can derive the existence of God from his creational works, as natural theology asserts. On the contrary, Romans 1 speaks so clearly and radically about the corruption of humanity and the wrath of God upon this passage (cf. vv. 18-19) supplies no basis at all for the idea of autonomous reason. This supposedly would be human reason uncorrupted by sin, and functioning independently of the state of the heart, that is, apart from faith or unbelief. The person here who has a "knowledge" of God (v. 21) does not owe this to the natural light of reason, but possesses this knowledge in the

---

14. Cf., e.g., "the power and coming" (2 Pet. 1:16), i.e., "the powerful coming."
15. Cf. Weber (1981, 210–13); Buri (1956, 226–29).
16. Cf. Berkouwer (1955, chapter 4); Henry (1976, 83–90; cf. also 104–23); Pannenberg (1991, 107–108).

greatest *foolishness* (v. 22). The portrait of God that the pagan possesses is not that of the scholastic "first cause" (Lat. *prima causa*) or "first mover" (Lat. *primum movens*, the *prōton kinoun* of Aristotle) but that of "images resembling mortal man and birds and animals and creeping things" (v. 23).

Of course, the expression "knowing God" must be understood contextually. With equal clarity, 2 Thessalonians 1:8 says that the pagans do *not* "know" God. Hosea 5:4 says of the wicked in Israel, which does possess a rich revelation of God, that they do not "know" the Lord (cf. Titus 1:16). In Romans 1:21, this "knowing" God cannot possibly extend beyond having caught a glimpse of God's eternal, divine majesty in creation. Subsequently, an idolatrous image is made from this glimpse according to the categories that are familiar to natural humans, an image confined to earthly creatureliness. Where is there any basis here for natural theology?

Romans 1 does implicitly speak of a natural *revelation*. However, it definitely does not speak of natural *theology*, but of a humanity that, to be sure, cannot escape the evidence of this natural revelation but knows only to respond to it in idolatry. We see here the activity not of natural reason arriving at deep insights, but of the corrupted heart, which abuses these intuitive insights in service to the most vile idolatry. The text does speak of a "perceiving intellectually" (Gk. *nooumena kathoratai*, v. 20 OJB), but the entire context of Romans 1 clearly shows what a *corrupt* insight this is. God's work-revelation has indeed become too strong for the natural human; such a person cannot escape the overwhelming impression of God's eternal majesty and glory. However, in the corruption of their transcendent heart, working through all immanent functions, including the thought function and the faith function, the only response that this person can think of is the most vulgar idolatry. Such a person employs their "knowledge" of God in the practice of idolatry, inventing and serving false gods that lead them away from the true God.

4.1.3 Awareness of God

There is another point worth mentioning. Romans 1:20 does not say that it is God's *existence* that is perceived from his works but rather his "eternal power and divinity." In identifying these attributes of God, his existence is already being presupposed. Humans have a natural knowledge of God, or as John Calvin called it, a "sense of the divine" (Lat. *sensus divinitatis*) or a "seed of religion" (Lat. *semen religionis*),[17] phrases that have become so encumbered with claims of a supposed natural theology. Therefore, Willie D. Jonker did not wish to speak here of a natural knowledge of God;[18] compare what he said about human conscience in connection with general revelation.[19]

This entire matter is rather complicated.[20] Thomas Aquinas spoke of a natural knowledge (Lat. *cognitio naturalis*) of God,[21] which, despite a certain confusion (Lat. *sub quadam confusione*), is inserted into us by nature (Lat. *est nobis naturaliter insertum*).[22] Martin Luther stated that all people have knowledge of the true God, including his power, justice, immortality, and goodness, and that this knowledge cannot be darkened, in spite of sin. He connected Romans 1:20 with 2:15 in order to link this knowledge of God with human conscience.[23] This view was followed by his collaborator, Philip Melanchthon.[24] It seems justified to speak here of some kind knowledge of God since in Romans 2:15 conscience (Gk. *syneidēsis*, from Gk. *oida* and Lat. *scire*, both meaning "to know") involves a certain measure of knowing. However, instead of some form of implanted knowledge(Lat. *notitia insita*), Jo-

---

17. Calvin, *Institutes* 1.3.1; cf. 1.3.3 and 1.4.1; cf. Heyns (1988, 52–54).
18. Jonker (n.d., 36, 41).
19. Ibid., 48–49.
20. Cf. Pannenberg (1991, 73–82, 107–113).
21. *Summa Theologiae* II.2.2 a 3 ad 1.
22. Ibid., I.2 a 1 ad 1.
23. WA 56:176–77.
24. *Loci communes*, 1521.

hannes Musaeus preferred the term "light of nature" (Lat. *lumen naturae*).²⁵ He recognized merely a certain "inclination" (Lat. *dispositio*) to knowledge of God, a "natural instinct" (Lat. *instinctus naturalis*), not an "actual knowledge" (Lat. *cognitio actualis*) of God. This may appear to be little more than a word play, but the purpose is to express in some way the confusing situation that natural humans without special revelation have a certain awareness of God, and yet do not know him.

Wolfhart Pannenberg argued that, by strongly toning down this knowledge in the way of Musaeus and others, we lose the insight of Luther and Melanchthon that a certain genuine knowledge of God is transformed into idolatry.²⁶ He, too, pointed to the significance of conscience in this respect,²⁷ and also mentioned Karl Rahner, who spoke of an "unthematic knowledge of God," and of a "mystery," such that "the silent and uncontrollable infiniteness of reality is always present [to humanity] as mystery."²⁸ Compare Pannenberg's comment, who pointed out that this is not innate knowledge (Lat. *notitia innata*) but acquired knowledge (Lat. *notitia acquisita*), that is, "a knowledge linked with [human] world experience and the knowledge acquired through this."²⁹ Although this knowledge is rooted in innate knowledge, it has been transformed into an awareness of God through the works of creation.³⁰

This is how complex this matter has become: we both accept the idea of natural knowledge (or awareness) of God and reject the idea of natural theology—whereas both of these notions were often viewed as identical in early Protestant theology. As I see it, this was a consequence of not clearly distinguishing between practical and theoretical (theological) knowledge; a (supra-theoretical, supra-rational) awareness in

---

25. *Introductio in theologia*, 1697.
26. Pannenberg (1991, 110).
27. Ibid., 124–26.
28. Rahner (1978, 21–23, 35).
29. Pannenberg (1991, 114–18).
30. Ibid., 131.

the heart is not the same as an articulated (pre-theoretical or theoretical) knowledge of reason.[31]

4.2 Natural Knowledge of God

4.2.1 Confusion of Revelation and Theology

Recall Calvin's assertion that because of their innate awareness of divinity, humans know in the depths of their hearts of God's existence, and because of this awareness, they now recognize in God's works his "eternal power and divinity." However, subsequently this knowledge manifests itself in the thoroughgoing corruption of paganism with its pervasive idolatry. To the extent that we are willing to speak of a sense of the divine (Lat. *sensus divinitatis*), this is no autonomous-rational organ of the knowledge of God, unaffected by sin, but only an inescapable impression, brought about by the intrusiveness of natural revelation in people's hearts. No matter how strange this may sound, not the argumentation of some natural theology but rather the idolatry that exists in this world constitutes the sure evidence of a sense of the divine or a seed of religion in human hearts.[32]

It is very important to distinguish carefully here. As we saw, people have often linked the idea of natural revelation inextricably with that of natural theology, as if the former would necessarily lead to the latter. This was done both by the adherents of natural theology, such as Roman Catholic theologians, on the basis of Romans 1:20, and by the opponents of it. The latter, such as Karl Barth, rejected not only natural theology, but also the notion of natural revelation, and thus threw out the baby with the bathwater. Conversely, American theologians Gordon R. Lewis and Bruce A. Demarest, for example, wrote that the reality of natural theology, though depreciated or denied in certain forms of Barthian and Reformed thought, is explicitly and repeatedly taught in Scrip-

---

31. Cf. ibid., 87; and see Ouweneel (1995, §§2.3, 4.1.3, 6.3.1; 2014; 2015).
32. Regarding Calvin's view, cf. Parker (1959) and Dowey (1965).

ture[33] — but what they apparently meant was nothing but the reality of general revelation! They are apparently unaware that certain Reformed theologians, and others sympathetic to them, including me, emphatically both maintain the biblical notion of general or natural or creational revelation and reject any form of natural theology. It is not only possible, but even essential, to make this fundamental distinction.

The important consequence of this viewpoint is that natural revelation is not grasped by natural (neutral, objective, unprejudiced) reason severed from faith, but is truly known and understood only when reason is renewed by regeneration and illuminated by the Holy Spirit, and when this renewed reason subsequently follows the light from scriptural revelation shining upon natural revelation. Only then will natural revelation be fully recognized as *revelation*, as *creational word*. And only then will its scope and significance be understood in the light of Christ, the incarnate Word of God, who is known to us from the inscripturated Word of God. Only in Scripture do we find the unmistakable testimony concerning God's existence and being, majesty and glory, power and love. Only here does the full light fall upon God as Law-Giver, and thus also upon the law-order that underlies created reality. Only in the light of Scripture can natural revelation be fully recognized and acknowledged as *revelation*.

4.2.2 Various Views

J. A. Heyns rightly pointed to the important fact that the so-called "nature psalms," such as Psalm 8, 19, 29, 93, and 104, are songs of *Israel*, God's redeemed people.[34] In these psalms, it is not pagans who are perceiving God's "eternal power and

---

33. Lewis and Demarest (1996, 75); their confusion becomes apparent later (76) when these authors speak of the Dutch Reformed and Barthian hypotheses that deny natural *knowledge* of God, but the denial involves natural *theology*. These authors betray the age-old scientist confusion of pre-theoretical, supra-rational knowledge of God and theoretical-rational theology.

34. Heyns (1988, 8).

divinity" in nature. The eyes being amazed by God's acting in nature are "enlightened eyes of the heart" (Eph. 1:18), opened by faith (subjectively) and by the Holy Spirit (objectively). The knowledge of God that comes to expression here is the knowledge of a heart enlightened by the knowledge of God's salvation. The experience of God's grace, within the framework of the covenant, also leads to the awareness of God's majesty and glory in the works of his hands.

Andree Troost pointed to the remarkable word "though" (Gk. *kai ge*) in Acts 17:27 (NKJV): ". . . so that they should seek the Lord, in the hope that they might grope for Him and find Him, *though* He is not far from each one of us." Why "grope for" God if he is not far from each one of us, and if we "live *in* him" (v. 28)? Why all this endless seeking, by all nations, throughout the centuries, when God is so near? Why this continual groping after, yet failing to grasp? Troost explained this by referring to the Fall:

> The answer to these questions lies in the great concealment of God, in his *wrath*, and thus in the *darkness in our human heart* (Rom. 1:18 and 21). Instead of a person re-finding God, and thus himself, as *by nature* is proper to him, his groping is a mis-groping, his seeking a not-finding, his autonomy is an equally tragic as ridiculous "losing himself," in the very thing that a person views as his grandeur: his *thinking*, his "reasonings" (Rom. 1:21 ASV). His nature has become unnatural; ". . . and *their foolish hearts* were darkened" (Rom. 1:21).[35]

The fact that people do not understand natural revelation, and do not believe it, is due not to the failure of their reason but to the foolishness of their hearts—it is the consequence of sin. However, this failure does not at all change the objective character of *revelation*. Cornelius Van Til expressed it even more strongly by speaking of the "sufficiency of natural revelation."[36] This revelation remains revelation, in the objec-

---

35. Troost (1978, 112).
36. Van Til (1946, 267); cf. Berkouwer (1955, 312).

tive sense even *sufficient* revelation, even though, as a consequence of their own fault, in the subjective sense it is not sufficient for *sinners*.

Philosopher Lorenz B. Puntel, too, did not seem to escape a certain form of natural theology in claiming that Christian theology presupposes a philosophical doctrine of God: God as the Absolute One, the ultimate Ground of interpretation, and thus the Ultimate Principle of comprehensibility. Only under this condition, said Puntel, can theology be truly rational.[37] He referred to Wolfhart Pannenberg, who launched the thesis that each theology must presuppose a "nominal definition of the concept of God" (notice the rationalistic overtones in such terms as "definition" and "concept"), and whose own formula was: God is "the all determining reality."[38] All these opinions, from more or less conservative theologians, are clear evidence of the continuing domination of scholastic-dualistic thought.

4.2.3 A Liberal Approach

So far, I have dealt with the notion of natural theology in a scholastic context. It is remarkable, however, that such a theology can be defended in a liberal theological context as well. An example of this was H. Kuitert[39] (unless one wishes to attribute his view to a residue of scholasticism in his theology). At any rate, Kuitert extensively developed the idea of religion as *the* presupposition of theology, and described this idea of religion in a purely phenomenal and rational way. Although he was familiar with the thought of Dooyeweerd and Vollenhoven, Kuitert never grasped — or refused to accept — the fundamental distinction between religion in the transcendent, supra-rational sense, and religion in the immanent, rational (pistical) sense.

As a consequence, Kuitert described humans as beings

---

37. Puntel (1988, 18–19).
38. Pannenberg (1976, 302–305).
39. Kuitert (1988, 42–65).

that (rationally or pre-rationally?) form a picture of reality, in which they assign meaning to their environment. This assignment necessarily implies an ultimate "meaning-assigning totality." Without such a totality, human life would be impossible. This totality is (rationally or pre-rationally?) ascribed to that power that we call God.

Kuitert himself referred explicitly to this interpretation as natural theology (thus implicitly underscoring its rational dimension), and saw nothing wrong with it. On the contrary, he blamed Karl Barth for having rejected natural theology.[40]

Kuitert offered here an excellent example, whether scholastic or humanistic, of deriving a notion of God without leaving any room for the Fall, by which human awareness of God was darkened (as we saw in Rom. 1:21; Eph. 4:18). Nor did Kuitert leave any room or necessity for regeneration and the enlightenment by the Holy Spirit, through which means alone people can have knowledge of God. He allowed even less room for the notion of *revelation* in his thinking. One of his best-known one-liners was this one: "All our speaking about Above comes from below, including the statement that something comes from Above."[41]

Interestingly, even his friend, Edward Schillebeeckx, wondered how theology, as Kuitert saw it, would be anything other than philosophy of religion, and what room Kuitert had for any form of "revelational offer" proceeding from God.[42] Regardless of possible objections to Schillebeeckx' own theology, at least he seems to have been aware of an objective revelation from God, some kind of address from God to people, no matter how people might respond to it.

---

40. Ibid., 79–80.
41. Part of this statement was used in the title of his biography: Peelen (2016).
42. Schillebeecks (1989, 222, 229).

General Revelation (2)

4.3 Creation "in Christ"[43]

4.3.1 Various Views

In addition to Romans 1:20-21, other Bible passages that play a central role in the theological study of natural revelation speak of the creation "in Christ" (cf. §2.7.1). Let us look first at the most prominent of these passages, "For in him [i.e., Christ] all things were created, in heaven and on earth, visible and invisible, whether thrones or dominions or rulers or authorities — all things were created through him and for him. And he is before all things, and in him all things hold together" (Col. 1:16-17).

The main problem here concerns the meaning of "in [Gk. *en*[44]] him," "through [Gk. *dia*] him," and "for [Gk. *eis*, ASV: unto] him." The small, purely lexicographical, differences between *en*, *dia*, and *eis* are not relevant right now. Our problem is rather of a theological nature: how should we understand that the world was created "in/through/for" Christ? In other words, what is the precise relationship between Christ's central creaturely position in the first creation and his redemptive position in the re-creation? If we formulate the problem this way, it can be grasped immediately how this problem is related to the problem of the relationship between creation and re-creation, that is, the relationship between general and special revelation (the central question in chapters 2-3 in this book).

Herman Ridderbos said regarding the phrase "created in him" that on this point "there is much uncertainty and difference of opinion,"[45] and continued with a description of the various interpretations: a *local-idealistical* view (in correspondence with the ancient Logos idea), a *local-cosmic* view (in correspondence with the Gnostic idea of the cosmos as a human

---

43. Regarding this, see specifically Troost (2004, 100–02, 120–21, 268–69, 272–73, 325–26).

44. Not "by," which would be Gk. *hypo*; KJV and others render both *en* and *dia* as "by," both of which are mistaken.

45. Ridderbos (1960, 139).

being), a *local-comprehensive* view (Christ as the unity in which all things are comprehended), and a *causal-instrumental* view (Christ as the conditioning cause of creation).[46] Ridderbos was correct to say that God

> has given in him to the entire creation its mutual existence, its mutual coherence. Outside Christ, each creature and every power are disintegrated. Only because, and insofar as,[47] they are upheld by Christ and stand under his rule, they have their coherent and meaningful connection with all other creatures. Here again, the apostle points to Christ as the undergirding basis and concentration point of every creature and every power.[48]

Here Ridderbos clearly indicates the real *problem* in each interpretation of these and similar passages. Many expositors see the cosmic significance of Christ only vaguely in Christ's power and rule over all things *without* indicating whether the scope of this rule is cosmological *or* soteriological, restricted to the redeemed world in agreement with Matthew 28:18, for example. In other words, are we dealing here with creation or re-creation, with the created world or the redeemed world, with general or special revelation? The commentaries ought to tell us whether this dominion of Christ is connected with the former or with the latter, *or they must explain that this is a false dilemma, and why.*

4.3.2 The View of Barth

This problem has been carefully formulated and answered by Karl Barth,[49] though not to everyone's satisfaction. Because of his fierce rejection of any idea of natural revelation, he approached each Bible passage about creation "in Christ" in an exclusively soteriological, infralapsarian way (i.e., pre-sup-

---

46. Ibid., 139–40.
47. To me, this seems to be a superfluous addition in light of "the firstborn of all creation" (v. 15) and "all things" (v. 16–17); cf. Troost (1978, 116).
48. Ridderbos (1960, 138–39); cf. also Ridderbos (1975, 82–84, 387–89) on Col. 1:16–17.
49. See especially Barth (*CD* III/1).

posing the Fall).⁵⁰ This was true for Colossians 1:16-17, but also for John 1:3 ("All things were made through him, and without him was not any thing made that was made") and Hebrews 1:2 (God's "Son, . . . through whom also he created the world"). Obviously, Barth's approach continued to presuppose the nature-grace dualism, but this time with all the emphasis on the pole of grace. This has been called Barth's "Christomonism" (or Christocentrism, Christocracy). As always happens with such dualisms, a strong emphasis on one pole in a dualism always provokes a strong reaction, in which all the emphasis is put on the other pole. In both cases, the underlying dualism itself continues to be presupposed. In the present case, the pendulum swings to and fro between the cosmological and the soteriological significance of the phrase "in Christ."

Barth's view clearly came to light in his comments on Colossians 1:16, John 1:3, and Hebrews 1:2. He wrote,

> It is not God or the world and their relation which is the problem of those passages but the lordship of Jesus Christ. The starting point is not that deity is so exalted and holy or that the world is so dark; nor is it the affirmation that there is something like a mediation between the two which bears the name of Jesus Christ. What they [i.e., these passages] have in view is the kingdom of God drawn near; the turning point of the times, revealed in the name of Jesus Christ, as the fulfilment of all the promises of the covenant of grace. To give to the Bearer of this name the honour due to Him, or rather to bear witness to the honour which He has, they venture the tremendous assertion that the world was created through Him and in Him as through God, and in God, in God's eternal will and purpose. . . . But now we may and must ask further whether it was the eternal Son (or eternal Word) of God as such in His pure deity that they [these Bible writers] had in mind; or whether, more inclusively and

---

50. Cf. also Ebeling (1979, 251-52).

mover concretely, it was the Son of God as the Son of Man, the Word made flesh.[51]

The point that Barth wishes to make is that, if the first interpretation were correct, it would be difficult to understand why Scripture would speak of such a *peculiar* causal position of the Logos in creation: *through* and *in* him. For, as Barth believes, such a *special* relationship involves more than the wisdom and power of God, which are also those of the Son, and therefore cannot refer to the pre-incarnate Logos. In other words, John 1:2 cannot be severed from verse 14 ("the Word became flesh"): "And in just the same way in this event [i.e., the incarnation] it [i.e., the Word] became historical reality, as the Word incarnate — how else? — this Word was in the beginning, i.e., in the divinely determined counsel with God before the world was."[52]

In other words, this is the way God wished to consider, know, and love, his only-begotten Son from eternity, namely, *in view of* the fact that he would become the Mediator, the Word in the flesh. And in view of this, he was the "rationale" (German: *Beweggrund*, "moving ground") of creation.[53] In fact, asserted Barth, we cannot speak of the Logos "as such." *Because* the Logos became flesh, John 1:1-3 can say of him what they do say. *Because* God, in his eternal counsel, decided to reconcile the world to himself, *therefore* the Word-that-became-flesh was in the beginning with God. Or as Marinus H. Bolkestein described Barth's view, God created in order that he would be able to redeem.[54] The Prologue (John 1:1-14) is not of a cosmological but of a soteriological nature. Although here clearly a cosmological function is ascribed to the Logos, this (supposedly) is not John's point; his point is purely soteriological. Here nothing is being projected back into eternity; each statement refers to the Word in the flesh. That is Barth's position.

---

51. Barth (*CD* III/1:53-54).
52. Ibid., 54.
53. Ibid., 50, 54-55; cf. also II/2, 102-109, where he deals with John 1:1-3; Col. 1:16-17; Heb. 1:1-2; cf. the comments by Berkouwer (1955, 239-50).
54. Bolkestein (1949, 5).

4.3.3 Comments

In my view, Barth's approach is a striking example of arguing in one's exegesis for a dogmatic position already adopted. The response by G. C. Berkouwer to this approach is that Barth's view is rooted in the false antithesis of "cosmological or soteriological."[55] On the one hand, no expositor doubts that John 1:1-13 points to Jesus Christ, and that the Prologue culminates in the incarnation in verse 14. In other words, the soteriological aspect lies on the horizon right from the beginning. John is not interested in cosmological and metaphysical insights as such, apart from the way and the knowledge of salvation. On the other hand, we cannot *begin* the Prologue with verse 14, and cannot give a soteriological turn to all pre-temporal aspects in the Prologue.

However, even though Berkouwer added the presumption that John transcends the cosmological-soteriological dilemma,[56] it seems to me that his own argument kept presupposing this dilemma. We find the same with Frederik W. Grosheide,[57] who, in his allegation that John does not sever the soteriological from the cosmological,[58] keeps presupposing this dilemma as well.

The consequences of this dilemma are still visible everywhere. Theologians do not wish to play off the cosmological against the soteriological; they plead for harmony and unity between the two aspects. However, these remain two antithetical aspects, such that the primacy keeps being ascribed to special revelation. As long as this is the case, we have no real defense against Barth, nor is there any genuine room for general revelation, except as part of a decent orthodox systematic theology.[59] In such a situation, insofar as Christian thought has any room for universal norms such as justice,

---
55. Berkouwer (1955, 242–45).
56. Ibid., 245.
57. Grosheide (1949, 75–76, 91–99).
58. Ibid., 76; cf. 83, 116.
59. Cf. Troost (1978, 114–15).

freedom, peace, altruism, and so on, these are treated in a biblicistic way from a soteriological viewpoint. That is, they are derived from the Bible in theological ethics, instead of being developed and positivized in all the different disciplines on the basis of a coherent Christian worldview: economic norms in Christian economics, juridical norms in Christian legal research, moral norms in Christian ethics, and so on (cf. §4.8).[60]

The reverse is equally undesirable. This is the situation where the primacy shifts from special to general revelation, which means in practice, from the soteriological to the cosmological viewpoint. Invariably, this implies a revival of natural theology, over against the common supernatural theology. In both situations, theology wrestles with the antithesis between creation and re-creation, between the two kingdoms of Lutheranism,[61] between the two supposed sources for our knowledge of God, and so on. The central error underlying all such struggles is nothing but the dualistic, antagonistic dilemma of general over against special revelation, which itself arises from the scholastic nature–grace dualism. This will be discussed further in the next sections.

I believe that we make progress here only if we proceed from Christ as the Root, the "beginning [Gk. *archē*] of God's creation" (Rev. 3:14b), the firstborn of all creation (Col. 1:15) as well as of the re-creation (Rom. 8:29; Col. 1:18; Heb. 1:6; Rev. 1:5). In this regard, we must constantly remember that we are speaking here of *one and the same* creation, which one day will be renewed. In Scripture, the biblical notion of all things having been created *in*, and their existing *in*, Christ (Col. 1:16-17), is being applied both soteriologically and cosmologically, without any distinction. This is possible because, in re-creation, we are not dealing with a different cosmos than in the first creation. Christ is the Root, the *archē*, of the *one* creation, as it came into existence at creation and will be renewed at the end. In such an approach, cosmology and soteriology

---

60. See extensively, Ouweneel (2014; 2015).
61. See extensively, Ouweneel (2017).

no longer constitute an antithesis because salvation concerns this very same world.[62]

We also must notice that, on the one hand, John 1:3 speaks of the Logos, and Colossians 1:13–16 and Hebrew 1:2 of the Son, which are both names that refer to Christ's eternal *deity*. On the other hand, in Colossians 1:15 this Son is described as "image of the invisible God," and as "firstborn of all creation," that is, emphatically according to his *humanity*. In Revelation 3:14, Christ is the "faithful and true witness" specifically as *Man*, and the *archē* ("beginning") of the creation specifically as *God*, but he is both at the same time: the God-Man. He is the "only begotten" (Gk. *monogenēs*) Son specifically as *God* (John 1:14, 18; 3:16, 18; 1 John 4:9 KJV), and he is the "firstborn" (*prōtotokos*) of creation (Col. 1:15; cf. v. 18; Rom. 8:29) specifically as *Man*. Again, he is the God-Man, by way of anticipation in the first creation, by way of reality in re-creation.

In other words, Christ in his capacity of anointed *Man* of God, who is God and Man in one person, the incarnate Son, may be called the Root of the cosmos, because the old cosmos and the renewed cosmos are one. In other words, Christ is the Root both cosmologically and soteriologically, in the sense of the transcendent-religious unity, fullness, and concentration of the cosmos in him who "upholds all things by the word of his power" (Heb. 1:3). This is what the apostle Paul expresses in the words, "in him we live and move and have our being," adding a quotation from a pagan poet (Aratus): "for we are indeed his offspring" (Gk. *tou gar kai genos esmen*), which he applies to *all* humanity (Acts 17:28).

4.4 Creation and Re-Creation

4.4.1 One World, One Kingdom

Regarding the issue of a double or a single divine revelation, Andree Troost wrote:

> In my view, this placing of God's supposed double revelational actions alongside, and subsequently inevitably under and

---

62. See extensively, Ouweneel (2017).

above, each other can, in its disastrous theological consequences, be stopped only through the alternative of acknowledging only the one revelation-in-Christ, the Word that from the beginning was with God. This self-revelation of God in his eternal Word retains its central position of source, fullness, and transcendence also within time, when it manifests itself after the Fall in the saving and liberating redemptive work of Jesus, the Christ. But then always *proceeding from* the divine Origin, who remains faithful to himself and to his creation within as well as beyond all times and history formation, until the "consummation" of "eternity."[63]

With these words I believe Troost has identified the proper theological path. This path leads us away from the remaining traces of the scholastic nature–grace dualism, and the false dualism of general *versus* special revelation that flows from it.[64] The dominion of Christ, that is, the kingdom of God, can and may never be severed from the creation order, in which God's creating and redeeming dominion is manifest as revelation of God's will in word and work.[65] The kingdom of God in which Christ is reigning—now in a hidden way, and one day in public glory—is *no other* kingdom than that of God's kingly reign from the beginning of the world.[66] Only if we maintain the unity of God's dominion, that is, the unity of creation and re-creation, do the full riches of the one and only revelation of God come to expression in the rich diversity of, the inner coherence of, and the deeper unity in, the divine laws for created things and for the many typical and characteristic acts and societal relationships of humanity in the

---

63. Troost (1978, 115–16); see also extensively, idem (2004, especially chapter 10).
64. Abraham Kuyper wished to eliminate this dualism. However, by maintaining the distinction between a "special principle" (Lat. *principium speciale*) and a "natural principle" (Lat. *principium naturale*) in theology (1898, 355–58), he nevertheless operated with this dualism, though he denied this (1898, 380–81).
65. Troost (1978, 116).
66. See extensively, Ouweneel (2017; 2018j).

course of history, from the creation to the consummation of the world.[67]

There is no contrast, no contradiction, no conflict, no antithesis, not even a tension between God's creational word and God's redemptive word. In Christ, they are absolutely one because Christ is the one and only Word of God for creation as well as for re-creation. He is not two Words: a creational Word and a redemptive Word. If there are any conflicts and tensions, they exist only on the human side because humans must respond to God's one and only Word. Preaching the redemptive word loses its power and foundation if it is not understood, as Troost insisted, that "the cross of Christ is erected *in* and *from* the creation in order that Christ would be able to freshly uphold, redeem, set free that creation from its un-nature, and would bring it to the fulfillment and consummation."[68]

The consequences of this view are far reaching. There can be no tension between creation and redemption if we realize that God's good creation, that is, before the Fall, in principle contained from the beginning blessing and bliss, the full and the perfect. It was the calling of humanity to walk in this way of blessing, which was the way of creation and its deployment, of "subduing" and "dominion" (Gen. 1:28), of farming and maintaining (2:15). Before sin entered creation, *this* was the "way of life" (Prov. 6:23; 15:24; Jer. 21:8; cf. Prov. 9:6; 16:17; Matt. 7:14; Heb. 10:20). And even after sin came in, this remained the same way of life, now in the power of Christ's redemption. In this way, the creation "in the beginning" and the eschatological future in Christ cannot be played off against each other. We may certainly point to the great emphasis that the gospel places on living in the power of, and on the way to, the future of Christ and his kingdom. But we are mistaken if we create a tension here with regard to God's creation revelation, because the kingdom of Christ refers to nothing other

---

67. Troost (1978, 117).
68. Troost (1976, 86; cf. 29–30).

than *this* created cosmos.[69]

4.4.2 The View of G. Spykman

These things have been poignantly expressed by Gordon J. Spykman.[70] In my words (with Bible references added), he wrote that the creation-Word remains God's first Word for the world. It is also an abiding Word (cf. 1 Pet. 1:23); God never withdrew or replaced it. It will stand forever (Isa. 40:8). This revelation has not lost any of its original force and clarity, although now, in a fallen world, this Word has become a two-edged sword (cf. Heb. 4:12) for creation, expressing not only the severity of its Author but also his goodness. The difficulty rather lies on the response-side. Therefore, that first Word, though still sufficient for its original goal and purpose, is no longer sufficient for our present need. Now, due to God's gracious condescension, that first Word is no longer his last Word. God reformulates his creation-Word in his redemption-Word. That first Word has neither been withdrawn nor mitigated.

One of the most basic themes in a non-scholastic and non-humanistic dogmatics is a clear insight in the relationship between creation and re-creation, and thus between general and special revelation. In spite of sin, there is a basic *continuity* that applies to our lives in the world as far as the *structures* of creation are concerned. The gospel is a redemptive *re*-proclamation of God's abiding Word. "Heaven and earth will pass away, but my words will not pass away" (Mark 13:31). God's second Word is a redemptively revised edition of God's creation-Word, now in the lingual and definitive form of Scripture. Thus, the will of God, the divine imperative for human relationships, was not proclaimed first in the Ten Commandments at Mount Sinai (or, I would add, even in the commandment that God gave to Adam and Eve [Gen. 1:26–28], or the *torot* that God gave to Abraham [26:5]). Rather, it is as old

---

69. Troost (1969, 12, 35–37; 1982, 189–92).
70. Spykman (1988, 142–43; cf. 1992, 88–90).

General Revelation (2)

as the everlasting hills (cf. Gen. 49:26; cf. Deut. 33:15; Prov. 8:25; Hab. 3:6). From the very beginning, God's Word served as the criterion for the creation order. Thus, speaking metaphorically, the law was not born but re-born at the Sinai. It was reformulated there on tables of stone, re-articulated, repeated, re-told in lingual form. I endorse Spykman's plea for a thorough review of the prolegomena of orthodox theology along the lines of Reformational philosophy (especially that of Dooyeweerd and Vollenhoven).[71]

This view has clear consequences for our understanding of the new creation in Christ. This new creation must never be viewed as an *independent*, new reality, separated from, or standing over against, natural life within *this* creation. When the apostle Paul describes the new self (new man, new person), he views this self as being manifested and realized practically within the spheres of God's created world: our faith community (with fellow believers), our home community (husband and wife, parents and children), and our labor community (masters and slaves, employers and employees) (Eph. 4:22-6:9; Col. 3:9-4:1; Titus 2:1-10; cf. 1 Pet. 2:13-3:9).

Here we are helped again by the important distinction between *structure* and *direction*. The new creation is not a new *structure* or *structural order*, which supposedly replaces the structure or structural order of the old creation. Rather, the new creation is a radical renewal of the *direction* of the human heart, so that humans live within the creation order in a totally *new* way, namely, not as sin-oriented but Christ-oriented persons.

4.5 Two Alternatives

4.5.1 *Creatio Continua*

Two alternative solutions must be rejected here (the first one discussed in this section, and the second one in the next sections).[72] The first one is the idea of "continual creation" (Lat.

---

71. See especially Spykman (1992).
72. Cf. Berkouwer (1952, 61–74); Troost (1969, 14–15; 1976, 30–31, 148–49).

creatio continua). This is the idea of a continual work of divine creation within time, more particularly: within human history, referring especially to structural changes of our own time. It is the humanistic idea that creation basically involves the idea that "the Creator creates creators." That is, the social and historical actions of humans are identified with God's creative action. It is not so much God but rather humanity that is the creator and re-creator of the world, specifically of historically determined society. In this view, God's assistance is all that is being confessed, but humans are in fact the acting persons.

This idea has led, for instance, to liberation theology, in which Christians grant theological approval to revolution, including armed agendas. The idea is that God makes all things new through people who improve their social structures. The guidelines for such changes are deduced from the new creation or the kingdom of God construed in a thoroughly humanistic way, *not* deduced from the unchangeable creation order, that is, the commandments of God. Thus, God is supposed to sanction humanity's own autonomous works.[73]

In such a view, the biblical truth that God remains faithful to his creation word once given, and subjects all human actions to the invariable norms of his one word of creation-and-re-creation, is totally twisted. Here there are no creation ordinances at all; instead, God supposedly (re-)creates the world, and thus his kingdom, through human activities. There is no creation order that must be maintained, and to which humanity is subject, but one that is continually evolving by human activity.[74] The essence of this error is the point just mentioned: a view of history that refuses to acknowledge both a transcendent normative structure and a transcendent root unity in Christ—unless one accepts the Barthian (dialectic-scholastic) distinction between the (eschatological, redemptive-revelational) "event" (Ger. *Geschichte*) and the (non-eschatological, secular) history (Ger. *Historie*).

---

73. Cf. Ouweneel (2018b, §9.3.3).
74. So Augustijn (1971, 204–205).

I will not investigate the views in which the idea of a continual creation is reduced to something like providence or sustenance, as with Dutch theologians Herman Bavinck and Abraham Kuyper.[75] I would observe only that G. C. Berkouwer rightly rejected this idea because it obscures the biblical distinction between creation out of nothing (Lat. *creatio ex nihilo*; cf. the force of the word "finished" in Gen. 2:1 and the calling into existence the things that do not exist in Rom. 4:17b) and the preservation/sustenance after creation (Lat. *conservatio post creationem*).[76]

Nor will I delve into the complex problem of *how* human responsibility under God's ordinances in the present sinful world must be precisely understood. Neo-Calvinism has dealt with this problem in the framework of its views concerning the cultural mandate (the divine command to human cultural work) and common grace.[77] This led to heated discussions, like the well-known debate between Oepke Noordmans and Klaas Schilder in 1936.[78]

4.5.2 Creatio Nova

In the idea of a brand new creation (Lat. *creatio nova*), we are dealing with the erroneous notion that the new creation is not a restoration and elevation of the original creation but a totally new creation, which *replaces* the previous one.[79] To be sure, restoration does *not* simply entail repairing what was broken, as if redemption would be essentially a reactionary act of returning creation to its state before the Fall. If this were so, nothing would have been gained, and creation could in principle fall into sin again. Restoration implies an enormous gain compared with mere repair, and this gain is related very

---

75. Bavinck (*RD* 2:606–608); Kuyper (*DD* 3:37–39).
76. Berkouwer (1952, 73–74).
77. See as a standard work Kuyper's *Stone Lectures: Kuyper* (2009); cf. the useful summary by Douma (2017).
78. Puchinger (1970); cf. also S. A. Strauss (1982, 68, 77).
79. See Ouweneel (2012, §14.1.1; 2017, chapter 9).

significantly to many topics in systematic theology. The new creation involves much *more* than Adam ever lost—but this does not mean that the new creation is a *different* creation.[80]

Compare the view of Philippus F. Theron concerning both the continuity and the discontinuity between the original creation and the *eschaton*: if the proper balance between the two is not maintained, confusion will arise in several chapters of systematic theology.[81] One example involves ecclesiology. Pieter C. Potgieter rightly emphasized the continuity between creation and re-creation, but drew the strange conclusion that, in the present age, the church must exhibit the same diversity as society does, which would imply a different church (as institution) for every nation.[82] This was an odd view against the background of the South African *apartheid* situation of the time! Potgieter's view has been rightly criticized by another South African theologian, Adrio König.[83]

The question of continuity and discontinuity, or of repair or replacement, touched one of the essential differences between the views of Emil Brunner (who defended the former) and of Karl Barth (who defended the latter), as has been beautifully summarized by British psychologist and theologian Alasdair Heron.[84]

The term "restoration" rightly involves the notion that God is restoring *this* creation through redemption in order to bring it to full development and unfolding, and to lead it to its full consummation and completion. God never abandons the present creation. If he would destroy it by replacing it, he would surrender creation to the power of sin and Satan. He would have to admit that he lost the creation to this power, and that he could respond to this loss only by making an entirely new creation. God does not replace the world but *re-*

---

80. Ibid.
81. Theron (1978, chapter 1).
82. Potgieter (1982, 107–09).
83. König (1982, 115–17).
84. Heron (1980, 84–88).

news and *exalts* it.⁸⁵ This is the force of the word "new" in the expressions "new self (man, person)," "new covenant," and "new creation." The fine lexicographic differences between the Greek words *kainos* and *neos* (Eph. 4:23–24; Col. 3:10) may be interesting,⁸⁶ but none of these implies a creation that is "new" in the sense of a substitute for the old one.

As is so often the case, the factual cause of the entire problem of the relationship between creation and re-creation is the scholastic nature–grace dualism, whether or not in its secularized, humanistic form of the nature–freedom dualism. In this case, it manifests itself in the so-called double order (Lat. *duplex ordo*) or the doctrine of the two kingdoms: the natural kingdom of earthly and human realities and the supernatural (spiritual) kingdom of God's revelation and (a part of) God's work. This roots in the well-known dualism of law and gospel, of the two regiments (in its Lutheran form the kingdom of God's left hand and that of his right hand), of the many constant commandments and the command of the moment (Ger. *Gebot der Stunde*; see §2.9.1),⁸⁷ of world and church, of body and soul (both viewed as immanent-modal-substantial function complexes),⁸⁸ of the secular and the sacred, of the human and the Christian, of reason and faith, and so on.⁸⁹ Even if some of these dualisms are no longer very popular in theology, nonetheless the same dualism remains very much alive under various names and in various versions.

4.5.3 Again: Structure and Direction

A basic problem in the scholastic dualism just described is that the *directional* antithesis between God and Satan, or between the Spirit and the flesh, has been replaced by a supposed antithesis that is perpendicular to it: an artificial *structural* antith-

---

85. See extensively, Ouweneel (2012, §14.1; 2017).
86. Cf. Ouweneel (2018l, §3.6.2).
87. Brunner (1937).
88. See Ouweneel (2008, chapters 6–8).
89. This entire subject is *the* theme of Ouweneel (2017).

esis *within* created reality. The directional antithesis between the Spirit and the flesh runs straight through the natural and the supernatural, that is, through the two supposed kingdoms. It manifests itself both within the church and within the world, both within the sacred and within the secular, both within faith and within reason (if we may use for a moment these largely false distinctions for the sake of argument). Creation and re-creation are not two *structurally* different words. The apostate creation and the redeemed creation are the *same* creation. Before its restoration, this one creation is, in an apostate way, *directed* toward sin and Satan, and through regeneration (re-creation) it is biblically restored, that is, *directed* anew toward God and his Word. There is no place here for a dualism of law and gospel: the redemptive word is enclosed in the eternal Torah, and the redeemed creation is subject to this same eternal Torah.[90] Any form of scholastic dualism of this kind drives a wedge between God's creational work and redemptive work, whose unity and center are given in Christ as the creation-and-redemption *Word*.

A dualism between the present (social and historical) world and the new creation (Lat. *creation nova*) cannot be bridged by some dialectical encounter. In such a view the natural social order, or marriage and family, supposedly does not stand under the dominion of God in Christ. The Christian is called to *bring* one's marriage, family, professional life, and societal life, and so on, under the rule of God. However, if we recognize the unity of God's word and work both in creation and in redemption, there is nothing in life or in the world that we could view *a priori* as *not* standing under God's dominion, and as something that should be *brought a posteriori* under it. The only thing that the Christian can do is to *recognize* (not bring about) this divine rule, and respond to it in obedience.

As soon as we have understood that the twofold order (Lat. *duplex ordo*) is untenable, we will be able to grasp why

---

90. See extensively, Ouweneel (2018a).

the dualism of general and special revelation, not this twofold revelation itself, is equally untenable.[91] In all conflicts between verticalism and horizontalism in theology, and in Christianity in general, people combat each other by one-sidedly emphasizing either special or general revelation. Both are equally wrong. Both by overemphasizing one of the two revelations and by accusing the opponent of overemphasizing the other one, the nature-grace dualism constantly remains presupposed. When will it penetrate into the deepest hidden corners of theology that *there is only one revelation of God in Christ*? In other words, when will theology give heed to the biblical testimony that literally *all things*, without exception, have been created by God in, through, and for Christ, that *all things* hold together in Christ, and that through him *all things* will be reconciled to God (Col. 1:16-17, 20), and *all things* in heaven and on earth will be headed up (Gk. *anakephalaiōsasthai*) under Christ (Eph. 1:10 NET)? *In the latter two quotations "all things" are exactly the same as "all things" in the former two quotations; there is only one creation, and only one revelation.*

Pieter C. Potgieter believed that such a view necessarily depreciated God's Word in Scripture, as if, for instance, mathematical laws would be on the same level as the law of Moses.[92] I know no theologian or philosopher who would make such an absurd claim. Behind Potgieter's statement is hidden a basic misunderstanding. The law of Moses is a written positivization of the one central (transcendent) Law of Love, and covers *all* of human life, whereas numerical and spatial laws are just a few of the typical modally delineated laws, just like, for instance, the physical, biotic, sensitive, logical, lingual, social, economic, or moral laws. In this sense, they can never be on the same level as the law of Moses. Furthermore, the central Law of Love (of which the Mosaic law is only a positivization) as *transcendent* Torah is *a priori* higher than all of its *immanent* forms, including the (positivized) law of Moses and

---

91. Cf. Troost (1978, 121-22, 124-25, 128).
92. Potgieter (1990, 16-17).

mathematical laws.

Moreover, does not Potgieter's criticism of Troost on these and other points run the risk of landing him in the very snare that Troost had so clearly identified, namely, the snare of the scholastic nature–grace dualism? Did not Potgieter's proposal to distinguish between the creational and the revelational function of God's Word strongly remind us of this dualism? Is not creation *itself* revelation? And does not Word-revelation *itself* participate in various creational forms, both in Scripture and in the physical body of Christ?

4.5.4 The Twofold Revelation

God's one and only revelation is *creational* revelation. This does not exclude Scripture, simply because Scripture is God's major creational work. Nor should we, conversely, limit revelation to Scripture (or to the person of Christ, for that matter). On the contrary, God's revelation encompasses the totality of created reality, in which Scripture, as the creaturely-immanent form in which it pleased the eternal, transcendent Word to be inscripturated, constitutes the radiating and directive center.[93]

This does not at all mean that we should not distinguish between general and special revelation. *On the non-theological level of faith and confession,* such a distinction between divine revelation in creation and history, on the one hand, and revelation in Scripture, on the other hand, is made in the Belgic Confession, Article 2. Problems arise when theology tries to supply a *warrant* for this distinction in a rational-theoretical way, as is its duty. In this case, theoretical thought falls all too easily into the snare of the age-old nature–grace dualism.

As we saw, the only *duality*—which is something very different from a *dualism*—that can be recognized here is the vertical duality of the transcendent unity and fullness, on the one hand, and the immanent-modal divergence and diversity of cosmic reality, on the other hand. That is, when it is a question

---

93. Troost (1978, 121).

of the transcendent unity and fullness of the creational revelation as we have it in Christ, we are dealing with God as the Origin and Fullness, who reveals himself in Christ in creation, redemption, and consummation. However, when the immanent-modal divergence and diversity as we find it in creational reality is in view, we are dealing with a *world history* of the creation, the Fall, and the renewal of God's creational revelation in view of redemption, leading to the consummation. Christ is the eternal-transcendent Root unity, from whom the entire immanent-historical reality, and the entire *history* of this reality, radiates in variation and diversity, and in whom the entire immanent-historical diversity is concentrated and integrated.

If this is understood, we can see why G. C. Berkouwer should not have had any trouble calling special revelation a "supplement" or "extension" of general revelation.[94] In the transcendent focal point of the revelation in Christ, there is indeed no supplement or extension but only absolute unity and integrity: an absolute fullness of love, grace, justice, beauty, glory, abundance, and so forth (cf. the Belgic Confession, Article 1: "God . . . eternal, incomprehensible, invisible, immutable, infinite, almighty, perfectly wise, just, and good, and the overflowing fountain of all good"). However, within immanent history, this integral fullness of God is deployed in many distinct and successive acts of God: in various manifestations of God's love and righteousness in the various successive dispensations of redemptive history.[95] Seen from this viewpoint, there definitely is "supplement" and "extension," in an ongoing deployment of everything that, from the beginning, was enclosed in God's revelation.

In this sense, it is also possible to retain the term "special revelation."[96] It is special because it reveals that, in spite of sin, God continues with his great creational purpose. It is

---

94. Berkouwer (1955, 311, 313).
95. Cf. Ouweneel (2018j, chapters 12–13).
96. Cf. Troost (1978, 121–25).

special because it refers especially to the work of redemption, that is, the redemption of *this* creation, in order that it will be restored, renewed, and exalted to the obedience to, and realization of, God's will. It is special because it is oriented toward the deployment—which, since the Fall, also involves deliverance—of creation until the ultimate completion, that is, the perfect manifestation of God's royal dominion of love in Christ, as the "God all in all" (1 Cor. 15:28; cf. Eph. 4:10). However, special revelation is *not* special in the sense that it entails anything other than the realization of God's universal law, as it comes to light also, but not exclusively, in the gospel (and has been inscripturated in the Bible); nor does it entail anything other than his universal redemptive purpose.

This emphasis on this universal character of special revelation (Rom. 3:23-24; 5:18; 11:32; 1 Tim. 2:5-6; Titus 2:11; 2 Pet. 3:9) does not minimize the truth of eternal election and predestination (Acts 13:48; Rom. 8:29-30; 9:23; 11:5; 1 Cor. 1:27-28; Eph. 1:3-5, 11; Col. 3:12; 1 Thess. 1:4; 2 Thess. 2:13; James 2:5; 1 Pet. 2:9).[97] On the subject-side of the pistical modality of creational reality, there is only limited response to this *universal* special revelation; but on the law-side of this modality, the universality and general validity of God's revelation is always fully maintained.

4.6 God and History

4.6.1 God of the Nations

It may be useful to add here a few words concerning the relationship between divine revelation and human history.[98] Scripture is clear that God is at work in history, and that he is concerned not only with Israel or the church but with all nations on earth. We find this initially in the Torah: "When the Most High gave to the nations their inheritance, when he divided mankind, he fixed the borders of the peoples according

---

97. See extensively, Ouweneel (2018d, chapters 10–14).
98. Cf. Troost (1969, 24–29; 1978, 120).

to the number of the sons of God" (Deut. 32:8[99]).

Elsewhere it says, "He makes nations great, and he destroys them; he enlarges nations, and leads them away" (Job 12:13). "God reigns over the nations" (Ps. 47:8). "Say among the nations, 'The LORD reigns! Yes, the world is established; it shall never be moved; he will judge the peoples with equity'" (96:10). "The king's [i.e., *Each* king's] heart is a stream of water in the hand of the LORD; he turns it wherever he will" (Prov. 21:1). Assyria is used in God's hand as a "rod (staff, axe)" against Israel (Isa. 10:5, 15); similarly, God "raises up" the Chaldeans, and uses them in his service (Hab. 1:6–11). "He changes times and seasons; he removes kings and sets up kings" (Dan. 2:21). To king Belshazzar, Daniel speaks of "the God in whose hand is your breath, and whose are all your ways" (5:23).

Through the prophet Amos God emphasizes that he has governed the history of other nations just as much as he did the history of his own people: "Are you not like the Cushites to me, O people of Israel? . . . Did I not bring up Israel from the land of Egypt, and the Philistines from Caphtor and the Syrians from Kir?" (Amos 9:7). Apparently, God is no less the God of the history of the Cushites, the Philistines and Aram than he is of Israel. He is the "God of all flesh [i.e., all people, all humanity]" (Jer. 32:27).

In the New Testament, we find the same picture. The apostle Paul says, "In past generations he allowed all the nations to walk in their own ways. Yet he did not leave himself without witness, for he did good by giving you rains from heaven and fruitful seasons, satisfying your hearts with food and gladness" (Acts 14:16–17). "And he made from one man every nation of mankind to live on all the face of the earth, having determined allotted periods and the boundaries of their dwelling place" (17:26). Even before the Messianic kingdom, God is the "King of the nations" (Rev. 15:3; cf. Exod. 15:18,

---

99. Note the ESV: "Compare Dead Sea Scroll, Septuagint; Masoretic Text *sons of Israel*'; on this point see Ouweneel (2018m, §2.1.3).

"The LORD reigns," present tense [NIV]; also see Num. 23:21; Deut. 33:5 with reference to Israel), and the Lamb is "Lord of lords and King of kings" (17:14; cf. 1 Tim. 6:15).

It is foolish to think that YHWH is a "god of the hills" and not a "god of the valleys" (1 Kings 20:23, 28), and thus to geographically limit his power and significance. It is equally foolish to believe that God is an ethnic God, the God of Israel only. The Old Testament describes him this way many times, but at the same time he is the God of *all* nations. This is expressed in a special way in the description "God of gods," which in my view is more than a simple Hebrew superlative (Deut. 10:17; Josh. 22:22; Ps. 50:1; 136:2; Dan. 2:47; 11:36). This description says that God is superior to all the "gods" (read: angelic princes[100]) of the nations. These gods govern the history of their own respective nations; for instance, Moab is called the "people of Chemosh," and this Chemosh "made his sons fugitives, and his daughters captives, to an Amorite king, Sihon" (Num. 21:29). However, over Chemosh is YHWH, the "God of gods," to whom ultimately all gods and all nations are subject.

4.6.2 God the Universal Judge

The judge Jephthah expresses this in a remarkable way.[101] He has a conflict with Sihon, the king of the Ammonites/Amorites, and says to him,

> So then the LORD, the God of Israel, dispossessed the Amorites from before his people Israel; and are you to take possession of them? Will you not possess what Chemosh your god gives you to possess? And all that the LORD our God has dispossessed before us, we will possess. Now are you any better than Balak the son of Zippor, king of Moab? Did he ever contend against Israel, or did he ever go to war with them? While Israel lived in Heshbon and its villages, and in Aroer and its villages, and in

---

100. See Ouweneel (2008, 79–86).
101. See Ouweneel (2018m, §2.1.4).

all the cities that are on the banks of the Arnon, 300 years, why did you not deliver them within that time? I therefore have not sinned against you, and you do me wrong by making war on me. The LORD, the Judge, decide this day between the people of Israel and the people of Ammon (Judg. 11:23-27).

Something quite extraordinary is happening here. At first glance, Jephthah seems to be speaking as though YHWH and Chemosh are equivalent deities, or at least comparable gods: YHWH governed the history of Israel, Chemosh that of Ammon. Jephthah accepts this as fact; this is more than just flattering. However, if Sihon remains unwilling to surrender, Jephthah threatens him that YHWH will be the Judge (Referee) between Israel and Ammon. Each nation as its own god: Israel has YHWH, Ammon has Chemosh. However, in reality YHWH is beyond all gods, including Chemosh; he will judge between Israel and the nations without Chemosh being able to do anything to oppose it. For this is the exciting thing: YHWH is the God of Israel, and at the same time he possesses a quality that hardly any nation has ever claimed for its own god: he is the God, and thus the Judge, over *all* nations.[102] He has given Canaan to Israel, and has allowed Chemosh to give Ammon its own territory. But if Ammon reaches out for Israel's territory, the same God will function as a Referee between the two nations.

It is good, though, to emphasize here that we must be careful with identifying "God's hand in history."[103] After the great failure of the Spanish Armada in 1588, during the Spanish-English War, the Dutch authorities had a commemorative coin made with the inscription: "God's breath scattered them." I suppose that many modern Christians would

---

102. Cf. how Celsus (quoted in Origen, *Contra Celsum*) emphasizes the local character of all religion: there is indeed one Supreme God, but under him there are many gods, who are strictly bound to their own regions (cf. the nation-angels, who are venerated as gods by the pagans!); see Ouweneel (2018m, §2.1.3).

103. Cf. Kuiper (1996); the expression comes from, or became known through, Guillaume Groen van Prinsterer (2008).

say something like this only with difficulty. (Incidentally, the defeated Spanish king Philip II agreed: he saw the failure of the Armada as God's punishment upon himself.) We are less quick to identify this hand of God in world events, certainly if our interpretation would be to our own advantage. We think of the specter of the phrase "God with us" (Ger. *Gott mit uns*) on the belts of German soldiers during the World Wars. Even the late-Roman and the Byzantine empires used the slogan "God with us" (Lat. *nobiscum Deus*). This phrase was used also by the Swedish king Gustav II Adolf during the Thirty Years' War, and appears in the coat of arms of the Prussian king Frederick I. In all such cases, God is annexed for people's own benefit.

It is also very superficial to claim that the conquest of so many European countries by the Germans (1940) was a punishment for the sins of these countries, and that the defeat of the Germans in 1945 was a punishment for their own crimes. Similar superficial explanations could be heard after the *tsunami* of Christmas 2004, and after various recent earthquakes (Fukushima 2011, etc.). Astonishingly large is the number of "Job's friends" who, in the face of calamity, think they can tell us immediately that serious sins must be involved.[104] "God's hand in history" is about much more than reward and punishment.[105]

4.7 Making History Autonomous

4.7.1 Modernism and History

We have seen that, in the sense of the transcendent fullness of the revelation in Christ, God himself is this Fullness, who reveals himself through Christ in creation, redemption, and consummation. However, in the sense of the immanent-modal variation and diversity within created reality there is a *world history* of creation, fall, redemption, and consummation. Christ is the Root unity, from whom the entire historical re-

---

104. See extensively, Ouweneel (2011b).
105. See extensively, Ouweneel (2018d) on the "counsel" and the "ways" of God.

ality radiates in diversity, and in whom the entire historical diversity is concentrated. History can never be reduced to history-in-itself because history is always history-of-something, and it is clear that this "something" cannot be history itself. In the fullest sense of the word, this "something" is the transcendent (supra-historical, plenitemporal) Root of history, that is, Christ as the one Creator, Redeemer, and Perfecter.

In all kinds of modernist theology, history is severed from this transcendent Root in a dualistic way. "Redemptive" history is entirely limited in time, and secularized in the (semi-)Marxist theology (inspired by German philosopher Ernst Bloch,[106] d. 1977), in so-called black theology (James H. Cone[107]), in feminist theology (theologian and philosopher Mary Daly,[108] d. 2010), in liberation theology (Gustavo Gutiérrez[109]), in the somewhat older theology of hope (Jürgen Moltmann[110]), of labor (Marie-Dominique Chenu[111]), of sexuality (Hermann Ringeling[112]), of history as such (Wolfhart Pannenberg[113]), and other "theologies of the genitive."[114]

We met this approach in our discussion of the idea of ongoing creation (Lat. *creatio continua*): the humanistic idea that equates human social-historical activity with God's creational work (§4.5.1). God supposedly makes all things new through people who improve their societal structures from the so-called perspective of the new creation or the kingdom of God, *not* on the basis of God's unchanging creation order. The notion of creation ordinances is replaced by the belief that God creates the world through humans.

---

106. Bloch (1954–59).
107. Cone (1969).
108. See, e.g., Daly (1998).
109. Gutiérrez (1971).
110. Moltmann (1967).
111. Chenu (1985).
112. Ringeling (1968).
113. Pannenberg (1968).
114. The expression comes from Kuitert (1988, 37).

As we have seen, the essence of this new view of history consists of ignoring the divine law-order. The activity of autonomous humans—God's (semi-)autonomous partners—is absolutized, severed from the transcendental ontic, *a priori* normative structure of created reality. One consequence of this is that no room is left for God's sovereign acting *against* humans, that is, for his judgment upon the norm-disobedient actions of humans, whether through his providence or his ultimate eternal judgment. If humans themselves determine the norms, and adapt these norms continually throughout history, then there will be no norms that could serve as the basis of God's judgment against them. Gordon J. Spykman spoke here of a "two-factor theology," which contains God and humanity, but leaves out God's Word or Law, above which God dwells and under which humanity stands.[115]

4.7.2 Rigidity?

One reason why the notion of creation ordinances and their realization in history has been neglected to such an extent is that people often think that such a notion necessarily implies static, rigid, sterile immutability. This immutability is dualistically placed over against the vital, dynamic changeability of history, which is ascribed to the actions of (autonomous) people. Such a view totally ignores the basic continuous dynamic embedded in the creation order *itself*, and which must be deployed by people during the developmental process we call history. Immanent-historical changes brought about by humans—and according to God's cultural mandate *must* be brought about—occur in obedience or disobedience to the ontic, *a priori* normative structures contained in the creation order.

Thus, the fixed, constant divine law-order does not exclude the developmental process of history. Quite the opposite. If this development occurs in obedience to this law-order, immanent-historical changes proceed from the transcendent

---

115. Spykman (1992, 44, 49, 59–61).

unity and fullness of history in Christ, and are brought about within time by the regenerated transcendent heart of the believer, and hence in the believer's immanent-modal-functional actions.

However, we sympathize with the widespread theological fear about creation ordinances and their realization in history. Usually, the traditional natural theology of the creation ordinances, just like scholastic thought in general, did not at all proceed from the ontic, *a priori* normative structures embedded in the creation order (on the law-side) but rather from the concretely existing forms of societal relationships (on the subject-side). Time and again, natural theology fell into the snare of trying to justify existing social structures (the societal and political *status quo*), and to maintain them with a false appeal to the so-called creation ordinances (or the logos, or some natural law, or substantial structures, etc.).[116] In reality, it was not appealing to the creation order at all, but rather to the *status quo*.

The worst examples in modern times are found in German-Christian national-socialism (Nazism) and other extreme forms of fascism, which in their days had all been legitimized by leading theologians. Such a justification of the *status quo* is absolutely objectionable. However, the overreaction of modernist theology is just as bad: it has entirely *severed* societal forms from any form of creation ordinances, and has absolutized and secularized them, entirely according to the demands of humanistic (read: pagan) thought, rooted in the apostate idea of human autonomy. Theology may try to slow down this fatal process of the secularization of societal life by issuing prophetic testimonies, or by disguising them with biblical terms such as "(theology of) hope," the "new creation," the "kingdom of God," and so on. But this does nothing but pull the wool over people's eyes. Along this road, the process of secularization will never be stopped, let alone be reversed.

---

116. Cf. Heron (1980, 9).

4.7.3 Conservatism and Progressivism

It may be useful to add here some remarks on the relationship between what is known as "progressive" and "conservative."[117] It is fascinating to notice that an appeal to creation ordinances can be used (or abused) to justify both a conservative and a progressive attitude. Thus, the appeal to some natural law has often been abused to justify the *status quo*, and even to declare it to be sacred. The defense of Nazi ideology by German churches and of the *apartheid* politics by South African churches with an appeal to creation ordinances (especially the idea of the *Volk*, "nation") were some distressing examples of this.

Conversely, however, a different appeal to such a natural (moral) law has often inspired people to a revolutionary engagement, such as happened during the American and the French Revolutions. Thus, the American Declaration of Independence (1776) begins with these words, "When in the Course of human events, it becomes necessary for one people . . . to assume among the powers of the earth, the separate and equal station *to which the Laws of Nature and of Nature's God entitle them* . . ." (italics added).[118] In their Declaration of the Rights of Man and the Citizen (Fr. *Déclaration des droits de l'Homme et du Citoyen*," 1789) leaders of the French Revolution spoke three times of the citizen's natural rights (Fr. *droits naturels*) rights.[119] In both cases, such an appeal was a defense of a revolution.

A *responsible* conservative attitude arises when Christians become aware again of God's immutable creation ordinances — immutable not in the sense that they ignore immanent-historical changes (on the subject-side) but because

---

117. Cf. Troost (1969, 26, 30, 33; 1976, 75, 146–49).
118. See en.wikipedia.org/wiki/United_States_Declaration_of_Independence#Text.
119. See textes.justice.gouv.fr/textes-fondamentaux-10086/droits-de-lhomme-et-libertes-fondamentales-10087/declaration-des-droits-de-lhomme-et-du-citoyen-de-1789-10116.html.

they find their focus in the transcendent creation order (on the law-side) as concentrated and integrated in Christ, the Root of creation and re-creation. Mistaken conservat*ism* rigidly absolutizes certain creation ordinances in the form (on the subject-side) in which they have been positivized within time by people, as happens in reactionary ideologies (see below).

A *responsible* progressive attitude arises when we follow the trajectory of the historical continuity guided by the divine creation order, that is, in a steadily continued disclosure and deployment of the potentials of this transcendent creation order within historical time, in obedience to God's revealed creation will, that is, the normative structures that are proper to created reality. Mistaken progressiv*ism*, as in revolutionism, strives for (drastic) historical change (on the subject-side) in disobedience to these normative structures (on the law-side).

If we would acknowledge and apply these principles, the entire distinction between conservative and progressive would become superfluous. The criterion for true Christianity has nothing to do with being either conservative or progressive, but with obedience to God's creation and re-creation will, as we know the latter from his creation revelation, of which Scripture forms the focus. It is regrettable that theology and the Christian world in general so often feel compelled to choose between a sterile, rigid conservatism, which simply defends the *status quo*, and a so-called progressive, but in fact *reactionary* slipping back into a scholastic synthesis with non-Christian thought. Conservative theology is usually nothing other than theology rooted in an *outdated secular* philosophy, whether scholastic (and thus Aristotelian) or humanist (e.g., Kantian, Hegelian, or positivist). Over against this, modernist theology is usually nothing other than theology rooted in some *current* (or recently) *secular* philosophy (e.g., existentialism, [neo]Marxism, post-modernism). But both attitudes are essentially secular.

4.8 Law-Order and Science

4.8.1 "Theological Ethics"

The extent to which Christian thinking has room for creation ordinances — universal norms like justice, freedom, peace, altruism, and so on — these are usually dealt with in a biblicistic way. That is, they are derived from the Bible in some kind of "theological ethics," instead of being developed and positivized in all the various disciplines on the basis of a strictly Christian paradigm: social norms in Christian sociology, economic norms in Christian economics, judicial norms in Christian legal research, moral norms in Christian ethics, pistical norms in Christian theology, and so on. Christian ethics is something basically different from theological ethics.

Strictly speaking, the term "theological ethics" can mean only one thing: just as social ethics studies the morals of social life, and medical ethics the morals of medical behavior (whether from a Christian or a non-Christian perspective), theological ethics studies the morals of *theological* behavior (whether from a Christian or a non-Christian perspective). A little less narrowly, the term "theological ethics" could be understood as the study of the morals of *faith* behavior. I am unable to see what other sensible meanings the term "theological ethics" could have. However, what people intend to suggest is that "the" discipline (Christian) ethics should be a constitutive part of theology.

The deeper background of the term "theological ethics" is that ancient scholastic dualism we already encountered in the dualism of cosmology *versus* soteriology, and the dualism of general *versus* special revelation. This time it is the supposed distinction between sacred theology (including theological ethics) and the other, profane (non-sacred) disciplines. As long as we grant validity to such dilemmas, there will be no real reformation of science, that is, no restoration of truly Christian scholarship.[120]

---

120. Troost (1976, 89–91, 136, 147).

If, in a biblicistic way, our knowledge of creation ordinances is limited to some "theological ethics," usually only four or five such creation ordinances are recognized: marriage and family, labor, authorities, church, and sometimes the cultural mandate (the divine command to do cultural work). However, due to an overestimation of theology, this is a rather impoverished approach to creation ordinances. At most, theology has the task of indicating the *nature* of the many creation ordinances for all creatures as the manifestation of the plurality and riches of God's creation will. However, various (Christian) disciplines must *elaborate* (determine, formulate, positivize) these various creation ordinances.[121] In a certain sense, the task of these disciplines is precisely that and nothing else.

The mistaken idea that this elaboration is supposedly the task of some "theological ethics" must be unmasked as a residue of scholasticism within theology. Christian psychologists, Christian economists, Christian art historians, and even Christian ethicists, and so on, must not beg theologians to supply them with Christian psychical, Christian economic, Christian aesthetic, and Christian moral norms, respectively. Theology is not at all equipped for this task. When it fails to resist the temptation to accept such requests, the best it can do is formulate some impoverished principles, drawn from the Bible, which will inevitably disappoint Christian psychologists, Christian economists, Christian art historians, Christian ethicists, and so on. The Bible is not the treasure trove for Christian psychical, Christian economic, Christian aesthetic, and Christian moral norms, but psychical, economic, aesthetic, and moral *creational reality* is the source for these. *Here* is where Christian psychologists, Christian economists, Christian art historians, and Christian ethicists should find the psychical, economic, aesthetic, and moral norms. Scripture is at most the (indispensable) light by which these norms can be recognized as belonging to God's creation revelation.

---

121. Troost (1978, 117).

4.8.2 The Law-Order and the Special Sciences

One of the central problems of the various disciplines (the special sciences, including theology) as well as philosophy involves their attitude toward the law-order that God has instituted for created reality. To express it more sharply: Are the special sciences and philosophy oriented toward God's word-revelation as *revelation*? To express it even more acutely: Does science produce real—though always incomplete and fallible—knowledge of *God* through the knowledge of nature, since nature is a revelation of God?

G.C. Berkouwer answered these questions with a clear "no":

> On this view the *Holy Scriptures* were regarded as the book of the *special* revelation of God and *nature* (with or without an appeal to [Belgic Confession] Article II) as the book of general revelation. It was thought that both theology and natural science were concerned with the revelation of God, theology dealing with special revelation and natural science with general revelation. . . . From this it follows that in the main we owe our knowledge of the revelation of God in nature to the natural sciences. . . . However, this view ignores the fact that it will not do simply to equate the knowledge of nature with the knowledge of God's general revelation, for this revelation deals with the knowledge of God *himself*. In our opinion, therefore, it is wrong to say, as is sometimes done, that the natural sciences "investigate" God's general revelation; and surely it is just as wrong to state that we owe our knowledge of God's revelation in nature primarily to the natural sciences. This, it seems to us, is a toning down of the idea and the reality of revelation, although that certainly is not intended. And we, of course, acknowledge wholeheartedly that it is our calling to investigate respectfully God's handiwork. But the revelation of God in his works is a matter of God's self-revelation, and that is not apprehended first of all by scientific investigation, but through faith, as is evident already in the Psalms of Israel. . . . The so-called nature psalms [Pss. 19,

29, 104, 147] are not concerned with the concept "nature" of the natural sciences; but they reveal the insight of faith into the works of God's hands. Consequently, the nature-psalms never deal with abstract aspects of cosmic reality, but rather with naive (in the good sense of the word) reality.[122]

This long quotation excellently describes the problems that must be dealt with in a discussion of the orientation of science toward created reality. However, even apart from this, this quotation shows again that many theological views fail because they are not rooted in a Christian-philosophical cosmology and epistemology. No doubt Berkouwer is right in saying that scientific investigation *itself* does not produce knowledge of God. Though oriented toward nature, it is not necessarily *directly* oriented toward God's revelation in nature. But, as Andree Troost rightly asked, "Did not Berkouwer overlook here the *depth dimension* of *all* knowledge, also of the knowledge of the (natural) sciences? Has not a *separation* been made here all too quickly between faith knowledge and scientific knowledge?"[123]

Berkouwer was perfectly right in saying that the knowledge of both general and special revelation is always *faith knowledge*. But he should not have played off this faith knowledge against the *scientific* knowledge of the natural sciences. In this way he ignored the important insight, which is not only a Christian-philosophical but also a modern-secular epistemological insight, that *all scientific knowledge is rooted in faith knowledge*. This has been discussed elsewhere extensively.[124] If we recognize this fact, then we can do justice to the two claims that God has revealed himself in nature, and the natural sciences are occupied with this same nature. Thus the *scientific* study of nature can very well be founded upon the *faith knowledge* of general revelation.

---
122. Berkouwer (1955, 287–89).
123. Troost (1978, 118).
124. Ouweneel (1995; 2013, chapters 1–5; 2014; 2015); cf. Strauss (1971; 2009); Chalmers (1976).

Therefore, Troost answered Berkouwer in the following way,

> The creatures that are investigated by, among others, the natural sciences — even if not under the *leading* viewpoint of faith but under that of theoretically deepened *thinking* — do they not yield *part* of their secrets to the investigators? Does not science bring to the outside world the result of its work as intended (theoretical) *truth,* and does not theoretical truth, according to its structure, also participate in the *full* Truth? And is not Christ the full Truth as the *Word of God*?[125]

Troost was thinking here on the basis of a deep-rooted (radical) Christian philosophy of science. He was not furnishing arguments for the purpose of identifying natural science and the faith knowledge of nature but neither did he want to separate them. Their inner coherence must be brought to light and analyzed. In this respect, there is no basis at all for making a fundamental distinction between theology and the other disciplines in a scholastic-dualistic sense. Theology, too, is occupied with God's *creation* revelation, of which Scripture forms the center. Conversely, as a matter of principle *all* the special sciences are occupied with Scripture, too, and this for two reasons. First, historians may be interested with biblical historiography, economists, sociologists, legal scholars, and ethicists with many aspects of, for instance, the Mosaic law, and so on. Second, Scripture is the light through which alone creation revelation can be truly understood. Word- and work-revelation are one, as God's Word and work are one.

4.8.3 Difference between Theology and Natural Science?

I wonder whether Berkouwer would have been prepared to apply the argument that he used for natural science *mutatis mutandis* for theology as well, but in connection with special revelation. If he would have genuinely and radically rejected the scholastic dualism between theology and the other spe-

---

125. Troost (1978, 119).

General Revelation (2)

cial sciences, I cannot see how he could avoid the following insights, which are implied by his own position. The reader is invited to compare these insights one by one with Berkouwer's own arguments, quoted in the previous section.

(a) We owe the knowledge of God's revelation in Scripture *not* mainly to theology but to the knowledge produced by God, through his Word and Spirit, in the regenerated heart.

(b) The (theological) knowledge of Scripture cannot simply be identified with the (faith) knowledge of God's special revelation, for this revelation is about knowledge of *God himself*, and such knowledge of God does not originate through theology but through faith.

(c) Strictly speaking, it is wrong to say — as scholastic theologians do — that theology investigates God's special revelation in contrast to general revelation. Theology investigates the totality of created reality — including the Bible — from a pistical viewpoint, that is, from the viewpoint of faith in the immanent-modal meaning of the term. In other words, it investigates immanent-religious phenomena, not only in Scripture but in all of created reality.

(d) The claim that theology investigates God's special revelation unintentionally blurs the notion and reality of revelation. God has given theology the task of reverently studying his redemptive activity. However, in God's revelation through that redemptive activity we are dealing with God's self-revelation, and, strictly speaking, the latter is not discovered through theological investigation itself but through faith. Thus, the claim that theology investigates God's special revelation fails to take into account the theoretical-analytical character of theological knowledge as distinct from supra-theoretical and supra-rational faith knowledge.

What should we think of this perfectly parallel argument? Claims (a), (b), and (c) are true in exactly the same way they are true for the natural sciences (*mutatis mutandis*). Moreover, claim (d), and to some extent also claims (b) and (c), are true but somewhat exaggerated in the same way as with the natural sciences. At any rate, it may be clear that, and why, the point mentioned at the start of this section is true: no matter how fallibly and indirectly (and often unintentionally), knowledge of the creation ordinances is acquired by *all* the various disciplines. This is even more evident and explicit if they are founded in a Christian-philosophical structural theory of reality, rooted in the biblical notion of the creation order. To say it in a concise way: philosophy is the theoretical study of the creation order as the structural order for the totality of immanent reality; the special sciences are the theoretical study of the various modal aspects (arithmetic, geometric, kinematic, physical, biotic, perceptive, sensitive logical, historical-formative, lingual, social, economic, aesthetic, juridical, ethical, pistical) of this creation order. Thus, each special science develops its own structural theory, in its own way and with its own method, and thereby discloses the ontic, *a priori* normative structures of created reality.

This emphasis upon the creation order is not appreciated at all in modern theology because of its (understandable) fear of metaphysics. However, the idea of the creation order degenerates into mere, dry metaphysics *only* if it is severed from the great Law of Love. The entire coherence of the great (immanent-modal) diversity of our daily lives finds its unity and concentration only in this transcendent-religious commandment. Indeed, severed from this service of the human heart to God, a truly biblical notion of the creation order is inconceivable. Metaphysics is the theory of the so-called "being-in-itself," of so-called "objective facts," that is, facts severed from their Origin and sustaining Ground. *This* metaphysics, in whatever of its numerous forms, is the basis for all supposedly neutral science, all supposedly neutral politics, all so-called "Christian humanism," all such notions as the solidarity of the church with the world, and so on.[126]

---

126. Troost (1976, 44–45).

In my view, the deep-rooted (radical) Christian response to this must be that we must return to a genuinely biblical view of the creation order, in order then to use this as a starting point for a Christian view of science and society. In the creation order, God reveals his will as a normative *principle*. This will is the beginning (the Lat. word *principium* means both "beginning" and "principle"), the creational starting point, the dynamic stimulus, and the religious guide that make human life possible, supply its contents, and direct it toward its center and integration in Jesus Christ. As *principium*, God's will leaves much room for human participation, as well as human elaboration and realization of that will, in responsibility toward God's creational-providential-redemptive word. Responsibility involves the human response to God's Word in elaborating the principles he has revealed, thereby shaping human life and human society by deploying and realizing all the potential embedded in God's wonderful creation, in service to him, out of love for him and for his creature.[127]

4.9 Law-Order and Positivizing[128]

4.9.1 The Positivizing Task

What we found in the previous section may lead to the following description of philosophy: it is the totality science concerning the nature and ground structures of created reality. The task of a Christian philosophy is the theoretical analysis of the biblical idea of the creation or law order. The various special sciences may be described as the attempts to *positivize* the various laws that belong to their respective fields of study. In other words, the task of the various disciplines is the human derivation, elaboration, determination, and formulation of the respective laws.

There is a basic difference between the law-order as such and this positivization of it by human beings. We must sharply *distinguish* between, on the one hand, the constant structur-

---

127. Ibid., 48–49.
128. See Troost (2004, 333–34, 337).

al principles of nature (read: the natural laws) and the constant normative principles of human mental life (read: norms) that God has anchored in the creation order, and, on the other hand, the concrete hypotheses, theories, natural laws, and norms that are the result of (fallible) positivizing work by humans. However, this does not mean that they should be *separated* from each other as if there were no connection between them. On the contrary, positivization is a divine commandment to humanity, which is entailed in the cultural mandate.

Thus, the position of humans in this positivization process is of great importance. First, as God's image and head of creation, they are the central reference point to which comes the commandment that is embedded in the divine creation order: "[S]ubdue [the earth] . . . and have dominion over" all creatures (Gen. 1:28), which also means: acquire knowledge about all creatures (cf. 2:19–20). "Knowledge is power," said Thomas Hobbes[129] (Lat. *scientia potentia est*); real dominion implies knowledge of that over which one has dominion. Second, this is the same reference point from which concrete scientific theories proceed.[130] Here, we see the fundamental mutual *orientation* of the creation order and the special sciences in that they intersect in humanity as the reference point of this knowledge.

In this connection, I wish to emphasize, too, that the creation order is a *transcendental, a priori condition* for the created reality, but also for the special sciences, and for *all* knowledge of reality. That is, the constant structural principles supplied in the creation order—principles of number, space, movement, energy, organic life, and perception—make nature *possible*, including human nature, and so too the natural sciences and psychology. In the same way, the creationally supplied sensitive, logical, lingual, historical-formative, social, economic, aesthetic, juridical, moral, and pistical norms make human mental life *possible*, and so too the mental sciences.

---

129. *De Homine* (1658), X (going back to Francis Bacon?).
130. Troost (1969, 5).

General Revelation (2)

There are no genuine natural, human, or mental sciences that do not, in some way, supply a concrete theoretical form to *these* natural laws and *these* normative principles, no matter how preliminary and fallible, and no matter their ideological background. Scientific research is a process of positivizing modal and structural-typical natural and mentalprinciples," which find their *principium* ("beginning") in God's creational word.[131]

4.9.2 Difficulties of Positivizing

We must realize that, as a consequence of sin, the human work of positivizing has become cumbersome and fallible in two respects.[132]

(a) *Subjectively* this is because the sinful nature in scientists and scholars rebels against the structural principles that God has given for the way human knowledge concerning God's law, or concerning anything, must be acquired.

(b) *Objectively* this is because sin has also affected the factual knowability of the creation order. That is, the structural principles of the creation order cannot be approached separately, apart from the subject-side of reality. These structural principles always consist of, and are only observable in, concrete experiential realities in which they are realized and embodied. In other words, they are always immanently present in natural phenomena and in human acts, situations, societal relationships, and events. We can observe the law only in concrete facts—but these facts are always beset with sin (i.e., anti-normative behavior).

It is not the creation order itself, nor its knowability as such, that has been affected by sin; objectively, God's revelation remains clear and visible, and free of sin. What *has* been seriously corrupted are our knowledge and our subjective knowing potential.[133] However, precisely because the creation

---

131. Ibid., 21.
132. Cf. Heyns (1976, 124).
133. Troost (1982, 189–90).

order itself remains knowable in principle, God's appeal to knowledge always remains intact. He has entrusted his revelation to our knowing functions; his revelation implies the commandment to endeavor to know it (the cultural mandate).

Already in the Bible, we find examples of such positivizing, and of the demand to positivize. For instance, it is beautifully illustrated in God's command to Adam to name the animals. In biblical parlance, this basically entails identifying their inner structure, and supplying that structure with a designation (Gen. 2:19-20; cf. Adam naming his wife, 3:20). Here, the single transcendent-religious Commandment of Love stands over against an immanent diversity of modal and structure-typical creation principles, which must be discovered and formulated by humanity. The general commandment that we are to love (Gk. *agapōmen*,[134] either "we love" or "let us love," DRA) is differentiated by Christ as the Commandment of Love toward God, and the Commandment of Love toward humanity (Matt. 22:37-40; cf. Deut. 6:5; Lev. 19:18), while the Ten Words (Commandments) of the Sinaitic covenant constitute a further positivization of God's covenantal word to Israel. In every cultural-historical context, from this root-law the differentiated diversity of ordinances must branch out, ordinances that God has instituted for the various facets of human living and that must be positivized by humanity one by one.[135]

4.10 Biblicism

4.10.1 Appeal to Bible Verses

In connection with our subject, South African philosopher Daniel F. M. Strauss identified an important exegetical-dogmatic point, namely, the danger of biblicism.[136] It is *not* true

---

134. Cf. 1 John 4:19, where, according to the best manuscripts, no object is mentioned; see Metzger (2005, ad loc.).
135. Strauss (1991, 9–11).
136. Strauss (1978, 99; 1979, 258, 263–64; 1991, 3–6, 74–80); cf. Smit (1980, 199).

that positivizing creation principles merely employs relevant Bible verses, as if such positivizing could be freely neglected if such verses were not available. Both the literalist use of certain Bible verses and the supposed silence of Scripture where no direct biblical statements are available, must be rejected. As a starting point for an approach that is more in line with the Bible, Strauss referred to Isaiah 28:26-29,[137] which tells us that

> God gave to humans the knowledge to do things as they ought to be done: dill and cumin are beaten out with a stick; grain is crushed for bread, and so on. Things must be handled in *this* or *that* way according to their God-given nature. Due to the *orderliness* of these things, we find the way to the order that God has instituted for the things! Through this, God teaches us how we must deal with his creatures—taking into account his will for their existence.

The important point here is that, according to verse 26, God instructs the farmer how he must do things; however, he does not do so through certain Bible passages, or through a voice from heaven. The farmer received from God the needed revelation, but not through God doing or saying something specific. No, what *God*, in his covenantal faithfulness, does is simply maintain his *law* for creation. And what the *farmer* does is simply pay attention to the *lawfulness* of creation, that is, the way creatures obey the laws, how things are or behave. In an entirely analogous way, the scientist receives insight into the structure of atoms or of living organisms, in the human mind, in thought and language problems, in technical, social, and economic matters, in juridical and ethical questions, and so on. He receives these insights *not* through an appeal to certain Bible verses, nor by listening to a direct voice from heaven, but by pursuing in scientific research into the *lawfulness* of reality (its functioning under the law-order), and by trying in this way to trace God's *law* for creation, and thus, gradually

---

137. Strauss (1991, 4); cf. Spykman (1992, 82).

to unfold God's general revelation.

Once in a while, a direct appeal to concrete Bible passages is definitely possible, but usually it is not. This often leads to the misunderstanding that Scripture has nothing to say about the matter concerned. As Herman Dooyeweerd put it,

> Would the laws that govern numerical and spatial relationships, the laws for the physical and chemical phenomena, the laws for organic life and the emotional life of feeling, the laws for your logical thought and for language formation, the laws for economical life and the norms for beauty, not all, without distinction, be founded in God's creation order? And can you find all these ordinances for the distinct aspects of reality directly in Scripture texts? If not, do you not recognize, then, that God has given to humanity the task of discovering these ordinances in cumbersome investigation?[138]

4.10.2 Principles and Positivizations

Not only is such a direct appeal to Bible verses usually impossible, but if it is possible, such an appeal may be misleading. This is because such verses usually — perhaps always — supply not a certain creational *principle* but only with a concrete *positivization* of the creational principle in a certain historical context. In my view, such a distinction between (timeless) principles and (often time-bound) positivizations leads to a better approach to the problem of biblical authority than the traditional distinction, stemming from the seventeenth century, between historical and normative authority (Lat. *auctoritas historiae et normae*).[139] J. A. Heyns rightly pointed out that *all* authority is normative, because it entails norms, and conversely, historical authority can never be strictly limited to the past.[140] He tried to solve the question by introducing

---

138. Dooyeweerd (1963, 56).
139. See, e.g., Bavinck (*RD* 1:459).
140. Heyns (1976, 104).

General Revelation (2)

a distinction between scopic and peripheral authority,[141] but Pieter C. Potgieter rightly identified several objections to this distinction.[142]

It is not biblical to separate certain concrete positivizations of the creation order from their biblical context, and to literally adopt them in practical life. On the contrary, we must rather search for the underlying creational principles. Thus, in light of various Bible passages (Gen. 2:20-24, Matt. 19:3-8; 1 Cor. 7; Eph. 5:22-33; Col. 3:18-21; Titus 2:3-5; 1 Pet. 3:1-7), the monogamous husband-wife marriage can no doubt be called a creational principle. However, in every age, the way marriages were conducted in the Bible (the wedding, relationships between husband and wife, number of wives, divorce arrangements, authorities conducting the marriages, etc.) is determined by the concrete cultural-historical context of the time. It would be biblicistic if we simply and naïvely adopted concrete biblical positivizations of the marriage ordinance in our own context. Such an indiscriminate adoption is not at all in the spirit of Scripture; rather it is biblicistic-literalistic, or more precisely, it ignores the distinction between general creation principles and their concrete historically conditioned positivizations.

Another example: it is biblicistic to adopt *a priori*, with a vague reference to the creation order, a negative position regarding contraception (claiming, for example, that it would be contrary to the creation order[143]), artificial insemination with donor semen (sometimes called "test tube adultery" or something like this[144]), women running for political office, or women in church offices (with reference to specific interpretations

---

141. Ibid., 106.
142. Potgieter (1990, 25).
143. This was the pope's argument in a Christmas speech on Dec. 22, 2008, to the Roman curia (www.katholieknederland.nl/actualiteit/2008/detail_objectID681655_FJaar2008.html).
144. This was argued by C. G. Clark in Wolstenholme (1963, 293); Thiadens (1969).

of 1 Cor. 14:34-35 and 1 Tim. 2:11-12[145]), church elders who identify as homosexuals ("homosexual marriages are wrong, so homosexual elders are also wrong"[146]). My point here is not to express any opinions on these matters; I am merely arguing that a simple appeal to the creation order in such matters is mistaken, or at least superficial.

4.10.3 Motivation and Judgment

The difficulty of this matter is implicitly illustrated by Daniel F. M. Strauss because his examples are not always felicitous. For instance, he gave the impression as if the law of Moses contains only legal liability for the consequences of actions, and does not take into account the trespasser's motivation.[147] In light of Numbers 35:15-25, this can be shown to be incorrect. Here, a distinction is made between the manslayer who kills inadvertently, and the manslayer who kills deliberately. (Compare the modern distinction between wrongful death, manslaughter, and murder.) Also see the difference between unintentional sin (which can be forgiven through a sin offering) and sinning "with a high hand" (AMP: "willfully and defiantly," cf. premeditated murder), in which case the trespasser must receive the death penalty (Num. 15:22-31).

We are dealing here with problems that of the highest theological importance. A creation principle is a constant, timeless starting point for time-bound positivizations in certain concrete periods and cultural-historical contexts. The creation principle retains its urgent, permanent appeal, even if its positivization may vary continually throughout history. This very important distinction offers another possibility for refuting conservatism (cf. §4.7.3). Conservatism wrongly clings to a certain time-bound tradition because it does not distinguish it from the underlying timeless creation principle.

---

145. See extensively, Ouweneel (2010a, chapter 12).
146. This was argued by P. Kerstholt, www.nd.nl/artikelen/2007/december/10/lesbisch-ouderschap-tegen-scheppingsorde.
147. Strauss (1991, 75, 78).

This is further clarified by Hendrik Hart, who blamed conservatism for confusing the principle and its positivization. As an example, Hart mentioned the constantly valid principle of social respect, which comes to expression in greeting habits, which can differ enormously in different times and cultural contexts.[148]

Finally, I emphasize that creation principles maintain their urgent appeal, but this does not mean that they are thereby in force. They appeal *to* humans, but they must be concretely implemented — positivized — *by* people, namely, by persons and institutions authorized to do so. This must be done in dependence on the norm that embedded in the principle itself, as well as on the demands embedded in the concrete cultural-historical situation. These demands are themselves governed by the normative principles of the creation order. There can be, and must be, no conflict between the positivized norm and the demands of the concrete situation.

---

148. Hart (1984, 58–63).

Chapter 5
The Inscripturation
of the Eternal Word

> . . . *the things which have been freely given*
> *to us of God:*
> *which also we speak,*
> *not in words taught by human wisdom,*
> *but in those taught by the Spirit,*
> *communicating spiritual [things]*
> *by spiritual [words].*
> 1 Corinthians 2:12–13 (DARBY)

Summary: *What is the relationship between revelation and inscripturation? Is special revelation an ongoing divine activity today? Among the views surrounding these matters, does a middle road exist between fundamentalism and liberalism? Are inscripturation and Christ's incarnation parallel, and if so, to what extent? What immanent forms can the transcendent Word of God take? Revelation has been called either "propositional" or "personal"; what is the difference between the two, and what is the correct approach?*

The terms idionomy, encapsis, *and* encaptic whole *are introduced; how do they apply to the Bible as a book? Four idionomies are distinguished: the idionomies that are qualified physically, historical-formatively, lingually, and pistically. Special attention is given to the latter one; its various modal aspects are investigated, and the connections as well as differences with the transcendent Word of God are explained. Here, the difference between the many "words" of the Bible and the "Word" as a transcendent notion is underscored; to this end, the difference between "concept" and "idea" is investigated. The modal* **ideas** *(both natural and mental) are used to shed light on the significance of the transcendent Word of God.*

5.1 Revelation and Inscripturation

5.1.1 The Word and Its Registration

Under God's guidance—one could say, "in the fullness of time" (cf. Gal. 4:4)—the eternal Word of God was inscripturated, recorded, registered, put down in writing; it became Scripture (from Lat. *scriptus*, "written"). As a paraphrase of John 1:14, we might say, "the Word became Scripture and resided among us" (see further §5.3). "Long ago, at many times and in many ways, God spoke to our fathers by the prophets" (Heb. 1:1), and afterward he spoke through Jesus and the apostles. But today, God speaks to us through Holy Scripture (which speaking cannot be severed from the work of the Holy Spirit). What was heard was always really God's Word: God *spoke*, sometimes even literally, through an audible voice. We find this clearly with Moses (Exod. 33:9-11; Num. 7:89; 12:6-8) and Samuel (1 Sam. 3:1-14), and presumably also with Isaiah (Isa. 6:8). God spoke, and what he spoke was his Word.

Can we say that the inscripturation (registration) of this Word in writings is also Word of God? Spoken words are instantaneous, they evaporate into the atmosphere. But words can also be recorded: on tape, in a digital form, or also—the most ancient way—in writing (on clay tablets, on papyrus, on parchment, on printed paper, etc.). One could argue that the Bible is not God's Word—the Word that he spoke at specific times—but at best the precipitate, the record of God's Word. But one could also argue that Scripture involves nothing but the once-spoken Word of God, and as such is definitely itself Word of God. Point to a *verbatim* report of the president's speech and ask: Are these the words of the president? Very few people would answer, No, this is only a record of his words.

It is not easy, though, to find Bible passages where the expression "Word of God" or "Word of the Lord" explicitly and unambiguously refers to Scripture. Examples are Mark 7:13 (". . . thus making void the word [Gk. *logos*] of God by your tradition that you have handed down") and John 10:34-35 ("Is it not written in your Law,[1] 'I said, you are gods'? If he called them gods to whom the word [*logos*] of God came — and Scripture cannot be broken — . . ."); here, Jesus apparently refers to the Old Testament as "Torah," "Word of God," and "Scripture." Also compare Romans 3:2 (NIV: "[T]he Jews have been entrusted with the very words [many others: oracles, Gk. *logia*] of God"). Various other passages may be related to the inscripturated Word of God, even though this is perhaps not (always) the first meaning of their statements (cf. Prov. 30:5; Rom. 9:6; Eph. 6:17; 1 Tim. 4:5; Heb. 4:12; 6:5; 1 Pet. 1:23, 25; 1 Joh. 2:14).

The term "Word of God" thus has a twofold character: it is "God's speaking" as well as "what God has spoken." This twofold meaning is also found, for instance, in the terms "creation" and "revelation." "Creation" is the (one-time) *act* of creating (e.g., "God rested from all his work that he had done in creation," Gen. 2:3; cf. Rom. 1:20) — "In the beginning, God created" (Gen. 1:1) — as well as the *result* of this act: "creation" is the created world (e.g., we are enjoying God's beautiful creation; cf. Mark 10:6; 16:15; Rom. 8:19-22; Col. 1:15, 23; Rev. 3:14). It is the same with the term "revelation": this can be the *act* of revealing at a certain point in time (e.g., God revealed himself there and then), but also the *result* of this act: "revelation" = what is revealed. God's Word is God's revelation

---

[1] Heb. *Torah*, here: the entire Old Testament (Jesus quotes from the "Torah" Ps. 82:6).

because it contains what God has revealed in the past.[2] In the former sense, the Bible as such is not revelation but at best the result of God *having* revealed himself, that is, the record of God's past revelations. In the latter sense, however, the Bible *can* be called "revelation," namely, the revealed things of God, what God wished to reveal to us in written form.

We have to consider here two things: *not* everything that has been revealed in the past has been inscripturated, and *not* everything that has been inscripturated goes back to divine revelation.[3] As to the former: in Jesus' seven miraculous signs that are mentioned in John's Gospel, Jesus "manifested his glory" (John 2:11). But John also tells us that Jesus had done many more things, which, however, have not been reported by John (21:25). Jesus revealed his glory on earth at many moments unknown to us because they have not been described in the Gospels. Also in other ways, John knew of received revelations that he was not allowed to write down (Rev. 10:4). New Testament prophets (e.g., 1 Cor. 14:3) received revelations that to a great extent have not been written down in the New Testament (see §§5.1.2 and 5.1.3).

As to the second point mentioned, the Bible writers sometimes quote from secular sources that do not go back to divine revelation but to very human utterances (e.g., Ezra 4:7–22). Or they simply send encouragements and exhortations, which as such do not possess a revelational character. The letter to the Philippians is a beautiful example of this (see further in chapters 7–8).

5.1.2 Any Further Revelation?

Now that the Word of God has been inscripturated, can there be room for any further divine revelation? For many Christians, the answer is apparently negative. This is because, to them, the concepts of "Bible" and "revelation" apparently coincide completely (apart from, perhaps, general or creation

---

2. Erickson (1998, 222).
3. Ibid., 226.

revelation). As we saw at the end of the previous section, the foundation of this thesis is mistaken: revelation and inscripturation coincide only partially.

People who do not see room for further revelation often connect their view with the notion of the closed canon (see chapter 6). They feel that, since the canon is closed, there can be no further revelation or prophecy. This type of argument is especially found among cessationists, those who believe that the *charismata* ("gifts of the Spirit") ceased with the closing of the canon.[4] Words of wisdom or knowledge, prophecies or revelation are no longer needed or possible, for everything that believers need in this respect is already contained in Holy Scripture.

Obviously, since the closing of the canon, everything that presents itself as prophecy or revelation must be evaluated in terms of Scripture. Ongoing revelation is necessarily built upon preceding divine revelation, and can never be in conflict with it.[5] What Jesus revealed after the prophets (cf. Heb. 1:1) could not conflict with the words of those prophets. And what the apostles revealed could not conflict with the words of Jesus. And since the apostles, what God may have revealed to or through believers, if it truly comes from the divine source, cannot conflict with the words of the apostles. Thus, works such as those by Augustine, Anselm, Calvin, or Wesley rightly have great authority because of their God-given position in Christianity, yet always *insofar* as these writings are in agreement with Scripture according to the judgment of other Christians.

The fact of ongoing revelation is evident. The apostle Paul prays that the Ephesian Christians may receive the "Spirit of wisdom and of revelation" (Eph. 1:17), but this can hardly be anything other than the illumination of the human mind, so that believer may understand the revealed truth (cf. §8.2). In

---

4. See Harinck (2006); for a refutation, see Ouweneel (2018c, §12.7).
5. Erickson (1998, 222–23).

1 Corinthians 14 the apostle Paul accepts as self-evident that in church meetings there is room for revelation: "When you come together, each one has a hymn, a lesson, a revelation, a tongue, or an interpretation. Let all things be done for building up.... Let two or three prophets speak, and let the others weigh what is said. If a revelation is made to another sitting there, let the first be silent" (vv. 26-30). Here, revelation seems to be esteemed more highly than prophecy.

Of course, there has been much discussion about what exactly the term "revelation" means here. But whatever conclusion one reaches, it can hardly be assumed that Paul is referring here to a phenomenon that would have suddenly ceased at the closing of the canon. In my view, this would only be a meaningful conclusion if we were to assume that *all* revelations in the New Testament time had ultimately been recorded in the New Testament. But of course, this cannot be true. Thus, Paul writes that, at a certain moment, he went up to Jerusalem "because of a revelation" (Gal. 2:2). This revelation has not been written down in Scripture—and this was not at all necessary. Therefore, I can think of no reason why *this* kind of divine revelation to Christian believers could not continue occurring after the closing of the canon. The two things simply have nothing to do with each other.

5.1.3 Prophecy

The same is true of prophecy. Agabus (Acts 11:27-28), the leaders of the church at Antioch (13:11), Judas and Silas (15:32), the daughters of Philip (21:9-11), and others, were prophets or prophetesses, but hardly any of their prophecies have been included in the Bible. Once this point is grasped, we can understand that, after the closing of the canon, precisely this type of prophecy can still occur today as in New Testament times.

Paul says, "Whoever has the gift of prophecy should use that gift in a way that fits the kind of faith they have" (Rom. 12:6 ERV). And, "[T]o another [believer] prophecy [is given by the Spirit] . . . . And God has appointed in the church first apostles, second prophets . . ." (1 Cor. 12:10, 28). To him, it was self-evident that there are prophets in the church; only with contorted reasoning can one argue that, after the closing of the canon, this ministry is no longer needed, or even possible. Again, the two matters are not really related.

Speaking of need, I refer to Ephesians 4:11-13, where we see that the ministry of prophets is needed until the intended goal has been reached, that is, "until we all attain to the unity of the faith and of the knowledge of the Son of God."[6] This indicates unmistakably that the church—also after the foundation of apostles and prophets has been laid (2:20)—will necessarily have the prophets among them as long as Christians are still on earth.

Thus, the idea that there could be new revelations today does not constitute any difficulty as long as these revelations (a) are in agreement with Scripture, (b) are not viewed as being on the same level (i.e., as equally authoritative) as Scripture itself, or (c) are not viewed as "new Scripture" (cf. the claims with regard to the Ku'ran and the Book of Mormon). Revelations may be useful to show a believer, or a group of believers, the right way (cf. again Gal. 2:2; Acts 11:28; 21:10-11). However, the revelation that *all* believers need at *all* places, and—since the closing of the canon—in *all* times is found exclusively in Holy Scripture.

5.2 Discussion Around the Bible

5.2.1 Three Reports

On their way to the Dutch church union of 2004, the General Synods of the Dutch Reformed Church and the Kuyperian Reformed Churches, as well as the Synod of the Lutheran Church, all three in the Netherlands, published a report under the title *De bijbel: Taal en teken in de tijd* (*The Bible: Language and Sign within Time*).[7] This might not be of great interest to

---

6. See Ouweneel (2010a, 310–325; 2010c, 81–84).

7. Generale Synode (1999).

the church worldwide, but let me use this report to illustrate certain points. In words intended for a broad audience, the three Synods explained their shared view of the Bible, the inscripturated Word of God. Their purpose was that seeking and reading the "book of the LORD"[8] would lead people to the "LORD of the book."[9] To this end, the "book" had to be dealt with first. Two earlier documents helped to clarify this for the three Synods: the report *Klare wijn* (*Clear Wine*) of the Dutch Reformed Church (1966),[10] and the report *God met ons* (*God with Us*) of the Kuyperian Reformed Churches (1979).[11]

When it was written, the report *Klare wijn* was adopted unanimously by the Synod of the Dutch Reformed Church in the Netherlands.[12] This occurred despite the report's attack on the doctrine of the mechanical inspiration (see §7.8) and fundamentalism (see chapter 9), as well as the indiscriminate plea for historical-critical theological research, with little attention for the anti-supernaturalism that unfortunately is embedded in much of this type of research (see chapters 11–12). In the meantime, the Dutch Reformed Church, and after the union, the Protestant Church in the Netherlands, has undergone a development that certainly has increased its level of orthodoxy. It would be worthwhile to know whether such a report, which speaks so vaguely of the Easter event, would be adopted unanimously today, too (despite the exodus of an orthodox contingent[13]). However, the way *Klare wijn* was criticized was not always satisfactory either. For instance, if people complain that *Klare wijn* had such an aversion against the orthodox doctrine of the inspiration of Scripture,[14] we fear

---

8. The expression is literally found in Isa. 34:16, where it presumably refers to Isaiah's own scroll.
9. Generale Synode (1999, 9).
10. Generale Synode (1966).
11. See *God met ons* (1981).
12. Generale Synode (1999, 11).
13. Afterward called the Hersteld Hervormde Kerk (Restored Reformed Church).
14. Quoted in Van Bekkum et al. (2003, 31).

that what is being defended is the mechanical inspiration meant here.

This question was even more acute regarding the report *God met ons* of the Kuyperian Reformed Churches. Elsewhere, I have extensively dealt with the relational concept of truth that this report presents as *the* answer to many difficult questions, whereas, in my view, this concept is beset with misunderstandings.[15] This report writes in an even more uncritical way about historical-critical theological research. I do say this, though, with appreciation for the many *good* things mentioned in these reports, and to which I paid too little attention at the time.[16] The 1999 report plucked some quite reassuring strings, such as this one: "Historical-critical Bible research . . . should not mean that the authority of the Bible is made dependent on human factors in general, or on human reason in particular."[17] Here, the Holy Spirit was seen as being of vital importance.[18] It was certainly laudable that the report sought a middle road between fundamentalism with its uncritical certainties and the type of biblical criticism that leaves the Bible in tatters. Yet, I wonder whether it really managed to find such a middle road.

This question is all the more urgent when we compare this report with the collection of articles entitled *De Bijbel betrouwbaar* (*The Bible Reliable*), which appeared at about the same time.[19] In these articles we hear voices of more conservative Dutch theologians such as J. C. Bette, Gijs van den Brink (not to be confused with the unrelated Gijsbert van den Brink), Jan van Genderen, Jan Hoek, J. W. Maris, and H. G. J. Peels. Here, a firmer language was spoken with which I feel more confident. A stronger stand was taken against modernist theolo-

---

15. Ouweneel (2013, chapter 14).
16. See Knevel et al. (1981).
17. Generale Synode (1999, 20).
18. Ibid., 26–31.
19. Hagoort (1998).

gians such as Nico ter Linden,[20] and both the Bible's authority and reliability were defended more powerfully.

5.2.2 Discussion Among the Reformed Churches (Liberated)

Again, I mention this discussion not because of its worldwide significance but as an example of how traditionally orthodox denominations are wrestling about the inscripturated Word of God. For instance, I appreciate the collection of articles by Dutch authors Koert Van Bekkum, Wim Houtman, Reina Wiskerke, all belonging to the Reformed Churches in the Netherlands (Liberated; corresponding to the heavily immigrant-populated American Reformed Churches and Canadian Reformed Churches). In my view, this collection found a better middle road than some of the publications mentioned in the previous section, without falling into fundamentalism.[21] In this book, Wiskerke discussed the same two reports mentioned above: *Klare wijn* and *God met ons*.[22] In the manner of journalists, not of theologians, the book gave a clear picture of the discussions about the Bible in the Netherlands in the first decade of the twenty-first century.

From the same Liberated Reformed circle, but then from theologians, came the collection of articles called *Woord op schrift* (*Word in Writing*), edited by Cornelis Trimp.[23] On the one hand, this book vigorously distanced itself from what it called the "Evangelical" doctrine of Scripture, both from the fundamentalist—as if there are no Reformed fundamentalists!—and from the "Neo-Evangelical" variety.[24] On the other hand, we find a contribution by J. J. T. Doedens, who plead-

---

20. Compare Generale Synode (1999, 46–47) with H. G. J. Peels in Hagoort (1998, 119–28).
21. Van Bekkum et al. (2003).
22. Ibid., 29–32.
23. Trimp (2002).
24. Ibid., 21–58.

ed for a rather free approach of Genesis 1.[25] His position is similar to that of J. Douma, who wrote a book on Genesis,[26] and both Doedens and Douma came under criticism within the Reformed Churches (Liberated). But during the Synod of Zwolle (2008), the objections against both authors were declared to be unwarranted.

In 2011, Douma protested against the doctoral dissertation by K. Van Bekkum on the book of Joshua (the conquest of the promised land), claiming that Van Bekkum had crossed the boundary of faithfulness to Scripture.[27] It is understandable that people would argue that Douma had gone far too far in his own book, and was now attempting to prove his orthodoxy by criticizing Van Bekkum. Thus, the Reformed natural scientist John Byl asked,

> [I]f modern secular science leads Dr. Douma to embrace a non-literal reading of Genesis 1, how can he object if that same science leads Dr. Van Bekkum to embrace a non-literal reading of Joshua 10[:12]? After all, Dr. Douma has already adopted the hermeneutical principle that it is sometimes permissible to let secular science trump the obvious (historical) reading of a biblical text. At issue now is merely the extent of its application. Since Douma advances no definite, biblically justifiable criteria, any limits on the application of this new hermeneutic are purely subjective.[28]

I do not mention these things as evaluations of the views of Douma or Van Bekkum (or Byl, for that matter). Rather I am seeking to show how, within a rather conservative denomination like the Liberated Reformed, the discussion about the authority and reliability of Scripture as the Word of God has become rather vehement. And of course, this applies as well to all sorts of other Reformational and Evangelical cir-

---

25. J. J. T. Doedens in ibid., 71–108.
26. Douma (2005).
27. See Van Bekkum (2011).
28. bylogos.blogspot.com/2010/06/doumas-doubts.html.

cles.²⁹ Such discussions are highly desirable. Time and again, theologians who view themselves as orthodox must try to find the middle path between fundamentalism (see chapters 9-10) and liberalism (see chapters 11-12). In doing so, they will receive—often vehement—criticism from *both* sides; this is inevitable. From the conservative wing in the older generation in the Reformed Churches (Liberated), Van Bekkum had to endure harsh criticism, but also from the progressive side, namely, from the journalist Marcel Hulspas, who heaped vitriol upon him.³⁰ Of course, this does not mean that, if one is criticized from both sides, one has necessarily adopted the correct position. This cannot be true because the middle path could still be very broad; it is possible for one to walk between the shoulders on the side of this middle road and yet risk falling off the path toward either side.

5.2.3 Discussion Necessary

In such a complicated matter as the authority and reliability of Scripture, ongoing discussion must be welcomed. We will not try to avoid it in the following chapters. In fact, the Bible itself *prompts* such a discussion. Thus, John Goldingay has placed much emphasis on Scripture as a "witnessing tradition,"³¹ in line with, particularly, this statement by Jesus: ". . . Scriptures . . . bear witness about me" (John 5:39). Goldingay argued that, as a witness, Scripture prompts us to investigate it evaluatively. These are two important statements in one. First, the nature of every witness entails the calling to interrogate the witness in order to determine whether their testimony agrees with the facts: "The judges shall inquire diligently, and if the witness is a false witness and has accused his brother falsely, then you shall do to him as he had meant to do to his brother. So you shall purge the evil from your midst" (Deut.

---

29. Regarding Genesis 1, see Ouweneel (2010d, especially 45–58), and my contribution (39–52) (and that of others) in Van Bekkum and Harinck (2010), and especially Ouweneel (2018l).
30. This internet source no longer exists.
31. Goldingay (1994, Part I).

19:18-19).[32] Scripture claims to be a divine witness, and it can withstand any scrutiny, not only about whether the facts are correct but also about the precise nature of its witnessing.

Second, as Goldingay emphasized, the nature of Scripture, as a document with divine authority, is that it renders a verdict on people's evaluation of Scripture. In other words, the Bible is not only a witness before a tribunal, but it is also a prosecutor and a judge; as Jesus said, "Do not think that I will accuse you to the Father. There is one who accuses you: Moses [read: the Mosaic Torah, the Pentateuch], on whom you have set your hope" (John 5:45). The same is true about the words of Jesus himself: "The one who rejects me and does not receive my words has a judge; the word that I have spoken will judge him on the last day" (12:48). These two claims are true simultaneously: the theologian renders judgment on Scripture, and Scripture — without being a philosophical or theological handbook — renders judgment on the theologian's judgments.[33]

A balance is required between these two claims, no matter how paradoxical this may sound: theologians submit the Bible to their most meticulous research, but they do so — hopefully — realizing that Scripture, through the Holy Spirit, at the same time investigates *them*:

> [T]he word of God is living and active, sharper than any two-edged sword, piercing to the division of soul and of spirit, of joints and of marrow, and discerning the thoughts and intentions of the heart. And no creature is hidden from his sight, but all are naked and exposed to the eyes of him to whom we must give account (Heb. 4:12-13).

Thus, theologians will always have to give an account for everything they have said about the Bible (cf. Matt. 12:36; Rom. 14:12; 1 Pet. 4:5). They must learn to live with this tension.

---

32. Ibid., 30.
33. Cf. §1.7 and Ouweneel (2018l, chapter 3).

5.3 Inscripturation and Incarnation

5.3.1 The Eternal Word in Temporal Form

I admit at the outset that the following argument is determined *a priori* by my belief concerning its conclusion. In other words, I cannot escape my hermeneutical circle.[34] Yet, I can still argue in the following way.[35] I consider it to be self-evident that God does not reveal himself to completely different people in entirely different ways. Rather, God reveals himself to all humanity in a single, unique form, which in principle is accessible to all people. In other words, I believe it to be self-evident that this Word of God to all people has been documented to us in a *book* (whether a literal book, or an audio, video, or digital version of it). For Christians, this book is the Bible (the Old and the New Testaments), since (a) this is the book that *presents* itself as the Word of God (a feature shared with other books, like the Kur'an and the Book of Mormon); therefore, a second reason must be added: (b) to the faith of the regenerated heart, illuminated by the Holy Spirit, this book *is* what it presents itself to be.[36]

I believe it to be more self-evident that the most direct, most unambiguous, most impressive, most evocative way in which God reveals himself is by clothing *himself* in human flesh, and thus coming to us *in person*. For Christians, this person is Jesus Christ, since (a) this is indeed the person whom the Bible *presents* as the incarnation (having-become-flesh) of God (John 1:14), and (b) for faith, it is indeed evident that he is what the Bible claims he is. God reveals himself through his *Word* (cf. 1 Sam. 3:21; Isa. 22:14), and this can be both the incarnate Word, that is, Jesus Christ, and the written Word, that is, Holy Scripture.

It goes without saying that this double revelation of God is something very different from the traditional duality of gen-

---

34. See previous note.
35. Cf. Ott (1972, 45); Potgieter (1990, 18).
36. Irenaeus seems to have been the first one who described the entire Bible as "revelation": *Adversus Haereses* I.3.6.

eral and special revelation. In chapter 4, we saw that scholastic thought often caused the distinction between work- and word-revelation to degenerate into a genuine *dualism*. In opposition to this, I have argued that, on the one hand, the entire creation (God's *work*) is nothing but the embodiment of God's *Word*; that is, the eternal Word of God has received a form within the immanent-empirical reality of God's creation. In the striking words of Andree Troost: "Holy Scripture ... is a form of God's revelational will, inspired by the Holy Spirit and 'positivized' by believing Bible writers, within the pistical mode of experience of human life."[37] Thus, creation revelation is ultimately *word*-revelation, namely, revelation that consists of God's creation word in Christ.

On the other hand, as a form that the uncreated, eternal Word of God has assumed, as inscripturated within immanent reality, Scripture too shares in the creation of God in Christ. Within the one and only creational revelation of God, Scripture constitutes the "radiating and guiding center" of this revelation, as we saw (§2.7.2). In this sense, the word-revelation is in fact *creation* revelation, since God's eternal Word comes to humanity in an inscripturated form, that is, in the form of "scripture" (Latin *scriptum, scriptura*, "written [matter]"), that is, in the form of a divine work of creation. It is this inscripturation (becoming scripture) of God's Word that is the subject of the present chapter. The Word existed before it became scripture, and in the "fullness of time," the eternal Word of God became scripture, and has resided among us (cf. Gal. 4:4; John 1:14).

In this way, the parallelism between Holy Scripture and the person of Christ has already been suggested: as Christ is perfectly divine and perfectly human, so too is the Holy Bible.[38] Peter Enns rightly stated that this also means that God,

---

37. Troost (1977, 179).

38. See Bromiley (1978, 372–89); Goldingay (1994, 238–41); Troost (2004, 258); Enns (2005, 17–18, 67, 111, 167–68); F. J. Matera in Brown (2007, 102–03).

in order to be able to reveal himself, had to accommodate himself.[39] In my words, the infinite Word limits itself to a format corresponding to the limited, finite understanding proper to human nature. Parallel with the fact that humans are not only spiritual (transcendent) but also corporal (immanent), the transcendent Word of God comes to us in a form that is not only spiritual (transcendent) but also corporal (immanent, material). This is true both for the Word that becomes scripture, and thus shares in the material world of books and letters, and for Christ, who is the Word of God, but in the incarnation has assumed the limitations of human existence.

5.3.2 Parallelism of Scripture and Christ

Christians confess Jesus Christ as the eternal Word that "has come in the flesh" (1 John 4:2-3; 2 John 1:7; cf. Rom. 8:3; 1 Tim. 3:16; Heb. 2:14), and parallel with this, they implicitly or explicitly confess the Bible as the eternal Word that has come in (the form of) scripture. In this regard, there is even more similarity between Scripture and Christ than between Scripture and (ordinary) humans. This is because we cannot describe an ordinary person as "having come in the flesh," since ordinary people are not pre-existent. But the pre-existent Eternal Word (Lat. *Verbum aeternum*) has come in the "flesh" of Scripture exactly like the pre-existent *logos*, the Son of God who is in the bosom of the Father (John 1:18), has "come in the flesh." We cannot say that ordinary people have "come in the flesh" because they exist in material form from their very beginning.[40] But we can say that the Word has *become* scripture and flesh, respectively, because it had existed beforehand, since eternity. The pre-existent, eternal, transcendent Word adopts an immanent-temporal-material form, in scriptural "matter" and in human "matter," respectively.

---

39. Enns (2005, 109–10); in *his* case, given the way he has dealt with Gen. 1–3, his use of the expression may be subject to suspicion, however; see Ouweneel (2018l, §§9.1.1 and 10.4.2).
40. See extensively, Ouweneel (2007, 248, 302, 320).

Since the earliest Christian times, at least since Origen, people have pointed to this parallelism between the *incarnation* of the Word and the *inscripturation* of the Word. During the twentieth century, this was done by, for instance, Abraham Kuyper,[41] Herman Bavinck,[42] and the Second Vatican Council.[43] From eternity, the eternal (transcendent, supratemporal) Word of God descended to our immanent-empirical reality, either in the temporal garment of the human flesh of Jesus Christ, or in the temporal "garment" ("the garment of creaturely reality"[44]) of human language, put down in human letters in a human book. Herman Dooyeweerd spoke of "the incarnation of the Word of God in the Holy Scriptures, in a collection of books composed by various people throughout the centuries, with regard to all modal aspects of our temporal experiential horizon."[45]

Through the incarnation, Christ, the eternal Son of God, the eternal Word of God, entered immanent reality from eternity. He was "manifested in the flesh" (1 Tim. 3:16), "coming in the flesh" (2 John 1:7), "begotten" by the Holy Spirit (Matt. 1:18; Luke 1:35). In an entirely parallel way, one can say that the eternal Word of God was manifested in the "flesh" of Scripture, has assumed a form in human language, in immanent matter of letters and paper, "begotten" by the Holy Spirit (cf. 2 Tim. 3:16; 2 Pet. 1:21). In both cases, the Word took part in all the modal diversity of the immanent creational reality, but God's Word itself abides forever (Isa. 40:8; cf. Ps. 119:89; Heb. 13:8; 1 Pet. 1:23). (A fascinating question, unanswerable at this point, is the extent to which Scripture abides forever in the form in which we know it today.)

The parallelism between inscripturation and incarnation also means, as Luis Alonso Schökel remarked, that misunder-

---

41. Kuyper (*DD* 2.1:59, 63–64, 75); (1898, 479).
42. Bavinck (*RD* 1:378, 435).
43. *Dei Verbum* III.13.
44. Barth (*CD* I/1:166).
45. Dooyeweerd (1958, 56; cf. *NC* 2:561; 1942, 767); Ouweneel (1986, 286–88).

standing Scripture exhibits a parallel with the great Christological heresies of the first centuries of church history.[46] He pointed out that there can be a kind of Docetism or Monophysitism that denies or decreases the human characteristics of the inspired Word. We also encounter a Nestorianism, which denies the divine character of it — or, I would add, concerning the parallel with Nestorianism, it separates the divine and the human sides of Scripture (cf. chapters 7–8). Schökel observed the former (Docetic, Monophysitic) danger especially among fundamentalist Christians, who recognize only the divine aspect of Scripture, or emphasize it one-sidedly at the expense of the human aspect. Schökel observed the latter (Nestorian) danger particularly among liberal Christians, who recognize only the human aspect of Scripture, or emphasize it one-sidedly at the expense of the divine aspect.[47]

With some caution, I present the following altered version of the Chalcedonian formula, now applied to the Bible:

> Following, then, the holy Fathers, we all unanimously teach that Holy Scripture is to us one and the same Scripture, the self-same perfect in divinity, the self-same perfect in humanity; truly divine and truly human; like any human book in all things, sin apart; acknowledged in two natures unconfusedly, unchangeably, indivisibly, inseparably; the difference of the natures being in no way removed because of the union, but rather the properties of each nature being preserved, and (both) concurring into one book; not as though the Word were parted or divided into two books, but one and the self-same Word of God.[48]

The divine and the human are inseparable with respect to both the person of Christ and Holy Scripture. In the remarkable formulation of Frederik O. van Gennep: "It has pleased

---

46. Schökel (1965, 53).
47. Cf. F. J. Matera in Brown (2007, 102-03).
48. Cf. https://en.wikipedia.org/wiki/Chalcedonian_Definition.

God to need humans."⁴⁹ Notice the intentional tension between "pleased" and "need": God "needs" humanity to reveal himself—whether in the person of the *Man* Christ Jesus or in Scripture written down by *humans*—but this "needing" is based upon his own sovereign choice. God does not wish to be, to work, to walk without humans. He chooses to make himself dependent upon humans, and to speak *to* humans *through* humans. Calling humans God's "partners" (cf. 1 Cor. 3:9) does not make them equal with God, nor does it at all diminish God's sovereignty. This is because God himself sovereignly decided to involve humans in his work.⁵⁰

5.3.3 Incarnation and Inscripturation: A Parallel?

G. C. Berkouwer has paid much attention to the traditionally assumed parallelism between incarnation and inscripturation,⁵¹ and levelled some criticism against it.⁵² Indeed, the parallels exhibit some clear deficiencies.⁵³

(a) In both cases, we can speak of a union (Lat. *unio*) between the divine and the human, but only in the incarnation are we dealing with a personal union (Lat. *unio personalis*), that is, with a *person* in whom the divine and the human have been united. Sometimes we find in Scripture that Scripture is personified, as in Romans 9:17 ("Scripture says to Pharaoh . . .") and Galatians 3:8 ("Scripture, foreseeing . . ., preached"; the "foreseeing" is especially remarkable here). However, this does not mean that Scripture *is* a person. For this reason alone, B. B. Warfield spoke of "only a remote analogy"; he seemed to be prepared to abandon the analogy altogether.⁵⁴

(b) Another difference is that, according to the testimony of the New Testament (e.g., John 5:18; 12:49; Rom. 9:5; Phil.

---

49. Quoted in Generale Synode (1999, 26).
50. See extensively, Ouweneel (2018d).
51. Berkouwer (1967, 117–34).
52. Ibid., 124–33, 139.
53. Cf. also Wentsel (1981, 213–14).
54. Warfield (1948, 162).

2:6; Titus 2:13; Heb. 1:8–12; 1 John 5:20), the incarnation of the divine Word emphatically underscores the divinity of Jesus, so that Jesus accepted worship, which in several cases unmistakably was divine worship (Matt. 8:2; 9:18; 14:33; 20:20; 28:9, 17; Mark 5:6; John 9:38; 20:28; by way of contrast, cf. Acts 10:25; Rev. 19:1). Inscripturation, however, does not imply the divinity of the Bible as book; therefore it may never lead to bibliolatry.[55] For instance, why would anyone literally bow down before the Bible as book? Believers bow down before the Word, not before a book. Any deification or idolizing of the Bible as a book would warrant the same judgment that was applied to the bronze serpent: king Hezekiah "broke in pieces the bronze serpent that Moses had made, for until those days the people of Israel had made offerings to it" (2 Kings 18:4).[56] At the same time we now realize the consequences of fully identifying the Bible and God's Word. For just as we should never deify the Bible as a book that "is" God's Word, at the same time we should maintain that the Word of God is divine, as the expression itself already indicates. Therefore, we *praise* God's Word (Ps. 56:10), and we *tremble* before it (cf. Ezra 9:4), but that is something very different from worshiping, or trembling before, a specific book, as people do with other things, such as worshiping an idolatrous image, and trembling before a lion.

(c) J. A. Heyns adduced a different reason for opposing the parallelism of incarnation and inscripturation, namely, the possible suggestion that Scripture is the incarnation of the Holy Spirit.[57] I do not see how this parallelism could ever lead to such a suggestion since Christ is no incarnation of the Holy Spirit either. The Scripture is the eternal Word inscripturated through the activity of the Spirit (2 Pet. 1:21), just as Christ is

---

55. Berkouwer (1967, 128–29); Wentsel (1981, 195).
56. Cf. the exceptional ("bibliolatrous") care that Muslims show to copies of the Kur'an (touch it only with clean hands, keep it in a beautiful cloth on a high shelf, with nothing on top of it, etc.).
57. Heyns (1988, 23–24).

the eternal Word incarnated through the activity of the Spirit (Luke 1:35). It is true, though, that sometimes the parallelism has been linked with the idea of an incarnation of the Spirit.[58] But then, we are no longer dealing with a parallelism between incarnation and inscripturation, but rather between the self-emptying (Gk. *kenōsis*) of Christ and that of the Holy Spirit. Berkouwer saw some room for such a parallel because it better underscores the close connection between Scripture and the Spirit of Christ.[59]

5.4 Forms of God's Word

5.4.1 Various Suggestions

Christian believers know the (transcendent) Word of God *in* their (transcendent) regenerated hearts, but on the one hand, *through* the (immanent) form of Scripture, and on the other hand, *through* their own (immanent) corporality (eyes, ears, perception, feeling, thinking, understanding). ("Corporality" has here the widest meaning as comprising the entire physical-biotic-perceptive-sensitive-mental mode of existence of humanity.) The encounter between believers and God's Word is of a *transcendent* nature, but within our immanent reality it always occurs in a mediate way, namely, in an *immanent* encounter between our corporal mode of existence and the tangible book called the Bible. Scripture *is* the eternal Word of God, but then in the temporal form of a book, just as Christ *is* the eternal Word of God, but then in the temporal form of a human. Only because Scripture and Jesus Christ share in our immanent-temporal reality is the encounter with the eternal Word possible, whereas basically this encounter is brought about in the transcendent heart of a human.

At this point, it must be mentioned that there are more

---

58. Haitjema (1933, 188–91); cf. Wentsel (1981, 212, 214). Haitjema spoke of the "crucifixion" of the Spirit (195), especially at the closing of the canon, where Scripture became the servant who became obedient to the point of death, as the continuation of Christ's humiliation (cf. Phil. 2:6–8).
59. Berkouwer (1967, 127).

forms of the Word of God than Christ and Scripture. Following Abraham Kuyper, J. A. Heyns distinguished no fewer than six forms of the Word (noting that the first three have been separated too much): (1) the creation word, (2) the sustaining or providential word, (3) the redemptive word, (4) the incarnate Word, (5) the inscripturated word, and (6) the preached word.[60] Regarding this last one: the thesis that the preached word is really Word of God is supported by the fact that the Greek term *logos* can also mean "preaching, proclamation" (see, e.g., Acts 8:4; 11:19; 1 Cor. 1:18; 14:36; 1 Thess. 1:8; 2:13; 1 Tim. 5:17; 2 Tim. 4:2; Heb. 13:7).

Paul Tillich also discerned six forms: (a) the principle of the divine self-revelation in the ground of Being itself, (b) the means of creation (cf. no. 1 in Heyns' division), (c) the manifestation of the divine life in the history of revelation (cf. Heyns' no. 2), (d) the manifestation of the divine life in the ultimate revelation, that is, Jesus Christ (cf. Heyns' no. 4), (e) the document of the ultimate revelation and special preparation of it, namely, the Bible (cf. Heyns' no. 5), and (f) the message of the church as proclaimed in its preaching and teaching (cf. Heyns' no. 6).[61]

Karl Barth distinguished only the last three meanings: the incarnate Word, the inscripturated Word, and the preached Word.[62] He linked this threefold form of the Word of God with the divine Trinity: Son, Father, and Spirit, respectively. This analogy is ingenious but hardly convincing.[63] First, the Son and the incarnate Word are identical (such that the Son was also the *pre*-incarnate Word), but the Father is not identical with the inscripturated, nor the Holy Spirit with the preached word. Second, there is no reason to link the Father in a special way with the inscripturated Word. Inscripturation is the work of the *Triune* God, as is the case with *all* divine works. It

---

60. Heyns (1976, 114; 1988, 146); cf. Strauss (1984, 115–18).
61. Tillich (1968, 1:175–76).
62. Barth (*CD* I/1:§4).
63. Cf. Van Genderen (2008, 32).

is just as much the work of the Holy Spirit (2 Pet. 1:21), who is the Spirit of Christ (1 Pet. 11:11), also in the work of inspiration. Nevertheless, Otto Weber adopted Barth's division by speaking of "the Word as event," "the Word witnessed to," and "the proclaimed Word."[64] James H. Olthuis distinguished three forms: the creational word, the Scriptural word, and the incarnated Word.[65] This arrangement was followed by Gordon J. Spykman as well.[66]

Gerhard Ebeling distinguished four forms, identified with Latin phrases: *Verbum praedicatum*, *Verbum scriptum*, *Verbum incarnatum*, and *Verbum aeternum*, that is respectively, the preached, the written, the incarnate, and the eternal Word.[67] Of course, these are all manifestations of the same Word of God, except the *Verbum aeternum*, for this *is* the Word of which the other three are manifestations. Thus, Ebeling's distinction cannot be correct: the first three forms are manifestations of the fourth, which is not an (immanent) form at all.

American theologians Gordon R. Lewis and Bruce A. Demarest made a different type of distinction; they spoke successively of (a) God's Word in eternity (i.e., the pre-incarnate Christ, John 1:1-3), (b) God's Word in time, namely, in (c) the incarnate Word of God, through (d) prophets and (e) apostles.[68]

5.4.2 My Own Proposal

If I were to identify these various forms, I would distinguish the following manifestations of the eternal Word.

(a) In light of the *one* creational revelation that I have distinguished in the previous chapters, I suggest that the creational word, the sustaining word, and the redemptive word are one continuous Word of God, which I would like to summarize

---

64. Weber (1981, 178–95).
65. Olthuis (1976, 9–10).
66. Spykman (1985, 13–19; 1992, 76–84).
67. Ebeling (1979, 258–59).
68. Lewis and Demarest (1996, 109–16).

under the one term *creational word*: God's Word *for* creation and manifested *in* creatures, both before and after the Fall.

(b) The inscripturated Word is not a separate Word alongside or in addition to the previous one, but, as I have quoted earlier from Andree Troost, it is the "radiating and guiding center" of this one and only creational word.

(c) The incarnate Word is a distinct manifestation of God's eternal Word. However, if we keep in mind that we know the incarnate Word only through the inscripturated Word, we can call the latter only the actual center of God's creational word.

(d) The preached word is the word as it has been processed *a posteriori* and subjectively by the preacher, and has been communicated to the listeners. Apparently, this is what Wolfgang Trillhaas described as "the tradition-stream of Christian preaching, Christian testimony, coming to us from Jesus Christ and the early church." He called the Bible "as it were only the first stage of Christian tradition . . . but at the same time a stage of the highest qualification, of decisive authority for everything that would further present itself as testimony, as Word of God, as Christian preaching."[69]

In my arrangement, the preached word is nothing other than the creational word as considered by people, and communicated by people to other people. However, for the listener this word can be the *a priori* word, that is, the very first divine word that he or she ever hears, the word that precedes his or her encounter with the eternal Word, which occurs in the power of the Holy Spirit who mediates this encounter.

Let us keep in mind here that we know all the forms of God's Word mentioned here only through the inscripturated Word. Through the enlightenment of God's Holy Spirit, this Word opens our eyes and hearts to Christ, the incarnate Word, and also to the creation word (or law-word[70]), which

---

69. Trillhaas (1972, 68–69).
70. Olthuis (1976, 191).

gives creation its structure and sustains creation on its way to the consummation of the ages.

5.4.3 Scripture and Humanity: Parallels

In order to better understand the relationship between the transcendent Word of God and the immanent Holy Scripture, it may be useful to pay further attention to the corresponding relationship between the transcendent human heart and the immanent corporality of the human person.[71] Of course, we also keep in mind the important difference: the eternal Word is uncreated and pre-existent, whereas the human heart (in the biblical metaphorical sense) was created together with the human corporal mode of existence, and thus was not pre-existent. Yet, the obvious ontological parallel between, on the one hand, the eternal Word and the written Word embedded in time, and on the other hand, the transcendent heart and immanent corporality, may help us to clarify some important points.

The human heart is the transcendent root of human existence, the point of unity and concentration (on the subject-side of reality) of all immanent-modal-function diversity of human corporality in the widest sense, that is, including the human psychical and mental life. The transcendent heart is the point of convergence of all immanent functions of human existence, just as, conversely, these immanent functions flow forth in refracted form from the transcendent heart. The heart is the human person in their transcendent fullness and unity, while the corporal mode of existence is the human person in their modal diversity. It is the same with Scripture as the Word of God. On the one hand, Scripture itself speaks implicitly of the eternal Word of God in the sense of a transcendent fullness and unity, when it says, for instance, that God's word abides forever (see §5.3.2). On the other hand, Scripture is itself the Word of God in its immanent diversity. Just as a human is more than their corporal mode of existence,

---

71. See extensively, Ouweneel (1986, chapter 5; 2008, chapters 6–8).

in the same way the Word of God is more than its immanent form in a human book. The eternal Word surpasses all immanence, including all human language and writing and books. At the same time, the human corporality *is* the human person (in their immanent form), just as Scripture *is* the Word of God (in its immanent form).

As a consequence of not properly distinguishing between transcendence and immanence, many theologians do not accurately describe the relationship between God's Word and the Bible. Thus, many theological battles have been fought over the word "is" (Lat. *est*) in the ancient confession that Holy Scripture is the Word of God (Lat. *Sacra Scriptura est Verbum Dei*).[72] Often those battles were meaningless from the outset because they were based on a lack of ontological precision. Theological statements rarely go beyond a vague thesis like that of Wolfgang Trillhaas: "The concept [!? 'idea' at best] of the Word of God surpasses the concept of the Holy Scripture."[73] That is, the Word of God is more than just the Bible.

Another example of a lack of clarity comes from Wolfhart Pannenberg.[74] He referred to early Lutheran theology, which emphasized the identity of God's Word and the gospel in its oral and written form, whereas John Calvin made a sharper distinction between the "heavenly teaching" (Lat. *coelestis doctrina*) and its written record.[75] This comes close to what I have called the transcendent Word and the immanent Bible words. Pannenberg *contrasted* — in my view rightly — the latter standpoint with the opinion that arose since the end of the sixteenth century, in which the view of God's Word more and more focused upon the divine inspiration that played a role in the written record of the Word. That is, the term "Word of God" became increasingly limited to its immanent form.

---

72. Cf. Berkouwer (1975, 17, 145 and *passim*).
73. Trillhaas (1972, 71).
74. Pannenberg (1991, 31–32).
75. Calvin, *Institutes* 1.6.3.

5.5 Revelation: Propositional or Personal?

5.5.1 Two Approaches

What exactly is the nature of special revelation? Does God reveal information in the form of propositions, logical theses like those in a philosophical treatment? Or does he reveal himself personally? Or is this a false choice?

In fundamentalism, the former view occupies the central place, but especially in neo-orthodox, existentialist, and postmodern theology, there is indeed the tendency to emphasize the personal character of revelation. Thus, John Baillie said that God does not give information through *communication*, but he gives himself in *communion*.[76] He also noticed that there seemed to be a remarkable range of agreement in recent discussion on revelation to the extent that what is basically revealed is God himself, not propositions about God.[77] Baillie also emphasized what, in his view, were the consequences of the two views: those who view God's revelation as the communication of propositional truths will describe faith as the act of embracing such truths.[78] Thus, faith would be a strongly *rational* matter. Those, however, who view revelation as the presentation of a person, will describe faith as the existential act of confiding in, and surrendering to, a person. In this case, faith is a *supra-rational* matter.

In a similar way, Emil Brunner, in a study in which the notion of personal encounter is central, argued that the Word of God is not a totality of doctrines, and that God in his Word does not say something true—about himself or anything—but reveals *himself*.[79] Knowledge of the truth does not originate through the critical analysis of logical propositions that are recognized and accepted as correct, but rather through the existential *encounter* with the One who reveals himself in the

---

76. Baillie (1956, 47).
77. Ibid., 49.
78. Ibid., 85–87.
79. Brunner (1964).

Bible. In a similar way, Bernard Ramm spoke of revelation as an encounter, even though he also argues that knowledge is involved.[80]

Erroneously, Gordon R. Lewis and Bruce A. Demarest called such approaches "non-cognitive" views of revelation, overlooking the fact that there is also existential, supra-rational, and supra-conceptual cognition.[81] Here lies the crux of the matter: the authors defended a cognitive view, which to them also meant rational and conceptual. Unfortunately, this is the general tendency within especially the *inerrancy* movement, which flourished in the seventies and eighties of the previous century. I will deal with this movement much more extensively in chapters 9–10, but here I want to alert readers to the claim that special revelation must be described as essentially propositional.

5.5.2 A False Dilemma

In the examples just given, inscripturation means that God has set forth his eternal truth in a totality of logically objective, intellectually superior, infallible propositions. We see this, for instance, in the Chicago Statement on Biblical Hermeneutics (for an extensive discussion of this, see §9.3.2), where we read in Article VI, "We affirm that the Bible expresses God's truth in propositional statements." This idea that the Bible is comprised of propositions occurs frequently in inerrantist literature but fails to take into account that the term "proposition" was particularly adopted from the sciences of mathematics and logic. Here, the impression is given that inerrantist theologians view Scripture as a collection of logical-analytical theorems, which need merely to be isolated and systematized by an unbiased, inerrantist theology.[82]

As has occurred so frequently in theology, the choice be-

---

80. Ramm (1971, 150–51).
81. Lewis and Demarest (1996, 1:122).
82. Regarding the many semantic problems with the term "proposition" with regard to the Bible, see extensively, Vanhoozer (1986, 56–75).

tween a propositional and an existential-personal revelation goes back to the scholastic nature–grace dualism. Again we encounter here the false dilemma of nature and supernature, of reason and heart, of thought and experience, of the objective and the subjective. In reality, the one is, of course, inconceivable without the other. These are correlative. On the one hand, embracing certain propositional truths does not by itself lead to salvation at all. A person may have the best conceivable theological knowledge of Scripture, but if one does not know the power of God's Spirit, which has touched one's heart and transformed one's life, in reality that person does not really know the Scriptures: "[Y]ou know neither the Scriptures nor the power of God" (Matt. 22:29; cf. Mark 12:24).

On the other hand, there can be no existential (*supra*-rational) encounter without a minimum of rational knowledge of what or whom one has encountered. Edward J. Carnell has stated that all "vital" faith, that is, putting one's confidence in a person, rests upon "general faith," that is, believing certain facts.[83] Millard J. Erickson emphasized this by arguing that believing *in* a certain person necessarily depends upon believing something *about* him or her.[84] In my words, an existential (*supra*-rational) relationship with a person presupposes a certain *rational* knowledge of this person; no *relation* is possible without some *information*.

However, Erickson and other theologians, who so strongly criticize what they call the neo-orthodox approach, should put as much emphasis on the reverse truth: information itself does not entail a relation, an encounter. Where the neo-orthodox and existentialist approach may emphasize too one-sidedly the existential side of revelation—though it is questionable whether we are doing justice in this way to, for instance, Karl Barth and Emil Brunner—the fundamentalist approach emphasizes too one-sidedly the propositional side of revelation. Revelation undoubtedly involves the communication

---

83. Carnell (1959, 29–30).
84. Erickson (1998, 218).

of certain propositional truths, and inscripturation undoubtedly entails the written recording of these truths. However, we would hopelessly diminish the value of the Bible if we reduced it to nothing more than, or as essentially, a collection of propositions that must be logically analyzed. The rationalism of fundamentalism is no better than the irrationalism of neo-orthodoxy and existentialism. Both fail to discern the proper ontological relationship between the rational and the supra-rational (not to be confused with the irrational).

5.5.3 Revelation and Relationship

Indeed, all revelation aims at the encounter between God and humanity, that is, at the formation of a relationship between God and humans. This encounter, this relationship, is of an existential, and thus of a supra-rational, and therefore of a supra-propositional character. To a large extent, the Bible is a description of such supra-rational, supra-propositional encounters, from Adam in Eden to John on Patmos. It is not simple, and in fact unwarranted, to draw a boundary between the Bible as (propositional) revelation and the Bible as description of (supra-propositional) revelations to people (Abraham, Moses, Isaiah, the twelve apostles, Paul, etc.), a description aiming at the reader receiving a similar existential encounter with the God who reveals himself. It is true that there can be no existential (supra-rational) relationship with God without a minimum of rational knowledge concerning that same God. But the reverse is true as well: propositions themselves do not entails an encounter with God, nor do they bring it about.

The apostle Paul says, "[I]f you confess with your mouth that Jesus is Lord and believe in your heart that God raised him from the dead, you will be saved. For with the heart one believes and is justified, and with the mouth one confesses and is saved" (Rom. 10:9–10). The *immanent* confession with the mouth basically has some propositional form; but such a confession *alone*, without the *transcendent* heart being involved, brings no salvation. Conversely, the existential faith of the *transcendent* heart is inconceivable without a minimum of *immanent* rational (propositional) knowledge that can be expressed by the mouth.

By the power of the Holy Spirit, Holy Scripture addresses humans in their transcendent *hearts* in order to produce in those hearts communion with God through their regeneration and renewal. By the power of the same Spirit, the same Scripture addresses them in the immanent functions of these hearts: thinking, wanting, feeling, and the like.[85] This is because such communion is inconceivable without the proper considerations, sentiments, and volitional decisions. To these belong truths that are (not exclusively) propositional, of which humans (pre-theoretically) take cognizance, and which are (theoretically) analyzed in theology. However, those who *only* take cognizance of these propositional truths, even profoundly analyze and intellectually embrace them, but no more than that, strictly speaking did *not* receive any revelation of (and from) God. Divine information has been communicated to them, and they may even have intellectually accepted its revelational nature. Their reason, and possibly even their feelings and will, have been addressed. However, their hearts have remained untouched. No existential, transcendent relationship with the revealing God has been created; the revelation *as revelation* did not reach its goal. Perhaps Simon the Magician was an example of such an event (Acts 8:9–24).

The Heidelberg Catechism, Q/A 21, seems to suggest both elements, the propositional and the existential:

Q. What is true faith?

A. True faith is not only a sure knowledge, whereby I hold for truth all that God has revealed to us in His Word (James 1:6), but also a hearty trust (Rom. 4:16–18; Rom. 5:1), which the Holy Ghost (2 Cor. 4:13; Phil. 1:19, 29) works in me by the Gospel (Rom. 1:16; 10:17), . . . [see *RC* 2:774]

---

85. See Ouweneel (2008, chapter 6) regarding the transcendent heart and it immanent functions..

The former element, sure knowledge, seems to suggest here a more proportional, rational character (*beliefs*); the latter element, wholehearted trust, seems to suggest here a more supra-proportional, existential character (*faith*). (I say this realizing that there is also a supra-proportional, existential knowledge of the heart, and conversely, there is also a trust or confidence of a purely logical-rational character.) Notice in the text of the Catechism the words "but also"; faith is never a matter of a purely propositional knowledge: something must happen in and with the *heart*.[86]

5.6 Coherent Structural Wholes

5.6.1 The Underlying Theory

As far as its immanent form is concerned, the Bible functions in all modal aspects of creational reality, just like human corporality.[87] Daniel F. M. Strauss argued that, for this reason, the Bible cannot be called "absolute."[88] Something is "absolute" if it (a) is inherently relationless, or (b) is not determined and restricted by conditions. In this sense, nothing within created reality is absolute. As the written Word, Scripture is (a) intertwined with all the dimensions of creation, and (b) entirely determined by the modal-functional diversity of creation.

One might object against condition (a) by asking how God can be called absolute if we consider his relationships with creation in general, and with humanity in particular. The answer is that God does not exist in his relationships; he is not determined by them, and dependent upon them. He existed before there was anything with which he now maintains relationships. Apparently, in his description Strauss referred to *relata* that belong to the same ontic order. That is to say, only God and his *eternal* Word are absolute, in the sense that he

---

86. The entire subject is closely related to what we understand by the term "truth." I have discussed this subject extensively in Ouweneel (2013, chapter 14).
87. Cf. Troost (2004, 276, 346–47).
88. Strauss (1984, 116–17).

and his eternal Word are not subject to the law-order that he has instituted for creational reality (see chapter 3).

In order to understand how Scripture, according to its immanent form, functions in all modal aspects, Herman Dooyeweerd's theory of modalities is insufficient.[89] At an early stage, he came to the conclusion that the dimension of the modalities and that of the entities intersect each other perpendicularly. This means that the theory of the modalities is different from the theory of the structural types, which determine the concrete things.[90] In this way, he developed his theory of the individuality structures — which I will refer to as idionomies[91] — as well as his theory of the encapsis, and his theory of the encaptic whole. Here is a very concise explanation: each class of entities has its own structure or idionomy, which determines its unique individuality or identity, and which always functions in all modal aspects (be it as a subject or as an object). Some modalities always stand out.[92] Thus, a painting has subject functions in the arithmetic, spatial, kinematic, and energetic modal aspects (i.e., it is subject to the arithmetic, spatial, kinematic, and energetic laws) as well as object functions in all higher modal aspects, for it functions as an object in the mental life of humans. The foundational function must be sought in the energetic modality (a painting is a physical thing), and the destination function in the aesthetic modality, for its value lies in the human experience of beauty (or ugliness).

In more complex cases, we observe a certain encapsis (intertwinement) of different idionomies: various idionomies may be intertwined, and thus constitute an encaptic whole, in which a physical, a biotic, a perceptive, a sensitive, and a mental idionomy are encaptically intertwined. Thus, I also

---

89. For a simple introduction to Dooyeweerd's philosophy, see Ouweneel (2014).
90. For the development of Dooyeweerd's thought, see Verburg (1989).
91. The term is from the Dutch linguist and philosopher, Pieter A. Verburg.
92. See note 86.

view human beings, according to their corporal mode of existence, as an encaptic whole, in which a physical, a biotic, a perceptive, a sensitive, and a mental idionomy are encaptically intertwined.[93] I emphasize again that *each* idionomy functions in *all* modal aspects, whether as a subject or as an object. The type of intertwinement that we encounter here is that of the so-called *foundational* encapsis, that is, each lower idionomy supports the higher ones (i.e., enables them to exist), and each higher idionomy rests on the foundation of the previous one, and would be inconceivable without the latter. Thus, the perceptive and sensitive idionomies of human beings could not possibly exist in our reality without their foundation in the physical and the biotic idionomies.

5.6.2 Scripture As a Coherent Structural Whole

In exactly the same way, the Bible as a book constitutes an encaptic whole, that is, an integrated totality of intertwined idionomies. We can think here of a *foundational* encapsis, which involves four mutually irreducible idionomies, that is, four intertwined structures, each of its own structural type, and each higher one resting on the lower one(s). The four idionomies that I discern in a bible[94] are in fact exactly the same as in any other human book. The enormous *difference* is that only in the Bible are we dealing with the immanent inscripturation of the transcendent Word. In other words, the Bible has a transcendent point of fullness, unity, and integration that no other human book possesses.

The four idionomies that I discern in a bible are successively a physical idionomy, a historical-formative idionomy, a lingual idionomy, and a highest idionomy. The latter is differently qualified, in each case in correspondence with the intrinsic destination of the book involved. In this case, the high-

---

93. See extensively, Ouweneel (1986, 186–260; 2008, 114–21; 2014; 2018l, chapter 6).

94. I refer to Scripture with the uppercase word "Bible"; I refer to a specific, particular concrete book bearing that title with the lowercase "bible."

est idionomy can be none other than the pistical idionomy: the Bible is a book of faith (see §5.8 for further explanation).

If I were to express myself as accurately as possible, I would have to write: idionomies that are *qualified* (i.e., their being-so-and-so is expressed) by the physical, the historical-formative, the lingual, and the pistical modalities, respectively. For, I repeat, *each* idionomy functions in *all* modal aspects. Thus, for instance, the lingual idionomy functions not only in the lingual modality but also in the physical, the historical-formative, and the pistical modalities, as well as in all other modalities. If we were to carefully investigate each of the sixteen modalities in which each idionomy functions, we would have a total of sixty-four modalities to consider.

In every idionomy, at least two modalities stand out. First, these are the foundational functions, which are always the highest subject functions; in this case precisely the four modal aspects mentioned: the physical, the historical-formative, the lingual, and the pistical modalities, respectively. Second, each of the four idionomies mentioned has a certain destination function, which indicates the intrinsic destination of the idionomy involved; in this case this is always the pistical function: all idionomies of the Bible are ultimately aimed at the human being as a being of faith.

Sometimes, a third idionomy is thought to stand out, in this case the historical-formative one in each idionomy, to indicate that the Bible is a cultural product, a work of human hands. As such, it stands in contrast to minerals, plants, lower and higher animals, which are natural products, characterized by the physical, the biotic, the perceptive, and the sensitive modalities, respectively.

5.7 The Three Foundational Idionomies

5.7.1 The Physical Idionomy

The physical idionomy is the idionomy of the materials used to manufacture of Bibles: clay tablets, papyrus/paper, parchment, leather, wood, linen, audiotapes, videotapes, CDs,

DVDs, and so on. Not to mention such a peculiar example as the "word of God" that came to King Eglon in the form of a sword (Judg. 3:20-21 DRA). This was a literal application of the figurative language of Jeremiah 23:29, "Is not my word like fire, declares the LORD, and like a hammer that breaks the rock in pieces?"

When the Word of Scripture is spoken with a human voice, it comes to people in the form of air vibrations (cf. Exod. 33:11; Num. 7:89; 12:8; Deut. 34:10; 1 Sam. 3:4-9; Isa. 6). As we have seen (§1.4.3), here revelation is simultaneously concealment: God's actual voice is hidden behind the air vibrations in which it expresses itself.

At other times, it is even said that God's Word was "seen" in some (visionary) way: "The word that Isaiah . . . saw" (Isa. 2:1; cf. 1:1; Amos 1:1; Micah 1:1). As a Jewish source (Metsudath Zion, eighteenth century) says, the prophet "sees" (perceives the divine message) with the eye of the spirit.[95]

This physical idionomy functions as a subject in the arithmetic, spatial, kinematic and energetic aspects. In practice, this simply means that the materials involved can be expressed in numbers, occupy space, exhibit molecular movements, and have weight, and are characterized by common energetic processes. This is not a trivial matter: there is no other way we could ever objectively receive God's revelation than through phenomena that are of an arithmetic, spatial, kinematic and energetic nature, that is, have a thing-like character.

5.7.2 The Historical-Formative Idionomy

The historical-formative idionomy is the typical idionomy of each book (or of a collection of scrolls, or audio-, or videocassettes, or CDs, or DVDs, or computer files, etc.) that is composed of the materials mentioned in the previous section. A book is a human cultural product, which is made according to a certain design, in which the size, materials, letter types, layout, and so on, have been determined. We can easily tell a

---

95. Slotki (1983, 1).

The Inscripturation of the Eternal Word

sixteenth-century from a nineteenth-century book. The eternal, infinite Word has entrusted itself, as it were, to a human cultural product: a temporal, finite book, with a form determined by time and culture.

Or should we say "books" (plural)? The word "bible" comes from the Greek *biblia*, which means "books." The first clear reference to the collection of holy books that resembles what we call "Bible" is Daniel 9:2, "I, Daniel, perceived in the books the number of years that, according to the word of the LORD to Jeremiah the prophet, must pass before the end of the desolations of Jerusalem, namely, seventy years" (cf. Jer. 25:11-12; 29:10). The article is important here: apparently, Daniel was already familiar with "*the* books," that is, the collection of sacred books, Scriptures (see further in §6.2.1).

The idionomy of this book functions again in all modal aspects, such as the arithmetic aspect (number of Bible books, or pages, or words, or letters), the spatial aspect (size), the kinematic aspect (weight), the sensitive aspect (the sentimental value of one's own bible), the historical aspect (each cultural period has its own types of bibles), the lingual aspect (the names: *bible, bijbel, bybel, bibel, bibele, biblia, bibbia, biblie, biblija, piibel*, etc.; various Bible translations and translational methods), the social aspect (wedding bible, family bible, church bible, school bible), the economical aspect (the commercial value of certain ancient or modern editions), aesthetic (beauty of an edition, craftsmanship), the juridical aspect (property, ownership), the moral aspect (love for one's own bible), and pistical (faithfulness toward one's own bible).

5.7.3 The Lingual Idionomy

The lingual idionomy is that of the text, the message, which (usually) has been printed on paper with ink. The thoughts of the Holy Spirit have not been impregnated in the paper, but have been "signified," that is, expressed in signs, that is, human letters and words. This is the specific nature of the lingual: the symbolic relationship between certain thoughts and certain characters. In other words, certain characters are symbols for certain thoughts. The eternal, infinite Word has entrusted itself, as it were, to human, temporal, finite languages (Hebrew, Aramaic, Greek; see below) with all their limitations and shortcomings.

The idionomy of this lingual text functions again in all modal aspects, in which the lingual one remains the qualifying aspect. As examples I mention the sensitive aspect (the emotionality and affection of the Bible language), the logical aspect (the grammatically logical structure of the text: its analyzability), the historical aspect (Bible language can be localized in certain phases of the history of Hebrew, Aramaic and Greek [see below]; the most ancient parts of the Bible have been hand copied for thousands of years before the invention of book printing), the social aspect (Hebrew is the cultural possession of Israel, *koinē* Greek that of the Hellenistic world), the economical aspect (e.g., the efficiency of *koinē* Greek for the purpose of the New Testament), the aesthetic aspect (the measure of literary beauty of the Bible's language),[96] and the pistical aspect (New Testament *koinē* Greek has its own specific forms and terminology, which have been partially formed by the Jewish faith tradition [think of the Septuagint!], and by the demands of the early Christian community of faith).

Let me add here a few notes about the languages in which the Bible was written.

(1) *Hebrew:* this is the language of the Jewish nation, and of by far the largest part of the Old Testament. We distinguish between Old- or Paleo-Hebrew, which we encounter especially in the song of Moses (Exod. 15:1–21) and the song of Deborah (Judg. 5), Standard or Classical Hebrew (the largest part of the Old Testament), and late biblical Hebrew (especially in Ezra and Nehemiah). Hebrew phrases occur in the New Testament as well, especially *Amen* (many times), *Hallelujah* (e.g., Rev. 19:1), *Hosanna* (lit., "Save please," Matt. 21:9), *Sa-*

---

96. See, e.g., Wielenga (1960).

baoth ("[of] hosts," Rom. 9:29; James 5:4 KJV); and *Corban* ("offering," Mark 7:11).

(2) *Aramaic:* the Aramaic Bible portions are Genesis 31:47 (*Jegar-sahadutha*); Ezra 4:8–6:18; 7:12–26 (quotations from documents); Daniel 2:4b–7:28 (in 2:4, the text also contains the word "Aramaic," indicating that what follows is in Aramaic); Jer. 10:11. Further, it has been thought that Aramaic words appear in Genesis 15:1 (*bammachazē*, "in a vision"); Numbers 23:10 (*roba^c*, "fourth part" or "dust clouds"); and Job 36:2a (according to Rashi). Aramaic phrases appear in the New Testament (in addition to many Aramaic proper names, from *Aceldama* [Matt. 27:8 WYC] to *Thomas*): *Abba* ("Father," Mark 14:36); *Ephphatha* ("Be opened!," Mark 7:34); *Eli, Eli, lema sabachthani* ("My God, my God, why have you forsaken me?," Matt. 27:46); *iota* (Matt. 5:18); *mammon* ("wealth," Luke 16:9–13); *Maranatha* ("Lord, come!" or "The Lord comes," 1 Cor. 16:22); *Rabboni* ("Teacher," John 20:16); *Raca* ("fool, empty-headed," Matt. 5:22); *sikera* ("strong drink," Luke 1:15; CEV: "beer"; and, *Talitha koum* or *kumi* ("Daughter, arise!," Mark 5:41). Because of the similarity of the two languages, it cannot always be determined whether a phrase is Hebrew or Aramaic.

(3) *Greek:* in the New Testament, and also in the Septuagint and the Greek church fathers, this is *koinē* Greek, the common Greek of the Hellenistic world, the *lingua franca* of the Roman world. It was not a sacred language, designed especially for the Bible, as people formerly sometimes thought.[97]

The Bible also contains loanwords.

(a) *Latin:* the number of Latin loanwords in the Greek New Testament is remarkable. In addition to proper names (e.g., *Aquila, Clemens* ["Clement"], *Iustus* ["Justus"], *Libertini* ["Libertines"], *Prisc[ill]a, Pudens*), the most important terms are: *assarion* (Lat. *assarius,* "penny," Matt. 10:29), *dēnarion* (Lat. *denarius,* Rev. 6:6), *kentyriōn* (Lat. *centurio,* Mark 15:39, 44–45), *kodrantēs* (Lat. *quadrans,* Matt. 5:26 DLNT), *kolōnia* (Lat.

---

97. E.g., Trench (1976; orig. 1880) many times speaks of "sacred Greek."

colonia, "colony," Acts 16:12), *koustōdia* (Lat. *custodia*, "guard," Matt. 27:65-66 [cf. custody]), *legiōn* (Lat. *legio*, "legion," Matt. 26:53), *lention* (Lat. *linteum*, "towel," John 13:4), *makellon* (Lat. *macellum*, "meat market," 1 Cor. 10:25), *membrana* (Lat. *membrana*, "parchment," 2 Tim. 4:13), *million* (Lat. *mille*, "mile," Matt. 5:41), *phragellion* (Lat. *flagellum*, "whip," John 2:15), *praitōrion* (Lat. *praetorium*, Matt. 27:27), *sikarios* (Lat. *sicarius*, Acts 21:38 MEV), *simikinthion* (Lat. *semicinctium*, "apron," Acts 19:12), *soudarion* (Lat. *sudarium*, "handkerchief," Luke 19:20), *spekoulatōr* (Lat. *speculator*, "executioner," Mc6:27), and *titlos* (Lat. *titulus*, "inscription," John 19:20). A strange mixture of Greek and Latin is *euraquilo* (Acts 27:14), from Greek *euros* ("east wind") and Latin *aquilo* ("north wind"), thus "northeaster" (seafarer's Latin).

(b) *Egyptian*:[98] e.g., *chartam* ("magician," Gen. 41:8); *abrēk* ("bow the knee!" v. 43) is possibly Egyptian, too.

(c) *Persian*: e.g., *achashtranim* ("satraps," Esther 3:12), *ganzak* ("treasure room," 1 Chron. 28:11), *pardes* (Gk. *paradeisos*, "paradise," e.g., Neh. 2:8 YLT), *pat-bag* ("rich, dainty food," Dan. 1:5 AMPC).

(d) *Late Accadian*: for instance, *sharbit* ("scepter," Esther 4:11), but also a well-known word such as *hekhal* ("temple, palace") goes back to Accadian, and from there to the (non-Semitic) Sumerian.

5.8 The Pistical Idionomy

5.8.1 Pistical *Versus* Religious

The pistical idionomy involves the content of the lingual message. This content is pistically qualified, that is, the Bible is above all a book of faith; it speaks the language of faith, it aims at bringing about and furthering faith (see below). Many subjects are dealt with in the Bible, such as physical, biotic, historical, social, economic, aesthetic, juridical, and ethical topics. However, the treatment of such matters is *never* an end

---

98. For (b), (c), and (d) cf. Mankowski (2000); Eskhult (2003).

in itself; it is always the faith aspect of these topics that matters.[99] Just as a theological (or any other scientific or scholarly) publication is logically-analytically qualified, a historical work historically qualified, a grammar lingually qualified, a book on good manners, house building, or traffic safety socially qualified, a commercial guide economically qualified, a law book juridically qualified, and an ethical handbook morally qualified, the Bible's content is pistically qualified.

Incidentally, the same is true for biblical diaries, collections of sermons, Christian websites, and so on, apart from the sacred books of other religions (Vedas, Qur'an, Book of Mormon). Each of these is a pistically qualified writing; the difference between them does not lie in this point. The difference is that we can say of the Bible alone that it is the immanent-temporal inscripturation (written record) of the transcendent-eternal Word of God.

As I have explained elsewhere,[100] this pistical character of the Bible does not mean only that it was especially written by religious people. It is much more than this: it was written with a transcendent-religious *purpose*. Please note that *every* book in our world is written by religious people in the sense that every book basically proceeds from the religious ground-motives that govern the author's heart.[101] Within immanent reality, the transcendent-religious expresses itself in a diversity of modal aspects. The pistical or faith aspect is just one of them, and must be carefully distinguished from the religious in its transcendent meaning. Thus, existing cookbooks, law books, books on aviation and gardening, as well as Bible books, have all been written in ways that expressed the religious ground-motives of their authors. However, law books are juridically, books on gardening biotically, but Bible books pistically qualified. They are *all* religious in the emphatic (transcendent) sense of the term, but they are qualified

---

99. See extensively, Ouweneel (2018l, chapter 3).

100. Ouweneel (1995, §2.4; 2014; 2015).

101. Cf. Ouweneel (2018l, chapter 6).

by very different modal aspects of our immanent world. Bible books are pistical because they were written with a *faith* purpose, namely, the regeneration, illumination, instruction, admonition, and consolation of believers with respect to God (2 Tim. 3:16-17; cf. 1 Cor. 14:3).

This means that, if we will distinguish the various modalities in the Bible's content (see the next section), each of these is continually viewed from the standpoint of faith; if one so wishes: from the standpoint of religious life in the limited, immanent sense of the term (the life of praying, Bible reading, preaching, offering, etc.). If we do not clearly discern this point, we will inevitably land in the snare of fundamentalistic scientism, which easily reduces the Bible's content to its logical-analytical or historical aspect, as we will extensively investigate (chapter 9). Fundamentalism treats the Bible like a natural-scientific or historiographical handbook, without people (sufficiently) taking into account the peculiar character of the Bible's faith language. Conversely, there is also a "theologism" (which could be called a form of "pisticism") that *reduces* the Bible to its pistical aspect, and makes it totally irrelevant as far as its statements about nature and history are concerned. We will return to this very important matter in the final chapters of this book.

5.8.2 Modal Aspects of the Pistical Idionomy

The idionomy of the Bible's actual content functions in all modal aspects. In so doing, the pistical aspect remains the qualifying aspect; that is, everything that will be said concerning the various modalities must be considered continually under the viewpoint of the biblical (or, for that matter, also the apostate) faith. Some examples:

(a) *Perceptive-sensitive:* reading or hearing the Bible's content brings about inner sensations, perceptions, feelings (positive and negative), affection and emotions, which are always related to faith (trust, confidence in God) or unbelief.

(b) *Logical:* the Bible's content is logically analyzable; otherwise, any theology would be nearly impossible. This does not mean, however, that humans would be able to completely comprehend every biblical thought. Sometimes, this content is illogical, for instance, when the Bible writer gets carried away with his emotions (e.g., Jer. 20). The Bible sometimes contains specifically logical arguments and reasoning (e.g., syllogisms in Rom. and Heb.), without ever becoming a logically-analytically *qualified* (theoretical, or even scientific, e.g., natural-scientific or historiographical, or even theological) handbook.

(c) *Historical-formative:* the Bible's content has undergone a long process of historical development. It lasted many centuries before the entire Word had been inscripturated, from the oldest parts of the Pentateuch to the last writings of the New Testament. This happened at many different places; as far as we have been able to ascertain, these were the wilderness between Egypt and Canaan, Canaan itself, Israel, Babylon, Persia, Asia Minor, Italy, Greece, Macedonia, and perhaps other places.

(d) *Lingual:* the eternal Word has been put into immanent, human words: ". . . in words not taught by human wisdom but taught by the Spirit" (Gk. *logois . . . didaktois pneumatos,* 1 Cor. 2:13; see §7.6.2). These words were adopted from certain human languages. They were not celestial or angelic languages (cf. 13:1), nor sacred languages, specially prepared (see §5.7.3), but ordinary language. What is involved is common words, everyday words with all their human nuances and restrictions, yet words that are carriers of the eternal Word.

(e) *Social:* just as the Bible language is the possession of a certain language community, the faith content of the Bible is the spiritual possession of a certain faith community. The Scriptures arose in the midst of God's people in the wilderness, in the promised land, in foreign (Asian and European) countries. They address God's people, or Christian churches, but in a wider sense even all humanity. Even Job was a member of a faith community (think of his friends), and also Theophilus (Luke 1:14; Acts 1:1), Timothy, Titus, Philemon, the "elect lady" (2 John 1:1, if she must be viewed as a literal individual), and Gaius (3 John 1:1) — individuals to whom Bible books were addressed — turn out to have been part of a faith community, and as such had to share the written Word to others. The Old Testament is the possession of *all* Israel — "the Jews were entrusted with the oracles of God" (Rom. 3:2) — and the entire Bible is the possession of *all* Christianity.

(f) *Economical:* the content of Scripture is balanced: it maintains the efficient equilibrium between the individual and the collective aspects, between God's sovereign counsel and human responsibility,[102] between the unity and diversity (three persons) of the Trinity, between the divine and the human natures of Christ,[103] between the temporal and the eternal, between grace and righteousness, between the natural and the spiritual, and so on.

(g) *Aesthetic:* not only the Bible's language, but the Bible's content — the depths and riches of its thoughts — is also magnificent. Seen from this viewpoint alone, many parts of the Bible (I just mention Job, Psalms, and John as remarkable literary examples) belong to the very best that human cultural history has ever witnessed (just as, seen from the viewpoint of faith, it *is* the very best).

(h) *Juridical-ethical:* above all, the Bible is a book of justice and morals; not only in the sense that the Bible *speaks* of justice and morals (for such a "speaking of" is something very different from functioning in the juridical and ethical *modalities*), but in the sense that the Bible *is* a righteous and morally lofty book. Micah 6:8 is a striking Old Testament example: the LORD "has told you, O man, what is good; and what does the LORD require of you but to do justice, and to love kindness, and to walk humbly with your God?" Again, we must realize

---

102. See extensively, Ouweneel (2018d).
103. See extensively, Ouweneel (2007, chapters 2–3 and 8–9).

that the terms "justice" and "morals" are not used here in a juridical and ethical sense only, but in a transcendent-religious sense (see the next section).

5.9 The Word and the Words

5.9.1 The Bible: God's Word or Expression of God's Word?

We must now enter more deeply into the very important relationship between, on the one hand, Scripture as an immanent-pistically qualified encaptic whole and, on the other hand, the transcendent Word of God. The eternal God has subjected the human transcendent heart to his eternal, transcendent Word. This is the one and only Word in its transcendent, integral fullness and totality, which, within the immanent form of the Bible, refracts into many different words. Just as the transcendent heart expresses itself in the many immanent functions, the one, undivided, eternal Word of God expresses itself in the many words of Scripture. Just as there is not one function in human existence in which the heart does not express itself, there is not a single word in Scripture in which the eternal Word of God does not express itself. Thus, in their transcendent-religious hearts, humans are subject to the transcendent-religious Word of God, and in their immanent functioning, humans are subject to the many distinct words of Scripture.

It is good to underscore again this distinction between the (transcendent) Word of God and the (immanent-empirical) Scripture. Bernard Ramm pointed to the opinion of Karl Barth,[104] in whose opinion the doctrine of the verbal inspiration and inerrancy involved a *materialization* of the inspiration doctrine. Such materialization means that the Word of God is literally reduced (solidified) to a concrete, material book that people can carry around in their pockets. The wicked King Jehoiakim could cut up the words of Jeremiah, and burn them in the fire (Jer. 36), but only — in Barth's view — because they

---
104. Ramm (1983, 118).

were Jeremiah's testimony concerning the Word of God, not the Word of God itself.

But this way of stating things is not sharp enough. In the immanent sense, the book of Jeremiah *is* (part of) the Word of God, as I will argue time and again. At the same time, Barth's point is clear, and it is correct when stated this way: the Word van God *cannot be reduced* to its immanent-empirical form. If all the Bibles in the world were destroyed, even then God's Word would abide forever (1 Pet. 1:23–25; cf. Matt. 5:18). But the reverse must be stressed, too: the Word of God is not something that evaporates into thin air, something disconnected from our tangible Bibles. My Bible is Word of God because in the immanent *words* that it contains God's eternal *Word* expresses itself.

This does not mean that the words of Scripture can be taken in an atomistic way; that is, it is not the separate words, each word alone, that count but *the* Word expresses itself in the Bible's words *in their coherence* (we will come back to this point when we discuss verbal inspiration; §8.5). Nor do all Bible words have equal authority; the authority of Bible words is determined by their functioning in the entire coherence in which they stand. Incidentally, the same is true of *all* human language.

5.9.2 No Separation Between Word and Words

We will consider this point more extensively, but at this juncture I wish to underscore the point that the immanent and the transcendent may never be separated. That is, each immanent word of the Bible has significance only if viewed within the scope of the totality of the transcendent Word (cf. §7.9.3). We may think here of Herman Dooyeweerd's well-known metaphor of prism and plant (§3.8.3).

(a) The immanent words of the Bible constitute the refraction of the imperishable, eternal Word of God; conversely, this Word is the transcendent point of concentration and integration (focal point) of all immanent words of the Bible.

(b) The eternal Word of God is the transcendent root-word, whereas the distinct words of the Bible, which the refraction of the root-word, constitute the immanent branches (ramifications).

In no way should we create here a dualism, as I have emphasized before.[105] Neither the heart and its functions, nor the eternal Word of God and the distinct words of the Bible, must ever be viewed in a dualistic way. It is naïve to assume that any dual*ity* is the same as a dual*ism*. A genuine dualism consists of two factors that have nothing in common, and stand in opposition to each other (antithesis). In contrast with this, in many dualities the two factors do have much in common, and are *not* opposed to each other; often on the contrary. In a good marriage, husband and wife are a duality but not a dualism. In the person of Christ, the divine and the human natures are again a duality but not a dualism. A and B cannot form a dualism if A is the focus of B, or B is the expression of A. As we have seen, the one transcendent Word of God *refracts* into all the various immanent words of Scripture; in other words, the immanent Bible words *are* the Word of God in its refraction. Conversely, the immanent words of the Bible *converge* into the one Word of God with its transcendent unity and fullness.

Think of the prism again (§ 3.8.3): the different words of the Bible are the refraction (radiation) *of* the one Word of God *itself*, just as the one Word of God is the focal point *of* the different Bible words *themselves*. The one Word *is* the totality of the various words of Scripture in their transcendent fullness, unity, and totality, just as the various words of Scripture *are* the Word of God in its immanent diversity and divergence. Here we have no room for any kind of dualism. Instead, we find — if one so wishes to express it — a *duality*. It is one that seems to me to be comparable to the distinction that Otto Weber made, though in a very different context, between the totality and wholeness (Ger. *Ganzheit*) that are ordered around a

---

105. Cf. Ouweneel (2018l, chapter 6).

middle or scope (Ger. *Mitte*), or between the qualitative "one" and unity (Ger. *Einheit*) and the purely quantitative totality and togetherness (Ger. *Gesamtheit*) or differentiation/differentiatedness (Ger. *Differenziertheit*).[106]

5.9.3 "Word" As Concept and Idea

As I have explained elsewhere,[107] we can speak of the one, eternal, transcendent Word of God — or of *any* transcendent subject, for that matter — only in terms that belong to our immanent experiential world. In such cases, the terms that are used function as border-concepts, or rather *ideas*, because they refer to matters that surpass the boundaries of immanent-empirical reality. The word "idea" goes back to the Greek verb *idein*, "to see." It refers to the "look" of a thing: you see it, but you cannot exhaustively describe it. Such ideas contain *modal* terms, used as ideas, which refer to *supra-modal* matters. These are matters that we can know only in terms that are logically definable but that themselves surpass logical definition. We are dealing here with supra-logical matters that can only be *approximated* with the help of logically definable terms. These lead to *ideas*, which have a regulative character, that is, regulate our thinking on a certain subject.

Such an idea is also the word "Word" (cf. what in §1.4.1 was said about "revelation"). When we speak of "word" in a common lingual way, we are dealing with a lingual *concept* because this concept encloses modal-lingual features as constitutive conceptual characteristics. Here the term "constitutive" means constituting the concept to be a concept. Constitutive conceptual characteristics are data that function within the boundaries of the lingual modality. In this case, a word is a separate conceptual lingual unit. An audible word is primarily a lingual sound, or a combination of lingual sounds, and a written word a lingual sign, or a combination of lingual signs. We can formulate a definition (delineation) of "word" as a

---

106. Weber (1981, 236–40).
107. Ouweneel (1995, §4.2.2; 2008, 24–35, 66–68, 148–49; 2015, chapter 6).

modal-lingual concept; and where the written term "word" occurs in the modal-lingual sense, we speak of a lingual unit, separately written (with spaces before and after it), forming sentences with other such units, often exhibiting declensions and conjugations (plurals, verbal forms, composite words), and so on.

The point is now that this lingual term "word" can also be used as an idea to refer to a supra-lingual matter (i.e., surpassing the lingual), such as when we speak of the eternal Word of God. The important point in such an idea is that *some* elements of the definition of the modal-lingual term "word" are, and others are not, applicable. What matters in the *idea* of "word" is still language, expression, communication, but not a lingual sound, or a lingual unit that is part of a written or spoken sentence. The reality of God's Word transcends the boundaries of created reality, whereas we can still speak of it with the help of immanent-modal terms, which in this case, however, are not used as concepts but as ideas. These terms *refer* to this transcendent reality but they do not "cover" it, so to speak. Thus, we believingly form for ourselves an idea of the Word, that is, we understand that it is a matter of God's speaking, communicating, bringing to expression. However, we cannot define it with, or enclose it in, our modal-rational concepts.

It is enormously important to understand this properly.[108] There is nothing vague, mystical, or irrational in the term "idea." This is because our rational knowledge is definitely not limited to conceptual knowledge, as rationalism has always asserted, also within theology. Rational knowledge also encompasses the knowledge that we have in the form of ideas. *Our knowledge of God and his Word is not only supra-rational but also rational, though not conceptual.* If this is not grasped or acknowledged, people must necessarily choose between two ways of escape. Either people declare that the knowledge

---

108. Cf. Strauss (1983, 53–54; 1988, 147–50).

of God and his Word is non-rational or irrational, and thereby fall into the snare of mysticism and bigotry. Or people declare that the knowledge of God and his Word is possible only because, and insofar as, God and his Word fall under the rational order to which the cosmos is subject. Thus, God and his Word are thought to be subject to the same logical laws that the Creator himself has instituted.

In short: the knowledge of God's Word in its transcendent meaning is thought to be either non- (or ir-)rational (mysticism), or rational-conceptual (either fundamentalism, or modernism). However, there is a third way between irrational and rational-conceptual, and this involves the knowledge that we have in the form of ideas. We can form rational *ideas* about the supra-rational Word of God.

Another consequence of such false dilemmas is that theologians began making a distinction between *incommunicable* (so-called essential) attributes of God (i.e., belonging to his essence) and *communicable* attributes of God (God's being insofar as he is able and prepared to reveal it to humanity).[109] One of the consequences of this distinction was that some people developed a so-called negative (or *apophatic*) theology (Lat. *via negativa*, Plotinus, Pseudo-Dionysius), which consisted only of propositions about what God was *not*, or drew the conclusion that we know God only in terms of the created relationships that he has used to reveal himself. This would imply that God has revealed only his relationships, not his being, not *himself*. In this case, we have no revelation *of God* at all but only a revelation of the form in which it pleased God to reveal himself to people.[110] I will return to this vital subject—do we have a revelation *of God?*—in a subsequent volume in this series about God.

---

109. Cf. Bavinck (*RD* 2:chapters 4 and 5).
110. Lewis (2001) recommended "negative theology" as a method to cleanse our thinking of errors concerning God, in order to then open it for the pure truth concerning God. Armstrong (2009) saw a revival of "negative theology" in post-modern theology.

The Inscripturation of the Eternal Word

We no longer need such ways of escape as soon as we recognize that there is rational *idea-like* knowledge, which surpasses the boundaries of rational conceptualization, yet remains rational. There is not only rational-conceptual but also rational idea-like knowledge. If this is grasped, it is no longer a problem to say that God has used *creaturely* terms to reveal his *being*, that is, *himself*. This does not mean that the knowledge of God and his Word can be *enclosed* in our rational knowledge. On the contrary, ultimately the truly existential knowledge of God (cf. John 1:18; 17:3; 2 Cor. 2:14; 4:6; 10:5; Gal. 4:9; Eph. 1:17; Col. 1:10; 2 Pet. 1:2; 1 John 4:6–7; 5:20) and his Word surpasses all rational knowledge, and becomes the possession of the supra-rational heart. However, read very carefully here: it is not *ir*-rational (which is an immanent term) but *supra*-rational (which is a transcendent term); rational idea-like knowledge is a knowledge of God and his Word that nourishes and enriches the supra-rational knowledge of the heart.

There is no purely rational-conceptual knowledge of God and his Word, but there *is* rational idea-like knowledge that does not enclose God and his Word but definitely approximates it, and ultimately finds its fulfillment in the transcendent, supra-rational, existential faith knowledge of the human heart. In summary, we will be greatly helped if we begin to distinguish between the (immanent) irrational-conceptual, the (immanent) rational-conceptual, the (immanent) rational idea-like, and the (transcendent) supra-rational; in short, distinguish between the *non-rational*, the *irrational*, the *rational*, and the *supra-rational*. Most confusions around this subject originate through not clearly distinguishing between two or more of these four expressions.

It is my conviction that, in this way, a fruitful model can be—and has been—developed to describe the relationship between the (eternal) Word of God and the (temporal) Holy Scripture. John D. Morrison described three approaches developed to grasp this relationship:[111] they are those of American theologians Donald G. Bloesch, Gabriel J. Fackre, and Clark H. Pinnock.[112] All three sought a pathway between, on the one hand, fundamentalism and inerrantism (with their inherent rationalism; see chapter 9), and, on the other hand, anti-supernaturalistic liberalism and the Barthian approach (see chapters 11-12). According to Morrison, all three came dangerously close to some dualism or dichotomy between the Word of God and the Holy Scripture. However, this tells us at least as much about Morrison's own approach, which equated the two too much. In my view, all four authors would have been helped with a profound consideration of the relationships between concept and idea, between dualism and duality, between the immanent and the transcendent, and between the temporal and the eternal.

5.10 The Modal Ideas

5.10.1 The Natural Modalities

Let us now look again at the modal aspects, this time with the intention of using the successive modal terms as ideas, in order to get a clearer picture of the supra-modal Word of God. It is very important to understand that *each* modal idea is a window on the *entire* Word of God in its transcendent fullness and unity, not on a certain aspect of that Word.[113] If we are dealing with God's Word in its transcendent fullness and unity, there is no question anymore of (modal) aspects in this Word. Thus, although the various ideas find their origin in the respective modalities, they each shed light on the Word of God in its integral totality.

The following descriptions will partly overlap with those of the so-called pistical analogies,[114] those of God's revelation

---

111. Morrison (2006, 188–204).
112. See especially Bloesch (1994); Fackre (1997); Pinnock (1984).
113. Cf. Strauss (1991, 128).
114. See on this, Ouweneel (1995, §4.4.1; 2013, chapter 12), and various introductions to Dooyeweerdian philosophy regarding "modal analogies."

(§1.4), and those of God's law (§3.9). The overlap mentioned first is almost inevitable because the pistical modal aspect, as the highest modality, is a border-aspect. That is, though it is immanent-modal, it touches upon the Word in its transcendent-supramodal meaning, more than any other aspect. The overlaps with God's revelation and God's law are even more obvious because of the close relationship between the notions of revelation, law, and Word. In order to avoid too much repetition, I will keep the descriptions concise.

(a) *Arithmetic:* the eternal Word is one, single, and unique, and in its fullness and totality it has only one primary author (Lat. *Auctor primarius*): God himself. But at the same time, there is a multiplicity and diversity enclosed in this Word that, in its immanent refraction, comes to deployment through a multitude of human authors (Lat. *auctores secundarii*), and a multiplicity of human words (see chapters 7–8 below).[115]

(b) *Spatial:* in the "supra" ("above") of the supratemporality of God's Word we clearly have to do with a spatial idea. We also speak in the form of spatial ideas when we refer to the Word's "(out)reach" or "extension," its "universal validity," also its "exalted" character (from Lat. *exaltare*, to raise, elevate). The eternal Word "descended from beyond" into our human world. It is obvious that we are dealing here with ideas, not concepts, because we cannot express these spatial measures in meters. At the same time, it is clear that these are not simple, arbitrary metaphors, but intrinsic creational data, for we discover that these matters cannot be possibly expressed in any other way than in spatial terms.

(c) *Kinematic:* strictly speaking, we already encountered kinematic ideas under the previous point, namely, when we speak of "extending," "exalting," or "descending." This "movement" in the idea-like sense is found also in a term such as the "transcendence" of the Word, which "surpasses"

---

115. This speaking of *auctores secundarii* does not necessarily mean a weakening of the contribution of the human authors; cf. Van Keulen (2003, 533).

our immanent world, or terms such as refraction (from the transcendent to the immanent) and convergence (from the immanent to the transcendent). Or think of our saying, for instance, that, at inscripturation, the transcendent Word of God entered into our temporal-immanent experiential reality. We speak of these movements in an idea-like manner, for they cannot be expressed in meters per second. But they are no arbitrary metaphors either, which might be easily replaced by very different metaphors.[116]

(d) *Energetic:* God's Word is dynamic (Gk. *dynamis*), has power (Heb. 4:12 KJV), is a force for the believer's entire life. It strengthens him or her (Ps. 119:28). The Word is also the light in which the believer can rejoice: "Your word is a lamp to my feet and a light to my path" (v. 105). "The unfolding of your words gives light; it imparts understanding to the simple" (v. 130). But it is also a fire and a hammer (Jer. 23:29). The latter belong more to the domain of metaphors, if one so likes; but the idea of power or strength—which cannot be expressed in newtons—is not an arbitrary metaphor. There is no other way to express the energetic influence that the Word has on people's lives.

(e) *Biotic:* the Word of God is the continual source of life for creation: "[T]he word of God is living and active" (Heb. 4:12); "the living and abiding word of God" (1 Pet. 1:23). It is also seed that falls in the earth and bears fruit (Luke 8:11; cf. Isa. 55:10-11); it is bread, nourishment for the soul (cf. the parallel in Matt. 4:4), milk for the babies in the faith (1 Cor. 3:2; Heb. 5:12-13; 1 Pet. 2:2); the Word can be "eaten" (Jer. 15:16; Ezek. 2:8-3:1; Rev. 10:9). In the latter examples, we are no doubt dealing with metaphors, but behind them is the basic thought that the Word is "life" (cf. John 1:4), and that it gives life. It is the Word of the "living God" (the expression occurs thirty times in the ESV, from Deut. 5:26 to Rev. 7:2), and this is far more than a mere metaphor. We may always assume that a

---

116. To this we must add the fact that "metaphor" is a literary (lingually qualified) term, and "idea" a logically qualified term.

term is more than a metaphor if a profound truth is involved that cannot be expressed in any other way than in the form of ideas. This way is not conceptual, because we are not dealing here with "life" that, for instance, exhibits metabolic processes in the common biotic sense.

(f) *Perceptive:* in all parts and aspect of reality, the Word causes itself to be concretely perceived, in a visible, audible, tangible, even "tastable" way: God's words are "sweeter also than honey and drippings of the honeycomb" (Ps. 19:10). "Oh, taste and see that the LORD is good!" (Ps. 34:8; 1 Pet. 2:3). It is the Word of God's "mouth" (Ps. 33:6; Isa. 45:23; 55:11; Ezek. 3:17; 33:7; Matt. 4:4), which is heard by all people, and obeyed or disobeyed.[117] I also mention here the "self-awareness" of the Word, which comes to expression in the testimony that the Bible gives of itself as Word of God (2 Tim. 3:16; 2 Pet. 1:21).

(g) *Sensitive:* the Word is also the revelation of God's great care and affection toward humanity, which moves people's hearts: "The law of the LORD is perfect, *reviving* the soul; . . . the precepts of the LORD are right, *rejoicing* the heart" (Ps. 19:7-8). The word (the law, the commandment, the precept) is a delight to the believer (Ps. 119:16, 24, 47, 70, 77, 92, 117, 143, 174; Rom. 7:22; cf. Job 22:26; 27:10; Ps. 37:4; Isa. 58:14).

5.10.2 The Mental Modalities

(h) *Logical:* the Word of God is logically coherent, the revelation of God's absolute rationality, which is reflected in the order and coherence (rationality) of the cosmos and its way of functioning, and also in the rationality of humans, through which they can obtain insight into the cosmos *and* into God's Word. Please note that people can acquire understanding of the rationality of the Word, but only in an idea-like manner, not in the conceptual sense. God's rationality, and thus that of his Word, is never *irrational* or *non*-rational, yet it surpass-

---

117. "Obey" comes from Latin *oboedire*, from *ob-* and *audire* ("to hear"); cf. Dutch *horen – gehoorzamen*; German *horchen – gehorchen*.

es human rationality; it is supra-rational: "[M]y thoughts are not your thoughts.... For as the heavens are higher than the earth, so are... my thoughts higher than your thoughts" (Isa. 55:8–9).

(i) *Historical-formative:* the Word of God is all-dominating; it is irresistible because it is the revelation of God's omnipotence and law-will. God's will-word gives to all things their specific form, exactly as it pleases God: "[M]y word that goes out from my mouth... shall not return to me empty, but it shall accomplish that which I purpose, and shall succeed in the thing for which I sent it" (Isa. 55:11). The "word of his power" (Heb. 1:3) is identical with the powerful Word of God (4:12 KJV).

(j) *Lingual:* the Word of God is *word*, speaking, expression, communication from God, "the word that goes out from my mouth" (see again Isa. 55:11), a very "telling" revelation of God. See above about the use of the word "word" as an idea. Also in our speaking of God as the "primary Author" of the Bible (see above) we are dealing with a lingual idea.[118]

(k) *Social:* the Word of God, which is communication, implies (the formation and furtherance of) communion between God and humans, and mutually between humans, a communion (fellowship) that is an extension of the inter-Trinitarian fellowship: "... the word of life... we proclaim also to you, so that you too may have fellowship with us; and indeed our fellowship is with the Father and with his Son Jesus Christ" (1 John 1:1, 3). "I do not ask for these only [i.e., the twelve disciples], but also for those who will believe in me through their *word*, that they may all be one, just as you, Father, are in me, and I in you, that they also may be in us, so that the world may believe that you have sent me" (John 17:20–21).

(l) *Economical:* the Word is God is perfectly balanced, effective, efficient, purposeful (cf. again Isa. 55:11), and has infinite

---

118. See Vawter (1972, 22) on various meanings that the Latin word *auctor* had in the early church.

value: "The words of the LORD are pure words, like silver refined in a furnace on the ground, purified seven times" (Ps. 12:6). "More to be desired are they than gold, even much fine gold" (19:10). "Therefore I love your commandments above gold, above fine gold" (119:127). Also compare Job 22:25, where the Almighty himself is "your gold and your precious silver." Such verses indicate that the value of God's Word cannot be expressed in conceptual-economical categories; we have to do here with the modal-economical *idea* of value.

(m) *Aesthetic:* the Word of God is perfect in peace and harmony, just as God himself — whose expression and revelation this Word is — is the "God of peace" (Rom. 15:33; 16:20; Phil. 4:9; 1 Thess. 5:23; Heb. 13:20; cf. 2 Thess. 3:16), an enemy of all disorder (1 Cor. 15:32).

(n) *Juridical:* the Word of God not only speaks of righteousness but *is* righteous in the sense that it assigns to all things in human life their own places that do justice to them: "I know, O LORD, that your rules are righteous" (Ps. 119:75; cf. vv. 62, 106, 144, 160, 164). "You have appointed your testimonies in righteousness" (v. 138). "Your righteousness is righteous forever, and your law is true" (v. 142). Again, we are dealing here with a term that is used as an idea: God's righteousness surpasses all human judicial principles.

(o) *Ethical:* in its highest sense, the Word of God is the Word of God's love, the loving revelation of his own perfect love, with which he carries his people in his arms (cf. Deut. 33:27; Isa. 40:11). It is a benevolent word: "[Y]our rules are good" (Ps. 119:39), like God is good: "You are good and do good; teach me your statutes" (v. 68). The Word shows God's love for his people, and insists that they, in their turn, love him and their neighbors (Deut. 6:5; Lev. 19:18), and even the Word itself (Ps. 119:47-48, 97, 113, 119, 127, 140, 159, 163, 167).

(p) *Pistical:* the Word of God is the revelation of God's faithfulness (Gk. *pistis*) toward his people, as implied in his covenant with them. His Word is credible because God is credible. God is trustworthy, therefore his Word is trustworthy (cf. Ps. 19:7 CEB; 1 Tim. 1:15; 4:9; 2 Tim. 2:11; Titus 1:9; 3:8).

Chapter 6
The Canon of Scripture

These are my words
that I spoke to you while I was still with you,
that everything written about me
in the Law of Moses
and the Prophets
and the Psalms must be fulfilled.
                                    Luke 24:44

. . . the revelation of the mystery
that was kept secret for long ages
but has now been disclosed
and through the prophetic writings has been
made known to all nations.
                                    Romans 16:25–26

Summary: *What does the term "canon" mean? How and when were Bible books first discerned to be canonical? In what sense are canonical books distinct? How does the notion of canonicity relate to the notions of divine inspiration and divine authority? In the process of canonization, how did God's providence relate to human responsibility (Israel and the church, respectively)? The two canons* *of the Old Testament are dealt with, as well as the notion of "deuterocanonical" books. The status of criteria of canonicity is investigated: are they rational or supra-rational?*

The criteria of canonicity are dealt with according to the various modal ideas, first and foremost the lingual idea: in canonical books believers are hearing God's own speaking. The second criterion is based on the historical-formative idea, that of divine authority. According to Protestants, authority is one of the properties of the Bible, the other main properties being the sufficiency, the perspicuity, and the necessity of the Bible. Lesser criteria of canonicity are the physical-biotic, the logical-analytical, and the social criteria.

Finally, the question is dealt with whether there are any post-apostolic books in the New Testament, whether they must be called forgeries, and whether this matters for our understanding of canonicity. The question is related to these: Is the boundary between Scripture and tradition vague? Are there degrees of canonicity? And what about the criterion of coherence?

6.1 Origin of the Canon

6.1.1 Stating the Problem

FOR A PROPER UNDERSTANDING of Scripture as the Word of God, it is important to discuss the matter of the *canon*, in coherence with that of the *inspiration* (chapters 7-8).[1] Christians believe that the Bible is a divine book, which, by God's providence, not only was faithfully delivered to them but originated through divine inspiration. In this acceptance of the Bible as the inspired Word of God, Christians differ fundamentally from Muslims, Buddhists, Hindus, and others, all of whom have their own sacred books. In the acceptance of the New Testament, Christians differ fundamentally from Jews, who consider as Holy Scripture only the Tanakh. (I would sug-

---

1. For this chapter, I have received help from Grosheide (1935); Harris (1957); Geisler and Nix (1968; 1974); Holwerda (1972); Carson and Woodbridge (1986); Metzger (1987); Bruce (1988a); Auwers and De Jonge (2003); McDonald (2007); in what follows, I will employ ideas drawn from their works without explicit documentation.

gest that Jews look at the Tanakh through the glasses of the Talmud, whereas Christians look at the Tanakh through the glasses of the New Testament.)

Christians differ among themselves about what belongs to Scripture; does the Bible contain either only the so-called canonical, or also the so-called deuterocanonical books (see §6.7.2)? Christians differ among themselves about the precise meaning of terms like "inspired" and "Word of God," which will be discussed especially in chapters 7 and 8.

According to Christians, in what respect do the thirty-nine books of the Old Testament and the twenty-seven books of the New Testament[2] differ from other religious books, such as the Rig-Veda and the Bhagavan Gita (Hinduism), the Pali-Canon (Buddhism), the Talmud (Judaism), the Qur'an (Islam), the writings of the Báb and Bahá'u'lláh (Bahá'í), or the Book of Mormon (Latter Day Saints)? In addition, in what respect do they differ from the writings of the so-called Apostolic Fathers: Ignatius, Polycarp, Clement of Rome, Papias, Pseudo-Barnabas, Hermas? In other words, what books belong to Holy Scripture, and thus can be viewed as the immanent-temporal expressions of the transcendent-eternal Word of God? What books do not? Why Esther, and why not Judith? Why the Gospel of Luke (who was no apostle, and not even born a Jew), and not that of Thomas (who was both an apostle and born a Jew)? Who decides that? According to what criteria? And who determines the criteria?

Questions related to these are the following: What does it mean that the Bible written by *humans* can nevertheless be called the Word of *God*, or can be viewed as inspired by God? How does this inspiration relate to that of, for instance, a great poet or novelist? Were not the writers of the Rig-Veda, the Talmud, the Qur'an, and even perhaps the writings of the

---

2. Is it a coincidence that these numbers return in Isaiah? The first part of this book contains 39, the second part 27 chapters (of which Isa. 53 forms the central chapter). Incidentally, in §6.5 we will find lower numbers because of the counting together of twin books.

Báb and the Book of Mormon, not inspired to a certain extent as well, that is, moved in a peculiar way by higher powers? Not to mention numerous other religious books, including Christian books. Many secular artists also speak of inspiration; they themselves have been inspired, for instance, by a beloved, or by nature, or also by their own religious experience.[3] Is inspiration a (deeply inspired, or different) dazzling idea, or is it more than that? If so, what is it?

6.1.2 A Starting Point

Many more questions could be asked about the matter of biblical authority, as well: What authority does Scripture, which after all is (also) a human book, have over the human living, thinking, feeling, believing, and acting of its readers? How does this authority relate to human authority, such as that of popes, councils, synods, bishops, priests, pastors, and other spiritual leaders—or even theologians? How does this authority "from above" relate to the listeners' own functions, such as reason, religious feeling, the sense of justice, moral consciousness, faith, and human existence?

Moreover, since the Bible was written by humans—so that in Scripture we may hear the voice of God as well as the voice of humans—we must wonder how God's voice relates to the human voices. This is because, in the past, the divine element in inscripturation was overemphasized at the expense of the human element. Nowadays, the danger is the opposite, namely, the human element is overemphasized so strongly that the divine element is pushed to the background. In addition, we must critically scrutinize this very language of "elements" as such, because it carries the stench of dualism.

If we try to answer these questions, our consideration must begin with what the Germans call the Bible's *Selbstverständnis*: its self-understanding, self-image, self-awareness. This is the way Scripture views itself, namely, as Word of God. In other words, we will seek the key to understanding the Bible not

---

3. See, e.g., Ursell (2012).

outside it, wherever it may be, but within the Bible itself. We are reminded here of the ancient Reformational adage: Holy Scripture is its own interpreter (Lat. *Sacra scriptura sui ipsius interpres*).[4] This means not only that each Bible passage must be understood in light of the Bible's totality, but also that the Bible must be the first to answer questions about what it is, and where it comes from. Scripture is the primary source for understanding Scripture; divine revelation is the primary source for understanding revelation. There is a hermeneutical circle involved here, which I discussed extensively in §1.7 (cf. also §6.6.3).

The questions just mentioned will be examined in two stages.[5] In the remainder of this chapter, I wish to show that certain books were considered to be *canonical*, that is simply, to belong to Holy Scripture, particularly because they were deemed to be *divine*: of divine origin, of divine reliability, and of divine authority. In chapters 7–8, I wish to show that calling certain books divine is the same as saying that faith recognizes them as divinely *inspired* ("breathed" by God). It is important to keep these two descriptions clearly distinct. Certain books are considered to be divine not simply because they belong to the Bible. Rather it is the opposite: they were included in the canon because the faith of early Christian generations recognized them as divine, which amounts to the same as saying that they were viewed as inspired. Because of this *a priori* acknowledgement, they were included in the Bible. However, it is equally true that, *for Christians today*, certain books are indeed considered to be divine because they belong to the biblical canon; for them this is an *a posteriori* criterion.

---

4. Cf. Luther, WA 7:97.
5. For the treatment of this subject, I have had help from Warfield (1948); Harris (1957); Geisler and Nix (1968, Parts I, *Inspiration of the Bible*, and II, *Canonization of the Bible*), and Geisler and Nix (1974, chapters 2–10, on inspiration and canonicity); Henry (1979b, 405–49); Metzger (1987); Bruce (1988a); Harris (1995, chapter 7); Kooij et al. (1998); McDonald and Sanders (2002); Auwers and De Jonge (2003); McDonald (2007); see also www.ntcanon.org.

6.1.3 Bible Quotations from Non-Biblical Sources

Let me begin with some brief remarks concerning the historical process of canonization. The clearest evidence for the Old Testament canon is found in the New Testament, which quotes almost every Old Testament book as divinely authoritative (although this is usually done implicitly). The only books that are not verbally quoted in the New Testament are Judges, Ruth, Chronicles, Esther, and Song of Solomon. However, stories from Judges (Heb. 11:32) and Chronicles (Matt. 23:35) are quoted as authentic, the person of Ruth after whom the book of Ruth is named is mentioned in Matthew 1:5, and Jesus presents himself as the bridegroom (Matt. 9:15) — in my view a clear reference to the Song of Solomon.[6] It seems that only the book of Esther is not mentioned in the New Testament; however, in my view, the typological significance of this book is so obvious that the book bears the divine stamp in a different way.[7]

The argument of quotation as validation must be used with reluctance, though, because sometimes an event from an apocryphal tradition, and thus the source from which this event is quoted, is presented as authentic as well. ("Apocryphal" means here: close to the Bible, but of doubtful authenticity; non-canonical; see §6.7.2.) Some examples:

(a) The reference to Jannes and Jambres, Moses' opponents (2 Tim. 3:8).[8]

(b) The phrase "Some were tortured, refusing to accept release, so that they might rise again to a better life" (Heb. 11:35) strongly reminds us of 2 Maccabees 6:18–7:42.

(c) The expression "sawn in two" (Heb. 11:37) is probably a reference to the prophet Isaiah.[9]

---

6. See Ouweneel (1973).
7. See Ouweneel (n.d.).
8. According to Origen (*Comm. Matt. 27:8*), there was an apocryphal *Book of Jannes and Jambres*, today unknown. The Targum of Jonathan mentions the two names in Exod. 7:11; 22:22.
9. *Ascensio Isaia* 1:9; 5:2, 6, 13–14.

(d) The dispute of the archangel Michael with Satan about the body of Moses (Jude 9).[10]

(e) The prophecy by Enoch (Jude 14).[11]

(f) Some expressions by Paul, such as "Satan as an angel of light" (2 Cor. 11:14) and "third heaven" (12:2) may have been adopted from the Jewish writing *Life of Adam and Eve* (in the Greek version known as the *Apocalypse of Moses*).

In addition to this, there are of course the quotations from, or allusions to, pagan authors: Aratus (Acts 17:28, "certain of your own prophets"; a quotation from *Phaenomena* 5), Epimenides (Titus 1:12–13, "One of the Cretans, a prophet of their own"; from the *Cretica*), and Menander (1 Cor. 15:33, from *Thais* 218).

A remarkable example is 1 Corinthians 10:4, where, according to some, the apostle Paul is referring to a Jewish legend:[12] the Israelites in the wilderness "drank from the spiritual Rock that followed them, and the Rock was Christ." This legend is supposedly first encountered in Pseudo-Philo (first century?),[13] who seemed to suggest that the rock followed the people through the wilderness. But even with Pseudo-Philo, it is not clear whether it really was the rock that followed, or the water from the rock, or the Lord himself. Later Midrashic and Talmudic literature also contains references to a "following rock." However, it cannot possibly be concluded from the short reference in 1 Corinthians 10:4 that such a legend existed already in Paul's days, that Paul knew that possible legend, and that he is really alluding to it in our passage. Moreover, Paul explicitly speaks of a *spiritual* rock, and identifies it with Christ. It seems instead that he intends to say that, already in the wilderness, the Spirit of Christ was with God's people,

---

10. *Assumptio Mosis*, to which Origen refers, *De Principiis* III.2.1.
11. 1 Enoch 1:9 (however, it is not clear which was first: this book or Jude's letter!).
12. Cf. Enns (2005, chapter 4), and the discussion by Beale (2008, 37–38, 49–50, 97–101 [including notes 28–33], 118–20).
13. *Liber antiquitatum biblicarum* 10:7; 11:15; 20:8.

taking care of them and meeting their needs.[14]

The underlying problem is obvious. Did the New Testament writers make use not only of the Old Testament but sometimes also of extra-biblical sources — including sources that contain spurious Jewish legends? In other words, does the New Testament contain Jewish legends, which have no basis in redemptive history? If so, what basis do we have for the claim that the New Testament is historically trustworthy? Whereas the New Testament indeed makes use of extra-biblical sources that definitely go back to historical material, in my view no case is known of which it can be proven that the New Testament appeals to non-historical stories. If the latter were the case, according to Peter Enns this would in no way affect the divine revelational character of the New Testament[15] — but in my view it would certainly cast doubt on the historical reliability of the New Testament.

6.2 Earliest Canon Suggestions

6.2.1 The Old Testament

The earliest suggestion of a canon, in the sense of a collection of certain books that were accepted as Holy Scripture, is found perhaps in Daniel 9:2, where Daniel encountered the prophecy of Jeremiah about the duration of Jerusalem's destruction (Jer. 25:11–12; 29:10) in "the books" (Heb. *bassepharim*).[16] *The books* is a reference to the sacred books belonging to what we now call the Bible, insofar as they were available to Daniel. Apparently, these were the books that he knew and accepted as divinely inspired and divinely authoritative.

The well-known tripartition of the Tanakh (i.e., T-N-K[h]) is that of the *Torah* (the law, i.e., the Pentateuch), the *Nebi'im* (the prophetic books, including the "former prophets," Josh. – Kings), and the *Ketubim* (the writings, Psalms – Chronicles; see §6.5). Jesus seems to refer to this tripartition: ". . . every-

---

14. Cf. Fee (1987, 446–49).
15. Enns (2005, 32, 35).
16. Bruce (1988a, 37–38).

thing written about me in the Law of Moses and the Prophets and the Psalms" (Luke 24:22). Of course, the third part included many more books than the Psalms; perhaps it was referred to this way because Psalms is the first and largest book of the *Ketubim*.

We seem to find this tripartition for the first time in the prologue written by the Greek translator (the grandson of the Hebrew author; 132 BC) of the deuterocanonical book Jesus Sirach or Ecclesiasticus[17] (c. 180 BC). Several times he refers to the law, the prophets, and the "other books":

> "Whereas many great teachings have been given to us through the law and the prophets and the others that followed them, ... my grandfather Jesus [read, Joshua[18]], after devoting himself especially to the reading of the law and the prophets and the other books of our fathers. . . . Not only this work, but even the law itself, the prophecies, and the rest of the books differ not a little as originally expressed" (RSV).

Apparently, during the author's time there was a certain awareness of a Hebrew canon, although it is not sure whether the term "other books" refers to a specific third part of the Tanakh, now called the *Ketubim*, or to other Jewish writings, not counted among the sacred books.

The Jewish-Alexandrian scholar Philo also recognized the authority of the sacred books,[19] and considered the Jewish apocryphal books known in his time (Baruch, Judith, 1 and 2 Maccabees, Sirach, Tobith, Wisdom) not to be divinely authoritative. This seems to indicate that these books were not viewed as canonical by the Alexandrian Jews, even though, remarkably enough, they were included in extant copies of the Septuagint (an Alexandrian work). Apparently, canonical or non-canonical, they were considered to be important enough for such inclusion.

---
17. Not be confused with the Bible book Ecclesiastes.
18. In Heb. 4:8, the name Joshua is also spelled as *Iēsous*, "Jesus."
19. *De Vita Contemplativa* 3.25.

Jewish historian Flavius Josephus wrote that the Jews acknowledge only twenty-two books as divine, and that the Jewish books written since the Persian king Artaxerxes, that is, Nehemiah's time (Neh. 2:1) — these were the apocryphal books just mentioned — did not possess this authority because in those days the prophetic continuity no longer existed.[20] Presumably, Josephus chose the number twenty-two because this is exactly the number of letters in the Hebrew alphabet. He referred to the five books of Moses, the thirteen prophetic books (probably Josh., Judg., Sam., Kings, Chron., Ezra-Neh., Esther, Job,[21] Isa., Jer., Ezek., Dan., and the Dodekapropheton [the twelve Minor Prophets]), and four books with praises and rules of life (presumably Ps., Prov., Eccl., and Song). Traditionally, Samuel, Kings, Chronicles, the Dodekapropheton, and Ezra-Nehemiah were each viewed as one book. Presumably, Josephus reckoned Ruth and Lamentations as appendixes to Judges and Jeremiah, respectively. In this way, we indeed arrive at a number of twenty-two instead of thirty-nine.

Josephus' remark that no divinely authoritative Jewish books were written after Artaxerxes must be noted. It means that chronologically the canon was closed with the prophet Malachi. This argument is found later in the Talmud as well.[22] Hendrikus Berkhof wrote, "Daniel was indeed included, but they did not know that it was a pseudepigraphical work."[23] However, this is less self-evident than it may seem to many present-day expositors, surely since we possess the Dead Sea Scrolls.[24] There are expositors in our time who date Daniel's

---

20. *Contra Apion* 1.38–41.
21. Job was possibly viewed as a prophetic book; cf. James 5:10–11 and Sirach 49:8–10.
22. Seder Olam Rabba 30; Sanhedrin 7–8, 24; after Mal. the Holy Spirit (of prophecy) departed from Israel (Joma 9b; Sotah 48b).
23. Berkhof (1986, 80–81). A book is pseudepigraphic if its author attributes it to, and hides himself behind, a much better known figure (usually someone in the past).
24. Peter Flint (1997) argued that Daniel was accepted as authoritative Scripture in the Qumran community, and that Daniel was viewed as a prophet (cf. Matt. 24:15).

book in the sixth century BC (in which Daniel lived).²⁵

The pseudepigraphic book Apocalypse of Ezra (see §6.7.2), written after AD 70 (!), mentions "twenty-four books" that ought to be made known publicly, and these seem to be the twenty-four books of the Tanakh: the twenty-two books referred to by Josephus, plus Ruth and Lamentations. There are also good reasons to assume that the Qumran community at the same time acknowledged a canon that contained the Torah, the Prophets, the Psalms, Daniel, and probably Job. On the whole, the Essenes in general agreed with the Pharisees as to the contents of the Hebrew canon, though we are not sure about one or two of the Ketubim.²⁶ In the first century of the present era, there was basic agreement on the Old Testament canon, also among the early Christians. Jesus did criticize the Jewish tradition in certain respects, but he is never reported to have disagreed with the Jewish leaders on the canon of the Hebrew Bible.

It is important that Jesus explicitly viewed this canon as a unity: "Scripture cannot be broken" (John 10:35). This was possible only if for him, as well as for the spiritual leaders of Israel, the term "Scripture" (singular; so almost always in John) was a well delineated concept. This actually holds for many places in the New Testament that refer to "Scripture" (Gk. *graphē*). This can be understood only if there was a clear common opinion on what was "Scripture," and what was not. In our terminology: what belonged to the canon, and what did not. Or, what were divinely inspired books, and what were not. Or, what were divinely authoritative books, and what were not. All these descriptions amount to the same thing.

6.2.2 The New Testament

The definitive formation of the New Testament canon took a significant amount of time, apparently because of the enor-

---

25. See, e.g., Harrison (1969, 1106–32); Archer Jr. (1985, 4–6); perhaps the final edition dates from the fifth century BC; cf. Slotki (1983, xiii).
26. Cf. Bruce (1988a, 38–42).

mous distribution of the books and the poor means of communication in those days. Already in the New Testament itself, the Greek term *graphē* ("Scripture") was used not only for the sacred books of the Old Testament but also for those of the New Testament. Thus, we read in 1 Timothy 5:18, "[T]he Scripture says, 'You shall not muzzle an ox when it treads out the grain,' and, 'The laborer deserves his wages.'" The first quotation comes from Deuteronomy 25:4 (cf. 1 Cor. 9:9), but the second one from Matthew 10:10 or Luke 10:7. Apparently, Paul places the two quotations on the same level as coming from "Scripture."[27] 2 Peter 3:15-16 speaks of the "letters" of "our beloved brother Paul," in which there are some things "that are hard to understand, which the ignorant and unstable twist to their own destruction, *as they do the other Scriptures.*" To Peter, Paul's letters were apparently just as sacred as the Old Testament Scriptures.

Especially in the light of Ephesians (3:1-10) and Colossians (1:24-28), I consider it to be quite likely that in Romans 16:25-26, Paul is also referring to New Testament Scriptures: ". . . Jesus Christ, according to the revelation of the mystery that was kept secret for long ages but has now been disclosed and through the prophetic writings has been made known to all nations, according to the command of the eternal God, to bring about the obedience of faith. . . ."[28] If I am right, these "prophetic writings (or, Scriptures)" are Scriptures of New Testament prophets because the Old Testament prophetic books do *not* reveal the mystery that was kept secret during the very days of the Old Testament.

In addition, the Apostolic Fathers, such as Ignatius and Polycarp, deal with quotations from the New Testament in a

---

27. Trillhaas (1972, 71) wrongly claimed that only 2 Pet. 3:16 is an example of the New Testament referring to certain New Testament books as "Scripture(s)."

28. See, e.g., Godet (1880, ad loc.); Grant (1901, 290); W. Kelly (*BT* 9:183; N4, 127–128). The term *graphē* is used both for certain passages (e.g., John 13:18) and for Scripture as a whole (e.g., 10:35).

The Canon of Scripture

way that shows that they must have been clearly aware of a sharp difference between their own writings and those of the apostles. In the second letter of Clement of Rome, five times a "Scripture" (Bible passage) is quoted; four times an Old Testament passage, and one time a New Testament passage (chapter 2): "And another Scripture says, 'I came not to call the righteous, but sinners.' [Matt. 9:13; Mark 2:17] This means that those who are perishing must be saved." Thus, Clement not only knew the written Gospels but he viewed them as being on the same level as the Old Testament Scriptures. Ignatius did the same in his letter to the Smyrnaeans (chapter 5): "Some ignorantly deny Him. . . . These persons neither have the prophets persuaded, nor the law of Moses, nor the Gospel even to this day, nor the sufferings we have individually endured."

Tatian's *Diatessaron* (c. 170), a harmonization of the four Gospels, implicitly shows that, in his days, Christians viewed the collection of the four Gospels as indisputable. In addition to this, we know dozens of other so-called gospels, all apocryphal (or less than that), and many pseudepigrapic (falsely attributed to well-known early figures: James, Joseph the carpenter, Judas, Mary, Philip, Thomas, "the Twelve," etc.).[29] We also note the great number of "oracles" (Gk. *logia*) of Jesus, handed down by the early church (since Acts 20:35), which do not appear in the New Testament Gospels; these are the so-called *agrapha*.[30]

Irenaeus (c. 180) makes clear that, in his day, the four Gospels, Acts, Paul's letters, 1 Peter, 1 and 2 John, were generally considered to be canonical, but James and Hebrews were not (yet),[31] and apparently 2 Peter and 3 John were also looked at with suspicion.

It is remarkable that the (Western) *Vetus Latina* — a collec-

---

29. See en.wikipedia.org/wiki/List_of_Gospels.
30. See en.wikipedia.org/wiki/Agrapha.
31. *Adversus Haereses* III–V.

tion of various Latin Bible translations before the Vulgate—does not contain some books that were particularly current in the East (Heb., James, 1 Pet.), whereas the Syriac Bible translation (in the East) does not contain some books that were particularly current in the West (2 and 3 John, Jude, Rev.). Apparently, it took some time before the missing books became known everywhere in the Christian world. However, together these two oldest Bibles contain the entire New Testament canon, except 2 Peter, which is lacking in both. The first complete canon is mentioned halfway between East and West: Origen (c. 230) in Egypt published a complete list of books that were universally acknowledged by Christians. He did add, however, that Hebrews, 2 Peter, 2 and 3 John, James, and Jude were disputed by some, but he supplied arguments against these doubts.[32]

6.2.3 Additional Notes

The Old and New Testament books that were accepted by all Christians from the beginning are called the *homologoumena*. The books that, despite being named after great men (and sometimes women) of God, were rejected by all Christians, are called the *pseudepigrapha*. The books that are today accepted by some and rejected by other Christians are called the *apocrypha*. They are similar to the Bible, but, according to most Christians, do not belong to the Bible. Some Jewish writings that Protestants call apocryphal books are called *deuterocanonical* by Roman Catholics, who view them as part of the Old Testament.

The books that were accepted by the majority, were disputed by some, and later were accepted by all are called the *antilegomena*. The latter are the Old Testament books of Esther, Proverbs, Ecclesiastes, Song of Solomon, and Ezekiel. These books seem to have been disputed by some only later, though, due to the rise of various rabbinical schools.

---

32. See especially his *De Principiis* and several of his *Commentaries* (Josh., Matt., Luke, John, Rom., Heb.).

The Canon of Scripture

The New Testament *antilegomena* are Hebrews, James, 2 Peter, 2 and 3 John, Jude, and Revelation. The main problems with these books were especially doubts because of anonymity (Heb.), or doubts concerning their authenticity (the others); that is, were they really written by the authors mentioned in them? Thus, there seemed to be apparent doctrinal conflicts with certain *homologoumena*: James seemed to conflict with Paul's reaching on the justification by faith;[33] Jude, because of his references to one or two pseudepigraphic sources; and Revelation, because of the millennialism of chapter 20, particularly after the Montanists had linked their teachings with it. I will discuss some of these books in §6.11.

6.3   Character of the Canon

6.3.1   Active and Passive Canon

The word *canon* came to us through the Vulgate, and goes back to the Greek word *kanōn*, which reminds us of Hebrew word *qanē*, "reed" (cf. the English *cane*).[34] A reed could be used as a ruler or a measuring rod (cf. Ezek. 40:3), so that the word also received the meaning of "rule, criterion." In this sense, the word occurs in Galatians 6:16 (". . . all who walk by this rule . . .") and Philippians 3:16 ("whereto we have already attained, let us walk by the same rule," KJV; NABRE: "course"; NET: "standard"). Hence, the word can also refer to a territory that has been delineated with a measuring rod: "area of influence" (2 Cor. 10:13, 16; lit., "measure of the rule," KJV; also, "area [or, sphere of service; or, measure of the work] assigned to us," CJB, NIV).

The word was used by the church fathers from the beginning with the meaning of "rule." Clement of Alexandria and Origen spoke of Scripture as "the rule of the church" (Gk. *kanōn tēs ekklēsias*), in the sense of a rule for Christian believing and living. In Latin, this was later described as a *regula*

---

33. See Ouweneel (2018e, chapter 5).
34. *TDNT* 3:596–602; Brown (1992, 3:399–402).

fidei, "rule of faith."[35] It was not before the time of Athanasius (fourth century) that the word "canon" began to be used in the same sense with which we are familiar, namely, a list of books considered to satisfy the "rule," the rule of canonicity, that is, books that are considered to be invested with divine authority due to divine inspiration.[36]

The two meanings are rather closely related, yet must be clearly distinguished. In the *active* meaning, a Bible book is canonical because it is an authoritative, divine *rule* for the Christian life. Far more common is the *passive* meaning: a Bible book is canonical because it satisfies a certain *rule* that determines whether a book has divine origin and authority, and thus belongs to the Bible. The two meanings are related in the sense that only canonical (divine, sacred) books have divine authority for Christian living.

Canonicity qualifies a book as Scripture since the latter word is explicitly reserved for books considered to be divinely inspired, and therefore divinely authoritative. During the Old Testament period, there was a clear public recognition that certain books proclaim God's Word; see Joshua 1:7-8, "[B]e strong and very courageous, being careful to do according to all the law that Moses my servant commanded you.... This *Book of the Law* [Heb. *sefer hattorah*] shall not depart from your mouth, but you shall meditate on it day and night, so that you may be careful to do according to all that is written in it" (cf. 8:31, 34; 23:6; 24:26; Deut. 29:21; 30:10; 31:26; 2 Kings 14:6; 22:8, 11; 2 Chron. 17:9; 34:14-15; Neh. 8:1, 3, 18; 9:3). However, this is not the same as canonization.[37] Only when the notion of canon (a list of sacred books) had been developed, no matter how preliminary and informal, certain books were distinguished as Scripture in contrast with other books, which were nonetheless highly appreciated. In the New Testament, the Greek word *graphē* (lit., "writing") is used exclusively for

---

35. See www.ccel.org/s/schaff/encyc/encyc09/htm/iv.vii.cxix.htm.
36. Cf. *TDNT* 3:596-602.
37. Cf. Bruce (1988a, 36-38).

Holy Scripture.[38] Sometimes, the Greek term *gramma* is also used to mean "Scripture" (John 5:47; 2 Tim. 3:15), but this word can also have other meanings.[39]

In the New Testament the expression "it is written" (Gk. *gegraptai*, from the same root as *graphē* and *gramma*, related to English terms like "graphic") always refers to what ancient English divines referred to as "Holy Writ" (an expression that interestingly does not occur in the Bible translations that I am aware of), from Matthew 2:5 to 1 Peter 1:16 (for the remarkable 1 Cor. 2:9, see the next section). In the Old Testament, this is somewhat less clear: see 2 Samuel 1:18 ("it is written in the [non-biblical] Book of Jashar"; cf. Josh. 10:13; see §6.6.1); Psalm 40:7 ("in the scroll of the book [i.e., the Torah, especially Deut. 17:14-20?[40]] it is written of me"); Isaiah 65:6 ("it is written before me," i.e., in the heavenly annals?[41]). Where the expression in the Old Testament refers to Bible books, these are always the books of the Pentateuch.

6.3.2 Spurious Sources

I do have to add here, though, that some quotations in the New Testament are introduced as if they have been quoted from Scripture, whereas their source can no longer be clearly identified.[42] Clear examples are the following:

(a) Jesus "lived in a city called Nazareth, so that what was spoken by the prophets might be fulfilled, that he would be called a Nazarene" (Matt. 2:23); ancient Christian sources thought the name "Nazareth" was derived from the Hebrew word *netser*, "branch," which is a Messianic title (Isa. 11:1;

---

38. *TDNT* 1:751–61.
39. Ibid., 765; Danker (2000, s.v. *gramma*).
40. Cf. Cohen (1985, 124); or the book of Ruth? See Rosenberg (1984, 90). Or it is a book of God's eternal counsels? Thus some older English divines (http://biblehub.com/psalms/40-7.htm).
41. Thus Kimchi, Ibn Ezra; see Slotki (1983, 315); cf. also Ellicott ("book of God's remembrance"), Gill ("book of his decrees"), etc. (http://biblehub.com/commentaries/isaiah/65-6.htm).
42. Cf. Bruce (1988a, 51–52).

60:12).

(b) "Whoever believes in me, as Scripture has said, 'Out of his heart will flow rivers of living water'" (John 7:38; some have seen here an allusion to Isa. 12:3).

(c) "... as it is written, 'What no eye has seen, nor ear heard, nor the heart of man imagined, what God has prepared for those who love him'" (1 Cor. 2:9; this seems close to Isa. 64:4).

Also compare passages where the expressions "Scripture," "prophets," or "it is written" do not occur but which seem nevertheless to be references to Scripture. Some examples:

(a) "Therefore go out from their midst, and be separate from them, . . . and touch no unclean thing; then I will welcome you, and I will be a father to you, and you shall be sons and daughters to me" (2 Cor. 6:17-18; passages that seem close are Isa. 52:11; Jer. 31:1; Hos. 1:10).

(b) "Therefore it says, 'Awake, O sleeper, and arise from the dead, and Christ will shine on you'" (Eph. 5:14; the quotation vaguely reminds us of passages like Isa. 26:19; 60:1).[43]

(c) "Or do you suppose it is to no purpose that Scripture says, 'He yearns jealously over the spirit that he has made to dwell in us'?" (James 4:5; the question where the quotation comes from evaporates if we translate quite differently; e.g., DARBY: "Think ye that Scripture speaks in vain? Does the Spirit which has taken his abode in us desire enviously?").

In all these cases, we can draw either of two conclusions. Either the authors are quoting Scripture, not literally but according to the gist of it: "This is what Scripture implicitly teaches." Or the authors are referring to books that they viewed as Scripture but that have not been included in the Hebrew canon as we know it. However, although we are familiar with numerous apocryphal and pseudepigraphic books, the quotations mentioned cannot be reduced to any of them. Perhaps, 1 Corinthians 2:9 and Ephesians 5:14 are the only exceptions; according to some church fathers, these

---

43. Cf. Bruce (1984, 376).

quotations come from a work called the *Apocalypse of Elijah*. Origen, Ambrosiaster, and Euthalius attribute 1 Corinthians 2:9 to this work, and Epiphanius does so with Ephesians 5:14. Of this work, two versions are known, a Coptic (fragmentary, Christianized) and a Jewish (Hebrew, abridged) version, but these both originated after the time of Paul. They might go back to a version with which Paul, too, may have been familiar.

It would certainly be spectacular if we could possess more certainty about the question whether Paul indeed would have drawn on this or a similar work, *and* viewed it as Scripture. So far, however, we have no such certainty; there are no plausible arguments that any of the spurious Scripture quotations mentioned above definitely come from a non-biblical source. It seems more obvious to assume that the passages mentioned do not intend to quote the Old Testament verbally but only to represent certain general Old Testament ideas, or to make only vague allusions to certain Old Testament passages, as I have indicated.

6.4 The Process of Canonization

6.4.1 Historical and Supra-Historical

Canonization was a *historical* process. At the same time, it was an act of God's providential care, belonging to his work of upholding his creation. Just as he preserves all of his creation, he has also preserved the inspired Scriptures, both in their canonization and in their transmission down through the centuries, and later by publishers and printers. Especially the faithfulness of Jewish people must be mentioned here; as Paul says, "[T]he Jews were entrusted with the oracles of God" (Rom. 3:2). Particularly through the Dead Sea Scrolls, we know now what a faithful work hundreds of godly Jews have performed, at least until the invention of printing.

In this sense of a divine work of preservation, canonization is also a *supra-historical* process, that is, one that transcends time. Just like revelation and inspiration, canonization has this dual (not dualistic!) aspect: it is a supratemporal act of God, which was manifested in the course of certain temporal-historical processes, in which godly Jews in particular have played an essential role.

To a certain extent, the view presented here can be compared with that of Fritz Buri, who emphasized that the notion of the canon must be distinguished sharply, on the one hand, from the idea of a strictly historically established fact, and on the other hand, from the reduction of the canon to some supernatural miracle.[44] Buri rightly argued that, in the former case, the canon would then no longer be an object of faith, while in the latter case, any historical investigation of the process of canonization is excluded *a priori*.

The process of canonization was very important for the unity of the early church. There may have been differences in the interpretation of the Bible, and indeed, such differences soon arose between East and West. But at least Christians agreed on the acceptable content of the Bible: the sixty-six books of the Old and the New Testaments.

6.4.2 The Old Testament

As far as the Old Testament was concerned, there was scarcely a problem because the Israelites had formed a relatively small and close community. Their books had not originated in a widely extended part of the ancient world. For the Jews, problems arose only after Jerusalem had been destroyed by the Romans in AD 70, and the Jewish community had been dispersed throughout all the nations of the world. Only then was the need for a formal canon of the Tanakh experienced, also in order to clearly delineate such a canon with respect to a great number of books written by Jewish authors that confessed Jesus. The New Testament writers were all Jews (Matthew, Mark, John, Paul, James, Peter, Jude, and the unknown author of the letter to the Hebrews), except Luke, but presumably he had already been a Jewish proselyte before he learned about

---

44. Buri (1956, 417).

Jesus (see §6.8.3).

All these authors who confessed Jesus wrote with the greatest respect about Scripture (the Tanakh), but also referred to some of their own writings as Scripture (see §6.2.2). To Jews who did not believe in Jesus, this must have been unbearable (at least as far as they were aware of it). The rabbis taught that after Malachi, no writings, even if they had been composed by very godly Jews, could be accepted as Scripture (see §§6.2.1 and 6.6.1).[45] This was true for the apocryphal books — in Jewish eyes it was even more true for the writings of the New Testament. Books had to be prophetic, and the last recognized prophet was Malachi. The fact that many Old Testament books are anonymous, so that it is difficult to assess their truly prophetic character, hardly constituted a difficulty; the rabbis were convinced of their prophetic origin — and so am I (see also §6.9.3.)

Christians had no difficulty at all accepting the Jewish canon of the Tanakh. Although the Roman Catholic Church later accepted the so-called deuterocanonical books as sacred (actually not before the Council of Trent in 1546; see §6.7.3), Jews and Protestants have always agreed on the Old Testament canon.

Interestingly, the early Christians never regarded the New Testament writings as additions to the Tanakh. On the contrary, they clearly distinguished the Old Testament from what they called the New Testament. This is clear already with the apostle Paul: "[T]o this day, when they [i.e., non-Jesus-believing Jews] read the old covenant [NKJV: Old Testament], that same veil [on non-Jesus-believing Jewish faces] remains unlifted, because only through Christ is it taken away" (2 Cor. 3:14). This verse certainly helped the early church to develop the habit of calling the Tanakh the "Old Testament." This was, so to speak, the collection of sacred books connected with the old (Sinaitic) covenant. Church father Tertullian

---

45. Cf. note 22.

(c. 208) wrote about "the two testaments of the law and the gospel" and "the Old and the New Testaments."[46]

6.4.3 The New Testament

The need for a formal New Testament canon was much greater for the widely dispersed Christians than the need for a formal Old Testament canon had been for the Jews. Let me mention here six reasons for such a need.[47]

(a) One cause of this need was that in many churches, especially in the East, certain books circulated that were highly respected but spurious; therefore, they were rejected by many other churches. The appreciation for these books explains why they are found in certain ancient Bible manuscripts such as the Codex Sinaiticus. Some manuscripts have a (pseudepigraphic) third letter by Paul to the Corinthians, or a letter to the Laodiceans. For the unity of the early church, it was important to reach agreement on what were to be considered the inspired books of the New Testament.

(b) A second cause of the need for a formal New Testament canon was the heretical canon of the Gnostic Marcion of Sinope (c. AD 140), who rejected the Old Testament, and limited the New Testament to Luke (which he called the *Evangelicon*) and the Pauline (except the pastoral) letters (which he called the *Apostolicon*). This implied a New Testament of only eleven books, which Marcion further purged of elements that did not agree with his views. At least, Marcion has had the merit of forcing the early church to form their thoughts about the real canon. Also the flood of Gnostic "gospels" and similar writings forced the church to confess the canon.

(c) There was also the missionary need to translate the Bible into other languages. The most ancient translations, those in Syriac and in Latin, date from the first half of the second century; the translations into Coptic (Bohairic and Sahidic), Ethiopian, Old Nubian, and Georgian are ancient. The first

---

46. *Against Marcion* III.14 and IV.6.
47. See Buri (1956, 409–10).

The Canon of Scripture

Germanic language into which the Bible was translated was Gothic (the fourth century translation of Wulfila or Ulfilas). The need for translations raised the question *what* books had to be translated, that is, which books were canonical.

(d) Almost from the beginning, there was the need for not only reading the New Testament but for expounding it. The earliest—what we would call today—Christian theologians (after the Apostolic Fathers), such as Justin Martyr, Irenaeus, Tertullian, Hippolytus, Cyprian, and the School of Alexandria (led by Clement and Origen), had to have a clear understanding of what was to be expounded, that is, what was Word of God, and what was not. Many of them indeed explicitly referred to this question.

(e) During the last great persecution of Christians under the Romans (beginning of the fourth century), Emperor Diocletian commanded the destruction of all New Testament writings.[48] To this end, all churches had to surrender their sacred scrolls. Christians considered such surrender to be direct apostasy from God, and therefore tried to mislead the authorities with other Christian, non-canonical books, hoping that the authorities would not notice the difference. It made the Christians themselves more aware of the distinction between canonical and non-canonical books.

(f) Less than a quarter of a century later, Emperor Constantine the Great instructed the Christian scholar Eusebius of Caesarea to make "fifty copies of the sacred (or holy) Scriptures."[49] This commission again demanded a careful sorting of the Christian writings, which by that time were already numerous. Such Bibles could be produced only on the basis of clear criteria for identifying which books were canonical, and which were not. These criteria will be investigated in §§6.6-6.10.

---

48. Eusebius, *Historia Ecclesiastica* VIII.2.4.
49. Schaff and Wace (1976, 549).

6.5 Ordering

6.5.1 Two Canons

It is remarkable that the Jewish people have left to us two canons: the one of the Hebrew Bible and the one of the ancient Greek translation of it: the Septuagint. The former contains the following order, as indicated in the acronym "TaNaKh": the T stands for the *Torah* (the Law, the Pentateuch), the N for *Nebi'im* (Prophets), and the K(h) for *Ketubim* (Writings):

I. The *Torah* (the five books of Moses).
II. The *Nebi'im* (the Prophets):
    A. The Former Prophets (four parts: Josh., Judg., Sam., Kings),
    B. The Later Prophets (four parts: Isa., Jer., Ezek., and the Dodekapropheton: Hos. - Mal.).
III. The *Ketubim* (the Writings):
    A. Poetic books (three parts: Ps., Job, Prov.),
    B. The Five Scrolls (*Megillot*) (five parts: Song, Ruth, Lam., Esther, Eccl.),[50]
    C. Post-exilic historical books (three parts: Dan., Ezra-Neh., Chron.).

Notice the interesting numerical order: 5 - 4 - 4 - 3 - 5 - 3, which is two times three, two times four, and two times five books: a total of twenty-four (if one takes for the Torah three books — Gen., Exod.-Num., and Deut. — then the series is 3 - 4 - 4 - 3 - 5 - 3, which is three times three, two times four, and one time five books: a total of twenty-two).

In the Septuagint, the order was changed significantly (in our eyes rather arbitrarily), which is of practical importance because this is the very order that has been adopted in the

---

50. These books form a group on their own because these are the ones that are read at Jewish festival times: *Pesach* (Easter), *Shavuot* (Pentecost), 9th of Av, *Purim*, and *Sukkoth* (Feast of Booths), respectively (at *Yom Kippur*, the book of Jonah is read).

Christian Bible:

I. The *Pentateuch* (the five books of Moses),
II. The *historical books* (twelve parts: Josh., Judg., Ruth, 1/2 Sam., 1/2 Kings, 1/2 Chron., Ezra, Neh., Esther),
III. The *poetic books* (five parts: Job, Ps., Prov., Eccl., Song),
IV. The *prophetic books*,
    A. The *Major Prophets* (five parts: Isa., Jer., Lam., Ezek., Dan.),
    B. The *Minor Prophets* (twelve parts: Hos. – Mal.).

Notice again the interesting numerical order: 5 - 12 - 5 - 5 -12, which is three times five and two times twelve books: a total of thirty-nine books. Of course, if we take some books (Sam., Kings, Chron., Ezra-Neh., the Dodekapropheton) together, we will again arrive at the number twenty-four.

6.5.2 The Old Testament Canon in the New Testament

Although the early Christians, beginning with Jerome in the Vulgate, decided to follow the order of the Septuagint, it is apparent from the New Testament that the earliest Christians did *not* follow the order of the Septuagint but rather that of the Hebrew Bible. We know this from at least two references.

(a) Luke 24:44 speaks of "the Law of Moses and the Prophets and the Psalms [i.e., the first and largest book of the *Ketubim*]." Here, all the prophetic books precede the book of the Psalms, whereas in the Septuagint the Latter Prophets come after the Psalms.

(b) In Matthew 23:35 and Luke 11:51, the Old Testament martyrs are summarized as a group ranging from Abel to Zechariah. This seems to be the Zechariah of whom we read in 2 Chronicles 24:21–22, which seems to presuppose the order of the Hebrew Bible: from Genesis to Chronicles. Matthew

23:35 speaks of Zechariah the son of Barachiah, though. This is either a confusion with the Zechariah of Zechariah 1:1[51] — interestingly, some manuscripts of Matthew omit the phrase "the son of Barachiah" — or Jesus really means the prophet Zechariah, whose supposed martyrdom is not narrated in the Old Testament, however.[52] In the latter case, the order of the Septuagint would be presupposed.

In a certain sense, the last position in the canon is a natural place for Chronicles. This post-exilic book is a kind of summary of the Old Testament: it begins with Adam (1 Chron. 1:1), and it ends with this significant statement: "The Lord, the God of heaven, has given me [i.e., the Persian king Cyrus] all the kingdoms of the earth, and he has charged me to build him a house at Jerusalem, which is in Judah. Whoever is among you of all his people, may the Lord his God be with him. Let him go up" (2 Chron. 36:23). The latter phrase is Hebrew *wey`aal*, from the root `-l-h, "to go up." From this verb, also the word *`aliyyah* is derived, which today is used for the "going up" (emigration) of Jews to Israel (*aliyah*). Thus, the Hebrew Bible ends with an appeal to return to the promised land, an appeal that, in my view, has great eschatological significance.[53] In Isaiah 44:28; 45:1-4, 13; and 46:10, king Cyrus is a Messianic figure, a type of him who will rebuild Jerusalem, and even the temple, and will restore the people of Israel in their own country. Thus, the end of the Hebrew Bible refers to the end times, the Messiah, and the Messianic kingdom.

In fact, *both* orders of the Old Testament books are interesting because of their respective endings.[54] The Septuagint, and thus also the Christian Old Testament, ends as follows: "Behold, I will send you Elijah the prophet before the great and awesome day of the Lord comes. And he will turn the hearts of fathers to their children and the hearts of children

---

51. France (2007, 880–81).
52. Archer Jr. (1982, 337–38).
53. Cf. Ouweneel (2012, especially chapters 7 and 13).
54. Bryan (2002, 77–78).

to their fathers, lest I come and strike the land with a decree of utter destruction" (Mal. 4:5-6). The reference here is not primarily to the second coming of Christ, but to his first coming: Elijah appears in the person of John the Baptist (cf. Matt. 11:14; 17:12; Luke 1:17). However, there is also an eschatological fulfillment of this prophecy (cf. John 1:21, 25; Rev. 11:1-13). If it is a reference to John the Baptist, the Gospels tie in seamlessly with Malachi 4. Both the Old Testament (in whatever order) and the New Testament point to the same Messianic end times.

6.6 Criteria of Canonicity

6.6.1 The Canon Determines the Canon

Now what exactly are the rules with which the measurements of the sacred books were taken in order to identify whether they were canonical (answering to the rule), that is, could be included in the collection that we now call the Bible?[55] Various older suggestions with regard to such criteria are only of subordinate importance; that is, they have meaning only in connection with criteria to be mentioned later in this chapter.

(a) The *age* of a book (according to Joh. Gottfried Eichhorn).[56] On the one hand, his criterion is understandable: for the Old Testament, the criterion was that a book could not be later than the prophetic period, that is, could not reach any further than Malachi, the last of the prophets (see §§6.2.1 and 6.4.2). For the New Testament, the criterion was that a book in principle could not be younger than the apostolic period: the books that had not been written by Paul or some of the twelve, that is, had been written by Mark, Luke, James, and Jude, were accepted because they stemmed from the immediate apostolic circle, so to speak. Some of these books were accepted relatively shortly after they had been written — that

---

55. Gk. *biblia*, "books," from *biblion*, "book" (Luke 4:17, 20; John 20:30; 21:25; Gal. 3:10; 2 Tim. 4:13; Heb. 9:19; Rev. 1:11; 5:1-9; 6:14; 20:12). The Bible is a collection of sixty-six *biblia*.

56. Eichhorn (1820).

is, at a *young* age—because they were obviously prophetic or apostolic in nature.

On the other hand, some Israelite books were *not* included in the canon despite their advanced age. These books are now lost; that is, they were not omitted from the canon because they got lost, but they got lost because they were not considered to be canonical. Some of these books are the following:[57]

(1) The book written as a memorial of the war against Amalek (Exod. 17:14).
(2) The "Book of the Wars of the LORD" (Num. 21:14).
(3) The "Book of Jashar" (or "Book of the Upright," YLT; Josh. 10:13; 2 Sam. 1:18; cf. §6.3.1).
(4) The book of Samuel about " the rights and duties of the kingship" (1 Sam. 10:25).
(5) The "Book of the Acts of Solomon" (1 Kings 11:41).
(6) The "Book of the Chronicles of the Kings of Israel and Judah" (1 Kings 14:19, 29; 2 Chron. 16:11; 27:7; cf. 24:27; 26:22; 32:32).
(7) The "Chronicles of King David" (1 Chron. 27:24; cf. 29:29).
(8) The "Chronicles of Samuel the seer" (1 Chron. 29:29).
(9) The "Chronicles of Gad the seer" (1 Chron. 29:29).
(10) The "History of Nathan the prophet" (2 Chron. 9:29; cf. 1 Chron. 29:29).
(11) The "Prophecy of Ahijah the Shilonite" (2 Chron. 9:29).
(12) The "Visions of Iddo the seer" (2 Chron. 9:29; cf. 12:15; 13:22).
(13) The "Chronicles of Shemaiah the prophet" (2 Chron. 12:15).
(14) The "Chronicles of Jehu the son of Hanani" (2 Chron. 20:34).

---

57. en.wikipedia.org/wiki/Non-canonical_books_referenced_in_the_Bible.

(15) The "Chronicles of the Seers" (other manuscripts: "of Hozai"; 2 Chron. 33:19).
(16) The "Laments" (2 Chron. 35:25).

(b) *The sacred Hebrew language* of a book (so Ferdinand Hitzig). This criterion cannot be decisive either; on the one hand, certain ancient writings in the sacred Hebrew language were not immediately viewed as canonical (Esther, Prov., Song, Ezek.), or not at all viewed as canonical (Sirach). On the other hand, also certain texts that had been written in Aramaic were included in the canon without translation (see §5.7.3), which, incidentally, for Hitzig was one of the reasons to reject the book of Daniel.[58]

(c) *Agreement with the Torah* (so Gerrit Wildeboer).[59] This criterion is quite insufficient. Of course, the prophetic books and the *Ketubim* are in harmony with the Torah (even though not every critic will agree with this on all points). However, on the one hand, some ancient Jewish books clearly are in harmony with the Torah, and yet are not viewed as canonical but as apocryphal (or at best as deuterocanonical). On the other hand, this criterion does not help us to understand why the Torah itself would be canonical. The latter may be self-evident, but theology has the task of supplying the warrant undergirding any form of (apparent) self-evidence.

(d) It is the same with the argument that books from the New Testament sphere are canonical if they *agree with the Old Testament* (so Albrecht Ritschl).[60] This criterion, too, is quite insufficient. Of course, all New Testament books are in harmony with the Old Testament (even though especially Jewish commentators will strongly argue against this). However, many ancient Christian books clearly are in harmony with the Old Testament, and yet are not viewed as canonical but as apocryphal.

---

58. Hitzig (2010).
59. Wildeboer (1900).
60. Cf. Buri (1956, 416–417).

6.6.2 A Supra-Rational Criterion

I see only one other really useful criterion for identifying a book's canonicity, one that is not of a rational, nor of an irrational, but of a supra-rational nature. This means that the faith of the believer's transcendent heart has heard the transcendent Word of God in the immanent words of the Bible books. That is, people came believingly to the understanding that these books addressed them with unique divine authority, which was explained as the consequence of divine inspiration. This agrees entirely with Jesus' statement in John 10:27, "My sheep hear my voice" — even though we realize that such a criterion always contains a subjective element. For instance, were those who, in early Christian times, viewed the *Didachē* or the *Letter of Barnabas* as canonical, bad sheep of the Good Shepherd?

Perhaps some readers would consider the argument just given to be rather mystical; they would prefer solid rational arguments for canonicity. Such readers must realize that until the Jewish Synod of Jamnia (AD 90), neither the ordinary Jewish people nor their leaders, and subsequently the leaders of Christianity, from the Synod of Rome (382) to that of Hippo (393) and those of Carthage (397 and 419), ever *bestowed* authority upon the Bible books, or ever *established* the canon. The only thing they did was to believingly acknowledge what books *possessed* divine authority. As Herman Bavinck put it, the decisions involving the church's recognition of the canon "were not self-willed, authoritarian acts but merely the codification and registration of the precedents that had long been operating in the churches with respect to these writings."[61] Kurt Aland described the canon as something that grew among believers, and only later was officially legitimized from above.[62]

To state it in my terms, godly Jews and early Christians

---

61. Bavinck (*RD* 1:400).
62. Aland (1962, 18).

knew with their *hearts* that the books concerned were sacred and divine—not because of certain logical-rational arguments. It cannot be proven that certain leaders in the past, during any council or synod, ever determined on their own authority what books had to be included in the canon. At best, they could formally identify what books apparently *did belong* to the canon because of their divine authority, as this was widely acknowledged within the Jewish and the Christian faith community, respectively.

Herbert E. Ryle developed the theory that the Old Testament canon had originated in three stages: the Pentateuch was supposedly declared to be canonical in the fifth century BC, the prophetic writings in the third century BC, while the *Ketubim* were accepted only at the Synod of Jamnia in AD 90), that is, after the rise of Christianity.[63] However, with many arguments, Robert T. Beckwith has made it plausible that the Old Testament could not have been completed any later than in the second century BC, that is, before the rise of various Jewish sects: Pharisees, Sadducees, and Essenes.[64] The reason is that the canon apparently never was an issue between these various sects. At any rate, in the New Testament, virtually every Old Testament book was quoted as divinely authoritative, that is, canonical (see below). Linking his position with the Jewish tradition and the early church, Hendrik J. Koorevaar believed that the Old Testament canon was completed around 400 BC.[65]

Karl Barth wrote about the process of canonization,

> [T]he Bible constitutes itself the Canon. It is the Canon because it imposed itself upon the Church as such, and continually does so. . . . And if we can only register this event (as such) as the reality in which the Church is the Church, nevertheless, when this is done, it is not impossible afterwards, exegetically, to state

---

63. Ryle (1892).
64. Beckwith (1985); cf. Paul et al. (2004, 3–4).
65. H. J. Koorevaar in Nullens (1997, 63–90).

in what this self-imposing consists and how far it sets a limit to the wisdom of our dialogue with ourselves.[66]

I would formulate it this way: though this process of imposing as such is transcendent and supra-rational, theology still has the task of supplying a logical-rational warrant for it *a posteriori*.

Otto Weber, too, emphasized the canonical authority of Scripture over the church—not the other way round[67]—although he did not go as far as Barth did.[68] Oscar Cullmann, too, stated that people cannot impose a certain canonical authority upon the Bible, but the authority of the canon must instead be derived from the Bible itself.[69] Again, I would formulate it this way: canonical authority is not imposed but submitted to. This is basically a supra-rational surrender of the heart, even if the reasons for doing so can be rationally analyzed *a posteriori*. This will be explained further in the next section.

6.6.3 Again, the Hermeneutical Circle

In fact, what we are encountering here once again is the hermeneutical circle that we discussed in §1.7. This time, we could formulate it as follows: the canonical books themselves determine what is canonical, and what is not. The only action that God's providence has assigned to humans in this regard is to believingly recognize and acknowledge such divinely authoritative books. Humans are called upon to receive the Word of God (1 Thess. 1:6; 2:13), not to judge it—but such acceptance is possible only if they indeed recognize the Word as *Word*.

It is important to emphasize that this recognition of the Word being Word is not founded upon some vague intuition.

---

66. Barth (*CD* I/1:107).
67. Weber (1981, 247–48, 252–54).
68. Ibid., 251.
69. Cullmann (1967, 270–77).

As I argued above, the acknowledgement of the Bible as the Word of God is based upon a supra-rational faith, which is something essentially different from a vaguely mystical or irrational faith. On the one hand, this means that such a transcendent-religious conviction of the heart can never be based upon, or derived from, rational arguments *a priori*. In other words, this faith does not arise in the heart because a person became convinced by certain logical arguments. Rather, God was speaking to the heart, and the heart was answering, "Speak, LORD, for your servant hears" (cf. 1 Sam. 3:9–10).

On the other hand, such a supra-rational faith can and must certainly receive a valid *warrant a posteriori*, as Barth indicated in the quotation given above: theology has the task of supplying the warrant for supra-rational things in a logical-analytical-rational-theoretical way. Faith in its transcendent-religious sense recognizes the Bible books as having divine authority, and therefore as being of divine origin, that is, as having been inspired. As Fritz Buri put it, "The canon represents such a complex, historical and dogmatic magnitude, which at the same time, other than historical or dogmatic, can be confessed only in an act of faith."[70] Faith knows these books supra-rationally *and* can supply a rational warrant for this knowledge. On the one hand, if the latter were not possible, faith would not be supra-rational but irrational (mystical). But on the other hand, this rational warrant for faith does not mean that faith as such is also rational. Just as faith itself is supra-rational, the inspiration and divine authority of the Bible books are also supra-rational matters of the heart. However, just as reason is an immanent function of the believing heart, and this heart expresses itself in the rational function, supra-rational faith can adduce rational criteria for its supra-rational convictions.

It is now time to explain these rational criteria in greater detail.

---

70. Buri (1956, 411).

6.7 The Question of the *Notae Canonicitatis*
6.7.1 Divine Providence and Church Responsibility

Of course, there has been much discussion concerning the so-called *notae canonicitatis* ("marks of canonicity") for the very reason mentioned: the problem of *accepting* what is *a priori* canonical *versus establishing a posteriori* what is canonical. Frederik W. Grosheide wished to avoid going in the latter direction, and therefore rejected the entire idea of "criteria" because these seem to suggest that the church would have the authority to judge the canonicity of a book.[71] In his view, we can do nothing but *receive* in faith the canonical books as God gives them. Compare the word *recipimus* ("we receive") in the Latin text of Belgic Confession Article 5:

> We receive all these books and these only as holy and canonical, for the regulating, founding, and establishing of our faith. And we believe without a doubt all things contained in them — not so much because the church receives and approves them as such but above all because the Holy Spirit testifies in our hearts that they are from God, and also because they prove themselves to be from God. For even the blind themselves are able to see that the things predicted in them do happen.

I do agree with the intention behind Grosheide's argument, as I agree with Article 5. Yet, I would state, with G. C. Berkouwer,[72] that the church — or should I not rather say theologians? — in order to be *able* to receive in faith (supra-rationally) the canonical books, should be capable of (rationally) indicating the differences between such a book and a non-canonical book. Otherwise, we run the risk of falling into mysticism. The *notae canonicitatis* are definitely a useful and necessary field of study; however, they do function *a posteriori*, not *a priori*.

Grosheide did speak, however, of a "recognition" of the

---

71. Grosheide (1935, 17–28).
72. Berkouwer (1975, 71–72).

canon,[73] and admitted that we can distinguish in history certain "factors" that have served "as means in God's hand" to bring the church to its confession of the canon.[74] He even admitted that these factors were sometimes identical with what others had called the marks of canonicity (Lat. *notae canonicitatis*).[75] But in this case, the entire problem has been reduced to a matter of definition. The *notae canonicitatis* must not be rejected but must be interpreted simply as criteria by which the early church was able to distinguish canonical from non-canonical books; that is, to supply a rationally valid warrant *a posteriori* for their *a priori* supra-rational belief about the canon.

Of course, this does not answer every question. This is because we cannot point out the precise boundary between a church that *passively* receives and acknowledges the canon (which does not exclude the church's extensive deliberations) and a church that *actively* identifies what books are to be included in the canon (which does not exclude God's guidance in the matter). Is not this entire distinction actually a false dilemma? As to inspiration, we will see that the deliberations, preparations, and decisions of the Bible writers do not at all exclude divine inspiration. In a similar way, the deliberations of the church fathers and the councils do not at all exclude divine providence regarding the canon. This transcendent providence of God was manifested within immanent-historical processes, both in the church's passive receiving and in the church's active identifying of the canon, such that the strict distinction between the two is ultimately irrelevant.

God's providence regarding the canonization process has

---

73. Grosheide (1935, 87, 132).
74. Ibid., 132. Cf. Kuyper (1909, 3:28), who spoke of a "motive" in the church fathers that took care of putting a book in the list, and emphasized that the fathers felt the need of a *principium canonicitatis* or "principle of canonicity"; 28, 41), which, however, in no way conflicted with the evident providence of God.
75. Grosheide (1935, 133).

been referred to as a "very special providence" (Lat. *providentia specialissima*), usually described as an "act of God concerning the canon" (Lat. *actio Dei circa canonem*). Apparently, we cannot turn to Scripture for hints regarding this very special providence. Thus, it is understandable that Herman N. Ridderbos rejected such an appeal to a special providence[76] because we encounter here a desire to identify *a posteriori* an authority that might legitimize the canon.[77] The historical, sometimes rather capricious course of the canonization process clearly shows how careful we should be in trying to derive from divine providence a *ground* for the acknowledgment of the canon.

The ground for such an acknowledgment does not lie somewhere *beyond* and *outside* the canon, neither in (transcendent) divine providence nor in (immanent) church history, but only in the *a priori* of the canon itself.[78] No theological theory concerning the canonization process can and should suppress the (pre-theoretical) *belief* in the canon. Such theories do not constitute any logical proof for the Christian belief in the canon; on the contrary, this belief constitutes the supra-logical proof for canon theories. Christians do not put their confidence in historical arguments concerning the canon—which belong to the subject-side of reality—but rather in the normative structure of the canon as such, that is, on the law-side of reality. This involves the divine authority that not only the early church encountered in the canon but that present-day believers, too, believingly find in the canon. This does not render the acknowledgment by the early church irrelevant; on the contrary, in the bond of faith we know ourselves to be united with the early Christians in the recognition of the divine authority of the Scriptures.[79]

---

76. Ridderbos (1988, 34–35).
77. Cf. Wentsel (1981, 229 and further).
78. Ridderbos (1988, 35–36).
79. As to the specifically Roman Catholic view, which maintains the notion of divine providence in the canonization process but also assigns to the church a great role in this process, and also newer views of the relation-

6.7.2 The Deuterocanonical Books

A few of the apocryphal books have been labeled as deuterocanonical by the Roman Catholic Church. The word *deutero-* (Gk. "second") does not mean here "second-rate" but "added later to the canon."[80] Thus, with respect to the supposed divine authority of the books, this designation makes no essential difference. "Apocryphal" means "secret," especially in the sense of "[book] of unknown origin." The term seems to have been used for the first time by Jerome.[81] He stated that they had to be read for the edification of the people, but not to confirm the authority of church doctrines.[82] Such recommendations were included in the first editions of the King James Version (1611) and the Dutch States Translation (1637) as well: the books are edifying but have not been divinely inspired. In the words of the Belgic Confession (Art. 6):

> All of which [apocryphal books] the church may read and take instruction from, so far as they agree with the canonical books; but they are far from having such power and efficacy that we may from their testimony confirm any point of faith or of the Christian religion; much less may they be used to detract from the authority of the other, that is, the sacred books.[83]

The deuterocanonical books are not part of the Jewish canon, but among the rabbis they do have a certain—if not formal, then at least moral—authority. They contain the following twenty-two books or parts of books. None of them is viewed as canonical by any Protestant denomination, but they are viewed as such by some other denominations (NPC = non-Protestant churches; books in **bold** are labeled as deuterocanonical by the Roman Catholic Church; these are also

---

ship between church and canon, see Berkouwer (1966, 97–108).
80. On this matter, see Bryan (2002, 76 and further).
81. *Prologus Sancti Hieronymi in Libro Regum* 54.
82. *Prologus Hieronymi in Libris Salomonis* 19–21.
83. *RC* 2:427.

the books that have been included in the Septuagint):[84]

1. **Prayer of Manasseh**: further acknowledged only by the Orthodox churches, but it does constitute an attachment in Vulgate (Vulg.) and Septuagint (LXX).

Additional Ezra (of Esdras) books:[85]

2. 1 Ezra/Esdras (LXX: Esdras A; Vulg.: 3 Esdras; Slavonic: 2 Esdras; also called Greek Ezra/Esdras): acknowledged by some Orthodox churches.
3. 2 Ezra/Esdras (Vulg.: 4 Esdras, also called Latin Ezra/Esdras), divided as follows:
    a. Chapters 1-2: also distinguished separately as 5 Ezra/Esdras.
    b. Chapters 3-14: also called 4 Ezra/Esdras, Jewish Apocalypse of Ezra/Esdras or Apocalyptic Ezra/Esdras: acknowledged by some Orthodox churches.
    c. Chapters 15-16: also distinguished separately as 6 Ezra/Esdras.
4. **Additions to Esther** ("Greek Esther"): acknowledged by all NPC except by the Coptic Church.
5. **Tobit**: idem.
6. **Judith**: idem.
7. Psalm 151: acknowledged only by Orthodox churches.[86]
8. **Wisdom of Solomon**: acknowledged by all NPC except by the Coptic Church.[87]

---

84. See en.wikipedia.org/wiki/Biblical_canon.
85. See en.wikipedia.org/wiki/Esdras.
86. See the text on http://bible.oremus.org/?ql=364191858.
87. Ratzinger (2011, 210) mentions an interesting New Testament allusion to Wisdom 2:18 ("[I]f the righteous man is God's son, he will help him, and will deliver him from the hand of his adversaries," RSV), namely, in Matt. 27:42-43 ("He is the King of Israel; let him come down now from the cross, and we will believe in him. He trusts in God; let God deliver him

9. **Sirach** (or **Ecclesiasticus**): idem.
10. **Baruch**: idem.
11. **Letter of Jeremiah**: idem (in Catholic Bibles: Baruch 6; in the Ethiopian Bible: remainder of Jer.).
12. 4 Baruch: acknowledged only by the Ethiopian Church (remainder of Baruch).
13. **Additions to Daniel** (Prayer of the three men in the fire, Susanna, Bel and the dragon): acknowledged by all NPC except by the Coptic Church.
14. **1 Maccabees**: acknowledged by all NPC except by the Coptic and the Ethiopian Churches.
15. **2 Maccabees**: idem.
16. 3 Maccabees: acknowledged only by some Orthodox churches.
17. 4 Maccabees: idem.
18. 1 Enoch: acknowledged only by the Ethiopian Church.
19. Jubilees: idem.
20-22. 1-3 Meqabyan:[88] idem.

6.7.3 Formal Recognitions

In several denominations, *formal* recognition of the canon occurred relatively late; for the Roman Catholic Church, this occurred at the Council of Trent (1546), especially after the Lutherans had rejected certain books (which they called apocryphal, by the Catholics deuterocanonical). The Reformed Protestants in the Netherlands formally indirectly identified the canon through their acceptance of the Belgic Confession (Art. 6; 1561), the Church of England (the Anglicans) did so in the Thirty-Nine Articles (1563), the Reformed Protestants in Great Britain did so in the Westminster Confession of Faith (1647), and the Orthodox Church did so during the Synod of

---

now, if he desires him. For he said, 'I am the Son of God'").

88. I.e., "Maccabees," but the protagonists have nothing to do with those in 1 and 2 Maccabees.

Jerusalem (1672).

Without doubt, the apocryphal books have an important historical-theological function because they fill the gap of four hundred years between the Old and the New Testaments. They give us some insight into the theological developments within Judaism during this period. This can help us to understand certain doctrines in Judaism during the New Testament period, especially in the field of eschatology (Messianic expectation, the notion of the "Son of Man"). Therefore, theologians regularly refer to these books, not necessarily as part of Holy Scripture, but as part of the Jewish tradition, which was one of the constitutive factors that shaped Christian thought.

As far as the New Testament is concerned, the situation is far less complicated because there are indeed many apocryphal books belonging to the world of the New Testament, but these have generally been rejected as non-canonical. An exception is the apocryphal book called the Acts of Paul, which is accepted as canonical by the Ethiopian Church. Conversely, the Assyrian Church, which has a Nestorian orientation, still rejects the canonicity of 2 Peter, 2 and 3 John, Jude, and Revelation (but views them as apocryphal). For the rest, there is universal agreement on the New Testament canon. On theological grounds, Martin Luther doubted the canonicity of Hebrews, James, Jude, and Revelation, but he did include them in the canon, as was clear from his German translation of the entire New Testament. The entire Lutheran tradition after him did so, too (cf. §6.12.2).

6.8 The Lingual Criterion

6.8.1 What Is It?

We can supply a theoretical warrant for the faith criteria mentioned in §6.6 by reminding the reader of what was said about the way we can speak about the Word of God in its eternal, transcendent sense: with the help of modal ideas (§5.10). Here I am making a selection of some particularly important modal ideas in this respect: the physical-biotic, the logical-analytical,

The Canon of Scripture

the historical-formative, the lingual, the social, the economic, the aesthetic, the juridical, the ethical, and the pistical ideas. I will change their modal order somewhat in order to underscore the most important canonical criteria.

The first and foremost criterion of canonicity is the inner faith conviction that the Word addressing people through the Bible comes from God. It is the persuasion that it is truly "word" or "speech" of God, "that goes out from my mouth" (Isa. 55:11; cf. Deut. 8:3). It is the modal-lingual idea of the "Word" that characterizes this criterion; therefore, I call it the *lingual* criterion. In practice, this means that the Bible writer must be acknowledged as someone who has spoken the words of God, or who has passed on the words that God spoke to him. Such a person is by definition a *prophet* (spokesman) of God, or an *apostle* (messenger, person sent forth, missionary) of Christ. In the next chapters dealing with inspiration, we will see that it does not matter if, in a certain Bible passage, God is directly speaking to people, or people are speaking about God, or people are speaking *to* God, as in the Psalms. In the written record of these things, it is always God addressing people.

Otto Weber called this the *criterion of originality*;[89] one could say, of authenticity. If a person had been acknowledged as a prophet of God, it was obvious that his prophetic writings had not been produced by human will but from being carried along by the Holy Spirit (2 Pet. 1:20-21; cf. the parallel in John 1:13, ". . . not of blood nor of the will of the flesh nor of the will of man, but of God"). In former times, *God* (Luke 1:70; Acts 3:18, 21; Heb. 1:1), that is, the *Holy Spirit*, spoke to the fathers through the prophets (Mark 12:36; Acts 1:16; 4:25; 28:25; 1 Pet. 1:10-12; 2 Pet. 1:20-21). This referred to the Old Testament. And when a New Testament book had been written by an apostle of Jesus Christ—Paul or one of the twelve (Mark 3:16)—it had to be accepted as canonical without fur-

---

89. Weber (1981, 258).

ther ado (cf., e.g., 1 Cor. 11:2; Gal. 1:1, 8-9, 11-12; 1 Thess. 2:13; 2 Thess. 2:2).

Conversely, on the one hand, we find that, to be sure, some apostolic letters may have been lost, such as the one or even two additional letters that Paul, according to some (but definitely not with certainty[90]), wrote to the Corinthian believers. However, no case is known in which a truly prophetic or apostolic book was *rejected* as non-canonical. Colossians 4:16 does refer to a letter that Paul had written to the Laodiceans, but presumably this is not a lost letter at all but rather the letter that we know as Ephesians, which possibly was a more general, circular letter.[91]

On the other hand, books that did not possess this prophetic or apostolic character were rejected outright by believers (2 Thess. 2:2; also cf. 1 John 2:18-19; 4:1-3; 2 Cor. 11:13). In some cases, the apostle Paul marked his own letters — which were often dictated (Rom. 16:22, "I Tertius, who wrote this letter...") — with his own signature to underscore their authenticity (1 Cor. 16:21; Gal. 6:11; Col. 4:18; 2 Thess. 3:17; Philemon 1:19). Of course, today such a special criterion of canonicity would no longer have any value because the *autographa* (the original manuscripts) no longer exist. And even if they did, we would no longer be able to recognize the handwriting of the apostle.[92] But this does not change the principle that Paul thought it essential to mark his letters as authentic.

6.8.2 The Old Testament

Seen in this light, we could state with caution that we find only prophetic books in the Old Testament. First, we have the five books of Moses, who was a prophet (Deut. 18:15, 18; 34:10). He is also called a "man of God" (Deut. 33:1; Josh. 14:6; 1 Chron. 23:14; 2 Chron. 30:16; Ezra 3:2; Ps. 90:1); such a person was always a prophet (cf., e.g., 1 Sam. 3:20-21 with

---

90. See the discussion in Guthrie (1990, 424–39).
91. See Bruce (1984, 184–85, 230–31); Medema (1991, 15–17).
92. Cf. Bruce (1988a, 255–56).

9:6-10). Next, we have the "former prophets," as Jewish tradition calls them. According to an ancient assumption—but not much more than that—these books were written, at least in part, by Joshua (cf. Josh. 18:8; 24:25), Samuel, Gad, Nathan (cf. 1 Sam. 10:25; 1 Chron. 29:29), Jeremiah, Ezra, or by prophetic men from their immediate surroundings. Or these books were composed later by drawing from writings left by these and other prophetic men. However, to a great extent we can only speculate on these things. Then we have the books of the latter prophets: Isaiah, Jeremiah, Ezekiel, and the twelve Minor Prophets (in the Jewish canon, Daniel is not part of this group). Our knowledge about these is much less certain than many would lead us to believe.[93]

Finally, there is the category of the Writings (*Ketubim*), which are for the most part also prophetic, even though they may not have been written by professional prophets. The authors were king David, who was also a prophet (2 Sam. 23:1-3; Matt. 27:35 KJV; Acts 2:29-30), and in the book of the Psalms we meet Asaph (Ps. 73), Heman (Ps. 88), Ethan (Ps. 89), Moses (Ps. 90), Solomon (Ps. 73 and 127), and the sons of Korah (many Psalms between 42 and 88). Apart from the Judean kings David and Solomon, these were all Levites; we read of them that they "*prophesied* [i.e., here: magnified God in ecstasy[94]] with lyres, with harps, and with cymbals" (1 Chron. 25:1). Further we find the political official Daniel, whom Jesus called "Daniel the prophet" (Matt. 24:14).[95]

King Solomon is the only one for whose prophetic status we have no direct or indirect indication. He was, however, one of the "wise men" (1 Kings 4:29-34), of whom it is known that they stood in a close relationship to the prophets. As Jer-

---

93. E.g., McDonald (2006, 32) says that the Bible was written over a period of 1500 years by forty different writers—which suggests that these authors would be known with any certainty.
94. See the Heb. root *n-b-'* in various lexica.
95. The so-called Florilegium (4Q174) also speaks of the "book of Daniel the prophet"; see Flint (1997).

emiah's opponents said, "Come, let us make plots against Jeremiah, for the law shall not perish from the priest, nor counsel from the *wise*, nor the word from the *prophet*" (Jer. 18:18). Jesus also linked the two categories: "I send you prophets and wise men and scribes" (Matt. 23:34). As a wise man, Solomon belonged to the circle of the prophets. Of course, Solomon's authorship of Proverbs, Ecclesiastes, and Song of Solomon has been heavily disputed; but see, for instance, Ronald K. Harrison for an excellent consideration of the arguments for and against.[96]

The prophetic character of the *Ketubim* indirectly follows from the fact that the main division of the Old Testament was not threefold (law, prophets, and writings; cf. Luke 24:44) but twofold: law and prophets. During and after the Babylonian exile, people spoke, though not yet conjoining them, of the "law (of Moses)" and "the prophets" (Neh. 9:14, 29-30; Dan. 9:2, 6, 11; Zech. 7:12), and this is the description that we find almost everywhere in the New Testament (Matt. 5:17-18; 22:40; Luke 16:16, 29, 31; 24:27; Acts 13:15; 24:14; 26:22; 28:23; Rom. 3:21). Thus, as far as we can assess, the Old Testament contains exclusively books that were written by men with a prophetic calling and capacity, that is, who were "carried along" by the Holy Spirit (2 Pet. 1:21).

6.8.3 The New Testament

The books of the New Testament were also written by men with a special prophetic calling and capacity. These were in the first place the apostles. Of the eight or nine New Testament authors—the number is imprecise because the letter to the Hebrews is anonymous—three belonged to "the twelve": twelve disciples or apostles of Christ (Luke 6:13-15): Matthew (one book), John (four books), and Peter (two books). Paul was the great apostle to the Gentiles, called by Jesus Christ apart from the twelve (see, e.g., Rom. 1:5; 1 Tim. 2:7; 2 Tim. 1:11). The letter writer James, the brother of Jesus, was also

---

96. Harrison (1969, 1013-18, 1049-52, 1072-78).

known as an apostle (Gal. 1:19). Some believe, but probably incorrectly, that he was James the son of Alphaeus, that is, one of the twelve (Matt. 10:3; Acts 1:13). The letter writer Jude was a brother of James (Jude 1). Some believe that he is the apostle Judas[97] son of James mentioned in Luke 6:16. He was likely the Judas who belonged to the circle of the apostles (cf. Acts 15:22, 27, 32).

The Evangelists Mark and Luke were not called "apostles," but they were close friends and co-workers of the apostles;[98] Mark had this position with regard to Peter (cf. 1 Pet. 5:13)[99] and Paul (2 Tim. 4:11; Philemon 1:24), and Luke with regard to Paul (ibid.; cf. also the "we" passages in Acts: 16:1-17; 20:5-21:18; 27:1-28:16). If the title of "apostle" was so easily applied to Paul's co-worker Barnabas (Acts 14:14), it can be said of Mark and Luke as well that they were apostolic figures. (Remarkably enough, Luke was not a Jew,[100] but according to Jerome, he was a proselyte before he came to know Jesus.[101])

Because of the importance of apostolic authorship, it is all the more remarkable that the four Gospels in the New Testament are anonymous; it is only through early tradition that we know the names of their authors. In opposition to this, there is a long list of pseudepigraphic "gospels" from the second and third centuries that explicitly claim to have been written by apostles and other eye witnesses (Thomas, Peter, Mary Magdalene, Judas, Nicodemus, Barnabas, Gamaliel, Philip, Andrew, Barnabas, Bartholomew; in addition: the Protoevangelium of James, the Infancy Gospel of Thomas, the Gospel

---

97. Both Jude and Judas are *Ioudas* in Greek, i.e., Heb. *Yehudah*.
98. Elsewhere I have defended the view that Mark and Luke (and others) were apostles of a lesser rank; see Ouweneel (2010a, 296–99).
99. As the writer of Mark's Gospel, Mark was called the "interpreter of Peter" (Papias, quoted by Eusebius, *Historia Ecclesiastica* III.39.15).
100. In Col. 4, Paul distinguishes between "men of the circumcision" (i.e., Jews; v. 11) and various Greek brothers, such as Luke (vv. 12–14); the style of his Gospel and of Acts shows that Luke was a native Greek speaker.
101. *Liber Hebraicum Quaestionum in Genesim* 46.

of Pseudo-Matthew, etc.).[102] Apparently, linking a book to an apostle was not a decisive argument for its canonicity, and the absence of such a link was not a decisive argument against canonicity. Moreover, the Gospels of Mark and Luke, and the book of Acts as well, did not appeal to apostolic authority, nor to divine inspiration. We may assume that they were accepted as divinely authoritative, and therefore canonical, simply because they were recognized as reliable witnesses of the redemptive events they report.[103]

An exclusively apostolic authorship was not decisive for accepting a book as canonical, since the Christian church is "built on the foundation of the apostles *and* [New Testament] prophets" (Eph. 2:20; cf. 3:5; 4:11; Luke 11:49; 1 Cor. 12:28-29; Rev. 18:20). Thus, men who themselves were not apostles in the actual sense but did possess a prophetic calling cooperated in building the foundation. Their books may not have come from an apostolic author but they do have apostolic authority and apostolic agreement. It was because of this very demand—the requisite prophetic character of a Bible book—that, for a long time, 2 Peter was reluctantly viewed as canonical. Only when the church fathers had become convinced that the letter was not fake (cf. 2 Pet. 1:1), it received its fixed position in the canon (cf. §6.11.3).

In many respects, the New Testament apostles clearly exhibited the characteristics of the Old Testament prophets.[104] Thus, Paul, too, had a special calling (Acts 22:17-21; 26:16-18; Rom. 1:1; 1 Cor. 1:1; Gal. 1:15-16; cf., e.g., Isa. 6; Jer. 1; Ezek. 1). He spoke of the irresistibility of the divine commission (cf. 1 Cor. 9:16 with Jer. 20:9), the foundation of this commission in his divine calling (Gal. 1; 1 Cor. 9:1), the authority that had been bestowed upon him due to this divine calling (1 Cor. 5:3; 2 Cor. 10:1-6), and so on. In the broad sense of the term, *every* New Testament writer possessed a prophetic character and

---

102. See extensively, en.wikipedia.org/wiki/List_of_Gospels.
103. Cf. Bruce (1988a, 257–58, 265–66).
104. Cf. Weber (1981, 237–38).

calling. In other words, the entire Bible is prophetic according to the original sense of the Greek word *prophētēs*, "spokesman," namely, of God. The words that prophets, as prophets, speak are the words of God himself.

6.9 The Historical-Formative Criterion

6.9.1 Authority

The Word of God consumes like a fire and smashes like a hammer (Jer. 23:39). In other words, it is supreme and irresistible because it manifests God's omnipotence. "Authority" is a historical-formatively delineated concept, as expressed in the intrinsic relationship between the two Greek terms *dynamis* ("power" in the sense of strength) and *exousia* ("power" in the sense of authority).[105] The latter term comprises the meanings of "power" (e.g., Acts 26:18; Jude 25; Rev. 9:19; 20:6) and "authority" (e.g., Mark 11:28-29, 33; Luke 7:8; 9:14; 2 Cor. 10:8; 13:10). In some passages, these meanings can scarcely be distinguished (Matt. 9:8; 10:1; 28:18; Luke 10:19; John 19:11; Acts 8:19; Rev. 13:12; 17:12-13).

In Protestant tradition, the *authority* of Scripture is one of the so-called attributes of Holy Scripture (Lat. *affectiones* [or *proprietates*] *Scripturae sacrae*).[106] Other important attributes are the *necessity*, the *efficacy*, the *sufficiency* (or *perfection*, here in the sense of "completeness"), and the *perspicuity* of the Bible (§1.2.1). Less important features (sometimes later classified along with the *affections*) are the *verity*, the *integrity*, the *purity*, and the *authenticity* of Scripture.[107]

---

105. In addition to Karl Barth, another person who has extensively investigated the matter of the Bible's authority is Carl F. H. Henry (1979b, 7–128), against the background of a thorough analysis of the idea of revelation (cf. 1976b; 1979a; 1979b).
106. See extensively, Kuyper (*DD* 2.1:19–160, 217–41).
107. Cf. Bavinck (*RD* 1:452–94), Wentsel (1981, 244–52), and Van Genderen (2008, 83–107) for the first four; Heyns (1976, 99–111, 122–36) for the first, third, and fourth; Weber (1981, 268–86) for the same and the fifth; regarding *authority*, see Bavinck (*RD* 1:455–65); Barth (*CD* I/2:538–85); Weber (1981, 268–74).

These five traditional Protestant *affectiones* are not accepted by the Roman Catholic Church, except for the attribute of the Bible's *authority*—and even this is viewed as inseparably linked with the authority of the church. At least, this has been the traditional opinion; several modern Roman Catholic theologians grant the Bible priority over the church and view church tradition at best as an addition to, and interpretation of, Scripture. No doubt, Hans Küng is the best-known representative of this view, although Pieter C. Potgieter has shown how Küng actually denied this priority by accepting the methods of historical criticism (see chapters 11-12 below).[108] Thereby he simply replaced one human, fallible authority—the church—with another one—secular science, based on the myth of neutrality, objectivity, and absence of bias.

6.9.2 Four Other *Affectiones*

As to the other four *affectiones*, in addition to the attribute of *authority*, I note the following:

(a) For traditional Roman Catholics, the attribute of *necessity* is unacceptable. This is because the term implies that the Bible is necessary for the church to be church, and for its dogmas, as well as for theology. In the Roman Catholic view, the church is church in its own right. This notion of necessity has been denied by Gnostics and other mystics also, as well as by German philosopher Gotthold E. Lessing, Friedrich Schleiermacher, and others.

(b) The attribute of *efficacy* refers to the effectual power of Scripture, which always realizes God's purposes, so that God's Word "shall not return to me empty [i.e., without any effect], but it shall accomplish that which I purpose, and shall succeed in the thing for which I sent it" (Isa. 55:11). In Hebrews 4:12, the Vulgate calls the Word of God *vivus* ("living") and *efficax* ("effective, efficient"). Again, the Word of God brings this about through the work of the Holy Spirit, without the need for the intervention of any church or denomination.

---

108. Potgieter (1990, 9, 32).

(c) The attribute of *perspicuity* refers to the clarity, the transparency, of the Bible to faith, over against the Roman Catholic doctrine of the essential obscurity of Scripture, which must be removed by the church. Protestants confess this perspicuity but have often misunderstood it. The Bible may be transparent to faith in the transcendent-religious sense, but not necessarily to reason, and certainly not to *theoretical* reason.[109] That is, the Bible's perspicuity involves the clarity of the biblical message of salvation by faith in Jesus Christ (cf. Matt. 11:25). But this definitely does not mean that each verse of the Bible is simple and clear.

Thus, this notion of perspicuity can never be transferred from the Bible to certain theological theories about the Bible, as if more perspicuous theories are more biblical. This was the mistake, for instance, of Hannes Venter,[110] who preferred a theology that is understandable for simple, non-informed believers. Basically, we must say that such a theology does not exist. The fundamental mistake here involves the true nature of theology as a logical-analytical-theoretical enterprise (something very different from the Bible itself) and of theological theory building.[111] This has been clearly grasped by South African theologian Gerrie Snyman,[112] who, however, unfortunately formulated his criticism within the framework of a certain modern, and in my view unbiblical, subjectivism.[113] I agree with Snyman's epistemological criticism, not with his alternative.

A second point is that one could link the Bible's perspicuity to its human character. Brooke F. Westcott is quoted as having said that the Bible is authoritative because it is the Word

---

109. Cf. Rossouw (1963, 246–48); Heyns (1976, 130–32); Goldingay (1994, 345–47).
110. Venter (1989, 170).
111. See extensively, Ouweneel (1995, chapters 4–6; 2013, chapters 11–14).
112. Snyman (1992).
113. Regarding this, see Ouweneel (1995, §6.1.1).

of God; it is understandable because it is the word of men.[114] I take this to mean that we would not have been able to understand God's Word if God had not put down his thoughts in human language and in human writing.

A third point is that, for by far the greatest part of humanity, what stands between the Bible and the reader is, first, the translator, and second, the expositor. Each translation, no matter how literal and accurate, always contains some measure of exegesis.[115] In this way, the translator does some thinking for the reader, and the expositor does so even more. In practice, the perspicuity that the reader experiences is not much more than what translator and expositor present to him as perspicuous.

(d) The attribute of *sufficiency* (or *perfection*) refers to the completeness of the Bible: nothing can or must be added to it. No tradition is required to complete it, as Protestants argue over against Rome;[116] Scripture is complete in itself. In the words of Seakle Greijdanus on Luke 16:27-31,

> Holy Scripture gives the revelation of God also for what is beyond death and grave, and concerning the way of life, of redemption, of salvation. To this Word nothing needs to be added. The only thing that matters is true faith in what God reveals in it, such a faith that entirely governs a person in their being and doing. Whoever who does not place faith in that Word would also not allow themselves to be truly led by anything else.[117]

Of course, here again we must not be naïve. Strictly speaking, the Reformational adage *sola Scriptura* (Scripture alone) is true. First, however, we should not overlook natural revela-

---

114. Quoted in Warfield (1973, 548).
115. A simple example is this: whether one translates Gk. *diakonos* in Rom. 16:1 (referring to a woman!) as "helper" (NCV), "servant" (KJV), "deacon" (NIV), "deaconess" (ESV), or even "minister" (NABRE), is a matter that tells us something of the translator's ecclesiological views.
116. See White (2004, 17–42).
117. Greijdanus (1955, 89).

tion (cf. Belgic Confession, Art. 2). The adage should be *Sola Scriptura et natura*.

Second, church tradition does not have the same authority as Scripture (*contra* Roman Catholic doctrine), but it does play an essential role. In understanding the Bible, where would we be without the sixty generations of Bible expositors that preceded us? Most Protestants belong to denominations that have accepted certain manmade creeds and confessions as authoritative. In other words, the way they read the Bible is strongly influenced by the expository tradition of their respective denominations. That is to say, the practice always involves *sola Scriptura et traditione*, even for Protestants!

Third, what effect could the Bible possible have apart from the work of the Holy Spirit, who enlightens readers or hearers (as well as translators and expositors)? In this sense, the Bible is insufficient, for the Spirit who interprets spiritual truths to those who are spiritual, as one rendering of 1 Corinthians 2:13 states. "[T]he Helper, the Holy Spirit, whom the Father will send in my name, he will teach you all things," said Jesus (John 14:26); and, "When the Spirit of truth comes, he will guide you into all the truth" (16:13). We might put it this way: *sola Scriptura et solo Spiritu*.[118]

Yet a fourth point has often been discussed: Do we need extra-biblical sources for the correct exposition of the Bible (which, in this case, would not be really sufficient in itself)? Joseph Ratzinger gave the example of Jesus' seamless tunic (Gk. *chitōn*), and opined that the apostle John was very certainly alluding to Jesus' high priestly dignity.[119] This is because Flavius Josephus tells us that the *chitōn* of the high priest had been woven from a single thread.[120] Without this detail, we would not have understood John's emphasis on Jesus' seamless tunic. The question is, of course, whether John

---

118. If we take the form as an ablative, as in *sola fide*; the nominative would be *solus Spiritus*.
119. Ratzinger (2011, 216–17).
120. *Jewish Antiquities* III.7.4.

is really alluding to the high priestly dignity of Jesus; such an approach is typical for the book of Hebrews but not at all for John's writings. But apart from this, is it the case that we can (properly) understand some Bible passages only if we know from other sources about the circumstances under which the described events occurred, or how the text came about? The answer must be in the affirmative. An obvious example is the enormous knowledge of the five ancient world empires (Assyrian, Babylonian, Medo-Persian, Greco-Macedonian, and Roman) that we possess through extra-biblical sources, without which many parts of the Old and New Testaments would not be easily understandable.

The four arguments that I have adduced do seem to imply a certain relativizing of the notion of the Bible's sufficiency and of the adage "Holy Scripture is its own interpreter" (Lat. *sacra Scriptura sui ipsius interpres*). However, we must remind ourselves here of the true meaning of these expressions; the Bible is sufficient for all those who wish to know the way of salvation, the path to the heart of God. And for understanding the Bible *with the heart*, we do need the Holy Spirit, but we do not need any extra-biblical sources that are basically foreign to Scripture.

6.9.3 Prophecy and Authority

In a sense, we might say that the criterion of the authority of Bible books is hardly a new criterion compared with the previous one. That is, if a Bible book had been written by someone who had been acknowledged as a prophet or an apostle, such a book automatically possessed divine authority. The Lord told Jeremiah, "I appointed you as a prophet to the nations" (Jer. 1:5), and he told Saul of Tarsus, "Go; I will send you far away to the Gentiles" (Acts 22:21). What more do we wish? They had a divine commission, which aimed at the world population in its totality.

In some cases, however, the calling of a prophet was less, or not immediately, obvious, or the authorship of a certain book (think again of Heb.) was unclear. In such cases, the authority criterion played a clear role. Each Bible book speaks with an authoritative tone, and in God's name, implicitly, and often even with an explicit "Thus says the LORD," "The Word of the LORD came to me," or "The LORD spoke to me." In the historical and the prophetic books, we find authoritative statements about *God's* past and future acts, in the doctrinal books we find authoritative statements on what *believers* do, or ought to do, and in the poetic books we find the subjective reflection upon what God and believers do. But, as I said, even if Bible writers address God, their writings are inspired words of God to the listeners.

The New Testament books possess an obvious apostolic authority, but as with the Old Testament books, this is nothing but derived authority. Ultimately, there is only one Authority, namely, God himself. The prophets and the apostles merely exercised the authority of their Master; as Paul says, "If anyone thinks that he is a prophet, or spiritual, he should acknowledge that the things I am writing to you are a command of the Lord" (1 Cor. 14:37). As "an apostle—not from men nor through man, but through Jesus Christ and God the Father, who raised him from the dead," Paul could say, "I did not receive it [i.e., the gospel] from any man, nor was I taught it [by others], but I received it through a revelation of Jesus Christ" (Gal. 1:1, 12).

This referring back to the Primary Authority might even be the reason why the author of the book of Hebrews remained anonymous, namely, in order to hide himself behind the authority of, and more broadly, behind the greatness of, "Jesus, the *apostle* . . . of our confession" (Heb. 3:1).[121] The four Evangelists did not mention their names either; that is, they did not present themselves as authors so that they could shine the light exclusively upon him who "was teaching them as one who had authority, and not as their scribes" (Matt. 7:29).

---

121. Ouweneel (1982, 1:7–10).

"When the crowds saw it [i.e., the miracle], they were afraid, and they glorified God, who had given such authority to men" (9:8). "And they were all amazed, so that they questioned among themselves, saying, 'What is this? A new teaching with authority! He commands even the unclean spirits, and they obey him'" (Mark 1:27).

When Jesus was on earth, it was not so difficult for open-minded people to recognize his authority. But with Bible books, it is not always that easy. Some apocryphal books also claim a certain authority, even divine authority, yet they were rejected because they did not possess the necessary prophetic or apostolic status. In some cases it was even worse: not only was the prophetic status of the book of Esther doubtful, but it was also unclear whether it spoke with divine authority; this was especially because it does not mention the *name* of God at all.[122] Only when it became generally evident that God's preserving providential acts with his people, and thus his counsels and purposes, are exceptionally obvious in this book, it received the place in the canon that it deserved.

The fact that in the case of some books there was reluctance is not necessarily an indication for their non-canonicity. On the contrary, it shows that Israel, and later the early church, dealt with God's Word not in a superficial way but rather with care and discernment. If they could not be convinced of a book's divine authority, it was rejected. Of course, the godly Jews and Christians were not always brilliant personalities. However, they were able to recognize the divine authority of a book if it indeed possessed such authority, just as the sheep can recognize the voice of the good shepherd (John 10:4, 27).

The New Testament supplies us with an important illustration of this principle. Jesus asked the chief priests and elders of the people whether John's baptism had a heavenly or a human origin, that is, whether John the Baptist had acted

---

122. In the Greek (apocryphal) version of Esther, this supposed defect was amply supplied.

on divine or human authority. They replied that they did not know. Therefore, Jesus was not prepared to tell them on what authority he himself acted (Matt. 21:23-27). In other words, if people are not able to recognize divine authority when it comes to them, no other (practical, theological, philosophical, scientific) argument will ever be able to convince them. In such cases, even miracles will have no persuasive power (cf. Matt. 16:1-4; Luke 16:31; John 2:23-25; cf. the seeming contrast with 4:48). Ultimately, this recognition is a supernatural matter of the believing heart, through the power of the Holy Spirit, even though this does not exclude rational *a posteriori* arguments. Thus, Jesus could adduce a *logical* argument in order to expose the *supra-logical* unbelief of the spiritual leaders. As Blaise Pascal put it, "There is enough light for those who only desire to see, and enough obscurity for those who have a contrary disposition."[123]

6.9.4 Misunderstanding the Bible's Authority

The question of the authority of Scripture can be easily misunderstood. Scripture's authority is a matter of its transcendent unity, fullness, and integrity, not of every distinct phrase or word (atomism). That is, if the Bible writers uttered words that are sinful, or bordering on evil (cf. Jer. 20:14-18), this has no authority for us in the sense that we are to follow this example. It *is*, however, Word of God in the sense that this is what God wished us to know.

Another example: the Word of the Lord to which the apostle Paul points in 1 Corinthians 7:10 — "I give this charge (not I, but the Lord)" — has more authority than the personal opinions of Paul: "Now as a concession, not a command, I say this ..." (v. 6). "To the rest I say (I, not the Lord) that ..." (v. 12). "Now concerning the betrothed, I have no command from the Lord, but I give my judgment as one who by the Lord's mercy is trustworthy" (v. 25). "Yet in my judgment she is happier if she remains as she is. And I think that I too have the Spirit of

---

123. *Pensées* 430 (http://www.ccel.org/ccel/pascal/pensees.txt).

God" (v. 40). Or take this example: the words of true prophets have been recorded in the Bible as well as the words of false prophets (e.g., Jer. 28). Or this: the speeches of Job's friends as such do not have any divine authority over us, as is evident from Job 42:7, where God rebukes these friends for what they have said. However, all these words *as recorded in the Bible* do have divine authority over us in the sense that, on the transcendent level, it is *always* God who, through Scripture, speaks to *us*, even if, on the immanent level, it is perhaps a person (i.e., the Bible writer himself, or the person he describes) who speaks to God, or a person who gives his personal views, led by the Spirit or not.

When, in the Word of God, it is a matter of revelation, the outbursts of Jeremiah, the personal opinions of Paul, the doubtful speeches of Job's friends, or the words of the false prophets were certainly not God's Word. However, seen from the viewpoint of inspiration, these words are part of Scripture, which in its entirety is Word of God, namely, for two very different reasons. First, it is this that God wanted us to know through the inspiration of the Bible. But also, second, God can speak to our hearts through *each* word, even that of unspiritual or wicked people. A striking example is found in 1 Corinthians 3:19, where Paul quotes a saying of Eliphaz: "He catches the wise in their craftiness" (see Job 5:13). This saying addresses us with divine authority in our responsibility — so that we would not fall prey to our own craftiness — even though this statement was made by a dubious character at the wrong time to the wrong person (see further §8.9.1).

Thus, we see that the matter of the Bible's authority must be dealt with very prudently, as I emphasized before in view of biblicism (§§4.8.1 and 4.10). Job's apparent description of an eclipse of the sun, which he — literally or literarily — ascribed to the work of dragons (Job 3:8), is not authoritative for astronomy. The biblical references to bringing forth children in pain (Gen. 3:16), or the spreading of gangrene (or cancer; 2 Tim. 2:17), are no authoritative commissions to medical science not to try to alleviate the pain of childbirth or to stop cancer. Jesus' statement that we will always have the poor with us (John 12:8; cf. Deut. 15:11) is no authoritative commission to social welfare not to try to alleviate poverty. And his statement that there are twelve hours in the day (John 11:9) is no authoritative commission to politics not to shorten the workday (a statement that, at the end of the nineteenth century, was still being adduced as an argument against the eight-hour workday).[124] We will return in chapter 10 to this question of the authority and reliability of Scripture.

6.10 The Lesser Criteria

6.10.1 The Physical-Biotic Criterion

We have seen that God's Word is dynamic (Gk. *dynamis*, "power"), and possesses vitality (Lat. *vita*, "life") (cf. Heb. 4:12; 1 Pet. 1:23; 2:2). The Word is a fire and a hammer (Jer. 23:29). These things can also function as a criterion for canonicity, though it is less decisive than the previous one, just as the latter was less decisive than the former. Each next criterion becomes really important only if and when the previous criterion, or criteria, are not directly, or not clearly, applicable, as in the case of Esther. In such a situation, it was quite important that people could testify to the divine power and vitality of the Word.

The inspired Scriptures are able to make people "wise for salvation through faith in Christ Jesus," for "[a]ll Scripture is breathed out by God and profitable for teaching, for reproof, for correction, and for training in righteousness" (2 Tim. 3:15–16). Open-minded people should be able to testify to this power of the Scriptures in their practical lives. Indeed, genuinely canonical books are characterized by the fact that they edify, encourage, strengthen, correct, nourish, grant new vitality, true renewal of the believers' lives (cf. 1 Cor. 14:3).

This property does not always come to light immediately.

---

124. Most of these examples come from Kuitert (1993, 279–80), who, however, abused them to reject *any* appeal to the Bible's authority.

Only when it was fully understood that the Song of Solomon is not superficial-sensual at all but rather lofty and profoundly spiritual—whether it is viewed typologically or not[125]—the book received its place in the canon. Here, too, this is ultimately a matter of believing recognition. However, the latter can be rationally warranted by pointing to the positive effects that the Word has had in the lives of people.

Of course, this criterion, too, possesses only a relative persuasive power, for there are many Christian books that build up, encourage, strengthen, correct, and nourish as well. It does not help very much if we would argue that such books (can) do so only because they are based upon the Bible, for one could argue just as well that the New Testament is based upon the Old Testament, and the Old Testament prophetic books based upon the Torah. The edifying, encouraging, strengthening, correcting, nourishing character of a book constitutes only circumstantial evidence; it is an auxiliary argument, supplementing the previous ones.

6.10.2 The Logical-Analytical Criterion

The logical criterion was applied especially in the negative sense. Each book that, judged by earlier revelation, contained inaccuracies was rejected as non-canonical. This was done on the basis of the simple consideration that God's Word must be true and consistent.[126] Thus the book of Judith was laced with historical inaccuracies.[127] In 2 Maccabees 12:38-45 we read, in contrast with biblical testimony, that Jewish believers of the second century BC prayed for their beloved ones who had died in order that they would receive forgiveness, and in 15:11-16, Judas the Maccabean dreamed that the deceased prophet Jeremiah and high priest Onias made intercession for Israel. Such praying for, and by, the dead is not in line with

---

125. See Ouweneel (1973).
126. Weber (1981, 259), who accepted only two criteria, spoke here of the *coherence criterion*, and Bruce (1988a, 260–61) spoke of the *criterion of orthodoxy*.
127. See, e.g., mb-soft.com/believe/txs/judith.htm.

the rest of the Bible.

If a book lacked such inaccuracies, this certainly did not mean that it was canonical; but if it did contain them, it could be rejected immediately. This was the reason why the believers in Berea "were more noble than those in Thessalonica; they received the word with all eagerness, examining the Scriptures daily to see if these things were so" (Acts 17:11); that is, they investigated whether Paul's doctrine was in harmony with previous divine revelation. Only in this way they could accept "the word of God, which you heard from us . . . not as the word of men but as what it really is, the word of God, which is at work in you believers" (1 Thess. 2:13).

Many apocryphal books were rejected because of their doctrinal errors and historical mistakes, even though they sometimes spoke with great authority. As far as the New Testament was concerned, the apostolic teaching had to be defended over against Docetic and Gnostic writings, which often claimed apostolic authorship, and unfortunately, acquired great influence in the second and third centuries of the Christian era. Especially Irenaeus developed a criterion of canonicity that involved an appeal to faith as it was maintained in the churches that had been founded by the apostles.[128] Thus, the so-called Gospel of Peter was rejected because its record of Jesus' death was laced with Docetism.[129]

6.10.3 The Social Criterion

We have seen that the Word of God aims at forming and furthering fellowship between God and humans, and mutual fellowship between humans, and that the Bible's content is the spiritual possession of a certain community of faith. The Scriptures originated in the midst of God's people, and address the people of Israel and Christian churches, respectively. The Old Testament is the possession of *all* Israel, and the entire Bible is the possession of *all* Christianity. Therefore, it

---

128. Cf. Bruce (1988a, 171–72, 260–61).
129. Cf. Eusebius, *Historia Ecclesiastica* VI.12.3.

was important to know how a certain book had been accepted by its original recipients. This criterion for the canonicity of books sometimes played a role if previous criteria could be applied less unambiguously.

The idea behind this is obvious. The original audience and recipients ought to have been the ones best capable of recognizing a document as God's Word. For this reason, later generations tried to discover whether, and how, a book had been received by its original recipients. However, because the news and the mail traveled very slowly in those days, obtaining this information often involved much time and effort. This was one of the main reasons why it took so long before certain New Testament books were universally acknowledged as canonical.

Moreover, this criterion was applied especially in a negative way: if a book had not been accepted immediately and generally by its original recipients, it was rejected immediately as non-canonical. Conversely, the fact that a book had been accepted by certain believers at a certain place did not necessarily imply that it was an inspired book. Some Christians living later, who were insufficiently informed about the original acceptance or rejection of a book, did accept non-canonical books as canonical, until they received clarification about these matters.

F. F. Bruce spoke here of the criterion of *catholicity*.[130] A book that was accepted by a large part of the worldwide church would probably, sooner or later, receive universal acceptance. Thus, the Western church ultimately agreed with accepting the book of Hebrews as canonical, one reason being that this church did not wish to be out of step with the remainder or orthodox Christendom. Athanasius of Alexandria probably convinced the Western church to walk in this respect in the same trail as their Eastern brethren.[131] Looking

---

130. Bruce (1988a, 261–62).
131. Ibid., 221.

back, we can only express our deepest gratitude about this decision—for what would New Testament theology be without the book of Hebrews![132]

6.10.4 Economic, Aesthetic, Juridical, Ethical, and Pistical Criteria

Of course, the other modal ideas concerning the Word of God also involve certain criteria for the canonicity of books. However, it is hardly necessary to explain them separately, because they can be easily understood as being enclosed within the criteria discussed in the previous sections, especially the second and the third ones. Believers experienced the tremendous balance, efficacy, and spiritual value of certain books (*economic*), their beauty and harmony, or also the divine peace that they contain and bring about (*aesthetic*), the exalted justice (*juridical*), morals and love (*ethical*), and trustworthiness (*pistical*) that these books radiate.

In a similar way, we can think of modal ideas that express the being of God as revealed in his Word. Books were acknowledged as penetrating manifestations of God's power (*physical*), God's life and vitality (*biotic*), God's affections and feelings (*sensitive*), God's omniscience (*logical*), God's omnipotence (*historical-formative*), God's speaking (*lingual*), God's longing for fellowship with humans (*social*), peace (*aesthetic*), God's righteousness (*juridical*), God's love (*ethical*), and God's reliability (*pistical*).

I must emphasize here again that the early Christians did not choose certain books to be canonical simply because these books pleased them. Theirs was not a cafeteria selection. Rather, these books *chose them*: through the power of the Holy Spirit, the early Christians were overwhelmed by the divine character of the books involved, so that in faith they recognized them as canonical. They did not *rule* over the books to select what they liked, but the books ruled over *them* with divine power. They did not pass a *judgment* on these books, but

---
132. See extensively, Ouweneel (1988, 90).

believingly submitted to the judgment that these books passed on *them*. In faith they entrusted themselves to these books because they knew they were, and are, God's own Word.

6.11 Post-Apostolic Books?

6.11.1 Forgeries or Not

Of course, the question may come up whether the process of canonization really occurred in such an ideal way as people might conclude from the previous sections. Therefore, we must now discuss a few critical points. Two of them are related to the assertion that some of the New Testament books are definitely post-apostolic (see §§6.11 and 6.12). The argument is that these New Testament books are certainly *not* apostolic in the sense of having been written by an apostle or by one of their close co-workers. Instead, they are viewed as originating with second generation Christians.[133] The importance of the argument is not only that the apostolic criterion can no longer be fully applied, but also that the choice of these books seems to involve a certain arbitrariness: why these books, and why not some other books from the second generation, such as the letters of Ignatius and Polycarp (no less than a pupil of the apostle John!), 1 and 2 Clement, the *Didachē*, the letter of Barnabas, and the Shepherd of Hermas?

At certain times in the history of biblical criticism, a great number of the Gospels and letters were considered to be post-apostolic, especially John's Gospel, the first and second letters to Timothy, the letter to Titus, the book of Hebrews, the letter of James, the second letter of Peter, the second and third letters of John, and Revelation. Fritz Buri represented this viewpoint, yet defended the canonicity of these so-called post-apostolic books on the basis of their catholic character.[134] In his view, the decisive factor was not their historical origin but their content and suitability to serve as an expression of, and support for, those beliefs that over time, had come to be

---

133. Cf. Weber (1981, 261); Berkhof (1986, 82–86).
134. Buri (1956, 410–11).

seen as catholic, that is, valid and useful for the worldwide church. We may wonder, however, why this argument would not be similarly true for 1 and 2 Clement, to mention an example.

Recently, this discussion has been reinvigorated by the work of Bart D. Ehrman, formerly an evangelical, now an agnostic theologian, if I understand correctly.[135] His argument is not only that a great part of the New Testament is pseudepigraphic, but also that people in antiquity judged such books exactly as we do today, namely, as forgeries. The latter point had already been refuted by, for instance, Terry L. Wilder, Richard Bauckham, and especially Karel van der Toorn.[136] The latter wrote in particular about the development of the Old Testament (as largely the results of *scribes*, writers, secretaries, who worked in the spirit of their great predecessors), but since the New Testament authors were virtually all Jewish, his arguments can be applied to the New Testament as well. It was a very common practice to entitle a book after the person who had supplied the first or main contribution to a certain tradition, *not* after the copyist who actually wrote the document (sometimes decades after the tradition had originated).

If the first and second letters to Timothy, the letter to Titus, the letter of James, the second letter of Peter, and Revelation, which suggest to have been written by Paul, James, Peter, and John, respectively, were actually written by their respective pupils, this would not have been viewed as forgery. This is because they would have adopted their materials from their masters, and they would have written in their spirit. One could call their books forgeries only if it could be shown that the actual authors hide themselves behind well-known masters from the past but teach things *contrary* to the thoughts of these masters. If some New Testament books would be shown to be such forgeries, the conclusion of Stanley E. Porter regarding the first and second letters to Timothy and the

---

135. Ehrman (2011).
136. Wilder (2004); Bauckham (2006); Van der Toorn (2007).

letter to Titus would be understandable. He argued that, if the church and its scholars are no longer prepared to accept the pastoral letters as written by Paul, they perhaps ought to eliminate them from the Bible as forgeries that once deceived but no longer will do so, rather than to create distorted theological justifications for their ongoing presence in the canon.[137]

6.11.2 Arguments for Apostolicity

The essential question is whether the books mentioned — and more recently Ephesians, Colossians, and 2 Thessalonians have been added to the list[138] — are post-apostolic. In some cases, expositors have returned to the acknowledgement of the apostolic character of the books concerned. Let us briefly look at some books that have been viewed by some, or many, to be post-apostolic.

(a) *Ephesians and Colossians*. It is fascinating to see how the argument works. People do not doubt Paul's authorship of the letter to Philemon; but both Philemon 2 and Colossians 4:17 mention Archippus, and in the greetings of Philemon 23-24 and Colossians 4:10-14 we find the same names (Aristarchus, Mark, Epaphras, Luke, Demas). One scholar sees this as clear evidence that both letters were written by Paul, during the same period; another scholar sees this as evidence of how clever a forger the author of Colossians was. In recent decades, the Pauline authorship of Ephesians and Colossians has been strongly defended by various authors, but this is not the place to enter into their arguments.[139]

(b) *2 Thessalonians*. It is remarkable that the author warns against false letters that would have been written in his name (2 Thess. 2:2), whereas, if the critics were right, he himself would be a forger — and a rather crafty one at that. Not all

---

137. Quoted in McDonald and Sanders (2002, 464); cf. Porter (1995) and the reply to this argument by Wall (1995).
138. See Van Kooten (2001).
139. Bruce (1984, 28–33, 229–33); Carson et al. (1999, 306–07); Hoehner (2002, 2–61); McCain (2002, 249); Wallace (2003).

that long ago, several theologians have defended the Pauline authorship of this letter.[140]

(c) *The so-called pastoral letters (1 Tim., 2 Tim., Titus)*. There are certainly remarkable differences between these letters and the (other) letters of Paul, but it is questionable whether these differences warrant the conclusion that they must have been written by one or more different authors. Some serious scholars still answer this question in the negative, and believe that there are no sufficient grounds to discredit the Pauline authorship of these letters.[141]

(d) *The book of Hebrews*. In his discussion of the canon, Paul Althaus wrote emphatically, "We know that [this letter] comes from an unknown man from the second Christian generation."[142] In my own commentary, I have argued extensively that, first, the possibility that the apostle Paul is the author of Hebrews cannot be excluded.[143] Second, if the author were not Paul, it still does not need to be an (unknown) second generation author (despite arguments for that position based on Heb. 2:3-4).[144] I believe the arguments for the apostolic character of this book are strong.[145]

6.11.3 Second Peter and Revelation

Paul Althaus added to his previous statement, "At least also the so-called second letter of Peter is post-apostolic, probably also a series of other parts of the New Testament . . . the pseudonymous second letter of Peter, stemming from the sec-

---

140. Green (2002); Beale (2003); Nicholl (2004); Jones (2005); Witherington (2006).
141. Edwards (1993); Bird (1997); Liefeld (1999); Mounce (2000); Towner (2006; with prudence); Holding (2009) (also important for other New Testament books); also see Guthrie (1990).
142. Althaus (1952, 157).
143. Remarkably, the revised version of the Dutch States Translation (2010) still calls Heb. a "letter of Paul."
144. Ouweneel (1982, 1:7-10).
145. See ibid., references; David Allen (2010) argued for Luke as the author of Heb.

ond century, is—as [German theologian] A[dolf] Jülicher [d. 1938] rightly says—the New Testament part 'least suitable for canonization'."[146] It is claimed that 2 Peter and similar New Testament books belong to the literature of the Apostolic Fathers, as testimonies from the time of the epigones (inferior imitators of the apostles). However, several authors have defended the Petrine authorship of 2 Peter.[147] In doing so, they do not neglect the clear external and internal, literary, historical, stylistic, and doctrinal problems of this authorship, but discuss them extensively.

Donald Guthrie concluded that the choice seems to lie between two fairly well-defined alternatives. Either the epistle is genuinely Petrine, with or without the use of an amanuensis (because of the remarkable literary differences with 1 Peter), in which case the main problem is the delay in its reception. Or it is pseudepigraphic, in which case the main difficulties are lack of an adequate motive and the problem of its ultimate acceptance. Both alternatives present some difficulties, but of the two, the former is easier to explain. If 2 Peter had been sent to a limited destination, it is not difficult to imagine that many churches might not have received it during the earlier history of the canon. When it did begin to circulate it may well have been received with some suspicion, particularly if by this time some spurious Petrine books were also beginning to circulate. That it ultimately became accepted universally must have been due to the recognition not merely of its claim to apostolic authorship, but also of its apostolic content.[148]

In my commentary on the book of Revelation, I discussed rather extensively the different theories concerning the book's authorship.[149] I adduced arguments against a post-apostolic author, like someone called "John the presbyter" (thus Gilles

---

146. Althaus (1952, 157–58).
147. Van Houwelingen (1988); Moo (1996b); Schreiner (2003); Davids (2006; with caution); Green (2008).
148. Guthrie (1990, 840–41).
149. Ouweneel (1988, 3–13).

Quispel,[150] d. 2006), or "John the prophet" (thus Robert H. Charles,[151] d. 1931), and *for* an authorship by John the apostle.[152]

I pointed to the remarkable fact that Revelation was one of the first New Testament books recognized as canonical in the writings of the early church fathers (*Didachē*, Shepherd of Hermas, Papias, Irenaeus; cf. the so-called Muratorian Canon, c. AD 170), but the very last book that was accepted by the *entire* church. The main reasons were of a doctrinal nature. My suggestion was that, even though most modern expositors reject the apostle John as the author of Revelation, this is still the most likely solution.

6.11.4 Summary

It is worthwhile to point here to the J. A. T. Robinson, who, despite his liberal background, strongly advocated a very early origin of *all* New Testament books. One of his arguments was that all these books must have been written before the fall of Jerusalem in AD 70, since none of the books seems to show any awareness of this event.[153] His view has been heavily criticized; if it is nonetheless correct, there is no question at all of any second-generation or post-apostolic New Testament books.

I wish to emphasize that, as I see it, there are still good arguments to maintain the traditional views concerning the authorship of several New Testament books, but that, for belief in the Bible as the Word of God, this is not *essential*. For instance, let us assume for a moment that it could be definitively *proven*—which in principle is never possible, of course—that the pastoral letters and 2 Peter were authored by

---

150. Quispel (1979).
151. Charles (1920).
152. In agreement with Justin Martyr (*Dialogue with Trypho* 81), Irenaeus (*Adversus Haereses* IV.20.11), Tertullian (*De Praescriptione Haereticorum* 36), and Hippolytus (*De Christo and Antichristo* 36); see Bette et al. (2000).
153. Robinson (1976).

pupils of Paul and Peter, respectively, writing in the spirit of their masters. Let us also assume that it could be proven that it was common practice in New Testament times to publish such books under the name of the honored master because it is *his* thoughts that are presented in them, and that no one considered this deceitful. In this case, these matters would not at all shatter our faith in the canonicity and inspiration of the books involved.

In principle, the situation might not be much different from that of Mark's Gospel, which, according to Papias of Hierapolis,[154] was in fact Peter's Gospel, with Mark being Peter's younger co-worker or pupil or secretary.

Even if there are post-apostolic books in the New Testament (which, in my view, is unlikely), these could still be canonical. Doubts would arise only, or especially, if the New Testament would contain books under the name of Paul, Peter, or John that actually present doctrines *contrary to* the teaching of these respective apostles. However, although some have indeed argued such things—for instance, the ecclesiology of the pastoral letters supposedly conflicts with that of Paul[155]—in no case have such arguments been generally accepted; on the contrary.

6.12 Additional Matters

6.12.1 The Vague Boundary between Scripture and Tradition

It cannot be denied that the boundary between what we know now as "Scripture" and the writings that arose directly after the Bible books were written is rather flexible. This argument also comes from Paul Althaus.[156] It goes as follows. If certain New Testament books belong to the post-apostolic period, and therefore must actually be assigned to the writings of the Apostolic Fathers, there cannot be a sharp boundary between

---

154. See note 99.
155. On this see Ouweneel (2010a, chapter 8).
156. Althaus (1952, 158, 169–70).

the inspired and therefore divinely authoritative books of the New Testament, and the non-inspired and therefore not divinely authoritative books of the Apostolic Fathers. In more general terms: there can be no sharp boundary between inspired and non-inspired ancient (or even more recent) Christian literature.

This argument basically entails the claim that there can be no such a thing as the divine inspiration of certain books, which supposedly are discontinuous with other deeply pious Christian books written by pupils of the apostles from the same period, or shortly afterward. For instance, what does the Gospel of Mark, who was a pupil of Paul and Peter, have that the touching letter of Polycarp, who was a pupil of John, does not have? (I am referring not to the importance of the context but to the spiritual power of the writing concerned.) The answer can only be this: the difference was not that early Christians had more respect for Mark than for Polycarp—even though this might have been the case—but rather that people heard the voice of God himself in Mark's Gospel in a way they did not hear it in Polycarp's letter.

The subject of inspiration will be discussed in the following chapters. I would mention here merely that, at an early stage in church history, the early church seems to have viewed the canon as a collection of books that clearly and discontinuously stood apart, and even actively *had to* be set apart, because these were the only books to which divine authority had to be attributed. American theologians Norman L. Geisler and William E. Nix wrote that, immediately after the time of the apostles, the writings of the earliest church fathers contained a recognition of the inspiration of all twenty-seven books. Their testimony was supported by the early translations, canonical lists, and statements by church councils. Taken together, they exhibited a continuous recognition from the first beginning of the canon in the time of the apostles until the ultimate confirmation by the universal church during the latter part of the fourth century. Just a little more than a generation after the end of the apostolic age, each New Testament book had been quoted as authoritative by a church father. Other confirmations of the first century canon are found in the translations and canonical lists from the second and third centuries. Translations could not be made unless there first was a recognition of a book that was to be included in the translation.[157]

This subject need not be elaborated any further. I would direct the reader to the arguments explained in the works mentioned, which show that the idea of a gradual transition between the canon and the early-Christian literature cannot be maintained. Let me limit myself to the conclusion of Geisler and Nix, with which I agree. They summarized their arguments by stating that the process of collecting authentic apostolic literature began in the New Testament era. In the second century, verification of this literature occurred when authors quoted the divine authority of each of the twenty-seven books of the New Testament. In the third century, doubts and discussions arose over certain books, which in the fourth century culminated in the decisions of influential church fathers and councils. Throughout the centuries since that time, the Christian church has maintained the canonicity of these twenty-seven books.[158]

6.12.2 Degrees of Canonicity?

In addition to the argument of the supposed post-apostolic character of certain New Testament books, other objections have arisen against the traditional canon idea. The first objection is that the canon itself involves degrees of canonicity. This involves a possible canon within the canon, which could serve, too, as an argument to relativize the notion of canonicity altogether.[159] The argument is that, if certain New Testament books are more canonical, that is, more inspired, and therefore more authoritative than certain other, deutero-

---

[157]. Geisler and Nix (1974, 107–108).
[158]. Ibid., 111–12.
[159]. Cf. Berkhof (1986, 84–86); Bruce (1988a, 270–83).

canonical books (possessing a second-rank canonicity), then the degree of canonicity ranges from highly inspired, through less inspired, to non-inspired.

If this were the case, we would be unable to draw a sharp boundary between inspired and non-inspired Christian literature. This would imply the absence of a clear discontinuity between inspired and non-inspired books. There would be a difference in the degree of canonicity between, for instance, Colossians and Philemon, but then between, for instance, Philemon and Polycarp, and subsequently also between, for instance, Polycarp and Thomas à Kempis's *De Imitatione Christi* or John Bunyan's *The Pilgrim's Progress*.

Now this entire idea of degrees of inspiration fundamentally conflicts with the biblical notion of inspiration, as will become clear in the following chapters. Let us nonetheless give some attention to the argument adduced to defend degrees of canonicity.

Both Emil Brunner and Paul Althaus appealed to Martin Luther in defense of their thesis.[160] Luther distinguished degrees of authority among different Bible books, and rejected some books (especially James) as non-canonical. This explains why he made very critical comments about certain Bible books, about their historical origin, the circumstances under which they were written, and so on. Ostensibly, "many of these views have been confirmed by the Biblical criticism of the last [i.e., nineteenth] century."[161] Althaus and Weber explained how this view of Luther was gradually dismantled through the work of German Lutheran theologians such as Martin Chemnitz, Johann Gerhard, Andreas Quenstedt, and David Hollaz. The latter finally declared that the distinction between the various canonical books, or between canonical and deuterocanonical books was unnecessary because all Lutheran theologians accepted the latter books as divinely

---

160. Brunner (1949, 111–113); Althaus (1952, 158–59, 163–64); cf. Weber (1981, 255).
161. Brunner (1949, 111).

authoritative anyway. Brunner said that, already before the end of the sixteenth century, Luther's view was largely dismissed.[162]

Both Brunner and Althaus regretted this development, and welcomed the fact that this view had been revived by historical criticism. Brunner wrote, "Thus Luther was the first to represent a Biblical faith which could be combined with Biblical criticism, and was therefore fundamentally different from the traditional, formally authoritarian view of the Bible, which culminates in the doctrine of Verbal Inspiration."[163]

What is the force of such an argument? First, Fritz Buri rightly emphasized that Luther never really suggested a change in the canon.[164] On the contrary, he attached great value to the entire Scripture (Lat. *tota scriptura*) as the foundation of the Christian faith. Moreover, Buri pointed out that Luther's critical judgments did not rest on historical considerations, unlike historical criticism, but on intrinsic, dogmatic considerations. In this respect, Luther's position was far different from that of later historical criticism.

Second, Brunner and Althaus had to recognize indirectly that, in this respect, as a thinker Luther stood rather alone among the Reformers. Brunner attributed this "traditional, formal-authoritarian Bible understanding" entirely to John Calvin,[165] who taught that the writings of the apostle must be regarded as oracles of God (Lat. *pro dei oraculis habenda sunt*).[166] Therefore, the believers must accept everything that has been handed down in the Holy Scriptures, without exception (Lat. *quidquid in sacris scripturis traditum est sine exceptione*).[167] The faith conviction that God is its founder/author (Lat. *auctorem*

---

162. Ibid.
163. Ibid., 111.
164. Buri (1956, 414–15).
165. Brunner (1949, 111); cf. Weber (1981, 256).
166. Calvin, *Institutes* 4.8.9.
167. Ibid., 1.18.4.

eius [= scripturae] esse deum) precedes all doctrine.[168] Brunner commented, "That again is the old view."[169] He was right: this is exactly what it is.[170] There is a long, almost uninterrupted current of opinion running from the early church to the eighteenth century concerning the canonicity and the inspiration of Scripture, in which Luther and a few of his direct successors, such as Martin Chemnitz, were lonely figures. The really new developments began with the rise of historical criticism, as we will see in chapters 11–12.

6.12.3 Loss of the Criterion of Coherence

The so-called criterion of coherence was both formulated and criticized by Otto Weber.[171] He referred to Ernst Käsemann, who wrote in a deprecating way about a canon in which 2 Peter could receive a place as a "most evident testimony of early Catholicism." Käsemann found his "canon within the canon" in the apostle Paul's theology of the cross (Lat. *theologia crucis*), and, according to this criterion, rejected Ephesians as bigotry — of all things — and the pastoral letters because of their supposed institutionalism.

This view was combated by Hans Küng,[172] who rejected it as sectarian and subjectivistic.[173] Hendrikus Berkhof basically followed Küng, especially because there are no criteria for identifying and isolating within divine revelation a central thought, which would not necessarily need to be Pauline.[174] To put it more strongly, I have argued elsewhere that the Pauline doctrine of the church as the body of the glorified

---

168. Ibid., 1.7.4.
169. Brunner (1949, 111).
170. Krusche (1953, 197), however, claimed that Calvin could not be called the father of the early Protestant doctrine of inspiration, *contra* Ritschl (1908, 1:63) and Seeberg (1920, 2:566). Cf. De Groot (1931) and Cramer (1926), who called Calvin "the father of scientific biblical criticism."
171. Weber (1981, 259–60); cf. Berkhof (1986, 81–86).
172. Küng (1963).
173. Cf. the reply by Käsemann et al. (1970).
174. Berkhof (1986, 86).

Christ, as expounded especially in Ephesians and Colossians, is more central than the theology of the cross because Christ's work on the cross is merely the foundation for the exposition of God's thoughts concerning God's kingdom, and especially God's church.[175] In this sense, Ephesians is more central than Romans because, no matter how important it may be, Romans is merely the road to Ephesians (cf. Rom. 16:25-26). This does not yet take into account whether, in a certain sense, John's ministry on the eternal Son and eternal life,[176] is more central (or basic) than Paul's ministry. I am not really defending this idea; I merely wish to point out more generally the futility of pointing to any center within the Bible.

Otto Weber argued along the same lines as Ernst Käsemann. He pointed to the content of Luke and Acts, and to the totality of Paul's writings (Lat. *corpus Paulinum*), in which the pastoral letters are viewed as documents belonging to emerging Roman Catholicism, just like Luke, Acts, and 2 Peter. Between 1 and 2 Corinthians, Galatians, and Romans, on the one hand, and Ephesians and Colossians, on the other hand, he also saw essential differences. Weber rightly noted that we should not view the results of exegesis as permanently valid. However, he believed that, with careful consideration and great self-criticism of exegesis, we cannot take it for granted today that the coherence criterion has been satisfied *a priori*. In other words, strictly speaking no book can be claimed as being absolutely coherent with every other book of the New Testament; the internal contrasts are too great to assert such a thing.

Personally, I believe that the difficulty of this entire argument is that coherence cannot be defined in an objective-logical way that would be univocal and acceptable among all theologians. That there are great differences within the New Testament, as within the Old Testament, is obvious, and is part of the great riches of the Bible. A real problem exists only

---

175. Ouweneel (2010a; 2010b; 2018j).
176. Cf. Ouweneel (2018l).

if, in an objective-rational way, clear doctrinal *contradictions* could be identified within the New Testament, or if certain books would clearly bear this character. Of course, many have attempted to identify such contradictions, but these have been effectively refuted by other theologians. In the end, we must conclude that the coherence criterion has little value in the theological assessment of the canon. This is all the more so because some writings of the Apostolic Fathers could also be viewed as coherent with the entire New Testament, while no one wishes on that basis to advocate their inclusion in the New Testament canon.

Chapter 7
Inspiration: Starting Points and Models

> . . . *the sacred writings, which are able to*
> *make you wise for salvation*
> *through faith in Christ Jesus.*
> *All Scripture is breathed out by God*
> *and profitable for teaching,*
> *for reproof, for correction,*
> *and for training in righteousness,*
> *that the man of God may be complete,*
> *equipped for every good work.*
>
> 2 Timothy 3:15–17

Summary: *The Bible is both a divine and a human book: inspired by God, written down by humans. It is a difficult task to precisely analyze the relationship between these two aspects. First, the main Bible passages on inspiration are discussed: those that say, "It is written" and "Have you not read?," and others (Matt. 22:29–32, on searching and power; 2 Tim. 3:16–17, on inspiration and purpose; 1 Pet. 1:10–11 on the role of the Spirit of Christ; 2 Pet. 1:19–21 on holy men carried along by the Spirit; 1 Cor. 2:9–16, on research, revelation, illumination, and inspiration).*

Eleven theories of inspiration are briefly discussed, classified according to the underlying modal ideas: spatial (the dualistic theory), kinematic (the widespread mechanical theory), energetic (the dynamic theory), biotic (the organic theory), perceptive (the scope theory), sensitive (the sensitivistic theory), logical (the intuition theory), historical-formative (the actualistic theory), lingual (the dialogical theory), aesthetic (the musical instruments theory), and ethical (the marriage theory). The practical value of all these theories as theories is limited because the supra-natural and supra-rational miracle of inspiration cannot be apprehended in any theological theory.

7.1 Introduction

7.1.1 The Divine and the Human Aspects

WE HAVE SEEN THAT Bible books were accepted as canonical because people heard in them the Word of God. What they heard was God speaking through them, God addressing them, appealing to them, in a way they did not hear through any other books. We can now state that this special character of Bible books comes from their having been *inspired* (literally, "breathed in").[1] In other words, the dilemma of whether a book is canonical or apocryphal is essentially equivalent to whether it is inspired. In our day, this matter is one of the most fundamental issues for Christian thought because many other issues depend directly on this characteristic, such as the Bible's credibility, infallibility, and authority, and its applicability to all kinds of modern practical issues.

These issues include whether the Bible presents us divine messages in a human, and therefore fallible, form. Or has every single word in the Bible been directly inspired by God, and is therefore infallible, each one of the same importance? Or do the biblical messages present to us merely human ex-

1. For this chapter, I have received help from Warfield (1948); Harris (1957; 1995); Young (1957); Geisler and Nix (1968; 1974); Vawter (1972); Pache (1977); Henry (1979c); Rogers and McKim (1979); Achtemeier (1980); Bloesch (1994); and Enns (2005); these sources will not be explicitly mentioned at every point in the following discussion.

periences of the divine, so that their authority is merely a human authority? Or does the truth lie somewhere between these options? Were the Bible writers mere human recorders, which blindly recorded what God dictated to them? Or human word processors, instruments with which God wrote what he wished to write, without any contribution by these instruments themselves (except features like formatting, font, and punctuation, to continue the metaphor)? Or did the writers contribute to the origin of the Bible books? And if so, what kind of contribution was this? And how does this human contribution relate to the divine contribution? How do we avoid here a dualism of the human and the divine? And how can the *entire* Bible be called *God's* Word if it resulted from a human contribution?

Once again, we acknowledge first of all that Holy Scripture is its own interpreter (Lat. *sacra scriptura sui ipsius interpres*) (see §§6.1.2 and 6.9.2). As Karl Barth put it, "When we adopt the Canon of the Church we do not say that the Church itself, but that the revelation which underlies and controls the Church, attests these witnesses and not others as the witnesses of revelation and therefore as canonical for the Church";[2] and "But even though it is in and with the Church that we ask what is that Holy Scripture which is the Canon given in the Church and forcing itself upon it by its own inspiration, we cannot take our answer from the Church but from Holy Scripture itself."[3]

7.1.2 Scripture on Inspiration

In many passages, Bible books tell us that they — or earlier Bible books — were inspired by God, even though they use very different terms to express this notion. Divine inspiration is not simply a kind of poetic inspiration or intuition underlying the Bible writers' work, the kind of inspiration we know in connection with visual, musical or literary artists. In what

---

[2]. Barth (*CD* I/2:474).

[3]. Ibid., 475.

follows, we will be seeing very clearly that biblical inspiration means that it was not the *writers* who were inspired, but their *writings* (cf. 2 Tim. 3:16, "All scripture is inspired by God," RSV). This is a fundamental distinction. As they were "[b]orne along (moved and impelled) by the Holy Spirit" (2 Pet. 1:21 AMPC), the Bible writers wrote words that came from God — this is the testimony of the Bible itself.

This truth can be seen most easily by examining some of the clearest New Testament passages on this point. I will do this despite the warning by Wolfgang Trillhaas that the inspiration doctrine for which 2 Timothy 3:16 and 2 Peter 1:19-21 have been adduced as proof texts (Lat. *dicta probantia*) has led to "ecclesiastical misfortune" (Ger. *kirchliches Schicksal*).[4] There simply is no other route we can follow, despite whatever errors our predecessors may have committed along this path, than to begin with the Bible's own testimony on inspiration. We cannot deduce a *theory* of inspiration from Bible quotations, but such passages do supply us with the material we need to develop our theories by way of our own scholarly thinking. Again, we are aware of the hermeneutical circle here (cf. §§1.7 and 6.6.3); the danger exists that a preconceived theory of inspiration theory will dominate the interpretation of relevant Bible passages.

Some might claim at the outset that the Bible cannot possibly testify about itself, about its own inspiration, because at the time of such testimony, the Bible was not yet finished. For instance, 2 Timothy 3:16 supposedly refers only to the completed Old Testament books. I reply to this that the same author who wrote this verse referred in 1 Timothy 5:18, written to the same co-worker Timothy, to Matthew 10:10 and/or Luke 10:7 ("The laborer deserves his wages") as "Scripture" (see §6.2.2). And Peter compared Paul's letters with "the other Scriptures" (2 Pet. 3:16). That is, to Peter, not only the Old Testament books were "Scriptures" but Paul's letters were

---

4. Trillhaas (1972, 76).

"Scriptures," too: equally inspired, equally canonical.

As Jesus said, "Scripture cannot be broken" (John 10:35). Therefore, if Scripture somewhere describes a property of "the Scripture," like its inspiration ("*All* Scripture is inspired"), this can be taken as being true for all newer (i.e., New Testament) Scriptures as well. In other words, it is not too far-fetched to claim that inspiration is a characteristic of Scripture in its entirety as we possess it with the completion of the canon.

The Scripture's talk about its own inspiration has a remarkable implication. If it is genuinely "Scripture," a passage cannot speak of the inspiration of Scripture without having been inspired itself. Through divine inspiration, the church received the first teaching about divine inspiration. Again we encounter here the hermeneutical circle: we believe in the inspiration of Scripture on the basis of what Scripture itself, due to inspiration, tells us about that truth. This is not a blind leap into the dark: those who, through faith and in the power of the Holy Spirit, know themselves to be addressed by God himself in the Bible have no difficulty accepting that the same Bible tells them that it has been inspired by God. Difficulties arise only when theologians, in a logical-rational-theoretical way, wish to supply a *warrant* for what exactly is involved in this notion of the inspiration. This is the task we are undertaking in these chapters (7 and 8).

7.2 The Gospels

7.2.1 God's "Speaking"

In Matthew 22:29-32, Jesus said to the Sadducees,

> You are wrong, because you know neither the Scriptures nor the power of God. For in the resurrection they neither marry nor are given in marriage, but are like angels in heaven. And as for the resurrection of the dead, have you not read what was said to you by God: "I am the God of Abraham, and the God of Isaac, and the God of Jacob"? He is not God of the dead, but of the living.

The remarkable key words, so easily overlooked, are the words "to you."[5] The words "I am the God of Abraham, and the God of Isaac, and the God of Jacob" were spoken by God to Moses in Exodus 3:6 (cf. Mark 12:26). However, Jesus said that, in his own day, *through Scripture*, these same words were *spoken by God* to the Sadducees. This means that, still today, these words are spoken by God to all those who read or hear them. Those who listen to Scripture are supposed to hear God's voice in it, as Jesus implicitly teaches. There may be uncertainty as to who wrote Exodus 3 (see §11.2.1), but there can be no doubt about the identity of the Primary Author (Lat. *Auctor Primarius*) of this chapter. Our interest is not only where this chapter comes from (from Moses or some later author?) but also who is speaking through these chapters, even today. Regardless of who the human authors were, the Bible comes from God, and God is still speaking through it to those who wish to listen.

Notice also the first part of Jesus' answer: "You are wrong, because you know neither the Scriptures nor the power of God." This sounds almost like a hendiadys, as if Jesus were saying: ". . . the divine power of the Scriptures." Genuinely knowing the Scriptures implies knowing the power of God. Conversely, those who do not know the power of God do not genuinely know the Scriptures; they have never truly heard his voice in it. Through the Holy Spirit, God is revealed in the Scriptures; it is God who speaks in them with power. In other words, the Bible has power because it is God who, through them, speaks with power. In this respect, the Sadducees were guilty before God. They searched the Scriptures but had failed to hear God's voice in it, and to experience God's power in it. Today, this is the worst that could happen to the theologian: professionally searching the Scriptures — as a liberal or as a conservative — without ever hearing God's voice in it. It is like the chemist analyzing the most delicious foods in his test tubes without ever tasting them.

---

5. Cf. Saucy (2001, 118); White (2004, 60–62).

We should not attribute to Jesus any *theories* of inspiration; but if we were to identify his view of the inspiration of Scripture, the answer must be: he had the highest conceivable view. According to him, in the Bible we hear the voice of God, the "Word of God," and "Scripture cannot be broken" (John 10:35). For Jesus, this was the profound meaning of the statement "It is written" (Matt. 4:4, 7, 10; 21:13; 26:24, 31; John 6:31, 45; 8:17), which to him meant the same as "God has said": "It is written, 'Man shall not live by bread alone, but *by every word that comes from the mouth of God*'" (Matt. 4:4; quoting Deut. 8:3). What is written is identical to what God had spoken at a certain time, and what he, through Scripture, still speaks to us. To Jesus, Scripture was so important that, as he said, not the smallest part would ever be lost: "Do not think that I have come to abolish the Law or the Prophets [i.e., the entire Tanakh]; I have not come to abolish them but to fulfill them. For truly, I say to you, until heaven and earth pass away, not an iota, not a dot, will pass from the Law [and similarly, from the entire Bible] until all is accomplished" (Matt. 5:17-18).

7.2.2 The Readers' "Reading"

It is noteworthy how often, without always mentioning the term "Scripture(s)," Jesus asks his listeners whether they have not "read."[6] This occurs especially in Matthew's Gospel, which is addressed to Jewish readers (12:3, 5; 19:4-5; 21:16, 42; 22:31). In Jesus' day, to a godly Jew and to Jesus himself, "reading" meant reading the Scriptures. Writing and reading are parallels: the "Have you not [or, never] read?" is scarcely less powerful than the "It is written." This critical question, addressed to his listeners, is understandable only from the enormous respect that Jesus had for the Scriptures. Basically, this respect equaled his respect for God himself. The reproach: "Have you not read?" meant to him exactly the same as: "Do you not give heed to what God himself has said, and actually is still saying?"

---

6. About Jesus' frequent use of questions, see Zuck (1995, 235–76).

In addition to Matthew 22:31, we read, "Have you not read what David did when he was hungry, and those who were with him . . .? [1 Sam. 21:6] Or have you not read in the Law how on the Sabbath the priests in the temple profane the Sabbath and are guiltless? [Num. 28:9]" (Matt. 12:3, 5). "Have you not read that he who created them from the beginning made them male and female [Gen. 1:27], and said, 'Therefore a man shall leave his father and his mother and hold fast to his wife, and the two shall become one flesh'? [Gen. 2:24]" (Matt. 19:4-5). "[H]ave you never read, 'Out of the mouth of infants and nursing babies you have prepared praise'? [Ps. 8:2]" (Matt. 21:16). "Have you never read in the Scriptures: 'The stone that the builders rejected has become the cornerstone; this was the Lord's doing, and it is marvelous in our eyes'? [Ps. 118:22-23; cf. Isa. 8:14; 28:16]" (Matt. 21:42).

In particular Matthew 19:4-5 is interesting because the Old Testament verse concerned (Gen. 2:24) is treated not (only) as a statement of the Bible writer (which of course it is), but as a direct statement of God himself. To Jesus, it was apparently self-evident that what the Bible is saying, God himself is saying.[7]

The reproach in Jesus' voice implies that a person who doesn't "read" doesn't give heed to what he reads (cf. Matt. 24:15c), and if one does not give heed, one is disobedient to God himself. "Blessed [is] he who reads" (Rev. 1:3 NKJV; or "reads aloud" ESV), for one who reads—and reads well—is the person who listens to the voice of God. Or one who reads aloud passes on the words of God himself to those who are listening. In John 5:39, Jesus said, "You search the Scriptures because you think that in them you have eternal life; and it is *they that bear witness about me.*" To Jesus, this apparently meant the same as saying: it is God who bears witness about me through the Scriptures. Incidentally, Revelation 1:3 seems thereby to be rendering an implicit self-testimony concerning

---

7. A. Baum in Stadelmann (2002, 46).

the character of the book of Revelation as Scripture.

7.3 Second Timothy 3

7.3.1 Introduction

The most conspicuous passage with regard to the inspiration of the Bible is 2 Timothy 3:16, "All Scripture is breathed out by God [or, inspired by God, God-breathed] and profitable for teaching, for reproof, for correction, and for training in righteousness." For the second part of this verse, compare Romans 15:4 ("whatever was written in former days was written for our instruction, that through endurance and through the encouragement of the Scriptures we might have hope"); 1 Corinthians 9:10 ("It was written for our sake"); and 10:6, 11 ("these things took place as examples for us, that we might not desire evil as they did. . . . Now these things happened to them as an example, but they were written down for our instruction, on whom the end of the ages has come").

The ASV renders 2 Timothy 3:16 as follows: "Every scripture inspired of God . . . ." This need not be understood in a limiting sense, as though it implies that some scriptures are non-inspired. By analogy, the phrase, "All children born of mothers," need not imply that some children are not born of mothers. The ASV rendering is certainly possible, though less felicitous. Grammatically, it is better to understand the Greek word *theopneustos* ("God-breathed") as a predicate adjective ("All/every Scripture is God-breathed") than as an attributive adjective ("All/every God-breathed Scripture").[8]

As to the rendering "all" or "every," it is correct that the Greek word *pas* followed by a substantive without the article usually means "every," and not "all," but there are exceptions: *pas Israēl* (Rom. 11:26) is "all Israel."

The apostle Paul uses here the term *graphē*, a well-known biblical expression, which is used in the New Testament to designate

---

8. Cf. Ridderbos (1967, 230–31); Berkouwer (1967, 7–8); Van Genderen (2008, 76); extensively, Towner (2006, 585–88).

(a) separate Bible passages (see Mark 12:10; 15:28; Luke 4:21; John 19:37; Acts 8:35);

(b) the Tanakh in general (see John 7:38, 42; 10:35; Acts 8:32; Gal. 3:8, 22; 2 Pet. 1:20);

(c) the New Testament (1 Tim. 5:18; 2 Pet. 3:16; possibly also Rom. 16:26; see § 6.2.2).

7.3.2 *Theopneustos*

Our text attributes a special feature to Scripture, namely, that it is *theopneustos* (from *theos*, "God," and *pneō*, "to breathe," or *pneuma*, "breath, wind, spirit"). A most literal rendering might be "God-breathed" (cf. AMP, CJB, NIV). The most common English rendering contains the verb "to inspire," derived from the Vulgate (see below). Luther rendered this term with *von Gott eingegeben*, which means something like "given by God into [the author]." This rendering was followed by the Dutch States Translation: *van God ingegeven*. Actually, the prefix *in-* is not contained in the Greek word *theopneustos*. The latter can be taken, first, to imply that the *graphē*, or the *hiera grammata* ("sacred/holy writings," v. 15), were "breathed *out*" by God. That is, they went out from him, they were *his* words, and were written down exactly as he wished. Second, they are the words that he has "breathed *into*" the ears and the hearts of the Bible writers; that is, he had them recorded in written form by holy men (prophets and apostles).

We are dealing here with what elsewhere is called the "breath of the Almighty" (Job 32:8; 33:4). The Bible came about by God's "breath," just like the "breath" of the LORD's mouth made the heavens and all their host (Ps. 33:6). Of course, these are metaphors, but not simply metaphors; in a lingual way, they express the logical idea (not concept!) of inspiration (see more extensively below).

The phrases "breathed in" and "breathed out" are much more concrete that the vague *durchweht* (something like "blown through" as by a wind) that we encounter with Otto

Weber,[9] or in the Dutch church report *God met ons*.[10] At the same time, we should not read too much in the term *theopneustos*. The early church fathers did not use the term to refer to a special feature of the Bible. It was sometimes also used for post-apostolic writings, such as the metric inscription of the Phrygian bishop Avircius, who described his visit to the churches between Rome and Mesopotamia, and even for the decree of the Council of Ephesus (431) that condemned Nestorius.[11] However, these statements were not *graphē theopneustos*, "God-breathed *Scripture*."

It seems that Tertullian introduced the Latin word *inspiratio* into our theological vocabulary. In the Vulgate, *theopneustos* is rendered as *divinitus inspirata* ("divinely inspired"); this translation also rendered the Greek term *pheromenoi* ("carried along") in 2 Peter 1:21 as *inspirati*. In this way, the term "inspiration" entered into our modern languages. Of course, a little element is added here, for the *in* in *inspiratio* is not present in *theopneustos*.[12] Thus, the more correct rendering would be *(divinitus) spiratus*, both in the sense of an "expiration" (here in the original sense of "breathing out") and of an "inspiration" ("breathing in"). Hence the title of Andrew T. B. McGowan's book,[13] *The Divine Spiration of Scripture*. "Spiration" does not mean that God breathed *into* the Scriptures,[14] nor that God has inspired (given inspiration to) the writers, but rather that the Scriptures are "God-spired," "breathed out by God" (ESV). The "in" in *inspiratus* (cf. *eingegeben, ingegeven*, mentioned above) runs the risk of placing a one-sided emphasis on the Bible writers rather than underscoring the *divine* origin of the Scriptures, as the Bible text does.[15]

---

9. Weber: *von God durchweht* (1995, 259).
10. *God met ons* (1981, 15); cf. Bavinck (*RD* 1:425); Heyns (1976, 46); Potgieter (1990, 22).
11. Bruce (1988a, 281).
12. Cf. Warfield (1948, 284, 296); Berkouwer (1967, 5–6).
13. McGowan (2007, see especially 38–43).
14. Cf. Warfield (1948, 296).
15. Cf. White (2004, 49–50). Van Keulen (2003, 539) understandably contrasts

For the proper understanding of *theopneustia*, the second part of 2 Timothy 3:16 must not be overlooked: the fact that all Scripture was God-breathed explains why it is "profitable for teaching [other people], for reproof, for correction, and for training in righteousness."[16] That is, the purpose of the God-breathed Scripture is very practical (see previous section). This passage is far removed from the idea that the God-breathed Scripture is profitable for drawing scientific and scholarly conclusions from it, such as in the field of the natural or the historical sciences,[17] or even the field of scholarly theology. God breathed the Scriptures in order that through it people would receive teaching (of practical truth), refutation (of falsehood), and practical correction of their way of life. Compare the next verse (v. 17), ". . . that the man of God may be complete, equipped for every good work." In other words, the emphasis lies here on the servants of the Lord in whose hand the Bible is the means to identify for the church the right way it must go, and to correct those who have strayed from this way. Early Christianity was called "the Way" (Acts 19:9, 23; 22:4; 24:14, 2), not "the Teaching."

7.3.3 Knowing *Versus* Doing

It is good to remember how much Christianity has developed into a religion of *knowing* ("What can I know?"), which was much more an effect of Greco-Roman culture than of Jewish culture. The Old Testament presents to us much more a religion of *doing* ("What must I do?"), as is still the case in present-day Judaism. For instance, note how a practicing Jew such as Marc Zvi Brettler deals with biblical authority; the Bible is used primarily not to support doctrinal tenets but rather to establish what the Eternal One expects from his people.[18] The

---

inspiration and theopneustia: "The core concept of Berkouwer's earlier view of Scripture is 'inspiration.' In his later work, the 'theopneustia' of Scripture is central."

16. Towner (2006, 590–94).
17. See, e.g., Ouweneel (2018l).
18. M. Z. Brettler in Brown (2007, 1–9).

Bible aims at "instruction in righteousness," says the apostle Paul (2 Tim. 3:16 KJV). This means primarily not that we learn from the Bible how to construct a theological theory about righteousness, but from the Bible we learn the proper way of the *tsaddiq* (the "righteous one"), of the "[wo]man of God" (cf. 1 Tim. 6:11; cf. "man of God" in Deut. 33:1; Josh. 14:6; 1 Sam. 2:27; 9:6-10; 1 Kings 13:1-31; 17:18, 24; 20:28; 2 Kings 1:9-13; 2 Tim. 3:16-17).[19] As we read in Titus 2:11-12, "[T]he grace of God has appeared, bringing salvation for all people, *training* us to renounce ungodliness and worldly passions, and to live self-controlled, *upright*, and godly lives in the present age." It is the "wise men" (cf. Dan. 11:33, 35; 12:3, 10) who "turn" God's people "to righteousness" (12:3), that is, to a righteous walk. God "has told you, O man, what is good; and what does the LORD require of you but to do justice [i.e., righteousness], and to love kindness, and to walk humbly with your God?" (Micah 6:8).

To be sure, this is no straightforward instruction, as if the text yielded no problems at all. The Bible may well have been inspired, but it must also be interpreted. A zealously practicing Jew such as Brettler can encounter all kinds of difficulties here.[20] For instance, if he wishes to celebrate *Sukkoth* (the Feast of Booths), he must decide whether he will celebrate the feast for seven days (Deut. 16:13), or whether he will attach an eighth day of "solemn rest" to it (Lev. 23:39).[21] He must also decide whether the prohibition of eating non-slaughtered meat refers to him (Deut. 14:21), or only to the priests, and whether as a non-priest he may eat a cow that was found dead alongside the road (see Lev. 17:15). Brettler viewed such passages as irreconcilable.

One may dispute the latter point, but at least we may agree that solutions must be found for the conflicts mentioned here.

---

19. Cf. White (2004, 52–53).
20. M. Z. Brettler in Brown (2007, 5).
21. Actually, I see no contradiction here: Lev. 23 is simply an extension of Deut. 16.

One can do this in the Orthodox Jewish way; that is, many centuries ago, rabbis decided once and for all how the texts must be explained (what is allowed, and what not). Or one does this in the modern scientific way, through grammatical-historical exegesis, as Brettler prefers. In the former case, the authority of the Bible threatens to be replaced *de facto* by the authority of spiritual leaders, especially those of long ago: the older they are, the more authoritative. In the second case, the authority of the Bible threatens to be replaced *de facto* by the authority of modern science: the more modern it is, the more authoritative. We seem unable to escape this dilemma. A third option might be to appeal to the guidance of the Holy Spirit. No matter how good this may appear, this is often only a pseudo-solution because, over against the authority of ancient leaders or of modern science, we now get the authority of purely personal hunches.

Of course, Brettler did not refer to 2 Timothy 3:16, but my own conclusion is as follows.

(a) In some way, the biblical text comes from God, through people, and thus possesses divine authority.

(b) However, the text, which is ancient and difficult—separated from us by many cultural barriers—must first be translated to our modern life situation. This occurs with the aid of a variety of authorities (wise leaders, scientists, one's own conscience—preferably a combination of them), which authorities inevitably stand between the text and one's own life situation.

(c) The text refers much more to what people must do than to what people must know. That is, its focus is far more ethical than theological. A few verses earlier, the apostle Paul speaks of "my teaching, my conduct, my aim in life, my faith, my patience, my love, my steadfastness, my persecutions and sufferings" (2 Tim. 3:10–11). Here, the first point mentioned, "my teaching" (Gk. *mou tēi didaskaliai*), is further qualified, so to speak, by the subsequent expressions: "my conduct" (Gr.

agōgē, "manner of life," KJV; "way of life" NIV), and so on. Here Paul is referring not to theological teaching, but to ethical teaching.

7.4 First Peter 1

7.4.1 The Spirit of Christ

Inspiration (*theopneustia*) is God's work, but this work is performed by the Bible writers. We find some further details about how this work is performed in 1 Peter 1:10-11, "Concerning this salvation, the prophets who prophesied about the grace that was to be yours searched and inquired carefully, inquiring what person or time the Spirit of Christ in them was indicating when he predicted the sufferings of Christ and the subsequent glories."

This passage does not deal in a direct sense with the inspiration of the Bible but more generally with the prophesying (testifying) by the (Old Testament) prophets. However, in this way, the text also teaches us indirectly about the *recorded* prophecies of the Old Testament.

Notice here the exceptional expression "Spirit of Christ," which is found only here and in Romans 8:9[22] (but cf. the "Spirit of Jesus" in Acts 16:7, the "Spirit of Jesus Christ" in Phil. 1:19, and the "Spirit of his Son" in Gal. 4:6). Presumably, the apostle Peter chose this description of the Holy Spirit to emphasize especially that it was the Spirit *of* Christ witnessing *about* Christ. Jesus said something similar about the "Spirit of truth" who was to be poured out very soon, and who was to proclaim and glorify Christ, who is the truth (John 16:13-15; 14:6). In Scripture, it is God/Christ testifying through his Spirit about God/Christ.

7.4.2 Four Lessons

From this passage, we learn at least four lessons that are important for a better understanding of the inspiration of Scripture.

---

22. Davids (1990, 62–63 including note 26); cf. Ouweneel (2018e, §§1.4.4, 3.3.2, and 3.6.1).

(a) Inspiration occurred *through the activity of the Holy Spirit* within the Bible writers; each prophet was (in Hebrew) an *ish haruach*, a "man of the Spirit"[23] (Hos. 9:7). Compare King David's statement, "The Spirit of the LORD speaks by me; his word is on my tongue" (2 Sam. 23:2; also see 1 Sam. 10:6; Isa. 61:1; Ezek. 2:2; Joel 2:28). Of course, it is the prophets who testify, but much more than that, it is the Spirit who testifies in and through them. Compare Jeremiah 1: not only "whatever I command you, you shall speak" (v. 7), but: "Behold, I have put my words in your mouth" (v. 9).

(b) The prophets wrote down infallible truth, whose fulfillment was certain, concerning both the sufferings that would come upon Christ and the subsequent glories, namely, his resurrection, his ascension and glorification, his second coming and kingdom. This is what Jesus explained to the Emmaus disciples, "Was it not necessary that the Christ should suffer these things and[24] enter into his glory?" (Luke 24:26).

(c) The inspiration through the Holy Spirit took place in such an overwhelming and authoritative way that the human authors themselves sometimes could not understand what the God-breathed words that they wrote down actually signified. If the Bible writers were the only authors, we would not be able to understand this. But if the Spirit is the Primary Author, we understand this very well. Clear examples are found in Daniel 8:27 ("I was appalled by the vision and did not understand it") and 12:8 ("I heard, but I did not understand").[25] Also compare Jesus' statement, "I tell you that many prophets and kings desired to see what you see, and did not see it, and to hear what you hear, and did not hear it" (Luke 10:24; cf.

---

23. This is so if we read an uppercase S here (cf. ERV, MSG, VOICE, YLT), i.e., if we should not think here of a man that is fervent in spirit (ecstatic), as we may expect from an Old Testament prophet according to the basic meaning of Heb. *n-b-'*; cf. Rom. 12:11, "fervent in spirit," *or* "fervent in the Spirit" (CSB, CEB).

24. Gk. *kai* epexegeticum: "and [thus]."

25. Blum (1981, 222).

Matt. 13:17). Or his statement to the disciple Peter: "What I am doing you do not understand now, but afterward you will understand" (John 13:7).

(d) Here again, inspiration is about *practical* matters of everyday life, not about theological teaching. The prophets' aim was to preach the way of salvation, the realization of redemption, well-being, peace, bliss, and the particular place that Christ's sufferings and glorification occupied in these blessings. Human reflection on these matters recorded in Scripture may well lead to soteriology and Christology. However, the purpose of the prophets was not the correct soteriological (or any other "-logical") understanding, but rather salvation itself. Inspiration is about God himself teaching people, through human instruments, about the way of righteousness (Heb. *tsedaqah*; 2 Tim. 3:16–17), and the road to ultimate peace (Heb. *shalom*, peace here in the broader sense of salvation). Theological reflection on these matters is a derivative activity arising from studying this content.

7.5 Second Peter 1

7.5.1 Three Lessons

In 2 Peter 1 we find another important passage that deals with biblical inspiration:

> [W]e have the prophetic word more fully confirmed, to which you will do well to pay attention as to a lamp shining in a dark place, until the day dawns and the morning star rises in your hearts, knowing this first of all, that no prophecy of Scripture comes from someone's own interpretation. For no prophecy was ever produced by the will of man, but men spoke from God as they were carried along by the Holy Spirit (vv. 19–21).

Of course, this passage is literally about "speaking," not about "writing" or "Scripture." But, as we have seen, in the broadest sense of the word all Bible writers were prophets, and God speaks through all the true prophets, including the Bible writers. Thus, it is no wonder that this Bible passage is adduced in every treatment of the subject of inspiration. We learn here, for instance, the following things.

(a) No prophecy "comes from someone's own interpretation" (Gk. *idias epilyseōs ou ginetai*, v. 20). This "own interpretation" does *not* refer to those *expounding* these prophecies but to the prophets themselves; see, for instance, the NIV: "[Y]ou must understand that no prophecy of Scripture came about by the prophet's own interpretation [others: understanding] of things." In other words, genuine prophecy comes not from (the inner feelings, intuitions, and deliberations of) the prophet himself but from God. As American theologians, father Cleon L. Rogers Jr. and son Cleon L. Rogers III, put it, the word "interpretation" (Gk. *epilysis*) here almost means inspiration. They claim that here the genitive form ("someone's own interpretation") indicates the source. Peter speaks of the divine origin of Scripture, not about its correct exposition.[26] This is also clear from the sequel: Peter emphasizes that the prophecies come not from people but from the Holy Spirit.[27] We are dealing here with the words of God himself, words that people may not manipulate according to their own ideas; hence the rendering "of private interpretation" in some translations.

(b) From a human point of view, the Bible books were certainly written down at the writers' own initiative (cf. Luke 1:1-4 as an impressive example).[28] They were rather *active*, for they were *men* who *spoke* — it was not just God speaking through them. However, viewed from God's standpoint, the prophets, including the Bible writers, were urged ("carried along") by the Holy Spirit. Take, for instance, Amos: "The lion has roared; who will not fear? The Lord GOD has spoken; who can but prophesy?" (3:8). Or, as David says, "The Spirit of the

---

26. Rogers and Rogers (1998, 584).
27. Cf. White (2004, 58–59).
28. Bruce (1988b, 384) also pointed out that Luke describes those parts of the missionary journeys during which he accompanied Paul much more extensively than the other parts, during which he was not present.

LORD speaks by me; his word is on my tongue" (2 Sam. 23:2; cf. Ps. 45:1c, "my tongue is like the pen of a ready scribe"). As a discouraged Jeremiah puts it, "If I say, 'I will not mention him, or speak any more in his name,' there is in my heart as it were a burning fire shut up in my bones, and I am weary with holding it in, and I cannot" (20:9).

(c) Thus, at the same time, the Bible writers were relatively *passive* in their work of writing: they were "carried along" (Gk. *pheromenoi*), or "borne along (moved and impelled)," like leaves in the wind (cf. *pheromenēs pnoēs biaias*: "a strong driving wind," Acts 2:2 NABRE). This is what the Bible's inspiration is: a being "borne, carried, driven, impelled" by the Holy Spirit. This process presupposes a certain power, one which does not eliminate the Bible writers' own deliberations, as we will see, but which ensured that they wrote down God's thoughts.

7.5.2 Finer Details

We can now refine our description of inspiration. Notice that I say "description," not "definition." Biblical inspiration cannot be conceptually enclosed within the boundaries (Latin *fines*) of a de-*fini*-tion; we can form only an idea of it.[29] When J. A. Heyns says that it is difficult to enclose the mystery of the inspiration in concepts,[30] I reply that this is simply *impossible*, at least if we take the term "concept" seriously here. Therefore, I would not like to suggest that everything that we can deduce from 2 Timothy 3:16, 1 Peter 1:10-11, and 2 Peter 1:20-21 is drawn out by some neutral logic, for such a thing does not exist.

Here again, I cannot escape my hermeneutical circle (see §1.7). I trust that my faith-idea of inspiration is formed by the Bible, but at the same time I cannot help but interpret these passages on the basis of my idea of inspiration. In brief, my exposition of Scripture influences my faith-idea of inspiration, and my inspiration idea influences my exposition of Scrip-

---

29. See §5.9.3 and Ouweneel (1995, §§4.2.1 and 4.2.2; 2013, §1.5; 2014; 2015).
30. Heyns (1976, 39).

ture; I cannot escape this circle, nor can other theologians. My inspiration idea is not the result of my theological research, and *cannot* be so; on the contrary, it necessarily and inevitably lies at the *basis* of my research. However, it is equally true that this research, in a continual interaction, refines my inspiration idea.

The Bible was inspired in the sense that men who were driven by the Holy Spirit wrote down God-breathed words, which therefore have divine authority for people. I emphasize again that neither 2 Timothy 3:16 nor any other passage says that the *writers* were inspired, but rather that *Scripture* is inspired. In some cases, the Bible writers might have written other books,[31] but these may not on that basis be viewed as inspired. Moreover, although the Bible writers were godly people, they definitely committed sins in their lives; think of Moses (Num. 20:10-12), David (2 Sam. 11), and Peter (Luke 22:54-62). *Only* the Bible books they wrote were God-breathed. Nonetheless, the authors were fully involved in their writing, for *they* were "carried along" (Vulgate: *inspirati*) by the Holy Spirit; and 1 Peter 1:11 says that "the Spirit of Christ" was "in them." In *this* specific sense, we can say that the writers, too, were "inspired," as the Vulgate clearly states. The Bible writers were, so to speak, "breathed *upon*" by God, and the result of their work, Holy Scripture, was "breathed *out*" by God.

We can compare this with several other Bible passages that speak of the activity of the Holy Spirit in both inspiration and preaching (Matt. 22:43; Rom. 15:18-19; 2 Cor. 3:6, 8; 4:13; 1 Thess. 1:5-6; Rev. 1:10; 4:2 [if "Spirit" is meant, and not "spirit"]; also see Isa. 48:16; 61:1; Ezek. 11:5; Micah 3:8).[32]

7.5.3 Summary

In summary, we may distinguish at least five components in

---

31. I have already mentioned other letters of Paul to the Corinthians, and his letter to the Laodiceans, unless this is the same as Ephesians (Col. 4:16; see §6.8.1).
32. Cf. Weber (1981, 229).

the process of the inspiration.

(a) *The divine Author.* The Word of God went out from God, was "breathed out" by him. The words that have been recorded in the Scriptures are his own words. He himself is the source and cause of the Bible.

(b) *The divine Instrument.* The Triune God was involved in the work of inspiration: the work went forth from the Father, it occurred "in" and "through" the Son (notice the expression "Spirit of Christ; also cf. 1 Cor. 8:6, "from" the Father, "through" Jesus Christ), in the power of Holy Spirit, who was the actual agent of the work.

(c) *The human instrument.* God used godly men[33] to write down his divine Word. These people did not function as "word processors," for each had his own style and vocabulary (see §§8.3 and 8.4). God fully maintained their personalities, and employed those personalities in order to reveal his thoughts through them.

(d) *The process of writing.* Godly men took the initiative to write, made their preparations (Luke 1:1-4), chose their words and sentences, and wrote them down. At the same time, it was the Holy Spirit who took the initiative, carrying these men along, giving them his words and sentences, and urging them to write these down. As we will see more extensively (chapter 8), there is only an apparent contradiction between these two statements.

(e) *The written result.* The product of God's "breathing" and the being "carried along" of the writers is a written book, which is thoroughly human and at the same time thoroughly divine, that is, invested with divine authority.

As 2 Peter 1 also teaches, the purpose of inspiration was to produce very practical matters: the prospect of the kingdom of God, which at the second coming of Christ will break

---

33. Although there were godly "prophetesses" (Exod. 15:20; Judg. 4:4; 2 Kings 22:14; Isa. 8:3; Luke 2:36), I am not aware of any female authors of any portion of Scripture.

through in full glory, the rising of the "morning star" in human hearts, and the encouraging role that the prophetic word plays in this. Driven by the Spirit, prophets speak on behalf of God, not (primarily) to arbitrate between our (theological or natural-scientific) theories but rather to show us the way we must walk in dark days until the day (of God's Messianic kingdom) will dawn (v. 19).

7.6 First Corinthians 2

7.6.1 First Series Leading to Enlightenment

Another passage of signal importance, emphasized as crucial by, for instance, Karl Barth,[34] is 1 Corinthians 2:9-16,

> But, as it is written, "What no eye has seen, nor ear heard, nor the heart of man imagined, what God has prepared for those who love him" — these things God has revealed to us through the Spirit. For the Spirit searches everything, even the depths of God. For who knows a person's thoughts except the spirit of that person, which is in him? So also no one comprehends the thoughts of God except the Spirit of God. Now we have received not the spirit of the world, but the Spirit who is from God, that we might understand the things freely given us by God. And we impart this in words not taught by human wisdom but taught by the Spirit, interpreting spiritual truths to those who are spiritual. The natural person does not accept the things of the Spirit of God, for they are folly to him, and he is not able to understand them because they are spiritually discerned. The spiritual person judges all things, but is himself to be judged by no one. "For who has understood the mind of the Lord so as to instruct him?" But we have the mind of Christ.

We may distinguish here the following five elements, in which the Holy Spirit plays the decisive role in five different operations: (re)search, revelation, illumination (twice), and inspiration. I will the use the classical Latin terms, which for the English reader will be easily recognizable.

---

34. Barth (*CD* I/2:515-16)

(a) **Scrutatio** (*scrutiny, [re]search*): "For the Spirit searches everything, even the depths of God. For who knows a person's thoughts except the spirit of that person, which is in him? So also no one comprehends the thoughts of God except the Spirit of God" (vv. 10b-11). This precedes all revelation and inspiration; the Spirit is the One who reveals and inspires, but he can do this only because he fathoms and knows the "depths of God" (of his being and his thoughts). And this he can do because the Spirit of God is God himself (just as the Son is God himself, and the Father is God himself).

(b) **Revelatio** (*revelation*): "'What no eye has seen, nor ear heard, nor the heart of man imagined, what God has prepared for those who love him' — these things God has revealed to us through the Spirit" (v. 10a). As far as this is possible, the Holy Spirit has revealed (disclosed, exposed, manifested, unfolded) to us the "depths of God." This revelation must be carefully distinguished from the inspiration (next section, point [d]). "Long ago, at many times and in many ways, God spoke to our fathers by the prophets" (Heb. 1:1) — this is revelation. But if all these prophets and apostles (the "us" in 1 Cor. 2:10) had simply written down their collective revelations, this would not automatically have yielded the "Holy Scriptures." To this end, in addition to revelation, inspiration was needed. Revelation is the divine *manifestation* of the truth, inspiration is the divine *recording* of the truth.[35] On the one hand, much has been revealed to the prophets that has not been recorded in inspired Scriptures (cf. Rev. 10:4, "Seal up what the seven thunders have said, and do not write it down"). On the other hand, there are many Bible passages, such as those of a hortatory nature, that do not contain any new revelation at all.

Therefore, it seems to me to be incorrect that Hendrikus Berkhof saw in Paul's letters an example of a virtual simultaneity between revelation and inspiration.[36] All these letters

---

35. This seems to make more sense than the confusing description of Erickson (1998, 226), who calls revelation a vertical, and inspiration a horizontal activity.

36. Berkhof (1986, 87).

were inspired, but large segments (e.g., Phil.) contain hardly any new revelation. Thus, in a certain sense, Berkhof is right when he quotes the well-known modernist view that the "Bible cannot be identified with the revelation. It is the human response to it. We encounter the revelation here indirectly, in the mirror of the human testimony."[37] However, this is correct *only* in the sense that revelation (usually) precedes its recording. My point is that not only revelation but also its recording, as a response to this revelation, is divine. This is the secret of inspiration: not only revelation but also inspiration is a work of God. The Scriptures are the human response to God's revelation, but at the same time they are the divine effect of divine inspiration. In brief: revelation is divine, its recording is divine as well as human. Yet, this does not prevent us from calling the recorded result "revelation of God" as well (about this, see §5.1).

(c) **Illuminatio** (*enlightenment of the prophets*): "[W]e have received . . . the Spirit who is from God, that we might understand the things freely given us by God" (1 Cor. 2:12). The "we" here must be the inner circle of the apostles and their intimate co-workers (cf. 1 John 1:1-4). The Holy Spirit not only unfolded the truth to those to whom God's revelation came, but also worked in them so that they not only heard the truth but also would know (acknowledge, understand) the things that God freely granted to them. With the Old Testament prophets, this was not always the case (see §7.4.1); therefore, New Testament apostles received more enlightenment than Old Testament prophets, whereas with regard to the inspiration of the books they wrote there was no difference between them.

7.6.2 Second Series Leading to Enlightenment

(d) **Inspiratio** (*inspiration*): "And we impart this in words not taught by human wisdom but taught by the Spirit, interpreting spiritual truths to those who are spiritual" (v. 13). The last

---

37. Ibid., 90.

phrase of this verse (Gk. *pneumatikois pneumatika synkrinontes*) has led to much discussion as to the correct translation and interpretation.[38] Does the verb mean "comparing" (KJV)?[39] Or "explaining" (CJB)? "Interpreting" (ESV)? If Mounce ("expressing spiritual truths in spiritual words") or DARBY ("communicating spiritual [things] by spiritual [means]") is right,[40] the apostle Paul is referring here to the proclamation of Christian truth, both the oral preaching (cf. 1 Thess. 2:13) and the *inspiration* of the New Testament books. That is, the spiritual truths (things, matters) of which the Bible writers speak are not enclosed in a defective form but in spiritual words. These are words that carry the same stamp of the Holy Spirit as the truths that are contained in them. The form is just as authoritative as the content—insofar as these concepts can really be separated, or even properly distinguished—for both are spiritual, that is, worked by the Holy Spirit.

If we render *synkrinontes* as "explaining" or "interpreting," namely, spiritual truths to spiritual people, we are dealing here not with inspiration but with *enlightenment*. If spiritual truths come to people who themselves are not spiritual, these truth avail nothing. Spiritual things can be explained only to spiritual people (see next point).

(e) **Illuminatio** (*enlightenment of the readers*). This is the fifth step, moving from the "depths of God" to the hearts of human beings. If this matter was not intended already in verse 13b (see previous point), then it certainly is intended in verses 14-16: "The natural person does not accept the things of the Spirit of God, for they are folly to him, and he is not able to understand them because they are spiritually discerned. The spiritual person judges all things, but is himself to be judged by no one. 'For who has understood the mind of the Lord so as to instruct him?' [Isa. 40:13] But we have the mind of

---

38. See extensively, Fee (1987, ad loc.); Thiselton (2000, ad loc.).
39. This rendering is not related to what Paul wishes to say here; see Fee (1987, 115).
40. See *TDNT* 3:953-54.

Christ." Not only the *revelation* of God's truth and the *inspiration* of Holy Scripture required the Holy Spirit, but also those who receive God's Word need the Spirit. The Bible reader must be spiritual, that is, open to the enlightenment by the Holy Spirit. The truth of God can be judged and understood only in a spiritual way, that is, by the light of the Holy Spirit. It is an amazing statement that those who possess this spiritual enlightenment in principle possess the same mind (insight, mentality, thought, way of thinking, attitude, Gk. *nous*) concerning the truth as Christ himself possesses. Through the revelation by the Spirit, the inspiration by the Spirit, and the illumination by the Spirit, the water that the believer drinks is as pure now as this water was in the original source, and the rays of light are as pure now as the moment they left the sun.

7.6.3 Comparison

Just as inspiration must be distinguished from *revelation* (see §7.6.1, point [b]), inspiration must be distinguished from *enlightenment (illumination)*.[41] The inspiration of Scripture alone is no guarantee that those who read it will understand it. To this end, the enlightenment of heart and mind is needed. Of the Emmaus disciples who encountered Jesus after his resurrection, we read, "And their eyes were opened, and they recognized him [i.e., Jesus]. And he vanished from their sight. They said to each other, 'Did not our hearts burn within us while he talked to us on the road, while he opened to us the Scriptures?'" A little while later, we read of all the disciples, "Then he [i.e., Jesus] opened their minds to understand the Scriptures" (Luke 24:31–32, 45).

As we have seen, even the (Old Testament) Bible writers themselves did not always understand what they were writ-

---

41. On the one hand, Wentsel (1981, 185–86) generalized the *theopneustia* too much, as if it were a general term for the guidance of the Spirit, while on the other hand, he hardly distinguished between inspiration and enlightenment because of the incorrect presupposition that inspiration refers to the pre-apostolic and apostolic eras, and enlightenment to the post-apostolic time.

ing down (1 Pet. 1:11; see §7.4.1). Yet, their Scriptures were fully inspired. Apparently, there are different degrees of enlightenment; but I am unaware of any biblical evidence that there are also different degrees of inspiration. The apostles were more enlightened than the Old Testament prophets. However, the words of the Old Testament prophets and the New Testament apostles that we encounter in Scripture are all equally inspired, equally divine, equally authoritative.

I wish to underscore here the significance of the enlightenment of the readers, a matter that is of the greatest importance for all biblical scholarship. Without this enlightenment, even the greatest academic scholarship will avail nothing. Joseph Ratzinger pointed to the ignorance not only of the Roman soldiers who crucified Jesus (Luke 23:33–34) and of the Jews who had handed him over to the Romans (Acts 3:14–17) but also to the learned Saul of Tarsus who had been "a blasphemer, persecutor [of the church], and insolent opponent. But I received mercy because I had acted ignorantly in unbelief" (1 Tim. 1:13):

> [H]e who had studied under the best masters [cf. Acts 22:3] and who might reasonably have considered himself a real expert on the Scriptures, has to acknowledge, in retrospect, that he was ignorant. . . . This combination of expert knowledge and deep ignorance certainly causes us to ponder. It reveals the whole problem of knowledge that remains self-sufficient and so does not arrive at Truth itself, which ought to transform man [cf. John 8:32].[42]

Ratzinger also pointed to the wise men from the east, who asked about the newborn King of the Jews, and wrote, "The chief priests and scribes know exactly where the Messiah is born [see Micah 5:2]. But they do not recognize him. Knowingly, they remain blind." Their problem was not only that they were blind but that they *thought* they could see. As Jesus told some of them, "If you were blind, you would have

---

42. Ratzinger (2011, 207).

no guilt; but now that you say, 'We see,' your guilt remains" (John 9:41). Only the blind who *seek* help can be helped (Mark 10:46-52). Some unbelieving theologians may have tremendous academic qualities; but a simple soul enlightened by the Holy Spirit will "see" more than they do.

The Bible was inspired by the Holy Spirit. However, such a God-breathed Scripture would avail nothing if there were no readers or listeners enlightened by that same Spirit. Without the enlightenment of the heart, the Bible reader receives no understanding. Paul prayed "that the God of our Lord Jesus Christ, the Father of glory, may give you the Spirit of wisdom and of revelation in the knowledge of him, having the eyes of your hearts enlightened" (Eph. 1:17-18). The Holy Spirit is both the Spirit of revelation and the Spirit of illumination. As Jesus said, "[T]he Helper, the Holy Spirit, whom the Father will send in my name, he will teach you all things and bring to your remembrance all that I have said to you" (John 14:26); and, "When the Spirit of truth comes, he will guide you into all the truth" (16:13).

7.7 Theories of Inspiration (1)

7.7.1 Introduction[43]

The inspiration of Scripture by the Spirit of God through human instruments was a miraculous event that surpasses human conceptualization. We certainly can speak about it in a rational way, but only as long as we keep in mind that (a) this can be done in the form of ideas only, not of concepts, and that (b) inspiration ultimately surpasses reason. Although inspiration is indeed a supra-rational matter, theologians have often endeavored to encapsulate it in a (logical-analytical) theory or model. This is understandable, for this is the very task of theologians: they must try to supply a logical-analytical warrant for the miracle of inspiration, or any miracle for that matter. Undertaking this is both a possibility and a duty—as long as theologians do not imagine that they would be able to *contain*

---

43. See Ouweneel (1997b).

this miracle in their concepts and theories.

We will briefly pay attention to several of these theories. Toward most of these I will adopt a rather negative attitude. Nonetheless they have some practical value because implicitly they express the various modal ideas that shed light on certain aspects of biblical inspiration. However, they run the risk of treating such ideas as concepts, as if the supra-rational, transcendent inspiration could be "pulled down" to the rational-immanent so that it is "caught" in rational-theoretical concepts. This is a fundamental error, which is characteristic of most, if not all, theories of inspiration, no matter how different they may (seem to) be.

This has been clearly discerned by several authors. For instance, Herman Bavinck wrote, "A [doctrine of] inspiration, therefore, is not an explanation of Scripture, nor actually a theory, but it is and ought to be a believing confession of what Scripture witness concerning itself, ... Inspiration is a dogma . . . not a scientific pronouncement but a confession of faith."[44] Otto Weber wrote, "[T]he concept [!?] of inspiration . . . serves the effort to ascribe to the Bible a tangible quality, inherently present in it, automatically given by its origin and means of development; that is, the certainty granted to us in faith in Christ is replaced by a security which is found in the tangible realm . . . ."[45] And G. C. Berkouwer wrote, "It would be incorrect to found this faith [i.e., faith in Scripture] upon an inspiration *theory*," and continued by pointing out that the inspiration metaphors that the church fathers used not necessarily imply or presuppose an inspiration *theory*, even less a supernaturalistic or mechanical theory (see §7.8).[46]

---

44. Bavinck (*RD* 1:436).
45. Weber (1981, 233). This distinction between *certainty* (Ger. *Gewissheit*) and *security* (Ger. *Sicherheit*) (about which see also ibid., 202, 296) may well be understood as analogous to the distinction between the certainty of practical, transcendent faith and the guarantee of some theory of immanent thought.
46. Berkouwer (1967, 20).

Thus, before beginning my summary of several theories, let me clearly state that the Bible is the infallible Word of God but no theory of inspiration (or any theological theory) is ever infallible.[47] No matter how orthodox the outcome of a discussion between, particularly, the mechanical and the organic *models* may be, people's *pre-theoretical* belief in the inspiration of Scripture is, as such, hardly touched by it. It is desperately perilous to make *belief* in inspiration dependent upon any ingenious (but fallible) inspiration *theory*.

7.7.2 *Spatial:* the Dualistic Theory

We come now to the first theory of inspiration, namely, the one in which the modal idea of the *spatial* is implied. It is the "dualistic" or "restricted" theory. This model views humans as being completely involved in the process of inspiration, such that they receive their own, autonomous place alongside the Holy Spirit. Matters thought to belong to the center[48] of Scripture, that is, which are viewed as necessary for people's knowledge of God and of his salvation, such as the Ten Commandments, certain prophecies, the teaching and life of Christ, are attributed to the Holy Spirit and are considered to be divine. Other matters are thought to belong to the periphery, that is, as unnecessary for people's knowledge of God and of his salvation. Supposedly, to this category belong many Bible stories, geographical and genealogical details viewed as less relevant; they are thought to be the product of purely human observation and research, and thus to be fallible, defective, and at any rate superfluous for the knowledge of God and of salvation.[49] In the reduction as applied by Johann Salomo Semler, entire Bible books are simply set aside as irrelevant, and thus as non-inspired (Ruth, Chron., Ezra, Neh., Esther, Song, Rev.).[50]

---

47. Troost (2004, 288).
48. German theologians often speak of the *Mitte* ("the middle"); see, e.g., Weber (1981, 237, 240, 265).
49. Cf. the analysis by Berkouwer (1967, 66–68, 77–79).
50. See Semler (1980).

Inspiration: Starting Points and Models

The nature of the distinction between center and periphery is clearly modal-spatial. As a spatial *idea*, pointing to the *transcendent scope* of Scripture (also see §7.9.3), it may be of some value. However, in this theory, this distinction is viewed as a *conceptual separation* between parts of the *immanent* Scripture: some immanent parts are supposedly inspired, other immanent parts are not. In my view, the objections against this view are simple.

(a) This view overlooks the evident *transcendent* unity and coherence of Scripture. It ignores, or even denies, the authoritative power of the "it is written,"[51] which is true for all portions of the Bible because "Scripture cannot be broken" (John 10:34-35). In its immanent divergence, the one and only eternal, transcendent "Word of God" (Mark 7:13; John 10:35; Rom. 9:6; Heb. 4:12), the one and only "Law of God" (John 10:34; 12:34; 15:25; Acts 25:8; Rom. 3:10-19; 1 Cor. 14:21), is expressed in all the temporal words of Scripture: the spiritual things of God are expressed in "spiritual words" (i.e., words of the Spirit, 1 Cor. 2:13; cf. §7.6).

(b) We are struck here by the scholastic nature–supernature dualism, in this case, the human natural *versus* the divine supernatural: the Bible contains human portions and divine portions. This dualism is created here *within* the temporal-immanent reality of Scripture by dividing the latter into a human natural portion and a divine-supernatural portion, a human element and a divine element, or a human factor and a divine factor, between which no real equilibrium is possible. This dualism creates a *horizontal* "spatial" separation within immanent reality, rather than identifying the *vertical* "spatial" duality (not dualism or separation!) of the one transcendent Word and the many immanent Scriptures. We will examine this dualism a little more closely in a moment (§7.8).

(c) Scripture is subordinated to an unacceptable subjectivism: by means of their own enlightened (or supposedly en-

---
51. Gr. *gegraptai*, dozens of times in the New Testament, from Matt. 2:5 to 1 Pet. 1:16 (see §6.3.1).

lightened) reason, *or* their religious intuition, *or* their religious experiences, theologians, or more generally Bible readers, must, decide for themselves what is the center of the Bible. In the light of this decision, they must determine which Bible portions do and which portions do not share in the *theopneustia*, that is, which portions must be viewed as divine, and which must not. Moreover, in such a view it is to be expected that the part viewed as infallible will become smaller and smaller as time passes, as modern(istic) scholarship discovers more and more (supposed) errors in the Bible.

7.8   *Kinematic:* the Mechanical Theory

7.8.1   Introduction

The mechanical theory of inspiration is rooted in the modal idea of the *kinematic* ("movement"). According to this model, the human part in the inscripturation of the Word is reduced to a minimum: the human writers were entirely passively moved by the Spirit (2 Pet. 1:21 KJV; cf. ESV: carried along [as leaves by the wind]). The Bible writers were only instruments or mechanisms (tools) in the moving hands of the Spirit ("mechanical" refers to machines, which are "operated" by humans).[52] Earlier, I made the comparison with typewriters, dictaphones, and word processors; I can add to them the traditional metaphor of the *calamus* ("reed, pen"), which goes back to Pope Gregory the Great.[53] This image was taken from Psalm 45:2, "I address my verses to the king; my tongue is like the pen [Septuagint: *kalamos*; Vulgate: *calamus*] of a ready scribe." Like the hand controlling a pen or a machine (such as a word processor), so the hand of God supposedly controlled the Bible writer, the latter remaining perfectly passive.

The mechanical model entails that the Spirit put into the hearts of the writers not only the subjects but also the specific words, and according to some, even the dots and the commas (cf. the jot and the tittle in Matt. 5:18 KJV), and, as to the He-

---

52. Cf. Goldingay (1994, 223–31).
53. *Moralia in Iob* 7.

brew, even the vowels. The only responsibility of the Bible writers was to record the dictation as accurately as possible. The Swiss creed called the *Helvetic Consensus Formula* (1675) put it this way:

> The Hebrew original of the Old Testament which we have received and to this day do retain as handed down by the Hebrew Church, "who had been given the oracles of God" (Rom 3:2), is, not only in its consonants, but in its vowels — either the vowel points themselves, or at least the power of the points — not only in its matter, but in its words, inspired by God.[54]

This was used as an argument against textual criticism, which (in the eyes of the opponents) threatens to relativize spelling and punctuation. The Helvetic Confession is the more remarkable because the vowel marks were added to the Hebrew text by the Masoretes (seventh to eleventh centuries) many centuries after the completion of the Hebrew canon. They were not always sure of the correct vowels, and occasionally differed from the text underlying the Septuagint. For instance, in Genesis 47:31b ("Israel bowed himself upon the head of his staff/bed") the Septuagint apparently translated *m-t-h* as *matteh*, "staff" (as sanctioned in Heb. 11:21), whereas the Masoretic text reads *mitteh*, "bed."

The theory of mechanical inspiration has had ardent Roman Catholic, Lutheran, Reformed as well as Evangelical adherents, to this day. C. Graafland once claimed that the postwar decline in the Kuyperian Reformed Churches began when the doctrine of mechanical inspiration was replaced by that of organic inspiration.[55] This conclusion seems far too simplistic, one arising from nostalgic longing for the time when the theolory of mechanical inspiration held sway. However, in my view it is inappropriate to fight for the truth with erroneous models.

In examining the theory of mechanical inspiration, we

---

54. *RC* 4:520.
55. Graafland (1981, 177).

must pay attention to its good intention (this section), but also to its relative character, its philosophical background, and its untenability (next sections).

(a) No doubt, those adhering to this theory had noble motives, namely, the defense of the Bible's absolutely divine origin, its divine authority, and its infallibility. However, even the noblest motives are no guarantee that people will reach a proper understanding of a certain matter. The very fear of a particular extreme teaching can easily drive people to the other extreme.[56] In a different context, Jesus warns against stressing certain detailed aspects instead of considering the complete picture: "Woe to you, scribes and Pharisees, hypocrites! For you tithe mint and dill and cumin, and have neglected the weightier matters of the law: justice and mercy and faithfulness. *These you ought to have done, without neglecting the others*. You blind guides, straining out a gnat and swallowing a camel!" (Matt. 23:23–24). In the present context this may be applied as follows: do stress the divine side of inspiration, but do not overlook the human side (see the following chapter).

7.8.2 Prudence

(b) Regarding the theory of mechanical inspiration, we must be prudent in trying to accuse certain authors of holding it. Someone who describes the Bible writers as "secretaries" (Johann Gerhard used the Latin word *notarii*[57]), and the Scriptures as the "dictates" of the Spirit is not necessarily an adherent to this theory. Thus, the Council of Trent (1545–1563) declared that the Bible books and the traditions were dictated either orally by Christ, or by the Holy Spirit" (Lat. *vel oretenus a Christo vel a spiritu sancto dictatas*).[58] The First Vatican Council repeated this statement.[59]

---

56. Cf., e.g., Ouweneel (2018d) on divine sovereignty *versus* human responsibility.

57. *Loci Theologici* loc. 1. cap. 2 § 18.

58. *Tridentinum* sess. 3.

59. *Vaticanum I* sess. 3.

Inspiration: Starting Points and Models

The idea of Scriptures as "dictates" goes back all the way to church father Irenaeus, who wrote that the Holy Scriptures are perfect because they are "dictated [or, said, spoken] by the Word of God [i.e. here, Christ] and his Spirit" (Lat. *a verbo Dei et Spiritu eius dictae*).[60] We find something similar with Augustine, who stated that Scripture entails dictates of the Spirit, so that the Evangelists were, as it were, only the Spirit's "hand."[61] Pope Gregory the Great used the term *dictare* as well.[62] We do remember, though, that *dictare* is derived from *dicere*, "to say." John Calvin also used the term *dictare*,[63] but often with the restrictive *quodammodo* ("to a certain extent").[64] He often referred to the personal liberty and activity of the Bible writers.

What may help us to find a way out of this apparent confusion is to distinguish carefully between the *method* of the Spirit, which does not involve dictation that would virtually exclude the activity and personality of the author, and the *result* of inspiration: what has been written down is not man-breathed but God-breathed. For instance, it may seem that, because of certain statements, Augustine could easily be accused of a holding to a theory of mechanical inspiration. However, in opposition to the Montanists (second to fourth centuries), who (according to their opponents) eliminated the factor of human consciousness in favor of divine inspiration (cf. §7.10.1), Augustine emphasized the important point that each of the four Evangelists described the life of Christ in his own manner.

How careful one should be in drawing conclusions from

---

60. *Adversus Haereses* II.28.2.
61. *De consensus evangelistarum* I.35.54.
62. *Moralia*, praef. 1.2: *Ipse igitur haec scripsit, qui scribenda dictavit.*
63. Calvin, *Institutes* 4.8.6: *dictante Spiritu Sancto.*
64. Ibid., 4.8.8: *quodammodo dictante Christi Spiritu*; see Berkouwer (1967, 20; cf. 22, 34); also see Calvin's commentaries on Matt. 22:43 and 2 Tim. 3:16; cf. Bavinck (*RD* 1:343–44); Barth (*CD* I/2:518–19); Althaus (1952, 183 note); Weber (1981, 232–33).

the use of the word "dictate" is illustrated by a letter Augustine wrote to that other great church father, Jerome.⁶⁵ Here, Augustine says of Jerome's Bible exposition that this was done through the "dictate" of the Holy Spirit.⁶⁶ This shows how freely some church fathers used the term "dictate." The same was true even for the term "inspiration," that is, they did not use the latter term exclusively for the inspiration of the Scriptures. Thus, Clement of Rome acknowledged that the apostle Paul wrote "in the Spirit" (1 Clement 47:3), but claimed of his own letter that it contained "words spoken by him [= Christ] through us" (59:1), and "things written by us through the Holy Spirit" (63:2). This does not imply that he placed his writings on the same level as those of Paul, but simply that Paul and he had received the same Spirit, who was active in a comparable way in bringing about their respective writings. Apparently, within Clement's thought, the *theological* idea of the inspiration of Scripture had not yet become formed into a doctrine.⁶⁷

7.8.3 Background

(c) The theory of mechanical inspiration clearly betrays a *Docetic* background because it respects only the divine nature of Scripture, and not the human nature of Scripture.⁶⁸ With regard to Christ, Docetism teaches that the Logos did not *really* become human flesh, but only apparently. Similarly, we may call it Docetic to believe that the Word id not *really* become human Scripture, but only apparently. We speak here of *monergism* ("unilateral activity"): it was the Spirit alone who was at work in inspiration; the Bible writers were only passively

---

65. Augustine, *Letter* 82.2 (= Jerome, *Letter* 116.2); quoted in Bruce (1988a, 266).
66. In http://www.newadvent.org/fathers/1102082.htm this word has been covered up.
67. Regarding inspiration through "mechanical dictation," see especially Henry (1979b, 138–42); his entire chapter (129–61) is worthwhile, in particular his arguments against the modernist views of James Barr (1973; 1981).
68. Cf. Du Toit (1990, 510).

receiving their content.[69] As G. C. van Niftrik put it, "The humanity [of Christ] (or humanness [of Scripture], respectively) evaporates [in Docetism] in the glow of the divinity."[70] John Calvin wrote that Scripture came from God alone, and that nothing human was mingled with this.[71] This is closely related to the scholastic dualism of nature and supernature, in which God or the divine are restricted to the sphere of supernature.[72]

The activity of this sphere within the natural sphere is viewed either as indirect and normal, or as immediate and miraculous. In the former case, the supernatural works *through* the natural, in the latter case it works *despite* nature (see more extensively, §3.7). According to this view, the natural itself cannot yield reliable knowledge, for such a knowledge would minimize the need for the supernatural, or make it superfluous. At best, the natural is the medium for the supernatural, and the constancy that is found in the natural sphere—in this case, Scripture—must be based upon and guaranteed by the divine reliability of the supernatural. In the theory of mechanical inspiration, the supernatural-divine is active, and the natural-human is passive. G. C. Berkouwer rightly remarked that, in the various forms of supernaturalism, we encounter a hidden longing to have at one's disposal a revelation so "pure" that one no longer needs to bother with all the complications of the creaturely, the human, and the historical.[73]

We must keep in mind here that rejecting the scholastic nature–supernature dualism does *not* necessarily imply, as some seem to believe, rejecting the supernatural in the sense

---

69. Cf. Berkouwer (1967, 14, 33, 62).
70. Van Niftrik (1961, 291).
71. *Comm. 2Tm3:16.*
72. See Vander Stelt (1978, 272–78, 305, 314–15, especially in connection with inspiration: 294–302, 323, 326); also see Berkouwer (1967, 24–27) and his references to Kuyper and Bavinck, who already criticized the nature–supernature dualism.
73. Berkouwer (1966, 91).

of a rejecting miracles and inspiration itself, as happens within humanistic theology. We need not choose here between fundamentalism (see chapter 9) and modernism (chapters 11–12); in the course of this book (see already chapter 8), I hope to identify a safe middle path.

7.8.4 Development

(d) The theory of mechanical inspiration fails to take into account how the Scriptures developed throughout history. In other words, it ignores the fact that the Bible was written by people with all their fallible creatureliness, and in human language with all its limitations. As many like to put it: God has made use of humanity and of human personality as the organ of the divine (see §7.9.2 and cf. §§8.3 and 8.4).[74] Thus, it is possible to discern within the Old Testament certain passages in early Hebrew and other passages in late Hebrew, and much in between (§5.7.3). As J. A. Heyns put it, "Luther supposedly said[75] that the sword of God's Word was put into the sheath of [human] languages — we might add to this also into the sheath of historical circumstances, and taking God's Word out of the sheath is the task of exegesis."[76] Of course, there is an important difference: putting the sword into the sheath is an ontic matter (inscripturation), whereas the taking the sword out of the sheath is a noetic matter (interpretation).

In the case of mechanical inspiration, the assumption seems rather obvious that all the Bible books should sound identical, but of course, this is not so. The style of the apostle Paul can be distinguished from that of the apostle John. In the occult sphere, for instance, in spiritism, we do find such "automatic dictation," in which the people involved are totally dominated by demons (cf. 1 Cor. 12:1–2). However, for the Bible writers, the statement is true: "[T]he spirits of prophets

---

74. Cf. Bavinck (*RD* 1:442–43).

75. See http://www.pajamapages.com/martin-luther-if-we-neglect-the-biblical-languages-the-gospel-will-perish/ (orig. from his work *An die Ratsherren aller Städte deutsches Lands*).

76. Heyns (1977, 141).

are subject to prophets" (14:32), that is, their prophecies are never expressed apart from their will, thoughts, and personality. A spiritistic inspiration is unworthy of both God and his human image-bearer.[77] This does not mean, though, that a theory of mechanical inspiration necessarily presupposes or requires a spiritistic or ecstatic explanation. On the contrary, the early forms of this theory were developed in opposition to the ecstatic view of the Montanists (§7.10.1).

Notice here that it is one thing to reject the theory of mechanical inspiration, but it is another thing to identify a proper alternative. For instance, P. C. Potgieter joined Calvin in stating that, according to its appearance and form, Scripture is indeed a human book, but according to its essential content and purpose it is the Word of God.[78] J. A. Heyns said almost the same thing: the *content* comes from God, the *form* comes from God *and* humans.[79] This is a better formulation than that of Potgieter—for, according to Heyns, both form and content come from God—but this formulation not yet sufficient; the remainder of my argument will explain clearly that such a distinction between form and content inevitably yields a false dualism. Did not Christ's servant Luke, *at his own initiative*, through diligent research, collect the material (the "content") for his Gospel (Luke 1:1-4)? Nonetheless, at the same time it was also *God's* initiative and *God's* material. There is no place here for any dualism of form and content. In my view, the only correct description can be none other than this: the content is just as human as it is divine; and the form is just as divine as it is human (see further in chapter 8).

7.9 Theories of Inspiration (2)

7.9.1 *Energetic:* the Dynamic Theory

The view known as the theory of dynamic inspiration is rooted in the modal idea of the *energetic* (or *physical*). In the Bible

---

77. Cf. Berkouwer (1967, 28–30) on "ecstasy" in the early church and the supposed parallels with inspiration.
78. Potgieter (1990, 23–24).
79. Heyns (1976, 19–20).

writers being "carried along" by the Spirit (2 Pet. 1:21), we are dealing with a modal-kinematic, or even a modal-energetic term, here as an idea referring to a supra-kinematic or supra-energetic state of affairs. Central is here the Greek concept of *dynamis*, "strength" or "power," that is, the dynamic of the Holy Spirit, who moved the Bible writers. We can easily imagine how such an idea occupies a central position within a theory of mechanical inspiration, but it can also function in an inspiration theory of quite a different kind. (For the *dynamis* of the Spirit see Luke 4:14; Acts 1:8; Rom. 15:13, 19; Eph. 3:16; as a hendiadys: Acts 10:38 ["with the Holy Spirit and with power"]; 1 Cor. 2:4 ["of the Spirit and of power"]; 1 Thess. 1:5 ["in power and in the Holy Spirit"].)

An example of a theory in which the energetic idea is elaborated in a non-mechanical way is the theory of dynamic inspiration, which goes back to the school of Friedrich Schleiermacher.[80] In a broad sense, it sees *theopneustia* not as the exclusive privilege of the Bible writers, but as the privilege of *all* Christians from the moment the Holy Spirit has been poured out. The Spirit is present and active everywhere. The Bible writers were merely the first to share in the *theopneustia*, but all post-Pentecost believers share in it as well, though perhaps to a lesser extent. Apparently, this was also the view of Paul Althaus,[81] who asserted that all church documents can be inspired as well, even if they are not canonical. He even reproached Karl Barth for not having grasped this.[82] Althaus worked with such a vague idea of biblical inspiration — which, in his view, also involved the copying, preservation, and translation of Scripture[83] — that theologically speaking the notion became virtually vacuous.

According to the theory of dynamic inspiration, the Bible writers bear witness to God's redemptive revelation in Christ,

---

80. See especially Schleiermacher (1998).
81. Althaus (1952, 160, 163, 180–89).
82. Ibid., 163.
83. Ibid., 180–81.

experiencing the inspiring *dynamis* of the Holy Spirit and, under this impulse, writing their books. Supposedly, these Scriptures themselves are not revelation but only a more or less faithful, sometimes defective, sometimes masterful record of God's revelation. To a greater or lesser extent, this *dynamis* is shared also by the believing copyists, keepers, translators, publishers, printers, expositors, and readers of the Bible.[84]

Here we encounter a confusion of inspiration with illumination (enlightenment), as described above. This theory is actually not about the inspiration of *Scripture* (cf. 2 Tim. 3:16), but rather about the inspiration (read: illumination) of the *writers*, and subsequently of the readers. In this view, there is no basic difference between the Bible writers and the writers of books *about* the Bible; at best, there is a gradual difference in enlightenment by the Holy Spirit. Here, the true character of the inspiration of *Scripture* is ignored or misunderstood. The point is this: writers were, and readers were and are, enlightened, but it is *Scripture* that is inspired, *not* the writers. By overlooking this important distinction, people discredit the true nature of Scripture itself.

Otto Weber argued that, though he personally rejected it, the doctrine of the verbal inspiration was superior to Schleiermacher's idea of personal inspiration because it maintained that God's Word comes to us in the *words* of Scripture.[85] Our theological attention should not shift from the inspired Bible words to the (supposedly) inspired Bible writers.[86] To be sure, these writers were "carried along" by the Spirit (2 Pet. 1:21), but it is *Scripture* that was *theopneustos* (2 Tim. 3:16). (However, I remind the reader of the confusing Vulgate rendering of 2 Pet. 1:21, *Spiritu Sancto inspirati locuti sunt sancti Dei homines*, "inspired by the Holy Ghost, holy men of God spoke.")

---

84. Cf. Sabatier (1916, 90).
85. Weber (1981, 236).
86. Cf. Berkouwer (1967, 44–45).

7.9.2 *Biotic:* the Organic Theory

In the *theopneustia*, that is, God's "breathing in" and "out" (2 Tim. 3:16), we are clearly dealing with a modal-biotic term ("breathing"). This term refers here, in the form of an idea, to a supra-biotic state of affairs: God's spiration of Scripture.

A special use of a modal-biotic idea is found in the so-called theory of organic inspiration promoted by Abraham Kuyper and Herman Bavinck. This view goes back to John Calvin, and nowadays it is defended in some Roman Catholic circles.[87] This theory attempts to avoid the errors of the theory of mechanical inspiration by emphasizing two things. On the one hand, it fully maintains the unique, divine inspiration of Scripture and carefully distinguishes that from the enlightenment of the writers. On the other hand, it tries to account for the fact that the Holy Spirit fully engaged the Bible writers in the process of writing.[88] The modal-biotic term "organic" means here that the Spirit used the writers as "organs" through which he expressed himself. The Spirit used the writers as human beings who thought for themselves, and acted by themselves, persons with their own deliberations and experiences, their own parlance and style, with their own cultural and geographical background, with their specific vernacular and ways of expression, with the limitations of their environments and their times. The Spirit made use not only of hands that could write (or mouths that could dictate to others; cf. Rom. 16:22) but of all the properties and special circumstances of the Bible writers.

In this sense, the Bible is a thoroughly human book. But at the same time, it is a thoroughly divine book; the proportion is not 50% + 50%, but 100% + 100%. Every phrase of Scripture bears, so to speak, both the divine and the human stamp. It does so in such a way that, just like in the incarnation of the Son, the Word shares in what is human, and thus in what

---

87. Cf. Wentsel (1982, 308–17).
88. Cf. Berkouwer (1967, 31–51).

Inspiration: Starting Points and Models

is weak and humble, but not necessarily in what is defective and sinful. The Word did indeed share in the weakness and limitations of the human nature, yet it is and remains infallible and reliable for the purposes that God had in mind during the inscripturation (see more extensively in chapter 10).

The question that may be asked here is whether the term "organic" adequately expresses all of this meaning. Herman Bavinck seemed so enthusiastic about the term that he sometimes told us that Scripture itself commands us to understand inspiration not in a mechanical but in an organic way.[89] Of course, Scripture does nothing of the kind; it is a typical example of reading a theological theory into the Bible in an era when people were scarcely aware of the epistemological underpinnings of theology. Scripture nowhere *mentions* the terms "mechanical" or "organic"; nor does it function as a referee between competing theological models. At best, we might say that Scripture's "data" — in itself a rather scientistic expression — seem to fit better in an organic view than in a mechanical view. But this is no guarantee that, first, the *term* "organic" most appropriately expresses the views of the organic theory,[90] and, second, that there might not be a third or a fourth model that explains the "data" even more elegantly, consistently, and coherently.

The term "organic" can be useful only if the idea behind it breaks radically with both the monergism of mechanical inspiration, and the strict dualism that speaks of a union of the divine and human factors or elements (cf. §7.11.3). In practice, however, it seems as if some conservative theologians, who ostensibly reject mechanical inspiration, nonetheless entertain "mechanical" ideas behind an "organic" disguise. Over against this, we find that, among Dutch theologians in the 1960s, not only G. C. Berkouwer[91] but even H. M. Kuitert

---

89. Bavinck (*RD* 1:431).
90. Cf. Ridderbos (1926); Berkouwer (1967, 31–33).
91. Regarding the development in Berkouwer's view of Scripture, see extensively, Van Keulen (2003, chapters 5–8).

and T. Baarda, who were far removed from Bavinck's views, could all describe their views as "organic."[92] This debasing of the term renders it rather useless nowadays.

The Greek word *organon* means "tool" (see, e.g., 2 Clement 18:2); secondarily, the derived term "organ" refers to a totality of animal or human tissues exerting a specific function in the body, that is, functioning as a "tool" in it.[93] In a certain sense, it cannot be denied that the Bible writers were "tools" of the Spirit. For instance, Jeremiah was a "hammer" in God's hand (Jer. 23:29), and, to mention also a negative example, the king of Assyria was in God's hand even a "rod," a "staff," an "axe," and a "saw" (Isa. 10:5, 15). However, a one-sided emphasis on this aspect may easily lead to a mechanical view (also Gk. *mēchanē* means, e.g., "tool"; cf. "mechanism, machine").

We may also wonder whether the theory of organic inspiration has really avoided the nature-supernature dualism. In this model, the natural-human is active but is never allowed to endanger the supernaturally active principle. The divine and the human aspects are indeed recognized, and a certain equilibrium is sought. However, a perfect balance is never possible in the theory of organic inspiration because the priority must ultimately be given to the supernatural.

If the organic model could rid itself of this dualism of the divine and the human elements, it could make a fruitful contribution to theological reflection on biblical inspiration. In my view, this would happen only if we realized that, when all was said and done, we are incapable of indicating in a theoretical-rational way how the supernatural inscripturation exactly occurred. We can speak about it in a rational way, both theoretically and practically, but at the same time, inspiration and inscripturation transcend all rationality. As Herman Bavinck rightly said in relation to the theory of organic

---

92. Cf. Potgieter (1990, 23).
93. This means that the term "organic," though biotically qualified, is in fact a retrocipation upon the energetic modality.

inspiration,

> There are intellectual problems (cruces) in Scripture that cannot be ignored and that will probably never be resolved. . . . Those who want to delay belief in Scripture till all the objections have been cleared up and all the contradictions have been resolved will never arrive at faith. . . . Those who do not want to start in faith will never arrive at knowledge.[94]

7.9.3 *Perceptive:* the Scope Theory

In the term "scope" (Lat. *scopus*, from Gk. *skopos*) we are dealing with a modal-perceptive term, which in modern theology is used as a modal idea to express a different aspect of biblical inspiration. In Philippians 3:14, the Greek word *skopos* means "goal," but this does not express its original meaning. The word is derived from *skopeō*, which means "to regard," "to give heed to," "to watch," "to direct one's eye to" (cf. Luke 11:35; Rom. 16:17; 2 Cor. 4:18; Gal. 6:1; Phil. 3:17). Compare words such as telescope, microscope, periscope, each of which involves a form of watching. The "scope" is what comes within our field of vision, our line of sight. It is that at which we must specifically look, on which we must focus, must fix our eyes, our special attention. In this sense, we can say that Jesus Christ, God's redemptive grace in him, and God's kingdom as established in him, constitute the central scope of the Bible. The idea behind the scope model is this: Keep your eye on this scope (the main subject, the core of Scripture), and do not be distracted by collateral matters (side issues).

In modern theology, the impression is often given that inspiration pertains only to the scope of the Bible, and thus not necessarily to all kinds of factual details.[95] This view resembles the one discussed in §7.7.2: the dualistic or restricted view. It runs the risk of creating a dualism between center and periphery, between content and form, between scope and

---

94. Bavinck (*RD* 1:442).
95. See extensively, Vroom (1979).

collateral issues. However, in chapter 8 I will emphasize that we should not generalize here, as if these kinds of distinction necessarily lead to dualisms. This is so because, as an act and gift of the Spirit of Christ, inspiration is definitely about the divine centrality of the person and work of Christ in the Bible, and of the kingdom of God.[96] Any emphasis on what is regarded as the core of the biblical message can never be inherently wrong.

The point is that such a *concentration* ought not to imply a *reduction* of the Bible's content. Reduction means that peripheral Bible portions can be ignored, and that it would not be problematic if these passages would turn out to be full of errors. However, this view is not necessarily intended when people speak of the scope of Scripture. On the contrary, in the scope we are not dealing with some kind of reduction, as if primary content is being emphasized *over against* secondary matters. Rather, we are dealing with the orientation, the intention, the special focus of the Bible as this focus is expressed in *each distinct Bible word* viewed in its context. As Abraham Kuyper put it, "Just as each droplet of water can be called water, every particle of air air, each glass of wine wine, every ray of light light, so each particle, each droplet from Scripture is *graphē*; . . . ."[97] This must not be taken in an atomistic way — we are not concerned with the *separate* words — but refers to the words in their contextual coherence, and even beyond that: the context of all these words within the totality of Scripture (see §8.4).

This emphasis on the Bible's scope does not, and ought not to, imply an escape from some human (fallible) form to some divine (infallible) content. Rather, it refers to the infallible *Word*, which finds expression in — weak but sinless — *words*. Here, we touch the heart of the matter: the Bible's scope is not some part *within* the boundaries of Scripture (in the temporal-immanent sense), distinct from other, less essential parts.

---

96. See extensively, Ouweneel (2018j).
97. Kuyper (*DD* 2.1:6).

Inspiration: Starting Points and Models

On the contrary; if we wish to use the word "scope" at all, we must think of the *supra-temporal* Word, of its eternal, transcendent essence, as the latter finds expression within our temporal-immanent reality in all the *temporal words* in which this transcendent scope has been inscripturated (see further chapter 8).

7.10 Theories of Inspiration (3)

7.10.1 *Sensitive:* the Sensitivistic Theory

Again, I think here of the school of Friedrich Schleiermacher, with its strong emphasis on religious experience. Here the term "experience" has the sense not so much of (German) *Erfahrung* (which is of a more rational nature) but more of *Empfindung*, which has the overtones of "sensation, sentiment, feeling," and has more of a sensitive, emotional nature (cf. the Dutch hyper-Calvinist term *bevinding*). In connection with the inspiration of Scripture, this entails the special, inspiring activity of the Holy Spirit within the Bible writers. According to this model, it is not so much Scripture that is inspired; rather, Scripture is the record of the inspired sensations (sentiments, feelings) of the Bible writers. For further discussion of this, I refer the reader to §7.9.1.

A perhaps even more striking example of sensitivism could be called the theory of "ecstatic" inspiration. Hermann Cremer has tried to show that the view of inspiration developed in the early church was rooted in ideas that arose in the context not of the Palestinian synagogue but of Hellenistic Judaism. Cremer claimed that it was Hellenistic to view the Old Testament prophets as "ecstatics," that is, people in whom the human mind (Gk. *nous*) had been silenced, that is, switched off during the act of their bearing witness. This "enthusiastic" view goes back all the way to Plato,[98] and is encountered, for instance, with early Christian writers such as Justin Martyr,[99]

---

98. *Ion* 534b.
99. *Apology* 1.36; *Cohortatio ad Graecos* 8.10.

Athenagoras,[100] and Theophilus.[101] The view was discredited especially through the rise of heretical Montanism because the latter tended to be ecstatic as well (§7.8.2).

By defending itself against this movement, the mainstream church became more and more critical of pure ecstasy, of "enthusiasm" (literally, the being-in-God). Thus, among later church fathers we observe a pendulum effect: in opposition to the ecstatic view, we see how the early forms of the theory of mechanical inspiration emerged. Here, the notion of an inoperative consciousness was replaced by another kind of passivity of the conscious: over against the ecstatic prophet, we now find the passive secretary, who received and wrote down a dictation (see §7.8).[102] The two types of prophets — the former very active, the latter very passive — may seem to be opposites, but they share a striking similarity: in both approaches, the inspiration of Scripture leaves the Bible writers' own thinking uninvolved. In the former case, thinking is overruled by feeling; in the latter case thinking is simply suspended.

7.10.2 *Logical:* the Intuition Theory

Millard J. Erickson mentioned the intuition theory as the first of the several inspiration theories that he dealt with.[103] He referred to certain liberal writers who viewed inspiration as a high degree of intuitive insight. In line with Reformational philosophy, I take intuition here primarily as a concept that is logical-analytically determined.[104]

In the intuition model, inspiration is linked to a specific attribute, a natural capacity, of the Bible writers. They were religious geniuses, just as the Israelites in general were superior to other nations, but not basically different from great

---

100. *Legatio pro Christianis* 9.
101. *Ad Autolycum* 2.9.
102. Cf. Weber (1981, 231).
103. Erickson (1998, 231–32).
104. Dooyeweerd (*NC* 2:472–85).

religious and philosophical thinkers such as the writers of the Gilgamesh epic, of the religious pyramid texts, of the Rigveda, of the Zoroastric Avesta, and of the Four Books of Confucianism, and further Plato (inspired by Socrates), Buddha, and Mohammad.[105]

In this view, the wonder of the inspiration does not necessarily lie in anything supernatural but in the wondrous (but basically natural-creaturely) talents of certain special people, similar to the wondrous talents of great musicians, visual artists, and literary geniuses. In the same way we regard the most exceptional talents among them as almost superhuman (e.g., Johann Sebastian Bach, Rembrandt van Ryn, William Shakespeare), we can imagine that millions of people have regarded the writings of the religious geniuses that are called "divine," or at least as originating in some higher world. That is the intuition theory.

This model differs only in degree from the second one that Erickson mentions,[106] and which he refers to as the illumination theory. Here, some activity of the Holy Spirit is indeed accepted, but only to the extent that it involves a strengthening of the natural powers and capacities of the Bible writers. Basically, this is the same theory as the one dealt with in §7.9.1 (on the dynamic theory).

7.10.3 *Historical-Formative:* the Actualistic Theory

The inspiration theory that can be called "actualistic" originated in the school of Karl Barth. Just as we encountered in §7.9.1 a confusion between inspiration and illumination, in the present theory the relationship between inspiration and revelation is at stake. According to Barth, divine revelation never becomes a "having-been-revealed," a given that ostensibly lies consolidated in the Bible as if we could say, This *is* the revelation of God, this *is* God's Word—which we could then freely dismiss. No, in Barth's view, the Word must be

---

105. Cf. Martineau (1889, 168–71).
106. Erickson (1998, 232).

repeatedly *actualized* (made actual or real). God never gives his revelation away. In other words, time and again he sovereignly and actually reveals himself in and *through* Scripture, *turns* the latter into his Word in his time and in his way (although only indirectly because in Barth's view, Christ alone is God's Word in the direct sense) in a personal encounter with a human being.[107]

In Barth's opinion, the Bible is in itself a human, and therefore fallible, book. Thus, he has no difficulty accepting all kinds of (supposed) results of modern Bible research. Through inspiration, the Word has become flesh, and in this way the Word participates in all the limitedness, defectiveness, and sinfulness that belongs intrinsically to the flesh. The Bible *is* not God's revelation, but only a (human, fallible) record of earlier, personal revelations of God to humans. Divine revelation is perfect, but its record (inscripturation) is fallible. However, the miracle is that the sovereign God wishes to use *this* book time and again to speak through it, so that, at that very moment, it *becomes* God's Word for humans. That was Barth's view.

In the more extreme form of this thinking, namely, in the demythologizing method applied especially by Rudolf Bultmann,[108] all biblical statements about the cosmos, nature, and history are rejected as irrelevant.[109] These statements form only the mythical shell, which must be peeled off the Scriptures in order to arrive at the true religious (existential) core of the biblical message. This core is referred to with the Greek term *kērygma* (literally, "heralding," "proclamation"). The Bible may become God's Word for us if and when it is correctly demythologized (which is the task of the theologian). In this way, the core of absolute love is exposed, as it is contained in the "myth" of the unselfish love of God in Christ.

---

107. See Ouweneel (1995, §5.2.3).
108. See, e.g., Bultmann (1952).
109. See extensively on this error, Ouweneel (2018l, chapters 3 and 4).

Whereas in the dynamic theory the enlightenment of the Bible readers is extended to the Bible writers (§7.9.1) — that is, inspiration is degraded to illumination — one might say that in the actualistic theory, the opposite occurs: inspiration is transferred from the Bible writers to the Bible readers. That is, the question whether, at a certain moment, the Bible *becomes* God's Word, depends (partly) on the reader, that is, on the reader being inspired at that given moment.

No doubt, Karl Barth has rightly drawn our attention to the fact that the Bible as God's Word is not a rigid, dogmatic "given," which could be theoretically manipulated. If the Bible is really God's Word, this is not only — or rather, not at all — a matter of dead orthodoxy, but of a living testimony, going out from Scripture and believingly received in the heart through the enlightenment of the Holy Spirit. We must guard here against any form of deistic objectivism, which severs Scripture, after the time of its inspiration, from the continual activity of God's Spirit.[110] The Word is inseparable from the Spirit, just as the Spirit is inseparable from the Word.

However, we should not fall into the other extreme — as did Barth — by denying the objective inspiration of Scripture and asserting that "the Word" is actualized only through the subjective enlightenment of the reader. The inspiration of the Bible must never be made to depend on the enlightenment (the supposed inspiration) of the Bible reader, and thus on subjectivism, and even, in the case of Barth and especially Bultmann, on the ideas of modern science and technology. The claims that "the Bible *is* God's Word" and "the Bible *becomes* God's Word" must not be played off against each other.

Perhaps we could describe a proper middle path between the two extremes this way: the Bible *becomes* subjectively God's Word in the heart of the believer, that is, finds its recognition as God's Word through the internal testimony of the Holy Spirit (Lat. *testimonium Spiritus Sancti internum*). This is

---

110. Cf. Bavinck (*RD* 1:427–28, 437–38); also see the criticism by Nicole (1984a, 130–36).

possible for the very reason that the Bible *is* objectively God's Word, apart from, and preceding, this believing recognition. The testimony of the Holy Spirit (Lat. *testimonium Spiritus Sancti*) in the believer's heart *through* the written Word is identical with the *testimonium Spiritus Sancti internum* that we find *in* the Bible *regarding* this written Word (cf. §1.9). "The Bible *is* God's Word even if nobody listens" is just as true as "the Bible *becomes* God's Word for those who do listen."

7.11 Theories of Inspiration (4)

7.11.1 *Lingual:* the Dialogical Theory

In the verb "to indicate" (Gk. *edēlou*) in 1 Peter 1:11, we are dealing with a modal-lingual term referring, in the form of an idea, to a supra-lingual state of affairs. Such a modal-lingual term is also the basis for the dialogical inspiration theory. This model was suggested by J. A. Heyns,[111] partly because of a certain (understandable) dissatisfaction with the term "organic" (§7.9.2). This approach emphasizes the human writer's will, his choices, or more generally his responsibility (a term derived from "response"), in brief, his true humanity. Humans are beings who are addressed by God in his Word, and are thus called upon to give a direct or indirect response. This is what Heyns meant by a dialogical relationship between God and humanity. In the response that God expects from people, his originally given Word must reverberate, find an echo, and come to rest.

In connection with the inspiration of Scripture, this theory involves the notion that God, for his part, called the Bible writers to writing, that is, to taking an initiative, whereas he, at the same time, drove them (carried them along) through the Holy Spirit. From the writers came a response to this, and this written response to God has become God's Word to *us*. This definitely does not mean that the Bible is an individual expression of faith, someone's own more or less independent understanding. The latter is the viewpoint of many

---

111. Heyns (1976, 14–45; 1988, 21).

modern(ist) theologians, who see in the New Testament an advanced stage of theological reflection in the early church, identified with German term *Gemeindetheologie* ("church theology"; Bultmann). No, the Bible is indeed a real response of human writers, which, however, was given to the Bible writers by the Holy Spirit, or elicited from them through their creaturely talents—a response that in certain respects surpassed their own understanding (1 Pet. 1:11). Thus, the words that they used were *their* words, which *they* sought and found (within their own historically determined perspective), even after consideration of various other words—but words that, at the same time, were *given* to them by the Spirit as a responding "re-action" to God's "action" with and in them.

Jacob Kamphuis pointed out that the dialogical relationship between God and humanity is governed by the Creator-creature relationship.[112] This means that humans have been created to hear, and hence obey, what God says.[113] However, this having been created for obedience must be distinguished from the *act* of hearing/obeying. I would like to emphasize this hearing/obeying even more strongly. The danger of the term "dialogue" could be that humans are viewed more as being too independent with respect to God, as God's partner, and less as standing under God's commandments, whereas they are always *obliged* to render an obedient response. Heyns, however, did not at all intend to convey such an idea of an independent partnership.[114] On the contrary, he denied that humans were involved in the *design* and *initiative* concerning the Bible's content.[115] However, this seems to go toward the other extreme, at least certainly as far as some Bible passages are concerned. Thus, Luke's Gospel seems to have originated as much from Luke's initiative (see chapter 1:1-4) as from *God's* initiative, as being *God's* Word (see §7.5.1).

---

112. Kamphuis (1982, 18–19).
113. Latin *oboedire*, "to obey," from *audire*, "to hear."
114. Heyns (1976, 14–45).
115. Ibid., 19, 57.

It seems to me that another comment by Kamphuis was more relevant. He argued that it is difficult to take, for instance, the phenomenon of being carried along (Gk. *pheromenoi*) by the Spirit in 2 Peter 1:21 as a (direct or indirect) speaking of God to the prophets, to which the speaking of the holy men would be the response. In this passage, their speaking is not a response to a preceding act of God. Rather, there is simultaneity, whereby the prophets *actively* speak while being *passively* carried along by the Spirit (see §7.5.1). This being carried along excludes any initiative by the writers independently of God. They were driven to speak, and also as they were speaking they were continually driven. This follows from the present tense of the Greek participle *pheromenoi*, which points to an ongoing process.

This idea of a response to God's speaking, though no doubt containing an element of truth, nevertheless does not do sufficient justice to the reality that God himself spoke *through* the writers; as Hebrews 1:1 says, "God spoke . . . by/through the prophets" (Gk. *ho theos lalēsas . . . en tois prophētais*, where the preposition *en* is instrumental: "through"). In Scripture, we *always* hear both forms of speaking: humans speaking in response to God (even where God himself is quoted), and God speaking to humans (even where humans directly address God). Kamphuis pointed out that this speaking of God through the prophets is so absolute that God could use even his opponents to this end, such as Balaam (Num. 22–24, called the "soothsayer" in Josh. 13:22 KJV) and Caiaphas (John 11:51 KJV, "being the high priest that same year"), or an overtly disobedient man of God (the "old prophet" in Bethel, 1 Kings 13:11, 21–22), or even an animal: Balaam's donkey (Num. 22:28). The free initiatives and choices of human beings must be underscored as emphatically as the truth that as the potter, God has all power over the clay (Rom. 9:21), in this case: all power over the Bible writers.

7.11.2 *Aesthetic:* The Musical Instruments Theory

We have seen that the men whom God used to write down his Word did not function as typewriters or word processors, for the inscripturated product exhibits their own style and vocabulary. God employed their varied personalities in order to reveal his thoughts through them. We could compare this with a trumpet, a horn, a violin, musical instruments that produce different tones—varying in pitch and timbre—while God was the One playing on these instruments, so that they produced the melodies he wanted in the manner he desired.

This comparison is very ancient;[116] it is found with Philo, who compared the divine Spirit with a musician playing on the vocal organism, and making sounds on it that clearly express his prophetic message.[117] This idea was adopted by the Christian author Athenagoras, who wrote that the Spirit moved the mouths of the prophets like people play musical instruments.[118]

Christians adopted the image from the apostle Paul: "If even lifeless instruments, such as the flute or the harp, do not give distinct notes, how will anyone know what is played?" (1 Cor. 14:7), although the context here is about speaking in tongues. Athenagoras[119] and Justin Martyr,[120] who developed precursors of a kind of inspiration theory, used this image. Justin believed that God's Spirit employed holy men like a zither player uses his zither: "In this way . . . they taught us with one mouth, univocally, consistently, and without [mutual] contradiction."[121] All musical instruments together form one harmonious and melodious orchestra, led by one conductor. (Notice that both the player and the conductor can be

---

116. Goldingay (1994, 224).
117. *De specialibus legibus* IV.8 (49); cf. I.11 (65).
118. *Legatio pro Christianis* 7.
119. *Legatio pro Christianis* 7 and 9.
120. *Cohortatio ad Graecos* 8.
121. Cf. Bavinck (*RD* 1:403–404); Barth (*CD* I/2:518–19); Brunner (1949, 107–108).

used as an image of the Holy Spirit.)

We are dealing here with a modal-aesthetic idea underlying the metaphor of the musical instruments. Of course, the notion has risks, since one might rightly wonder about the essential difference between the images of a typewriter and a musical instrument. For instance, typewriters and word processors produce different fonts. This is correct, and it indicates that the image of musical instruments could easily lead us back to the theory of mechanical inspiration. Therefore, in my view, the only (prudent) use for this image is to clarify that different instruments (Bible writers) produce different sounds (styles, vocabularies). However, the metaphor hardly identifies how each instrument contributes to the melody.

Typically the notion of the aesthetic is associated with the idea that Scripture contains literary compositions,[122] in which the various parts, as well as the total design, always have a theological purpose (more correctly, a religious purpose). In other words, Scripture does not present photographs of reality but paintings, which disclose much about not only the painted object, but also the painters.[123] Abraham Kuyper spoke here of impressionism.[124] This does *not* mean that, because the Bible books are religious compositions, they contain the writer's imagination.[125] The portrait of the described object, such as Jesus in the Gospels, must *resemble* him, otherwise it is useless. The supposed contradictions between the Gospels cannot be used as an argument against the authenticity of the described events, just as the significant differences between

---

122. Regarding the Gospels, see Verkuyl (1992, 192); for the remainder of this § see much more extensively, Ouweneel (2007, §6.3).

123. Cf. Macquarrie (1981, 30); Pentecost (1981, 24); Van de Beek (1998, 124); Loonstra (1999, 68).

124. Quoted in Harinck (2001, 113).

125. See for the Gospels, Den Heyer (2003, 21–24). Guthrie (1990, 107) says, "No one would deny that Luke's purpose is theological. But this is quite different from saying that the history has been conformed to the theology,... It is truer to say that Luke brings out the theological significance of the history."

three (imaginary) portraits of the same person painted by, for instance, Vincent Van Gogh, Paul Cézanne, and Paul Gauguin do not imply that these portraits could, and do, not resemble that person.

7.11.3 *Ethical:* the Marriage Theory

Finally, I wish to mention the approach, or one of them, Abraham Kuyper followed to explain the miracle of inspiration.[126] He spoke of a mystical union (Lat. *unio mystica*), a covenant or marriage between the divine and the human factors involved in inspiration, parallel with the way the Mediator's divine nature was wedded to his human nature (cf. §5.3).

Kuyper also compared the divine factor involved in inspiration to a vein of gold.[127] One could think here of the idea of the modal-economical because of the apparent notion of value represented here. He also spoke of the human form of Scripture as the "bearer of the Divine factor";[128] this involves a modal-physical idea, namely, the foundation or lower story bearing a higher story; or even a modal-biotic idea, namely, that of a mother carrying a baby (*draagster,* "carrier," is feminine in Dutch). Yet a fourth image Kuyper employed was that of the telephone, which seemed to imply a modal-lingual idea (cf. §7.11.1).

The usual sense of the word "marriage" entails an ethically qualified concept; that is, love indicates the actual quality of the marriage bond. In our case, the term is used in the form of an idea as a reference to the supra-modal loving marriage bond between the divine and the human in the work of inspiration. The (aesthetic) attractiveness of this metaphor is larger than its (logically) explanatory power, though. I mention this model only to complete my summary of modal approximations of biblical inspiration that are consistent with the nature of an idea.

---

126. Kuyper (*DD* 2.1:59; 2.2:8); (1898, 478).
127. Kuyper (1898, 474).
128. Ibid., 479.

The most complete and coherent *theories* of inspiration are the dynamic, the mechanical, the organic, and the dialogical theories, which for our purpose are the most relevant ones. However, it is more important to realize that inspiration is a *supra-theoretical*, even *supra-rational* matter, which ultimately cannot be contained in any theological *theory*. In this sense, *all* inspiration models that we have dealt with are, strictly speaking, wrong insofar as they would claim to exhaustively explain, and supply a warrant for, the truth concerning biblical inspiration. In my view, the best thing one could do with such theories is to use them *all* (or most of them) because each of them does shed some light on a certain aspect of the inspiration of Scripture. To put it more precisely, *all* modal ideas together shed light on what ultimately is totally *supra-modal* but can be approximated only through the modal ideas.

In this sense, one could just as well defend the idea that, because of their strong claims, complete, coherent ,and consistent inspiration theories are the *least* suited to approximate the miracle of inspiration. Perhaps the less consistent and coherent, more vague models, such as the marriage idea, or the scope idea, or the *dynamis* idea, are ultimately more satisfactory than any *theory* that inherently promises *a priori* far more than it can deliver.

Chapter 8
Inspiration: A New Approach

Concerning this salvation,
the prophets who prophesied about the grace
that was to be yours
searched and inquired carefully,
inquiring what person or time the Spirit of
Christ in them was indicating
when he predicted the sufferings of Christ
and the subsequent glories.
It was revealed to them that they were serving
not themselves but you,
in the things that have now been announced
to you
through those who preached the good news
to you
by the Holy Spirit sent from heaven,
things into which angels long to look.
         1 Peter 1:10–12

. . . knowing this first of all,
that no prophecy of Scripture comes from
someone's own interpretation.

> *For no prophecy was ever produced by the will of man,*
> *but men spoke from God*
> *as they were carried along by the Holy Spirit.*
> 2 Peter 1:20–21

Summary: *When it comes to the authority of Scripture, I reject all three options that Heinrich Ott distinguished: the fundamentalist, the dualist, and the Barthian approaches. They are based on not (sufficiently) distinguishing between (a) the immanent and the transcendent, (b) inspiration and illumination, and (c) the objective (the Bible **is** God's Word) and the subjective (the Bible **becomes** God's Word to people).*

Another problem is the human versus the divine aspects of the Bible, which also entails the historical versus the supra-historical aspects. Many human aspects of Scripture are enumerated and analyzed. God employed the human with all its weaknesses and limitations, but not its sinfulness. I defend belief in verbal inspiration, but not its inherent atomistic nature and its theoretical quality.

Other problems include the midrashic, typological, and homiletic reasons why the New Testament often cites very loosely from the Old Testament, as well as textual-critical questions concerning the Old and the New Testaments.

Finally, the matter of the divine authority of Scripture is investigated: its exact meaning, the examples of Jesus and the apostles, the relationship between authority and inspiration, possible contradictions in the Bible, and the unity and the center of the Bible.

8.1 The Immanent–Transcendent Problem

8.1.1 Ott's Three Options

HEINRICH OTT STATED THAT, if the Bible possesses any real authority, there are basically three possibilities to describe this authority:[1]

---

1. Ott (1972, 37, 46–48).

(a) The entire text of the biblical canon is authoritative; every phrase in the Bible imparts truth, and therefore is binding upon the Christian. Ott called this the fundamentalist approach, linked to the theory of verbal inspiration (cf. §8.5).

(b) Scripture speaks binding truth only in certain parts and statements; only in these does it have authority. The rest is human writing, historically limited, not binding for modern humanity. Ott called this the "elimination method," which corresponds more or less with what I have called the dualistic theory (§7.7.2).

(c) The third option is a blend of the previous two, in agreement with dialectic (Barthian) theology. In the Bible, what is time-bound and what is of continuing validity are completely interwoven. The Bible must be viewed primarily as a purely historical, human writing from a certain time period. However, at the same time, if we conduct a historical investigation of the Bible, we must be prepared for a sudden encounter with an ultimate divine appeal, which will come from God himself. This is what Ott called the existential interpretation of the text.

Ott could scarcely conceive of a fourth option,[2] and thus spoke only of these three conceivable possibilities,[3] and chose the third one. It is worthwhile to look a bit more closely at the three options before we adopt Ott's claim that only these three are available to us. He did not use an ontological frame of thought in order to analyze these three options a little further. Otherwise he might have discovered that some of them in fact contain more than one alternative, and thus that more options are conceivable. Personally, I would rather prefer a division that flows from carefully distinguishing between (a) the immanent and the transcendent (§8.1) and between (b) illumination and inspiration (§8.2).

---

2. Ibid., 37.
3. Ibid., 46.

8.1.2 Three Erroneous Views

Let us first pay attention to the view concerning the immanent *versus* the transcendent. Such a view could go astray in three respects.

(a) *Absolutizing the immanent.* This is the first approach that Heinrich Ott overlooked, or perhaps he ignored *a priori* this thoroughly secular view. This view acknowledges only the immanent form of Scripture, and ignores or flatly denies its transcendent point of convergence and integration, namely, the vertical dimension: the eternal Word (Lat. *Verbum aeternum*). This view may attribute authority to Scripture, but this authority is at most that of a venerable ancient book, in which venerable people described their venerable religious experiences of God, or more broadly, the *numinous* (cf. §§7.9.1 and 7.10.1 on the dynamic and the sensitivistic approach). This position allows no basic difference between the Bible and other venerable religious writings.

(b) *A dualism within the immanent*, that is, a separation within the immanent form of Scripture, namely, between the (supposed) "Word of God" and the (supposed) "word of men." This is what I have called the dualistic theory (§7.7.2), which seems to be identical with what Ott referred to as the elimination method.

(c) *Absolutizing the transcendent.* Ott described this approach as fundamentalistic, characteristic of the theory of mechanical inspiration (§7.8). This approach acknowledges only the transcendent *Verbum aeternum*, and equates or confuses this with the immanent form of Scripture. In other words, it ignores that the latter is merely the immanent divergence (refraction) of the *Verbum aeternum* within our temporal-empirical reality. Thus, this approach ignores the course of Scripture's development within human history; the (passive and active) preparation of the Bible writers for their task; the very human (sometimes decidedly weak, almost sinful) words that in the Bible are addressed *to* God; the sometimes enormous

Inspiration: A New Approach

differences in style, way of writing, vocabulary, sphere of interest, emotional mentality, spiritual strength, development, and subject matters among the writers; the direct incentive to writing that was often present within the human circumstances themselves; the many different literary genres in the Bible, and so on (see §§8.3 and 8.4).

Whatever approach to biblical inspiration is preferred, we must avoid these three erroneous approaches concerning the immanence–transcendence relationship (along with the wrong approaches concerning the illumination–inspiration relationship; see §8.2). Neither the immanent nor the transcendent must be absolutized, and a dualism of these two does not help us grasp the true character of Scripture, either. The only way open is the view that accepts both the transcendent-divine *Verbum aeternum*, which is the point of convergence and unity of all immanent words of Scripture, and the immanent-historical-human form of Scripture, which represents the divergence and diversity contained in the eternal Word.

8.1.3 No New Dualism

Speaking of the one transcendent-divine *Verbum aeternum* and the immanent-historical-human form of Scripture, we can avoid any danger of a new (in this case, vertical) dualism if we are aware of two things.

(a) *Within* this immanent form of Scripture, we reject any form of dualism between a center and a periphery, or between an *immanent* Word of God and an *immanent* word of men (cf. §§7.7.2 and 7.9.3).

(b) A *duality* can exist only between the *transcendent* Word of God (which does not express itself in any other way than *by means of* the immanent-human word, and *through* this word of men) and the *immanent* Scripture.

These can never become a *dualism* as long as we remain aware that the *Verbum aeternum* is nothing but the convergence and integration *of the human words themselves*, and that the immanent-human Scripture is nothing but the refraction of *God's Word itself*. The eternal Word *is* the words of Scripture in their unity and fullness, and Scripture *is* the Word of God in its multiplicity and diversity. To speak here of a dualism betrays a basic misunderstanding concerning the tremendous difference between duality (two-ness) and dualism (bipolarity).[4]

Someone who sensed this problem, and tried to map it out thoroughly, was J. A. Heyns. He rightly rejected the dualistic notion that, according to its essence, Scripture is the Word of God, and according to its nature it is a word of men. But I am not happy with his alternative that, according to its essence, Scripture is the Word of God, and according to its nature, Scripture is the Word of God in human words (cf. §7.8.4, where I mention a similar pair of words that was used by J. A. Heyns and P. C. Potgieter: content and form). It is not clear how essence and nature must be precisely distinguished. But speaking of essence especially in this context had too many substantialistic overtones to be useful.

8.2 The Illumination–Inspiration Problem

8.2.1 Objective and Subjective

When it comes to understanding the miracle of biblical inspiration, several mistaken paths can be followed. One of them involves not grasping correctly the relationship between illumination and inspiration. This mistake occurs in two ways.

(a) *Inspiration is viewed as illumination*. In the theory of dynamic inspiration (§7.9.1), the Spirit's illumination is transferred from the Bible readers to the Bible writers, as if the reader's illumination were identical with the writer's inspiration. Readers and writers are placed on the same level when it comes to receiving divine revelation.

(b) *Illumination is viewed as inspiration*. In what was called the actualistic theory of inspiration (§7.10.3), which is identi-

---

4. See extensively, Ouweneel (1986, chapters 5–6; 2014).

cal with the approach preferred by Heinrich Ott, inspiration is transferred from the Bible writers to the Bible readers, as if the Bible's inspiration were dependent on the reader's illumination.

I do not wish to emphasize the distinction between (a) and (b) because the similarity they share is that both views blur the distinction between illumination and inspiration. The two ideas more or less merge, so that the idea of biblical inspiration is robbed of its specific character, and the Bible books of their uniqueness. We find a similar form of confusion in various articles by philosopher Nicholas Wolterstorff,[5] which have been quoted and criticized by C. F. H. Henry.[6]

The combination of these two views with the three views explained in §8.1 yields a total of five approaches. Of these five, only three were mentioned by Heinrich Ott, who said he could scarcely imagine a fourth one. In principle, I would *reject all five*: the former three because they ignore the proper relationship between the immanent and the transcendent, and the latter two because they ignore the proper relationship between illumination and inspiration. Let me summarize.

(1) *Inspiration* is an objective event; this involves the God-givenness of Scripture as it comes to humanity, independent of readers and listeners being illumined. It is like the light of the sun, shining on human eyes, whether or not they are blind.

(2) *Illumination* is a subjective event, occurring within humans through the power of the Holy Spirit. It is like blind eyes being opened, whether or not the sun is shining.[7]

Scripture may or may not be God-breathed, but this has nothing to do with people's (subjective) knowledge of the matter, nor with their relationship to the Bible. We may extensively and critically investigate Scripture's being God-

---

5. Wolterstorff (1969a–1969d).
6. Henry (1979c, 14–20).
7. Cf. Ouweneel (1995, §6.1.1).

breathed, but these subjective considerations do not change anything in its objective status. At any rate, it has nothing to do with *people's* being inspired (i.e., illumined) by Scripture.

However, in order to be able to *receive* Scripture, a person must be illumined with respect to Scripture. In other words, one's acceptance of Scripture as the Word of God is always subjective, or existential. But this does not affect whether or not Scripture *is* the Word of God, even if there were no person on earth who has been spiritually illumined about this matter. If the objective biblical inspiration is reduced to subjective illumination — or to the inspiration of the reader — there is no *a priori* reason why God's Spirit could not grant this illumination (inspiration) to people through any other religious, or even non-religious, or even anti-religious book. At best, Scripture would differ *only in degree* from other books because people's illumination includes the existential experience that the Bible is a book that is closer to God than other books. However, in this case, there is no *a priori* reason why other people might not have such an existential experience with regard to a very different book, or books. In the eyes of some, this may be a respectable view, but we cannot agree that such a view corresponds with the Bible's own self-testimony regarding inspiration and illumination (see §7.6).

8.2.2 Being and Becoming

To make myself perfectly clear I add here that, of course, I do not deny the desirability and even the necessity of an existential relationship between the Bible and the reader. It would be of no use, and even impossible, to speak of the inspiration of Scripture if no people on earth had been illuminated by the Holy Spirit regarding this fact. However, what I do deny is that such a relationship would add to, or detract from, or replace, the notion that the Bible is God-breathed in an objective sense.

For instance, the confusion between illumination and inspiration is clearly illustrated by Wolfgang Trillhaas:

This proclamation coming from Jesus Christ, this message or also tradition, becomes Word of God when it hits me, when it forces me to a response, when I recognize anew my own being in its light, when I believe this word, or reject it in unbelief. Without this subjective, personal side, the Word of God cannot be understood.[8]

Dialectical theologians seem to be so remarkably unaware of the inner logical contradiction in such a statement. On the one hand, it is asserted that the message *becomes* Word of God, namely, *through* the reader's faith. On the other hand, the person recognizes, believes, and understands that what is coming to them *is* the Word of God (cf. especially the last phrase in the quotation). Both cannot be true. There are only two options. *Either* the message coming to people *is* Word of God. They can accept or reject it as the Word of God, but this does not change the fact that Scripture *is* the Word of God, that is, that God *has* spoken. *Or*, at the moment the message comes to people, it *is not yet* Word of God but *becomes* so only through their faith.

In fact, Trillhaas says, by believing that it *is* the Word of God we make it to *become* the Word of God. This is an outright confusion of the objective and the subjective. I fully accept that the Word of God remains sterile, inactive, infertile as long as nobody is affected by it, is moved to respond to it, and recognizes anew their own identity in the light of that Word. I fully accept the necessity and importance of the soul's illumination by the Holy Spirit regarding the Word of God. However, all these things do not alter the ontic status of Scripture, as being inspired by the Holy Spirit and thus the eternal Word of God in an immanent form. God *has* spoken (objectively), (long) before anyone may (subjectively) respond to this speaking.

As I see it, it is basically no different with the existence of God. God would exist, even if no human would accept and honor this fact. God existed for an entire eternity before

---

8. Trillhaas (1972, 69).

there *were* any humans who could begin to believe in him. It would be absurd to claim that God *"becomes"* in the moment that a person begins to believe in him. God's existence is an objective matter, irrespective of people's beliefs. However, this does not at all diminish the importance of the Holy Spirit opening people's hearts to God's existence; this is the subjective aspect. What kind of God would the Creator be if he had created beings none of which/whom was ever led to accept his existence and worship him? The objective and the subjective are inseparable; the one must not be played off against the other.

8.2.3 No Deism

At this point, I wish to repeat my warning against a Deistic approach to biblical inspiration (§7.10.3). Deism does recognize God as the Creator of the world but does not acknowledge his providential rule. In a similar way, a sterile, Deistic doctrine of inspiration views God's Word after its inspiration *apart from* the continual activity of the Holy Spirit (cf. §1.10.3 and the quotation from Walter Kreck). Creation occurred once and for all; we read in Genesis 2:1 that it was finished. This occurred through the Spirit who was hovering over the face of the waters (Gen. 1:2) — but this Spirit still hovers over the globe (cf. Ps. 104:30). Inspiration occurred through the Spirit as well, and again once and for all; it was finished at the moment the last words of Scripture were written down.

However, here again, we can say that God's Spirit is still hovering over the Scriptures. Throughout the centuries, God the Holy Spirit carefully preserved the Bible; moreover, all over the world, the Spirit constantly addresses people through the Scriptures. How else than through Scripture can the Spirit bear witness with people's spirits that they are children of God (Rom. 8:16)? This is the well-known internal testimony of the Holy Spirit (Lat. *testimonium Spiritus Sancti internum*; see §1.9), which is mentioned by Trillhaas.[9] However, in the

---

9. Trillhaas (1972, 76–77).

same passage he again confuses Scripture's having been inspired once and for all with the present, continual activity of the Spirit *through* the inspired Scriptures.[10]

Though the inspiration of the Bible is an objective ontic given, Scripture would remain sterile and infertile without the work of illumination by the Spirit hovering over the Bible, who continually applies Scripture to the hearts of people. However, this is not an excuse to confuse the two; God's (objective) inspiration *of Scripture* and God's (subjective) illumination *of people* must be carefully distinguished.

Emil Brunner's argument that the term "revelation" is sometimes used also for the internal event in the receiving subject, as in the cases of Peter (Matt. 16:17) and Paul (Gal. 1:16),[11] seems to me hardly relevant here. This is because in none of these cases does revelation entail an internal illumination regarding an already given message (a "Scripture") but an entirely new, or at least essentially enriched, message *itself*. Peter and Paul *received* new revelations; they did not only receive the Spirit's illumination in order to understand revelations given before. This is not on the same footing as what happens to a person to whom Christ or the Father reveals himself through the Bible. Such a revelation—if at least the word is correctly used in this way (cf. Matt. 11:27; Eph. 1:17)—is nothing but Spiritual illumination regarding what had been objectively revealed centuries earlier.

8.3 The Humanity of Scripture

8.3.1 God's Word and Human Word

Earlier I emphasized that we can speak rationally of biblical inspiration but that, at the same time, it is a phenomenon that surpasses rationality. Inspiration is a work of the Holy Spirit, and as human beings we are unable to fathom the work of

---

10. In addition to mentioning Rom. 8:16, Brunner (1949, 30) refers to 1 Cor. 12:3 ("[N]o one speaking in the Spirit of God ever says 'Jesus is accursed!' and no one can say 'Jesus is Lord' except in the Holy Spirit").
11. Ibid., 23, 34.

the Spirit. Jesus himself pointed to this fact when he spoke of regeneration: "The wind [Gk. *pneuma*] blows where it wishes, and you hear its sound, but you do not know where it comes from or where it goes. So it is with everyone who is born of the Spirit [Gk. *pneuma*]" (John 3:8). This passage reminds us of the God-breathed or God-blown quality (Gk. *theopneustos*) mentioned in 2 Timothy 3:16, and the quality of being carried along by the Holy Spirit (Gk. *hypo pneumatos hagiou pheromenoi*), like leaves carried by the wind, mentioned in 2 Peter 1:21. The question of Nicodemus concerning the manner of regeneration is rationally unanswerable. Basically it is just as foolish as the question concerning the manner of the resurrection of the dead (1 Cor. 15:35-36), which is also an unfathomable work of God's Spirit (Rom. 8:11), or the question concerning the manner of the Spirit's work of inspiration.

This being carried along by the Spirit, or the Scripture being breathed, is not a kind of whispering in the writer's ear; that is, it is not something that can be captured immanent-conceptually. If we would look at this differently, we might easily end up with a theory of mechanical inspiration. Or at least we might end up with a theory in which we try to capture inspiration in an immanent-logical concept. However, this is impossible. Biblical inspiration occurred in a way that is supra-temporal, transcendent, unable to be conceptualized, in the heart of the writer, while at the same time *all* his immanent-modal functions—feeling, thinking, willing, formulating, believing, and so on—were fully and very actively involved in the process.

It is of essential importance to understand this correctly. We are dealing here not simply with an activity of the Spirit in the writer's feeling, thinking, willing, formulating, and believing. Rather, we are dealing with an activity that surpasses all these modal functions; that is, it is an activity in the *heart*. Inspiration moves (drives) the heart of the Bible writer at a level that transcends all our logical-rational-(pre)theological conceptualization, but at the same time emanates from

Inspiration: A New Approach

there to permeate *all* the writer's immanent functioning. The thoughts that he wrote down had been formed by his own mind, his own feeling, his own ratio, his own will, his own creativity, his own character, his own aesthetic taste (poetry!), and so on. All these functions and dispositions were *fully* involved in the process, so that the end result is a typical product of the kind of personality *he* was. And at the same time, the end result is *fully* the product of the Holy Spirit's activity in the writer's heart, which activity permeates all his functions and dispositions.

8.3.2 Historical and Supra-Historical

J. A. Heyns summarized the matter rather adequately: "The words of the Bible *are* and *remain* human words, sought by humans and found by humans, but *in*, *with* and *under* these written words, yes, *as* human words, God's Word is present."[12] In my view, we cannot possibly conceptualize this process, this cooperation between the human mind and God's Spirit; we can approximate it only through modal ideas.

In order to look at this matter from a different viewpoint, let me put it this way: *biblical inspiration was not a historical event*. It cannot be analyzed or discussed in terms of any common historiographical categories because it belongs to the transcendent, not to the temporal-immanent "sphere." (Using the word "sphere" here is, I am afraid, unavoidable, even though dualistic overtones easily creep in with such a term. I refer here again to my extensive discussion of the relationship between the transcendent and the immanent, and my rejection of any form of dualism, even though certain expressions may seem to point into this direction.[13])

History, too, certainly has its own transcendent point of unity and concentration, namely, personally in the human heart, and supra-personally in the first and the last Adam, respectively. However, history itself occurs within time, is im-

---

12. Heyns (1976, 39).
13. Ouweneel (1986, chapters 5–6; cf. 413; 2014; 2015).

manent-empirical. Therefore, I would never say, as does Emil Brunner,[14] that the (transcendent, and thus supra-historical) revelation itself is historical (Ger. *geschichtlich*). Revelation is supra-historical, even if the Word is *expressed* in historical, therefore immanent-empirical forms, that is, in the historical Scriptures and in the historical Jesus.

The same applies to biblical inspiration. It is transcendent, even though it was *expressed* in the (immanent-empirical) historical event of the actual writing of the books by the authors. Inspiration is just as transcendent, that is, supra-historical, as

(a) *the act of creating*, even though the latter was expressed in the immanent-historical formation of things, plants, animals, and humans;

(b) *the Fall* (as far as the human heart was concerned), even though this Fall was expressed in certain immanent-historical sinful acts;

(c) *redemption*, even though the latter was expressed in the immanent-historical events of the sufferings, death, resurrection, ascension, and glorification of Christ.

Now the transcendent is always — by definition — also *supra*-rational, but it is not thereby *ir*-rational (that which conflicts with the immanent laws of logic). Therefore, theological investigation of Scripture can certainly adduce rational arguments for the fact and the character of biblical inspiration. Even though this inspiration cannot be conceptualized (i.e., contained within concepts), it can certainly be approximated in the form of an idea — and therefore rationally! — even if it surpasses the rational. Therefore, rational ideas and arguments can never bring about belief in inspiration; only the Spirit of God can do this. Nor can they exhaustively explain it. However, rational arguments can certainly support this supra-rational faith. Therefore, let me give some of those considerations, in addition to those that I have already described.

---

14. Brunner (1949, 16–17).

8.3.3 Humans Employed by God

God has equipped humans in a very special way, for he created them in his image and after his likeness (Gen. 1:26-27; 9:6; 1 Cor. 11:7; James 3:9). Therefore, it is no wonder that he fully employed human capacities and personality, which he himself had granted. However, the superior power of the Spirit—not to be confused with being overwhelmed by the Spirit[15]—ensured that, in the end, humans wrote down those words that God wanted to see recorded. This was also the view of the Second Vatican Council:

> The divine revelation, which is written, and exists, in Holy Scripture, has been recorded by the breath of the Holy Spirit... For the manufacture of the sacred books, God chose people whom he, while they applied their capacities and powers, used as true authors for passing on in writing all that, and that alone, which he—working in and through them—wanted to be written.[16]

God did not employ a medium as his instrument (see §7.8.4 on Spiritism), no person in trance, no human whose own thinking, feeling, and willing had been inoperative. He wanted to use the entire person, complete with all his modal-functional life. As Otto Weber put it,

> [I]f the work of God in the biblical witnesses is a work of the Holy Spirit, then this means that the witnesses themselves are at work. It is a mechanistic or ecstatic misunderstanding of the Holy Spirit to view him as a kind of competitor to human action. He is not the mechanical "cause" of human behavior and activity; rather, he is the one who liberates us so that we can act.[17]

The humans in whom God breathes are not bound for this purpose but liberated.

---

15. This is what evil spirits do; cf. 1 Cor. 12:2.
16. Grillmeyer (1966, 3:11).
17. Weber (1981, 234).

In this process, God warded off human sin. Thus, in a unique way, his preserving hand over the human writers kept them from lies or subterfuges. The Bible writers do render the lies and loopholes that some of their protagonists employed, but they themselves do not lie or deceive. Lying does not belong to the creaturely-weak and defective in humans, but to the sinful in them — this is something essentially different. Again, we must carefully distinguish here between *structure* and *direction* (see §§2.8.2 and 2.9.2). Weaknesses and limitations belong to the horizontal *structure* of what is human. This structure was not affected by the Fall, otherwise humans would not have been humans after the Fall anymore. Structure is what is proper to the creatureliness, the humanness of humans. However, lying and falsehood involve the vertical *direction* of the human heart; in this case, the downward direction.

God employed the creaturely structure of the human personality, with all the limitations that belong to it. However, as far as the direction was concerned, the Bible writers were filled with the Spirit, not with the flesh (cf. Gal. 5:16-24). Sometimes they touch upon what is sinful in what they say to God (Jer. 20:14-15), but they do not sin toward their readers through lying and deceit. To put it more sharply, when Jeremiah uttered the words of chapter 20:14-15 ("Cursed be the day on which I was born! The day when my mother bore me, let it not be blessed! Cursed be the man who brought the news to my father, 'A son is born to you,' making him very glad") he was not very spiritual — but when he, guided by God, recorded these words, he was filled with the Spirit.

God was not hindered by the personality differences among the Bible writers; on the contrary, he made full use of them. He used the Jewish collaborator Matthew (a tax collector for the Romans, thus collaborating with the occupying force; Matt. 9:9) to write the Gospel of the Jewish King-Messiah, who one day will subjugate all Israel's enemies. The unfaithful servant Mark, who was afterward restored (Acts

12:25; 13:5, 13; 15:37-39; Col. 4:10; 2 Tim. 4:11; Philemon 24; 1 Pet. 5:13), wrote the Gospel concerning the true Servant. The "beloved physician" Luke (Col. 4:14) describes Christ as the true Man, who came to manifest God's healing mercy (see Luke 1:50, 54, 58, 72, 78; 4:22; 6:36; 7:13; 10:33, 37; 15:20). And the beloved apostle John, who had been reclining at table on the bosom of Jesus (John 13:23; 19:26; 20:2, 7; 21:20), describes him in his highest glory as the Son of God, in the bosom of the Father (1:18), the full manifestation of God's love.

God's employment of humans and humanness as organs of the divine must be taken very seriously. The humanity of Scripture is just as essential to the Bible as its divinity. Recall here what was said earlier about the danger of Docetism (§7.8.3), which is the actual denial of the human form in which the Word of God was inscripturated. As a variant of 1 John 4:2-3, I would say: By this you know the Spirit of God: every spirit that confesses that the Word of God has come in the "flesh" of human writing is from God, and every spirit that does not confess the Word of God as having come in this "flesh" is not from God.

8.4 Human Aspects

8.4.1 Five Aspects

It was one of the merits of Herman Bavinck that in his day he recognized the problem surrounding the humanity of Scripture, and underscored some of the following points,[18] which I formulate here in my own words.

(a) First, consider the developmental course of Scripture within human history. On the transcendent level we are dealing with the one, eternal, unchangeable Word of God. But on the immanent level, a collection of books grew and increased gradually, to which continually new books were added, such that later books commented upon earlier books. This is true not only for the New Testament with regard to the Old Testament (numerous times), but also for the later Old Testament

---

18. Bavinck (*RD* 1:431-35).

books with regard to the Torah (see Josh. 1:7-8; 8:31-32; 22:5; 1 Kings 2:3; 2 Chron. 25:4; Neh. 8:15; Dan. 9:13), or to other books (e.g., Dan. 9:2 referring to Jer. 25:11-12; 29:10).

(b) Next, consider that Scripture was written by people with all their limited creatureliness, and in human language with all its limitations. The eternal, transcendent Word is clothed in the garment of temporal-immanent-human words, with all the weaknesses and limitations of what is human, and more generally: of what is creaturely. God's Word became Scripture, "and as scripture subjected itself to the fate of all scripture," said Bavinck.[19] Abraham Kuyper wrote, "... we do not deny that the quality of what is humanly weak [Dutch *menschelijk-gebrekkige*] clings to Scripture."[20] I will return to the matter of the supposed weakness of Scripture in the following chapters.

(c) When quoting from the Old Testament, the New Testament writers often refer to the transcendent Primary Author (Lat. *Auctor Primarius*; see §5.10.1); this is important because it underscores the divine character of Scripture (see Mark 12:36; Acts 1:16; 4:25; 28:25-27; Heb. 3:7-11; 10:15-17). However, it is equally important that the writers often refer to the immanent secondary authors (Lat. *auctores secundarii*), such as Moses, David, and Isaiah (Matt. 13:43; 22:43; John 1:23, 46; 5:46; 12:38; cf. Acts 1:16; 3:18; 4:25; 28:25; Heb. 4:7). Sometimes this involves words that originally had been spoken by God himself, but which nonetheless are quoted as those of the secondary author (cf. Deut. 32:21 and Isa. 65:1 with Rom. 10:19-20). The Bible writers were led to refer both to God and to certain men as the authors of the Bible (see more extensively §8.6).

(d) Often, the Bible writers were set apart, prepared, and qualified for their task (Exod. 3:4; Isa. 6:1-8; Jer. 1:5; Gal. 1:15). This preparation did not involve, for instance, merely that Moses was instructed in all the wisdom of the Egyptians (Acts

---

19. Bavinck (*RD* 1:434).
20. Kuyper (*DD* 2.1:64); cf. also Bavinck (*RD* 1:434).

Inspiration: A New Approach

7:22) and Saul of Tarsus received a rabbinical training (22:3; Gal. 1:14). A great part of their capacity as Bible writers often enabled them to write very *differently* from that for which they had been trained.[21] They were trained in *God's* school, which for both Moses and Paul required not sitting at a school desk but dwelling in the wilderness (Exod. 3:1; Gal. 1:17). The power of God in biblical inspiration did not exclude the gradual preparation of the human writer. On the contrary, the true character of inspiration, because it involved the full employment of the human personality, presupposed and demanded such a preparation.

(e) In Scripture, many Bible writers speak to *God* from the fullness of their hearts (e.g., Neh. 13:14, 22, 29; Jer. 18:19-23; 20:7-12; and many Psalms), or speak to others in a deeply emotional way (e.g., Lev. 26; Deut. 28-29; Gal. 3:1-5; 4:12-20; 5:12; Rev. 2-3). Sometimes their words to God are even sinful, or border on the sinful (e.g., Num. 11:11-15; Job 29-30; Ps. 88; Jer. 20:14-18). We encounter many quotations from unbelievers; remarkable are the occasional long quotations from (as such obviously non-inspired) letters and documents of pagan people (e.g., Ezra 4:11-22; 5:6-17; 6:2-12; Dan. 4:1-37; 6:26-28; Acts 23:26-30). We find statements of the devil (Job 1:7-11; 2:2-5; Matt. 4:3, 6, 9). The matter of the Bible's inspiration has nothing to do with the kind of persons who express themselves in the Bible. These persons were not inspired—often we must say, on the contrary—but the *Scriptures* are inspired; in them we find these statements recorded exactly as God desired, because they are important for us.

On the transcendent level, God is *always* speaking through Scripture to people; but on the immanent level, it could happen that (a) God is speaking to himself (Gen. 1:26; 11:7; Ps. 110:1; Isa. 6:8), that (b) God is speaking to people ("thus says the LORD"), (c) a person (i.e., the Bible writer, or the person about whom he writes) is speaking to God, or (d) a human is

---

21. *Contra* Van Genderen (2008, 81).

speaking to other humans. On the other hand, in the wider sense, as a thoroughly human book, Scripture *in its entirety* could be viewed as a human response to God.[22]

8.4.2 Five More Aspects

(f) The Word of God does not lie hidden somewhere within the biblical testimony. This *entire* testimony has power because it has been totally saturated and permeated by that about which it testifies. At the same time, the witnesses are no passive or neutral reporters, but fully involved in what they describe (cf. Isa. 43:10, 12; 44:8; John 8:12-19; 15:26-27; 18:37), to such an extent that one described by the Greek word *martys* ("witness") can become a "martyr" (a word derived from *martys*). Thus, in the book of Revelation the meanings of "witness" and "martyr" can hardly be distinguished (Rev. 2:13; 11:3; 17:6; cf. 1:9; 6:9; 12:11, 17; 20:4). The Bible writers, too, were witnesses who were personally strongly involved; many of them became martyrs for their faithfulness to the Lord, something true of Isaiah, Jeremiah, Matthew, Peter,[23] Paul, James, Jude, and possibly Zechariah (cf. Matt. 23:35). They did not just write about "matters of fact," but about him with whom they had had a personal encounter of faith, and to whom they were dedicated with all their zeal and energy, and sometimes even with their lives.[24]

(g) As we saw, the various authors exhibit clear, and sometimes enormous differences with regard to style, way of writing, vocabulary, sphere of interest, emotional disposition, spiritual power, development, and topics. Inspiration did not at all exclude these personal traits of the human writers. On the contrary, the true character of inspiration, which entailed the full employment of the human personality, presupposes

---

22. Cf. Barr (1990, 120).
23. All of the Twelve died as martyrs, except the apostle John (although authorities *tried* to kill him); tradition tells us he supposedly died at Ephesus shortly after AD 98.
24. Cf. Weber (1981, 199, 205–08).

and demands that these very traits would become clearly evident in Scripture. For instance, the early church wondered how it was possible that the apostle Peter wrote his first letter in a style very different from that of his second letter. Was the literary form of 1 Peter perhaps influenced by Silvanus (see 5:12), and that of 2 Peter perhaps by a different secretary? How is it possible that 2 Peter quotes many times from the Septuagint, which one might expect from a Hellenistic author but not from a Galilean fisherman? If Peter did use a secretary (as Paul did, Rom. 16:22), this underscores the importance of the human aspect in producing the biblical text.

(h) The transcendent urge to write — which ancient authors called the *impulsus ad scribendum* (see §8.5.1) — was only rarely based on a direct divine command to write (Exod. 34:27; Deut. 31:19; Jer. 30:2; 36:2; Rev. 1:11, 19; 2:1-3:14; 14:13; 19:9; 21:5). Much more often, this urge was based upon the immanent circumstances, which provided the authors a reason to write of their own accord (cf. Luke 1:1-4; 1 Cor. 7:1; 2 Cor. 2:9; Philemon 8-10; 1 John 2:26; Jude 3). However, this did not exclude the guidance of the Holy Spirit in all these things. On the contrary, none of the immanent circumstances under which the Bible books arose conflicted with, or competed with, the transcendent work of the Spirit.

(i) Sometimes, the Bible writers speak of such details of their personal lives that a mechanical view of inspiration is rendered totally inadequate. A well-known example is 2 Timothy 4:13, where Paul writes to Timothy, "When you come, bring the cloak that I left with Carpus at Troas, also the books, and above all the parchments." Bible scholar William Kelly suggested that the parchments intended here (expensive material!) had not yet been written upon, and that Paul, who knew that his martyrdom was near, had a great desire that these parchments would be used for copying his letters.[25]

(j) Scripture contains all kinds of literary genres, identical

---

25. *BT* N5, 287.

to those found in other literary works, such as prose and poetry, epic and drama (Job!), ode and hymn, lyrical and didactic poems (the Psalms!), letters, historiography and prophecy, vision and apocalyptic, parable and fable (Judg. 9:7-15; 2 Kings 14:9). None of the common immanent-human literary traits that are normally found in a literary work are absent in the Bible books, nor does this fact contradict the continual transcendent supervision of the Spirit over the origin of these books.

8.4.3 Human Limitations

Luke based his Gospel on a careful personal preparation and thorough investigation (Luke 1:1-4).[26] He and the others considered and deliberated during the entire time they were writing (John 14:26). For instance, they referred to personal memories, both collective and individual (1 Cor. 1:14-16; 2:1-5; 3:1-2; Gal. 1:11-24; 2 Pet. 1:16-18). Sometimes, their memories were so ordinarily human that they had forgotten certain details of their story: "Beyond that, I do not know whether I baptized anyone else" (1 Cor. 1:16). This verse is a beautiful example of an afterthought: in verse 14, the apostle Paul says that, among the Corinthians, he only baptized Crispus and Gaius; but in verse 16, he also remembers the household of Stephanas. Sometimes, he did not know the true nature of a situation: "I know a man in Christ who fourteen years ago was caught up to the third heaven—whether in the body or out of the body I do not know, God knows" (2 Cor. 12:2). Or he did not know what to choose: to depart or to remain in the flesh (Phil. 1:22). With respect to Acts 20:7-12, F. F. Bruce wrote that Paul's ministry in Troas some two years before had apparently yielded more fruit than he had realized at that time (2 Cor. 12:12-13).[27] Others have suggested that the apostle Paul was firmly convinced that he would live to see the second coming of Christ (cf. 1 Thess. 4:15, "*we* who are

---

26. Cf. Berkouwer (1967, 219-21); cf. Green (1997, 33-46).
27. Bruce (1988b, 384).

alive . . ."), and that he erred in this respect.[28]

We also discover that the Bible writers sometimes did not know the *precise* facts. Thus, John 6:19 speaks of "twenty-five or thirty stadia"; would the Holy Spirit not have known the exact distance? The same occurs in Acts 19:7, "*about* twelve men," though in the case of such a small group it could not have been difficult to identify the *exact* size. Apparently, Luke did not know the precise number. He does something similar elsewhere: Anna was "about" eighty-four years old (Luke 2:37), the daughter of Jairus was "about" twelve (8:42, so perhaps she was 11 or 13?), the transfiguration on the mountain was "about eight days" later (9:28, so perhaps seven or nine days later, or between seven-and-a-half and eight-and-a-half?), whereas providing an exact number could not have been a problem for the Holy Spirit. Of course, in many other cases the word "about" is very suitable because an accurate number was not needed (cf., e.g., Luke 1:56; 9:14; 22:41, 59; 23:44). All the more remarkable are those cases in which a very precise number *is* given, where we might think such precision would have been unnecessary, as with the 153 fish mentioned in John 21:11, and 276 persons mentioned in Acts 27:37, unless these numbers have a special meaning.[29]

On the basis of the theory of mechanical inspiration, such ignorance or imprecision regarding details would be incomprehensible. Such ignorance belongs to the weakness and limitation of humanity, and was not suppressed by the work of the Spirit. None of the common immanent-human processes that normally occur during the writing of a book were absent in the writing of the Bible books, and this did not at all conflict with the Spirit's continual transcendent supervision

---

28. Cf., e.g, Benson's Commentary and Meyer's New Testament Commentary, http://biblehub.com/commentaries/ 1_thessalonians/4-15.htm.

29. Amazingly, just like the number 666 (Rev. 13:18), the numbers 153 and 276 (the only three-digit numbers in the New Testament that were not rounded off) are triangular numbers (cf. https://en.wikipedia.org/wiki/Triangular_number). This can hardly be a coincidence, although we can only speculate about the spiritual meaning of this.

of this work of writing.

I do not think that many Christians today would accept the view of Gisbertus Voetius, or Johannes Andreas Quenstedt, that preparatory investigation by the Bible writers was completely unnecessary, or that differences in language and style, and even Paul's "I do not know," must be attributed entirely to the sovereignty of the Spirit. This would imply that the Spirit created a different style for every Bible writer (which was not *their own* style at all), or that the Spirit moved Paul to write "I do not know," totally irrespective of what Paul in reality did or did not know. Such a view sounds too much like wishing to save a theory at all costs, instead of *basing* a theory upon, and adapting it to, these and many other biblical data. It seems to me the view of Quenstedt and Voetius is of the same category as the (still occurring?) belief that God created the fossils in the earth in order to test his children's belief in the divine creation of the world.[30] Similarly, would the thoroughly human impression that Scripture makes supposedly have been created by God to test his children's belief in the theory of (mechanical!) inspiration?

8.5 Verbal Inspiration: Faith and Theory

8.5.1 An Ancient Belief

Because of the transcendent character of inspiration, it is impossible to express its precise nature in concepts. This is often overlooked by both strong defenders and ardent critics of the concept of verbal (word-for-word) inspiration.[31] We can fully maintain that inspiration is expressed in the distinct words of Scripture *without* trying to contain this idea within a theological theory.

Belief in the verbal quality of inspiration is very ancient; traces of it are found in the writings of Clement of Alexan-

---

30. The most infamous example of this view came from the English scientist Philip H. Gosse (2003).
31. Cf. the discussion in Berkouwer (1967, 41–49).

dria,³² Origen,³³ and Jerome.³⁴ Yet, this *belief* was not automatically linked with a *theory* that should supply a logical-analytical warrant for this belief. Such a theory, which far surpassed the *belief* in inspiration, was the early Protestant view of the three—successive!—actions of the Spirit in the inspiration event: supplying the urge to write (Lat. *impulsus ad scribendum*), the subjects, contents, or topics (Lat. *suggestio rerum*), and the words (Lat. *suggestio verborum*).³⁵ This triad betrays a desire to know more than one can possibly account for. It conceptualizes and historicizes what is basically a *supra-historical* event that had a *supra-rational* character. This approach is symptomatic of the rationalism that permeates (or permeated) Western science, and with which early Protestant theology was saturated as well.

The *belief* in verbal inspiration is not necessarily linked with the *theory* of mechanical inspiration, or with any inspiration theory at all.³⁶ A theory of organic or dialogical inspiration can also be based upon *belief* in verbal inspiration, but the link with the theory of mechanical inspiration seems the most obvious.³⁷

Belief in verbal inspiration implies that not only the *kerygma*, the biblical message or content, but also the words, the form, in which the message comes to people, proceed from God (we are using the conceptual pair of form and content with caution, since for some it might imply a false dualism). Thus, we read that Moses wrote down all the *words* of the Lord (Exod. 24:4; cf. Josh. 24:26; Dan. 9:11-12). God laid his *word* on David's tongue (2 Sam. 23:2; cf. Ps. 45:1). God put his *words* in Jeremiah's mouth (Jer. 1:9; cf. 26:2; 36:2, 4, 18, 27, 32; 45:1; 51:60; Deut. 18:18). The Preacher wrote "*words* of

---

32. *Protreptikos* IX.82.1.
33. *In Psalmos comm.* on Ps. 1:4.
34. Mentioned in Bavinck (*RD* 1:405).
35. Cf. Weber (1981, = Ger. 256).
36. Cf. Webster (2003, 37–38).
37. Berkouwer (1967, 43–44).

truth" (Eccl. 12:10). God entrusted his "oracles" (Gk. *logia*, related to *logos*, "word") to Israel (Rom. 3:2, which referred to the Old Testament). The apostles spoke with *words* that the Holy Spirit had taught them (1 Cor. 2:13). And finally, let no one take away "from the *words* of the book of this prophecy" (Rev. 22:19). This emphasis on the words of Scripture, and not just on the general sense of Bible passages, is undeniable, and must be accounted for in some way.

The last two New Testament quotations mentioned are important over against Emil Brunner, who was prepared to defend a kind of verbal inspiration of the prophetic word in the Old Testament, but asserted that the New Testament revelation, in contrast to the Old Testament, cannot be understood unequivocally as Word revelation,[38] and that the apostles, in contrast to the prophets, could not claim that their "teaching words" were inspired by the Holy Spirit.[39] Brunner seemed to overlook the existence of New Testament prophets (Acts 11:27; 13:1; 15:32; 21:10; Rom. 12:6; 1 Cor. 12:28; 14:29; Eph. 2:20; 3:5; 4:11; 1 Thess. 5:20; 1 Tim. 1:18; 4:14), and that the apostle John refers to Revelation as "prophecy" (Rev. 1:3; 22:18-19), thus counting himself among the prophets, that the apostle Paul placed in 1 Timothy 5:18 an Old Testament text (Deut. 25:4) and a New Testament text (Luke 10:7) on the same level of "Scripture,"[40] and that the apostle Peter places Paul's letters alongside "the other Scriptures" (2 Pet. 3:16).

Strangely enough, Otto Weber, too, claimed that the Greek term *graphē* in the New Testament always refers to the Old Testament,[41] which is incorrect. In Romans 16:26 Paul seems to refer to the *apostolic* writings as "prophetic writings" (see Eph. 2:20 and 3:3, 5 for reference to the New Testament foundational "prophets"[42]), but commentators do not uniformly

---

38. Brunner (1949, 31–32).
39. Ibid., 32.
40. But cf. the critical discussion of this point in Towner (2006, 364) and references.
41. Weber (1981, =Ger. 208).
42. Cf. Godet (1880, ad loc.); Grant (1901, 290); Kelly (*BT* 9:183; N4, 127–28).

defend this exegesis.[43]

Verbal inspiration renders more than the words as important. Jesus referred to the letters (the very small Hebrew *yod*) and the "tittle" (or "stroke," Gk. *keraia*) when speaking of the inviolability of Scripture (Matt. 5:18). This argument was used by Clement of Alexandria.[44] Karl Barth referred to him, and significantly commented, "Here too, in the light of Mt. 5:17-20 we must be on our guard against trying to say anything different."[45] In this context, he defended the notion of verbal inspiration, though carefully distinguishing this from being verbally inspired (Ger. *Verbalinspiriertheit*),[46] and approvingly quoted Martin Luther and John Calvin in this respect.[47]

Emil Brunner, too, acknowledged that verbal inspiration was defended both by pre-Christian Judaism and by Paul and other apostles[48] — even though he praised Luther for not having developed a doctrine of verbal inspiration.[49]

8.5.2 A-Contextual Atomism

Difficulties with the idea of a verbal inspiration arise only if this *pre-theoretical belief* is enclosed within a theory that requires a rational warrant for such a belief. In this case, theologians easily be trapped in the snare of literalism, for instance, by asserting that, in Scripture, each word or each letter *itself* apart from its context, would have exactly the same value and significance because of inspiration. This literalism can be compared with the way Israel dealt with the Law: as a matter of the letter, not of the Spirit (Rom. 2:27, 29; cf. 7:6; 2 Cor. 3:6). The one, eternal Word of God (Lat. *verbum Dei*) is thus re-

---

43. Cf., e.g., Murray (1968, 2:242); Moo (1996a, 939–40).
44. *Protreptikos* IX.82.1.
45. Barth (*CD* I/2:517).
46. Ibid., 518.
47. Ibid., 520–22.
48. Brunner (1949, 107).
49. Ibid., 109–110.

duced to a collection of many words of God (Lat. *verba Dei*).⁵⁰ In this way, people forget that the letters of Scripture function only in words, words only in sentences, sentences only in contexts.

In the Nestle-Aland edition of the New Testament, the apparatus mentions numerous readings involving spelling differences that are inconsequential for word meanings. Various readings are mentioned involving word differences within sentences that are inconsequential for the exegesis of these sentences. What is important are not the letters themselves, but how they function in the words. What is important are not the words themselves, but how they function in the sentences. The assertion that the important feature is not the form (the actual words) but only the *kerygma* is objectionable. But the view that exalts the mere form (letters, words, punctuation) into a kind of *kerygma* is equally objectionable.

In agreement with Herman Bavinck's view of organic inspiration,⁵¹ Otto Weber emphasized that an organic understanding of inspiration assigns to each distinct word of Scripture its own place within the *totality* of the biblical testimony.⁵² Each separate word has been inspired in relationship to this totality, to the scope of Scripture. Such a statement may disquiet adherents of a mechanical view, Weber argued, but in reality no discerning believer has ever clung to an arbitrary word of Scripture apart from its relationship to the scope of Scripture. Weber himself gave this—rather trivial—example: no one would ever cling to the words "There is no God" (Ps. 14:1; 53:1) without reference to the context.

We could think of less trivial examples. In a Dutch translation of a pious booklet by John Owen, I found on the frontispiece this quotation: "No man also having drunk old wine straightway desireth new: for he saith, 'The old is better'"

---

50. Cf. Ebeling (1979, 32).
51. Bavinck (*RD* 1:431–48).
52. Weber (1981, =Ger 261–62).

(Luke 5:39 KJV). Apparently the publisher recommended this ancient book, implicitly claiming that the publications of modern theologians fall far short of those of the seventeenth-century giants. However, Jesus said this with a negative purpose: the Pharisees and the scribes were clinging to the old, refusing the new things Jesus was bringing. Thus, by dealing with Scripture in an atomistic way, people can make it say the very opposite of what it intends!

Many similar examples of an a-contextual use of Scripture could be added. Thus, there are good grounds to argue that, in (the complex passage of) 1 Corinthians 11:2-16, the apostle Paul intended to say that women in church should not behave differently from how they behave at home or in public; so if their heads are covered at home or in public, then the same should happen where believers meet together. By claiming today that women—who at home and in public are usually bareheaded—should cover their heads in church, people seem to be following Paul's rule literally, but in fact they are doing the very *opposite* of what he intended! They are doing exactly what Paul wished to prevent: women in church behaving differently when not in church. (This apart from the point that Paul wished them to have their heads covered when they pray or prophesy [v. 5]—whereas today in churches where women are required to have their heads covered they are neither allowed to pray [aloud], nor to prophesy![53])

Another example is Romans 7:14-26, especially verse 24 ("Wretched man that I am!"), which is often seen as Paul's description of the normal Christian life: a believer remains a "poor wretched sinner" until death. However, the entire context of Romans 5-8 shows that we are dealing here with a person who is indeed born again but has not inwardly appropriated what it means to be "set free from [the power of] sin" (cf. 6:18, 22; 8:2), namely, a person who is not living through the power of the Holy Spirit (8:1-17).[54] Viewed in the entire

---

53. See Ouweneel (2010a, §12.4.2).
54. See extensively, Ouweneel (2018c, chapter 8).

context, the "wretched man" of 7:24 describes the very opposite of the normal Christian life!

8.5.3 God and Scripture

Christians who have considered inspiration more closely have never *lived* with a verbal inspiration in the sense of a strict *theory* of mechanical inspiration. In practice, no believer attributes the same existential significance to 2 Timothy 4:13 ("When you come, bring the cloak that I left with Carpus at Troas, also the books, and above all the parchments") and, for instance, verse 7 ("I have fought the good fight, I have finished the race, I have kept the faith"). These statements are equally "words of God," but this fact does not give them equal spiritual weight, for they are not equally close to the scope of Scripture (cf. §§7.9.3 and 9.11.2).

At any rate, such a verse does not form an argument against the inspiration of the *entire* New Testament. R. Laird Harris argued that in the Old Testament God's interest extended to bodily ailments and unclean bugs and animals in the Hebrew household. Those who speak denigratingly of 2 Timothy 4:13 are perhaps forgetting that the God who cares for the sparrows was far more concerned with warm clothes (2 Tim. 4:13) and adequate housing (Philemon 22) for his aged apostle. Actually, the tiny detail about the cloak left behind in Troas, if accepted as authentic (which most modernists refuse to do), forms the key to Paul's later history. It proves that the view is correct that he was released from his first Roman imprisonment, that he travelled around — at least to Troas — before he was imprisoned a second time, before his execution shortly after 2 Timothy was written. That was the view of Harris.[55]

The *belief* in verbal inspiration implies that the words of Scripture, in their context and coherence, are ultimately words (oracles, Gk. *logia*) of God; in more theoretical terms: they are the immanent refraction of the one and only transcendent

---

55. Harris (1995, 63).

Inspiration: A New Approach

Word of God. Because of divine inspiration, not only do the Bible writers speak *about* God—and sometimes *to* God— on the immanent level of Scripture, but on the transcendent level God himself is always speaking to *humanity*. This is true not only for the passages in which God (on the immanent level) is directly quoted by the Bible writer but it is true for the totality of Scripture. In this respect, we can discern four categories of Bible passages.

(a) What *God* says in the Bible to people can be quoted as a word of *God*. Thus, God says in Psalm 2:7, "You are my Son; today I have begotten you," and in Hebrews 1:5 this is quoted as a word of God. This is the most obvious example.

(b) What a *human being* says in the Bible to God can be quoted as a word of that human; thus, David's words in Psalm 110:1 ("The LORD says to my Lord . . .") are indeed attributed to him (Matt. 22:43-45). This, too, is an obvious example. The really fascinating examples are found under (c) and (d).

(c) The Bible is a thoroughly *human* book. This means that what is said to Isaiah by God ("I was ready to be sought by those who did not ask for me; I was ready to be found by those who did not seek me," Isa. 65:1) can be quoted in Romans 10:20 as words of Isaiah because he is the human author of this biblical statement.

(d) The reverse is possible as well (and this is the most interesting example): the Bible is a thoroughly *divine* book, so that in Matthew 19:5 Jesus attributes what in Genesis 2:24 the author (Moses?) says directly to God himself. In Acts 13:35, what in Psalm 16:10 David says *to* God is attributed to God himself. *The moment David's words to God had been written down they had become God's Word to humanity.* The same occurs with the various quotations in Hebrews 1, which are all attributed to God, whereas almost none of them was a direct utterance by God.

Apparently, it does not matter whether a human speaks in the Bible to God or to other people, or whether God speaks to himself or to people—the record of it in Scripture can always be quoted as a word that God is speaking from that time forward to all of humanity. No matter who is speaking in the Bible to any other person, the believing reader always hears in those words the voice of the Holy Spirit. Even if the greatest evildoers, or the devil himself, or foreign rulers, are speaking, we hear in the *record* of those words the voice of the Spirit: *this is what the Spirit wishes us to hear.* The Bible writer speaks "in the Spirit" (Matt. 22:43), or "by [Gk. *en*] the Holy Spirit" (Mark 12:36 KJV), or even more strongly: the Holy Spirit speaks "by [Gk. *dia*] the mouth of" the Bible writer (Acts 1:16; cf. Heb. 3:7; 9:8). It is one and the same to say that David or Isaiah spoke in the power of the Spirit or to say that the Spirit spoke (and speaks) by the mouth of David or Isaiah.

Also fascinating are those passages in which Scripture is more or less personified, and thereby identified with the Holy Spirit. Thus, it is "the Scriptures" that, so to speak, are the eye and ear witnesses of Jesus (John 5:39), which is the very same as saying that the Holy Spirit testifies of Jesus through the Scriptures. It is the same thing to say that "Scripture says" as to say "God says (through Scripture)." This can lead to peculiar situations. Thus, we read in Romans 9:17 that "the Scripture" speaks to Pharaoh, even as an "I" ("For this very purpose I have raised you up . . ."), whereas it is obviously *God* who speaks here, and this at a time when the Scripture involved did not yet exist. "The Scripture says" is the same as "God says."

Even more peculiar is Galatians 3:8, "And the Scripture, foreseeing that God would justify the Gentiles by faith, preached the gospel beforehand to Abraham, saying, 'In you shall all the nations be blessed.'" Words such as "foreseeing" and "preached"—again referring to a time when the Scripture involved did not yet exist—point to the strongest imaginable form of personification of Scripture. The words "the Scripture preached" are identical with "God preached" or "the Holy Spirit preached." Again, what Scripture says is what God says. In Paul's mind, God's speaking and Scripture's speaking coincide so completely that he can say, "the Scripture says," where he intends to say, "God, as recorded in Scripture, says."

8.6 Old Testament Quotations in the New Testament

8.6.1 Midrash and Typology

One argument often adduced against Scripture's verbal inspiration in quite different contexts is the remarkable way the New Testament often quotes passages from the Old Testament. The fact that this often occurs in a non-literal way, or that Bible passages are quoted only according to their general thrust, is taken to suggest that the New Testament writers did not attach that much value to the specific wording of the Old Testament text but more to the gist of the text. This is taken as an argument against verbal inspiration. Usually, those with this opinion share with others an emphasis on the literal (grammatical-historical) exegesis of Scripture, exhibiting little interest in a midrashic (homiletic and/or typological) approach to the text.

Some expositors may indeed exhibit little interest in typology, whereas others seem to go to the other extreme. For instance, Joseph Ratzinger gave this typological explanation of the sour wine that Jesus drank on the cross (Matt. 27:48):

> The vineyard of Israel [Isa. 5:2] fails to yield for God the noble fruit of justice, which is grounded in love. It yields the sour grapes of man, who is concerned only for himself. It yields vinegar instead of wine. God's lament, which we hear in the song of the Prophet, is brought to fulfillment as the vinegar is proffered to the thirsting Savior.[56]

Such an interpretation seems rather far-fetched. But, as a lover of typology myself, I admit that it is often difficult to know when the boundary has been crossed.

Let me provide some examples of quotations, which I

---

56. Ratzinger (2011, 218).

summarize under different categories (see this and the two following sections). First, in the New Testament we encounter references to Old Testament passages that we cannot identify. Apparently, such quotes refer to the general gist of the Old Testament as a whole. One example is John 7:38, "Whoever believes in me, as the Scripture has said, 'Out of his heart will flow rivers of living water.'" The problem is that the quoted words are found nowhere in the Old Testament. At best we may think this is an allusion to Proverbs 18:4 ("The words of a man's mouth are deep waters; the fountain of wisdom is a bubbling brook"), or to Isaiah 12:3 ("With joy you will draw water from the wells of salvation"), or 58:11 ("[Y]ou shall be like a watered garden, like a spring of water, whose waters do not fail"). There may even be a typological reference to the rock that gave water to Israel in the wilderness (cf. the use that Paul makes of this rock in 1 Cor. 10:4).

Another example is 1 Corinthians 14:34, where Christian women are called upon to "keep silent in the churches. For they are not permitted to speak, but should be in submission, as the Law also says." The problem is again that "the Law" — the Torah (Pentateuch) or the entire Old Testament[57] — nowhere says anything close to this "quotation"; a reference to Genesis 3:16 ("your husband . . . shall rule over you"), which does not describe a divine commandment but rather a consequence of sin, seems quite far-fetched. Here it seems that a vague and general reference is being made to the thrust of the Old Testament concerning the position of women.

8.6.2 Passages Not Quoted Word for Word

Matthew 2:23 says that, according to the prophets, the Messiah would be called "Nazarene." This is not found anywhere in the Old Testament. Generally, interpreters explain this as a reference to the Hebrew word for "shoot" or "branch," *netser*, like in Isaiah 11:1 ("a branch from his [i.e., Jesse's] roots shall

---

57. Given the preceding references (mainly from the Psalms and Isaiah), "the Law" in Rom. 3:19 apparently refers to the entire Old Testament.

Inspiration: A New Approach

bear fruit"). Thus, Matthew actually says that the Messiah would be called a *netser*; if we assume that the name "Nazareth" (Heb. *Natsrat*) comes from *netser* (which is not accepted by all etymologists), then *netser* can be explained as "Nazarene." We may view this as an example of popular etymology, just as the Bible explains the names Jacob (Gen. 25:26; real meaning perhaps "he will protect") and Moses (Exod. 2:10; probably an Egyptian word: "child") in a popular etymological way.

In Exodus 3:6, it is the LORD who says, "I am the God of your father, the God of Abraham, the God of Isaac, and the God of Jacob." But in Luke 20:37, Jesus renders this verse in such a way as if it were Moses who, in the story of the burning bush, called the LORD "the God of Abraham, the God of Isaac, and the God of Jacob." In itself, this is correct, of course, for Exodus 3:15-16 and 4:5 imply that Moses indeed described the LORD in this way to Israel. In fact, the two passages, Exodus 3 and 4, are freely intertwined here.

Psalm 40:6 ("ears you have dug for me") is rendered in the Septuagint as "a body have you prepared for me." (the rendering we find in Heb. 10:5 as well). Apparently, the Septuagint understands "ears" as part for the whole (Lat. *pars pro toto*), that is, as a reference to the entire body.[58]

In Romans 11:26-27 Paul says, "'The Deliverer will come from Zion, he will banish ungodliness from Jacob'; 'and this will be my covenant with them when I take away their sins.'" Here, several Old Testament passages are altered and intertwined. The first phrase reminds us of Psalm 14:7 and 53:6, "Oh, that salvation for Israel would come out of Zion!" (Isa.

---

58. Cf. the strange reasoning of Ratzinger (2011, 233): "Obedience had already replaced the Temple sacrifices here [Heb. 10]: living within and on the basis of God's word had been recognized as the right way to worship God. . . . So here the idea of spiritual sacrifice, or 'sacrifice in the manner of the word', was formulated: prayer, the self-opening of the human spirit go God, is true worship." I would rather believe that, in Heb. 10:5, the animal offerings of the Old Testament are replaced not by some "word offering" or prayer but by the "bloody" offering of Jesus' own body.

59:20-21 says, "And a Redeemer will come *to* [or, *for*] Zion"). The second phrase reminds us of Isaiah 27:9 ("by this the guilt of Jacob will be atoned for") and 59:20 (". . . to those in Jacob who turn from transgression"). The third phrase reminds us of Isaiah 59:21 ("as for me, this is my covenant with them") and Jeremiah 31:33-34 ("this is the covenant that I will make with the house of Israel after those days . . . : I will forgive their iniquity, and I will remember their sin no more"). It is as if Paul had Isaiah 59:20-21 in mind but, as he quoted this, was thinking at the same time of several other passages. What he quotes is entirely scriptural, but it is not a word for word quotation of any Old Testament passage.

Second Corinthians 6:16b-18 is equally complicated: "'I will make my dwelling among them and walk among them, and I will be their God, and they shall be my people.' Therefore '"go out from their midst, and be separate from them," says the Lord, "and touch no unclean thing; then I will welcome you, and I will be a father to you, and you shall be sons and daughters to me," says the Lord Almighty.'" In verse 16b, Paul gives a free rendering of a combination of Exodus 25:8, Jeremiah 32:38, and Leviticus 26:11-12. Verse 17 is a free rendering of Isaiah 52:11, while the last words ("I will welcome you") remind us of Ezekiel 20:34 (Septuagint; cf. vv. 40-41). Verse 18 is a reminder of 2 Samuel 7:14 (but there it is "him," not "you" [plur.]), and possibly Isaiah 43:6 ("my sons . . . my daughters") and Jeremiah 31:9 ("I am a father to Israel"). The last words, "the Lord Almighty," remind us of Amos 3:13; 4:13 (Septuagint).

In all these cases, Old Testament passages are not quoted word for word but (very) freely, and sometimes mingled with other Old Testament verses. The emphasis on the (distinct) "words" of Scripture is appropriate, but it did not seduce the New Testament writers to verbalism and atomism. That is, it did not prevent them from sometimes quoting Old Testament passages not separately and word for word, but jointly according to their overall gist.

8.6.3 Quotation According to Application

In this section I give some examples of references in which the meaning of the quoted passages is altered. That is, they are not quoted according to their original intention—as established by common grammatical-historical exegesis—but according to free applications made by the New Testament writers. In rabbinic language: the New Testament writers were interested not only in *Peshat* (the straight, direct meaning of the text), but also in the deeper *Remez* (allegorical or symbolic meanings), the still deeper *Derash* (the midrashic meaning, or homiletic application), and the deepest *sod* (the esoteric or mystical meaning of the text).[59]

Good examples of *Remez* and/or *Derash* are the following. The LORD told Abraham, "[I]n your offspring shall all the nations of the earth be blessed" (Gen. 22:18); here, "offspring" refers either to Isaac personally, or to the entire progeny of Abraham, and of course to Israel in particular. The apostle Paul quotes this as follows: "Now the promises were made to Abraham and to his offspring. It does not say, 'And to offsprings,' referring to many, but referring to one, 'And to your offspring,' who is Christ" (Gal. 3:16). Of course, Paul knows very well that "offspring" (Heb. zēra, Gk. *sperma*) can have a collective meaning. But using a midrashic approach, he emphasizes the singular form of *zēra/sperma*, and freely applies this to Christ. This is not arbitrary: to Paul, like to other New Testament writers, not only is Isaac a clear type of Christ (cf. Heb. 11:17-19), but Christ is a type of the true Israel, or is himself the true Israel (cf. the LORD's Servant in Isa., who in 49:3 is Israel, while in Isa. 52-53 the Messiah emerges as the true Israel).

This also explains how Hosea 11:1 ("out of Egypt I called my son"), which obviously refers to the "son" Israel (Exod. 4:22; Deut. 1:31; 8:5; cf. 14:1; Hos. 1:10), can be applied to

---

59. Cf. https://en.wikipedia.org/wiki/Pardes_(Jewish_exegesis). The first letters of these words form the acronym *PaRDeS*, which is Hebrew for "Paradise."

Christ personally (Matt. 2:15). Again, the underlying thought is that Christ is the true Israel.

Another example: in Jeremiah 31:5 we meet Rachel crying because her (grand)children, Ephraim and Manasseh, have been deported along with the other Northern tribes to Assyria. In Matthew 2:17-18 this verse is applied to the cruel infanticide that Herod perpetrated in Bethlehem. The link is that the tomb of Rachel was near Bethlehem (Gen. 35:19); from the elevated place of her tomb, this "mother in Israel" watched as it were the horrible event at Bethlehem, and wept over the little boys who had to die there. Again, this is a typically midrashic application of the original text.

Other examples are the application of Israel passages to converted Gentiles. See, for instance, Isaiah 49:8 ("In a time of favor I have answered you; in a day of salvation I have helped you"), quoted in 2 Corinthians 6:2. Or Hosea 1:10 ("Yet the number of the children of Israel shall be like the sand of the sea, which cannot be measured or numbered. And in the place where it was said to them, 'You are not my people,' it shall be said to them, 'Children of the living God'"), quoted in Romans 9:26 and 1 Peter 2:10. Or Hosea 2:23 ("I will sow her for myself in the land. And I will have mercy on No Mercy [*Lo ruhama*, cf. 1:6], and I will say to Not My People [*Lo-ammi*, cf. 1:9], 'You are my people'; and he shall say, 'You are my God'"), quoted in Romans 9:25.

Of course, cessationists have used these quotations to defend their claim that the church is the true, spiritual Israel, an error that I have refuted elsewhere.[60] This claim confuses grammatical-historical explanation and midrashic application. Paul loves the latter type of approach. For instance, Psalm 19:4 says, "Their voice goes out through all the earth, and their words to the end of the world," referring to the celestial bodies. But in Romans 10:18, Paul freely applies this to the voices of the apostles going out through all the earth. Of

---

60. Ouweneel (2010a, §3.3.3).

Inspiration: A New Approach

course, this is not all that amazing: there is a close connection between general revelation, as it comes to us in nature, and special revelation, as it comes to us through the apostles (see chapters 1-4 above).

In all the cases mentioned, the New Testament quotations of the Old Testament generate problems for all those who insist that verbal inspiration requires an exclusively grammatical-historical exegesis. For orthodox Jews, there is no doubt that the Torah was verbally inspired, whereas Jewish tradition nonetheless spoke of every verse having seventy meanings.[61] Consider as but one example the book *Ayin Panim ba-Torah* ("Seventy Faces [i.e., Meanings] in the Law") written by Abraham ben Samuel Cohen of Lask (1797). The *Peshat* (the literal and most obvious meaning of the text) comes first, followed by many other exegeses, or applications, of the text, distributed among *Remez*, *Derash*, and *Sod*. (In other words, we should not believe that Jewish tradition suggests that there are seventy different *grammatical-historical* exegeses of each verse, which would be absurd!) This is also the—genuinely Jewish—way the apostles apparently deal with the Old Testament, without this approach necessarily diminishing their appreciation for the literal words of the text. The same apostle Paul who quotes so freely—which basically means that he has an appreciation for *Remez*, *Derash*, and *Sod* besides *Peshat*—implicitly teaches that the Bible writers are using the *words* of the Holy Spirit (1 Cor. 2:13).

8.7 Textual-Critical Aspects

8.7.1 The Old Testament

One consequence of the doctrine of verbal inspiration is that textual criticism—the scholarly establishment of the original text of Old and New Testaments—gains importance. This is because the inspiration refers to the *autographa* (the originally written documents), not to the many copies of it, with all their mutual differences. We no longer possess these *autographa*;

---

61. Cf. Talmud: Shabbat 88b; further Num. Rabbah 13–15.

that is, we no longer possess the original documents which contained the text of the inspired Scriptures. At best we can try, through textual criticism, to come as close as possible to the original text—and we are under the impression that textual criticism has managed to do so very well.

However, we will never arrive at a text that corresponds one hundred percent to the *autographa*; or more correctly, any *possible* success in producing such a text would be unknowable because we would not be able to compare our result with these *autographa*. This definitely implies a certain relativizing of the notion of verbal inspiration (at least in the traditional version thereof); apparently, the Holy Spirit is not concerned about our using a biblical text that comes extremely close to the original but is not identical with it.

Thus, the Masoretic text of the Old Testament, no matter how carefully composed by the Masoretes (rabbis from the seventh to the tenth centuries), does not automatically coincide with the *autographa*. We know this through comparison with the Bible manuscripts found among the Dead Sea Scrolls, especially the Isaiah scroll, and other ancient versions of the Old Testament, such as the Septuagint (the Greek translation of the Old Testament, third and second centuries BC) and the Peshitta (the Syriac translation of the Old Testament, second century after Christ?). All these versions together show how highly accurate the available Masoretic text of the Old Testament is, but also that this text is not perfect.

Thus, we now know—to use a well-known example—that the inspired version of Isaiah 53:11 in translation very probably sounded like this: "he shall see light," and not simply "he shall see." Nonetheless, we will always wonder whether the former version *added* the word "light" to avoid the awkward lack of an object, or whether the latter version inadvertently *omitted* the word "light."

8.7.2 The New Testament

For the New Testament, the battle about the correct original

Inspiration: A New Approach

text still continues. Some scholars prefer the so-called majority or Byzantine text, which forms the basis of, for instance, the (N)KJV.[62] This is the text that is encountered in the great majority of available Bible manuscripts. However, these manuscripts are relatively young (the great majority of them are from the fifth century or later). Since the discovery of much older manuscripts, in particular the Egyptian papyri, some of which go back to the second century, many textual critics began to give preference to the *oldest* manuscripts instead of the *majority* of manuscripts. Nowadays, the great majority of Bible translations are based upon an eclectic text, usually referred to as the Nestle-Aland text.[63] In this text, all available variants are evaluated according to age, number, and probability. In general, an older variant is preferred to a younger one, a frequent variant is preferred to a rare one, and a more difficult variant is preferred to an easier variant, considering that copyists (consciously or inadvertently) would have replaced a more difficult variant with an easier one rather than the other way around.[64]

For the doctrine of inspiration, this involves, for instance, the following question: Are the words "For Yours is the kingdom and the power and the glory forever. Amen" in Matthew 6:13 inspired or not? Because they are lacking in important ancient manuscripts, scholars presume that these words were a later addition made for liturgical purposes in the early church.[65]

Another well-known example is the so-called *Comma Johanneum* in 1 John 5:7-8, where the Nestle-Aland text reads (in

---

62. The NKJV mentions textual variants in footnotes; the most important ones are referred to as NU-text, that is, the critical text of the 26th edition of the Nestle-Aland Greek New Testament (N; see next note) and the United Bible Society's third edition (U).
63. Edited by Eberhard Nestle, his son Erwin Nestle, and his successor Kurt Aland; their *Novum Testamentum Graece* is currently in its 28th edition (NA28).
64. Regarding this fascinating evaluative process, see Metzger (2005).
65. Ibid., ad loc.

translation), "For there are three that bear witness: the Spirit, the water, and the blood," whereas the majority text reads, "For there are three that bear witness in heaven: the Father, the Word, and the Holy Spirit; and these three are one. And there are three that bear witness on earth; the Spirit, the water, and the blood." Which text was inspired by the Holy Spirit? The textual witnesses unambiguously point to the shorter variant (as the ESV note says, "Only four or five very late manuscripts contain these [i.e., the additional] words in Greek"). Here again, we are very probably dealing with a much later insertion, made for doctrinal and apologetic reasons.[66]

Regardless of the answer people may give to this question, the textual variant has nothing to do with the *truth* of what the broader text says. All orthodox expositors agree with its truth, but this is not the point. A little surfing on the Internet teaches us that we can find two opposite opinions about this. Some suggest that the insertion is *omitted* in modern Bible translations because certain theologians and translators wished to cover up the truth of the Trinity. Other authors suggest the exact opposite, namely, that the (in their view) erroneous doctrine of the Trinity was *smuggled* into the Bible text of 1 John 5:7-8. Of course, neither of the two allegations is correct. Scholars choose for the longer or—far more often—for the shorter reading purely on the basis of textual-critical considerations. In my view, the Bible supplies us with enough evidence for the doctrine of the Trinity, even without the longer reading of 1 John 5:7-8. People can be fully convinced of the truth of the Trinity, and yet be convinced that the insertion mentioned was not part of the original Bible text. Words can have a perfectly true content without belonging to the inspired text of the Bible.

8.7.3 The Ending of Mark's Gospel

Inspiration becomes still more important in connection with a textual portion as long as Mark 16:9-20 (the entire ending of

---

66. Ibid., ad loc.

Mark's Gospel), which is lacking in important ancient textual witnesses.[67] The following four chief explanations of this phenomenon are given.

(a) Mark certainly wrote these (inspired) words, even though they disappeared from ancient textual witnesses. However, such a disappearance can hardly be accounted for. Moreover, the style and vocabulary of verses 9–20 are quite different from the rest of Mark's Gospel.[68] Further, there is a strange transition from verse 8 to verse 9. Therefore, many assume that theses verse did not come from Mark. One exception is William Kelly, who said that this passage enjoyed its present textual position already in the second century, before any textual witnesses existed that omit it or doubt its authorship. He argued that thoughts and expression in these verses point to Mark alone, and that therefore the passage must be genuine and authentic.[69]

(b) Mark's Gospel accidentally lost its last page before it was copied; verses 9–20 are a later addition, and thus do not belong to the inspired Bible text. However, for those who believe in the divine inspiration as well as the divine preservation of Scripture it is very hard to believe that a page of the Gospel could simply get lost.

(c) For some reason, Mark did not complete his Gospel; verses 9–20 are a later addition, and thus do not belong to the inspired Bible text. Bruce M. Metzger, specialist in textual criticism, defended the option that verses 9–20 are an extract from a very different document, possibly from the first half of the second century.[70]

(d) For some reason, Mark did not complete his Gospel. Shortly after it was written, verses 9–20 were added to the

---

67. Ibid., ad loc.; some less important textual witnesses have a shorter ending; others contain vv. 9–20 in a slightly more extended version. Another longer passage that is questionable is John 7:53–8:11; see ibid., ad loc.
68. See extensively, Bratcher and Nida (1961, 519).
69. W. Kelly (*BT* 16:336).
70. Metzger (2005, ad loc.).

Gospel by another writer to complete it; they definitely belong to the inspired Bible text. But it is scarcely conceivable that Mark really wished to end his Gospel with verse 8, that is, with the trembling and fear of the women. Joseph Ratzinger claimed that we cannot possibly accept that the Gospel would have ended with the silence of the women. This is because the mentioning of this silence presupposes their imminent encounter with the Risen One.[71] Thus, we can imagine that an ending was added to the Gospel at a somewhat later stage that, to be sure, does not exactly tie in with the previous text, and also has a different style and vocabulary, but whose divine authority we need not deny.

This is indeed the final judgment of several authors. J. A. C. van Leeuwen concluded,

> The portion that, original or not, constitutes the ending of Mark's Gospel, and deserves a place in the canon just as much as the rest of the Gospel. Its content corresponds with the other Gospels; it is a brief summary of several appearances of the Risen One. According to its form, it fits perfectly into the framework and the scope of Mark's writing.... From ancient times, it was acknowledged and accepted in the church as part of Holy Scripture. This part, too, is canonical, and was given to God's church as a part of his Word, and is acknowledged as such by the church.[72]

The conclusion of F. F. Bruce with respect to verses 9–20 was that, even though we cannot regard them as an integral part of the Gospel to which they have been attached, no Christian should hesitate to read them as Holy Scripture.[73]

8.8 The Authority of Scripture

8.8.1 Urging Versus Forcing

Because of its divine inspiration, Scripture has a self-evident and unassailable authority. This authority can be defined as

---

71. Ratzinger (2011, 261–62).
72. Van Leeuwen (1928, 215).
73. Bruce (1945, 181).

follows: the Bible is the expression of God's will to people, and thus is entitled to tell them what they must believe, and how they must behave.[74] Clearly, Scripture never possesses this authority apart from God; on the contrary, it is *God* who exercises his authority *through* Scripture.[75] This also means that Scripture possesses no authority apart from Christ, which concretely is the authority that Christ exercises as the One who has received all authority in heaven and on earth (Matt. 28:18), that is, in the kingdom of God. In other words, the authority of Scripture functions within the framework of God's kingdom.[76] Nor does Scripture possess any authority apart from the Holy Spirit; if Scripture has authority, it is because it is the Spirit who speaks in and through it (see Mark 12:36; Acts 1:16; 4:25; 28:25; Heb. 3:7; 10:15-17).

Authority is not the same as power or compulsion. True authority is based on *justice*; however, in practice justice is combined with the power to apply this justice, though some exercise of power is not based on justice. Scripture *rightly* exercises authority (i.e., based on justice) because it is God's own Word. People are *urged* to acknowledge this authority, but not *forced* (Dutch: *gedrongen*, but not *gedwongen*); people are expected to accept Scripture's authority voluntarily. In other words, Scripture is *authoritative* but not *authoritarian*. This does not imply that God will never *impose* his will; on the contrary, on the day of judgment, God will use force to subjugate people to his power (Isa. 45:23; Rom. 14:11; Phil. 2:10). However, in the meantime, God presses people but does not force them. Biblical language is sometimes strong: "Go out to the highways and hedges and *compel* [Gk. verb *anankazō*] people to come in, that my house may be filled" (Luke 14:23), but generally the emphasis is rather on entreating than on enforcement: "[T]he love of God controls [Gk. verb *synechō*, others: compels, constrains] us . . . . [W]e are ambassadors for

---

74. Cf. Ramm (1957, 10–12); Erickson (1998, 267–69).
75. Wright (2005, 23).
76. Ibid., 28–30, 33.

Christ, God making his appeal [others: begging, beseeching, entreating] through us. We implore you on behalf of Christ, 'be reconciled to God'" (2 Cor. 5:14, 20).

The authority of Scripture must not be played off against comparable authorities. Thus, the church is "pillar and buttress of the truth" (1 Tim. 3:15); Christ gave to his church prophets and teachers, who necessarily possess prophetic and teaching authority, respectively (Acts 13:1; 1 Cor. 12:28; Eph. 4:11; cf. 1 Tim. 5:17), not to speak of the Holy Spirit's authority, who guides and leads believers (John 16:13; Rom. 8:14). However, Scripture is always the authority by which all statements made by the church or by its prophets and teachers must be evaluated. Also the true guidance of the Holy Spirit can never conflict with the statements of Scripture. However, it is equally true that the Bible must be *expounded*, an activity in which the teachers of the church do have a God-given role. Even then, we are dealing with an interaction in which it is Scripture, not the church or theology, that has the last word.

Bernard Ramm referred to this interaction as a "pattern of authority"[77] in the sense of an interaction between the objective Word of God and the subjective illumination of the Holy Spirit. The (over)emphasis on only the Bible easily leads to the kind of objectivism that we encounter, for instance, in Protestant scholasticism and modern fundamentalism (see the next chapter). It often ends in a rationalistic confessionalism and theologicism. The (over)emphasis on the Spirit easily leads to a subjectivism that we encounter, for instance, in hyper-Calvinism and in charismatic Christianity (two extremes that find each other in this subjectivism). As has been said, emphasizing the Bible and neglecting the Spirit breeds Pharisees; emphasizing the Spirit and neglecting the Bible breeds fanatics. In other words, those having the Bible without the Spirit will dry up, while those having the Spirit without the Bible will blow up, but those having both will grow up.[78]

---

77. Ramm (1957, book title: *The Pattern of Authority*).
78. Erickson (1998, 278).

8.8.2 The Example of Jesus

Jesus Christ is the great example of dealing with, and speaking of, Scripture on the basis of believing that Scripture is the Word of God himself. To Jesus, Scripture is the authoritative Word; as we saw (§6.3.1), for Jesus the "it is written" (Gk. *gegraptai*) is of decisive significance in all matters (e.g., Matt. 4:4, 6–7, 10; 11:10; 21:13; Mark 7:6). He never theorizes about the Word, nor provides an explanation of its inspiration, but shows in all his life what the divinely inspired and authoritative Word means practically and concretely to him. During the temptations in the wilderness, he silences the devil three times by this simple but powerful "it is written." He is convinced that everything about his life will be fulfilled exactly as they have been foretold in the Bible (Matt. 26:24, 31, 54, 56, 64; Mark 9:12; Luke 22:37; 24:44; John 13:18; 19:28). The apostles deal with Scripture in the same way (Acts 1:16; 13:29–30; 26:22–23; 28:25–27; Rom. 3:4, 10–18; 11:8–10, 26; 1 Cor. 15:3–4; Gal. 3:10, 13).

Jesus spoke with great authority (Matt. 7:29; Mark 1:22; Luke 4:32, 36). Nonetheless, he himself says in John 5:45–47, "Do not think that I will accuse you to the Father. There is one who accuses you: Moses, on whom you have set your hope. For if you believed Moses, you would believe me; for he wrote of me. But if you do not believe his writings, how will you believe my words?" This is a typically Jewish *kal w'chomer* argument (in Western logic called an *a fortiori* argument; e.g., if you can handle a lion you will *a fortiori* be able to handle a cat). It means: if A, then all the more B; if not A, then even less B. This can be said only if the probability of A is greater than the probability of B. What Jesus says here in so many words is that it is more convicting to believe Scripture than his own statements; that is, the *written* Word goes beyond his own *spoken* words. He says, if you do not believe Moses, even less you will believe me. The written Word of God has more authority than Jesus' spoken words (although the latter are now part of Scripture, and thus are part of the authoritative written Word to us).

In a similar way, the apostle Peter implicitly places the (written) prophetic Word above his own experience on the mount of transfiguration: ". . . And we have the prophetic word more fully confirmed, to which you will do well to pay attention as to a lamp shining in a dark place, until the day dawns and the morning star rises in your hearts" (2 Pet. 1:17-19). The authority of the written Word is even greater than that of a person risen from the dead: "If they do not hear Moses and the Prophets, neither will they be convinced if someone should rise from the dead" (Luke 16:29–31).

An authority greater than that of Scripture cannot be imagined. If a person speaks of a vision he has had, or if someone rises from the dead and relates his experiences, these things are worthless if they conflict with the Bible (a matter that must be carefully evaluated, of course). As Paul says, "[E]ven if we or an angel from heaven should preach to you a gospel contrary to the one we preached to you, let him be accursed" (Gal. 1:8; cf. 2 Cor. 11:4). Also when the experiences mentioned do not conflict with the Bible, even then the testimony of Scripture always has greater value and authority than any visions and experiences that people may claim. It surpasses that of a risen person, an angel, an apostle, and even the spoken words of Jesus. Of course, saying this is not to denigrate Jesus in any way, for we realize that the Holy Spirit who spoke through the prophets was none other than the Spirit of Christ himself (1 Pet. 1:11). We could express this is follows: what the Spirit of Christ made the prophets write down has greater authority that what the Holy Spirit made Christ speak on earth (but the same Spirit made the Gospel authors write down Jesus' words, so that now they are written Word, too).

8.8.3 The Example of Paul

If we are aware of these things (see previous section), we will understand how the apostle Paul in 1 Corinthians 7 can make a distinction between what he himself said (vv. 6, 12, 25) and what the Lord said (v. 10). As long as we keep in mind the distinction between revelation and inspiration, there is not the slightest difficulty here. All the things we find in Scripture have been *inspired*, but not every word of Scripture goes back to a direct *revelation* from God. Concerning the wife being bound to her husband, Paul had an explicit revelation from the Old Testament, a commandment from the Lord (1 Cor. 7:10; cf. 11:13; 14:37; also Matt. 5:31–32; 19:3–9). In other cases, no such explicit commandment was available to him; but as someone who was convinced he "[had] the Spirit of God" (v. 40) he could give information about God's judgment in certain cases (v. 17b; cf. 4:17).

Now it is undeniably true that even what apostles of the Lord, filled with the Spirit, pass on to people as their personal opinions possesses only relative authority. However, the crux of the matter here is that we have received 1 Corinthians 7 as *inspired Scripture*. We do not easily accept personal opinions, even if they come from the respected apostle Paul—but we do accept everything that *Scripture* says. Whether Paul possessed a special revelation, or passed on his personal conviction, everything he wrote in 1 Corinthians 7 is inspired Scripture. The Holy Spirit "breathed" in him what he had to write about various matters, whether the explicit commandment of the Lord, or his own thoughts, granted to him by the Spirit. The *exegesis* of this passage must establish the significance and import of Paul's instructions, and the degree to which they have the same validity for us as they had at the time they were written. However, with respect to the quality of inspiration, we cannot distinguish between the authority of the Lord's commandments and the authority of Paul's inscripturated opinions.

Therefore, it seems to be insufficiently precise for A. Troost to distinguish between "God's Word" and Paul's opinion in 1 Corinthians 7.[79] The former is revelation of God, and the latter supposedly is not; but seen from the viewpoint of inspiration

---

79. Troost (1983, 32).

both are "God's Word" for us as part of the inspired Scripture. The distinction that we must make is not between God's Word and Paul's word, but between God's directly revealed commandments and Paul's Spirit-led views. Through inscripturation, *both* are now Word of God for people.

It seems to me equally unfortunate that Gisbertus Voetius wished to restrict the authority of Scripture to the direct statements of God and to the imperatives of prophetically and apostolically speaking persons.[80] Here, the authority of Scripture is limited to commandments and prohibitions. See the next section on the narrative character of the Bible, which for us has equal divine authority.

Also unfortunate is a remark that Herman Dooyeweerd reportedly made in an interview, when he said that it would be foolish to say that 2 Timothy 4:13 was inspired.[81] What he apparently intended to say is that this verse does not contain any direct revelation from God, and/or that it does not have the same divine authority as so many other verses. This, and another unfortunate error resulting from Dooyeweerd's lack of theological interest and knowledge, were sufficient for Harold Lindsell to dismiss Dooyeweerd altogether,[82] without investigating the philosopher's thought in order to determine whether this condemnation was justified in the light of his other publications.

8.9 Authority *Versus* Inerrancy

8.9.1 The Specific Nature of Inspiration

The Old Testament, too, offers examples of the distinction between divine revelation and other kinds of statements, all of which involve inspired Scripture. Thus, we hear about the sharp confrontation between God's Word preached by the true prophets and the (often equally ecstatic) words of the

---

80. *Selectae disputationes theologicae* I.30 and further; cf. Weber (1981, =Ger 301).
81. Van Dunné et al. (1976, 57–58).
82. Lindsell (1979, 89).

false prophets (e.g., 1 Kings 22; Jer. 23 and 28). As far as revelation is concerned, the words of the false prophets are definitely not Word of God. However, viewed from the standpoint of inspiration, these words belong to Scripture, which is entirely Word of God, which God wanted to communicate to us through the inspiration of Scripture.

Another example are the Psalms, in which God only rarely addresses people, but in which people speak *about* God, and often *to* God. In this human response to God's Word, we hear the inscripturated Word of God as well. This is evident from the fact that (a) the poets of the Psalms are called prophets (Matt. 27:35 KJV; Acts 2:30), and (b) it is the Spirit who speaks to people through the Psalms (Matt. 22:43; Acts 1:16; Heb. 3:7). In §8.4.1, I referred to the literal quotations from non-biblical written sources, such as the Persian archives or the letter from Claudius Lysias. Of course, it was not the contents of the original documents that was inspired, but their inclusion in Scripture was. Thus, through inspiration God communicates the contents of such documents to us, so that "even" in such passages we are dealing with the Word of God.

Another example are the many speeches by the friends of Job (see earlier in §6.9.4). Their spoken words were definitely not inspired by God; they did not speak on the basis of some revelation, though Eliphaz does seem to suggest so (Job 4:12-21). Generally speaking, we must conclude that Eliphaz and his friends did not speak what was right, which the LORD made very clear at the end:

> After the LORD had spoken these words to Job, the LORD said to Eliphaz the Temanite: "My anger burns against you and against your two friends, for you have not spoken of me what is right, as my servant Job has. Now therefore take seven bulls and seven rams and go to my servant Job and offer up a burnt offering for yourselves. And my servant Job shall pray for you, for I will accept his prayer not to deal with you according to your folly. For you have not spoken of me what is right, as my servant Job has" (Job 42:7-8).

However, the book in which these words have been recorded *was* inspired. As a result, many words spoken by Job's friends, though totally out of place in Job's situation, can have practical value for believers today in their own situation.

A remarkable example is the apostle Paul's approving quotation of a statement from Eliphaz, "He catches the wise in their own craftiness" (Job 5:13), cited in 1 Corinthians 3:19; he even introduces this with the significant words "it is written." The words of these friends as written down in the Bible are for us Word of God, even if the thoughts that they expressed were not from God. This is the power of the inspired, inscripturated Word of God. This example of Eliphaz makes clear that the Bible's authority does not mean that the Bible is a collection of commandments, norms, and rules, but it is especially a *narrative* book: a book of *stories*, which have an implicitly normative character.[83] These norms can be implied in stories, similar to the teaching that Jesus gave to his followers in the form of parables (little stories). But these norms can also be alien to the stories in which they function, just as, within the framework of the actual story of Job, the statement by Eliphaz was mistaken, whereas the same statement can be very meaningful outside this framework.

8.9.2 Contradictions

Many authors have tried to discredit biblical inspiration by pointing to various supposed contradictions in the Bible. These seem to conflict with the idea of a divine "breathing" of the entire Bible, for how could God contradict himself? I will return to this matter in chapters 9 and 10. For now we will identify several categories of supposed difficulties, and briefly indicate how we can deal with them.

(a) Errors occur in the various Bible manuscripts (which usually can be solved through textual criticism) and errors or weaknesses in Bible translations. For instance, certain words, nuances, and turns of phrase in the original text are not (suf-

---

83. Wright (2005, 25–27).

ficiently) expressed in translation, which may lead to unintended and unnecessary contradictions (e.g., compare Acts 9:7 and 22:9, where some translations [KJV] have a contradiction, and others [ESV] do not).

(b) Often, expositors, translators and readers encounter specific ancient and Eastern expressions and renderings that they misunderstand due to lack of knowledge of the contemporary circumstances (recall our earlier mention of the need for extra-biblical sources, which may clear up certain points of misunderstanding).

(c) Expositors, translators, and readers can encounter pre- and supra-theoretical parlance, for instance of a metaphorical nature, which they read in a literalistic way, which in turn generates further questions (e.g., Job 3:8 and 26:13 may be references to popular mythology, according to which mythical beings can produce a darkening or eclipse of the sun or the moon — here not to be taken literally but as examples of poetic expression).

(d) Often people distinguish inadequately between different revelations, acts, and words of God in different phases of redemptive history. God remains the same (Heb. 1:12) but he does not always *act* in the same way. For instance, he forbade many things to Jewish believers (e.g., the food laws) that he did *not* forbid to Gentile believers in the New Testament.

(e) We often encounter ignorance regarding the fact that the very same matter may be reported by different writers from different viewpoints: they often supply us with very different aspects of this matter, or omit different things. The four Gospels are the most obvious examples of this category. These differences yield contradictions only for literalist or scientistic readers; in reality, the different descriptions complement each other.

(f) Many passages can be read in different ways; it is disappointing to see how often they are read in a way that yields (apparent) contradictions.

Of course, these brief remarks serve merely to introduce the categories. To be honest, we must note here that the persuasiveness of any proposed resolution of many alleged contradictions will be minimal at best. We will discuss this problem much more extensively in chapter 10.

8.9.3 What Biblical Authority Is Not

For clarification, it may be useful to delineate the authority of Scripture a little more precisely by indicating what this authority does *not* involve.

(a) The entire idea of inerrancy as derived from the notion of inspiration ("Scripture was inspired, *therefore* it is inerrant") is a *non sequitur*. John Goldingay compared it with other such unfounded theological conclusions: Christ has paid the ransom for us, *therefore* we must establish to whom the ransom was paid. From eternity, God has chosen some for redemption, *therefore* from eternity he must have chosen the others for damnation. God is Father, *therefore* he must be masculine and not feminine.[84] In all four instances, the conclusion may seem perfectly obvious, yet in all four instances the conclusion is wrong. This is so for a reason Goldingay does not mention, namely, that ideas are viewed here as concepts,[85] or sometimes are simply described in a wrong way. The question whether inerrancy is necessarily implied by inspiration depends on the preconceived view of inspiration as well as on the definition of inerrancy being used. Various inspiration models are conceivable that do *not* imply a Bible that is inerrant in the sense of the natural or historical sciences, and thus do *not* imply that the Bible has authority in purely scientific questions, as we will see in the following chapters.

(b) Biblical authority must never be reduced to a "letter" that "kills" (2 Cor. 3:6).[86] As we have seen, the authority of Scripture does not mean anything without the working of

---

84. Goldingay (1994, 275.
85. See extensively, Ouweneel (2008, 24–32; 2015, chapter 6).
86. Goldingay (1994, 93).

the Holy Spirit. James Barr pointed out that, according to Romans 7:7-13, a totality of instructions and commandments, in a written form, coming from God, and explicitly "holy and righteous and good," can nonetheless furnish an opportunity and cause for evil.[87] The Bible must be used as a "sword of the Spirit," not as a sword of the flesh (Eph. 6:17). Scripture contains "healthy doctrine" and "healthy words" (cf. 1 Tim. 1:10; 6:3; 2 Tim. 1:13; 4:3; Titus 1:9; 2:1), but healthy food does not *make* someone healthy if the quantity is too great, or the ingredients are imbalanced, or it is eaten by someone with a specific food allergy.

(c) The authority of Scripture must never be confused with the (supposed) authority of *preachers*.[88] There are moments when a Christian can simply appeal to the Bible's "it is written." However, such an appeal always presupposes a certain exegesis, or even a complete view of Scripture. Where such a view is not made explicit, grave misunderstandings may arise. Between the absolute (divine) authority of Scripture and the relative (fallible human) authority of the preacher, there is always the relative (fallible human) exegesis of Scripture. As a consequence, we can think of hardly any controversy that might be decided once and for all by a simple reference to one or a few Bible verses, because such references always imply certain hermeneutical and exegetical presuppositions. Therefore, the simple "The Bible says . . ." may have a great preaching effect, but usually has hardly any persuasive effect for the somewhat more critically thinking person. Scripture has authority, but our appeal to Scripture does not. To put it more strongly, a single Bible word has authority only within the word's context, and within the totality of Scripture; but identifying this context implies a fallible human activity (cf. the hermeneutical circle; §§1.7 and 1.8).

(d) Thus, the authority of a certain word of Scripture is always qualified; it depends on the context within which the

---

87. Barr (1984, 119).
88. Cf. Wright (2005, 91).

statement is found. Although Christians acknowledge the divine authority of each Bible statement, including that of Leviticus 11:7 ("[T]he pig, because it parts the hoof and is cloven-footed but does not chew the cud, is unclean to you"), the great majority of Christians have no difficulty eating pork because they believe that the verse stands in a certain context that is not theirs. And although they acknowledge the authority of 1 Corinthians 11:3-15, the great majority of Christians have no difficulty with the fact that women sit in church with their heads uncovered. Similarly, the great majority of Christians do not believe at all, despite 1 Timothy 5:14, that young widows must necessarily remarry and have children. And despite Acts 15:20-29, the great majority of Christians have no difficulty with eating blood pudding. Or, to mention another type of error: *narrative is not normative*; that is, a biblical story itself does not have normative authority as if, for instance, because early Christians did this or that, therefore, modern Christians must do the same.[89]

(e) The connection between the authority and the interpretation of Scripture must not lead to a well-known logical error, quite characteristic of postmodernism. People argue that, if all authority of Scripture is a matter of interpretation, then one interpretation is as good as any other.[90] Of course, that cannot be true. To be sure, exegesis is more than a strictly rational activity; affections, emotions, memories, experiences, values, and cultural horizons play a role in exegesis, along with many other factors. However, we refuse to allow postmodernists to rob us of the conviction that, according to academic standards, one exegesis is definitely better than another. The norm for exegesis is not how a person experiences the text—no matter how much emotions may play a role in one's exegesis—but whether the text is *telling* the reader something.[91] The principal question is whether a person is

---

89. Cf. Goldingay (1994, 108-15).
90. Cf. Wright (2005, 111).
91. Ibid., 103; cf. the book title of Vanhoozer (1998; also see 2002): *Is there a*

aware of being *addressed* by Someone through the text.

(f) Appealing to the authority of Scripture is of little value if we take some parts of the Bible very seriously—and use them to pummel our listeners—but ignore other parts. Some Christians put great emphasis, for instance, on what the Bible says (or what they think the Bible says) about the position and clothing of women (especially in church), or about the death penalty, or about homosexual behavior, or about the truly biblical baptism, or the true interpretation of Genesis 1-3. All of these are very important. However, the same Christians often seem to neglect what the Bible says about wholehearted forgiveness, about loving one's enemies, about discrimination against foreigners, about other grave sins (such as greed, envy, slandering, sectarianism, and oppression), or about social justice (recall the ancient liberal maxim, "Everyone for himself, and God for us all").[92]

(g) The appeal to the authority of Scripture seems often to be nothing but an attempt to confirm one's own opinions. As N. T. Wright put it, people try to prove that the Bible is right mainly with the intention of enabling them to continue thinking as they always have thought. That is, they do not take the Bible so seriously that the Bible is allowed to tell them things that they have never heard before, things that they actually do not *like* to hear.[93] In all such cases, people let the Bible say what they want it to say, and in this way they make the Bible subservient to their own theological and ecclesiastical strategies and agenda. This is not real submission to the authority of Scripture but rather a manipulation of Scripture for one's own goals.

8.10 The Unity of the Bible

8.10.1 Comparing Scripture with Scripture

Seakle Greijdanus has argued that, in hermeneutics, the belief that the Bible is the inspired Word of God leads first and

---

meaning in this text? Cf. Fowl (1998); Thiselton (2008–09).

92. Cf. Wright (2005, 93).

93. Ibid., 95.

foremost to the conviction that Scripture is a *unity*, and that it intends to be accepted and understood this way.⁹⁴ The International Council on Biblical Inerrancy (see chapters 9–10) also emphasizes the significance of the unity of Scripture as a hermeneutical starting point.⁹⁵

It is true that the Bible books were written by many different human authors, who, moreover, wrote about an enormous diversity of subjects. It is true that the Bible books were written in very diverse times and locations, and from very diverse backgrounds. It is true that the various Bible books were written in very different styles, and with very different intentions. However, all these matters refer to the *immanent-empirical form* in which the eternal-transcendent Word of God was inscripturated. The absolute unity of the Bible is a *transcendent* matter, which surpasses all immanent diversity, divergence, and differences. In other words, the unity of Scripture is rooted in its one and only Primary Author (Lat. *Auctor Primarius*). When we say that the Bible is God's Word, we intend to say that its entire *immanent* form, however diverse and divergent it may be, was written down by secondary authors (Lat. *auctores secundarii*) who brought to expression in an *immanent* form what was in the *transcendent* thoughts of God. They did so under the perfect guidance of the Spirit, and insofar as the Spirit would and could express these depths of God.

As a starting point for hermeneutics, the unity of Scripture has some important consequences, some of which I mention without discussing them all too extensively (see this and the next sections).

From 2 Peter 1:20–21 we learn secondarily—the primary meaning seems to be another one (see §7.5)—that the interpretations of Bible passages should not be one's own, that is, without paying attention to a passage's context and coherence with other Bible passages. The rule of comparing Scripture

---

94. Greijdanus (1946, 47).
95. See http://www.alliancenet.org/the-chicago-statement-on-biblical-hermeneutics, article XVII.

with Scripture, never isolating it from its context, is a rule that is broken most frequently. Of course, this rule applies to *any* literary text; we must not assume beforehand that a certain author contradicts themselves until we have gathered independent and unassailable evidence for this conclusion. In the Bible, this rule applies as well to writings of different (human) authors, precisely because of the divine unity of Scripture.

Scripture must be compared with Scripture with great care in cases of seeming contradiction, for instance, between John 10:30 ("I and the Father are one") and 14:28 ("the Father is greater than I"). Such passages can be understood properly only if the tension that exists between them is resolved in a way appropriate to Scripture, that is, with the help of other Bible passages. In general, the application of this rule involves explaining more difficult passages in the light of simpler passages, not the other way around. For example, what the New Testament reveals about existence in the intermediate state (i.e., the time between physical death and resurrection) cannot be dismissed on the basis of certain difficult verses in Ecclesiastes (e.g., 9:5, "the dead know nothing"); this is a mistaken approach.[96] This example illustrates a preference for living by the question marks of the Old Testament rather than living by the exclamation marks of the New Testament.

An example of a seeming contradiction that arises through an atomistic use of Scripture, but is resolved by comparing Scripture with Scripture, is what the New Testament teaches about being like children. On the one hand, Paul reproaches the Corinthian believers (1 Cor. 3:1-3), and the author of Hebrews 5:11-14 reproaches the Hebrew Christians, for behaving like immature children when they should have been spiritually mature. On the other hand, Jesus admonishes his disciples that they should lay down their presumed maturity and become like children (Matt. 18:1-4). Only when both statements are viewed in the broader context of New Testa-

---

96. Thus, e.g., Telder (1960).

ment teaching can the paradox be resolved: believers must put away *some* characteristics of children, such as childish behavior, and they must retain, or return to, *other* characteristics, such as simplicity, admissibility, and plainness. To this example many others could be added.

8.10.2 The Center of Scripture

Because of its absolute divine unity, Scripture also has one specific center. This center is Christ, or God's self-revelation in him, in view of the ultimate glorification of God.[97] Therefore, Martin Luther used as a criterion for the canonicity of books whether a book promotes Christ (Ger. *ob sie Christum treiben*).[98] This is equivalent to asking whether Christ occupies the central position in a book, whether he is glorified in that book, whether the main focus of the book is his person, explicitly or implicitly. Luther also spoke of Scripture as "the Crib wherein Christ lieth."[99]

Jesus himself said to the Jewish spiritual leaders, "You search the Scriptures because you think that in them you have eternal life; and it is they that bear witness about me" (John 5:39). J. A. Heyns linked this verse to the notion of the scope of Scripture.[100] The scribes had accepted the inspiration and divine authority of each Old Testament word. They even searched the Scriptures because they hoped in this way to receive a share in eternal life (cf. Luke 10:25, "a lawyer [i.e., Torah scholar] stood up to put him to the test, saying, 'Teacher, what shall I do to inherit eternal life?'"). But they did not find eternal life because they did not search the Scripture in terms of him who was and is the scope, the center of the Scriptures. By leaving him out, they had nothing at all. Similarly,

---

97. Cf. Greijdanus (1946, 50); Weber (1981, =Germ 334–41); Heyns (1976, 69); Davis (1984b, 649–50).
98. WA 7:384, 26–27; see Bornkamm (1967, 177–78).
99. Ger. *die Krippe, darinnen Christus liegt*; quoted by Brunner (1949, 34) from Luther's *Vorrede auf das Alte Testament* ("Preface to the Old Testament").
100. Heyns (1976, 68).

Herman Dooyeweerd pointed to Jesus' expression "the key of knowledge," which Jesus used in his speech to the Torah scholars (Luke 11:52).[101] They had a perfect theological knowledge of the creation, the Fall, and the promise of the coming Messiah as articles of the orthodox Jewish faith, which are also articles of the Christian faith. But they had severed these from the true, pre-theological, transcendent-religious "key of knowledge": "the radical meaning of God's Word as the central, driving force of his life in Jesus Christ," that is, the life of the theologian, the philosopher, and every believer.

Heyns has formulated this in a beautiful way:

> He who does not use the scope as a key can commune with Scripture without communing with God; can read Scripture without feeling the claim of God's rule and submitting to it in obedience; can walk the way to Calvary without meeting the Man of God; and can come to Jesus without knowing that he is the Christ.[102]

Of course, in John 5:39 Jesus speaks of what we call the Old Testament. Not only the New Testament but also the Old Testament Scriptures write about him, as he himself explained to his disciples:

> [H]e said to them, "O foolish ones, and slow of heart to believe all that the prophets have spoken! Was it not necessary that the Christ should suffer these things and enter into his glory?" And beginning with Moses and all the Prophets, he interpreted to them in all the Scriptures the things concerning himself. . . . [Shortly afterwards he said,] "These are my words that I spoke to you while I was still with you, that everything written about me in the Law of Moses and the Prophets and the Psalms [i.e., the entire Tanakh] must be fulfilled" (Luke 24:25–27, 44).

The Old Testament refers to Christ both through direct prophetic language and through types, whose explanation is

---

101. Dooyeweerd (1960, 145–46).
102. Heyns (1976, 73).

supplied by the New Testament (cf. Rom. 5:14 [Gk. *typos*]; 1 Cor. 9:9-10; 10:1-11; Gal. 4:21-31; Heb. 7:1-10; 1 Pet. 3:20-21). Without typology, how could we understand such books as Ezra, Nehemiah, Esther, Job, Proverbs, Ecclesiastes, and Song of Solomon to be truly Christocentric?

In addition to this, from its beginning to its end the Bible deals with many other subjects. But ultimately, all of them come to be concentrated in the scope of Scripture. Nobody can deny that, *within* the immanent form of Scripture, Jesus Christ is *one* of the main subjects. However, when it is a matter of the *transcendent scope* of Scripture, Jesus Christ is *the* subject: the creation is God's creation in Christ, the Fall is the fall of the first man as opposed to the Second Man, redemption is by the last Adam as opposed to the first Adam, the reconciliation of all things unto God occurs through Christ, the covenant is God's covenant in Christ, the kingdom is God kingdom in Christ, the church is God's church in Christ.

Of course, the Father and the Holy Spirit are not excluded from this, for it is my conviction that here the term "God" always refers to the *Triune* God, who has revealed himself, acts and will act in and through the Man Christ Jesus, who himself is God the Son. Not a single work of Christ is independent of the Father and the Spirit (see, e.g., Matt. 3:15-17; John 5:19; 2 Cor. 13:13; Heb. 9:14).[103]

8.10.3 The Unity of the Old and New Testaments

John J. Davis has summarized objections usually adduced against the unity of Scripture, involving especially the unity of the Old and New Testaments.[104] Some of these modern objections go back to the Gnosticism of the first centuries of church history. They refer, for instance, to the (supposed) conflict between the Old Testament imprecatory psalms and God's alleged mercilessness, and the New Testament spirit of love and compassion. Since antiquity, these arguments have

---

103. Cf. Ouweneel (2007, 290–91).
104. Davis (1984b, 651–54).

been adequately refuted many times. Biblically speaking, it is simply untenable to create a conflict between the lower Creator-God (alleged author of evil) of the Old Testament, and the higher Redeemer-God (author of the good) of the New Testament. This is because the God of the Old Testament *is* definitely the "merciful and gracious" God, "slow to anger, and abounding in steadfast love and faithfulness" (Exod. 34:6; Neh. 9:17; Ps. 86:15; 103:8; 145:8; Jonah 4:2; cf. 2 Chron. 30:9; Neh. 9:31; Ps111:4; 112:4). At the same time, the God of the New Testament is definitely also the God of judgment and revenge (Rom. 3:6; 1 Cor. 4:5; 5:13; 2 Tim. 4:1; Heb. 13:4; Jude 1:4; Rev. 14:7). Davis also referred to modern opponents such as Roy L. Honeycutt Jr., Ernest S. Armstrong, Alfons Weiser, William E. E. Oesterley, and Rudolf Kittel, and to many authors of his time and before who have refuted the arguments mentioned.

Actually, the problem of the relationship between the Old and New Testaments is too large to be treated extensively here. I will limit myself to a summary. Uwe Gerber mentioned the following solutions for this problem:[105]

(a) Set aside the Old Testament completely (Marcion of Sinope, Adolf von Harnack).

(b) Dehistoricize the Old Testament so that what remains is only the law (Emanuel Hirsch), or only failure (Rudolf Bultmann), or only some general basic promise (Friedrich Baumgärtel).

(c) Depreciate Old Testament history in a Christological-suprahistorical way (Wilhelm Vischer, Martin Kähler), or in a Christocentric, primordial-historical (*urgeschichtliche*) way (Karl Barth).

(d) Promote a typological ordering of the two Testaments (Gerhard von Rad, Hans Walter Wolff), or a universal-historical or tradition-historical interpretation (Wolfhart Pannenberg), or a linear, redemptive-historical summary (Oscar

---

105. In Ott (1972, 54; cf. 51–58).

Cullman).

Paul Althaus, Otto Weber, Wolfgang Trillhaas, and Jan van Genderen, to mention just a few authors, have also dealt with this problem.[106] The last-mentioned author claimed that a problem exists only for those for whom the canon has no self-evident divine authority, or for whom the question of divine authority has become irrelevant.

One of the objections is that, especially in the Sermon on the Mount, Jesus seems to correct certain parts of the Old Testament, or even to reject them. This concerns in particular the expression, "You have heard that it was said . . . but *I* say to you" (Matt. 5:21-22, 27-28, 31-34, 38-39, 43-44). People have suggested that here Jesus is rejecting the (Jewish) morals of the Old Testament in favor of a newer, higher (Christian) morality. *In reality Jesus is not rejecting any commandment of Moses.*[107] Instead he does three other things.[108]

(a) Jesus brings to light the true spiritual depth of these divine commandments (i.e., the eternal Torah in its fullness; e.g., "You shall not kill" or "commit adultery" fundamentally means, You shall not do such things even in your *heart*).

(b) Jesus levels sharp criticism, not of the commandments themselves but of the wrong interpretations of, omissions from, and additions to these commandments by the Pharisees.

(c) Jesus presents himself as the fulfillment of the Torah. He says that he did not come to abolish (cancel, annul) the law or the prophets but to fulfill them (bring them to their fullness) (Matt. 5:17-20).

Davis referred in this connection to opponents such as Bennett Harvie Branscomb and Roy L. Honeycutt Jr., and refutations by John W. Wenham, Roger Nicole, and Pierre-Charles Marcel.

---

106. Althaus (1952, 189–212); Weber (1981, 316–41); Trillhaas (1972, 84–96); Van Genderen (2008, 63–69).

107. *Contra*, e.g., Weber (1981, = Ger 322).

108. Ouweneel (2018a, chapter 6).

In an important addition to Davis, Robert D. Preus investigated the history of the idea of the unity of Scripture.[109] He mentioned especially some critics of his own day, and pointed to the enormous diversity of, and contradictions in, their views. Often, the critics do maintain the idea of the unity of Scripture as an indispensable hermeneutical principle. However, they seek this unity in the applicative, not in the explicative meaning of the Bible. According to Preus, the orthodox Protestant theological idea of the unity of Scripture rests upon four pillars: (a) the divine authorship of the Bible, (b) the agreement between Old Testament prophecy and its New Testament fulfillment, (c) the Christocentricity of the entire Bible, and (d) the doctrinal agreement that we find throughout Scripture.

Preus called these four pillars thoroughly biblical because each of them is based exclusively upon the exegesis of Scripture itself. This seems to me a little naïve and all too optimistic, because (a) *every* theologian can claim such things for their own theology, and (b) Preus overlooks the peculiar character of theological theory building, also with regard to the unity of Scripture. Nonetheless, in my view it is correct to prefer this view to the explanation of Scripture's unity promoted by historical criticism. The latter imposes on Scripture an idea of a *rational-immanent* unity, derived from autonomous humanistic thought, because of the critics' resistance against any suprarational-transcendent idea of unity. Preus believingly stated that, when we stop reading something into the words of another, even if these words seem absurd or contradictory to what he said elsewhere, and when we simply accept the clear and evident significance of that person, then we consciously or unconsciously admit that this person's thinking and expression are superior to our insight or critical judgment. This, Preus added, is simply our attitude toward the Scriptures, and toward the Scriptures alone, because Scripture differs from all other books in this respect: it is the Word of God.[110]

---

109. Preus (1984).
110. Ibid., 687.

Chapter 9
The Fundamentalist View of Scripture

[B]ehold, the wicked bend the bow;
they have fitted their arrow to the string
to shoot in the dark at the upright in heart;
if the foundations are destroyed,
what can the righteous do?
                                  Psalm 11:2-3

Summary: *From a movement defending the foundations of Christian faith, fundamentalism developed into an infallibilist and inerrantist movement believing that the Bible's errorlessness can be scientifically proven. Its scientism, exhibited by the two Chicago Statements on Biblical Inerrancy, appears in appeals made to "solid facts" and "factual" or "objective" evidence — which basically do not exist. Facts always function within the framework of worldviews and basic beliefs.*

Such fundamentalism suffers from at least three inherent dualisms: an epistemological, an anthropological, and an ontological dualism. Fundamentalism's scientism is evident also from its penchant for attributing theories to the Bible, such as the notion that the Bible teaches what is called the "correspondence theory" of truth.

This is disastrous, not only because it entails theoreticalizing the Bible, but also because the correspondence theory of truth is philosophically untenable.

One specific form of scientism is biblioscientism: the Bible is so reliable that it is always scientifically correct — a tremendous overestimation of science. Inerrantism lacks a radically Christian ontology and epistemology. In its scientism, it has much more in common with modernism than it would likely be prepared to admit.

9.1 Historical Background of Fundamentalism

9.1.1 Early History

I HAVE ARGUED ELSEWHERE that the main difference between fundamentalist and modernist theology is that the former is rooted in an outdated, strongly *Aristotelian* philosophy, namely, medieval and early Protestant scholasticism, while the latter is rooted in modern *pagan* philosophy, of whatever humanistic coloring.[1] Directly related to this, we notice that the two kinds of theology share a commitment to *scientism*, the overestimation of scientific thought and expression in comparison with everyday thought and expression, including those of Scripture itself.[2] In this and the following chapter, we will investigate the effects of scientism on the fundamentalist approach, and in the last two chapters, the effects of the modernist approach (biblical criticism) on the doctrine of Scripture.

Let us begin with a brief look at the history of fundamentalism.[3] Originally, it was an American revival movement that opposed theological modernism arising from the Enlightenment. The roots of this movement lay in the revivals and Bible conferences that occurred at the close of the nineteenth century. It was based upon the serious concern of many Christians in many different denominations regarding the teaching of God's Word. Thus, fundamentalism was in particular an attempt to maintain the fundamental truths of Christiani-

---

1. See extensively, Ouweneel (1995; 2014; 2015).
2. Cf. Buri (1956, 118–20).
3. Cf. Berkouwer (1966, 21–26); Shelley (1974); also see note 10.

ty over against the devastating effects of modernism. Most prominent here were truths such as the deity, virgin birth, and bodily resurrection of Christ, his vicarious atonement, his physical return, and the authority and infallibility of Scripture. The powers that were being combated were especially evolutionism, biblical criticism, and the emerging social gospel. Around the turn of the century, two different movements arose in various denominations: on one side were the progressives (or liberals, modernists) and on the other side were the conservatives (or fundamentalists).

The attacks by the fundamentalists were carried out in various ways, both in publications and in public debates. In 1910, they began their own magazine, *The Fundamentals*, which ultimately became a series of twelve booklets, published from 1910 to 1915, with articles defending the fundamental Christian truths.[4] Of these booklets, three million copies were sent for free to theology students and Christian workers. In this project, eschatological millennialists like American evangelist Reuben A. Torrey and Reformed men like B. B. Warfield collaborated fraternally. The magazine was noted for its scholarly thoroughness and its absolute submission to Scripture.

The designation *fundamentals* was being used more and more, and in 1920, Baptist preacher Curtis Lee Laws, editor of the Baptist magazine *Watchman-Examiner*, suggested the terms "fundamentalist" and "fundamentalism" as designations for the person who, and the movement that, respectively, maintained the fundamental truths of the Bible. In that same year, a group of Baptists adopted this name for the first time. They were linked neither with millennialism, nor with dispensationalism, nor with a crusade against evolutionism. Quite simply, they emphasized maintaining the central tenets of traditional orthodox Protestant Christianity. Only later did other fundamentalists in their movement get involved with the battle against evolutionism.

---

4. Torrey et al. (2003).

Soon, the term "fundamentalism" became a slogan in the battle between progressives and conservatives on both sides of the Atlantic. In some extreme cases, it led to church splits, as, for instance, in the Netherlands, with the division in the Kuyperian Reformed Churches (Synod of Assen, 1926) over the question raised by J. G. Geelkerken whether the serpent in Paradise had really spoken.[5] Among the American Reformed, it was especially J. Gresham Machen of Princeton Theological Seminary who played a main role in fundamentalism. In this battle, he was condemned for insubordination toward his superiors.[6] Out of this conflict, the Orthodox Presbyterian Church was born, and later, the Bible Presbyterian Church.

9.1.2 Later History

In later years, the term "fundamentalism" fell into disuse because of the predominance of militant, narrow-minded leaders who lacked scientific training. As a consequence, more and more people saw fundamentalism characterized by a mistrust toward all science (obscurantism), by a lack of thorough knowledge of the Bible, of church history (especially the history of theology), of cultural and ethical matters, and by biblicism and fanaticism. During the 1950s, more and more conservatives separated from this type of fundamentalism, and at the initiative of Harold J. Ockenga, began calling themselves "Neo-Evangelicals."[7] They rejected what they viewed as degenerated fundamentalism, and began emphasizing scholarly integrity, social involvement, and a cooperative attitude. The magazine of this movement is, until the present day, *Christianity Today*.

Karel Blei described the mindset of fundamentalism in the broad sense as follows:

> Finding a handhold in faith, a certainty, a foundation to build upon, does not itself yet mark a person as a "fundamentalist."

---

5. See extensively, Harinck (2001).
6. See extensively, Gatiss (2008).
7. See extensively, Rosell (2008).

The Fundamentalist View of Scripture

For *each* believer it is true that faith is about fundamental matters. . . . But "fundamentalism" begins where a certain use is made of these fundamental matters of faith. Namely, where they must serve as a "foundation" to strengthen a very specific defensive position: to undergird and establish a bulwark behind which people seek refuge. Indeed, "fundamentalism" is first and foremost a defensive response, coming from a dark, negative judgment about what is going on in the modern world. The "fundamentalist" emphatically thinks in black-and-white contrasts. "Of course," fundamentalists themselves stand on the "white" side. There is no room for nuance. Nuance would by definition imply a "betrayal" of the "good side."[8]

From a historical point of view, conservative Protestants in non-American continents are unconnected with fundamentalism in the narrower sense of the term. Strictly speaking, neither can the rise of "Evangelical" forms of Protestantism in Europe, including conservative Calvinists, Lutherans, Anglicans, and free-church Christians, be associated with fundamentalism, although these are often called "fundamentalist." This is so because, when these movements arose, American fundamentalism had already died a peaceful death. However, the more conservative part of the Evangelical movement in North America is still called "fundamentalist" because it stands for the same fundamental truths as the early fundamentalists. In fact, the term has become a label for all Christians who oppose higher criticism and evolutionism.

At the same time, we are confronted with the confusing phenomenon that certain conservative Calvinists—who are freely referred to as "fundamentalists" by modernists—use the term "fundamentalist" to refer to others, namely, to Evangelical Christians in general, and to millennialists and creationists in particular.[9] We could put it this way: each Chris-

---

8. Blei (1996, 31).
9. Back in 2003, Liberated Reformed journalist Reina Wiskerke counted me among the fundamentalists; see Van Bekkum et al. (2003, 35).

tian can freely use the term "fundamentalist" for those who stand to the right of them; modernists do this with Calvinists, Calvinists do it with Evangelicals, Neo-Evangelicals do it with older Evangelicals, and so on. Not to mention the fact that the now commonly used phrase "Muslim fundamentalism," often linked with terrorism, has made the term almost useless with respect to Christians (except, perhaps, violent Christians attacking abortion clinics, etc.). Therefore, it will be necessary to enter somewhat more deeply into Christian fundamentalism, and to try to arrive at a precise definition.

9.2 An Attempted Description

9.2.1 Extreme and Moderate

In more or less recent times, several authors have been occupied extensively with fundamentalism, and have tried to give a meaningful description of it.[10] On the basis of the sketch given in §9.1, we can easily see in what sense both an extreme and a moderate fundamentalism might be distinguished.

(1) *Extreme:* fundamentalism in the stricter sense of the term, also called ultra-fundamentalism.[11] American historians Sydney E. Ahlstrom and Stewart G. Cole saw *the* characteristic of this form of fundamentalism in its *reactionism*. It is a militant, partly even obscurantist and separatist protest against the (supposed or real) subversion of Christian faith. American historian George Marsden, too, pointed especially to its militant character. This concerned especially the pre-World War II American fundamentalism, but this extreme, militant form still exists, also in the Netherlands.

By obscurantism we understand the aversion to, and resistance against, every form of science (including the humanities), which proclaims: "Away with all your scholarship! We

---

10. Packer (1958); Cole (1963); Sandeen (1970); Marsden (1980); Barr (1981, chapter 1); Wentsel (1982, 572–90); Montsma (1985, 151–65); Ahlstrom (*RGG* 2, 1178–79); Carpenter (1997); Velema (1997); Brasher (2001); in a wider context: Percy (1996); Ruthven (2005); Armstrong (2008). I will refer to some of these authors without always supplying references.
11. The term is from Robert Marzano (1993–94).

are simply sticking with the Bible." N. T. Wright correctly pointed out that people who talk like this forget that they owe to scholars first their Bible translation, but then also their biblical dictionaries and encyclopedias. Nor would they understand much of the Bible if they themselves or their teachers had not been shaped by scholarly Bible commentaries. It is true that scholars are often wrong, and that their assertions must be constantly refined, or even replaced, but fallible scholarship is infinitely better than no scholarship, or anti-intellectualism.[12]

(2) *Moderate:* fundamentalism in the broader sense of the term. James Barr and Jan A. Montsma saw the clearest characteristic of fundamentalism in its conservative or infallibilist view of Scripture ("the Bible is inerrant"). This feature is encountered not only among (ultra-)fundamentalists in the narrower sense but also among older and newer Neo-Evangelicals, and among conservative Lutherans and Calvinists. As far as this point is concerned, we can further distinguish between:

(a) A *less moderate* form, which comes close to ultra-fundamentalism by absolutizing its own view of Scripture, and not taking their opponents seriously. We will meet this form below when we discuss the inerrantist movement.

(b) A *more moderate* form, which in important respects maintains the traditional view of the infallible Scripture, but sees its own view on this point as fallible. Therefore, this form has some basic objections against (the Chicago brand of) inerrantism, as we will see. The credibilism that we will discuss in the next chapter could be considered to be a most moderate form of fundamentalism in its widest sense (if one insists on retaining the term).

9.2.2 New Terminology

In order to get some clarity in the discussion, please consider the following terms:

---
12. Wright (2005, 91).

1. *(Ultra-)Fundamentalism.* This designation corresponds excellently with its recent use in the media. The term "fundamentalism" is used today in particular for extremist and militant forms of Islam.[13] The qualities of extremism and militancy seem to be so characteristic of modern forms of fundamentalism that it seems useful to apply the term within Christianity exclusively to extremist, militant fundamentalism, what we are calling ultra-fundamentalism. In this chapter, I will use the term fundamentalism also in a somewhat wider sense, however, namely, in order to include inerrantism (see 2.).

2. *Inerrantism* refers to the movement that promotes the inerrancy or errorlessness of the Bible. This designation is suitable because the movement itself has adopted this self-description. The inerrantists of the *Chicago Statements* (see §9.3.2) sometimes like to distinguish themselves from "fundamentalism" in the extreme, militant sense (so, e.g., James I. Packer). Fundamentalists are always inerrantists, but inerrantists are not always (ultra-)fundamentalists. It seems that this group of inerrantists roughly corresponds with the (older) Evangelicals in North America.

3. *Credibilism.* I am introducing this term to identify the view that considers the Bible to be divinely inspired, and therefore divinely authoritative, and therefore absolutely credible (Lat. *credibilis*). All fundamentalists and inerrantists are credibilists, but not all credibilists are inerrantists in the scientistic sense as intended under a. below, and far less are they (ultra-)fundamentalists. It seems that this group, at least with regard to its view of Scripture—not necessarily its social and political views—corresponds generally to the Neo-Evangelicals in North America.

In brief, I distinguish between:

a. *fundamentalist,* inerrantist credibilists (fundamentalists in the narrower sense of the word);

---

13. See Harrison (2007, chapter 10) on the (possible) connections between Jewish, Christian, and Muslim fundamentalism.

b. non-fundamentalist, *inerrantist* credibilists (inerrantists in the narrower sense of the word);

c. non-fundamentalist, non-inerrantist *credibilists* (credibilists in the narrower sense of the word). As I hope to make clear (see the next chapter), I sympathize with inerrantism on the faith level, but I do not fit within the credibilist category, especially because of the inherent scientism of the Chicago type of inerrantism.

9.2.3 Significance

The distinctions mentioned above are rather important because often the impression is given as if there is be no other choice than between (basically anti-supernaturalist) Enlightenment modernism and (ultra-)fundamentalism. By the way, these two movements themselves like to give this impression. Some liberal theologians exhibit the tendency to automatically label as fundamentalists all those who reject (the anti-supernaturalist tendencies within) biblical criticism as well as the general theory of evolution. According to James Barr, the image of fundamentalism seems to require fundamentalists to be very hostile toward modern theology and biblical criticism, and to be convinced that those not sharing their views are not true Christians.[14] This image is fortified by Barr himself, though with some nuances.

Remarkably, many fundamentalists make exactly the same categorical mistake. They exhibit the tendency to automatically label anyone who criticizes their view of Scripture as "Bible critical" (liberal). This is a consequence of the exclusivist nature of their view of Scripture, as we will see. Thus, the Chicago Statement on Biblical Inerrancy (1978) exhibits this tendency in its somewhat menacing Article XIX:

> We affirm that a confession of the full authority, infallibility, and inerrancy of Scripture is vital to a sound understanding of the whole of the Christian faith. We further affirm that such

---

14. Barr (1981, 1).

confession should lead to increasing conformity to the image of Christ.

We deny that such confession is necessary for salvation. However, we further deny that inerrancy can be rejected without grave consequences, both to the individual and to the Church.[15]

All the more refreshing is the statement by inerrantist Harold O. J. Brown. He argued that one way to aggravate the inerrancy controversy, and to create a position with which many inerrantists would be unhappy, is to suggest that inerrantists view biblical inerrancy as the central doctrine of Christianity. The moment inerrantists give the impression that they view this cardinal doctrine as central to the Christian faith, they will necessarily alienate from themselves those who rightly recognize that Scripture first and foremost proclaims Christ, and not itself. Even though Scripture proclaims Christ inerrantly, its first concern is that *he* is proclaimed, not that its own inerrancy is acknowledged.[16] In principle I can wholeheartedly agree with Brown's assertion.

9.3 The Inerrantist View of Scripture

9.3.1 What Is an Error?

I agree with James Barr, Ernest Sandeen, Bert Montsma, and others that, in the discussion between fundamentalism, inerrantism, and credibilism, the position of Scripture plays the central role. In the 1970s and 1980s, a certain view of Scriptural inerrancy[17] was strongly advocated.

At the outset, I would assert that applying term "inerrant" to Scripture is quite strange. If we say that a set of galley proofs, or the phone book, is errorless, everyone understands the intention. But, as John Goldingay asked, what would it mean to say that a certain song, or a certain novel, is errorless? The point is not whether there are errors in a song or a novel,

---

15. http://www.alliancenet.org/the-chicago-statement-on-biblical-inerrancy.
16. Brown (1984b, 391).
17. Excellently summarized by Paul Feinberg (1979).

The Fundamentalist View of Scripture

but that applying this category to such writings is strange.[18] At the outset, we feel uncomfortable with even asking whether the Bible's authority, credibility, and reliability depend on whether the Bible contains errors. What kind of errors could it possibly contain? What category of error? Or does this not matter? And who determines whether a certain element is an error? According to what criteria? And is *each* conceivable error equally devastating for the status of Scripture? Who are the authoritative referees in such matters? We will discuss these and related questions extensively in the next chapter.

The International Council on Biblical Inerrancy (ICBI), established in 1977, gave the term "inerrancy" heavy emphasis. Members of this Council, which was abolished in 1988 after fulfilling its temporary task, included a number of Christian scholars who had taken up the gauntlet against some theologians who had strongly criticized the traditional inerrancy view. ("Traditional" refers here especially to the views of the—formerly Reformed—Princeton Theological Seminary in Princeton, NJ, and of Presbyterian Westminster Theological Seminary in Philadelphia, PA, which was founded in 1929 due to disaffection with Princeton.)

One such critical theologian was G. C. Berkouwer, whose Dutch work appeared in English translation as *Holy Scripture*.[19] In this work, he clearly moved further to the left (if I may put it that way) of inerrantists, but also of many credibilists. By opening the door for the results of (anti-supernaturalistic) biblical criticism, Berkouwer was teetering on the edge of modernism. However, his simultaneous criticism of fundamentalism deserves our attention. It is no wonder,

---

18. Goldingay (1994, 339).
19. Berkouwer (1966; 1967); *Nota Bene*: the 1975 English volume has been included in the bibliography only for the sake of completeness; because it contains the English translation of only two-thirds of the original Dutch volumes, careful scholars need to consult those Dutch volumes for accurate access to Berkouwer's thought.

therefore, that several other authors in North America immediately defended Berkouwer, such as Donald K. McKim, J. Ramsey Michaels, Clark H. Pinnock, Jack Rogers, and Roger R. Nicole.[20]

9.3.2 The Chicago Statements

In 1978, the ICBI published a statement called The Chicago Statement on Biblical Inerrancy,[21] written after its Summit Conference held in Chicago. In 1982 this was followed by a second statement: The Chicago Statement on Hermeneutics.[22] The latter declaration was published on the occasion of a congress organized by the ICBI on inerrantist hermeneutics. In my comments, I will discuss the large publication that contains the lectures of the congress,[23] but also into older and newer publications.[24] We will pay some attention to the earlier theology of the Princeton and Westminster Seminaries, to which, in the nineteenth and twentieth centuries, great names were attached, such as those of Archibald Alexander, Charles Hodge, B. B. Warfield, J. Gresham Machen, and C. Van Til. Their extensive work forms a substantial component of the work of the ICBI.

Philosopher John C. Vander Stelt has dedicated an inter-

---

20. See, e.g., Rogers (1977); Nicole and Michaels (1980); McKim (1983); Pinnock (1984).
21. See note 15; and further Geisler (1979b, 493–97); Henry (1979b, 211–19); see the extensive commentary by Sproul (2005, 121–74).
22. See http://www.alliancenet.org/the-chicago-statement-on-biblical-hermeneutics; see further Radmacher and Preus (1984, 881–87); also see the *Journal of the Evangelical Theological Society* 25, 397–401 (1982), and Youngblood (1984, 230–39).
23. Radmacher and Preus (1984).
24. More recent publications in which the inerrancy is defended (partly in a nuanced way) are, e.g., Saucy (2001); Schirrmacher (2001); Stadelmann (2002), both as a response to Hempelmann (2000); further Sproul (2005); Beale (2008); see for critical objections, e.g., Goldingay (1990, chapter 19); Trimp (1992); Percy (1996); Carpenter (1997); Maris (1998); Webster (2003); Enns (2005); Wright (2005); Bovell (2007); McGowan (2007); Sparks (2008).

The Fundamentalist View of Scripture

esting dissertation to the earlier Princeton and Westminster theology.[25] He was a student under Berkouwer, and like the latter, he sometimes went too far (though not to the extent suggested by Hendrik Krabbendam[26]). However, Vander Stelt's arguments cannot be brushed aside that easily.

To complete this survey, I note that in 1986 a third statement appeared, The Chicago Statement on Biblical Application,[27] dealing with the following practical subjects: the living God, the Savior and his work, the Holy Spirit and his work, the church and its mission, sanctity of human life, marriage and the family, divorce and remarriage, sexual deviations, the state under God, law and justice, war, discrimination and human rights, economics, work and leisure, wealth and poverty, and stewardship of the environment. Some of its conclusions are highly debatable—not only theologically, but also psychologically, economically, politically, sociologically, and ethically—and have little to do with the notion of an inerrant Bible. But to deal further with this would take us far beyond our present purposes.

9.3.3 The View of J. I. Packer

At the outset, I wish to emphasize that, at the supra-rational, pre-theoretical level of faith, I feel very sympathetic to inerrantism, especially in the battle against Enlightenment modernism. The collection mentioned of the 1982 congress lectures contains an appendix written by J. I. Packer.[28] In this article, Packer gave a summary of a conservative hermeneutic with whose main points I can agree. My only reluctance concerns some formulations by Packer that, in my view, are not free of scientism. Examples are: a phrase such as "the rational, verbal, cognitive character of God's communication to us," "propo-

---

25. Vander Stelt (1978).
26. Krabbendam (1984).
27. http://www.alliancenet.org/the-chicago-statement-on-biblical-application.
28. Packer (1984); also see Henry (1979b, 162–255) for one of the best and most balanced treatises on biblical "inerrancy."

sitional revelation,"[29] and in particular: "Scripture interprets *scientific* knowledge" (italics added).[30] However, I hasten to add that this scientism is encountered much more frequently in other places in the collection of congress lectures. My summary at this point is a bit more concise,[31] because my point is not Packer's view of the principles of hermeneutics but rather his view of Scripture.

In his article, Packer argued that God speaks to us in his Son Jesus Christ, and through his written Word. Therefore, Christians must endeavor to expound Scripture as well as possible, so that the divine message is understood. This Bible interpretation must be based upon the convictions that (a) the Bible is continually true and reliable, (b) hermeneutics plays a crucial role in modern discussions of Scripture's authority, and (c) the exposition of Scripture must determine the scope and significance of biblical inerrancy.

Next, Packer argued that God gave humanity the gift of language, and in Scripture he communicates perfectly with humans in understandable human words, despite the limitations of human language. The Bible is a thoroughly human book, and at the same time God's reliable self-revelation. Scripture's authority is closely linked to the authority of Jesus Christ, who himself has testified concerning the authority of the Old Testament, as well as concerning the words that the apostles would speak later. The Holy Spirit moved the human writers to write the Bible books, and now accompanies these books with his power, and gives insight to the church to understand and expound the Word.

According to Packer, Scripture can be understood and expounded if this occurs not on the theoretical but on the faith level; that is, if people have a vital communion with the God of Scripture, and are enlightened by the Holy Spirit. In this,

---

29. Packer (1984, 907); regarding propositions, see §9.2.3 above.
30. Ibid., 912.
31. Cf. Ouweneel (1987b, 67–69).

the believer must adhere to (a) the simple, literal meaning of the Bible text, (b) the principle of the inner harmony of the text, and (c) the following central principles.

(1) Jesus Christ and the saving grace of God in him constitute the Bible's central scope. Each approach to Scripture that ignores this central place of Christ is mistaken.

(2) Within this scope, Scripture often speaks of nature and history, and always does so in a reliable way, though not in the language of the natural or historical sciences but in the language of faith, in the words of ordinary life. Scripture is the revelation about God, and is never a treatise about scientific subjects themselves.[32]

(3) Scripture offers us eternal truth but applies this within very different cultural and situational contexts. Scripture itself determines which of its principles remain invariably valid, and which are culturally bound.

On the level of faith I fully agree with Packer's presentation, apart from those few scientistic formulations mentioned. We now must enter into this matter somewhat further.

9.4   Scientistic Dualisms within Inerrantism

9.4.1   Epistemological Dualism

By now, I have used the term "scientism" several times.[33] This term identifies an overestimation of scientific thinking and speaking, compared with ordinary thinking and speaking. Science (the natural sciences and the humanities) is supposedly more accurate, and thus more impressive and credible, than ordinary parlance. With regard to the problem of scientism, there is a remarkable similarity between, on the one hand modernism and liberal theology, and on the other hand, fundamentalism, because those committed to the former believe they can show, *through science*, that the Bible is wrong,

---

32. In my view, the term "scientific" also includes "theological" here because I reject any scholastic division between (sacred) theology and other (profane) sciences (see §4.8); cf. Ouweneel (1995; 2014; 2015).

33. Cf. Ouweneel (1987a, 82–84, 86–92, 130–31, 140–56).

and those committed to the latter believe they can show, *through science*, that the Bible is right. We will consider this more extensively in a moment.

This is beautifully expressed in a document entitled "Environmental Analysis" (Dutch *Omgevingsanalyse*) by the Dutch Reformed Church in the Netherlands (1993):[34] the fundamentalist "has given preference to an unholy alliance with functional rationality, which, on the one hand, is viewed as a threat to religion, and on the other hand is drawn within the world of faith as a starting-point for the way the faith is translated."

Historically speaking, this absolutization of the scientific method was a consequence of the scholastic nature–grace dualism, the separation between the natural, material, visible world and the spiritual, ecclesiastical, invisible world.[35] This dualism permeates scientism in several ways. First, we discern an *epistemological dualism*. In medieval scholasticism, science was localized in the neutral realm of nature, whereas religion belonged to the higher realm of grace (or supernature, which is beyond nature). In later, secularized thought, grace was actually replaced by the freedom of modern, independent, autonomous humanity.

However, due especially to William of Ockham, and later, Immanuel Kant, this separation between the two worlds was maintained. In Kant's language: the realm of pure reason (Ger. *reine Vernunft*) is home to neutral science and philosophy, and the realm of practical reason (Ger. *praktische Vernunft*) is home to religion, theology, and ethics. This division between the profane disciplines and sacred theology, between science and Scripture, and between reason and faith, has had a disastrous effect on Western thought, both in the past and at present.

In the Chicago type of inerrantism, too, this dualism plays an import role as a consequence of the overestimation of sci-

---

34. P. 7; quoted by Blei (1996, 35).
35. See Ouweneel (2017, chapters, 1, 2, and 11).

entific thinking and speaking. Thus, great emphasis is placed on the "solid facts" and "objective evidence" established by science (so-called), and to which proponents and opponents can appeal equally (see below). People have a strongly optimistic expectation of true science (which can never conflict with the Bible). This science is viewed explicitly or implicitly as purely objective, which in turn lends pure objectivity to one's own conclusions based upon this science. It is amazing how self-evident the main tenets of scientism are to many fundamentalists: good (i.e., true, genuine, real) science is neutral, objective, and unprejudiced. Interestingly, both modernists and fundamentalists appeal to this *very same* good (i.e., true, genuine, real) science, and few people seem amazed that a strange situation occurs. Or people simply and naïvely say, "The science of our opponents is not good (true, genuine, real) science." In the remainder of this chapter, I will supply some striking examples of this circular type of reasoning.

I have combated this epistemological dualism in this volume and elsewhere, strongly emphasizing that every science is religiously biased. No matter how solid the facts and objective the evidence may appear, such claims are scientific nonsense. Facts and evidence always function within a theoretical framework, and are therefore always rooted in someone's pre-theoretical worldview, which itself is rooted in the transcendent faith of one's heart.[36]

9.4.2 Anthropological Dualism

In scholastic thought, this epistemological dualism was closely related with an anthropological dualism. This is still the case, both in secularized, humanistic thought and in fundamentalism. In this anthropological dualism in its medieval and early Protestant form, the substance of the natural, material body stands over against the substance of the soul, which was viewed especially as the *rational* soul.[37] The latter notion,

---

36. See extensively, chapter 1 above, and Ouweneel (2014; 2015).
37. Cf. Ouweneel (1986, chapters 5–6; 2008, chapters 6–8).

derived directly from Aristotelianism, crept into Christian thought at a very early stage. The Athanasian Creed tells us that Jesus Christ is "completely God, completely human, with a rational soul [*anima rationalis*] and human flesh," and also that any "human is both rational soul and flesh."[38] If we take this Creed's assertions seriously, then anyone not believing in this notion of the "rational soul" "will doubtless perish eternally."

Understandably, this thinking led directly to the scientistic view of humans as primarily rational beings, and to the idea of autonomous reason: through this independent, absolutized reason, humanity is thought to be able to fathom all of cosmic reality. In opposition to this, deep-rooted (radical) Christian philosophy has emphasized the insight that humans are, first and foremost, *religious* beings, and *that reason is just one of many immanent functions of the transcendent heart*. This will also help us to better understand the epistemological dualism: neutral, objective, unbiased reason *does not exist*, and therefore purely objective facts do not exist. What does exist is human reason governed by the religious condition of the (reborn or apostate) human heart.[39]

John Vander Stelt described how this scholastic view entered fundamentalist Princeton and Westminster theology.[40] The latter placed within its apologetics a strong, semi-Arminian emphasis on neutral rationality that is shared by both believers and unbelievers, and on the rational subjectivity of Scripture. Rationality was viewed as the essence of all reality as well as of all revelation, both general and special revelation (see chapters 1–4).[41] In this view, orthodoxy speaks first of all in the indicative mood, not the imperative mood, which means that it declares to us first and foremost how things *are*,

---

38. https://www.crcna.org/welcome/beliefs/creeds/athanasian-creed.
39. See extensively, Ouweneel (2014; 2015, 2017, chapter 2; 2018l, chapter 6).
40. Vander Stelt (1978, 283–94, 306–308, 310–11).
41. Cf. C. Trimp (1992, 132), who with respect to inerrantism spoke of a "glow of rationalism" and an "afterburner of a mechanical inspiration doctrine."

and not how they *ought to* be. In line with the entire rationalist tradition originating with the Greeks, scholastic orthodoxy is concerned primarily with right doctrine, pure thinking, the proper understanding of the truth, and the need to ascertain the entire system of truth (or truths) in a logical-analytical way. Think again of the Chicago Statement on Biblical Inerrancy, Article XIX (see §9.2.3): for increasing conformity to the image of Christ (a very *practical* matter), you must have the proper (i.e., inerrantist) view of Scripture (a very *theoretical* matter); if you deny this inerrancy (in the inerrantist sense!), this will have "grave consequences" whose nature is not further described.

Notice the rationalism and scientism in such an attitude. Through persuasive evidence and inductive reasoning, this theology thinks it can rationally prove the divine authority and reliability of Scripture. The Bible is viewed here as a totality of logically objective, intellectually superior, infallible propositions. If you do not accept this *theory* this will supposedly have grave *practical* consequences. This is the spirit of the Athanasian Creed, even if the latter goes further: if you do not accept the notion of the "rational soul," you are lost forever.

I have endeavored to refute this approach by exposing the underlying rationalism and scientism. Reason is *not* the highest property, or even the essence, of being human, but nothing more than one of the many immanent functions of the human heart. This heart is the transcendent, *supra-rational* (*not ir-*rational!) concentration point of *all* functions—of which reason is just one—by concentrating them in the transcendent-religious sense upon God (or, in the case of apostate humanity, upon one or more idols). Of course, this does not exclude reason, since it is a function of the heart, but then this reason is determined entirely by a person's faith or unbelief. Humans are not primarily rational beings but religious beings, either in the biblical or in the apostate sense. Both modernists and fundamentalists appeal to objective facts, but both are wrong. They do not have the same facts before them because modernists view all facts in a modernist light, and fundamentalists in a fundamentalist light. I will try to elucidate this further.

9.4.3 Ontological Dualism

The third form of scholastic dualism within inerrantism is the ontological dualism between the natural and the supernatural. Here, God or the divine is localized in the realm of the supernatural.[42] I dealt with this point already in §§7.7.2 and 7.8.3 above, and identified the danger of severing God from the natural. Those who, consciously or (usually) unconsciously, work with this ontological dualism are constantly obliged to form for themselves an idea of how the supernatural realm in some way or another is operative within the natural realm. We have seen that people conceive of this happening in one of two ways: either the supernatural works indirectly, normally, providentially, that is, *through* the natural, or it works directly, miraculously, that is, *despite* nature (Lat. *contra naturam*).

In opposition to this scholastic-rationalist interpretation of the relationship between Creator and creature, I assert the conviction—mentioned several times before—that this relationship can never be entirely understood or defined in a theoretical-analytical way. I repeat, this has nothing to do with mysticism, neo-Kantianism, irrationalism, existentialism, or postmodernism, qualifications that rationalists (including inerrantists) love to attach to this type of argument (see the next chapter). For such people, there are only rationalists and irrationalists; the Bible praises reason—all too easily equated with the practical wisdom of the book of Proverbs, for example—so irrationalists must be dead wrong. God created humans as rational beings, not irrational beings.

Apparently, rationalists who argue this way have never really studied a deep-rooted (radical) Christian ontology. My relativizing of reason—claiming that reason is *only* an immanent function of the transcendent heart, governed either by

---

42. Vander Stelt (1978, 272–78, 305, 314–15).

faith or by unbelief—stands over against the Greek-scholastic tradition, and has to do with the true biblical revelation concerning God, religion, and the human Ego. This relationship does not demand a logical-analytical (philosophical or theological) explanation, but rather obedient dedication and confessional recognition, as Vander Stelt argued as well. As Creator and Law-Giver, God can never be contained within the rational order that he himself has instituted for the cosmos, that is, be enclosed within a theoretical-analytical frame of thought (see §§3.4–3.6 above). In this case, this means, among other things, that God can in no way be localized in, or identified with, some supernatural sphere, kingdom, or realm, precisely because he is the Creator of all spheres, kingdoms, and realms, and therefore surpasses all spheres, kingdoms, and realms.

In chapters 7 and 8, we have seen that the scholastic dualism between the natural and the supernatural has great consequences for the theological doctrine of inspiration. Not only the theory of mechanical inspiration, but also every kind of theory of organic inspiration that is rooted in this dualism—as comes to expression in the terminology of a "divine" and a "human element" or "factor" in the Bible—must be rejected.[43] Of course, I do *not* reject the supernatural itself—understanding this to refer to all that surpasses the normal categories of *science*—in the sense of many biblical miracles, or the bodily resurrection of Christ, or the verbal inspiration of Scripture, as does liberal theology. However, I do reject the scholastic nature–supernature *dualism* itself. Frequently, inerrantists are caught so tightly in this dualism that they easily explain the rejection of it as a liberal anti-supernaturalism. For them, the choice is either inerrantism or modernism (errantism). They cannot see how anyone—like me—can reject *both*.

---

43. Ibid., 294–302, 323, 326.

9.5 Scientism and "the Facts"

9.5.1 Facts and Glasses

There is one aspect of scientism that I briefly mentioned above, but that must now be discussed a bit more extensively. It follows directly from the scientistic view of neutral, objective, unbiased science, a view many Christians still hold because they are unaware of all the developments in the philosophy of science during the twentieth century, both in secular and in deep-rooted (radical) Christian philosophies. A neutral, objective, unbiased science is a science that is (ostensibly) unaffected by certain philosophical or religious biases but limits itself to objective facts. A good illustration of this is the classic *Systematic Theology* written by Charles Hodge. He wrote that the Bible is for the theologian what nature is for the man of science. It is his "storehouse of facts"; and his method to establish what the Bible teaches is the same method followed by the natural philosopher (meaning: the natural scientist) to establish what nature teaches.[44]

What strikes us here is Hodge's description of the Bible as a "storehouse of facts," a phrase that is not different from the way positivism would speak about nature. However, as I have argued elsewhere,[45] modern philosophy of science — whether secular or deep-rooted (radical) Christian philosophies — has emphatically eliminated the idea of an objective, unbiased collection of facts, and has done so, according to my strong conviction, quite correctly. When people read in the Bible about angels, prophets, the ark of Noah, the resurrection, the inspiration, miracles, and so on, their observation of these matters is colored by the knowledge they have, or think they have, arising from their memories, biases, feelings, affections, imagination, mentality, cultural and denominational background, and especially: their faith or unbelief. According to people's amount of knowledge, and according to the col-

---

44. Hodge (1872, 10).
45. Ouweneel (1995, chapter 6; 2014; 2015).

oring of this knowledge, they will read or hear very different things when they encounter the matters mentioned.

Therefore, it is of the utmost importance to grasp that people's ordinary observation, including their awareness of what comes to them through Scripture, occurs within the framework of what has been called a certain "cognitive structuring." By far the greatest part of this, though not everything, is of a non-theoretical nature,. Through the great influence of science in society—including the influence of theology in church life—theoretical knowledge permeates the everyday observation of all people to a greater or lesser extent. Thus, no (Western, and by now also many non-Western) Bible reader can ever read the Bible without the coloring of their reading as a consequence of certain doctrinal or theological insights that they have acquired, consciously or (very often) unconsciously. Thus, there is a non-theoretical, but also a certain theoretical "cognitive determination" of people's observation.

The cognitive structuring of people's knowing activity, including both their common, ordinary Bible reading and their theological investigation, implies that the notion of objective facts is a mere illusion. This cognitive structuring functions like glasses of varied color and power through which we see things. Moreover, we must take into consideration that this cognitive structuring involves not only preceding knowledge, memories, and biases but, on the deepest level, it involves especially the orientation of people's hearts. This ultimately determines how we observe facts. This means that people ultimately choose between fundamentalism, inerrantism, credibilism, moderate or extreme modernism, and so on, on the basis not of objective facts but of the faith choice of their hearts. To put it another way, people choose on the basis of facts—but they see these facts through the glasses of their *a priori* faith choice.

No doubt, this choice itself is not independent of people's observation and rationality; we are certainly dealing here with a certain interaction. That is, faith choices are justified *a posteriori* on the basis of people's observation and rationality. However, this can occur safely only if they remain carefully focused on the priority of their faith choices. Here again, we see the enormous importance of the hermeneutical circle, which I have mentioned several times already (first in §1.7 above).

9.5.2 The Second Chicago Statement

Regarding the points just mentioned, several Christian apologists have trespassed by believing that, in opposition to liberal theology, they could freely appeal to supposed objective facts, which ostensibly could be accepted by both believers and unbelievers if people were only fair and honest. This can be clearly seen in the Chicago Statement on Biblical Hermeneutics,[46] which, generally speaking, deserves our sympathy but, unfortunately, clearly exhibits scientistic features. Thus, we read for instance in Article VI: "We affirm that the Bible expresses God's truth in propositional statements, and we declare that biblical truth is both objective and absolute." This idea that the Bible's truth is contained in propositions (logical theses, as we find in a philosophical or mathematical treatise) suggests, as we saw earlier (§5.5), that Scripture is a collection of logical-analytical theorems, merely needing to be isolated and systematized by an unbiased inerrantist theologian (apparently of the Chicago type). Inerrantism and errantism are each a theological *theory,* are in constant discussion within the scientific community, and must never be confused with the pre-scientific *faith* or *unbelief* in an infallible, supra-theoretical Scripture.

Another typically scientistic expression is the reference to "genuine scientific [!] facts" in Article XXI, where it is denied that such "facts" could ever be "inconsistent with the true meaning of any passage of Scripture." At the transcen-

---

46. http://www.alliancenet.org/the-chicago-statement-on-biblical-hermeneutics.

The Fundamentalist View of Scripture

dent level of faith, if it were seasoned with a dash of goodwill, such a statement would be quite palatable. But at the scientific level, it is completely senseless. This is because the question rises immediately what "genuine scientific facts" are, or what is the "true meaning" of a Bible passage. Who decides that? Such a statement is a purely circular argument. On the one hand, it is argued that "genuine facts" are those that are consistent with people's exegesis of Scripture. On the other hand, it is claimed that "genuine facts" cannot be inconsistent with Scripture. Stated more briefly: what agrees with Scripture cannot conflict with Scripture. Such a tautology is not very fruitful.

Scientists hardly fare any better. Scientists have come up with numerous "genuine scientific facts" that conflict with the Bible; at least this is what they claim because natural scientists often operate with the very same positivist errors that plague the inerrantists. Both parties claim they have the "scientific facts" because both look at the world through their own, very different glasses. Each side accuses the other of an "unscientific" approach because the "genuine scientific facts" of one side do not coincide with the "genuine scientific facts" of the other. This is because both sides are operating with the same positivist notion of a neutral, objective, unbiased science—and both are wrong in this respect. *Occasionally*, the sides retreat somewhat in the face of overwhelming new "genuine facts," but usually each stands his ground because their pre-scientific *starting points of faith* are unassailable.

Even if we are so kind as to assume that the second Chicago Statement actually does not mean "scientific facts" but "facts of nature"—which to every non-scientistic mind are very different—the question remains *who* decides *what*, according to *which* objective observation and *which* objective reasoning, are the "genuine facts of nature." People clearly and objectively observe in ordinary experience that the earth stands still, and that the sun rises and sets. Is each of these therefore a "genuine fact"? This is how the Bible speaks about the earth and the sun, and fundamentalist geocentrists take this literally, even today.[47] Or is this an optical illusion, and is it actually a "genuine fact" that the sun stands still with respect to the earth, and that the earth rotates around its axis, as physical cosmology teaches us? What are the "genuine facts," and how do they relate to our ordinary parlance, which is also the biblical parlance? If we do not apply a careful and thorough philosophical analysis here in order to determine what we must understand by "genuine facts," this bold inerrantist claim remains suspended in the air.

This kind of references to "the facts," even "genuine" or "objective" facts no less, is also encountered in Articles VI, XIII ("factual"), XIV ("historical fact"), and XXII ("Genesis 1-11 is factual").[48] During the congress, American hydrologist Henry M. Morris spoke of the "scientific accuracy of Genesis 1-2,"[49] and theologian and philosopher Norman L. Geisler implicitly claimed that the language of Genesis is "scientific."[50] In opposition to this, I state emphatically that, even though I believe that Genesis 1-2 is historically fully reliable, this book does not contain any "scientific facts" or "scientific theories."[51] I would add that this is both obvious and fortunate.

9.5.3 A Debate

In 1967 and 1968, Arthur F. Holmes and Norman L. Geisler had an interesting debate on the relationship between theological theories and "the facts."[52] Holmes suggested that some — personally I would rather say, *all*[53] — theological theories are not simply deduced from the "facts" of Scripture, or

---

47. Van der Kamp (1985); Sungenis and Bennett (2009).
48. Cf. Geisler's comments in Radmacher and Preus (1984, 902–03); cf. Nullens (1997, 216–20).
49. Radmacher and Preus (1984, 337).
50. Ibid., 314.
51. See extensively, Ouweneel (2018l, especially chapters 3–5).
52. See the reprints: Holmes (1984a; 1984b); Geisler (1984b).
53. Cf. Ouweneel (1995, §6.2.2; cf. 2014; 2015).

obtained as the result of inductive study of the phenomena. He called such theories "theological constructs of the second order," which are adduced for systematic-theological reasons, and he mentioned inerrancy as an example. Doctrines of the first order, however, such as the doctrine of revelation, supposedly were based upon direct statements of Scripture.

I find Holmes's standpoint far from satisfactory, first because, in the strict sense, *all* theological *theories* are of the second order; they are invented to account for the observed data.[54] But second, and even more importantly, Holmes failed to clearly distinguish between faith ideas—and as such, inerrancy is entirely acceptable, and based directly upon our ordinary experience with Scripture—and theological *theories*. As to the latter: both a *theory* of revelation and a *theory* of inerrancy are theological constructs, and therefore fallibly formulated ("invented," to use Karl Popper's term), though based upon relationships and coherences that have been discovered in Scripture.

Nevertheless, despite these points of criticism, Holmes intuitively sensed certain very important matters clearly. To me, it is all the more remarkable to see that an authoritative theologian such as Geisler seemed not to grasp these matters. He wanted certitude that there is a "factual or textual basis," which demands that the data are interpreted in a given manner.[55] He defended the traditional inductive (Baconian) or positivist way of deducing theological constructs from the "facts" of Scripture, failing to realize that positivism has long been refuted, also by those advocating a deep-rooted (radical) Christian philosophy.[56] Geisler greatly feared that inerrancy as a *faith* idea would be lost—which indeed would be disastrous—so much so that he defends the status of the inerrantist theological *theory* of the Bible's errorlessness as if people's

---

54. See ibid.
55. Geisler (1984b, 140).
56. Cf. Dooyeweerd (1984).

faith depended on any theological *theory* at all.[57]

This is rationalism *par excellence*. One searches in vain for a clearer example of inerrantism's (or at least Geisler's) scientism. Geisler was not content with the faith idea of inerrancy — in his view, this idea had to be *scientifically correct*. Science had to come in to salvage the Christian belief in the Bible's perfection. We will discuss this point extensively in the next chapter.

9.6 The Correspondence Theory in the Bible?
9.6.1 Taught by the Bible?

Asking what theory (!) of truth is presupposed in Scripture is also incredibly scientistic.[58] Robert D. Preus claimed that without a correspondence theory of truth there can be no such a thing as *informative* language or *factual* meaning. The Eighth[59] Commandment collapses entirely unless it is based upon the correspondence theory of truth. In fact, the Bible is full of evidence that it everywhere presupposes this theory.[60]

John Feinberg also wondered what theory (!) of truth is taught (!) in the Bible.[61] But fortunately, he himself gave the correct answer by asking why an actual *theory* of truth and error must be deduced from Scripture instead of being deduced from a philosophical discussion. This is exactly correct! He also noted that various *uses* of the term "truth" do not necessarily imply that a certain *theory* of truth is *taught* by the Bible writer when the latter uses the term in a different way. He underscored that the Bible writers nowhere *teach* a concept or

---

57. See extensively, Ouweneel (1995, chapter 6).
58. For a more meaningful and responsible (and more recent) approach to this question, see Padgett and Keifert (2006), especially the contributions by N. Wolterstorff and S. T. Davis.
59. This reflects the Roman Catholic and Lutheran numbering; it is the Ninth Commandment according to other Christians and Jews.
60. R. D. Preus in Montgomery (1973, 2:24); see more recently also Saucy (2001, 148–55); he, too, insists that truth entails objective correspondence with reality (149).
61. Feinberg (1984, 13).

theory of truth. They definitely did not intend to give a philosophical treatise on the nature of truth, nor did they. Feinberg pointed out that, of course, Jesus says he is the truth (John 14:6), but neither he nor the Bible writer assert that his claim represents a *theory* of truth, which would seek to explain the qualities of the truth or untruth of a statement.[62]

A bit later, however, Feinberg weakened this correct approach by asserting that, although the Bible writers do not teach any truth theory, they do presuppose one as they write;[63] and this supposedly would be a form of the correspondence theory of truth.[64] His co-referent, Norman L. Geisler, made matters worse by asserting that Feinberg weakened his case for a correspondence view of truth by claiming that such a view is not taught in the Bible. It may not be taught *directly*, but then neither is the Trinity. However, Geisler insisted that both the Trinity and a correspondence theory of truth are *indirectly* taught in the Bible.[65]

In my view, this is comparing apples and oranges: the Trinity is not a theory, *in contrast* to a correspondence *theory* of truth. In addition to this, here again we encounter a striking example of the enormous importance of distinguishing between theoretical and practical knowledge. Feinberg and Geisler both suffered from a typically scientific confusion of a philosophical correspondence *theory* with people's immediate ordinary experience of reality.[66] Apart from considerations relating to the Bible and theology, there are serious philosophical objections to the correspondence *theory* of truth, which asserts that for a statement to be true means that it corresponds with reality. One such objection is very simply *that we have no independent access to reality whereby we would be able*

---

62. Ibid., 16–17.
63. Ibid., 17–18.
64. Ibid., 19.
65. Geisler (1984a, 55).
66. See extensively, Ouweneel (1995, §§6.1.3, 6.2.3 and 6.4.1; 2014; 2015).

to determine whether our judgments correspond with reality.[67]

9.6.2 Ordinary Experience

Indeed, philosophically speaking the correspondence *theory* is untenable simply because we have no means to test it. In their ordinary experience—which is also that of Scripture—people are (unconsciously) convinced that their perceptions constitute a picture of reality around them, and rightly so. To ordinary people, the (theoretical) problem of truth does not exist at all. Consciously, and usually unconsciously, every person knows *pre-theoretically* an external objective reality. In ordinary life, "I see a squirrel in the yard" is a meaningful statement if and only if it corresponds with the actual presence of a squirrel in the yard. In the Bible, it is exactly the same with, for instance, the (imaginary) statement "I see an angel in the yard."

In the ordinary (pre-theoretical) world, there is no problem. However, as soon as people wish to cast this ordinary experience of truth into the mold of a philosophical *theory* they no longer have any ground to stand on. This is because immediately the theoretical, unanswerable question arises as to what *evidence* or what solid *arguments* exist for such a notion of correspondence between subjective perception and objective reality. It is a belief—one that for ordinary experience is indispensable, but one that cannot be proven in a logical-empirical way.

In the ordinary experience of life, people accept as self-evident that their judgments correspond with reality; it does not occur to them—unless they are philosophers—that it might be different. Every person has an intuition of the pre-theoretical conviction that, when one says, "There is a cat on the mat,"[68] this statement corresponds with an objective cat on an objective mat, which is the same reality for any other person. However, such an ordinary correspondence *idea* does not

---

67. See extensively, Kirkham (1992).
68. The famous example is from John Searle (1979).

mean that, first, in *theoretical* experience, we defend a correspondence *theory*. Second, even less would we wish to claim that Scripture presupposes such a theory. Third, even more absurd is the thought that Scripture teaches such a theory. *Scripture does not teach any theories at all*, whether scientific, philosophical, or theological theories.

By claiming the opposite—on the basis of their scientistic biases—Feinberg and Geisler placed imprison the Bible within a theoretical construct. In this way, they unintentionally destroy the Bible's life, for a correspondence *theory* is basically untenable. Theoretical judgments are rooted in achieving a certain abstract distance from reality,[69] so that *in the full, integral sense* these judgments can never correspond with reality. Therefore, if Scripture is theoreticalized, it can no longer be true in this full, integral sense. Or, if the Bible were to teach or presuppose a correspondence *theory* of truth, it would be erroneous, for the correspondence *theory*—as theory—is erroneous. Feinberg and Geisler had the noble intention of defending the truthfulness of the Bible. But the manner of their defense unintentionally yielded the opposite result. In order to defend the Bible's inerrancy they postulated a philosophical theory that turns out to be errant, and in this way they achieved the very opposite of what they intended.

9.6.3 Praxis and Theory

We are dealing here (see previous section) with a scientistic error that I have discussed more extensively elsewhere.[70] Only with our pre- or supra-theoretical faith do we truly *know* creational reality. However, theories—theological, philosophical, scientific—contain at most certain moments of truth. These are disclosed only if, in the *supra*-theoretical, transcendent attitude of faith, they are based on creation in its integral fullness, unity, and coherence, and hence on the Creator as the Root and Ground of this creation.

---

69. Ouweneel (1995, §4.1).
70. Ibid., chapter 6; cf. Ouweneel (2014; 2015).

Dutch sociologist Hijme Stoffels wrote, "Religious orthodoxy is linked with an *absolute and universal claim of truth*: what is asserted is, in the opinion of its adherents, unassailably true and, in principle, is valid for all times and places."[71] Dutch philosopher Jan Hoogland rightly criticized this statement,[72] but overlooked its core: orthodoxy has always believed in absolute truth, but often had great difficulty relativizing its (fallible) *theological formulations* of this truth (Stoffels: "what is asserted"). In other words, *of course* religious orthodoxy claims to have a basic knowledge of absolute truth. This is not the problem at all. The problem arises when this faith conviction is theoreticalized, and people think they can scientifically prove, or at least scientifically undergird, their claims. I believe God's Word to be true—but theological (and philosophical) *theories* contain at best only elements of truth.

In fact, the claims of orthodoxy were strengthened when French philosopher Jean-François Lyotard introduced the word "postmodern" into Western thought, namely, in the sense of mistrust (Fr. *incrédulité*, cf. English "incredulity") toward all "grand narratives" (Fr. *grands récits*).[73] Many Christian thinkers protested against this because, as Christians, they wanted to defend absolute divine truth. However, they failed to make a basic distinction between the absolute Word of God and the perpetually relative (fallible) *meta-narratives* that Christian movements constructed on the basis of this absolute divine truth. Postmodernists do not necessarily oppose Christianity itself—although some of them did—but they oppose (rationalistic) modernism with its optimistic, self-assured certitudes. This includes rationalist movements within Christianity, whether in liberalism or in fundamentalism (which in *this* optimistic-rationalist respect strikingly

---

71. Stoffels (1995, 29); J. D. Caputo (2006, 8) quoted a witty person who said that philosophy deals with *unanswerable questions*, and theology deals with *unquestionable answers*.
72. J. Hoogland in Van den Brink et al. (1997, 142–43).
73. Lyotard (1979; cf. Caputo (2006, 49–50).

resemble each other).

9.7 Other Philosophical Theories in the Bible?

9.7.1 Prejudices of the Opponents

By not being (sufficiently) conscious of the philosophical and religious presuppositions of all science, inerrantists repeatedly fell, and continue to fall, into the snare of scientism. This is observed also in their conviction that their own hermeneutics is objective, whereas their opponents—consistently called "errantists" by them—are the ones plagued by all kinds of philosophical prejudices. First, this is highly unfair because those who reject the inerrancy view of the inerrantists are *not* automatically errantists (just as those who reject atheism are not automatically religious people). Second, it is highly naïve to think your opponent is biased and subjective whereas you are unbiased and objective. Where and when in the history of thinking has such a situation ever existed?

Consider this example. German-American philosopher Winfried Corduan spoke exclusively of the humanistic, especially language-analytical, presuppositions that supposedly influence liberal theological hermeneutics.[74] In this respect, he may have been perfectly right. But why did he ignore the possible Christian, or perhaps not all that Christian, philosophical presuppositions of his own allegedly biblical hermeneutics? Only the naïve, simple-minded Christian may be convinced that he is automatically right "because he sticks to the Bible." But Christian theologians and philosophers should always be aware of the fallible character of all their theories, and their personal biases attached to these theories arising from their cultural and ecclesiastical background.

A wiser example was provided by the thoroughly orthodox Frederik W. Grosheide, who wrote a study on the biases that are present in all exegesis.[75] All Bible commentaries, including those of Grosheide, betray the presuppositions of the

---

74. Corduan (1984).
75. Grosheide (1948).

expositor and of the school of thought that formed the expositor. So far, so good. However, Grosheide stated that the true bias of exegesis is the self-testimony of Scripture, and the only *seemingly* unbiased approach begins with setting aside this very self-testimony. In a certain sense this is correct, but (the Chicago type of) inerrantism could easily endorse this viewpoint by claiming that its only bias is nothing other than this self-testimony of Scripture. It might do so without noticing how strongly its bias (its idea about what this biblical self-testimony entails) is influenced by, for instance, scientism, scholasticism, positivism, and rationalism, all of which are foreign to the self-testimony of Scripture.

In Grosheide's time (1948), his position was understandable because the philosophy of science, including those advocated by both secular and deep-rooted (radical) Christian philosophy, was still in its infancy. However, it is astonishing that someone like Norman L. Geisler and others could still defend in the 1980s such an unabashed positivism, with its emphasis on "solid facts" and its "objective" stance. I do hasten to add, though, that the opponents of inerrantism often did not fare any better when they claimed, in an equally positivistic way, that it is precisely biblical criticism that allows the Bible to speak for itself (see chapters 11–12 below). They often commit(ted) the same mistake as the inerrantists, claiming that it is their opponents who are imposing ideas upon Scripture that are basically foreign to it.[76] This conflict will never be resolved as long as both parties refuse to reconsider their basic pre-theological (philosophical) views involving the status of theoretical thought as compared with ordinary thought, the status of scientific and scholarly *theories* (especially theologians dislike having their work described with the word "theory" because they believe that their conclusions simply and objectively restate Scripture), and the absoluteness of Scripture as compared with the fallible status of all philosophical and theological thought, and so on.

---

76. See Achtemeier (1980, 95); Barr (1980, 79).

9.7.2 "Factual Evidence"

Let us return to the inerrantists themselves. Norman L. Geisler edited a book on the philosophical presuppositions of biblical errantism,[77] and spoke about this subject during the first inerrantist congress. In his lecture, he placed the humanistic philosophies of the errantists in opposition to the factual evidence (!) that, in his opinion, existed for inerrantism on the basis of the Bible.[78] Apparently, he did not see that the scientism, scholasticism, positivism, and rationalism underlying the Chicago type of inerrantism are just as humanistic *or* scholastic (or a bit of both) in nature.

Insofar as Geisler himself accepted a philosophical foundation for his hermeneutics, he claimed that this foundation was theism, supranaturalism, and metaphysical realism. We encounter such a view elsewhere; J. A. Heyns wrote that theism is "the biblical standpoint"[79] — as if the Bible teaches any "-ism" at all, or acts as a referee between different "-isms." This is not a matter of nitpicking but of carefully distinguishing between ordinary and theoretical thought. The Bible does not teach any "-ism" (theory, model, ideology, or even religion) concerning God, but it presents *God*. It does not argue about him — he is simply there: "In the beginning God . . ." (Gen. 1:1; cf. John 1:1).

Here is another regrettable example. After Dutch-American philosopher Cornelius Van Til had told us how pleased he was with the work of Christian philosophers Dirk H. Th. Vollenhoven, Herman Dooyeweerd, and South African philosopher Hendrik P. Stoker, he showed how little he had learned from them by continuing to point out that the Bible does indeed contain a *theory* of reality, and that this *theory* propounds two levels of being: first, God as infinite, eternal, and unchangeable, and second, the universe as derived, fi-

---

77. Geisler (1981).
78. Geisler (1979a, 333–34).
79. Heyns (1977, 121; cf. 1976, 12).

nite, temporal, and changeable.[80] All these, and many more, examples of theoreticalizing our faith knowledge, and even the Bible itself, show how much even the most Christian of philosophers and theologians often remain under the influence of scholastic (and in fact also subsequent humanistic) thinking.

So Geisler did not stand alone in his assertions; this is a widespread disease, occurring in every sector of Christianity—perhaps more in the Anglo-Saxon world than in the European world because the latter has enjoyed a stronger philosophical tradition. Be this as it may, Geisler went one step beyond many others by asserting that the "-isms" he mentioned were not only presupposed in, but even *taught* by, Scripture.[81]

Another example is Donald A. Carson, who was far too facile in speaking of the solid phenomena of the Scripture, and who placed a certain *interpretation* of the phenomena of the Bible text (by the errantists) in opposition to the phenomena *themselves*.[82] Again we are struck by the naïveté of such a positivist view. For what human on earth has access to the phenomena themselves—the brute facts—without any presuppositions or any (conscious or unconscious) interpretation of the facts? What thinker is audacious enough to claim that he and his fellow believers are the only ones capable of seeing the facts *without glasses*?

9.7.3 The Biases of Inerrantism

Opponents of the Chicago type of inerrantism have often returned the accusations of the inerrantists, identifying the philosophical presuppositions—foreign to the Bible—that play a role in this inerrantism. One of the examples mentioned is scholastic dualism,[83] or what is called the "scientific model,"

---

80. Van Til (1955, 235).
81. Geisler (1984a, 55).
82. Carson (1986, 23).
83. Vander Stelt (1978).

The Fundamentalist View of Scripture

which involves Baconian[84] inductivism, as well as Scottish Common Sense Realism.[85] Gerrie Snyman sought to identify neo-Platonism, positivism, and naïve realism in the work of the Theological School in Potchefstroom (South Africa).[86] Presumably, he might have had a similar evaluation of the theological work done at the Dutch theological universities in Apeldoorn and Kampen (Broederweg), or about Westminster Theological Seminary (Philadelphia, PA, USA) or Westminster Seminary California (Escondido, CA, USA), and quite a few others.

Many more examples could be mentioned. But I remind the reader that both inerrantists and errantists often overlook two things. First, the "-isms" that errantists and inerrantists attribute to the others' approach tell us as much about their *own* philosophical and theological biases. And second, both sides must be blamed for too rapidly *theoreticalizing* the opponent's biases, including their pure faith biases. Not every bias is an "-ism" in any theoretical sense; most are probably not.

Alas, in this theoreticalizing of ordinary, including biblical, parlance—that is, in this scientism—the more fundamentalist and the more liberal theologians share remarkable similarities. We therefore do not need to expect that American errantists fare any better than the inerrantists. Thus, Jack B. Rogers and Donald K. McKim tried to prove that their Evangelical-errantist view had always been the traditional view of the Christian church.[87] They distinguished between a so-called "functional" and a "scholastic" theology, or, to keep it simple, between errantism and inerrantism. The word "func-

---

84. This refers to Francis Bacon, who developed the inductive method of science.
85. Marsden (1980, 214–15); the basic idea of Common Sense Realism is that common sense is the foundation of philosophy; it influenced Thomas Jefferson, and the American political ideas of his time.
86. Snyman (1992).
87. Rogers and McKim (1979); cf. also Rogers (1977, 18–23), and the response by Woodbridge (1982).

tional" was intended to express that biblical inspiration refers to the divine goal, the usefulness, the function of Scripture in the sense of 2 Timothy 3:16-17 (cf. chapter 10 on credibilism). The authors counted among the "functional" theologians (their own party) Augustine, Anselm, Martin Luther, John Calvin, Abraham Kuyper, Herman Bavinck, Karl Barth, and G. C. Berkouwer. Among the "scholastic" theologians they counted Thomas Aquinas, Philip Melanchton, Theodore Beza, Charles Hodge, and B. B. Warfield.

Such a view is acceptable as far as it goes (although one may wonder how precise such a division can be). However, it is remarkable that Rogers and McKim not only called the "scholastic" theologians Aristotelian(-Thomist) — which in a certain sense was correct — but called their own "functional" theology Platonic(-Aristotelian). In this way, these neo-Evangelicals placed themselves without any hesitation on the same pagan-scientistic foundation as the inerrantists. In opposition to this, I strongly claim that neither Plato nor Aristotle can be accepted as a guide when it comes to biblical inspiration or a hermeneutic that seeks to remain faithful to the Bible's self-testimony. We cannot allow any foreign influences here. If we allow any philosophy to come between the Bible and our theological theories it can be nothing other than a deep-rooted (radical) Christian philosophy, instead of any scholastic or humanistic mixture with Christian ideas that so many Christian theologians unfortunately embrace.

9.8   Fundamentalism and Biblicism

9.8.1   Some Natural Modalities

South African philosopher Daniel F. M. Strauss wrote that, when biblicism implements the consequences of its own position by entering into a scientific debate concerning the infallibility of Scripture, it opens the door for the most dangerous enemy of the authority of Scripture. This is because (so-called) "science" can just as easily "prove" that Scripture *cannot* be the Word of God, or at least is not infallible at all.[88] Science is a two-edged sword! This is similar to the Bible itself: it can be used as a "sword of the Spirit" (Eph. 6:17), but also as a sword of the flesh. Science is not a neutral referee, to whom fighting parties can appeal in controversies; science is rather an axe that can be wielded by either party at its own discretion.

We will now enter somewhat more deeply into this biblicism about which Strauss wrote, for it is a vital concept.[89] This discussion will not be easy, for the terms "biblicism" and "fundamentalism" are equally vague and thereby capable of a variety of widely different meanings.[90] I will mention what I consider to be the most important meanings, and will arrange them according to the underlying modal ideas.

(a) **Kinematic:** *mechanicism*. This view bases the absolute authority of the Bible on a doctrine of verbal inspiration, which is understood to be explicitly mechanical; Gisbertus Voetius was one of its most outspoken adherents. See our earlier discussion in §7.8 (cf. also §8.5). German theologians Adolf von Harnack and Otto Ritschl attributed such a view of mechanical inspiration to Augustine and Martin Luther, and therefore called them "biblicists."[91] This mechanical paradigm ignores the human character of Scripture, that the Word has entered historical time, has undergone cultural-historical development, and has become subject to humanness with all its limitations. This view of mechanical inspiration engenders the practice of harmonizing the text in order to smooth out presumed inconsistencies in the text.

(b) **Perceptive:** *anti-empiricism*. This is an overestimation of special revelation in comparison with general revelation (cf. chapters 1–4). It is the definition of biblicism that is pre-

---

88. Strauss (1978, 97).
89. Cf. Ouweneel (1995, §1.2.2).
90. On this, see De Klerk (1937); Bijlsma (1964, 84–90); and Wentsel (1982, 562–72).
91. Harnack (1958, 102); idem (1900, 235); Ritschl (1908, 50).

ferred by Andree Troost.[92] The Bible is viewed as the exclusive source of true knowledge, whereas logical-empirical knowledge, derived from a study of created reality (i.e., of general revelation), is disavowed. This form of biblicism affirms that everything in the Bible is true and that all truth is in the Bible.[93] Anti-empiricism works with slogans such as the "all-sufficiency of the Bible" or "true science is found in the Bible alone." Of course, both slogans are mistaken. The Bible is all-sufficient with regard to God and salvation.[94] But anyone wishing to build a computer, bake a cake, repair a car, lay out a garden, remove an appendix, or heal a psychosis, will receive little help from the Bible. We could not expect otherwise. God has equipped humanity with both his Word and with logical-empirical creational gifts, so that humans themselves can invent these things.[95] Broadly stated, we may say that the Bible tells us what we could learn in no other way but definitely ought to know; it *rarely* tells us the things we *could* learn by ourselves (even if such learning often took centuries).

As to the second slogan, "true science is found in the Bible alone," this one is based on an ambiguous use of the word "science" (cf. Lat. *scientia*, which also entails ordinary knowledge). People confuse the theoretical knowledge belonging to science with the ordinary knowledge of the truth. Biblicists who are enamored of this type of slogan ultimately acknowledge to be science only what is derived directly from the Bible. In this way, Christians have developed a "biblical" psychology came about, and a "biblical" economy, a "biblical" ethics, a "biblical" psychiatry, and even a "biblical" theology,[96] whereas, strictly speaking, the Bible does not contain a

---

92. Troost (1978, 121).
93. Cf. Holmes (1977, book title: *All Truth Is God's Truth*).
94. This matter is related to the ancient doctrinal issue of the *sufficiency* of Scripture (see §6.9). In opposition to the Roman Catholic emphasis on the church, the Reformation claimed that Scripture is sufficient for people's salvation and for the true knowledge of God; cf. Weber (1981, =Ger 302–309).
95. Cf. Heyns (1976, 122–29).
96. I mention only Chambers (1995; 1998).

single item of psychology, economics, ethics, psychiatry, or even theology, if these terms are understood to refer strictly to theoretical disciplines.

A striking example was Henry M. Morris, who deduced a cosmogony, an astronomy, a thermodynamics, a chemistry, a physics, a geophysics, a hydrology and meteorology, a geology, a paleontology, a biology, an anthropology, a demography, a linguistics, and an ethnology from the Bible, which were all called "biblical."[97] All of these are mistaken. The Bible does contain very important knowledge concerning humanity, the soul (healthy or sick), economic relationships in ancient Israel, morality, and faith. And I do believe that this knowledge is of essential importance for the Christian practitioner of each scientific discipline. However, this knowledge is not identical with these disciplines as such. It is not of a scientific but rather of a pre-scientific nature; that is, it precedes scientific knowledge, and constitutes a pre-theoretical foundation for it.

9.8.2 Some Normative Modalities

(c) **Logical:** *anti-logicism*. This is an attempt to arrive at a kind of "biblical" theology, which is directly based upon Scripture, without a basic theoretical consideration of the starting points, the methodology, and the nature of such an enterprise. Even less does it supply a valid *warrant* for these matters. Such an irrational theology is frequently offered as the result of rejecting all current doctrines—considered to be corrupt—and of a return to the plain teaching of Scripture, under the direct guidance of the Holy Spirit (appealing often to John 16:13!), without any human intervention. Often, people resist calling such an approach theology because to them, "theology" is a dirty word.[98]

This well-intended path is a perilous road because it looks scriptural but *never* is. The reason is that a theology—

---

97. Morris (1984).
98. Cf. Davis (1984a, 57–58).

or a system of Bible doctrines—that does not weigh its presuppositions and starting points has no other choice than to blindly (and unconsciously) work with the presuppositions and starting points that are automatically given with modern culture, and which we have all imbibed from early youth. And these are never purely Christian presuppositions and starting points. Think of rationalism and positivism, or alternatively, irrationalism and postmodernism, which permeate popular culture and influence Christian thinking (usually unconsciously). This form of biblicism threatens not only fundamentalism but also each Evangelical, Lutheran, or Calvinist theology that does not provide sufficient warrant for its prolegomena.[99] Such a "biblical" theology or a "just the Bible, nothing but the Bible" mentality is self-deceived, and will lead to scholasticism or humanism, or to both simultaneously.[100]

(d) **Historical:** *anti-historicism*. This is closely related with the previous, the anti-logical form of biblicism. Anti-historicism is an attempt to obtain access to Scripture in an arrogant and headstrong way without giving heed to almost twenty centuries of Christian exegesis of Scripture, and to the great teachers of the church, with the exception of the few leaders of one's own faith community (sectarianism).[101] Valentijn Hepp distinguished between a *grave* form of biblicism, which rejects all church dogmas and confessions, and all theological theory building, (2) a *lighter* form, which allows the formulation of confessions but insists on regularly reviewing church dogmas, and (3) the *lightest* form of biblicism, which leaves the confession untouched but is not concerned with the scope of each phrase in the confession.[102]

The question naturally arises whether Hepp's own ap-

---

99. See extensively, Ouweneel (1995, §§1.2.2 and 2.1; 2014; 2015).
100. One example is the Pentecostal theology of Duffield and Van Cleave (1996), into which various traditional scholastic elements could sneak in surreptitiously because it lacks a philosophical-theological filter.
101. See Ouweneel (2010a, chapters 13–14).
102. Hepp (1936).

proach traveled the proper middle path between biblicism and confessionalism. On the one hand, the dangers of this kind of biblicism include individualism and pride, which conceal stubborn personal opinions. In short, it ignores the guidance of the Spirit in church history (see again John 16:13). On the other hand, there are the dangers of confessionalism: a rigid conservatism, enclosing Scripture in one's own tradition, and walling oneself off against new insights in Scripture. In short: it camps within the safety of its own oasis without seeing — or wishing to see — the cloud moving forward (Num. 9:17-23).

9.8.3 Absolutizing Positivizations

(e) **Juridical:** absolutizing time-bound "positivizations" (a juridical term) of certain timeless biblical principles. This is a form of biblicism that we met already in §4.8. Biblicism forgets that each positivization of certain biblical principles, because of their concrete circumstances, always has a unique historical character. Therefore, such a concrete positivization cannot be uncritically applied to different historical circumstances, which clearly differ from previous ones. In this way, biblicism achieves the opposite of the view that declares the Bible to be time-bound. The latter throw out the baby with the bathwater: they reject not only the concrete positivizations but also the underlying immutable divine principles, and invent such principles according to their own taste and insight. Over against this, biblicists accept the underlying principles, but confuse them with the concrete positivized forms in which they come to us.

Here is a positive example: the South African report *Die Reformatoriese Sola Scriptura* ("The Reformational *Sola Scriptura*") rightly argued in 1980 that affirming the perpetually valid *principles* of Christian communion does not obligate us to imitate the concrete positivizations of this principle that we read about in the New Testament. The report mentioned examples such as the voluntary sharing of possessions (cf. Acts

2:45; 4:32), foot washing (cf. 1 Tim. 5:10), the brotherly kiss (cf. Rom. 16:16), love feasts (cf. Jude 12), and so on.[103] As such, historical states of affairs in Scripture never have normative meaning. For instance, think of the Roman Catholic appeal to the forty days of fasting of Moses, Elijah, and Jesus (Exod. 34:28; 1 Kings 19:6-8; Matt. 4:2) as a basis for the church's practice during *Lent*, the forty days of fasting between Ash Wednesday and Easter. But I could also mention the argument of Baptists, based on New Testament examples, of baptizing adults only. Or the argument of Plymouth Brethren against leadership by a solitary pastor because New Testament churches had no such leadership. Or the argument of Pentecostals that all Christians must speak in tongues because the early Christians spoke in tongues. And so on.[104]

Here is another example: in politicology (the science of politics), people should not wish to derive, from the fact that in the Old Testament God gave a king to Israel, that Scripture prescribes monarchy as the proper form of the state, and rejects, for instance, a republic. The *principle* here is the social-juridical demand of ordered authorities, instituted by God (Rom. 13:1-7; Titus 3:1; 1 Pet. 2:13-14). The concrete *positivization* of this principle entails the nature of these people in authority: tribal heads (the patriarchs), leaders (Moses, Joshua), judges (as in the time of the Judges), kings, emperors, presidents, prime ministers, heads of state. In the same way, the social, economic and juridical ordinances in the law of Moses each have their own historical context, which can never be literally transferred to different times and circumstances.

However, this is only half the story. Beyond the concrete positivizations within the law of Sinai, we must search for the underlying, universally valid creational principles, for these remain valid both for our ordinary Christian life and for the Christian social, economic and juridical sciences. In §4.10.2, I mentioned the example of marriage as a creational institution

---
103. *Reformatoriese Sola Scriptura*, 1980, 11-12.
104. Cf. also Brillenburg Wurth (1951, 152-53); Ridderbos (1975, 275-78).

of God, which remains valid but assumes many different outward forms in different times and cultures.

Consider as well what the Bible teaches about stewardship, about the relationship between humanity and labor (labor must not be viewed as a commodity, apart from the laborer), between labor and reward (reward according to need or to achievement), about personal and collective property, about the treatment of the poor and foreigners, about labor and rest, about laziness and burnout, about humans as producers and consumers, about the relationship between crime and punishment, between retribution and remediation of the evildoer, between responsibility and guilt, and so on.[105] Some New Testament instructions about these matters are given in exhortations to masters and slaves (Eph. 6:5-9; Col. 3:22-4:1; Titus 2:9; cf. 1 Pet. 2:18). In this teaching, we find important *principles*, which we encounter here in a concrete (and objectionable) *positivization* of the relationship between employer and employee. But (hopefully) nobody would think of drawing the conclusion from this teaching that it is God's will that people have slaves. Not long ago, however, many Christians did draw this conclusion.[106]

Biblicistic fundamentalism has often tried to work certain "biblical principles" into existing, secular disciplines, believing that, in this way, the latter could be Christianized. The result is a peculiar mixture of a thoroughly secular-humanistic discipline and certain Christian insights. Instead we need to elaborate these biblical principles in a responsible, coherent, pre-theoretical Christian life- and worldview, and from there draw the lines to a deep-rooted (radical) Christian philosophical cosmology. From that position, these principles can then be developed into a Christian natural philosophy, philosophical anthropology, social philosophy, philosophy of history,

---

105. Cf. Ouweneel (1987a, 47-58).
106. A striking example was Dutch Bible teacher and poet Isaak da Costa (1823); see http://www.dbnl.org/tekst/cost002bezw01_01/cost002bezw01_01_0004.php.

aesthetic philosophy, philosophy of jurisprudence, moral philosophy, and so on. In this way, they ultimately can permeate our concrete special-scientific investigations. I have tried to elaborate this with respect to the fields of psychology[107] and theology.[108]

9.9 Biblioscientism

9.9.1 In the Natural Sciences

There is a peculiar form of biblicism that one could view as a kind of crossbreeding with scientism. For this I have coined the word "biblioscientism."[109] This view overestimates (natural) science when it claims it can find accurate (natural) scientific statements and theories in the Bible. This spiritual attitude goes back to early British Enlightenment, when natural science began to make great progress and scientists still had great respect for the Bible. Infallibility became the trademark of the natural sciences. The scientific method sought to remove all errors from naïve thinking, and out of reverence for the Bible, this method was applied to it as well. As devoted people concluded, God was so perfect that he would never commit scientific errors.

This purely rationalistic and scientistic attitude survives to this day. It does so especially among certain North American creationists who read scientific models into the Bible. This view can be summarized in a statement by one who was a leading creationist, Henry M. Morris: "The Bible *is* a textbook of science."[110] I do believe that the Bible speaks in a thoroughly reliable way, also when it speaks of nature, the cosmos, and history.[111] But this claim is essentially different from identifying the Bible as a "textbook of science." I can think of no way to render Morris's statement true and meaningful. When

---

107. Ouweneel (1984; 2016).
108. Ouweneel (1995; 2015).
109. Ouweneel (1987a, 86, 130–31, 136, 140–56).
110. Morris (1966, title of chapter 11: *The Bible is a Textbook of Science*).
111. Cf. Ouweneel (2018l, chapter 3).

I studied biology, I had biology textbooks. They differed from the Bible in every respect. The Bible is not even a textbook of theology. The Bible teaches us truths about *God* and his *creation*, about *Christ* and about *salvation*. Theologians can develop these truths into theological models, and sometimes biblical statements about nature may be useful in biological models. But this is essentially different from the Bible being a "textbook of science," including theology.

Biblioscientism treats expressions and statement from the Bible as if they were of a scientific character. Elsewhere I have described variations of these,[112] which I arrange here according to the underlying modal ideas.

(a) *Physical* biblioscientism is a "physicalism" (absolutization of the physical or energetic modality) that defines a believing attitude toward the Bible according to the measure in which a person takes the Bible's statements to describe what is physically literal. People fail to discern here that the Bible speaks of physical matters exclusively from the viewpoint of faith, not from the logical-analytical viewpoint of scientific physics. For instance, such a physicalism demands that the days of creation are taken to be "ordinary days," and fails to explain everything that might be implied in such an expression. Herman Bavinck rightly spoke of "extraordinary, cosmic days" and "the workdays of God."[113] The six days of creation are primarily God's working days in the pistical sense, as days in *God's* "time." What do we gain if these days are further theoreticalized by defining them as days of twenty-four (!) hours?

Other examples include various physical or astronomical theories: those of the nuclear forces, of the field of gravity, the second law of thermodynamics, the theory of the isostasy of the earth, and so on, which have all been read into the Bible.[114] For each of these physical theories, Bible verses are

---

112. Ouweneel (1987a, 142–51).
113. Bavinck (*RD* 2:499–500).
114. Cf. Morris (1968, especially chapter 1: *Modern Science in the Bible*; also see 1984).

adduced which allegedly presuppose, or teach, the things just mentioned, long before physics became aware of them. This is the essence of biblioscientism: the Bible is sufficient (divine, trustworthy, authoritative) to such an extent that it tells us about nuclear forces, gravity, thermodynamics, isostasy, and does so in a perfectly accurate way.

Another author, Dutch-Canadian astronomy amateur Walter van de Kamp, suggested that those who do not believe that the sun circles around the earth, instead of the other way around, do not take Genesis 1:1-19 seriously. This implies that those who are not geocentrists are not faithful to the Bible.[115] However, the statement, "He set the earth on its foundations, so that it should never be moved" (Ps. 104:4), is no more an argument *for* geocentrism than the statement, "[A]ll the foundations of the earth are shaken" (82:5), is an argument *against* it.

9.9.2 In Historical Science

(b) *Historical* biblioscientism is the attempt to degrade the Bible into scientific information, whether in the fields of the natural or the historical sciences. I do believe that Scripture must be taken seriously, when it speaks — *always strictly under the viewpoint of faith* — about nature or history. For instance, I take the story of Noah's Flood seriously, also in historical respect. However, this does not automatically imply the "flood model" advocated by many creationists, which is supposed to explain the origin of earth strata and fossils. The biblical story of the Flood is inspired truth, also from a historical point of view. But the flood model is a human, scientific construct whose validity must be established and evaluated on the basis of extra-biblical criteria. This view is a human attempt to link our belief in the Flood story with our knowledge of earth strata and fossils.

This attempt may or may not be successful; but we can never evaluate a person's faithfulness to the Bible in terms of

---

115. Van der Kamp (1985, especially chapter V).

their accepting or rejecting the Flood model. The history of the Flood does not constitute a few random pages from world history, nor is it a story about the origin of the earth's crust. It is the story of human apostasy, of God's holy judgment, and of his saving grace for a small remnant with whom he continued the redemptive history of humanity. Genesis 6–8 is a true story, not because it comports with the viewpoint of the natural and historical sciences, but because the story really happened, *and* because these chapters point to the Truth, as it received its ultimate form in the person of Jesus Christ (cf. John 14:6; Eph. 4:21).

9.9.3 In Theology

(c) *Pistical* biblioscientism is the opposite of the previous two forms just discussed. In contrast to physicalism and historicism, we could call this form of biblioscientism "pisticism" or "theologism." I mention this form especially to indicate that not only certain fundamentalists fall prey to biblioscientism. Pisticism is the attempt to reduce the Bible content to its pistical aspects. The fact that Scripture considers the totality of cosmic reality, of nature and history, under the viewpoint of faith is abused in order to argue that the trustworthiness of what the Bible says about nature and history is irrelevant. Scripture is treated so "reverently" that it is exalted above nature and history.

British Darwinist Thomas H. Huxley sarcastically predicted in 1890 that the day would come when faith would be severed from facts, especially from pre-patriarchal history, and that faith would then advance in ever growing triumph; quoting from a Bampton Lecture, he approvingly wrote: "No longer in contact with fact of any kind, Faith stands now and forever proudly inaccessible to the attacks of the infidel."[116]

This is a remarkable statement. Huxley foresaw that theologians would one day think that theology could be sustained

---

116. Huxley (1894, 237–38); https://archive.org/details/sciencehebrewtra-00huxl_0); cf. Ouweneel (1978, 18).

only by severing faith from nature and history. This prediction has been fully realized, especially in the dialectical, existentialist, and postmodernist theology of the twentieth century (see chapters 11–12). For many people, faith has become an existential experience whose content can be neither evaluated nor transferred to others, and which therefore cannot be criticized. Huxley must have viewed this as a particularly amusing development, for he understood that a faith severed from history would have as much value as some Eastern meditation, an LSD hallucination, a sexual experience, or any kind of unverifiable sensation.[117]

9.10 Fundamentalism and Modernism

9.10.1 Scientism

Let me return once more to the remarkable similarities between fundamentalism and modernism. Of course, neither of these wishes to hear about these similarities; they would rather stress their enormous differences. But to me these resemblances seem undeniable. They illustrate the truth of the slogan "the extremes touch each other" (Fr. *les extrèmes se touchent*).[118]

First, with regard to *scientism*, I have argued that both fundamentalism and modernism are characterized by scientism, the overestimation of scientific thinking and speaking in comparison with ordinary thinking and speaking, including Scripture's own parlance. Whereas Roman Catholicism has tried to anchor the credibility of its theology in the authority of the *church*, both fundamentalist and modernist theology (Protestant as well as Roman-Catholic) anchor credibility in the authority of *science*. It is a form of chutzpa to claim that the very same science can be employed as an ally of both sides, either to prove that the Bible is God's Word and inerrant (even

---

117. Schaeffer (1982, 1:257; 2:122; 4:31, 332–33).

118. Cf. Murphy (1996), who earlier discovered the foundation of inerrantism in modernism, and tried to find a way going beyond the fundamentalism–liberalism dispute; see, in his line, also Perry (2001).

The Fundamentalist View of Scripture

in the fields of the natural and the historical sciences), or to prove that the Bible is full of scientific errors, and therefore cannot, in any credible sense, be God's Word.

To put it in different words: fundamentalist theology appeals to science in order to demonstrate the inerrancy of the Bible from a *scientistic* viewpoint, and modernist theology appeals to science in order to demonstrate the errancy of the Bible from a *scientistic* viewpoint. One could also say that modernism finds its scientific credibility in the inerrancy of *history* from a *scientistic* viewpoint.[119] In opposition to the (allegedly scientifically established) slogan "the Bible is always right"[120] stands here the (allegedly scientifically established) slogan "the history (of Western thought) is always right." That is, modern thinking can never regress to pre-modern (i.e., pre-Enlightenment) thinking. Both standpoints—fundamentalism and modernism—appeal as loudly as possible to the solid facts of true science, whether the natural or the historical sciences.

Regarding this relationship between fundamentalism and modernism, Andree Troost saw a historical aspect, too: each modernist theology has an orthodox past, in which the rationalistic seeds of corruption were present at the outset.[121] These seeds merely required adequate time and suitable conditions in order to germinate. In other words, skepticism always arises from faulty conservatism (just as, e.g., the rise of socialism arises from faulty capitalism). Thus, a theologian who moves from fundamentalism to so-called biblical criticism—and the twentieth century has known many such scholars—often hardly needs to change his rationalistic methodology. Rarely, the opposite occurs: a modernist theologian who is converted very easily ends up in fundamentalism because, in so doing, he or she need not abandon their scientistic methodology

---

119. Cf. Weber (1981, =Ger 199–201).
120. Cf. Keller (1983, original book title: *Und die Bible hat doch recht* ["And the Bible was right after all"]).
121. Troost (1977, 140, 193; cf. 2004, 335–36).

(even if they are not conscious of this fact). German Protestant theologian Eta Linnemann, who converted from modernism to fundamentalism, clearly seemed to exhibit a tendency in this direction.[122]

9.10.2 Scholasticism

I have also argued that the scientism mentioned above has a peculiar *scholastic* character. Scientism and scholasticism are often closely linked. The connection lies in views such as the autonomy and priority of human reason, the neutrality and objectivity of facts, and thus also of science, and (therefore) the necessary separation between faith and science. Unfortunately, these views seem to be ineradicable from Western thought, whether we are dealing with fundamentalists or with modernists. Although this type of epistemology has been refuted within the philosophical world, these views persist in the various disciplines, in which the practitioners—including the theologians—often have no idea of what is involved in that specific part of epistemology that we refer to as the philosophy of science ("What is science? How does scientific knowledge differ from practical knowledge? How do we obtain reliable scientific knowledge?" etc.).

Earlier I tried to show how fundamentalism is trapped in the nature–grace dualism of scholastic thought. Daniel F. M. Strauss demonstrated the same thing with respect to the theology of German-speaking theologians Karl Barth, Emil Brunner, and Rudolf Bultmann.[123] At the same time, he described the differences between them in terms of the relationship between rationalism and irrationalism.[124]

(a) *Fundamentalism*. On the one hand, fundamentalists are confident that (rationalistic) science will salvage the reliability of the Bible (the *nature* motif). On the other hand, they accept timeless, universally valid principles, which are supposed-

---

122. Linnemann (1992; 2001).
123. Strauss (1978).
124. Cf. Wentsel (1982, 553–54).

ly deduced from the biblical data (the *grace* motif). Through theological analysis, these principles must serve to shed light upon natural life. This approach is a characteristic example of a rationalistic casuistic ethics.

(b) *Karl Barth*. Barth believed that, in its immanent limitedness and defectiveness, Scripture encloses the Word of God in a disturbingly restrictive way, and sometimes even contradicts it. On the one hand, without any reluctance he subjected the Bible to the historical criticism of (rationalistic) science (*nature*). On the other hand, Barth claimed that we do not encounter God's commandment as universally valid principles but as concrete, purely historical, that is, time-bound, rules. Thanks to God's sovereign good pleasure, these can become for people God's-Word-for-the-moment (*grace*). This approach to the Word of God as well as to the discipline of ethics is purely *irrationalist*.

(c) *Rudolf Bultmann*. A similar distinction can be observed in the work of Bultmann. On the one hand, he was confident that rationalistic (objectifying) science could demythologize the non-authoritative, objectifying (historical-)biblical parlance (*nature*). On the other hand, like Barth he rejected the notion of universal, unchangeable principles, since, in his view, it is only the (*irrational*) existential-historical (Ger. *geschichtliche*) appeal of God's love, consisting in the transcendent (timeless) moment (*grace*), which dialectically stands over against nature.[125]

(d) *Emil Brunner*. In nature, Brunner found a point of contact for hearing God's Word, for as Creator, God demands our obedience to the external natural ordinances (*rational*). However, as Redeemer God demands that we surpass these rigid ordinances in obedience to the internal appeal of God's commandment of love of the timeless moment (Ger. *Gebot der Stunde*) (*irrational*).

---

125. Strauss (1978) pointed to Ernst Fuchs (1963), who pressed the fundamental dialectic of nature and grace so strongly that revelation (read: grace) annuls history (read: nature).

9.10.3 Dehistoricization

As I have just described, the dialectical tension between nature and grace in scholastic dualism leads to a rationalistic view of God's Word within fundamentalism, and to an irrationalistic view of God's Word in dialectical and demythologization theology. However, in a different respect there is a remarkable similarity in the way fundamentalist theology and critical theology view the "upper story" of grace (also called: supernature) where God's Word supposedly resides.

Daniel F. M. Strauss has formulated this as follows:

> Even the rationalistic program of biblicism exhibits clear correspondence with dialectical theology and the demythologization program. For both Barth and Bultmann c.s. the *actual meaning* of God's Word revelation cannot enter into the (common) historical experience of the everyday person—this because [according to them] the Word did not become flesh, did not die on the cross, and did not rise after three days. Although biblicism does *not* wish to demythologize these biblical data, we have seen that, nonetheless, it also exhibits a little the ideal that God's Word could not have entered into time. At the 'pole of nature' within their dialectical thought, Barth and Bultmann appeal to the rationalistic natural and historical sciences to deroot the mythological worldview of the Bible, for the objectifying terms in which it speaks have no revelational authority. It is the very same (supposedly neutral) rationalistic science that, at the 'pole of nature' within biblicism, is applied to salvage the very authority of the Bible! Both make use of the same method, but hope to reach opposite results! At the pole of nature, there is even no difference when it comes to the *confidence* in the truth claim of rationalistic (objectifying) science![126]

As we saw under the previous point, there is also a clear similarity with respect to the element of grace within the dualism, in the sense that both fundamentalist and dialectical theology assign an exceptional status to theology — a typically

---

126. Strauss (1978, 107–108).

scholastic attitude.[127] According to Strauss, with respect to the element of grace the basic distinction between fundamentalist and dialectical theology is that the former chooses a rationalistic, and the latter an irrationalistic (existentialist) position. Each has a certain timeless, ahistorical view of God's Word. The difference is that fundamentalism holds a rationalistic view of timelessness, which in a casuistic way, deduces from concrete positivized biblical data supposed biblical principles that are valid for all times (see §§4.8 and 4.9).[128] The irrationalistic response of existentialistic theology leads to the opposite, so-called situation ethics, in which what counts is the contingent, timeless moment, the *nunc aeternum* ("eternal now") of philosopher Søren Kierkegaard.[129]

9.11 Other Similarities

9.11.1 Elimination of Scripture

Yet another similarity between fundamentalism and modernism has been identified by philosopher Hendrik Hart.[130] I call this *elimination*; it is the attempt to place the Bible in effect outside our common creaturely life. If I understand Hart correctly, he was thinking of critical theology when he said that we must avoid claiming that what holds authority for us is not the Bible but merely the Word. However, the fact that the eternal Word (Lat. *verbum aeternum*) always surpasses the Scriptures does not mean that the Word actually *exists apart from* the Scriptures, or should, or could, be *severed* from the latter. The Scriptures have been specifically given to us as an authoritative source of teaching. If people undermine the authority of Scripture, they simultaneously cause the Word to vanish into thin air.[131]

---

127. We find the very same attitude toward theology in so-called two–kingdom theology; see Ouweneel (2017, chapter 2).
128. Cf. also Du Toit (1990, 510–11).
129. Regarding the two types of ethics, cf. Troost (1958).
130. Hart (1968, 120, 131).
131. Ibid., 131.

As a consequence of this, the Bible is eliminated from our practical lives.[132] Hart argued that, if Scripture is made divine (I take it: as in fundamentalism), it transcends our creatureliness, and we would not be able to look at it for fear that it would kill us in all its glory (cf. Exod. 33:20; Deut. 5:26; Judg. 6:22-23; 13:22; 1 Tim. 6:16). If God deems it necessary to reveal to us his Word in a creaturely way (through incarnation or inscripturation), we must not be wiser than God. That is, on the one hand, if we push aside this creaturely dimension (intended to place the Word fully within our experience), we place the Word outside our creaturely experience (as happens in dialectical theology). On the other hand, if we identify the Word and Scripture (I would add: and thus ignore the transcendence of the Word) so strongly that we turn the Word into a mere creature (as in fundamentalism), we place Scripture outside our lives, too. God intends to bring the transcendent Word in a creaturely way (i.e., in the form of the immanent Bible) into our lives.

If we separate the Word from the Bible, we violate Scripture's intention to be the inscripturated Word among us. Therefore, what we think Scripture is becomes highly important, for if we identify Scripture wrongly, then we endanger the correct functioning of our Bible reading. This is Hart's position.[133]

For the relationship between the eternal, transcendent Word and Scripture as the temporal-immanent form of this Word, see chapter 5 above. Hendrik Hart wrote about this subject, too,[134] in a good, but not entirely satisfactory way. In distinction from Hart, I have no difficulty saying that inscripturation means that the Word has become Scripture. I do this without accepting Hart's assertion that this would mean that the Word would be reduced to sentences. The parallel, also used by Hart himself, can help us here: the incarnation of the

---

132. Ibid., 120.

133. Ibid., 131.

134. Ibid., 118-19.

Logos (John 1:14) does not mean that the eternal Word is *reduced* to flesh and blood (for more on this, see §5.3 above). The Word remains infinitely more than the flesh it has assumed (in the incarnation), or the human material form it has assumed (in inscripturation), respectively.

9.11.2 Separating Scope and Periphery

We have seen that both fundamentalism and modernism exhibit the tendency to, in effect, sever Bible portions from the scope of Scripture. Fundamentalism sometimes emphasizes the (correct) idea that the Bible speaks reliably about nature and history so strongly that it creates the impression as if this feature is all, or at least is *the* most important feature, that really matters in the Bible passages involved, such as the stories of creation and the Flood. I have emphasized that in the Bible the point that matters is *always* God's salvation and human faith, in the widest sense of the scope of Scripture. This scope is *always* Jesus Christ, and the realization of God's counsels in him. Only *within this scope* does the Bible speak so often about history, nature, and the cosmos. We take these Bible passages seriously, *also with regard to their historical feature*. However, we never do so from the theoretical viewpoint of Western, modern natural and historical sciences, but only from the practical viewpoint of faith.

For example, when we read that in Joshua's days, the sun "stands still" (Josh. 10:12–13), we take this historically seriously. In opposition to modernist pisticism, we maintain not only the *redemptive* historical, but also the redemptive *historical*, significance of this story. Indeed, the sun *stood* still, and the day *was* lengthened. At the same time, we cannot avoid various questions arising in our minds. The believing scientist will not manage to suppress his curiosity as to *what exactly* happened on that day from a (natural and historical) scientific viewpoint. Do we have to believe that, for a couple of hours, the earth stopped turning on its axis? Or was it "only" a matter of the refraction of sunlight?

In opposition to fundamentalist historicism or physicalism, we maintain that (a) this question is definitely not what this story is really about, and (b) the narrative itself contains no clue to satisfy our curiosity; that is, in no way does it choose among competing *theoretical* models, say, between the geo- or heliocentric model. We do believe in the "that" of the sun standing still, but we can only speculate about the "how."

In such cases, fundamentalism and modernism suffer from the same ailment: scientism. That is, fundamentalism does not rest before it has found a scientifically satisfactory solution for the question what actually happened that day. This is because the story must be scientifically acceptable, otherwise the scientific reliability of the Bible—whatever this means—might be at stake. In turn, modernism never tires of trying to convince us that a sun literally standing still, and a day literally lengthened, is scientifically untenable. No modern *thinking* human could ever conceive of a sun that stood still and a day that was lengthened.

Both opponents enlist science as an ally[135]—and, in my view, both go astray. Faith is a transcendent-religious matter of the heart, and as I have argued before, faith is neither rational nor irrational, but it is supra-rational. If faith can wrest itself free from the bonds of scientism, it is unimpressed by both the scientific speculations of fundamentalism and the scientific counter-speculations of modernism. Faith *knows* about the lengthened day recorded in Joshua, and faith is not distressed about probably never having a satisfactory explanation for it.

---

135. See the Dutch Reformed quotation in §9.4.1 (note 34).

Chapter 10
The Credibilist View of Scripture

Jesus said to them,
"Is this not the reason you are wrong,
because you know neither the Scriptures
nor the power of God?"
Mark 12:24

Now these Jews [in Berea] were more noble
than those in Thessalonica;
they received the word with all eagerness,
examining the Scriptures daily to see if these
things were so.
Acts 17:11

Summary: *In this chapter, we seek a way between "errantism" and (the scientistic form of) inerrantism. We believe we have found that path in "credibilism" (or "qualified inerrantism"): the Bible is perfectly trustworthy, but not necessarily in every chronological, numerical, genealogical, and grammatical detail. This does not mean that it* **may** *err in these domains, but rather that alleged errors in such domains usually cannot be proven to be errors. It is not a good* idea to theoreticalize the Bible first, and then find possible theoretical errors, which must then scientifically be argued away.

On the level of faith, we believe that the Bible is perfectly credible, but on the theoretical level such a claim can never be substantiated: as a scientific postulate, inerrantism is neither verifiable nor falsifiable. This is because (a) the **autographa** no longer exist, (b) many alleged errors cannot be proven to be errors, and (c) an objective criterion that can distinguish between inerrancy-threatening errors and not-inerrancy-threatening errors cannot be formulated (a number of alleged errors belonging to the latter category are investigated). If falsifiability is a feature of a truly scientific theory (as Popper claimed), then inerrantism is not scientific.

Moreover, in what way can (supposed) irregularities in the text really present a problem? Faith does not acknowledge an (in-)errancy problem; if we think otherwise, this is probably due to the theoreticalization of everyday life: science is our highest authority, even in matters of biblical credibility. In opposition to this rationalism, we posit not irrationalism but rather a view of the human heart as the supra-rational, transcendent concentration point of human existence.

Finally, our speaking of the scope of Scripture does not imply a **reduction** of the latter's content, but its **concentration**. This scope is expressed in every part of the Bible, also in those parts that speak specifically of matters of nature and history.

10.1 The Central Problem

10.1.1 Contra Errantism

IN THE PREVIOUS CHAPTER, I sought to explain my dissatisfaction in several respects with the entire North American orthodox Protestant debate between so-called errantists and so-called inerrantists. In opposition to both movements, I claim that among both of them I encounter authors who have clearly fallen into the snare of scientism, and who thereby endanger the possibility of a sound hermeneutic. In other respects, I sometimes feel more at home with the one group, at other times with the other party. Let me explain.

First, together with the inerrantists, and in opposition to the errantists, I maintain the following theses:

(a) The way God employed human features in the process of inscripturation must be expressed in terms of *adaptation*, namely, to human weakness and finitude, which is proper creatures. It must *not* be expressed in terms of *accommodation*, if this term must include God adapting to human sinfulness, or any defect caused by the Fall.[1] (Accommodation can also be understood, as Calvin does,[2] in the sense that God stoops down like a mother who adapts her language to the level of the child.) The Bible exhibits many consequences of the Fall, even in the lives of the Bible writers, but not in the writings themselves.

(b) Contrary to the maxim "to err is human" (Lat. *errare humanum est*), the human contribution to inscripturation need not imply that the Bible contains human errors.[3] The alternative maxim is "to err is human, but humans need not always err" (Lat. *errare humanum est, sed homo non errandus est*). However, this and similar statements must be carefully weighed against the background of asking: What *are* (possible) errors in the Bible? The question "Are there errors in the Bible?" is preceded by the question "What *is* a (possible) error?," in contrast to mere weaknesses, which is something quite different. In other words, can we speak in an unequivocally scientific way about errors or non-errors in the Bible?

(c) The Bible speaks in a true and reliable way, also when it speaks about matters of history, nature, and the cosmos—at least if we view such speaking strictly from the viewpoint of faith rather than of the natural and historical sciences with their specific terminology and specific claims of precision. The text of the Bible is *always* reliable, but *never* scientific, as I will seek to clarify.

---

1. Cf. Rogers and McKim (1979, 9–10); Hannah (1984, 28–30, 52, 146, 157, 166, 186, 226, 402); and very extensively, Berkouwer (1967, 62–113).
2. Calvin, *Institutes* 1.14.3.
3. Brown (1984b, 389–90).

10.1.2 Contra Inerrantism

Second, together with the errantists, and in opposition to the inerrantists, I maintain the following theses:

(a) The Bible is not a collection of *scientific* truths (in the fields of the natural or the historical sciences), that is, truths concerning nature and history formulated in a scientific way and evaluated according to modern scientific criteria (as the Chicago Statements seem to claim).

(b) The inerrancy of Scripture must be sought in its absolute truth and trustworthiness, its being free of all lies, deceit, aberrations, fallacies, deception, falsehood, and untruthfulness. It must not be sought in the domain of all kinds of (real or supposed) technical inaccuracies and discrepancies (see §10.4 below).

(c) The divine origin of Scripture need not imply denying original (real or alleged) discrepancies between parallel Bible portions like Samuel and the books of the Kings compared with Chronicles, or between the four Gospels, or between historical references in the apostolic letters and in the book of Acts.

The inerrantists have endeavored to protect themselves against claims (b) and (c) with the important Article XIII of the Chicago Statement on Biblical Inerrancy:

> ...We further deny that inerrancy is negated by Biblical phenomena such as a lack of modern technical precision, irregularities of grammar or spelling, observational descriptions of nature, the reporting of falsehoods, the use of hyperbole and round numbers, the topical arrangement of material, variant selections of material in parallel accounts, or the use of free citations."[4]

Later we will extensively discuss these various points (§10.4).

---

[4]. http://www.alliancenet.org/the-chicago-statement-on-biblical-inerrancy; cf. Geisler (1979b, 496); Nullens (1997, 214).

However, by way of contrast, recall Gleason L. Archer Jr., who emphatically stated that, for Jesus, matters of technical precision were of real importance.[5] These are the two ways out for an inerrantist when they encounter a (real or alleged) technical inaccuracy in the Bible:

(a) The *Chicago reply* is this: Indeed, we have a technical inaccuracy here, but this is not an error that would threaten the Bible's inerrancy. That is, there are two types of errors: errors that do not threaten inerrancy (possibly occurring in the Bible), and errors that do threaten inerrancy (not occurring in the Bible). Later we will explain why this is a striking example of a circular reasoning.

(b) The *Archer reply* seems to go something like this: There can be no errors in the Bible — as Jesus himself implicitly stated — and technical inaccuracies are definitely errors. Therefore, if we think we encounter a technical inaccuracy in the Bible, we must be mistaken. In fact, this too is a circular argument. For this reason, the Archer reply is just as unhelpful as the Chicago reply.

10.1.3 The Heart of the Matter

Here we come to the heart of the matter: the Bible's inerrancy has been called a vital Christian doctrine — but is it a doctrine that can be scientifically substantiated? Can it be elevated above all circular reasoning? Will it be possible to develop a scientific (supposedly neutral, objective) criterion of errorlessness with which to measure the Bible, yielding the conclusion that the Bible is free of any errors whatsoever?

The Chicago reply and the Archer reply may seem to be different, but they agree in one important feature (in addition to the one already mentioned). The ultimate background of inerrantism is the quite sympathetic view that the honor, the power, and the primacy of God, or Jesus, are at stake when it comes to the Bible's inerrancy.[6] Thus, Harold O. J. Brown

---

5. Archer Jr. (1979, 58).
6. See Vander Stelt (1978, 229, 323–24).

wrote that the statement "the Scriptures are inerrant" (at least as far as the *autographa* are concerned) is essentially a confession of faith regarding the nature and character of God, and thus regarding the nature of Scripture as God's Word. Therefore, Brown asserted that the doctrine of inerrancy was essentially a theological doctrine concerning the character of God, and only secondarily a bibliological doctrine concerning the nature of the Bible. He called this doctrine of the inerrancy "doxological" in the sense that it is an expression of praise toward the God whom we know as the Author of Scripture.[7]

Again, this is the core question, now formulated a bit differently: Is there a direct coherence between the trustworthiness of God and the technical accuracy of the Bible? Would God be less trustworthy than we thought if we were to encounter a technical inaccuracy in the Bible? There are three possible answers:

(a) God's trustworthiness is absolute; it cannot countenance any inaccuracies in the Bible. So yes, the Bible *cannot* contain technical inaccuracies because this would shock our faith in God's perfection. A perfect God produces a perfect Scripture.

> Response: This answer must be wrong, because God *is* absolutely trustworthy, nonetheless there *may be* technical inaccuracies in the Bible, as we will see.

(b) God's trustworthiness is absolute; it cannot countenance any errors. However, the technical inaccuracies that we do—or that some claim to—find in the Bible are insignificant; that is, they do not threaten the Bible's inerrancy.

> Response: At a minimum, this answer is inaccurate, even self-contradictory: it basically says that there *are* errors in the Bible, but that these do not threaten the Bible's errorlessness. In other words, the Bible is sometimes erroneous, yet it is inerrant.

(c) God's trustworthiness is absolute but exists on a level

---

7. Brown (1984b, 389).

other than matters that might comprise technical inaccuracies. I fully trust my wife, even if I sometimes encounter inaccuracies in the things she says. The two things simply have little to do with each other.

> Response: This answer is unsatisfactory to many: is God trustworthy for instance in his promises, but not when it comes to contradictions (e.g., between the books of Sam. and Kings, and Chron.; see §10.6.1), erroneous descriptions of nature (e.g., the hare chewing the cud, Lev. 11:6; insects that walk on four legs instead of six, v. 21), the use of hyperbole (e.g., the furnace was heated "seven times" more than earlier, Dan. 3:19) and the use of vague descriptions (see §8.4.3, "about" so many). We must now enter a bit more deeply into this matter of God's trustworthiness.

10.2 "Trustworthy" Is Not "Inerrant"

10.2.1 The Faith Level

Starting from an ontological dualism of the natural and the supernatural (see §9.4), inerrantism defends an infallible and inerrant Bible that arose from the supernatural sphere. Personally, I accept the supernatural as such, on the level of faith. I accept the errorlessness of the Bible, and I believe that the Bible speaks with divine authority and reliability about all kinds of matters, including matters in the fields of history, nature, and the cosmos. Nonetheless, I prefer to call my view "credibilism." That is, I believe in the credibility, the complete trustworthiness, the perfect reliability, and the divine authority of Scripture on the level of *faith*, but not necessarily in any *scientific* respect (whether in the field of the natural or of the historical sciences). To me, a reliable Bible need not be a scientifically accurate Bible (whatever this phrase may mean).

For inerrantists this is insufficient, however. They ground the supernaturality of this perfect product of divine activity — the Bible — in a rationalistic, scientistic concept of inerrancy, such that the smallest error — or merely something viewed as erroneous—would annul this supernaturality and credibility of Scripture. The notion of inerrancy is insufficient; the notion must be *scientifically warranted*. Only a scientifically correct Bible is thought to be fitting for God—as if any scientific theories could serve as the criterion to establish what is and is not fitting for God.

In many different ways, inerrantists throughout the centuries have warned against the danger of casually accepting errors in the Bible. This is because, in their view, the slightest error would affect the Bible's credibility. We need only think here of the sixteenth-century adage: "false in one (point), (then actually) false in all (points)" (Lat. *falsus in uno, falsus in omnibus*).[8] If just one small error could be shown in the Bible, this would be enough to ruin its inerrancy, for how could we know whether there might not be (many) other small, or larger, errors in the Bible? We would not be able to trust the Bible at all. It is like a hydraulic system: the smallest oil leak renders the entire system worthless.

Wolfhart Pannenberg mentioned Andreas Quenstedt and Melchior Leydekker as examples of this line of thinking.[9] They were part of early Protestant scholasticism. A twentieth-century example was Edward J. Young. He defended the thesis that either Scripture is infallible in *everything* it says, or we can no longer be certain that it is infallible in *anything* it says. He also argued that claiming errors or mistakes in the *autographa* is the same as claiming errors or mistakes in God himself.[10]

10.2.2 The Theoretical Level

The ideas mentioned in the previous section are notions with which I can wholeheartedly sympathize *on the level of pre-theoretical,* even *supra-rational faith*. I confess that God's Word is perfect because God is perfect. "The law of the LORD is perfect,

---

8. Erickson (1998, 253) prefers the slogan "false in one, uncertain in all"—which, in fact, is just as untenable.
9. Pannenberg (1991, 32, 34–35).
10. Edward Young (1957, 103, 123; also see 5, 48, 54, 88, 109, 185, 269).

The Credibilist View of Scripture

reviving the soul; the testimony of the LORD is sure, making wise the simple" (Ps. 19:7). However, as soon as such a statement of *faith* becomes a *theological postulate*, I believe that highly overrated human reason is again overruling the wonder of biblical inspiration. Thus, Edward J. Young stated explicitly that the *autographa* are infallible and inerrant, not only from a confessional but also from a scientific point of view.[11]

This is an incredible overestimation of science; in other words, this is *scientism*. The point that disturbs me is not so much the *idea* of the infallible functioning supernaturally, miraculously in a fallible world. Rather it is the scientific rationalism of Young's postulate. Ultimately, science becomes the referee to establish the perfect inerrancy of the Bible: Scripture is so perfect that *even science* cannot find any errors in it. Out of a longing for logical-analytical, theoretical-scientific evidence, any conceivable uncertainty is excluded *a priori* by placing the Bible, so to speak, in the supernatural and therefore unassailable sphere. This line of thinking seeks to exclude any scientific error that human reason might believe to be able to point out in the *autographa*.[12] Scripture is placed in a realm of unassailable supernatural perfection—but the gateway to judge this perfection is human, fallible, defective science. How could people ever invent such a thought?

This scientific certainty is based upon the following argument: God is perfect and cannot lie; God has revealed himself to humanity in Scripture; therefore the written Word must be perfect, that is, free of lies, of all falsehood; errors and mistakes are basically forms of lies; therefore the written Word cannot contain any errors or mistakes; if errors are identified in the Bible, they invariably are the kind of errors that do not threaten inerrancy. Science is accepted as the great referee to prove to the so-called objective mind that the theses just mentioned are indeed perfectly true.[13] There are no errors in God,

---

11. Ibid., 64.
12. Cf. Berkouwer (1966, 32–33).
13. Beegle (1973, 199).

so there can be no errors in his Word—and science has the task of proving this, is able to prove this, and actually does prove this.

B. B. Warfield's definition of inspiration was, "What the Bible says, God says." Of course, we basically agree with this. However, it is not without reason that Clark H. Pinnock said with respect to this slogan that Warfield's *arguments* for it, given the context in which he said it, were based on a deduction from *a priori* theological assumptions rather than on a conclusion founded upon Scripture itself.[14] In other words, what Warfield was basically doing was proclaiming a theological thesis, not the Bible. Maybe this sounds like a harsh judgment by Pinnock—but it is hard to see how we can avoid or contradict it.

10.2.3 Infallibility and Inerrancy

Indeed, Scripture is the Word *of God*. But if we too easily equate the two—God and his Word—then we easily ignore the humanness of the Bible. *God speaks*, but he does so through human words. When God speaks, he does so perfectly. But when he speaks in and through human words, is it self-evident that these human words are just as perfect? Can *perfect* human vernacular exist? If words are human, they cannot be perfect; if they are perfect, they cannot be human. These are the central questions of the chapters 9 and 10 of this book. Bruce Vawter argued that, if God really condescended to the human sphere without the human Scripture containing errors, this would mean that God had altered this human sphere into something else. A piece of human literature without any error would indeed be an inner contradiction, since nothing is more human than to err.[15] In other words, to be human and to be errorless are incompatible. If this is true, in what possible way could we speak of an errorless Scripture?

In view of this line of argument, some would prefer the

---

14. Pinnock (1984, 158–59).
15. Vawter (1972, 169).

term "infallibility." The two terms, infallibility and inerrancy, are sometimes viewed as synonymous, and at other times they are distinguished. In the latter case, infallibility is taken in a somewhat narrower sense than inerrancy. As Carl F. H. Henry put it, inerrancy refers only to the *autographa* as the tremendous achievement of divine inspiration, whereas infallibility is a more qualified or conditional perfection of the copies (Lat. *apographa*) of the *autographa*.[16] This means that copies communicate to humanity in a reliable and authoritative way the revealed truth and purposes of God. The copies or transcriptions of the original writings retain the epistemic consequences of the divine inspiration of the inerrant prophetic-apostolic *autographa* in such a way that they authoritatively communicate the truth about God and his purposes.[17]

I cannot find this a very satisfactory presentation of things. Bert Loonstra rightly asked, "What purpose could the Holy Spirit have had with inspiring an inerrant Bible, which he subsequently surrendered to the mistakes of fallible copyists? In this case, the unity and the perfection of God's works would be lost."[18] Indeed, this basic and obvious objection must arise in the mind of every person who hears inerrantists appealing to perfect *autographs* that no longer exist, and thus cannot be checked: *Why did God produce inerrant autographs without taking care that these would be preserved?* A second question that arises here is: *If God allowed the autographs to get lost, why did he not ensure that inerrant copies would be made?* In other words, why take the trouble of producing inerrant *autographs* in the first place, if today we possess only erring copies? At this point we must discuss these questions somewhat more extensively.

10.3 Unverifiability

10.3.1 Three Shortcomings

I repeat that my objections involve a theological postulate, not

---

16. Henry (1979b, 243).
17. Ibid., 246.
18. Loonstra (1999, 29).

a belief. Christians accept Scripture as the authoritative, reliable Word of God. They read the Bible as their daily food in order to know and serve God and his Son Jesus Christ ever better. As such they do not care at all about whether there might possibly be scientific shortcomings in the Bible. Faith itself does not even *know* this problem. None of the great heroes of the Bible, if they had Scriptures at their disposal, ever bothered about their scientific accuracy. Even if certain questions could have been raised, these would be the bones on which theologians can ruin their teeth, whereas the meat is for believers[19] (of course, we realize that some believers are theologians, and vice versa). Their conviction concerning the trustworthiness of the Bible is not affected at all by such questions.[20]

However, as we have seen, what is at stake in the inerrantist movement is not only a faith presupposition but a theoretical postulate, which is primarily based upon rationalistic *a priori* assumptions, and on an optimistic scientism. Not only are these philosophical roots invalid, but they are methodologically shaky as well. The inerrantist postulate—"Scripture is inerrant also scientifically"—suffers from at least three methodological shortcomings:

(a) As we just saw, this postulate is neither verifiable nor falsifiable, because the *autographa* are lacking; there is nothing scientific about an appeal to evidence that is no longer available to anyone (see §10.3.2 below).

(b) The inerrantist postulate is neither verifiable nor falsifiable, because it is impossible to formulate clear, universally acceptable, objective criteria for the distinction between errors that threaten inerrancy and errors that do not. Therefore, the postulate can only exist as a circular argument: because the Bible is *a priori* inerrant it cannot contain any errors that threaten inerrancy (see §§10.4 and 10.5 below).

---

19. The image is old; it goes back at least to Heinrich Frauenlob (c. 1300) and Hans Rosenplüt (fifteenth century).
20. Cf. Van Bruggen (1986, 98–101).

(c) This inerrantist postulate is not at all the pivotal point when it comes to the credibility of the Bible (see §10.6 and following).

10.3.2 The Missing *Autographa*

It is not difficult to explain the first shortcoming mentioned in the previous section. The point is that the inerrantist postulate does not refer to our modern Bibles, for these do contain a number of translational and printing errors. Nor does it refer to the original text on which these translations are based. As far as textual criticism has been able to establish, we have a Hebrew, Aramaic, and Greek text that has been handed down in an exceptionally accurate way. However, this text is not perfect, since at numerous (albeit minor) points, there are doubts about the precise original text. Therefore, the inerrantist postulate refers only to the *autographa*;[21] these writings provide the basis for the logical-theoretical certainty of the inerrantist. Therefore, in certain cases of (supposed) errors in the Bible, the inerrantist will take refuge in the *autographa*. The inerrantist will quietly assert that the error cannot have been in these original writings, even when the supposedly correct reading has been preserved in not a single extant Bible manuscript.

No matter how strange this may sound, the *autographa* no longer exist. The inerrantist foundation is vacuous. The absolutely scientific inerrancy of the *autographa* can be neither demonstrated nor refuted. Thus, on the one hand, they provide scientific certainty for the inerrantist, and on the other hand, like a valuable treasure, the *autographa* are safely beyond the reach of science.[22] This too is scientism, a "faith in science" of which inerrantists (rightly) accuse liberal theology without realizing that they adhere to basically the same faith. Therefore, what Harold O. J. Brown wrote is correct on the level of faith, but not on the theological level. He argued

---

21. See, e.g., Bahnsen (1979).
22. See Loetscher (1954, 25).

that, insofar as the Bible's inerrancy is unverifiable *a posteriori*, it must be defended *a priori* on the basis of the evidence collected from the extant, not-autographic texts, starting from knowledge that believers already possess or to which they are committed by faith.[23]

Please note, I am not saying that because the *autographa* no longer exist, it does not matter whether they contained errors. This is what Gleason L. Archer wrongly suggested with respect to those who emphasize that the *autographa* no longer exist.[24] What I am saying is that the notion of inerrant *autographa* is based on a postulate of faith, one that is not necessarily wrong or right, but one that, because of its unverifiability, cannot, and ought not, serve as a *theological* postulate (see §10.4 below).

However, even as a postulate of faith this notion is hardly anything more than a rationalist conclusion from a theoretical reasoning concerning God's perfection and Scripture's inerrancy that should follow from this perfection. Moreover, this is not at all how Scripture speaks about its own credibility. The Bible rarely refers to its *autographa*, and certainly not to inerrant *autographa*. The entire notion is a nothing but a theological construct. Bible passages such as 2 Timothy 3:16-17 (see §7.3) and 2 Peter 1:19-21 (see §7.5), classical proof texts regarding the doctrine of biblical inspiration, refer to copies of the Old Testament that were available to Paul and Peter at that moment, not to *autographa* that might differ from transcribed copies. Moreover, a passage such as 2 Timothy 3:16-17 is not at all a theoretical statement about the nature and possible inerrancy of Scripture but about its divine origin and its practical effects in believers' lives.[25]

10.3.3 Inerrant Copies and Translations

Again, we may wonder why, if the inerrant *autographa* are

---

23. Brown (1984b, 388).
24. Archer Jr. (1982, 28).
25. Pinnock (1984, XVIII, 40).

The Credibilist View of Scripture

so crucial for the logical-theoretical certainty of inerrantism, these have not been preserved by God's providence. Or, if God allowed these manuscripts to be lost, why did God not transfer this inerrancy to the copies, or even to the translations?

In fact, this is exactly what the most extreme North American inerrantists believe. They are convinced that, by God's miraculous providence, the text of the inerrant *autographa* was preserved fully in the Masoretic text of the Old Testament, and the Byzantine text of the New Testament (which coincides to a large extent with the Received Text [Lat. *Textus Receptus*], the first printed Greek text of the New Testament [1516]). I dealt with this matter in §8.7 above, and I tried to show that neither the Masoretic text nor the Byzantine text can be viewed as perfect. These texts are astonishingly accurate—but this is something essentially different from being inerrant. A little knowledge of textual criticism and its scientific starting points suffices to understand that neither text is inerrant. The Masoretic text differs from the Septuagint and from the Dead Sea Scrolls (and who can determine which of these preserved the original text in any disputed passage?), and the Byzantine text differs from the Alexandrian text and the Western text (and we have seen why the latter texts often must be preferred).

This kind of extremism can go one step further to claim that the King James Version is an absolutely inerrant translation of the Bible. A remarkable example of this is the astronomer Gerardus D. Bouw, who is also a geocentrist.[26] He believes that the KJV is the inspired Word of God for English-speaking people. I once asked him how many errors in the KJV I should show to him, but he was not interested. The NKJV has corrected many of the errors of the KJV, and of course has introduced some new ones, because every Bible translation is fallible. Being of Dutch descent, Bouw must be familiar with the highly

---

26. http://www.geocentricity.com/bibastron/bouw_bio.html.

venerated Dutch States Translation (1637, twenty-six years younger than the KJV). The two translations are quite similar, yet differ on many points, just as both of them differ from Luther's German translation (1545) or the—so much better—Italian Bible of the Calvinist Giovanni Diodati (1649), or the French Bible of the brothers Lemaistre (1695). None of these versions is identical. My question to Bouw was, and still is: Why would God give an inerrant Bible only to English-speaking people, and not to any other nation of the Reformation? The entire idea is a romantic illusion.

Personally, I feel far more at home with the following words by the thoroughly orthodox Herman Bavinck:

> Scripture does not satisfy the demand for exact knowledge in the way we demand it in mathematics, astronomy, chemistry, etc. This is a standard that may not be applied to it. For that reason, moreover the autographa were lost; for that reason the text—to whatever small degree this is the case—is corrupt [i.e., contains errors]; for that reason the church, and truly not just the layman, has the Bible only in defective and fallible translations. These are undeniable facts.[27]

So it is. But our translations (especially the most literal ones) are remarkably close to what the Bible writers must have written.

10.4 Unfalsifiablity

10.4.1 Errors That Do Not Threaten Inerrancy

According to common epistemological criteria, the theory of inerrant *autographa*—that is, emphatically as a *theory*—is unscientific and therefore theologically useless, since it is neither verifiable nor falsifiable, because the *autographa* are missing. However, there is an even more important reason why the theory is unfalsifiable, and therefore unscientific. This is the absence of clear, universally acceptable criteria regarding what exactly must be understood by "error" and "(in)erran-

---

27. Bavinck (*RD* 1:444).

cy." The inerrantist should indicate *a priori* the criteria that determine what certain errors can be accepted in Scripture without affecting its inerrancy, and what errors definitely should *not* be accepted in the Bible because they *would* affect its inerrancy. In this way, the inerrantist must indicate precisely the essential difference between these two categories of (supposed) errors: those that threaten inerrancy and those that do not.

It may seem harsh to demand that the inerrantist supply such objective criteria, but we must not forget that it is the *inerrantist* who has adorned the notion of inerrancy with a halo of scientific accuracy. Any person who does so must be the first to endeavor to satisfy solid methodological criteria.

In order to illustrate how and why it is impossible to make a scientific distinction between errors that threaten inerrancy and errors that do not, let us recall what was quoted earlier from Article 13 (see §10.1.2 above): inerrantists "deny that inerrancy is negated by Biblical phenomena such as a lack of modern technical precision, irregularities of grammar or spelling, observational descriptions of nature, the reporting of falsehoods, the use of hyperbole and round numbers, the topical arrangement of material, variant selections of material in parallel accounts, or the use of free citations." I will discuss these points in summary fashion, and also add a few examples that the authors apparently had in mind.

The first case mentioned is a *lack of modern technical precision*. An interesting example here is 1 Kings 7:23, where the "sea of cast metal" (the priestly washing basin) in Solomon's temple is described this way: "It was round, ten cubits from brim to brim, and five cubits high, and a line of thirty cubits measured its circumference." This gives for π a value of 3, which is indeed rather imprecise (π is 3.14159265358...). Harold Lindsell "solved" the problem through the (forced) assumption that the circumference (thirty cubits) was measured on the inside of the basin, and the diameter (ten cubits) on the outside. The diameter on the inside would then be about 9.55 cubits (or 30 divided by π) 9.55 cubits, and the rim would thus be 0.45 cubits wide (between 7.87 and 9.45 inches, which is very wide).[28] Of course, the text says nothing about an inside and an outside; moreover, it would be quite unlikely to measure the circumference on the inside of the basin.

We could also think here of the examples mentioned earlier (§8.4.3), such as the *"about* twelve men" mentioned in Acts 9:17 (with such a small group, why not provide the precise number?). Actually, this has little to do with technical precision, but rather with the fact that the author Luke apparently did not know exactly how many men there were. Of course, one could argue that it does not really matter for understanding the story whether there were, eleven, twelve, or thirteen men. But this is not the point. The point is that a *scientifically* inerrant Bible would have either omitted the number or provided the precise number. It is the same with Luke elsewhere: Anna was "about" 84 years of age (Luke 2:37), the daughter of Jairus was "about" 12 (8:42), the transfiguration on the mountain was "about eight days" later (9:28), whereas the Holy Spirit could easily have supplied an exact number.

Please note, I must repeat that my point is not that there *are* errors in the Bible; my point is that a *scientific* inerrantism is obliged to show less indulgence toward such inaccuracies. The Bible's numbers must be perfect, or else it is not inerrant.

10.4.2 Observational Descriptions of Nature

The biblical descriptions of nature must not be judged according to criteria drawn from modern natural sciences. For instance, the water in Egypt changed into blood (Exod. 7:17–21), but who believes that this was *literal* blood: a biotic, liquid tissue full of erythrocytes, leukocytes, and trombocites? Scientifically speaking this was an error: the changed water *looked like* blood but it was not real blood. Job 29:18 speaks of a phoenix

---

28. Lindsell (1976, 165–66).

(Heb. *chol*),[29] but such an animal does not really exist, just like the unicorn in Numbers 23:22 (KJV; Heb. *re'ēm*), the basilisk in Psalm 91:13 (DRA; Heb. *peten*), and the satyr in Isaiah 34:14 (KJV; lamia in DRA; Heb. *sair*). We should not think that the latter are simply wrong translations; maybe the other translations did not dare to render what the Hebrew text really says!

Acts 27:27 contains an "error" that scarcely any translation renders honestly, except Darby (also cf. DLNT, YLT) ". . . the sailors supposed that some land neared them." Almost all translations have something like this: "the sailors suspected that they were nearing land" (ESV; cf. "even" the KJV).This is of course what happened; but it is not what the original text says. Scientifically speaking, this is an error: the land was not nearing the ship, but the ship was nearing the land.

In Luke 23:45, the text says that the sun "stopped shining" (thus many translations; Gk. *tou hēliou eklipontos*), which scientifically speaking—and this is what inerrantists want—is simply wrong. The translation "the sun was darkened" (ESV) is inaccurate because it suggests an eclipse of the sun (a mistake enhanced by the Gk. *eklipontos*, the word from which the English word "eclipse" was derived). However, there was a full moon, and a common eclipse of the sun is possible only at new moon.

Other mistakes—at least scientifically speaking, but this is the way inerrantists want to have it—are the notion that the grain of wheat, when it falls into the earth, literally "dies" (John 12:24; 1 Cor. 15:36), or that the mustard seed "is the smallest of all the seeds on earth" (Mark 4:31). I have not the slightest problem with such statements, and would not even call them "errors." But according to the scientistic demands of the inerrantists they are definitely "errors." They even admit this (see again Article 13) but declare that these errors do not threaten inerrancy. I would not know why not, except for the inerrantist circular argument: the Bible is *a priori* without er-

---

29. If this is the correct translation (CJB); others read "sand" (KJV, ESV).

rors, so all errors in the Bible are non-errors.

Not all such errors can be attributed to ordinary, everyday observation. The latter *is* the explanation for such common expressions such as "the sun rises" and "the sun sets." But this cannot be true, for instance, when it comes to expressions such as the "pillars" (Heb. *ammudim*) of the earth (Job 9:6; Ps. 75:3; cf. Job 26:11). No ordinary, everyday observer has ever seen anything that resembles such a thing like "pillars" under the earth. Some render the word as "foundations," but mistakenly so, because everywhere in the Old Testament the meaning is "pillars." The next step is to apply this term to the earth's lowest strata, which no Bible writer ever thought about, of course. But even this does not really solve the problem because no ordinary observer has ever observed these "foundations." Moreover, with such a rendering, what could possibly be the "pillars/foundations" of *heaven* (Job 26:11)? Rather, we must say that these "pillars" seem to be a reminder of the (creative) worldview of antiquity, which, according to modern cosmology, is thoroughly erroneous.

10.4.3 Other Cases of Possible Errors

Irregularities of grammar or spelling. Especially in the book of Revelation we find a number of remarkable grammatical errors, which can occasionally be easily explained.[30] Thus, Revelation 1:4 literally says, "... from the being [One] and he who was, and he the coming [One]," that is, "he" instead of "him," plus a participle (twice) and an imperfect (once). No Greek teacher would accept such things in any student's exam. The explanation is that, apparently, the writer takes the expression "he the being [One] and he who was, and he the coming [One]" as a standing name of God (cf. 1:8; 11:17; 16:5).[31] But this does not change the fact that this is a grammatical error.

---

30. Cf. Ouweneel (1988, 8–9; 1990, 36, 39, 72, 121, 160).
31. In Hebrew, the phrase would be something like this: *hahoweh wehayah weyabo*; see the Hebrew New Testament published by the United Bible Societies (1976).

Further, anyone consulting the apparatus of Nestle-Aland (see §8.7.2) can see how many spelling variants there are in the text of the New Testament, only one of which in each case could have been the original reading. Apparently, this kind of error constitutes no problem for the Holy Spirit.

The topical arrangement of material. As far as the synoptic Gospels are concerned, a careful comparison leads many to assume that Mark follows most, and Luke least, the chronological order of events. Sometimes, Luke arranges the stories in a way suggesting that they follow in chronologically sequence (e.g., 23:45-46).[32] At every place where the author departs from the correct chronological order without accounting for this, we would have to say, according to our criteria of historical-scientific accuracy, that the text is erroneous. However, only the scientistic inerrantist should be bothered by such supposed errors.

The use of free citations. Some striking examples are the quotations in John 7:38; 1 Corinthians 2:9; 2 Corinthians 6:17-18 from the Old Testament, for which we can find at most some vaguely similar statements (see §6.3.2). According to the scientistic demands of inerrantism, such quotations are simply wrong, for the text says, "Scripture says," whereas in reality Scripture (i.e., the Old Testament) says nothing of the kind.[33]

10.4.4 Variant Selections of Material in Parallel Accounts

A study of parallel parts in the Bible is worthwhile to give us an idea of variant selections of material. We find many examples of this in the Gospels, and also in the parallel parts in Samuel/Kings and Chronicles.[34] One of the conclusions from such comparisons is that, in some cases, supposedly erroneous impressions are created. In Acts 9:26, it seems as if the apostle Paul's visit to Jerusalem took place very shortly after his conversion, whereas we must conclude from Galatians

---

32. See Ouweneel (2007, 208).
33. For an answer, see Silva (1983); Nicole (1984b).
34. See the extensive examples mentioned by Loonstra (1994, 29-41).

1:15–18 that there were three years in between.³⁵ According to scientific standards, Luke is inaccurate.

Recall the famous words of Abraham Kuyper about the very words (Lat. *ipsissima verba*) of Jesus (his own words, which he literally spoke):

> When in the four Gospels Jesus, on the same occasion, is made to say words that are different in form of expression, it is impossible that He should have used these four forms at once. The Holy Spirit, however, merely intends to make an impression upon the Church which wholly corresponds to what Jesus said.³⁶

An examples of this is Matthew 19:17 ("Why do you ask me about what is good? There is only one who is good") *versus* Mark 10:18 and Luke 18:19 ("Why do you call me good? No one is good except God alone"). Matthew seems to weaken Jesus' words, presumably in order not to give the impression that Jesus would deny his own goodness.

There are more occasions where Matthew seems to weaken Mark's wording. For instance, Mark 6:5 says, "And he could do *no* mighty work there," but Matthew 13:58 says regarding the same occasion, "And he did *not* do *many* mighty works there."

Other problems involved in harmonizing parallel Bible stories belong to a similar category. Thus, we find considerable discrepancies in the accounts of Peter's denial of Jesus. Harold Lindsell suggested that we solve these discrepancies by an "additive" harmonization, based on no fewer than six denials by Peter.³⁷ In this way, all the three reports (in the synoptic Gospels) are salvaged! But no, Jesus clearly foretold to Peter that the latter would deny him *three* times, not four, five,

---

35. See Ouweneel (1997a, 79–80).
36. Kuyper (1898, 550); quoted by Bavinck (though with some differences in the English translation) (*RD* 1:444) and Berkouwer (1966, 218).
37. Lindsell (1976, 174–76).

or six (Matt. 26:34; Mark 14:30; Luke 22:34).[38] Here we see the contortions of inerrantists who need to satisfy their own scientistic demand of smoothing all the wrinkles.

Bluffing does not help us very much here. For instance, B. B. Warfield wrote that not a single error has ever been demonstrated in the Scriptures, namely, in the sense that no evidence whatsoever can ever transform an apparent difficulty into a proven error.[39] British theologians Richard P. C. Hanson and Anthony T. Hanson wrote the following parody of this: not a single error has ever been encountered in the Scriptures that could not be explained away by applying the inventive imagination and assuming the most improbable conjectures.[40] Indeed, the statement by Warfield was meaningless because he never told us in advance what evidence he considered acceptable. In this way, he could simply brush from the table any kind of (apparent or real) evidence. His thesis was, and is, unfalsifiable; it is always possible to invent ingenious hypotheses to explain (away) alleged errors.

We seldom hear about those cases for which, in my view, such a method of explanation is absolutely impossible. Thus, Jesus says in the parable of the tenants (Matt. 21:40–41): "When therefore the owner of the vineyard comes, what will he do to those tenants?" They [i.e., the spiritual leaders] said to him, "He will put those wretches to a miserable death and let out the vineyard to other tenants who will give him the fruits in their seasons." However, in Luke 20:15–16, the dialogue is presented as follows: "What then will the owner of the vineyard do to them? He will come and destroy those tenants and give the vineyard to others." When they [i.e., the spiritual leaders] heard this, they said, "Surely not!" In Matthew, the suggestion about giving the vineyard to others comes from Jesus' opponents; but in Luke, Jesus himself makes this suggestion,

---

38. Regarding the problem of harmonization, see Blomberg (1986).
39. Warfield (1948, 225).
40. Hanson and Hanson (1990, 54); see the discussion by Goldingay (1994, 268–73).

and the opponents respond to this with indignation.[41] At best, one of the two authors can have transmitted the correct version; according to the inerrantists' own scientific logic, the other version thus is simply wrong. I could not imagine how the two versions could be plausibly harmonized in a way that does reasonable justice to both of them.

10.5   Conclusions

10.5.1   What I Am *Not* Saying

What is my message in the previous sections? There are two claims that I am *not* making.

(a) I do not deny that, at least for some "errors," plausible explanations might be given—although I must say that in many cases the offered solutions seem rather twisted and forced.[42] We can only admire the ingenuity of many authors, who diligently supply us with such explanations, even though we cannot with a good conscience accept many of these subterfuges.

(b) I did not make my remarks with the intention of demonstrating that there *are* apparent mistakes in the Bible, as if this were in the interest of my argument. On the contrary, to me the Bible is the absolutely trustworthy Word of God. What I do argue is that those who construe a *theory* in with the Bible's reliability is linked to the non-occurrence of errors in the Bible are simply making a claim that is scientifically void. This is because any opponent who chooses to do so could refer to all the points mentioned as errors in the Bible. The inerrantists will categorically contradict him, but they will not be capable of refuting their opponent's arguments. The reason is that they *do not have a scientific criterion* by which to distinguish between errors that are acceptable (i.e., they do not threaten inerrancy) and those that are unacceptable (i.e., they do threaten inerrancy).

---

41. See Ouweneel (2007, 212).
42. See the "encyclopedia" of Archer Jr. (1982), and the similar work by Geisler and Howe (1992), although in both volumes a discussion of some of the most embarrassing "problems" is lacking.

10.5.2 The Falsifiability Criterion

The Austrian-British philosopher Karl R. Popper (1994) sought the criterion for good science in (a) the principal falsifiability of a theory, and, we may add, (b) in the number of falsification attempts that a theory has survived.[43] Verified theories do not exist, for verification would demand an infinite number of tests. The thesis "all swans are white" can hardly be verified, for in that case we would have to examine all swans in the universe. However, in principle the thesis can be very easily falsified: we need only one swan of a different color to refute it.

A good theory is a theory that allows for risky predictions about the outcome of scientific problems that have not yet been investigated — risky because they might not come true. The thesis "all swans are white" satisfies this criterion, for it has the following implication: "each next swan that is encountered will turn out to be white as well." This is a risky prediction, which is falsified by the very first swan of a different color that is encountered.

According to this — by now famous — criterion of Popper, inerrantism is a bad theory because it is a basically unfalsifiable theory. This means, it is *a priori* impossible to discover an error in Scripture that would refute the notion of its inerrancy. If such an error were found, inerrantism would either argue this error away, or declare it to be an error that does not threaten inerrancy.

If inerrancy were only a matter of faith, then I too believe in an absolutely reliable Bible. However, the inerrantist tries to elevate it to the level of a scientific theory. This leads to problems for the theory, for in this case it is unfalsifiable, and thus, according to Popper, a *bad* theory. That is, a theory that explains everything (in this case, every irregularity in the Bible), explains nothing. *Faith* knows that the Bible is perfectly credible. A *theory* that wishes to demonstrate this has no

---

43. Popper (2002a; 2002b).

basis. Possible errors are immediately reduced to either the category of the "merely apparent errors" or the category of those that do not threaten inerrancy. Thus, the entire theory is a circular argument: the Bible is God's Word – therefore it cannot contain any errors – all errors that nonetheless are encountered are declared to be non-real errors.

The inerrancy theory can prove anything the inerrantist wishes, and thus it proves nothing. The sad thing is that this can damage even the viewpoint the inerrantist so eagerly wishes to defend. For if the inerrancy theory itself is refuted – which is not so difficult, as I am trying to demonstrate – people might easily conclude that *therefore* the Bible is errant. This is the intention of neither the inerrantists themselves nor believing theologians who refute their theory. Yet, inerrantists are responsible for the fact that such a mistaken conclusion indeed may be drawn.

10.6 "Errors Are Allowed"

10.6.1 Irregularities

On the level of faith, the Christian does not have – or ought not have – the slightest difficulty with irregularities encountered in the Bible. This is not because a Christian simply believes everything. A man once told me that he believed that although the whale swallowed Jonah, if the Bible had told him that Jonah had swallowed the whale, he would have believed that. I hope this is not characteristic of the average Christian. Casper Labuschagne wrote, "That one should believe certain things blindly, and thus sideline one's intellect, is not only an unreasonable demand; it is also harmful for one's faith."[44] And, I would add, for one's intellect.

A thinking Christian does not believe everything. A Christian would find Scripture very untrustworthy if it would declare that the earth was carried on the back of elephants, which are standing on a great turtle swimming in the cosmic

---

44. Labuschagne (2000, 17).

ocean, as a Hindu tradition has it.[45] A Christian would find Scripture very untrustworthy if the biblical story of Noah's Flood would resemble the Babylonian version, with its cube-shaped, and thus totally unseaworthy ark, its quarreling, immoral gods, humans elevated to divinity, and so on.[46] It is an outright miracle that, in contrast with so many ancient writings, the Bible is free of this kind of ideas. Faith sharply senses the differences between the irregularities in the Bible and the kind of nonsense encountered in so many ancient writings.[47] Moses was instructed in all the wisdom of the Egyptians (Acts 7:22), but the Holy Spirit kept him from introducing any Egyptian mythology and pseudo-science into the Torah.

However, for the inerrantist this is insufficient. The inerrantist demands that the Bible's high quality be *theoretical-scientifically* established. This implies that one cannot allow the smallest discrepancy because, as we saw, to the inerrantist one single error would annul the credibility of the entire Bible.[48] It is important that we try to imagine what this entails. Take, for instance, the contradictory numbers in the stories of Israel's kings.[49] In 2 Samuel 8:4, David takes captive 700 or 1,700 horsemen of Hadadezer (depending on the translation; cf., e.g., KJV and ESV), but according to 1 Chronicles 18:4 there were 7,000 horsemen (as the Septuagint has in 2 Sam. 8:4). Similarly, did he kill 700 Aramean charioteers (2 Sam. 10:18), or 7,000 (1 Chron. 19:18)? Did Joab count 800,000 fighting men in Israel, and 500,000 in Judah (2 Sam. 24:9), or were they 1,100,000 and 470,000, respectively (1 Chron. 21:5)? Did the bronze basin hold 2,000 bath (i.e., about 44,000 liters) (1

---

45. https://en.wikipedia.org/wiki/World_Turtle.
46. Cf. Ouweneel (1978, 80).
47. See many examples in Hobrink (2005).
48. Cf. one of Van Keulen's summary statements of G. C. Berkouwer's view (2003, 533): "Scripture may not be measured with a concept of reliability that is characterized by exactness, precision, accuracy, and neutrality."
49. Harris (1995, 94–95) points out that some of these contradictions have disappeared through study of the Dead Sea Scrolls (see the NIV notes at the relevant Bible verses).

Kings 7:26), or 3,000 bath (2 Chron. 4:5, about 66,000 liters)? Was Ahaziah 22 when he became king of Judah (2 Kings 8:26), or was he 42 (2 Chron. 22:2)?

I could continue like this.[50] Please notice that these are cases in which discrepancies can be discovered only because of the parallel historiography that we find in Samuel/Kings and in Chronicles. But what about all the numbers in Bible stories for which we have no biblical or other parallels? How can we know whether *these* numbers are correct?

It is obvious that inerrantists cannot simply brush such discrepancies from the table because, according to them, one of these little contradictions would be sufficient to endanger the credibility of the entire Bible. Therefore, as we saw, in such cases they take refuge to (often very sophisticated) interpretations, or assume copying errors—usually without any manuscript evidence—or errorless *autographa*, which is rather unfair since the latter can no longer be consulted. Gleason L. Archer said that there is nothing that proves that such discrepancies existed in the original manuscripts of Samuel and Chronicles.[51] This is entirely correct—but the opposite is also true: there is no proof that such (supposed) discrepancies did *not* exist in the *autographa* of Samuel and Chronicles. The entire argument is void and meaningless.

10.6.2 Restrictiveness

Andree Troost summarized and answered the underlying problem very well:

> Also think ... of the differences or "flaws" (an obscuring term!) between the books of Samuel, Kings and Chronicles. It would be a mistake to view these "*stories*" as exact scientific presentations of facts, in order to speak subsequently either, in a biblical-critical sense, of "contradictions in the Bible," or, in a fundamentalist sense, to "harmonize" the stories concerned. The latter is

---

50. Cf. Blomberg (1986, 162–66) for other differences between Kings and Chronicles.
51. Archer Jr. (1979, 60).

done because, on the basis of a *rationalistic* (scientistic) *version* of our Christian faith in the inspiration, in scientific-historical respect they could not or *may* not conflict with each other. As if Scripture would use a scientific concept of truth instead of a practical *faith* idea of truth, in direct orientation upon the *fulness* of the truth that is "in Christ": "*I am* the truth" [John 14:6].[52]

What strikes me in the entire argument of the inerrantists is the kind of restrictive attitude to which their rationalistic view of inerrancy leads. Every irregularity must be smoothed out at all cost with sometimes very ingenuous arguments, sometimes even with an appeal to inaccessible sources. In opposition to this, Jakob van Bruggen rightly pleaded for a certain relaxation.[53] He argued that, as a consequence of the great distance in time and culture, we should not be amazed if many irregularities are problematic for us that perhaps were not so for the original readers. This is an important point. In opposition to the inerrantists, who make a scientific postulate of the inerrancy of the Bible, I claim that this postulate is unfalsifiable because in many cases we do not even know whether real errors are involved, and today we *cannot* know.

Van Bruggen also warned against the restrictiveness of the inerrantists, who apparently believe that the trustworthiness of Scripture stands or falls with the smallest irregularity: "As if this belief [in the canon] really would *have* to disappear if just one error were encountered."[54] I myself would prefer to speak of *supposed* errors, and emphasize the fact that it is *a priori* impossible to find an error that would falsify the inerrancy of Scripture in the sense of epistemology. Because this point is so important I wish to summarize again why this is the case. It is impossible to falsify the (supposed) inerrancy of the Bible for the following reasons:

(a) In many cases we cannot know for sure whether we are

---

52. Troost (2005, 260).
53. Van Bruggen (1986, 103–105).
54. Ibid., 98–101.

dealing with what was a real error in the *autographa* (this is the main argument of the inerrantists themselves).

(b) No clear, objective criterion can be supplied for distinguishing between errors that do, and errors that do not, threaten the (supposed) inerrancy of the Bible.

(c) For every (supposed) error that is encountered, no matter how serious, an explanation can be imagined — no matter how sophisticated — such that the (supposed) inerrancy of the Bible is not threatened by it.

Once more: the theory of the biblical inerrancy, taken in the sense of the inerrantists, is a non-theory, epistemologically speaking, because it cannot be falsified. In this sense, it belongs to the same category as Marxism, (Neo-)Darwinism, and Freudianism, with apologies for the comparison. This is because Marxists, (Neo-)Darwinists, and Freudians are equally able to "explain" each possible phenomenon such that it fits into their theories.[55] Just try to demonstrate that a cultural phenomenon is *not* related to economic relationships (i.e., *contra* Marxism), or that a phenotypical change in a species did *not* arise through natural selection (i.e., *contra* [Neo-]Darwinism), or that a psychical phenomenon is *not* related to the (supposed) unconscious (i.e., *contra* Freudianism). These theories are unfalsifiable, and therefore useless and meaningless. Inerrantism is an unscientific theory, and *as a theological theory*, it is therefore useless and meaningless.

10.6.3 Refutation

My point is that I do not consider the unscientific character of inerrantism to be problematic. On the contrary, the postulate of the Bible's inerrancy is a venerable presupposition of faith. If it can be liberated from every rationalistic and scientistic stain, I can wholeheartedly live and die with this faith presupposition. However, I cannot live, and I certainly cannot die, with any *theory* about the Bible's inerrancy. My problem with the inerrantists is their scientism, that is, their belief that they

---

55. Popper (2002b, 33–39).

The Credibilist View of Scripture

can contain this presupposition of faith within a scientific theory that is pervasively reasoned. In this way, they maneuver themselves into a position that is scientifically untenable, in which they become vulnerable to justified scientific criticism.

What is worse is that inerrantists judge a person's faithfulness to Scripture according to the criteria of their untenable theory. However, faith and faithfulness can never be judged by human, fallible theological theories. *This is true for all domains of theology.* Unfortunately, in the past this has happened thousands of times, and as a consequence Christians have been martyred for it. Thus, we find that the credibility of Scripture is a delicate matter.

Here is the other negative consequence: if a good belief is defended with the help of a bad theory, the moment this bad theory is refuted, many people will conclude that this good belief has been refuted as well, and therefore reject it. This has happened, for instance, with the so-called proofs for the existence of God formulated by Italian philosopher Thomas Aquinas. By claiming that such proofs could be scientifically established and grounded, and by undertaking to do so, Thomas became vulnerable to scientific criticism. Indeed, David Hume and Immanuel Kant thoroughly debunked these so-called proofs.[56] By itself it is not such a serious matter if these proofs turn out to be scientifically untenable. But one serious collateral effect could be that many people will think that such a refutation of arguments for God's existence proves that God does not exist. This is a logical blunder, but it does occur, and understandably so.

The same thing might happen when it comes to the trustworthiness of Scripture. By elevating its inerrancy to a scientific postulate, the inerrantists do a disservice to the Bible. This is because, if it could be shown that this postulate is unscientific — which I think is not all that difficult — many might draw the mistaken conclusion that therefore Scripture is not

---

56. Cf. Pannenberg (1991, 84–95).

trustworthy. Logically, this is an unwarranted conclusion, but the inerrantists carry a certain responsibility for people drawing such a conclusion.

10.7 Views of Inerrancy

10.7.1 Inaccuracy *Versus* Deceit

Several authors have endeavored to relieve the notion of inerrancy, as applied by inerrantists, of its scientistic load. G. C. Berkouwer argued that we should make a sharp distinction between error in the sense of inaccuracy, mistake, and error in the sense of sin, misleading, lie.[57] He believed that it is not the (supposed) occurrence of factual inaccuracies that should be the criterion for inerrancy, but the non-deceitfulness of Scripture. In his view, possible irregularities—say, of a chronological, numerical, genealogical or grammatical nature—would not turn the Bible into a deceitful, misleading, sinful book. Of course, inerrantists themselves see this as the primary criterion of inerrancy, too. This is clear from the Chicago Statement on Biblical Inerrancy, Article 12: "We affirm that Scripture in its entirety is inerrant, being free from all falsehood, fraud, or deceit"—but subsequently, this inerrancy is extended to the "fields of history and science." Please note, not "the field of nature," but that of "science"! Real adherents of scientism will probably argue that this is the same.

David A. Hubbard argued that a view of error in the sense of deliberate deceit—instead of departure from formal (scientific!) criteria of accuracy—agrees far more with Scripture itself.[58] As Bruce Vawter put it, the root idea of biblical truth entails reliability (trustworthiness), durability, firmness (stability). The opposite of this is not error, but deliberate falsehood.[59] Scripture is without errors (mistakes, fallacies) in the sense that it never carries us away from the will of God, or away from the knowledge of truth in Christ. A good person

---

57. Berkouwer (1967, 90; cf. also 124–26).
58. Hubbard (1977, 167–68).
59. Vawter (1972, 150); cf. also Pannenberg (1970, 203).

makes errors and mistakes, but such a person does not deceive his friends; he may say things that, strictly speaking, are incorrect or inaccurate, but he does not lie.

10.7.2 Qualified Inerrancy

In connection with our previous considerations, it is helpful that Richard S. Taylor distinguished three types of inerrancy.[60]

(a) The adherent of *salvational inerrancy* acknowledges inerrancy only in matters of faith (as do, e.g., many dialectical theologians and Neo-Evangelicals).

(b) *Total inerrancy* is the view that admitting any error of any type is fatal for the authority of the whole (this is the very view of the ICBI).

(c) *Qualified inerrancy* is errorlessness in all matters related to God, salvation, the cosmos, and humanity, but not necessarily in every chronological, numerical, and grammatical detail (this is the view of Swiss theologian René Pache [d. 1979],[61] and it also seems to be implied in the well-known Evangelical Lausanne Covenant[62]).

Apparently, Clark Pinnock belonged to category (a); he pleaded for the notion of a "focused inerrancy," that is, inerrancy with regard to the "focus" of Scripture as a covenantal book, whose primary purpose is to bring people into a saving relationship with God.[63] This seems to be the same as what

---

60. Taylor (1980, 33–34); cf. also Erickson (1998, 248–50), who distinguishes no fewer than seven types, which, however, have more to do with the various underlying theories of inspiration (see chapters 7–8 above).
61. Pache (1977, chapter IX, §III).
62. See www.lausanne.org/covenant, Art. 2:
   We affirm the divine inspiration, truthfulness and authority of both Old and New Testament Scriptures in their entirety as the only written word of God, without error in all that it affirms, and the only infallible rule of faith and practice. We also affirm the power of God's word to accomplish his purpose of salvation.; Cf. also the explanation by John R. W. Stott: www.lausanne.org/all-documents/lop-3.html.
63. Pinnock (1984, 127).

others have referred to as the "scope" of Scripture (§7.9.3). Presumably, however, Pinnock would not have accepted Taylor's "qualified inerrancy."

What exactly does the latter entail? Qualified inerrancy means that in Scripture God does not intend to reveal to us the precise value of π, or to present to us geological teaching about the "foundations" of the earth, or to offer us historiography according to scientific criteria of accuracy (see the examples in §10.4 above). This is because all these matters do not contribute to our salvation or to a deepening of our knowledge of God or of humanity. Where Scripture speaks *within the framework of salvation* about nature and history—that is to say, *always* from a pistical, not a scientific viewpoint—it always speaks in a reliable way. That is, it speaks with that kind of reliability that is demanded *in view of salvation*, the knowledge of God and of divine things, but not necessarily with the precision that is demanded by modern criteria of the natural and the historical sciences.[64] In the Bible, such a precision is simply not *needed*.

Donald G. Bloesch was even more outspoken in his distinction between the two types of inerrancy. He stated that the Scriptures did not err in what they proclaimed, but this does not mean that they were inerrant in their recording of historical data, or in their worldview, which is now obsolete.[65] Peter Enns said he believes in the inspiration and trustworthiness of Scripture, yet stated that the creation story of Genesis is firmly rooted in the (mythical) worldview of the time.[66] In other words, according to our modern criteria, Genesis is not inerrant in its representation of physical reality.

10.7.3 Inerrantist Protests

The notion of a Bible that is inerrant with respect to its scope but not necessarily in all kinds of factual details provoked

---

64. Cf. Bavinck (*RD* 1:445–46); Weber (1981, 268–74).
65. Bloesch (1983, 135).
66. Enns (2005, 27); see Ouweneel (2018l, §§9.1.1 and 10.4.2) on Enns.

The Credibilist View of Scripture

fierce reactions among the inerrantists. They were afraid that a dualism is introduced between center and periphery, between content and form (cf. §7.9.3). Often, this objection was, and is, perfectly warranted; a clear example is found in the Dutch report *God met ons* (*God With Us*).[67] However, G. C. Berkouwer argued that we should not generalize here.[68] He pointed out that inspiration itself, as an act and gift of the Spirit of Christ, *refers* to such a centrality, a divine concentration in the person and the work of Christ.

This *concentration* is something very different from a *reduction* of the content of Scripture in the sense that certain peripheral parts would remain outside this reduction, and therefore may certainly contain all kinds of errors. In §7.9.3 I have argued that this is not necessarily implied, and ought not to be implied, in the notion of the scope of Scripture. This notion does not imply a flight from a fallible form to an infallible content (the *kerygma*), but pertains to the infallible, transcendent *Word*, which manifests itself in the immanent *words* (see further in §10.10 below).[69]

I would prefer a qualified version of Taylor's qualified inerrancy ([c] above), with this explanation and addition: I would not say that correctness in every chronological, numerical, genealogical, and grammatical detail does not matter, but that such a correctness is simply neither verifiable nor falsifiable. It thus falls outside the domain of theological testing. I believe that Scripture is perfectly trustworthy, even in its details. However, this is a presupposition of *faith*, not of a scientific nature, a presupposition that cannot be scientifically verified — nor scientifically falsified, for that matter.

Perhaps the parallel with the incarnation of God's Son (recall §5.3 above) can be helpful here.[70] Some Evangelical theologians have claimed that, in a moral respect, the human Jesus

---

67. *God met ons* (1981).
68. Berkouwer (1967, 57; cf. 77–100).
69. Cf. ibid., 97–98.
70. Cf. Beale (2008, 39–40, 81).

was perfect but this does not necessarily mean that at school he earned only As, or that he never forgot something, or as a carpenter apprentice of his father never made a mistake in his woodworking. By analogy, in a moral respect, Scripture is perfect, but this is not the same as perfect in the fields of the natural and the historical sciences.

I would prefer to avoid this line of reasoning, however. First, we know nothing about Jesus' school and woodworking achievements, and thus it is both useless and risky to speculate about these things. Those who enter this arena will never be able to draw an acceptable boundary between errors that Jesus would have been allowed to commit, and errors that Jesus would *not* have been allowed to commit, without affecting his perfection. Second, even if we were able to draw such a boundary, we cannot claim that what is true for Jesus is *mutatis mutandis* true for Scripture, and vice versa.

10.8 Faith Is Oblivious to Any (In-)Errancy Problem

10.8.1 The Theoreticalization of Ordinary Life

To believers, it is self-evident that they hold a perfect Bible in their hand, but also that it is irrelevant whether they are capable of resolving, for instance, the numerical differences between Samuel/Kings and Chronicles. There are hardly any ordinary believers for whom such irregularities constitute a serious faith difficulty. It is the inerrantist who *turns* them theoretically into difficulties; they elevate these irregularities to the status of scientific problems. This is perfectly in order — this is what theologians are for. However, the inerrantist tries to sell these scientific problems to us as *faith* problems; ordinary believers should also consider them problems.

Actually the inerrantist does not appear to do this deliberately; he simply appears to be insufficiently aware of the philosophical differences between the concrete-practical experience (in this case, the practical faith reading of Scripture) and the abstract-theoretical thought- and knowing-attitude (in this case, that of theology). It is the same with the myth that every believer is a little theologian; here again, the essential difference between practical and theoretical knowledge is erased. Practical knowledge may lead to a faith conviction of the heart; theoretical knowledge is at best a preliminary and temporal rational conviction, valid only as long as it has not yet been refuted, and then replaced by a new theory.

Theoretical research creates problems—this is its task—that do not exist for faith. *Not* because faith is naïve but because it is not characterized by the abstract-theoretical thought attitude. Therefore, such theological problems should not be imposed upon believers, as if *they* should be concerned whether all kinds of (supposed) discrepancies in Scripture can be resolved. Their faith does not depend on this—*unless the ordinary believer, too, is infected by the theoreticalization of ordinary life*. This awkward situation resembles, for instance, that of the abortion debate that is dominated by the question at what moment in the fertilization of the ovum a human person exists. Ordinary believers know little about fertilized ova, but only about expecting a baby.

Or, for instance, creation theology is dominated by the question whether the modern theory of evolution can be reconciled with Genesis 1. The moment the fundamentalist believer is caught in modern-scientific ideas he *must*, in order to salvage his faith, believe that the fertilized ovum is a human person, and that Genesis must be taken literally, whatever this means.[71] These convictions play no role for ordinary believers when they are reading the Bible, and within the Bible they certainly play no role either. They arise only for ordinary believers in a strongly scientistically oriented culture, where they seem to have only two options: either allow modern science to dominate their pre-theoretical faith—and in this way many often lose this faith—or take refuge in the fortress of fundamentalism, which, *mirabile dictum*, enlists this very same science as its ally.

---

71. See extensively, Ouweneel (2018l, especially chapters 3–5).

10.8.2 The Idea of Truth

In reality, pre-theoretical faith in its transcendent-religious sense does not at all depend on this kind of (pseudo- or genuine) scientific discussions. Neither modernists nor inerrantists have the right to impose their (usually unconscious) scientism on ordinary believers, and to make the credibility of Scripture depend on their respective theoretical reasonings. Both parties will not salvage the faith of ordinary believers with their scientific arguments *for* either the errancy or the inerrancy of Scripture, respectively, because the arguments of neither party hold water.

For the believer, the credibility of Scripture is not an abstract-theoretical matter, but a matter of faith confidence, through which one, in the power of the Holy Spirit, entrusts oneself to the Word of God, or rather, to the God of the Word. Inerrantists do their best to prove that Jesus and the apostles extensively testified to the inspiration and infallibility of the Old Testament[72] — even if only implicitly — and I agree with them. However, this *never* involved chronological, numerical, genealogical, or grammatical details; problems of this nature will never shock any ordinary believer, except if — partly as an effect of inerrantism! — their worldview has been unhappily theoreticalized. What does affect the ordinary believer when it comes to the inspiration and infallibility of the Bible are exclusively those subjects that really matter in each Christian's daily faith reading of the Bible: salvation, God, humanity, the church, the kingdom of God, power, consolation, instruction, exhortation, edification — all matters that deepen and enrich one's faith.

In this connection, J. A. Heyns rightly remarked,

> For the Greek, truth is rather the pure representation of the objective reality, but in the Bible, truth is that quality of reality that addresses me so evidently that I have confidence in it, and know that it will not disappoint me but will lead me to my God-given

---

72. See, e.g., Archer Jr. (1982, 21–22); Wenham (1979); Blum (1979).

purpose. We might also represent this as follows: for the Bible, truth is not yet truth in the mere establishment of facts, that is, a truth statement is not automatically identical with a reality statement; only if the reality statement also includes a destination statement, we have to do with truth. . . . In Scripture, God did not wish to scientifically instruct us concerning the reality around and in us [as such], but he wished to show the proper relationship of this reality to him.[73]

In other words, the truth idea of the inerrantists is more related to the ancient Greek notion than to the biblical truth idea.[74] For instance, is it not a typically scientific form of logic to conclude from Jesus' testimony concerning the trustworthiness of the Old Testament that *therefore* the discrepancies between Samuel/Kings and Chronicles *cannot* have existed in the *autographa*? The testimony of Jesus and the apostles exists on the *practical-pistical* level; the conclusions of the inerrantists exist on the *theoretical-logical* level. To put it in somewhat black-and-white terms: inerrantists give the impression as if Scripture must be Word of God because it is perfect (read: scientifically correct). According to credibilism, Scripture must be Word of God because it is perfect (read: brings people into a relationship with God). Of course, the inerrantist may believe the latter, too; yet, their emphasis on the former is disquieting.

10.9 Inerrantist Response

10.9.1 Rationalism *Versus* Existentialism

It is not difficult to predict the response of the inerrantists to the counter-arguments as just given. One such a response comes from Millard J. Erickson. He argued that attempts to reconcile difficult passages (like in the parallel Bible portions mentioned) are viewed by the opponents as examples of rationalism. Erickson, claiming his and others' familiarity with

---

73. Heyns (1988, 31; cf. also 1976, 116–18).
74. See extensively, Ouweneel (2013, chapter 14).

the motives of existentialism, saw behind such objections the common existentialist emphasis on the paradoxical (that is, irrational!) nature of reality, the absurdity of the universe, and the impossibility to capture reality in the solid and rigid categories of logic.[75] In other words, if you refuse to be a ratio-nal*ist*, you must necessarily be an irrationalist.

This is a highly interesting response. To Erickson—at least the Erickson of 1982—there were only two alternatives: either inerrantist logic, or modern-liberal, existentialist (today he would perhaps say, "postmodern") logic. Unfortunately for him, things are far more complicated than these two simplistic options. I totally reject modernism with its anti-biblical, humanistic, scientistic, either rationalist or existentialist roots, including those of postmodernism. However, the tragic of inerrantism is that it does not see that, in many respects, it is caught in the very same scientism, as well as in a scholastic dualism—"-isms" that are not at all of a biblical, but of a secular, origin. We do not wish to get caught in such an awkward dilemma of having to choose either Erickson's rationalism or his opponents' irrationalism. We do not wish to be bitten either by the dog or by the cat (to use a Dutch proverb).

Indeed, just as simplistic as the contrast inerrantism–(post-)modernism is the contrast rationalism–irrationalism. Where Erickson hears the reproach of rationalism, he retorts immediately with the reproach of irrationalism—as if there are no other options. Apparently, he is of the opinion that only an irrationalist can accuse him and other inerrantists of being a rationalist. In this way, just like most of his opponents, he remains caught in the ancient contrast between reason and feeling. In other words, Erickson does not seem to see that a person could place great emphasis on rational thinking without being a rationalist (i.e., someone who *absolutizes* rational thinking).

---

75. Erickson (1982, 391); cf. Ouweneel (1995, §1.2.1).

10.9.2 Conquering the Contrasts

How can such contrasts (inerrantism *versus* modernism; rationalism *versus* irrationalism) ever be overcome? This is possible only through a radically Christian ontology and epistemology, which is also able to unmask all kinds of false philosophical roots, in both liberal and orthodox theology, and all sorts of false problems, which arise from false presuppositions. The forced smoothing out of errors in the Bible is an example of such a false problem, rooted in such scientistic presuppositions. We have seen that, because of their (unconscious) scientism, the inerrantist wishes to make the entire trustworthiness of the Bible dependent on their theoretical arguments. This shows us how far orthodox theology can drift away from ordinary Christian faith as a consequence of this theology's inherent rationalism.

Without the help of a radically Christian ontology, theologians will feel pressured time and again to choose between either a theoretical-*rational*-conceptual approach, like inerrantism, or a theoretical-*irrational*-conceptual approach, like existentialist or postmodern theology. Only if we expose the roots of the underlying, largely pagan thought patterns can we overcome this kind of dilemma. In my view, the problem of inerrancy can be approached in a manner that is both rational and supra-rational (not irrational!), and this can be done not conceptually, but idea-wise. That is, of inerrancy we cannot form a (logical) concept, but we *can* form a (logical) idea of it. It is not primarily a theoretical matter but it surpasses theoretical, and ultimately rational, thought. It is a matter of our transcendent-religious faith, which only afterward can and must be accounted for by, but not enclosed in, rational-theological arguments.

For our simple supra-theoretical, supra-rational faith, at least as long as the latter is not corrupted by false theoretical reasonings that are imposed upon it, it is a literal folly that certain (supposed) irregularities could detract from the inspiration, the divine authority, and the absolute trustworthiness of Scripture, and of the God of Scripture. According to the viewpoint of faith, such (supposed) inaccuracies can never imply a danger for the scope of the Bible: salvation as prepared by God for fallen humanity, accomplished throughout the centuries through promise and fulfillment, redemption and consummation, which culminate in the kingdom of God. This salvation is realized in and through our great God and Savior, Jesus Christ, by whom humans, through faith, are eternally elevated to fellowship with, and the service of, God. Scripture is word for word imbued with this redemptive plan of God. Therefore, by God's Spirit we confess the infallibility and trustworthiness of the entire Bible.

10.9.3 Against Scientism

Let me refer here to Philip E. Hughes, who strongly argued against any form of scientism.[76] I am quite happy with his approach, and would like to refer at some length to his arguments. He admitted that it would be nice if we had the *autographa*, but also argued that their loss is no disadvantage. No good purpose is served by fleeing for refuge to *autographa* that are not at our disposal; it is much healthier for us if we simply, positively, and confidently speak of the Bible as the Word of God without any limitation of this idea (for instance, by appealing to these lost *autographa*). The Bible that we have in our hands is the Word of God.

In fact, argued Hughes, the Bible does not need our protection. In 2 Samuel 6:6, Uzzah put out his hand to steady the ark to prevent it from falling. We might likewise be tempted to stretch out the arm of our human intellect in order to prevent the ark of Scripture from falling. But instead, we should approach Scripture with simplicity, reverence, and expectation, and always with gratitude, knowing that the written Word of God is an inexplicable mystery. We acknowledge its teaching as absolutely true and highly authoritative. We will not lean on our limited logical abilities, or on the testimonies

---

76. Hughes (1983, 193–94).

of experts and scholars—no matter how valuable these may be in their own right—for our conviction that Scripture is the Word of God. It is not through any kind of scholarly proof that we know the Bible to be the Word of God. Rather it is through the inner working and testimony of the Holy Spirit that this conviction is unshakably established in our heart and our mind.

Here I would call to mind Romans 8:16, "The Spirit himself bears witness with our spirit that we are children of God." Without any hesitation, I would like to offer this variant: "The Spirit himself bears witness with our spirit that the Bible is the Word of God." And as long as we are not tending towards scientism, I would gladly add: the infallible, trustworthy, and authoritative Word of God.

Hughes argued that those who cherish the orthodox and evangelical faith have become *too defensive* as far as the Bible is concerned. They confess the worthy premise, "The Bible is the Word of God," but then jump to a negative conclusion: "... therefore it is *in*errant," that is, errorless. In itself this may be correct, but Hughes suggested that this conclusion reflects the position into which orthodox Christians had maneuvered themselves. The Word of God is the sword of the Spirit (Eph. 6:17), and Christians must learn to use this mighty weapon in an offensive and bold way. That is, they must proclaim to the world in a *positive*—and thus, more biblical—way that the Bible is the Word of God, and therefore living, dynamic, penetrating, and infallibly effective, because it cuts with the edge of redemption for the believer, and with the edge of judgment for the unbeliever (Heb. 4:12). This is the view of Hughes.

How true are these thoughts. We do not believe the Word of God primarily because it is *without* errors but because it is *loaded with* enormous divine power—the power of the Holy Spirit—to transform the hearts and lives of people.

I am under the strong impression that no person will ever be convinced of the trustworthiness of God's Word by the scientistic arguments of the inerrantists. Rather, this conviction comes from the Holy Spirit alone. This does not mean that rational and theoretical arguments might not be useful. On the contrary; one cannot be a theologian without accepting and advocating the proper function of theoretical thinking. Yet, people discover that the Bible is God's Word not through arguments, or arguments alone, but through their daily reading God's Word on the practical level of faith. They are taught by the Word, reproved, corrected, trained, and in this way they become equipped — not for the defense of a theoretical bibliology but — "for every good work" (2 Tim. 3:16-17).

10.10 The Scope of Scripture[77]

10.10.1 Concentration *Versus* Reduction

Several times so far, I have brought up the subject of the scope of Scripture. Let me add a few further remarks here. The term "scope" is rather old. Martin Luther said, "Christ is the scope of the entire Scripture" (Lat. *Christus universae scripturae scopus est*).[78] And John Calvin wrote, "Thus it rightly takes us to the faith in Christ, as to the scope and summary of it" (Lat. *proinde non immerito nos ad fidem Christi revocat, tanquam ad scopum atque adeo summam*).[79]

Several have attempted to formulate this scope. Herman Dooyeweerd spoke of creation – Fall – redemption.[80] Some see the person of Christ as the scope of Scripture, others select God's self-revelation, or the covenant, or the kingdom of God (my favorite), or the theocentric and Christocentric motif, and so on. One formulation that I especially like is that of J. Heyns: "[T]he center of Scripture is God's kingdom, and the center of

---

77. For these last sections, see extensively, Bavinck (*RD* 1:445–48); Berkouwer (1966, 178–80); 1967, 56–59, 85–87, 95–100).
78. *WA* 24:16.
79. *CR* 52.382; cf. also CR 47.321–22; 50.45; Luther and Calvin quoted by Rossouw (1963, 191, 193).
80. E.g., Dooyeweerd (1963, 28–31, 35–38, 104–05).

this center is Jesus Christ."[81]

Of course, we must remember that every rational-immanent formulation can at best be a weak human attempt, which can never capture the supra-rational, transcendent scope of Scripture in certain modal-logical concepts; at best, it can be approximated in the form of an idea. Incidentally, this is also my objection against Herman Dooyeweerd's formulation of the four ground motives that he thought dominated Western thought throughout the centuries: the matter-form, the nature-grace, the nature-freedom, and the creation-Fall-redemption motive. These are *rational* formulations of motives that themselves are *supra-rational*. In my view, if we wish to express this supra-rational, transcendent-religious character, we should distinguish only two ground motives. These could be described as the *anastatic* ground motive (an idea-wise approximation of this can be done in the manners mentioned above) and the *apostatic* ground motive (the matter-form and the nature-freedom motives) as well as mixtures of these (such as the scholastic nature-grace motive, but also mixtures of the anastatic and the nature-freedom motive since the Enlightenment).

No matter how we view this, the emphasis on central themes in the Bible may never lead to a distinction within the Bible between more and less important portions. The specific identification of a scope must be sharply distinguished from a dualism like those that have unfortunately been introduced in modern theology: between center and periphery, or between content and form (cf. §7.9.3). Scripture is concentrated in the person and work of Christ, but we have seen that this *concentration* is very different from a *reduction* of the Bible content such that supposed peripheral parts fall outside this reduction, and could therefore easily be incorrect or untrustworthy from the viewpoint of the natural or the historical sciences. Just as no droplet of ocean water lacks sea salt, no portion of

---

81. Heyns (1976, 70); cf. Ouweneel (2018j).

Scripture lacks Christ.

10.10.2 Again, the Center–Periphery Dualism

No, the scope is not a reduction or summary of Scripture, but the *transcendent* orientation, directedness, intention, specific goal of the Bible, as it comes to expression in *each* Bible passage, and in *each* of the separate *immanent* words, viewed in their context and in the coherence of all the words of Scripture together. In this scope, we are not dealing with some infallible content wrapped securely in some fallible form, but with the infallible Word that is manifested in all the separate words.[82] *Each* Bible portion is related to the scope of Scripture, and must be dealt with as such, even though, of course, the New Testament story of the sufferings of Christ are closer to the scope than the Old Testament genealogies.

This matter of distinguishing between concentration and reduction is of the greatest importance, and therefore I will try to formulate it a little more sharply in terms of transcendent *versus* immanent, or eternal *versus* temporal. We have seen that the human mode of existence must not be divided into two temporal, hypostasized function complexes: the soul substance (comprising the mental functions, from the logical to the pistical) and the body substance (comprising the natural functions, from the arithmetical to the sensitive).[83] In a precisely analogous way, the Bible as the temporal-immanent form of the eternal-transcendent Word of God, must not be divided into two temporal parts: the center (i.e., the part relevant for salvation) and the periphery (i.e., the part not relevant for salvation).

In a radically Christian anthropology, the heart (or the soul, the spirit, in the emphatic-transcendent meaning of these terms) is the transcendent concentration point of all temporal-immanent functions. This is true not only for the mental but also for the natural functions, which are all viewed as im-

---

82. Cf. Berkouwer (1967, 77–100, especially 97).
83. See Ouweneel (2008, chapters 6–8; 2016; 2018l, chapter 6).

manent aspects of the temporal human mode of existence. In an analogous way, the scope of the Bible is the latter's transcendent point of concentration, the eternal Word of God, just as, conversely, this eternal Word comes to expression in *all* the distinct temporal-immanent words of Scripture, without exception.

On the one hand, it must be clear that not a single Bible passage could ever be severed from the scope of Scripture, as has been tried so often in modernism. On the other hand, fundamentalism sometimes wishes to emphasize so strongly that the Bible speaks in a reliable way about nature and history that it gives the impression that this was the explicit goal of the Bible passages involved. In this way, it actually makes the same mistake as modernism: a Bible passage is severed from its scope. The false impression is created (probably unconsciously) that the Bible at times speaks of salvation in Christ, and at other times about nature and history. However, the Bible is *always* about salvation, in the widest sense of the word, and *always* about faith, in the widest sense of the scope of Scripture, and *never* about nature or history *as such*.

10.10.3 Nature and History

Nature is described in the Bible insofar as it is relevant within the framework of salvation and faith in Christ, and is therefore seen exclusively from this viewpoint. In the Bible, history is viewed exclusively as *redemptive* history. Scripture's goal is always the unfolding of God's counsel and of the ways along which this counsel is realized in Christ within the history of this world.[84] The center of Scripture is *always* Jesus Christ and the realization of God's counsel in him. It is only *within this scope* that the Bible sometimes speaks about history, nature, the cosmos; and of course, we take these Bible passages absolutely seriously. We do the same with Genesis 1, both as a historical description of creational events and as a description of nature, but viewed exclusively from the scope of Scripture:

---

84. See extensively, Ouweneel (2018d, chapters 2–5).

the realization of God's counsel in Christ. Those who would wish to learn cosmology, astronomy, and biology from Genesis 1 *would emphatically denigrate and reduce Christ*, and would violate the intention, goal, and nature of Scripture.

The worldview of the Bible is always the viewpoint of faith, and never, according to its own nature, physical or biotic in the strict sense of the terms. In principle, it is quite possible that certain parts of this worldview are rooted in some ancient physical worldview, but in fact this is irrelevant because the Bible's aim is never to impose a physical worldview upon us. The only worldview it presents to us is of a faith nature. Therefore, it cannot be God's intention that we would adopt historical, physical, or biotic data from the Bible that we have first severed from the latter's scope. Those who nonetheless do so ventriloquize Scripture. It may look reverent to use the Bible for such a purpose, but in fact it is a depreciation of Scripture.

J. A. Heyns emphasized that the notion of the scope underscores the organic character of the Bible, and fully excluded by definition any atomistic or mechanical interpretation of Scripture.[85] Fundamentalism often seems to view Scripture as an comprehensive arsenal of texts that can be simply and immediately applied to all circumstances of life, including the domains of science.[86] The notion of the scope, if properly understood, can help us to demonstrate that such an approach and usage affects Scripture in its essence, and effectively paralyzes its message. The Bible addresses us through its scope, which is expressed in the many statements of Scripture. But it does *not* address us through isolated statements, that is, words of Scripture that have been naïvely and biblicistically severed from Scripture's scope. The Bible does not, explicitly or implicitly, offer us a treatise on natural science, the arts, politics, economics, and so on, and not even on ethics and

---

85. Heyns (1977, 172–73).

86. Cf. the quotation from Hodge in §9.5.1 about Scripture as a "storehouse of facts."

The Credibilist View of Scripture

theology. Isolated Bible verses can never serve as a referee in any purely special-scientific, political, economic, or even ethical or theological controversy. But at the same time *it touches upon all these matters*, without exception, through the universal perspective of its scope. In this, the dynamics of the reforming and transforming powers of the gospel are contained.

Once again, this scope *never* implies a reduction of the Bible content, but underscores the radical significance of Scripture, which refracts into *all* the variability and multiplicity of its words, sentences, and passages. This does not mean that all words and sentences of Scripture stand in the same vital relationship to its scope, just as, for instance, the arms and legs in the human body are not equally vital for human existence as, for instance, the lungs or the intestines.[87] At the same time, arms and legs are not superfluous or trivial; they are a *person's* limbs, of vital significance for that person's full identity. In a similar way, the identity of Scripture is expressed through its scope.

It is important to point out that the fundamentalist tendency to sever Bible passages from their scope threatens to bring about exactly what the fundamentalist tries to avoid at all costs. That is, it endangers the inerrancy of the Bible. At least, this is what was argued by Gerhard Lohfink: "Each book, every text is free of error, at least if it is read in the framework of the great totality. However, as soon as a word or a sentence is isolated from this wide coherence, there is no guarantee for the inerrancy anymore."[88]

---

87. Cf. Heyns (1976, 67).
88. Quoted by Miskotte (1966, 158).

Chapter 11
The Modernist View of the Old Testament

[Y]ou do not have his word abiding in you,
for you do not believe the one whom he has sent.
You search the Scriptures
because you think that in them you have eternal life;
and it is they that bear witness about me,
yet you refuse to come to me that you may have life.

John 5:38–40

Summary: *So-called "biblical criticism" refers not to criticism leveled at the Bible, but to a critical analysis of the Bible. It comprises lower (textual) and higher criticism, the latter including literary and historical criticism. Current biblical criticism is heavily beset with naturalism, rationalism, historicism (including evolutionism). No expositor can avoid dealing with underlying literary questions (post-Mosaica, contradictions, authorship, **vaticinia ex eventu**), but ideological prejudices play a great role in this.*

Special attention is paid to the Pentateuch, in particular the documentary hypothesis (especially Wellhausen, with his historicist prejudice). In opposition to such fragmenting, others have defended the essential unity especially of Genesis.

Special attention is given to the underlying prejudices, from Enlightenment modernism (including historicism) to post-postmodernism. Newer approaches are described, such as form criticism. In particular the role of archeology is emphasized (Albright, Kitchen, Dever, and many others). The debate continues, but to a certain extent the traditional view has been vindicated.

11.1 What Is Biblical Criticism?[1]

11.1.1 Misunderstandings

SEVERAL TIMES, THE PHRASE "biblical criticism" or "historical criticism" was mentioned in previous chapters. In the strict sense of the word, the phrase "biblical criticism" is a literary phrase, referring to the discipline dealing with the origin and the present state of the text of an (ancient) writing, in this case the Bible. "Biblical criticism" is a "critical" — which means here: a scholarly profound and accurate — investigation of the form and content of Scripture with the help of the literary and historical sciences. Thus, strictly speaking this discipline is not at all about leveling criticism *at* the Bible, even if some Christians do experience some results of biblical criticism more as a criticizing the Bible (being critical of the Bible) than as a critical analysis of the Bible.

Unfortunately, this misunderstanding is deeply rooted, even among theologians. Thus, Jan van Genderen wrote, "[Hendrikus] Berkhof refers to this verse [i.e., Matt. 28:19] as a product of subsequent reflection and even thinks of it as fiction.[2] This is an extreme form of biblical criticism [i.e., criticism leveled at the Bible]."[3] Interestingly, this very Berkhof

---

1. Among the older dogmatic theology textbooks, Buri (1956, 315–406) offered one of the most extensive treatments of the problem of historical criticism; see more recently Waltke et al. (1997); Barton (2007).
2. Berkhof (1986, 353, 382).
3. Van Genderen (2008, 788).

The Modernist View of the Old Testament

made the same mistake. He wrote, "'Biblical criticism' must also, first and foremost, be Scripture's criticism leveled at us!"[4] This may sound nice, but it starts from the same misunderstanding, namely, that the word "criticism" in "biblical criticism" is not a critical analysis *of* the Bible but criticism leveled *at* the Bible. Unfortunately, J. Douma used the term in this sense in his criticizing Stefan Paas's views in the history of religions field.[5]

If theologians themselves use the phrase "biblical criticism" in such a sloppy way, it is no wonder that non-theological Christians do the same. The expression is just as strange as if a creationist were to say of evolutionist biology: "We are dealing here with a grave form of biology." Biology, biblical criticism, and *all* literary criticism are scientific disciplines, which do not occur in "grave" or "less grave" forms. At best, one might dislike some of their (alleged) results. Biblical criticism is part of the Bible (Old or New Testament) scholar's profession, and such a scholar is necessarily occupied with critical problems that require a solution.

As Casper Labuschagne wrote, the Bible scholar must

> approach his object of investigation with the same methods of literary, historical, and philosophical criticism that are common in the other comparable humanities. For this discipline, there are no domains with the sign "No trespassing," no questions that may not be asked, no answers that may not be formulated. The only thing that makes theology different from all other sciences is that, in addition to investigating the relevant, concrete, tangible and visible reality, it is also explicitly occupied with thinking about "that which is invisible" [Rom. 1:20; Col. 1:15-16; 1 Tim. 1:17; Heb. 11:27], that which in the language of faith is called "God": the deepest ground of reality, the origin of all being.[6]

---

4. Ibid., 93.
5. Douma (2009) (https://www.nd.nl/nieuws/dossier/dissertatie-stefan-paas-botst-met-godsopenbaring.173597.lynkx); cf. Paas (1998).
6. Labuschagne (2000, 16).

The word "critical" in biblical criticism does not necessarily have a pejorative meaning, but in fact has a meaning that is not much different from "scientific" or "scholarly." Immanuel Kant used the term in 1781 in the title of his first main work: *Critique [i.e., critical analysis] of Pure Reason* (Ger. *Kritik der reinen Vernunft*). When Carl R. Holladay called his introduction to the New Testament a "critical" introduction, he meant that his introduction was critical in the sense that it dealt with exegetical questions regarding the literary, historical, social, and religious dimensions of the New Testament.[7]

11.1.2 Two Types of Criticism

Usually, people make a distinction between:

(a) *Lower* or *textual criticism*. This is the discipline that deals with the *form* of the text, that is, with establishing as accurately as possible, by means of the available manuscripts, the correct wording of the original text. This is a very useful and important investigation, which provides scholarly textual editions of the Old and New Testaments (cf. §8.7).[8]

(b) *Higher criticism*, or biblical criticism in the narrower sense, or historical criticism (historical-critical investigation). This is the discipline that deals with the *content* of the text on the basis of the nature and the forms (literary genres) and the themes of the various Bible books, the coherence of the various parts of the Bible, the circumstances of the (presumed) authors and of the (presumed) addressees (historical backgrounds). This investigation also involves the credibility, authenticity, and integrity of the various Bible books.

The phrase "historical criticism" is not always necessari-

---

7. Holladay (2005, 1).
8. The most recent and most accepted standard edition of the Old Testament is the *Biblia Hebraica Stuttgartensia Quinta* (fifth scientific edition of the Hebrew Bible), which has been published since 2004 until (presumably) 2020; see Schenker (2004–20). For the New Testament, it is Nestle-Aland (1984): *Novum Testamentum Graece*, 27th ed.; the most recent, the 28th edition, is now available on the Internet: http://www.nestle-aland.com/en/read-na28-online/.

The Modernist View of the Old Testament

ly identical with "biblical criticism," if the latter is primarily understood as "literary criticism" (identifying literary genres, etc.). Thus, Fritz Buri placed "historical criticism" in opposition to many Bible views that he considered to be a-historical: not only the Roman Catholic and the early Protestant view, but also the rationalist view (from Enlightenment rationalism *via* speculative liberal theology until Albert Schweitzer), the "pneumatic-suprahistorical" view (Albrecht Ritschl and his school, Wilhelm Herrmann, Georg Wobbermin), and the so-called "theological" or "Christological" exegesis (Karl Barth). These are all "biblical-critical" in the broader sense of the term, but, according to Buri, they are "a-historical."[9]

Though this may have been Buri's opinion, this does not alter the fact that, *methodologically*, these were all forms of historical criticism. We are dealing here with a terminological confusion between the terms "a-historical" (i.e., at odds with historical norms) and "non-historical" (not belonging to the domain of the historical) (cf. a-social and non-social, unethical and non-ethical). In the remainder of this chapter, I will use the phrases "historical criticism" and "biblical criticism" as more or less identical because biblical criticism almost always is not just literary criticism but includes the historical dimension.

Obviously, I cannot offer here an exhaustive treatise on biblical criticism; such an investigation would belong to the domain of biblical (Old and New Testaments) scholarship. As a systematic theologian, it is my purpose instead to ask in what respect, and to what extent, biblical criticism has contributed to our understanding of the *locus de Scriptura*, the doctrine of Holy Scripture, as part of systematic theology.

11.1.3 Underlying Bias

Recall my central thesis that fundamentalism and modernism (the latter insofar as they are based on biblical criticism) exhibit an important similarity. To a large extent, both are based

---
9. Buri (1956, 326–46, 359–76).

upon certain philosophical schools that are foreign to what I consider to be the essence of the Bible. Just as I did in the previous two chapters for fundamentalism, it is my present purpose to expose the philosophical roots of modernism, which has used — or if one so wishes, has abused — biblical criticism to reach conclusions that are foreign to the Bible. It is crucial to root all literary and historical investigation of the Bible in a Christian ontology and epistemology that are congruent with the Bible's own character, or with the transcendent-religious faith of the Christian who wishes to live by the Bible. The fact that this necessarily involves a hermeneutical circle has been dealt with in several previous chapters, especially in §§1.7 and 1.8.

One of the characteristics of such a radically Christian approach is that by maintaining the distinction between theoretical and practical thought, we avoid the problem that afflicted Karl Barth,[10] Rudolf Bultmann,[11] and Fritz Buri.[12] What I am referring to is the painful conflict between, on the one hand, preaching the Bible as the Word of God and, on the other hand, investigating Scripture in terms of the presuppositions of modernist biblical criticism. In other words, the conflict between the infallible Word that is preached, and the fallible Scripture that is investigated. In the following sections, I hope to make this matter somewhat more transparent.

If we take biblical criticism in the strict sense of a literary- and historical-critical analysis of the Bible, *in principle* nothing is wrong with this practice. This kind of critical analysis is applied to *all* ancient writings. Even if we believe that the Bible possesses a special character as the inspired Word of God, this does not change the fact that, at the same time, it is an ancient book, written by a number of human writers in various countries at various times, a book with its own history of origin and development. Therefore, there cannot be

---

10. Barth (1933, "The Preface to the Second Edition").
11. Bultmann (1969, 131).
12. Buri (1956, 354–55).

any basic objection against a discipline that investigates the various literary genres in, and the origin and development of, the Bible, or even—were the investigated material to point in this direction—the different sources underlying the books. I am unaware of any *a priori* reason why such an investigation would be disallowed.[13]

So when J. A. Heyns claims that biblical criticism is basically impossible because people are thereby "judging" the content of Scripture by means of human reason,[14] he seems to have forgotten that *all* theological work is nothing but precisely this: forming judgments about the content of Scripture with the help of human reason. Insofar as there is a problem with biblical criticism, the problem is not this judging nor the use of reason—how else should it be done?—but the *pre-theoretical, transcendent-religious attitude of the heart* underlying such judgment and use of reason. What is active is either the allegedly autonomous reason that *rules over* Scripture by its own wisdom—a type of wisdom foreign to Scripture—or the Spirit-led reason, which *submits* to God's Word beforehand, and arrives at its scholarly judgments along this route. The error lies not in the critical analysis of Scripture, but in the *apostatic* analysis of Scripture.

A similar confusion is encountered with George E. Ladd. On the one hand, he stated that the historical-critical method, strictly interpreted, is based on a rationalistic view of history.[15] "Strictly interpreted"—to use Ladd's terms—this is incorrect: historical criticism is certainly rational but as such does not need to be rationalistic at all. On the other hand, Ladd pleaded for a "historical-theological criticism" that acknowledges the revelational dimension in biblical history, as well as the revelational character of the Bible.[16] There might

---

13. Cf. Payne (1979, 85–87); Du Toit (1990, 516); Labuschagne (2000, chapter 1).
14. Heyns (1976, 105 note).
15. Ladd (1967, 53).
16. Ibid., 40.

be a confusion here between revelational history *in* the Bible, and the developmental history *of* the Bible (historical criticism is concerned with the latter), but for the rest this is a correct statement: everything depends on the pre-theoretical and theoretical presuppositions that underlie biblical criticism.

Carl F. H. Henry wrote helpfully about these presuppositions.[17] For instance, he argued that what is objectionable is not the historical-critical method as such, but rather the foreign presuppositions — that is, foreign to Scripture — to which neo-Protestant scholars subject the Bible. If the historical-critical method is combined with an anti-supernaturalistic bias, this is not implied by the method as such but it is nothing but a bias of the historian concerned.[18] Carl Henry extensively summarized what historical criticism can do, and what it cannot do.[19]

11.2 Unavoidable Questions

11.2.1 Genesis and Deuteronomy

Even the most conservative theologians cannot avoid literary and historical questions, and thus implicitly confirm the *raison-d'être* of biblical criticism. Let me mention a few of them, nothing more than a small anthology of legitimate theological questions that demand thorough historical-critical investigation. These and many more questions were raised not only under the influence of the Enlightenment, but already at the time of the Reformation, or even before. Thus, Martin Luther ventured to question features of the books of Esther, Hebrews, James, Jude, and Revelation ([in]famous is the fact that he called James an "epistle of straw"[20]). His (former) friend and collaborator, Andreas Karlstadt, claimed that, because of internal differences in style, the books of the Pentateuch could not possibly have been written by Moses, but that Ezra, as ed-

---

17. Henry (1979b, 385–404); see extensively, Linnemann (1987).
18. Henry (1979b, 393).
19. Ibid., 403; cf. Geisler (1999); Morrison (2006, chapter 4).
20. *Luther's Works* (1960, 362).

itor, may have compiled the five books from older sources.[21] The idea was elaborated by Andreas Masius, and adopted by Benedict Pereira (or Pererius) in his commentary on Genesis.[22] Campegius Vitringa was impressed by the arguments adduced, and referred to Masius.[23]

An obvious objection against Mosaic authorship comes from the so-called *post-Mosaica*, the passages in the Pentateuch that must have been written (long) after Moses:

(a) If Moses were the author of Genesis,[24] how could he have written: "At that time the Canaanites were in the land" (12:6b)? In fact, this could have been written only sometime after the conquest of the promised land, when the Canaanites had largely disappeared. Thus, Genesis 14:14 ("in pursuit as far as Dan") could have been written only by a person who lived after Judges 18, when the Danites had conquered Laish, and had then given the city the name of their forefather, Dan (v. 29). In Genesis 14, this Dan was not yet born (see 30:6), nor his father Jacob or even his grandfather Isaac. The name "Dan" is an anachronism; it is like speaking of the "New York of the middle of the sixteenth century," whereas in reality the city was then called "New Amsterdam."

Genesis 34:7 speaks of "an outrageous thing in Israel," which presupposes the existence of Israel as a nation; but this was not the case before Exodus 1:7. In Genesis 36:31–39, we find a list of Edomite kings, "who reigned in the land of Edom, before any king reigned over the Israelites" (v. 31). This passage seems to date from the time when people were familiar with kings in Israel (from Saul and later).[25] In Genesis 40:14,

---

21. Karlstadt (1520); also cf. Talmud: Sukkah 20a (cf. Sanhedrin 21b, where a comparison between Moses and Ezra is made).
22. Pererius (1591–1599).
23. See more extensively, Saebø (2008, 973).
24. The only New Testament evidence for this is the expression "Moses and the prophets" (Luke 16:19, 31; 24:27, 44; Acts 28:23; cf. John 1:46; Acts 26:22), in which the name "Moses" refers to the entire Pentateuch.
25. In order to strictly maintain the Mosaic authorship of Genesis, Abraham

we hear about the "land of the Hebrews," which could hardly have been written before the conquest of the promised land.

(b) That Moses was the author of Deuteronomy seems to be suggested in John 1:45 and 5:46 (if referring to Deut. 18:16), Matthew 19:7-8 (referring to Deut. 24:1) and 22:24 (referring to Deut. 25:5). However, if Moses were really the book's author, how can we explain chapter 2:12, "The Horites also lived in Seir formerly, but the people of Esau dispossessed them and destroyed them from before them and settled in their place, as Israel did to the land of their possession, which the LORD gave to them."[26] This must have been written after the conquest of the promised land. In chapter 3:14 we find the expression "as it is to this day," which points to a time (long) after the conquest. Chapter 34 is the chapter about Moses' own death, which must have been written after the event.[27] Only those who defend mechanical inspiration have no problems with such matters.[28] They might answer that God could very well have whispered the story of Moses' death into his own ear. In §7.8 I explained the inadequacy of this approach.

Please note, I am not saying that there are no possible explanations for (some of) these *post-Mosaica*; for instance; they may betray the hand of later editors. Nor am I saying that they demonstrate that Moses cannot have been the writer of the bulk of the Pentateuch[29] — nor that he *was* the writer, for that matter. I mention these things especially to show that *any* attempt to formulate an answer to such questions is a form of literary criticism (historical criticism, biblical criticism). For instance, assuming the work of editors is a typical element in

---

Ibn Ezra and Obadiah ben Jacob Sforno wanted to see in the term "king" a reference to Moses—a typical emergency solution; see Cohen (1983, 218).

26. Sforno (see previous note) thinks of the countries that had been taken from Sihon and Og during Moses' time; see Cohen (1983, 998).
27. According to Ibn Ezra, Deut. 34 was written by Joshua; according to Rashi from v. 5 by Joshua; see Cohen (1983, 1182).
28. Unfortunately, Bible scholar John N. Darby (*CW* 6, 359–364, "Inspiration of the Scriptures") went quite far in this direction.
29. Cf. McDowell (1975, 91–116); Archer Jr. (1982, 45–54); Craigie (1976).

The Modernist View of the Old Testament

the discipline of literary criticism. At the same time, such an assumption would be a great problem for those committed to mechanical inspiration. This is because such editors would have altered the Holy Writings that had already been verbally inspired. Moreover, if we assume that editing of the sacred text occurred at *some* places, how can we be sure that it did not occur at *many* places, including where this is not immediately obvious?

11.2.2 Other Problems

(c) If Moses really were the author of both Exodus and Deuteronomy, how can it be explained—as many authors have wondered—that there are such remarkable contradictions between these books? Normally in such a case, literary critics would assume that one tradition came to the addressees along two very different ways, and that during the process several differences arose. Jewish Bible scholar Marc Zvi Brettler mentioned several examples (see §7.3.3).[30] For instance, if one wished to celebrate *Sukkoth* (the Feast of Booths), one would have to decide whether to celebrate the feast for seven days (Deut. 16:13), or to add an eighth day of "solemn rest" (Lev. 23:39). One would also have to decide whether the prohibition against eating non-slaughtered meat refers to him (Deut. 14:21), or only to the priests, and whether as a non-priest, he may eat a cow that was found dead alongside the road (see Lev. 17:15).

Brettler viewed such passages as irreconcilable. This might not necessarily be the case; but the problem itself can hardly be denied: there are difficult differences within the Sinaitic Torah. One reason for the origin of the Mishnah (the oldest part of the Talmud) was to establish how God's commandments had to be obeyed, for instance, in cases where different parts of the Torah seemed to contradict each other.

Brettler's examples are only a few. We will always encoun-

---

30. M. Z. Brettler in Brown (2007, 5).

ter expositors who manage to iron out such wrinkles, but the question becomes how convincing they are. Usually, they are convincing most of all to the people who "knew" the proper answer already beforehand. At any rate, people cannot simply ignore or deny this kind of literary problem. Not just the rabbis who contributed to the Mishnah, but also present-day scholars are obligated to try to find a scientifically reasonable and plausible solution to them.

(d) Of a very different nature, yet a typically literary-critical matter, is the consideration that the Hebrew of the song of Moses (Exod. 15:1–21), just like that of the song of Deborah (Judg. 5), exhibits certain archaic traits. Therefore, it is assumed that this Hebrew represents a (much) older stage in the development of the language than the Hebrew in the rest of the Pentateuch.[31] This would mean that the song of Moses goes back to a very old source, whereas the rest of the Pentateuch would stem from a later time. However, the Hebrew that Moses spoke must necessarily have been the same as that of Exodus 15. If this argument is valid, large parts of the Pentateuch must stem from a time much later than that of Moses.

No Bible scholar can escape doing historical or literary criticism—and why would such a scholar wish to escape doing such criticism? In such a scholarly enterprise, questions in the domain of the historical and literary sciences must not be argued away with a superficial appeal to the supernatural. On the contrary, they must be answered with arguments derived from these same historical and literary sciences. Scottish theologian I. Howard Marshall referred to the beautiful example of the thoroughly orthodox English theologian Joseph B. Lightfoot,[32] who followed this very approach.[33] Lightfoot wrote that abjuring reason is not a demonstration of faith but the surrender to despair.[34] In modern parlance: the appeal by

---

31. See extensively, Young et al. (2008).
32. Lightfoot (1889).
33. Marshall (1977, 112).
34. Lightfoot (1865); quoted by Cassels (1874) at the beginning of his book,

The Modernist View of the Old Testament

fundamentalists to the supernatural—in this case, to divine inspiration—is not an *answer* to the questions that have been posed but a *fleeing from* the questions, for fear of confrontation. Lightfoot fully believed in the divine inspiration of Scripture; however, he answered historical questions with historical arguments, as is proper. Only in this way can justice be done, not only to the text but to opponents, and only in this way can the latter be won over. This is what the apostle Paul did: in opposition to the Corinthians who did not accept the (bodily) resurrection, he did not say: "You simply must believe it," but he provided a number of solid, rational *arguments* for the resurrection (1 Cor. 15).

Thus, there is nothing wrong with the disciplines of historical or literary criticism as such. On the contrary, these are an important instrument for obtaining a better understanding of the Bible text and its backgrounds. *The only problem lies in the starting point, the presuppositions with which these disciplines begin their investigations.* Are these presuppositions foreign to the Bible as the object of investigation, adopted from extra-biblical thinking, and sometimes outright anti-biblical thinking? Or are these presuppositions consistent with the believing confession of Scripture as the Word of God?

This is not intended as a naïve question. Such a believing confession does not automatically establish (a) what criteria determine whether presuppositions are foreign or proper to Scripture, (b) how the literary and historical investigations must be performed, and (c) whether as part of a (post-)modern culture, the reader is influenced by forces foreign to Scripture.

11.2.3 Criticism Alien to the Bible

About the starting point for any form of biblical criticism there can be no doubt; it is well described in Luther's adage men-

---

which was the book that was combated by Lightfoot (1889).

tioned before: Holy Scripture is its own interpreter (Lat. *sacra scriptura sui ipsius interpres*). The investigation of Scripture must never be dominated by pagan and humanist influences imposed upon it from the outside, which are entirely alien to the Bible. In fact, the approach that I propose is nothing but the usual treatment of ancient literature, namely, a congenial, harmonizing approach, in which seeming discrepancies are explained as much as possible from the context, and in which the unity of the text is maintained as long as the opposite has not been clearly demonstrated.

The practice, however, is less than the ideal. Even the strictest *literary* criticism, which is occupied with literary genres only, is often linked with philosophical views that are alien to the Bible's own spiritual world. Otto Weber emphasized that the right of historical-critical investigation as such is undisputed, but this investigation has so often been attacked because of its link with the biases of rationalism, and especially of (theological) liberalism.[35] He questioned whether this link was necessary, and whether historical criticism in fact belongs to the Christian self-understanding as radically historical. This seems to me rather hypothetical; the reality is that biblical criticism seems to have been invariably associated with philosophies that are alien to the Bible, such as Platonism and Aristotelianism, scholasticism, the more modern rationalism, Romanticism, historicism, evolutionism, (neo-)positivism, existentialism, structuralism, neo-Marxism, postmodernism, and so on.

The first literary-historical criticism with respect to the Pentateuch and the authorship of Moses was closely linked with British empiricism and deism, with continental rationalism, and later with the German and French Enlightenment. It was in this spiritual climate that the documentary hypothesis concerning the Pentateuch originated. We think here of Henning B. Witter, Jean Astruc, or, especially since the Enlighten-

---

35. Weber (1981, 330–33).

ment, Johann Gottfried Eichhorn (he was called the father of Old Testament criticism, and was influenced by the anti-supernaturalism of German thinkers such as Johann Salomo Semler and Johann Philipp Gabler, and the Romanticism of Johann Gottfried Herder), Wilhelm M. L. de Wette, Abraham Kuenen, and Julius Wellhausen. Each of the latter three adhered to a strictly evolutionist view of the history of Israel's religion, as we will see. Then there was Ferdinand C. Baur, who, like De Wette, was active in New Testament criticism, and like Wellhausen, was heavily influenced by the dialectical historicism of Georg W. F. Hegel. Thus, Baur viewed the New Testament dialectically as a synthesis of the earlier Petrine theology (thesis) and the later, Pauline theology (antithesis).[36] I will return to discuss these influences that are alien to Scripture; my point here is that a strictly neutral literary-historical approach does not exist, and never did.

Thus, it is no wonder that orthodox theology has often strongly protested against current biblical criticism. Johan Verkuyl rejected all forms of historical criticism that arose from hatred toward the Bible, and even called them a "scientific scandal."[37] However, he did believe that there is a believing historical criticism, which has solved many difficulties in the Bible text, has better explained the background of the Bible books, has shown that the Bible writers were not infallible in their worldviews and in their rendering of historical events, and so on. But were all of these indeed positive developments? And is not all scholarly Bible research being simply identified with historical-literary criticism? And is not Verkuyl's distinction between a believing and an unbelieving historical criticism too idealistic? All these questions will be discussed below.

---

36. Baur (1831); also cf. Adams and Horrell (2004, 13–16, 51–59).
37. Verkuyl (1992, 36–38).

11.3 Other Literary Questions

11.3.1 Deutero-Isaiah

In the previous sections, we have dealt especially with some questions concerning the Pentateuch. However, more of this kind of questions may be asked concerning other books of the Old Testament. Let me give two well-known examples (in this and the next section). The first involves the so-called Deutero-Isaiah. Since the end of the nineteenth century, Bible scholars launched the thesis that Isaiah 40-66 could not possibly have come from the same author as chapters 1-39. They referred to the unknown writer of chapters 40-66 as Deutero-Isaiah (i.e., Second Isaiah). Some even believe that Isaiah 56-66 came from another unknown prophet, whom they call Trito-Isaiah (i.e., Third Isaiah).

Conservative theologians responded to this by pointing to various New Testament passages where portions from Isaiah 40-66 are attributed to the prophet Isaiah (e.g., Matt. 3:3; 8:17; 12:17-21; Luke 4:17; John 1:23; Acts 8:28, 30; Rom. 10:6, 20). This is certainly a point to be taken into account. However, such theologians did not thereby answer the literary-critical questions that had arisen, such as:[38]

(a) How can it be that the name "Isaiah" occurs sixteen times in chapters 1-39, but never in chapters 40-66?

(b) How can the obvious change in style and subjects after chapter 39 be explained?

(c) How can it be that several passages in chapters 40-66 refer to events that did not occur during Isaiah's time, but much later, such as the establishment of Babylon as a world empire, the destruction of Jerusalem, and especially the rise of the Persian king Cyrus, who is named (Isa. 44:28; 45:1), and who conquered the Babylonian empire and established the Persian empire?

The point is not only whether a prophet could mention the

---

38. See, e.g., Lemche (2008); Kugel (2008, 538-68); a recent plea for Isaiah's authorship Isa. 40-66 is offered by Beale (2008, chapter 5).

name of a person several centuries before that person's birth; to deny this would be nothing but a rationalistic anti-prophetism (*the* example of such mentioning is 1 Kings 13:2, where a prophet predicts the name of future king Josiah). The question goes deeper. How can it be that Isaiah 40-55 not only refers to events that took place long after Isaiah, but that the prophet concerned *writes as if he himself lives during the time of the events*? (See especially the Babylon passages: Isa. 43:14; 47:1; 48:14, 20.) Even the most conservative expositor cannot get around the latter question.

My point here is not to engage in a deep discussion about Deutero-Isaiah; this is a task for Old Testament scholars. I merely wish to indicate that not (only) some rationalistic prejudice but (also) the Bible text itself generates literary questions that cannot be solved by a simple appeal to some New Testament quotations.

11.3.2 The Dating of Daniel

Literary questions are generated by the Bible text itself. This is also clear from my second example: the dating of the book of Daniel. Some expositors have claimed that the arguments for a dating shortly after the death of king Antiochus IV Epiphanes (164 BC) are overwhelming.[39] In opposition to this, other expositors claim that there are still good arguments for a dating in the sixth century BC (the time of Daniel).[40]

Whatever theory people may prefer, even the most conservative expositor must face the underlying literary questions. This particular question must be answered: How must we explain

(a) that the book supplies us with so many details about the history of the world empires after the death of Daniel, but not later than the Seleucid king Antiochus IV Epiphanes;

(b) that the book tells us extensively about the latter in

---

39. E.g., Brown et al. (1999, 448).
40. See, e.g., Harrison (1969, 1110–27); Archer Jr. (1985, 4–6).

particular (see Dan. 8, especially vv. 9–14 and 23–25; Dan. 9, especially v. 27; and Dan. 11, especially vv. 21–35);

(c) that it nevertheless tells us nothing about the death of this king and about the time after him, apart from eschatological passages about the Son of Man (the Messiah) and his kingdom (especially in Dan. 2 and 7)?

In this case, too, we may presume that rationalistic biases may play a role with many expositors. They consider long-term prophecies to be impossible, and conclude that the book of Daniel necessarily offers predictions made after the predicted events had occurred (Lat. *vaticinia ex eventu*). And here again, one might simply reply with an appeal to the New Testament, where Jesus attributes the book to "Daniel the prophet" (Matt. 24:15). Here, too, various linguistic and historical objections have been raised that other scholars consider unpersuasive. Again, this is a matter for Old Testament scholars to resolve.

For now, the single literary question of importance is: Why do the detailed predictions (see especially Dan. 11) stop precisely with king Antiochus IV Epiphanes? In each dating of the book, traditional or modern, expositors must account for this problem.

This kind of question illustrates the legitimacy of literary criticism applied to Scripture. The real problem is not literary criticism as such, but the philosophical presuppositions that play a role in performing such criticism. Are the critics, not only the modernists but also the fundamentalists, always sufficiently unbiased and methodologically pure in the way they perform their task? It is even *possible* to be unbiased and pure in such matters? Because of such questions and because of the complexity of the investigation itself, debating the results of literary criticism will probably continue indefinitely. This debating is not a problem, but rather is proper to any scientific debate.

11.4 Development of Biblical Criticism[41]

11.4.1 Earliest Development

One of my main theses in these chapters is that the historical development and philosophical presuppositions of biblical criticism go hand in hand. Thus, during the time of the Reformation we see humanism rising alongside the Reformation. Sometimes, the two overlapped, as with Ulrich Zwingli and Philip Melanchthon; John Calvin has also sometimes been reckoned among the Christian humanists of his time.[42] However, because of the increasing emphasis that humanism placed on human autonomy, it became estranged from the Reformation. The rising Enlightenment left little room for a belief in miracles, in divine revelation, in the inspiration of Scripture, and in the supernatural generally. Thus, the Bible books were declared by some to be important pieces of ancient literature, of a particular religious quality, but no more than this. In the science of comparative religion, they were explained alongside other examples of pagan cultures and religions.

We think here especially of the British deists and thinkers sympathetic to them, who rejected biblical inspiration and the Bible as the Word of God, such as Isaac (de) la Peyrère, Baruch Spinoza, Thomas Hobbes, and Richard Simon. In these circles, one of the chief topics was the historical-critical analysis of the Pentateuch and (the rejection of) its Mosaic authorship. In the early eighteenth century, this criticism gave birth to the documentary hypothesis, particularly with regard to the Pentateuch. This theory believes aims to discern various sources (Ger. *Quellen*, i.e., earlier writings and traditions) of

---

41. For the history and claims of biblical criticism, see Berkouwer (1938); Kraus (1969); Maier (1974); McDowell (1975); Brown (1976); Wenham (1976); Harrison (1978; 1979); Guthrie (1978; 1979); Wentsel (1982, 456–561); Geisler (1999); Osborne (1999). Here are some works on (the history of) biblical criticism by authors with presuppositions alien to Scripture: *RGG* 1:1184–90; Roessingh (1914–1929); Knight and Tucker (1993); (ex-inerrantist) Ehrman (2005).

42. See, e.g., N. Wolterstorff in Zimmermann (2017, chapter II.4).

the Pentateuch.

In the eighteenth century, the Enlightenment moved from Great Britain to Germany. Great influence was exerted by the views of Hermann S. Reimarus. He rejected miracles, called Jesus an idealizing Jew without future aspirations, and called the disciples immoral because they had stolen Jesus' body and had begun preaching the resurrection out of their own self-interest.[43] Johann Salomo Semler (see §11.2.3) was equally radical and influential.[44] He did wish to retain what he considered to be the essential parts of the Christian religion, but to this end made a distinction between the divine content (Word of God) and the human form (Scripture). He declared certain parts of the canon to be non-authentic. The third leading theologian in those days was Johann Philipp Gabler (§11.2.3), who introduced the concept of myth (a story about one or more supernatural beings) into historical criticism, especially with regard to Genesis 1–3.[45]

It is quite remarkable that the beginning of the history of biblical criticism does not consist of objective scientific work, but rather of arguing certain types of philosophical thought. These philosophers excluded *a priori* the possibility of divine revelation, thereby rejecting the Bible's self-testimony. Also in the nineteenth century, we observe this close interwovenness of biblical studies with philosophy. Thus, Johann Gottfried Eichhorn (§11.2.3) was influenced by the Romantic philosophy of Johann Gottfried Herder.[46] At the same time, we notice the influence of Hegel's dialectical idealism, especially in the new Tübingen school of Ferdinand C. Baur (see above). This school was founded upon Semler's view concerning a contrast between the Jewish and the Gentile Christianity in the early church, and applied to this Hegel's dialectical idea of historical development: through the thesis (Jewish [Petrine]

---

43. Regarding him, see Strauss (1862).
44. Regarding him, see Hornig (1996).
45. See, e.g., Gabler (1790).
46. See, e.g., Herder (2010).

Christianity, also, e.g., in Rev.) and the antithesis (Gentile Christianity, rooted in Paul's ministry), the synthesis of Catholic Christianity (e.g., Acts) came about (cf. §11.2.3).[47]

11.4.2 The Pentateuch Documentary Hypothesis[48]

Henning B. Witter seems to have been the first who claimed the existence behind the canon of various documents or sources, from which the Bible books would have been composed.[49] Like Astruc and Eichhorn, he used the various names of God as a starting point for a documentary hypothesis. Eichhorn distinguished in Genesis between the Jahwist (J), the document that uses the name YHWH, and the Elohist (E), the document that uses the term *Elohim* ("God").[50] Eichhorn also introduced new criteria, such as (supposed) parallel stories and doublets, like the two (supposed) creation stories in Genesis 1-2 (the first one using only *Elohim*, the second one also YHWH), and the two Flood stories in Genesis 6-8, which reflect different documents that were editorially blended in these Bible passages.

The great uncertainty about the identification and application of the various chosen criteria soon led to a great diversity of documentary hypotheses concerning the Pentateuch (Karl D. Ilgen, Alexander Geddes, Johann Severin Vater, Heinrich Ewald, Wilhelm M. L. de Wette).

In 1853, German Orientalist Hermann Hupfeld brought about a great breakthrough,[51] which has been called the "Copernican revolution" in the history of the documentary hypothesis.[52] He laid the foundation for the modern documentary hypothesis by arguing that J originally had been one document; that E was actually a composition of two doc-

---

47. See note 36.
48. Cf. Holwerda (1972, 12–17); Houtman (1980, 60–67).
49. Witter (1711).
50. Eichhorn (1820).
51. Hupfeld (1853).
52. Archer Jr. (1964, 77).

uments, E¹ and E²; that an editor had put these three documents together to form the present book of Genesis; and that De Wette's D document (Deuteronomist) was indeed a separate document (this thesis in fact came from Hupfeld's pupil Eduard K. A. Riehm, who dated D in the second half of the rule of Manasseh[53]). Later, E¹ was referred to as P (Priestly Code), and E² simply as E.

According to Hupfeld, the chronological order of documentary origin was P–E–J–D. This was doubted by Alsacian theologian Édouard G. E. Reuss[54] and his renowned pupil, Alsacian theologian Karl H. Graf, who believed that P was the latest document.[55] With the powerful support from Dutch Old Testament scholar Abraham Kuenen,[56] the order of the four documents now became J–E–D–P. Here again, the decisive arguments were not of a strictly literary or historical nature, but of a philosophical nature. Kuenen was occupied in particular with the evolutionist reconstruction of Israel's history. In this respect, he was followed by the most important representative of the Pentateuch documentary hypotheses, Julius Wellhausen.[57] In fact, the latter did not add any new elements, but he formulated and revised in a brilliant way the theory of Graf and Kuenen, and gave it the classical form that has become so well-known. Due to him, the theory became very quickly the position of the majority of Old Testament scholars in Europe, later in North-America.

It has been claimed that his classical work[58] gave Wellhausen a status comparable to that of Charles R. Darwin in biolo-

---

53. Riehm (1854).
54. Reuss (1881, VII) claimed that, already in 1834, he had suggested the thesis that the law is younger than the prophets. The enormous consequences of this view for Old Testament theology are dealt with in the next section (§11.5).
55. Graf (1866).
56. Kuenen (1874).
57. Wellhausen (1963; 1987).
58. Wellhausen (1994).

The Modernist View of the Old Testament

gy.[59] The reason is that Wellhausen's literary criticism formed the framework for his historical criticism, which was of a thoroughly evolutionist nature (see below). Today we would say that Wellhausen gave a definitive form to a genuine paradigm shift in Old Testament scholarship.

11.4.3 Philosophical Foundation

At this point, the examples given so far — later I will give some more — may suffice to illustrate that, from the beginning, biblical criticism was based on a philosophical framework that was rooted in the humanistic ground-motive. In my view, the main elements in this framework are the following:

(1) *Naturalism*, which accepts only explanations that fit in with the natural laws such as the natural sciences (rising rapidly to prominence at this time) discovered and formulated them. This was the same as *anti-supernaturalism*, that is, the basic rejection of everything supernatural, everything that surpasses the natural laws as we know them in the world in its entirety, and certainly in the Bible. This led to:

(2) An *evolutionist* approach, especially inspired by the historicism of German philosopher Georg W. F. Hegel and the biological evolution theory of English naturalist Charles R. Darwin, both with respect to (a) the development of the individual Bible books, and (b) the development of a theology of Israel, as well as (c) the later development of the theology of the early church (Ger. *Gemeindetheologie*, "church [produced] theology," the [de]formation of the story and message of Jesus).

Some specific consequences of (1) and (2) were:

(a) The distinction within the text of Scripture between an essential *center* (focus, scope) and a non-essential *periphery*, or between content and form (cf. §7.9.3).

(b) Alleged identification of the *mythical* element, whether in the peripheral parts of the Bible (see a), or in the church

---

59. Douglas (1974a).

theology woven around Jesus.

(c) Alleged identification of the ancient *worldview* of the Bible writers (and readers), which is unacceptable to modern readers and undermines the credibility of the Bible.[60]

11.5 A Case Study: Julius Wellhausen[61]

11.5.1 Wellhausen and His Forerunners

Julius Wellhausen dated the J document in the ninth century BC in the southern (or two-tribe) kingdom. He claimed that this Jahwist had been the first author who had merged the legends, myths, poems, and well-known stories of other nations, such as the Babylonians, into one large history of God's people with the help of oral traditions and written sources. Further, he dated the Elohist document around 750 BC, and assumed that the latter, too, had intended to merge existing traditions into one history. The E document supposedly employed the traditions current among the northern (ten) tribes, some of which were the same as those available to J. The E document used only the name *Elohim* for God in stories dated before Moses' time because he supposed that the name YHWH had first been revealed to Moses later (cf. Exod. 6:1-2). After the destruction of Jerusalem (586 BC), an editor merged J and E into one history, in which he sometimes preserved both versions of a story, even if these differed in details, or he used only one version, adding details from the other version.

P, the so-called Priestly Code, supposedly came from a priest, or a group of priests, who lived in Babylon during the exile. They designed for the people a holiness code, or a form of the worship service, and the laws that pertained to these. At first, P was a separate work. In the fourth century BC, this writing was merged with certain parts of the JE work. It was as if someone took a fascinating account of American history, and at essential points larded it with the American constitu-

---

60. Cf. Ouweneel (2018l, §§3.5, 3.6, chapters 4 and 5).
61. See extensively, Holwerda (1972, 25–71); McDowell (1975, chapter 8); Houtman (1980, 76–80); Nicholson (2003).

tion or parliamentary laws.[62] This JEP work contained what we today would call the first four books of the Pentateuch.

Later, D was added, the work of the Deuteronomist, which supposedly was composed during the revival under king Josiah (621 BC) (cf. 2 Chron. 34:13–33). To D is linked forever the name of Old Testament scholar Martin Noth.[63] He launched the theory of the "Deuteronomist history": the theory that the books Deuteronomy, Joshua, Judges, Samuel, and Kings form one coherent historiography. The basic idea is that the sojourn in the promised land was linked to two conditions: (a) the worship of YHWH alone, and (b) such worship only at the one central place of worship, first announced in Deuteronomy 12 and culminating in Solomon's temple at Jerusalem.

In the Anglo-Saxon countries, the Pentateuch documentary hypothesis was strongly popularized by William R. Smith, Charles A. Briggs, and Samuel R. Driver.[64] During the twentieth century, scholars kept suggesting limited additions to, and changes in, the theory, but these did not find general recognition. On the contrary, the tendency of twentieth-century Old Testament theology was to replace the documentary hypothesis with even more radical theories (see below).

As I said, the significance of, and the explanation for, the rapid success of Wellhausen's theory lies in the fact that he placed the documentary hypothesis in a wider historical-critical framework. Others, such as Wilhelm M. L. de Wette, Johann Friedrich L. George,[65] and Johann K. Wilhelm Vatke,[66] had attempted this before Wellhausen. However, these could not be successful as long as the literary aspects of the documentary hypothesis had not been established to the satisfaction of the critics. Wellhausen himself noticed that De Wette,

---

62. Pedersen and Cumgerlege (1947, 14).
63. Noth (1960).
64. Smith (2009); Driver (1892); Briggs (1897).
65. J. F. L. George exhibited the strong influence of Hegel; he divided the history of Israel into a mythical phase, a religious phase, and a rational phase.
66. De Wette (1806–07); George (1835); Vatke (1835).

George, and Vatke had correctly discerned the historical problems, but that the critics rightly had been occupied first with the compositional problems. However, it had been their mistake to believe that discerning the various sources implied the solution of the historical problem as such.[67] In reality, the historical question "had been merely put to sleep" — so said Wellhausen — and it had been Graf's achievement, after a long period of lethargy, to have awakened them. What Graf and Kuenen had begun, Wellhausen had completed: he had placed the documentary hypothesis in the framework of a (in my words, evolutionist) view of history. To this end, through Vatke he appealed to the evolutionist historicism of Georg W. F. Hegel.

In 1835, Vatke had published a work featuring a synthesis between the idealist evolutionism of Hegel and the literary criticism of Eichhorn and De Wette. In a typically Hegelian manner, Vatke distinguished a pre-prophetic (natural-religious), a prophetic (after Moses), and a post-prophetic phase (after Jeremiah). Vatke asserted that the religion of the Hebrews had developed from relatively primitive historical phases into the monotheistic faith of later Judaism. During the time of Moses, the Israelite society had still been basically pre-historical, Vatke suggested, whereas the Torah obviously was the product of an established and developed state. Half a century later, Wellhausen acknowledged how much he owed to the work of Vatke. He called it the most important attempt ever undertaken to understand ancient Israel in strictly historical categories.[68]

11.5.2 The Alleged Evolution of Israel's Religion

This had become the new goal: explaining the history and religion of ancient Israel as a gradual development through a natural evolutionary process. At first, Eichhorn, De Wette, and others, had considered this developmental process from the

---

67. Wellhausen (1994, 10).
68. Harrison (1969, 423).

viewpoint of Romanticism. Later, George, Vatke, and Ewald had done so from the viewpoint of Hegel's dialectical idealism. Within the natural sciences, Darwin's concept of natural selection resembled the Hegelian notion of dialectics, just like his evolutionism resembled Hegel's historicism.[69] The evolution theory referred to the development of life, but could be applied to culture as well.[70] Darwin's doctrine conquered the entire scientific world, including theology. The theory of a development from a primitive animism to a highly developed monotheism fit excellently into the framework of Hegel's dialecticism as well as that of Darwin's evolutionism.

Wellhausen himself was well aware of this, as has been shown or emphasized by the works of Samuel R. Külling, Herbert F. Hahn, Paul D. Feinberg, William F. Albright, Gleason L. Archer, and Roland K. Harrison.[71] Purely on the basis of anti-supernaturalism, dialecticism, and evolutionism, Wellhausen worked from the unproven presupposition that Israel's religion, just like any other one, was of a purely human origin, and, in the spirit of historicism, had to be explained exclusively in an evolutionary way. This historical development, as Wellhausen saw it, can be summarized as follows:

(1) **Pre-Prophetic period** (Abraham until about 760 BC). This is the supposed period of:

(a) *Animism:* stone worship (Gen. 28:18; 31:17), tree worship (12:6; 14:3), superstition (Exod. 20:25; Lev. 19:9), and so on.

Of course, nothing in the texts suggests any *worship* of stones or trees.

---

69. Back in 1890–1891, David G. Ritchie investigated the relationships between Hegel and Darwin; see Ritchie (2015); cf. §11.8.
70. See rather recently Distin (2010); Mesoudi (2011); Lewens (2015).
71. Külling (1964, 153); Hahn (1966, 9–10); Feinberg (1968, 3); Albright (1966, 15); Archer Jr. (1964, 79); Harrison (1969, 351–53 56, 423). Cf. also Houtman (1980, 80); remarkably, Houtman does not mention Darwin.

(b) *Animal worship:* the golden calf (Exod. 32; 1 Kings 12), the bronze serpent (Num. 21:8-9; 2 Kings 18:4). The critics venture to say that Moses and other leaders *must* have approved of this idolatry.

However, see Amos 3:14; 4:4; 5:5-6, where the early prophet Amos condemned calf worship in Bethel.

(c) *Child sacrifices,* based on Exodus 22:29b, "The firstborn of your sons you shall give to me," in which the critics think they have found an implicit justification, or even the demand for, child sacrifices.

But again, if the prophets were before the Torah, see the strong condemnation of such sacrifices in Jeremiah 19:5 and Ezekiel 16:20; 20:31. If the Pentateuch was largely invented in the prophets' time, why would the inventors accuse ancient Israel of such misbehavior? For what purpose?

(d) The first *ritual laws,* which allegedly can be found in Exodus 34:11-26; these are thought to presuppose that, in those days, still all Israelites could become priests (cf. 19:6, and the young men in 24:5).

However, if there was any change in this respect, it was within the book of Exodus itself (Exod. 28:1).

(e) *Polytheism,* as seems to be suggested by the plural *Elohim* (lit., "gods"), from the recognition of other gods (Exod. 12:12; 15:11; 18:11; Num. 21:29; Judg. 11:24; 1 Sam. 26:19) and of *asherahs* (sacred poles) and *teraphim* (household idols; see, e.g., Hos. 3:4). During this period, the god of pre-prophetic Israel was supposedly viewed as a tribal god, whose power was limited to Palestine (see for a similar misunderstanding, 1 Kings 20:23, 28).

However, back in Genesis 18:25, God is the "Judge of all the earth," and in Joshua 3:11 and 13, he is the "Lord of all the earth." (Of course, the critics salvage their theories by viewed all such annoying Bible verses as later insertions.)

The Modernist View of the Old Testament

(2) **Prophetic period** (760–586 BC). According to the theory presented here, the monotheistic idea was introduced by Amos, the first writing prophet. Of course, there is not the slightest evidence for this; it is merely speculation on behalf of the critics' cause. Amos' enthusiastic followers were allegedly Hosea, Isaiah, and Micah. During the time of Jeremiah, their monotheism was recorded in Deuteronomy, which was attributed respectfully to Moses. In reality, the literary structure of the book allegedly suggests that it did not originate in the second, but in the first millennium BC.

During this period, the priesthood in Israel was limited to the tribe of Levi, but not yet to the family of Aaron (as it is believed, in spite of the clear statements in Exod. 28:1; Deut. 27:9, 12; 1 Kings 8:4). It was a period with strong emphasis on a liberal gospel of social justice and redemption through good works. Meanwhile, the image of God as a cruel, jealous spirit, roaring out of a volcano (Sinai; cf. Exod. 19:18; Deut. 4:11; 5:23), developed into the image of an exalted person of love and mercy. *This* God would abhor bloody sacrifices (for this idea, Amos 5:21–26; Micah 6:6–8; Isa. 1:11–17; and Jer. 7:22–23 are quoted).

However, the biblical picture is rather that the prophets call upon the people to return to the very God of the Exodus (Hos. 11:1; 12:10, 14; Amos 2:10; 9:7; Micah 6:4; 7:15). On the one hand, the God of the Exodus is "merciful and gracious, slow to anger, and abounding in steadfast love and faithfulness" (Exod. 34:6). On the other hand, the God of the prophets is still the avenging God (see, e.g., Isa. 1:24; 5:9, 29; 34:8; 35:4; 59:17; 63:4; Jer. 50:15; Ezek. 25:12–17; Nah. 1:2). And as to the sacrifices, the prophets obviously speak only of God abhorring *hypocrite* sacrifices (see, e.g., Isa. 66:3; Mal. 1:6–14).

(3) **Priestly period** (since the Babylonian exile). After the fall of the kingdom of Judah, and Israel's giving up their last political aspirations, the priestly tribe of Levi came to the fore. From Ezekiel (1:3; cf. 44:7–16), the priesthood was limited to

the family of Aaron, while Aaron himself was viewed as a fictional figure (despite Micah 6:4). The worship service was now gradually set forth in rules, and ultimately in the P document. In this way, an explicit, universal, cultic monotheism was created.

In order to support this model, all legal rules in earlier Old Testament books had to be argued away. In reality, there are abundant indications that the P parts must be very old.[72] First, archeology has shown that the specific terminology of the worship service was known among other nations at a very early stage.

Second, at the time of the exile, many P segments would have been rather anachronistic because we find many elements in P that are sometimes described in great detail but were lacking after the exile, or were not mentioned again: the tabernacle, the ark, the Ten Commandments, the Urim and Thummim, the Day of Atonement, the avenger of blood and the cities of refuge, the wave offerings, the significance of sacrificial blood, the Nazirites, and so on. Why would post-exilic writers take the trouble to invent so many early-Israelite matters that to post-exilic Jews were no longer relevant?

Third, conversely, important post-exilic elements are totally lacking in P: the name YHWH *Tsebaoth*, "the LORD of hosts" (first in 1 Sam. 1:3), singing and playing music during worship (first mentioned in 1 Chron. 25); the class of the scribes (Heb. *sopherim*[73]); the term "temple";[74] and so forth.

11.5.3 Reading into the Text

The fact that, in reality, no religion in antiquity has ever developed into a genuine monotheism — the monotheism of the Egyptian Pharaoh Akhenaton was temporary and disput-

---

72. See, e.g., Külling (1964).
73. The oldest meaning was "secretary"; see, e.g., 2 Sam. 8:17; 20:25; after the exile, the *sopher* became the Torah-scholar (cf. Gk. *grammateus* in the New Testament).
74. Heb. *hekhal* first occurs in 1 Sam. 1:9.

The Modernist View of the Old Testament

able—did not matter to Wellhausen. His evolutionist bias meant that Israel *could* not have begun with anything but animism, fetishism, and gross polytheism. The overwhelming indications that Israel's religion was refined from its very beginning in Genesis, and was monotheistic from the start, were simply dismissed as later additions and textual changes. This is the well-known, epistemologically completely reprehensible circular argument: *the text is used to support the theory, but where the text contradicts the theory, the theory is used to "correct" the text*. One could mock such a procedure, but the matter is far too grave for that.

One of the far-reaching theological consequences of Wellhausen's theory was that the biblical order—first the law, then the prophets—was reversed: the law (i.e., especially D and P) originated a long time *after* the activities of the prophets. Thus, the entire biblical picture was abandoned, namely, the portrait of YHWH giving his Torah to his people at the beginning of their history, and some considerable time later, sending his prophets *to lead the people back to the Torah*. Instead, a view is presented to us in which the prophets discover, or even invent, this one God, after which a newly formed priestly class *a posteriori* place the Torah on the lips of this (real or imaginary) God.

This is claimed despite the clear statements of Scripture itself as to how the prophets seek to lead the people back to the Torah, and to the God of the Exodus. As to the Torah, here are some examples from the oldest prophetic books: the people have "rejected the law of the Lord of hosts, and have despised the word of the Holy One of Israel" (Isa. 5:24); "they are a rebellious people, lying children, children unwilling to hear the instruction [Heb. *torah*] of the Lord" (30:9); "since you have forgotten the law of your God, I also will forget your children" (Hos. 4:6); "they have transgressed my covenant and rebelled against my law" (8:1); "they have rejected the law of the Lord, and have not kept his statutes" (Amos 2:4).

About the Exodus, the oldest prophetic books are equally clear: "[O]ut of Egypt I called my son" (Hos. 11:1, i.e., Israel; cf. Exod. 4:22). "By a prophet [i.e., Moses] the LORD brought Israel up from Egypt" (Hos. 12:13). "Also it was I who brought you up out of the land of Egypt and led you forty years in the wilderness" (Amos 2:10; cf. 9:7). "I brought you up from the land of Egypt and redeemed you from the house of slavery, and I sent before you Moses, Aaron, and Miriam" (Micah 6:4).

It is of the greatest importance to establish the fact that the new picture that Wellhausen and his forerunners created of the history of Israel's religion did *not* arise from a critical analysis of the Bible text itself. On the contrary, the text presents to us a very different picture. No, the entire model can be explained entirely and exclusively from the anti-biblical biases of the Old Testament scholars involved. In this way, the critics created a fundamental and irreconcilable contrast between the chronology of Israel's history and its theological development. What had traditionally been viewed as the inspired and trustworthy Word of God was degraded to a defective mixture of half-mythical and historically unreliable literary fragments. This was not concluded from the literary analysis of the text itself but on the basis of historicist and evolutionist biases.

This view has enormous consequences for our perspective of the New Testament and of Christianity as well.[75] This view turns the Old Testament into nothing more than a great literary forgery: the history of Israel and its religion is merely an afterthought, a fiction called into existence through the manipulation of older sources, and a systematic representation of earlier events in the light of much later times, with the intention of presenting them as original and authentic. However, if we can no longer believe in the God of the Exodus and the God of the Sinai, what basis do we have to believe in the God of Jesus Christ and the God of Calvary, since Jesus him-

---

75. See Orr (1906, 56–62).

The Modernist View of the Old Testament

self appealed constantly to Moses (Matt. 8:4; 19:8; 23:2; Mark 7:10; 12:26; Luke 16:29, 31; 24:27, 44; John 3:14; 5:45–46; 6:32; 7:19, 22–23)?

11.6 The Unity of Genesis

11.6.1 *Toledot*

These philosophical biases have led to an ever-continuing fragmentation of the Pentateuch. Refuting this procedure requires not only the antithetical combating of the underlying philosophical biases, but also the thetical emphasis on the comprehensive intrinsic unity of the Bible text. The text *itself* supplies the best antidote to this poison of fragmentation.

As an example of this unity, which is entirely disturbed by the documentary hypothesis, I choose the book of Genesis. This unity is remarkable through the book's *toledot* structure, which is unique in the Bible.[76] The expression "(and) these are the generations" (Heb. *(we)*ēleh *toledot*) occurs ten times in Genesis (2:4; 6:9; 10:1; 11:10, 27; 25:12, 19; 36:1, 9; 37:2), together with the phrase "this is the book of the generations" (Heb. *ze sēfer toledot*; 5:1).

The Hebrew word *toledot* (sometimes spelled *toldot*) comes from the root *y-l-d*, "to give birth" and "to make give birth," "to father" (as in 25:19b); the derivative *yeladim* means "children." At the eleven places mentioned, the word usually means "descendants," but in 2:4 it means "origins." Rabbi Obadiah Sforno translated the word in 25:19 as "life story," that is, the totality of the events that were "born" from Isaac's days.[77] Actually, in all eleven cases this would make good sense: "This is the life story (or, the history) of . . . ."

From there, we easily arrive at the rendering "book," especially because this Hebrew word (*sēpher*) occurs in 5:1.[78]

---

76. Regarding this, see Wiseman (1960); Cassuto (1961–64); Holwerda (1971); Wenham (1987, 1994); Hamilton (1990); Sailhamer (1990).
77. Cohen (1983, ad loc.).
78. So Paul et al. (2004, 17, 20).

The expression *"book* of the generations"[79] might point to a very ancient, distinct document (5:1-6:8?). We could even speculate that (a large part of) Genesis is composed of several such documents from antiquity. (Please note that this is something very different from the alleged J, E, and P documents, which [a] are thought to be very much later in origin, and [b] are viewed as comprehensively interwoven in Genesis.) Our speculation must not be stressed too much, though, because the successive *toledot* portions form a clearly coherent totality.

The *toledot* structure leads to a division of Genesis in exactly twelve parts (the number of the sons of Jacob) of very different length, namely,

(1) the book of the creation of *heaven and earth* (1:1-2:3);
(2) the book of *heaven and earth* (2:4-4:26);
(3) the book of *Adam* and his progeny (5:1-6:8);
(4) the book of *Noah* and his progeny (6:9-9:29);
(5) the book of *Noah's sons* and their progeny (10:1-11:9);
(6) the book of *Shem* and his progeny (11:10-26);
(7) the book of *Terah* and his progeny (11:27-25:11);
(8) the book of *Ishmael* and his progeny (25:12-18);
(9) the book of *Isaac* and his progeny (25:19-35:29);
(10) the book of *Esau* and his progeny part I (36:1-8);
(11) the book of *Esau* and his progeny part II (36:9-37:1);
(12) the book of *Jacob* and his progeny (37:2-50:26).

11.6.2 Other Aspects

In addition to the *toledot* structure, many other aspects of the unity of Genesis can be mentioned.[80] First, the very consistent parallelism between 1:1-6:8 ("books" 1-3; see previous section) and 6:9-11:26 ("books" 4-6). Successively, we find in *both* parts:

---

79. Cf. the beginning of the New Testament in Matt. 1:1: "the book of the generation" (Gk. *biblos geneseōs*).
80. See extensively, Rendsburg (1986); cf. the summary in Paul et al. (2004, 16-19).

The Modernist View of the Old Testament

(a) the *tehom* (Hebrew for the "deep"; the primordial ocean, 1:2 and 8:2);

(b) a new beginning (with Adam and Noah, respectively);

(c) sin (3:6; 9:21), nakedness (3:9; 9:22), and subsequent curse (3:17; 9:25);

(d) the role of the youngest son: Abel (4:1-6) and Japheth (9:23);

(e) the sinful son and his progeny: Cain (4:1-6) and Ham (9:22), respectively;

(f) the chosen son and his progeny: Seth (4:25-26; 5:3-8) and Shem (9:26-27; 10:21-31; 11:10-11), respectively;

(g) rebellion (6:1-4 and 11:1-9);

(h) a short introduction of the next protagonist: Noah (5:29-32) and Abr[ah]am (11:26), respectively.

The stories of Abraham, Jacob, and Joseph each exhibit a remarkable chiastic structure, whose details I will pass by here, providing only the key elements. In Abraham's story (11:27-22:24) there are the two covenants (15:1-16:16 and 17:1-18:15). In Jacob's story (25:19-35:22) there are the two kinds of descendants: his sons (29:31-30:24) and the young of his flocks (30:25-43). In Joseph's story (37:2-50:26) there are the two stages in the core encounter with his brothers (44:1-34 and 45:1-28). Between these three stories, we find two connecting parts (23:1-25:18 and 35:23-36:43), which again exhibit a certain parallelism.

In addition, note that Abraham's story is characterized by four altars, Isaac's story by four wells, Jacob's story by four pillars, and Joseph's story by four garments.

From all these examples, the striking intrinsic literary structure of Genesis is evident. It can hardly have been the work of an editor; rather it must have been that of one author. This unity is of such a nature that no separation can be made between the (supposedly mythical, legendary) primordial history of Genesis 1-11 and the ordinary history of Genesis 12-

50, such that we should take only the second part historically seriously (at least to some extent).[81] Given the compositional unity of Genesis, such a separation cannot be maintained. The God who was at work in the stories of the patriarchs is the same as the One who was at work in the story of the creation and the Flood.[82] In my view, these *factual* states of affairs — no matter how carefully we should handle the subjective concept of "fact" — speak more forcefully than any refutations of the philosophical biases in current biblical criticism that we might adduce.

11.7 Naturalism and Other Postulates

11.7.1 Biases

Wolfgang Trillhaas wrote, "As important, even indispensable, as historical criticism may be for a conscientious exposition and disclosure of the text, faith is nonetheless independent of the correctness of historical-critical judgments."[83] These words may perhaps sound reassuring, but actually they are not at all. The great danger embedded in such a statement is that faith supposedly independent of science and science supposedly independent of faith increasingly grow apart. The fantasy is then born that, whatever biblical criticism may assert, faith remains unaffected. This comes close to the fundamentalist willingness to believe anything (even that Jonah swallowed the whale; §10.6.1), no matter how unscientific it may be. What Trillhaas seems to suggest is that whereas science asserts A to be true, faith may know non-A to be true. Life is lived in two separate worlds. The reality that genuine faith is not at all separated from science, nor does faith need to fear science. The kind of science presented by Vatke, Graf, Kuenen, and Wellhausen tells us more about their own faith than about science in any epistemological sense.

Please note the essential difference between what I am

---

81. See Ouweneel (2018l, chapter 4).
82. Paul et al. (2004, 20).
83. Trillhaas (1972, 84).

saying here and what inerrantists are saying (see chapters 9 and 10). The latter claim that "science really says . . .," and "science is on our side." But to what science are they referring here? As we saw, they seem to believe that all the biases exist on the errantist's side, whereas theirs is a neutral, objective, unbiased science. I reject the supposedly neutral, objective, unbiased science of both the errantists and the inerrantists, and of modern biblical criticism as well. *What we need is a radically Christian ontology and epistemology,* which are able to expose the presuppositions of both errantism and inerrantism, as well as those of modern biblical criticism.

Indeed, the influence of the evolutionist bias within the documentary hypothesis is as conspicuous as it is arbitrary.[84] Take, for instance, the alleged historical order of J, P, and E. All critics before Graf said that J is younger than E, for the name YHWH is later than the term Elohim. No, say Kuenen and Wellhausen, J is older than E because J contains more primitive ideas than E. The P document is the Elohist that differs most from J in topics and style, so P must be the oldest document, said the older critics. But no, P is the youngest of all, for this fits better with the idea of the evolutionary development of Judaism, from primitive polytheism to the monotheism dominated by priests. Instead of the evolutionist approach being the *result* of careful historical criticism, which is rooted in the results of literary criticism, things have been turned upside down. Literary criticism has been made subservient to historical criticism, and the latter has been made dependent on the evolutionist bias.

This conclusion is very significant for evaluating the results of modern biblical criticism. It is important to note that this conclusion originated not with opponents but with the critics themselves. Vatke was not ashamed of making his literary criticism subservient to his historical criticism. Thus he wrote, "[S]ometimes the main reasons to attribute a book to a

---

84. Cf. McDowell (1975, 54–57).

later period are of a dogmatic nature."[85] Otto Eissfeldt therefore said that Vatke was more concerned with insights that were viewed intuitively and determined by material and historical postulates than with literary-critical proofs.[86]

The most important of these postulates was the evolutionistic one, which was based upon the naturalistic postulate of the Enlightenment. Abraham Kuenen openly recognized this by saying, for instance, that, to him, the intimate communion of the Godhead with the patriarchs — which he considered impossible — was one of the decisive arguments *against* the historical character of these stories.[87] Julius Wellhausen wondered who could seriously believe the miracles that occurred at Mount Sinai, when God gave the law to Moses.[88]

In this way, the possibility of a transcendent, supernatural origin of Israel's religion is dismissed *a priori*. Such an origin is simply viewed as inconceivable on the basis of the (anti-super-)naturalistic postulate.[89] This postulate is unjustified because the question that is really at stake here cannot be decided *a priori* by a philosophical bias. This is the question whether the religion of Israel is of divine origin. That is, as to its origin, does it differ essentially from any other religion? With this very same question, Christianity stands or falls, as well. If, as naturalism asserts, Judaism is a religion like any other, then Christianity also contains nothing transcendent and supernatural.

From a strictly scientific viewpoint, a measure of respect is due the investigator who does not accept *a priori* an anti-supernaturalist standpoint, and yet, during their investigation, concludes that an explanation of Israel's religion from purely naturalistic principles is most in agreement with the biblical data. However, it is difficult to respect the investigator who

---

85. Quoted by Rupprecht (1898, 102).
86. Eissfeldt (1965, 165).
87. Kuenen (1874, 108–113).
88. Wellhausen (1994, 12).
89. See extensively, Orr (1906, 12–14); McDowell (1975, 3–16).

The Modernist View of the Old Testament

knows beforehand what the Bible is allowed to say, and who excludes *a priori* the possibility of miracles, of divine revelation, of biblical inspiration, in short: of a transcendent explanation of the Bible's origin. The idea that such an approach is more scientific than the traditional orthodox approach is based upon mere scientism, and constitutes a faith-dogma as imposing as that ascribed to the conservative investigator by Bible critics.

11.7.2 Survey

In summary, one can have some appreciation for the theologian who rejects any bias, and wishes to carry out their literary and historical criticism with as much neutrality and objectivity as possible (if such is at all possible). However, it is far more difficult appreciate the critic who believes beforehand their (anti-super-)naturalist standpoint to be more scientific than the supernaturalist standpoint. What follows is a brief survey of the chief philosophical movements that, in addition to naturalism, have played a role in the origin and history of biblical criticism.[90]

(a) The *rationalism* of the Enlightenment, and its precursors. Some philosophers who have greatly influenced theology were, within continental rationalism, Gottfried W. Leibniz, and within British empiricism, John Locke, John Toland, and Matthew Tindal.[91]

(b) *German idealism*, especially Immanuel Kant. Particularly important are his division between knowing and believing (related to pure reason and practical reason, respectively, based on the humanistic nature–freedom dualism), his distinction between the doctrinal and the authentic exegesis of Scripture (governed by the same dualism), and his pioneer work in demythologizing Scripture.[92] The influence of Georg

---

90. Among the dogmaticians, especially Wentsel (1982, 456–561) has paid much attention to this matter.
91. See Jongeneel (1971).
92. See De Vos (1968); see also Dooyeweerd (1963, 165–70), and his *NC* espe-

W. F. Hegel, at least as important, was already mentioned before.[93]

(c) *Romanticism*, especially the influence of Johann Gottfried Herder.[94]

(d) *Positivism*, and afterwards *neo-* or *logical positivism*. Especially philosopher Ludwig J. J. Wittgenstein must be mentioned here, who, for instance, has strongly influenced Paul Van Buren (d.1998).[95]

(e) *Pragmatism* has influenced theology particularly through American philosopher William James.[96]

(f) *Existentialism* and the precursors of it: Søren Kierkegaard, Friedrich Nietzsche. Martin Heidegger greatly influenced theologians Rudolf Bultmann, Ernst Fuchs, and Gerhard Ebeling,[97] and to some extent Karl Barth.[98]

(g) *Structuralism*, especially that of linguist Ferdinand de Saussure.[99] This philosophy gave rise to a structure-analytical school in theology, which investigates the structural, autonomous coherence of the texts in order to find their deeper significance, viewed as an integrated unity.[100]

(h) *Postmodernism*, especially that of philosophers Jacques Derrida and Jean-François Lyotard, as well as philosopher Richard Rorty.[101]

Note also the rationalistic bias that genuine prophecy in

---

cially 1:325–402; 2:491–541).
93. Cf. De Sopper (1948); Heron (1980, 38–51).
94. Regarding this, see Brown (1984a), who also classifies Schleiermacher under this heading.
95. Van Buren (1963).
96. James (1904).
97. See Zuidema (1956); De Jong (1958).
98. Zuidema (1953; 1955).
99. De Saussure (1916).
100. Regarding the intrinsic unity of the Bible text, see Fokkelman and Weren (2003).
101. See Derrida (1979); Lyotard (1987); Rorty (1989); cf. Kitchen (2003, 369–72).

The Modernist View of the Old Testament

the sense of prediction is impossible. Predictions are thus reduced to prophecies given after the events they predict (Lat. *vaticinia ex eventu*). On this basis, Isaiah 40–66 is dated after the appearance of the Persian king Cyrus (cf. Isa. 44:28; 45:1), and the book of Daniel is dated after the Maccabean revolt to which the book alludes several times (see §11.3). We must properly distinguish here, lest the reproach of rationalism be made too hastily. If Isaiah 40–66 and Daniel are dated late because of a rationalistic anti-prophetism, we cannot agree. However, purely literary arguments have been adduced for this late dating, with which even the most conservative expositor will have to deal.

11.7.3 Theological Post-Postmodernism

I must clearly emphasize here that exposing the philosophical biases of Enlightenment modernism does *not* necessarily imply a return to a premodern approach. Reactionism has hardly ever led to something sensible. Neither reactionism, nor modernism, nor, for that matter, a postmodernist pluralism that relativizes all thought, is the solution for the literary and historical questions mentioned, but serious new investigation. A new approach is needed, which, if so desired, could be referred to as "post-postmodernism," a term, however, that does not tell us very much, and betrays little creativity.

To introduce this matter, let me begin with N. T. Wright. He argued that we must go further with serious historical work than modernism (for its own reasons) was prepared to do. In doing so, we will discover time and again that many of the problems or supposed contradictions that were discovered by modernist critical study resulted from projecting worldviews on the text that were alien to it. Today we have much better lexica than modernism had; new editions of more numerous ancient texts; more archeological and numismatic discoveries than most of us can handle. We must gratefully use all of these historical resources. In doing so, we will discover that much of the old modernist consensus falls apart on the basis of what it originally appealed to, namely, serious historical reconstruction.[102]

Wright quoted philosopher Michael J. Inwood to the effect that critics of Enlightenment have no choice but to use the Enlightenment's own weapons against itself.[103] In other words, it is in the spirit of the Enlightenment to critically and diligently pursue thorough historical investigation, even if this results in earlier assertions of modernism being thereby refuted. We should not promote the rationalism and evolutionism of modernism, but we should certainly defend its critical attitude. This involves the following rejections:

(a) Rejection of *premodernism* (ended about 1750), which limited itself to uncritically appealing to the authorities of former days: the church, tradition, the confession, the Bible expositions that had been established once and for all by the great leaders of an earlier time.

(b) Rejection of *modernism* (1750-1950), insofar as it concerned its naturalistic and rationalistic biases. For lack of sufficient historical sources, the results of Enlightenment modernism were inspired by such biases rather than by rigorous historical and literary investigation.

(c) Rejection of *postmodernism* (began about 1950), which on the basis of its pluralism and relativism basically deems all interpretations as equally valid. Here, the only question is how the text affects me, not whether something or someone objectively addresses me through the text.

Modernism *rightly* rejected the simplistic authoritarianism of premodernism. The great leaders of old do not decide what and how we must think; we ourselves are responsible for this. Postmodernism *rightly* rejected the universalist rationalism of modernism: the *sola ratio(ne)* is no more the solution than the earlier blind authoritarianism with its *sola ecclesia, sola tradi-*

---

102. Wright (2005, 95).
103. M. J. Inwood in Honderich (1995, 237).

tio(ne), or *sola confessio(ne)*.[104]

Apart from these things, I *defend* the positive elements in the "-isms" mentioned:

(a) *Premodernism:* in my view the formal authority of Scripture comes first, but not any formal authority of church leaders, creeds, expositors, or Bible scholars.

(b) *Modernism:* I defend the demand of modernism, namely, the necessity of rigorous critical literary and historical investigation, but only on the basis of paradigmatic biases consistent with Scripture.

(c) *Postmodernism:* I defend the room that postmodernists have created again for *all* conceivable presuppositions and starting points, as long as these are consistent with Scripture and produce useful results.[105]

In the theological "post-postmodernism" as I describe it here, supra- (not ir-)rationalistic and supernaturalistic presuppositions are allowed again, while at the same time the requirement of rigorous critical literary and historical investigation is maintained.

Let me refer here to the wise words of Joseph Ratzinger:

> If scholarly exegesis is not to exhaust itself in constantly new hypotheses, becoming theologically irrelevant, it must take a methodological step forward and see itself once again as a theological discipline, without abandoning its historical character. It must learn that the positivistic hermeneutic on which it has been based does not constitute the only valid and definitively evolved rational approach; rather, it constitutes a specific and historically conditioned form of rationality that is both open to correction and completion and in need of it. It must recognize that a properly developed faith-hermeneutic is appropriate to

---

104. *Ratio, traditio,* and *confessio* mean "reason," "tradition," and "confession"; *ratione, traditione* and *confessione* mean "by reason," "by tradition," and "by the confession" (cf. *sola fide*, "by faith alone").

105. Cf. the "anything goes" of Paul Feyerabend (2008).

the text and can be combined with a historical hermeneutic, aware of its limits, so as to form a methodological whole.[106]

11.8 Historicism

11.8.1 The Enlightenment Influence

Julius Wellhausen was convinced that Charles R. Darwin, through the latter's evolutionary doctrine, had offered him a well-founded scientific basis for his religion-historical theories.[107] Evidently, in the nineteenth century, the age of optimistic and positivistic-scientistic overestimation of the natural sciences, each practitioner of the humanities was glad if his theories turned out (or, seemed) to stand on a solid natural-scientific foundation.[108] A remarkable example of this was Karl Marx, who, shortly after the appearance of Darwin's book (1859), wrote to Friedrich Engels (1860), "Darwin's book is very important, and serves me as a foundation in the natural selection for the class struggle in history."[109] In a similar way, Darwin unknowingly influenced the evolutionistic view of Wellhausen.

In reality, the basic idea of Darwin's theory, the idea of natural selection, had not been discovered by scientific research either. We could call it a paradigmatic prejudice, which formed the foundation of his theory (and the similar theory of sympathetic scientist, A. Russell Wallace). Darwin seems to have adopted the idea of natural selection from the British economist and clergyman Thomas R. Malthus.[110] The latter claimed that he had discovered the idea with American scholar Benjamin Franklin, who presumably had adopted it from the French Enlightenment philosophers.[111]

---

106. Ratzinger (2011, xiv–xv; cf. 240: "The mystery of atonement is not to be sacrificed on the altar of overweening rationalism.").
107. See Hayes (1941, 127, 138); Archer Jr. (1964, 79); Pearce (1974, 363).
108. See extensively, Ouweneel (2018l, chapter 2).
109. Quoted by Zirkle (1959, 85–86); cf. Ouweneel (2000a, 408).
110. Malthus (1926).
111. See Ouweneel (1978, 76–84).

This same Enlightenment was also the breeding ground of German idealism: Immanuel Kant, Johann Gottlieb Fichte, Friedrich W. J. Schelling, and finally Georg W. F. Hegel. The latter elaborated historicism — *the* characteristic of *all* great nineteenth-century philosophical schools[112] — into a complete evolutionary philosophy of history.[113] Hegel believed that it was the main task of philosophy to determine the meaning of history. Because the history of Israel comprises more than three thousand years, it seemed an excellent starting point for historicistic considerations. In his *Lectures on the Philosophy of Religion*, Hegel attributed to Judaism a well-delineated and necessary place in the evolutionary development of Christianity.[114]

More recently, there is a certain tendency to belittle Hegel's influence upon Wellhausen, or to deny it completely.[115] And if such philosophical influences are recognized at all, they are easily brushed aside by asserting that the obtained scientific results are solid enough to be maintained, apart from such philosophical influences. (Of course, the same is said about Darwin's doctrine of natural selection, and the possible philosophical influences that gave rise to it.) In my view, such a view betrays a lack of epistemological insight.

11.8.2 Form Criticism

I feel Cornelis Houtman was only partially right when he said,

> No investigator is without prejudices, and the possibility must not be excluded beforehand that philosophical presuppositions can open the eyes to noticing certain connections, which have a

---

112. Cf. Troost (2004, 402–03); Strauss (2009, 260–63).
113. I use the word "evolution(ary)" here anachronistically because neither the German idealists, nor Darwin in the first edition of his *The Origin of Species* (1859), used the term. The first who applied it in the biological sense seem to have been Robert Grant in 1826, and Charles Lyell in 1832; see Hall and Hallgrimsson (2007, 4–5).
114. See Hegel (1990); Hodgson (2005).
115. As does Perlitt (1965, 153).

basis in historical reality. However, the available material data will have to support the correctness of the philosophical presuppositions.[116]

In my view, this statement is partially mistaken, and partially irrelevant. As to the first point: Houtman's statement contains a clearly positivistic danger by suggesting that "material data" normally support or refute philosophical presuppositions. The modern philosophy of science rather suggests the opposite: there *are* no neutral, objective scientific facts, but facts always function within the framework of a certain worldview or philosophy.[117] Instead of supporting or refuting presuppositions, the perspective within which the "material data" are viewed is strongly determined *a priori by* the presuppositions.

As to my second point — the irrelevance of Houtman's remark — I claim that the documentary hypothesis managed to survive not at all because of its objective historical basis but because of its philosophical presuppositions. Subsequent critics have heavily attacked the documentary hypothesis, and very little of the "material data" on which it was supposedly based has survived.[118] I mention here in particular the form criticism (Ger. *Formgeschichte*) of Hermann Gunkel and Hugo Gressmann.[119] This school rejected the idea of well-defined written J-E-D-P documents, and thought it best to discern in the Pentateuch oral traditions which underlay the writings. This was done by distinguishing certain literary genres (Ger. *Gattungen*), each with its own characteristic life situation (Ger. *Sitz im Leben*). These studies were assisted significantly by investigations into the history of religions, which concentrated upon parallel forms of religion and literature among Israel's neighboring nations, especially the Egyptians and the Meso-

---

116. Houtman (1980, 80).
117. Cf. Wright (2005, 14, 16, 89–90).
118. It is all the more remarkable, then, that Paas (1998) unabashedly employed the JEDP model.
119. See especially Gunkel (1910); Gressmann (1913).

potamians. Thus, Genesis was allegedly a collection of sagas, which had been handed down in a rather variable, oral form, and only during or after the Babylonian exile had been put in a written form.

Gunkel and sympathetic researchers have done to us a great service by clearly showing how unfounded and contrived the documentary hypothesis was. Their own results in the field of history of religions are often very valuable, but only when they are disconnected from the philosophical presuppositions of these researchers themselves. I will return to this in chapter 12, where I will try to explain the middle path between fundamentalism and modernism. In fact, Gunkel traveled a very different path because, although he demolished the so-called "material data" of the documentary hypothesis, he nonetheless adhered to the same modernist framework of historicism, positivism, scientism, naturalism, and evolutionism.

11.8.3 Friedrich Schleiermacher

Briefly in passing, I must mention the renowned Friedrich Schleiermacher, one of the most influential Christian thinkers of the nineteenth century. He was a father of the history of religions school since he was among the first to investigate the essence of religion and its forms of appearance. Moreover, he was a pioneer of modern hermeneutics by presenting his discipline as the art of contextually interpreting the Bible's contents. In this respect, there is a direct line running from Schleiermacher to the theologians who were also influenced by Heidegger: Rudolf Bultmann, Ernst Fuchs, and Gerhard Ebeling (§11.7.2).[120]

It is of little value to discuss further the developments in Old Testament biblical criticism, because the frame of thought shared by Wellhausen and Gunkel continued to dominate the discipline. I pause only to mention the Uppsala school with Johannes Pedersen and Ivan Engnell, which emphasized the

---

120. Cf. Wentsel (1982, 486–92); Packer (1983, 332–44); Klooster (1984).

history of tradition (Ger. *Traditionsgeschichte*).[121] Note should also be taken of the Leipzig school with Martin Noth and Gerhard von Rad, which put great emphasis upon the Bible's theological contents (the "matter" [Ger. *Sache*], the *kerygma*), more than upon literary genres and the historical sources of the Old Testament, as well as upon the necessity of a new hermeneutic.[122]

Of course, the underlying philosophical presuppositions have assumed forms different from those of the nineteenth century or the first half of the twentieth century. Quite some time ago, the assumptions of optimistic social evolutionism, German idealism, and positivism died a quiet death (although the news seems not to have reached many natural scientists and theologians). However, phenomenology, structuralism, and the various schools within existentialism, along with analytical philosophy in the twentieth century usually had a scientistic-naturalist basis as well. The same is true for modern critical theologians who were inspired by these and other contemporaneous philosophical schools.

11.9 Old Testament Scholarship and Archeology

11.9.1 Worlds Apart

Today, many scientists of all kinds — except, perhaps, theoretical physicists — do acknowledge that there is no such thing as a neutral, objective fact. What we call a fact always functions within a certain cognitive perspective; and what are called scientific facts function within a context of various philosophical, special-scientific, and methodological biases.[123]

Some may claim that the problem is never the facts, but only how scientists view them (cf. §9.4.1). But this is not very accurate. As certain as it is that facts are never neutral and objective, and always function within a certain paradigm, it is equally certain that new facts may arise that do consti-

---

121. Pedersen and Cumberlege (1947); Engnell (1954).
122. See Noth (1960); Von Rad (1962–65).
123. See the standard work by Kuhn (1996).

tute a significant challenge to the paradigm in which they are viewed. If documents would be found from, say, the eighth century BC, which would turn out to have a content corresponding more or less with J or E, this would certainly be a blow not only to the fundamentalist view of Scripture, but also for the form critical school. Conversely, it would be a blow to the modernist view of Scripture if we were to find a document from, say, the tenth century BC that corresponded generally or entirely with what we today call Genesis.

Both cases involve *archeological* findings. Here we are encountering the strange effect of specialization in science. In evolutionary theory, population geneticists and paleontologists hardly know what is going on in each other's discipline; people are fully occupied with their own specialization. As a consequence, the results of such disciplines do not at all correlate. A similar phenomenon occurs with Old Testament scholars and archeologists, who work in different fields. This is amazing because archeology is so important for Old Testament scholarship. Here we face the astonishing fact that, in their literary and historical criticism, the biblical critics have placed more confidence in their subjective biases, and ignored the less bias-dependent and more verifiable information supplied by archeology.[124] As soon as their theories had acquired a more or less stable form, they were no longer concerned with newer results of archeology. Biblical criticism and archeology are separate realms of discourse, with scarcely any meaningful communication between them.

It was the archeologists *par excellence* who have repeatedly delivered evidence that was crucial to the critics. I mention here especially the Tyndale Fellowship in Cambridge (UK) that, on archeological and exegetical grounds, defended the historical trustworthiness of the Old Testament. Let me just name archeologists such as William F. Albright, Alan R. Millard, linked with Donald J. Wiseman, James K. Hoffmeier[125]

---

124. Regarding Wellhausen, cf. Houtman (1980, 81).
125. Millard and Wiseman (1980); Millard et al. (1994); Hoffmeier (2009).

and David W. Baker, and others, and the expositor Gordon J. Wenham, in cooperation with V. Philips Long[126] and David W. Baker, and others. The great archeologist Albright made the forthright claim that, through a Hegelian analogy with pre-Islamic and Islamic Arabia, Wellhausen had attempted to build a system for the development of Israel's history, religion, and literature that would agree with his critical analysis. However, all of this occurred in the infancy of archeology, and was of very little use for interpreting history.[127] Much earlier he had written that, in the light of the ancient Orient, nothing seemed more artificial, and more in conflict with the analogy, than the postulated evolution of Hebrew religion within the boundaries of time and circumstance allowed by the school of Wellhausen.[128]

11.9.2 Some Examples

Let me mention a few aspects that have been clarified by archaeological excavations, just to make my point.[129]

(a) It has been convincingly shown that, back in the centuries before David, not only in Israel but also in the neighboring countries religion was basically monotheistic, even if in those countries is was intermingled with various forms of polytheism. Only in Israel did monotheism exist in a highly moral form.[130]

(b) It has also been shown that the so-called P portions of the Pentateuch could definitely be very old because, according to the excavations, at an early stage the specific terminol-

---

126. Long et al. (2002).
127. Albright (1966, 15).
128. Albright (1938, 182).
129. See extensively, McDowell (1975, 17–22, 52–83; also cf. 2006); Harrison (1978, 6–20; 1979, 232–39); and especially much more recently, Kitchen (2003).
130. Cf. Albright (1940, 271–72, 313; 1942, 178); Wright (1947, 90); Free (1956, 334–35); Archer Jr. (1964, 133–34); Kitchen (1966, 113–14); Youngblood (1971, 9); Harrison (1969, 399–403).

The Modernist View of the Old Testament

ogy of the worship service was known among other nations as well.[131]

(c) Purely on the basis of their evolutionistic bias, early critics asserted that the art of writing was practically unknown until David (despite, e.g., Judg. 8:14, where we are told that even a common boy could write). The conclusion was that Moses could not have written (parts of) the Pentateuch. Today we know that the art of writing existed at least 1,500 years before Moses in the Middle East. Discoveries in (the now Syrian) Ebla have confirmed this in a remarkable way.[132]

(d) Critics held the stories of the patriarchs to be untrustworthy, and often ahistorical. However, the excavations at Ur of the Chaldeans, those at Shechem, Bethel, and many other places in the Holy Land, as well as the famous clay tablets of Mari, Nuzi, Ebla, and so on, have shed light on many details in the stories of the patriarchs.[133]

In the light of these and many other discoveries, many authors have severely and understandably criticized the conclusions of the average critics in light of the archeological data. Think of Archibald H. Sayce and Kenneth A. Kitchen, Paul Volz and Wilhelm Möller, Abraham S. Yahuda, Edward J. Young and Brevard S. Childs, and Ronald K. Harrison.[134] Several of these authors have received far too little attention in Europe, where German theologians have seemed to dominate the field.[135] Even in cases where these Bible scholars left room for a possible late dating of the books of the Pentateuch, they

---

131. Cf. Free (1950, 112); Unger (1954, 154–57); Archer Jr. (1964, 161–63); Külling (1964); Yaron (1969, 1–2); Houtman (1980, 80–83).
132. Cf. Albright (1960, 132, 187); Archer Jr. (1964, 157–58); Wilson (1977); Houtman (1980, 207).
133. Cf. Albright (1940, 2, 179, 183; 1952; 1960, 236; 1965, 3–5); Wright (1947, 43, 87, 148); Free (1950, 53, 62–63); Unger (1954, 105, 114, 120–27); Wight (1955, 61–62); Archer Jr. (1964, 158–61); Frank (1971, 74).
134. See Sayce (1894); Möller (2010); Volz (1989); Yahuda (1935); Young (1969); Kitchen (1966; 2003); Harrison (1969); Childs (1979).
135. Cf. Houtman (1980, 82–83).

did emphasize that the historical material contained in these books offered a credible picture of the times of the patriarchs and of Moses.

11.10 Kenneth A. Kitchen

11.10.1 General Criticism

I would like to draw special attention here to the monumental work of the eminent Egyptologist and connoisseur of the ancient Middle East, Kenneth A. Kitchen. This work is of a rather recent date, and deals with the trustworthiness of the Old Testament.[136] Kitchen is convinced that the Pentateuch did not arise in the first millennium BC but is largely a work from the third and second millennium BC, even if he leaves room for a certain measure of post-Mosaic editorial work. Kitchen's work is not of a dogmatic but of a purely historical and literary nature. His goal was (and is, I suppose) to show especially two things:

(a) *Historical reliability*. In the light of the overwhelming material that we know from other sources about the second and third millennia BC, the events that have been described in the Old Testament—I am now referring especially to the Hexateuch (Gen. - Josh.)—must be considered to be historically absolutely trustworthy. Of course, we cannot scientifically *demonstrate* that these events really took place, but the arguments of the earlier critics that they could *not* have taken place have been totally refuted.

(b) *Literary accuracy*. The authors of the Hexateuch exhibit such an enormous knowledge of numerous details of the world of the Middle East in their day that they must have been very close to the events described. Therefore, it would be hard to believe that the books were written long after the events described took place.

This is not a form of reactionism, as though Kitchen had ignored more than two centuries of scientific research, and

---

136. Kitchen (2003).

The Modernist View of the Old Testament

had simply returned to the old, conservative view concerning the Hexateuch, as some of his critics assert. On the contrary, his conclusions are *based* upon two centuries—especially the last fifty or sixty years—of scholarly research concerning the ancient history of the Middle East. His point is precisely that the earlier schools of Old Testament literary-historical criticism were *not* based upon much knowledge of the ancient Middle East but rather on certain philosophical biases. This had to do less with the historical and literary sciences, and all the more with ideology. Any literary-historical criticism not incorporating an extensive archeological knowledge as thorough as that of Kenneth Kitchen—in his field he is a superb authority—is little more than a puff of smoke. Thus, Kitchen easily refuted Wellhausen's denial that the tabernacle ever existed, a denial made without even the slightest knowledge of the advanced Eastern art in the second millennium BC.[137]

11.10.2 The Times of Moses

Actually, Kitchen did not agree with conservative Old Testament scholars. For instance, he believed that the Exodus took place during the time of Ramesses (Ramses), and not in the fifteenth century BC. The latter dating is mainly based upon 1 Kings 6:1, "In the four hundred and eightieth year after the people of Israel came out of the land of Egypt, in the fourth year of Solomon's reign over Israel, in the month of Ziv, which is the second month, he began to build the house of the LORD." If the building of the temple began in or around 969 BC, as is generally assumed, the Exodus should have taken place around 1449 BC. However, there are reasons to question this dating, both textual-critical and chronological reasons (especially the chronology of Egypt).[138]

At any rate, modern expositors date the Exodus in the thirteenth century rather than in the fifteenth century BC. Very important here is the reference to Israel on the stele of Pharaoh

---

137. Ibid., 495.
138. See various comments on http://biblehub.com/1_kings/6-1.htm.

Merenptah, which describes Israel as dwelling in Canaan.[139]

Kitchen pleaded for dating the Exodus in the time of the Nineteenth Dynasty, that is, the time of the Ramessides during which many Semites sojourned in Egyptian society, on all levels, from Pharaoh's court to the slaves. The stories in Exodus–Deuteronomy about the Hebrew people present a kind of picture that has become very well-known from the thirteenth century BC. Many details in Exodus–Judges point to an accurate knowledge of local circumstances, which have nothing to do with book learning in seventh (!) century BC Babylon or Jerusalem, or later, a date to which Pentateuch criticism loved to assign the Pentateuch.[140]

In addition, the tabernacle built in Moses' time was not an invention of post-exilic Israelite priests, but rests upon an ancient Semitic concept, linked with Egyptian technology, dating from (several centuries) before 1000 BC. Further, according to Kitchen, the form and contents of the Sinaitic covenant fit only the late second millennium BC, as is evident from many firsthand sources. Kitchen also pointed out that brick-making slaves were no diplomats: the format of the covenant demands a leader from court circles in that time who *had* learned about such things at the court. We would have to invent a Moses if one were not available.[141] Kitchen concluded that his arguments had not demonstrated that the Exodus and the Sinai events had indeed occurred, or that the tabernacle and the covenant, and so on, had existed at that time. However, their similarity not only to documented realities (not fantasy in Sargon style[142]) but also to well-known customs from the late second millennium BC and earlier, does favor the conclusion that the tabernacle, the covenant, and so on, must definitely

---

139. Kitchen (2003, 206–207).
140. Ibid., 311.
141. Ibid., 311–12.
142. The Assyrian king Sargon II ruled in the late eighth century BC, the date that current Pentateuch criticism assigns to parts of the Pentateuch.

The Modernist View of the Old Testament

have had a historical basis as well.[143]

11.10.3 The Times of the Patriarchs

Kitchen went even further back in biblical history, to investigate the time of the patriarchs, Abraham, Isaac, and Jacob with his twelve sons, in the early centuries of the second millennium BC. According to Kitchen, the archeological results necessitated the definitive rejection of Wellhausen's overconfident assertion that the patriarchs were only a glorified mirage projected backward from the time of the Hebrew monarchy. Kitchen insisted that there is not a shred of evidence for such a view; instead, all the background material that he was able to adduce contradicts the assertion.

Kitchen concluded that it should finally be evident that the events of the patriarchal stories either could have occurred in the first half of the second millennium BC, or were at least compatible with that date.[144] All the features of the patriarchal stories point to the Canaan of the early second millennium BC, and *not* to the period of the Hebrew monarchy (David and later. Kitchen argued that the oft-repeated assertion of a consensus that the patriarchs have never existed is itself a case of self-deception; this view was in fact a "con-nonsens-us"![145]

Kitchen concludes that, in terms of general trustworthiness, the Old Testament manages remarkably well, as long as its writings and their writers are dealt with in a fair and impartial way, consistent with independent data accessible to everyone.[146] This conclusion might seem identical to the conclusions of traditional Bible expositors—but the great difference is that Kitchen undergirded his conclusions with both exegetical arguments and archaeological arguments.

---

143. Ibid., 312.
144. Kitchen (2003, 371–72).
145. See previous note.
146. Ibid., 500.

11.11 Newer Viewpoints

11.11.1 Dever and Others

Of course, not all Old Testament scholars agree with Kenneth Kitchen. The seed of liberalism, with its biases, has taken root so deeply in our Western culture that it is impossible to exterminate it. Kitchen himself mentioned several examples: theologians Thomas L. Thompson, Philip R. Davies, Keith W. Whitelam, and Niels P. Lemche.[147] He and others referred to such scholars as "minimalists" because they recognize as authentic only a minimum of Old Testament history. In his great work, Kitchen has powerfully refuted such minimalists—he even spoke of "fraudulent postmodernism"[148]—but has also been heavily criticized himself.

Someone with views close to those of Kitchen is archeologist William G. Dever.[149] The fascinating thing about Dever is that, as he said himself, he is not a Christian, scarcely a theist. His view is that the biblical narratives are indeed stories, often fictional, and almost always propagandistic, but here and there they do contain *some* valid historical information. This hardly makes him, as he put it, a "maximalist."[150] Nonetheless, like Kitchen he emphasized that the only context in which the Old Testament stories, from Genesis to Kings, are understandable is that of neither the Persian nor the Hellenist (i.e., post-exilic) era, but that of the Iron Age, that is, pre-exilic.[151] Whatever people may think of the historicity of these stories, they are much older in date than biblical criticism, following Wellhausen, believed for a long time, according to Dever.

William Dever saw certain "convergences" between the biblical text and archeology, but emphatically argued that this

---

147. Thompson (1992; 1999); Davies (1992); Whitelam (1996); Lemche (1998).
148. Kitchen (2003, 463).
149. Dever (2001; see also 2003).
150. www.bibleinterp.com/articles/Contra_Davies.htm.
151. Dever (2001, 295–96).

has nothing to do with what in earlier times was called "biblical archeology." What he implicitly said here is that he did not want to prove the Bible right, nor provide warrants for its theological claims. He was simply stating that, at certain points, the biblical text and the archeological discoveries run along the same line, and ultimately arrive at the same conclusions. He did not try to demonstrate this; it simply turned out to be the case. Numerous historical sources, including the Bible and archeology, together point to what may be called "core history." Dever claimed a thousand-page book could easily be written about ancient Israel in the Iron Age and the early Persian period (about 1200–500 BC).[152] In his view, both the revisionists (those who rewrite the entire history of ancient Israel, i.e., reduce it to practically nothing) and the fundamentalists are utterly mistaken.[153]

The debates are fierce, as has always been the case since the beginning of Old Testament scholarship.[154] Moreover, the discussion is complicated, since the diversity is much larger than that between maximalist and minimalist views, and significant methodological and ideological differences exist. In addition to Kitchen and Dever, I mention two Old Testament scholars who tended toward the maximalist view: Umberto Cassuto[155] and Gleason L. Archer.[156] The debates will persist until new, dramatic findings move them into one specific direction. As it looks now, this direction will be more maximalist than minimalist, for this has been the tendency during the last fifty years, as important investigators like Cassuto, Archer, Kitchen, and Dever have shown. Christian tradition has always adopted a maximalist position—but it is encouraging that this is now supported by a discipline that suffers far less

---

152. Ibid., 296.
153. Ibid., 297.
154. See the discussion in Ahituv and Oren (1998); Finkelstein et al. (2007); Hess (2007).
155. See especially Cassuto (1961–1964; 1967, 1973–1975, 2006).
156. See especially Archer Jr. (1994).

from ideological biases like those of Wellhausen and his disciples.

11.11.2 The Debate Continues

We turn now from historical criticism to literary criticism. Regarding the latter, Roger N. Whybray pointed out that three explanations for the origin of the Pentateuch.[157]

(a) The *documentary hypothesis*. The books of the Pentateuch, especially Genesis and Exodus, are compilations of originally distinct, but integrally complete documents (JEP).

(b) The *supplementary hypothesis*. Each of the books originated approximately as we know them today, but with later omissions and many additions.

(c) The *fragmentary hypothesis*. Each of the books originated from many small fragmentary writings and editorial changes.

Whybray argued that the first of these three—the still popular documentary hypothesis—is the least likely. One of his arguments is this: why would the final books be allowed to contain various duplications, whereas the original documents were not allowed to exhibit this feature? Why would the supposed writers of the proposed documents have been consistent, whereas the editors were not?

Since Whybray, there have been other dissenting opinions, yet the documentary hypothesis remains very popular. Thus, Richard E. Friedman wrote an extensive reply to Whybray.[158] At the same time, he departed fundamentally from Wellhausen by dating P in the time of king Hezekiah, thus overthrowing Wellhausen's developmental model, in which P is necessarily late.

Ernest Nicholson was of the opinion that Pentateuch studies were ripe for a thorough revision, but that, nonetheless, Wellhausen's approach remained the safest starting point.[159]

---

157. Whybray (1987).
158. Friedman (2003; see also 1987).
159. Nicholson (2003).

However, Rolf Rendtorff wrote that though Wellhausen's documentary hypothesis was passé, nothing had arisen to replace it except a confusing multiplicity of hypotheses.[160]

It seems to me that what remains unaffected are at least the two conclusions by Kenneth A. Kitchen (see above):

(a) *Historical:* the Old Testament stories, including those about the patriarchs, are much more reliable than the critics had thought for a long time.

(b) *Literary:* the historical books about pre-exilic Israel are, at least in their core, much older that the critics had thought for a long time. The thesis that the bulk of the Pentateuch can be dated in the time of Moses (and Joshua) cannot be proven, but neither does any widely supported refutation of this claim exist.

Among Evangelical Pentateuch expositors, for instance, Earl S. Kalland and Walter C. Kaiser maintained the Mosaic authorship of Deuteronomy and Exodus, respectively.[161] R. Laird Harris and Ronald B. Allen did the same with respect to Leviticus and Numbers, but at least they took the trouble of also discussing the views of biblical criticism.[162] For Genesis, John H. Sailhamer followed the tradition regarding the Mosaic authorship of the book, but did remark that we should not forget that the Pentateuch comes to us as an anonymous work, and apparently was meant to be read this way.[163]

---

160. Rendtorff (1993); summaries are provided by Rofe (1999); Mendenhall (2001); Garrett (2003); Kugel (2008); and among the Evangelicals especially Wenham (2003).
161. Kalland (1992, 3); Kaiser (1990, 287–88).
162. Harris (1990, 502–13); Allen (1990, 663–68).
163. Sailhamer (1990, 5).

Chapter 12
The Modernist View
of the New Testament

As it is written,
"What no eye has seen,
nor ear heard,
nor the heart of man imagined,
what God has prepared
for those who love him" –
*these things God has **revealed** to us*
through the Spirit.
For the Spirit searches everything,
even the depths of God.
                    1 Corinthians 2:9–10

Summary: *New Testament criticism deals largely with literary (e.g., the origin of the Gospels) and historical questions (the historical Jesus). Because of the current critics' prejudices, they have sought for parallels between Jesus and mythical figures in other religions. A cleft was imagined between the historical Jesus (of whom we allegedly can hardly still know anything) and the kerygmatic Christ, largely a product of the early church's pious imagination. (Naturalism and scientism were responsible for creating this cleft.)*

This First Quest for the historical Jesus was followed by a Second Quest (with new interest for possible historical elements in the Gospels), and even a Third Quest (with special interest in Jesus the Jew).

This chapter scrutinizes the methodology of the critics: I see Western presumption, no objective (independent) evidence, epistemological ignorance, a disintegrative approach, circular reasonings, a high degree of speculation, failing to satisfy common methodological criteria.

The early apostolic letters support the Christology of the Gospels. Apart from historical reasons, the authenticity of the Gospels has been doubted for literary reasons, such as alleged contradictions. Against this, I argue that the differences between the Gospels (obscured in harmonies of the Gospels) are theologically highly significant: the Gospels are theological compositions (portraits) of Jesus' life and teaching, interesting because of their different views of Jesus, yet basically one through the work of the Holy Spirit.

12.1   New Testament Criticism

12.1.1 Striking Parallels in the Gospels and Epistles

JUST AS IN THE OLD TESTAMENT (see previous chapter), the New Testament presents all sorts of literary problems that even the most conservative New Testament scholar cannot avoid. Thus, many scholars have wondered how the synoptic Gospels (Matthew, Mark, and Luke) could exhibit such remarkable parallels, with wordings that are sometimes (almost) entirely identical. This is the so-called "synoptic problem." This *problem* demanding a solution undeniably exists, even if one need not agree with the current answers.[1] The questions force themselves upon us: Did the Evangelists know each other's work? If so, which of the three Gospels was the first, and how did the other two authors make use of it, and possibly also of the other Gospels?

Every New Testament scholar encounters this problem.

---
1. I regret that in her (overall impressive) study (1992) E. Linnemann does not even acknowledge the *problem,* unlike, e.g., Van den Brink (1999, 9).

Even the solution provided by the doctrine of mechanical inspiration (see §7.8) is a form of literary or historical criticism: this solution is that the Evangelists did not necessarily know each other's work, but that God was able to whisper into the ears of each of them the words of their respective Gospels — which were sometimes identical words. However, these conservative Christians, too, must offer an explanation not only for the remarkable similarities between the synoptic Gospels but also for the — often insoluble — contradictions; back in §10.4.4 I mentioned a striking example. Such contradictions can hardly be explained by means of a notion of mechanical inspiration; one would make God a liar in this way.

We encounter a similar problem when comparing 2 Peter 2 with the letter of Jude, which strongly resemble each other. Here again, the doctrine of mechanical inspiration has a simple solution: God whispered more or less the same text into the ears of both writers. This is easily stated — but it does not tell us *why* two times (more or less) the same text occurs in the New Testament epistles. One can hardly claim that the content of these passages is so exceptionally important that God had to tell us the same thing twice. Those who reject the doctrine of mechanical inspiration usually claim that either Jude depends on 2 Peter 2, or (more frequently) that 2 Peter 2 depends on Jude. At any rate, we are dealing here with a literary *problem*, which requires a solution and cannot be simply brushed aside.

As we saw in the previous chapter, critics soon attempted to explain the Bible books from other religions. Thus, certain Bible books were declared to be important pieces of ancient literature, of a special religious quality, but easily reducible to parallels in Judaism or pagan religions. In the discipline of comparative religions, parallels for the New Testament were sought in Jewish literature (John Lightfoot[2]), or in classical

---

2. Lightfoot (1979).

literature (Hugo Grotius[3]), or in both (Joh. Jakob Wettstein[4]). This approach necessarily placed certain parts of the canon in doubt: do they really belong there, given their (alleged) non-Christian origin? Thus, indeed, Grotius objected to 2 Peter and 2 John.[5]

John Locke distinguished between the essential doctrines of Jesus and the apostles, and what he judged to be non-essential doctrines of the New Testament epistles.[6] Others taught that Jesus had been merely a simple moralist, concerned only with his own teaching, whereas the later Gospel writers constructed a theology around his person, and began to place more emphasis upon his person than upon his teaching. Georg L. Bauer investigated the so-called "mythological" character of the New Testament.[7]

12.1.2 The Critics' Biases

In the previous chapter, we noticed that, from the outset, Bible critics engage not in objective-scientific work, but rather in philosophical thought. Many forms of the latter exclude beforehand the possibility of divine revelation in written form, and thereby reject the Bible's self-testimony (see §11.4.1). *Thus, as we saw*, Joh. Gottfried Eichhorn was influenced by the Romanticist philosophy of Joh. Gottfried Herder.[8] He declared the pastoral letters to be non-authentic, that is, non-Pauline, and believed that even within Bible books he could distinguish between the original parts (for instance a "primitive gospel" within the synoptic Gospels) and later additions.[9] Wilhelm M. L. de Wette, working within the same sphere of influence, doubted the authenticity of 2 Thessalonians and

---

3. Regarding him, see Nellen (2007).
4. Wettstein (1962).
5. Grotius (1646).
6. See Locke (1988).
7. Bauer (1800–1802).
8. See Herder (2010).
9. Eichhorn (1804–1812).

Ephesians (cf. §6.11.2).¹⁰

We have witnessed the influence of Hegel's dialectical idealism within the school of Ferdinand C. Baur (see §§11.2.3 and 11.3.1). On the basis of Hegel's model of thesis (here: Jewish Christianity), antithesis (here: Gentile Christianity), and synthesis (here: catholic Christianity), he believed he could identify the authentic parts of the Pauline letters. This approach, which was applied to the epistles in the first half of the nineteenth century, was applied in the second half of the century to the Gospels. The interest of the critics became more and more focused upon the latter, which gave rise to the New Testament documentary hypothesis.

Earlier we encountered the theory of the "primitive gospel," with whose help theologians such as Eichhorn and Gotthold E. Lessing tried to solve the synoptic problem, which involves the numerous similarities and differences between the synoptic Gospels. Joh. Carl L. Gieseler, and later Brooke F. Westcott, believed that, the apostles' preaching yielded a somewhat fixed oral gospel.¹¹ This supposedly received a more stable form, until finally the three synoptic Evangelists, each in his own way, wrote down this primitive gospel, and elaborated upon it. Other critics believed that the Gospels depended on each other, even though theologians like Joh. Jakob Griesbach,¹² Ferdinand C. Baur, Hampden G. Jameson,¹³ and William Lockton,¹⁴ disagreed widely about the order of the mutual influencing of one Gospel writer by another.

In the nineteenth century, the view defending the priority of Mark gained increasing acceptance; it almost became a dogma. The two primitive sources assumed by this view were Mark, or an earlier form of it (*Ur-Markus*, "primitive Mark"), as well as a Q-source (*Quelle*, German for "source," also called

---

10. De Wette (1826).
11. Gieseler (1818); Westcott (1902).
12. Griesbach (1789).
13. Jameson (1922).
14. Lockton (1922).

Logia because Q was thought to contain mainly sayings of Christ[15]). It was believed that both Matthew and Luke quoted from these two sources, each in his own way. In the twentieth century, this two-document theory, which had been developed especially by Heinrich J. Holtzmann,[16] was transformed into a four-document theory. What was added were the two assumed sources M and L, from which Matthew and Luke, respectively, adopted the material that each mentions alone. Despite its totally speculative character, this theory became very popular in the Anglo-Saxon world. Many, however, wished to probe further to determine how these sources had originated (see §12.3).

12.2 The Historical Jesus

12.2.1 Jesus an Ordinary Man

In addition to considering the *literary* problem of the origin of the New Testament books, New Testament criticism is dominated especially by the problem of the reconstruction of earliest Christian *history*, that is, the history of Jesus and his apostles, and of the earliest Christian congregations. I have discussed this matter elsewhere,[17] and limit myself here to the notions of biblical criticism that were linked with this investigation.[18]

Early on, the critics believed that the Gospels offer us a distorted picture of the historical Jesus. Under the strong influence of the Enlightenment rationalism of Hermann S. Reimarus, as well as Joh. Philipp Gabler's notion of myth, it was especially David F. Strauss who, in his sensational work *The Life of Jesus Critically Examined* (Ger. *Das Leben Jesu kritisch bearbeitet*), claimed that the New Testament had to be read as a collection of myths.[19] According to him, the Gospels are

---

15. Thus Weisse (1838).
16. Holtzmann (1863).
17. Ouweneel (2007, 117–25); also see Van Segbroeck (2004).
18. An extensive (two-volume) introduction to New Testament criticism is Baird (1992; 2003).
19. Strauss (1973a; cf. 1973b).

The Modernist View of the New Testament

only the account, developed after Jesus' death, of the mythical faith that the disciples had woven around Jesus, particularly after they began viewing him as the fulfillment of the Old Testament. Strauss claimed that the only thing of value in this myth was the idea embedded within it, that humanity must be aware that it is an incarnated god, a union of the finite and the infinite. Humanity is destined for a state of perfection, which must be reached along an upward trajectory. In the New Testament, this state is described through the symbols of death, resurrection, and ascension. Ultimately, Strauss reduced religion to a pious veneration of the ordered universe, viewed entirely in a Darwinistic way.[20]

Strauss set in motion a totally new development of thought. Along these lines, Ferdinand C. Baur asserted that John's Gospel is totally unhistorical, and describes only the idea of Christ.[21] Therefore, the critics could only hope to find something of the historical Jesus in the synoptic Gospels. Wilhelm Wrede formulated the theory that Jesus did not at all view himself as Messiah; the Messiah idea, too, was claimed to be an invention of the early church.[22] Therefore, said Wrede, Mark had to write a Gospel to explain how Jesus could still be the Messiah, even though he had never claimed this himself. This explanation involved the assertion that Jesus had definitely viewed himself as the Messiah, but had forbidden others to make this public (cf. Mark 1:34, 44; 3:12; 5:43; 7:36; 8:26, 30; 9:9). In a similar way, Julius Wellhausen claimed that Jesus was nothing more than a Jewish teacher, who did call himself "Son of Man," but only with the simple meaning of "I, human"[23] — totally in conflict with the special significance that Jewish apocalyptic had meanwhile given to this title (see below).[24]

---

20. Strauss (1872).
21. Baur (1847).
22. Wrede (1971); cf. Ouweneel (2007, 147–48).
23. Wellhausen (1987).
24. Cf. Ouweneel (2007, 173–74).

12.2.2 Religious Parallels

As mentioned earlier (§11.4.1), during the same time, around 1900, the discipline of history of religions began. It was thought that Christianity could be explained from the parallels in the culture and religion of the Greeks and Romans,[25] the Persians and the Egyptians. This was the view, for instance, Richard A. Reitzenstein.[26] Wilhelm Bousset began explaining the book of Revelation in a way consistent with the history of religions approach,[27] and others, such as Carl Clemen, tried to explain baptism and the Lord's Supper, along with the structure of the early church, in the light of pagan rites and societies.[28] This is all the more remarkable because baptism and the Lord's Supper are clearly rooted in Jewish rites and congregational structures: the *mikveh* and *Pesach*, respectively.[29] The same is true for the structure of the early church.[30] These evidences seem to be irrelevant, however, since bias is again dominating the debate.

On the basis of such studies, people tried to reconstruct the life of Jesus and that of the early Christian congregations. Thus, the "consistent eschatological" school tried to explain Jesus entirely from Jewish apocalyptic.[31] It was claimed that Jesus' predictions had not come true, that this would have brought him to the cross, and that the early church had to cope with the frustration of Jesus not returning.

In a similar way, Bousset reconstructed the gradual development of Christology in the early churches.[32] According to him, the Palestinian early church began confessing Jesus as Son of Man, a notion developed in Jewish apocalyptic. After

---

25. Wendland (1907).
26. Reitzenstein (1921).
27. Bousset (1906).
28. Clemen (1924).
29. See Ouweneel (2010b, chapters 8–9; 2011a, §5.1).
30. See Ouweneel (2010a, chapter 8).
31. Weiss (1964); Schweitzer (1966); see Ouweneel (2007, 453; 2010b, 471–73).
32. Bousset (1913).

The Modernist View of the New Testament

this, the Greek church began worshiping Jesus as the Lord (Gk. *Kyrios*) who is present in the worship service, just like these converted pagans had been accustomed to the presence of pagan gods in the cult. Paul supposedly had elaborated these two elements into a supernatural doctrine of redemption, whose center was Jesus. Under Greek influence, the apostle John in turn exalted Christianity to an intensely mystical doctrine. In this Jewish-pagan mixture, the essence is nothing but Jesus' simple preaching about the gracious God who forgives sins, according to Bousset.

Thus, virtually nothing remained of the actual life and work of Jesus Christ as traditional faith had known and cherished it. The historical Jesus can no longer be reconstructed, so that, henceforth, Bible readers can be occupied only with how the early church *confessed* Jesus. This confession consists of the message or preaching (Gk. *kerygma*) at the core of the Gospels. The critics also tried to find links with Qumran and the Essenes,[33] and with the supposed early-Jewish Gnosticism.[34] They gave their special attention to the apostle John, who supposedly had made use of the myth of the descending "revealer," who, by his mere descent and ascension, brought the redeeming knowledge (Gk. *gnosis*) to humanity. Others assumed more influences from Plato's idealism.[35] At any rate, they all agreed that John does not offer an account of historical events from the life of Jesus, and actually did not *intend* to offer such.

12.3 Founders of Form Criticism

12.3.1 The Form-Critical Method

Just as happened in the case of the Old Testament, so too with the New Testament we naturally encounter the rise of the form-critical (Ger. *formgeschichtliche*) school. This is because the theologians for whom little of the historical Jesus

---

33. Dupont-Sommer (1960).
34. See, e.g., Bultmann (1963).
35. Dodd (1946).

remained, especially Rudolf Bultmann, are the same as those who propagated the form-critical method.[36]

John P. Meier saw here a similarity between Bultmannians and die-hard fundamentalists: both groups view the quest for the historical Jesus as irrelevant, or even as damaging for the true Christian faith. The Bultmannians claim that the historical Jesus cannot be found anymore, so be satisfied with the kerygmatic Christ. The fundamentalists claim that the historical Jesus is identical with the Jesus of the four Gospels, so any quest can only lead one astray from this fixed conviction.[37] Either the Gospels are largely the pious imagination of the early church, or the Gospels are historical biographies. But neither view is correct. The Gospels are neither fantasy sketches nor photographs; they can best be compared to paintings (see §§7.11.2, 12.11.3).

The critics came to believe that the Gospels describe not the historical Jesus but the mythical Jesus, the Christ of the post-Easter *kerygma*, as confessed by the early church. The first Christians allegedly put words into the mouth of Jesus and attributed acts to him that he — according to the naturalistic critics — could never have said and done. The early congregations also attributed to him the Jewish title of Messiah (Anointed One), and various Gnostic myths, such as the virgin birth, the title "Son of God" or "Kyrios," and so on, concepts that also permeated the written Gospels, and thus the earliest Christian theology.

Once the critics adopted these views, the Gospels became interesting to them in a new way. No longer was it a matter of finding out something about the history of Jesus — which, they claimed, was no longer possible — but to reconstruct the thought history of the early church. Each of the various literary forms has its own life situation (Ger. *Sitz im Leben*), that

---

36. Bultmann (1952; 1963).
37. Meier (1991, 196).

is, being situated in the circumstances and needs of the early church. The form-critical school viewed its task to require tracing the origin of these literary forms, and to determine their original life situation. It sought to probe behind the four documents postulated by the documentary hypothesis (see §12.1.2), and to determine how tradition developed in the decades between the death of Jesus and the origin of the first written sources.

12.3.2 Mythical Influences

The critics believed that, from the very beginning, pagan-mythical elements were seeping into the thinking of the early Christians. B. Wentsel presented the counter-argument that, in those days, the orthodox Judaism from which the early church issued took great care that no pagan influences would enter. For instance, the thinking of the apostle Paul was based not upon the general religiosity of his time but upon the Old Testament and the tradition concerning Jesus.[38] Wentsel emphasized that the central question at stake is the recognition of God's self-revelation in Christ Jesus. He also pointed out that the form-critical school, too, just like older critical schools, went back through the history of religions school to the historicist philosophy of Georg W. F. Hegel and Joh. Gottfried Herder.

The modern scientific worldview, whatever this may be, urged the first form-critics to demythologize the Gospels, that is, isolate from them the first-century mythical elements that do not stand the test of modern science. In this broad sense, that is, of all things that supposedly cannot be fitted into the conceptual-rational knowledge of the critics and into their naturalist picture of the world and of history, all essential matters of Christianity are simply downgraded to myths (ahistorical stories about gods): theophanies, the incarnation,

---

38. See Wentsel (1982, 533–45).

revealed truth, divine history, miracles, the resurrection, ascension, second coming, and so on.[39] By purging all these elements, the critics wished to reach the essence of the gospel, which lies hidden in the literary forms. Thus, their task amounted to (a) discerning the various literary forms (parables, miracle stories, speeches, sagas, legends, myths, passion stories), (b) determining the life situation of each, along with the form-giving community involved, and (c) assessing their historical value on the basis of the critics' naturalist bias.

Around 1919, this was how three founders of the New Testament form-critical school approached their discipline: Karl L. Schmidt,[40] Martin Dibelius,[41] and later especially Rudolf Bultmann.[42] Whereas Dibelius still assumed the essential historicity of the tradition, Bultmann denied it outright, with the exception of a limited number of sayings of Jesus. He attributed the tradition entirely to the imagination of the early church. His deeply rooted prejudices included, in addition to omnipresent naturalism and scientism, especially the existential philosophy of philosopher Martin Heidegger,[43] and the science of comparative religions (see the discussion about Reitzenstein and Bousset in §12.2.2 above). As a consequence, it had become impossible for Bultmann to view the Gospels as serious history. He could see them only as the products of a church-produced theology (Ger. *Gemeindetheolgie*) that was rich in imaginative power.

---

39. Buri (1956, 201).
40. Schmidt (1964).
41. Dibelius (1966).
42. Among the dogmatic-theological textbooks, there are several extensive introductions to Bultmann's thought: Weber (1981, 334–45); Berkouwer (1966, 157–70; 1967, 226–40); Wentsel (1982, 533–55). See also the later volumes by Barth (*CD*, e.g. III/2:442–47).
43. See especially Heidegger (1962), a work that Lackey (1999) considered to be one of the most important philosophical works of the twentieth century.

12.3.3 Literary Forms

The forms that Bultmann distinguished were the following: (a) *apophthegmata* (short stories with a moral, more or less corresponding with what Dibelius called "paradigms"), (b) *miracle stories* (by Dibelius called *novellas*), (c) *sayings*, by Bultmann divided into words of wisdom (proverbs), "I" words: alleged sayings of Jesus about himself, in fact invented by the early church), prophetic and apocalyptic statements, laws and prescriptions, and finally parables, which are all viewed as mainly non-authentic. And (d) *legends:* edifying stories in the widest sense, including *myths*, such as the story of the temptation in the wilderness, the transfiguration on the mount, that is, stories in which it is suggested that the supernatural intervenes in a special way in the natural world by the occurrence of spiritual powers or God-men coming from the "Beyond" (Ger. *Jenseits*) In brief, Bultmann distinguished three main categories of myths:

(1) A pre-scientific cosmology (the ancient worldview).

(2) The Redeemer myth (attributed to the Persian religion of Zoroastrism) of a celestial being that enters into our empirical world in a dramatic way.

(3) An interpretation of God as a being that behaves in an anthropomorphic way, that is, in a way comparable to beings with whom we are familiar.[44]

The only materials in the Gospels that Bultmann viewed as authentic were about forty "words" (sayings of Jesus), plus the fact (the *Dass*) of Jesus' life and his death on the cross. All the other materials have been elaborated or invented by the early church.[45] Bultmann did not have the slightest trouble with this view because he had completely severed faith from the historical facts. On the one hand, he believed that the historical Jesus, whoever or whatever he may have been, has been dead since more than nineteen centuries. On the oth-

---

44. Cf. Heron (1980, 103.
45. Cf. France (1976) for a positive view of the authenticity of Jesus' sayings.

er hand, he proclaims that the essence of Christianity is the existential encounter with Christ, who is not to be confused with the dead Jesus. For Bultmann, this existential aspect had a specific significance, which he had adopted from Heidegger. The New Testament statements must be pressed into the mold of Heidegger's existential philosophy; everything that does not fit within that mold is mythical.[46]

12.4 Consequences

12.4.1 Kerygma and Mythology

The consequences of the view just described are disastrous; all essential elements of the gospel have simply been brushed aside. The apostle Paul says, "[I]f Christ has not been raised, your faith is futile and you are still in your sin" (1 Cor. 15:17). Bultmann said that Christ was raised only in the *kerygma*, not in empirical reality. In that case, believers' sins have been forgiven in the *kerygma*, but not in empirical reality. The object of faith is a dream, not facts.

Interestingly, Paul Althaus argued that Bultmann is not entirely consistent in this respect.[47] Radical demythologizing ought to involve the exclusion of *every* theology that is still an expression of faith in Jesus Christ. Therefore, Bultmann's own theology should also be demythologized until nothing is left that cannot stand the test of the modern scientific worldview (whatever this is).[48] In this case, we may wonder whether any element of an existential encounter with Christ could possibly survive. Only on the basis of the humanist nature-freedom dualism, going back to the scholastic nature-grace (or nature-supernature) dualism, can Bultmann maintain this schizophrenia (see below).

Eduard Buess argued that the biblical *kerygma* and the mythical cannot possibly go together, but that in this way a problem did arise, namely, how, within the New Testament,

---

46. Cf. Bruce (1976).
47. Althaus (1952, 175).
48. Cf. Weber (1981, 337–40).

we could and should possibly draw the boundary between the two:[49] "The boundary between kerygma and mythology was in the New Testament a battle field." In the thought of the critics, the domain of the mythical has been constantly growing, and the kerygmatic was pushed back more and more. Alasdair Heron said that some of Bultmann's followers have been more radical than he was; they argued that, since faith is an event in the present, the idea of God itself must be demythologized all the more radically, and must essentially be understood as the power and dynamics of the faith event as it takes place here and now.[50]

Bultmann and his followers never explain how the early church ever managed to unleash its imagination to such a large extent, and could tolerate this cognitive divorce. They *knew* who Jesus was, yet *created* the Christ. This is the first difficulty, created by the Bultmann school: how could this imaginative power of the early church bring about such an enormous distortion and embellishment of the facts, and this within an extremely short period, namely, until the first written sources?[51] Second, must we believe that this imagination could continue unhindered in the presence of so many (often hostile) ear- and eyewitnesses of Jesus' life and death who were still alive during the first period of the church's existence? Third, must we assume that this imagination could continue unimpeded despite the early Christians' great interest in the facts of Jesus' life? Fourth, did all of this occur despite the great learnedness, and therefore critical attitude of some of these witnesses (Paul!)? Fifth, did all of this occur despite the lofty integrity and moral standard of the first disciples?[52] And sixth, must we believe that the apostles were prepared to undergo hardships, persecutions, and even mar-

---

49. Buess (1953, 23).
50. Heron (1980, 113).
51. Here, we must consider that today we possess fragments of the Gospel manuscripts that go back to the beginning of the second century, such as the John Rylands Papyrus (p^{52}).
52. Cf. Wentsel (1982, 541–45).

tyrdom for their pious fantasies?

12.4.2 The Second Quest for Jesus

Despite these objections, the influence of Bultmann was enormous. But it was of short duration. Already in the fifties, a new movement arose in reaction to Bultmann's pervasive historical skepticism. This movement involved theologians like Joachim Jeremias, Ernst Fuchs, Günther Bornkamm, and Ernst Käsemann, and J. A. T. Robinson.[53]

If the nineteenth-century quest for the historical Jesus was called the First Quest, since about 1954 the men just mentioned began the New[54] or Second Quest for the historical Jesus. This movement went searching again for historical sayings and acts of Jesus in the Gospels, but did no longer manage to find the connection between the historical Jesus and the *kerygma* of the early church.[55] One of the fascinating aspects of the New Quest was that, just as with Karl Barth, there was room again for the concept of revelation (especially with Fuchs) and the factuality of the resurrection. Although the resurrection lies outside the reach of historical investigation, Bornkamm argued that not a myth but the appearances of Jesus and the word of witnesses formed the basis for faith in the resurrection. Jeremias emphasized that there definitely is a historical basis for the Christian faith, and that it can be scientifically established.

There were additional positive points. Jeremias emphasized that theologians should be required to demonstrate not the authenticity but the non-authenticity of a saying of Jesus. We must begin with accepting the Gospels to be what they pretend to be, namely, a representation—no matter how subjective—of what Jesus really said and did, until scholar-

---

53. Käsemann (1954); Bornkamm (1956); J. A. T. Robinson (1959); Fuchs (1960; 1971); Jeremias (1971).
54. Also notice the title of J. M. Robinson (1959): *A New Quest of the Historical Jesus*.
55. For the most recent development, see Evans (1992); Chilton and Evans (1994); Borg (1994b); Witherington (1997); Barnett (1998); Theissen and Merz (1998); Knight (2004).

ly analysis demonstrates, or makes plausible, that the opposite is the case.[56] C. H. Dodd argued that the teaching of Jesus was simply too brilliant to have been invented by the early church. A genius was needed for this—and the New Testament describes such a genius. Why should we not take the New Testament seriously on this point?[57] The traditional view that the teaching of Jesus came from Jesus himself is far less problematic than the view that attributes this teaching to the early church.

During the same period, other critics extended their critical investigation to the totality of the New Testament, such as Ernst Lohmeyer and Ernst Haenchen.[58] Just as in Old Testament theology, interest arose in redaction criticism (Ger. *Redaktionsgeschichte*, the history of collecting the materials for, and the editing of, the Gospels).[59] The critics searched for the life situation not only of Jesus and the early congregations, but also of the actual Gospel writers (read: composers). Instead of producing church theology, the Evangelists had their own intentions and needs in collecting and editing the material, according to Hans Conzelmann and Willi Marxsen.[60] At the same time, just as with the Old Testament, a new kind of New Testament hermeneutic was developed, instigated by Bultmann himself,[61] and elaborated in the 1960s by Oscar Cullmann, Ernst Fuchs, Gerhard Ebeling, and others.

12.5 The Third Quest

12.5.1 A New Search for the Historical Jesus

Elsewhere I have argued that, during the last two centuries of Christology, there was a remarkable pendular movement.[62]

---

56. Marshall (1977, 200).
57. Dodd (1952, 109–110; 1971, 49).
58. Lohmeyer (1957, 1958); Haenchen (1968).
59. Cf. Erickson (1998, 85–104) on both form and redaction criticism; see also 108–14 about reader-response criticism.
60. See especially Conzelmann (1993); Marxsen (1968; 1969).
61. Bultmann (1952).
62. *EDR* 2, §§4.1–4.2.

If the nineteenth-century liberalism (First Quest) meant a shift to the left, Karl Barth meant a shift to the right (although not as far as many theologians who were more conservative would have desired). Rudolf Bultmann and his followers (non-Questers) inaugurated another enormous shift to the left—though very different from earlier liberalism because Bultmann at least retained the kerygmatic Christ, whatever this meant. As we saw, this could be followed only by a new shift to the right: a renewed interest in the historical Jesus (Second Quest).

What was the significance and the result of these Quests? Let me emphasize again that no serious New Testament scholar can escape the questions that the Questers asked. Even the theologian who believes in the inspiration of Scripture and in the supernatural (virgin birth, miracles, bodily resurrection) cannot avoid the historical questions—and these can only be seriously answered according to the criteria of the historical sciences. Only in this way can justice be done to the opponents, and only in this way could these ever be convinced. Thus, theology investigates, among other things, the historical context of Jesus and his functioning in this context (the "historical Jesus") as well as the ecclesiastical-Christological development around his person (the "kerygmatic Christ"). Such a theology is always culturally determined; if theologians flee to an island ("we simply believe what the Bible says"), they are fully entitled to do so—but that would be the end of theology as an academic discipline.

Therefore, when, during the Enlightenment, the historical-critical approach arose within Western culture as a whole, no theologian who took his discipline seriously could avoid the challenges presented by the historical approach as such. One could safely accept these challenges, as long as one was not seduced into accepting the anti-supernaturalist biases of the Enlightenment; that is, as long as one refused to accept the fallacy that, for the modern mind, anti-supernaturalism was the only proper attitude that satisfied the criteria of the

The Modernist View of the New Testament

modern scientific worldview, whatever this was.

The usefulness of the search for the historical Jesus, a Jesus of flesh and blood in a concrete historical context—"born of the Virgin Mary, suffered under Pontius Pilate," as the Apostles' Creed says—is multifaceted. First and foremost, it may keep us from every form of Docetism, which exalts some "kerygmatic Christ" to an ahistorical, timeless, mythical, existential level. This occurs not only in liberal theology, but also in orthodox Christianity, where the (basically Docetic) danger exists of identifying a Christ whose divinity is emphasized both one-sidedly and excessively. As an example, I mention the complaints in certain Reformational circles, especially where cessationism (replacement theology) is still very strong, against the emphasis upon "Jesus the Jew" in the Third Quest. A remarkable example is the Jewish [!] Calvinist Baruch Maoz, who has vigorously opposed everything that he called a Judaizing of Christianity.[63]

I myself am rather concerned about the opposite danger: the neglect of Jesus' Jewishness. This is the Jewish Jesus, the historical Jesus, the non-conformist Jesus, was the One who protested against the hidebound traditionalism and the religious hypocrisy of the Judaism of his days. It is precisely this Jesus who can keep us from a staid *bourgeois* Christianity, which resembles this first-century Judaism. This kind of Christianity does not allow any challenge to its own risks of rigid traditionalism and of an exclusively outward religiosity.

Orthodox Christians have nothing to fear from a search for the historical Jesus, who was the genuine Jesus who belonged inseparably to his Jewish historical setting, "born under the Torah" (Gal. 4:4). On the contrary, they have much to learn from such a search. The only thing they must fear is the mistaken philosophical biases of many critics, which biases are alien to their field of investigation. Such biases exist today among those theologians who still work in the spirit of En-

---

63. Maoz (2003); cf. Ouweneel (2001).

lightenment rationalism and naturalism. Indeed, it resurfaces repeatedly, as in Bultmann's demythologization program. At the same time, there is a general awareness, which hardly existed during the Enlightenment, that all science, including all theology, is paradigmatically determined, as well as that naturalism (or anti-supernaturalism) is not *a priori* better (more scientific) than supernaturalism.

12.5.2 The Jesus Seminar

In the Anglo-Saxon world, the quest for the historical Jesus was the project of the Jesus Seminar, begun in 1985 by Robert W. Funk. This involves a large group of New Testament scholars and sympathetic theologians who wished (and wish) to discover in particular what, according to their criteria, Jesus *really* did and *really* taught.[64] Their goal was to liberate Jesus from the dogmatic prisons in which he had been allegedly held captive: the bleak, bloodless, iconic Jesus, who compares meagerly with the crass reality of the genuine Jesus.[65] Their reality is supposedly that of Jesus the philosophical teacher of Greek wisdom; the Jesus Seminar blamed the synoptic Evangelists for inventing the myth of the Jewish Jesus.

This is a strange idea. Recall that the apostle Paul, *the* main contributor to the New Testament, called Jesus no one less than a descendant of king David (Rom. 1:3; 2 Tim. 2:8). From the beginning, he proved to the Jews that Jesus was the (Jewish) Messiah (Acts 9:22; 17:3; 18:5, 28). He wrote that Jesus was "born under the Torah," that is, as a Jew (Gal. 4:4), and that he had come "to confirm the promises given to the patriarchs" (Rom. 15:8). Paul not only preached the Jewish Jesus but testified that he himself had lived as an orthodox Jew, even after he had come to faith in Jesus (Acts 28:17). Paul knew no other Jesus than the Jewish Jesus. He contrasted Jesus, who is the "wisdom of God," with the wisdom of the Greeks

---

64. Funk and Hoover (1993); Funk (1998; 1999; see also 1996; 2002). For a critical evaluation, see Witherington (1997, 42–57, 272–76).

65. Funk (1996, 300).

(1 Cor. 1:20-24).

In addition to Funk, other important representatives of the Jesus Seminar were John Dominic Crossan and Marcus Borg.[66] They all began with what James D. G. Dunn has rightly called a dubious starting point: mistakenly thinking that the genuine Jesus ought necessarily to be a Jesus separate from faith.[67] This Jesus of faith contrasts with the Jesus of the Gospels — whereas in fact we cannot have any other access to the historical Jesus than through the first disciples. Therefore, the scientific findings of the Jesus Seminar have been fiercely combated by Evangelical authors.[68] It is fascinating to see the sympathetic-critical way in which Marcus Borg and N. T. Wright have structured their more liberal and more conservative Christology (respectively) in a comparative manner.[69]

The Christologies of New Testament scholars and of dogmaticians between, say, 1990 and 2010 differ significantly. However, here and there they exhibit a new trend: they no longer emphasize how the Gospels differ, but how they are similar. Several of these theologians are no longer afraid to find in New Testament research evidence for Trinitarianism and the doctrine of the two natures of Christ. On the contrary, people increasingly realize that first-century Christology was much more uniform, and related to the New Testament much more closely, than people had thought for a long time. Raymond E. Brown wrote that a "moderate conservatism" is perhaps the scholarly approach to Christology about which scholars agree most.[70] And Richard Bauckham proposed an end to the longstanding divorce between the historical Jesus

---

66. Crossan (1991; 1995a; 1995b); Borg (1987; 1994a; 1994b; 1998); see also the discussion between Borg and Wright (1999); regarding Borg, see Witherington (1997, 93–108).
67. Dunn (2005, 22).
68. Wilkins and Moreland (1995); Johnson (1996); Wright (1996); Witherington (1997); Craig (1998); Wright in Borg and Wright (1999); Dunn (2003; 2005).
69. Borg and Wright (1999).
70. Brown (1994, 102).

and the kerygmatic Christ by replacing it by the "Jesus of the testimony," that is, the Jesus of the ear- and eyewitnesses, as we encounter them in the Gospels.[71]

Today it is possible to make such conservative claims again. Of course, we must avoid being reactionary and ahistorical by seeking a return to premodernism, to the paradigm existing before the Enlightenment. Perhaps we should not desire such a return—we have no other choice than to move forward. At the same time, we note that, in our postmodern times, the Enlightenment paradigm, with its emphasis on universal reason and its corresponding anti-supernaturalism, is clearly past its prime.[72] As we try to learn lessons from the past, one lesson could be that, had the liberal approach prevailed, this ultimately would have entailed the end of the Christian faith. To say it in a positive way: not only in the non-Western but also in the Western world, Christianity will survive if it manages to continue declaring what it believed one thousand years ago. However, it will have to do so in a way that is both self-critical and relevant for the present time.[73]

12.5.3 Conclusions

In an extensive study on Jesus, New Testament scholar Klaus Berger came to the following interesting conclusions with respect to the trustworthiness of the Gospels.[74]

(1) Many facts in the Gospels must, also on the basis of the Dead Sea scrolls, be viewed as historically certain, and thus as true—many more facts than people considered to be possible fifty or sixty years ago.

(2) Whereas scholars viewed everything found only in the New Testament as incorrect, many of them assume today that the New Testament stories must be taken as historically correct until the opposite has been demonstrated. (Such demon-

---

71. Bauckham (2006).
72. Dulles (1992, 3–15) speaks of a "post-critical" theology.
73. Cf. Van de Beek (2006, 253).
74. Berger (2004, 41–52).

stration is possible only through other documents, which have been demonstrated to be more reliable that the New Testament.)

(3) When Evangelists report the same matters in different ways, this is not a reason to doubt the historical veracity of these matters.

(4) The time when the Gospels originated was closer to the earthly life of Jesus than was formerly believed.

(5) The (what Berger calls) "mystical" stories (visions, angelic appearances, and the like) do not necessarily plead against the historicity of the Gospels. (I add, they would do so only if the supernatural is excluded beforehand on the basis of a philosophical bias.)

Interestingly, such a plea for the basic historicity of the Gospels received support from an unexpected direction, namely, from an orthodox Jewish scholar. The rabbi David Flusser was one of those who, in recent decades, led us back to the historical Jesus. With his knowledge of first-century Judaism and local circumstances, Flusser claimed that the Jesus sketched in the synoptic Gospels was the historical Jesus, and not some ahistorical kerygmatic Christ.[75] This orthodox Jewish thinker believed that we are allowed to return to where we were before: the portrait of Jesus in the Gospels is both theologically colored and incomplete, but it is historically trustworthy.

12.6 Misunderstandings

12.6.1 Jesus the Jew

In the light of what we just discussed, it is important that James D. G. Dunn recommended restricting the name "Third Quest" to the search for Jesus *the Jew*.[76] Indeed, as I've explained elsewhere, in the wider sense the Third Quest does involve especially the new interest for the Jewish roots of Je-

---

75. Flusser (1998; cf. 1987; 1988; 2013).

76. Dunn (2005, 62; see extensively, 2003; 2005); for a Dutch view, cf. Duvekot (1998).

sus and his teaching.⁷⁷ The Redeemer of millions of believers among the Gentiles was first of all the Messiah of Israel. This is what was announced to the shepherds: "[U]nto *you* is born ..., Christ [i.e., Messiah] the Lord" (Luke 2:11), and this the One whom the "wise men from the east" came seeking: the "king of the *Jews* ... the Christ" (Matt. 2:2, 4). Notice again the order of purposes in the following statement by the apostle Paul: "Christ became a servant to the *circumcised* to show God's truthfulness, in order to confirm the promises given to the patriarchs, and in order that the *Gentiles* might glorify God for his mercy" (Rom. 15:8-9). To the question, "Are you the Christ, the Son of the Blessed?" Jesus answered unequivocally, "I am" (Mark 14:61-62).

At a minimum, Jesus' own statement, "[S]alvation is from the Jews" (John 4:22), means that we will never truly understand salvation apart from its Jewish context. And of course, when Paul says, "[T]he Jews were entrusted with the oracles of God" (Rom. 3:2), he is thinking of the Old Testament, but the same statement is true for the New Testament. The New Testament books were all written by Jewish men, except for Luke—but he was probably a Jewish proselyte before he was converted to Christ. Much of Jesus' teaching, such as the Sermon on the Mount, can be properly understood only against the background of the Judaism of his days. As Markus Bockmuehl stated so well, the Christian faith *in* Jesus is organically and inextricably connected with the Jewish faith *of* Jesus.⁷⁸ As far as the New Testament as a whole is concerned, any serious and credible New Testament scholarship today requires a thorough knowledge of intertestamental Jewish apocalyptic as well as first-century Judaism.

At the same time, we must also be alert as to "over-Jewishifying" Jesus. Sometimes, the emphasis on the Jewishness of Jesus' person and teaching is so strong that the redemptive

---

77. See extensively, Ouweneel (2007, §§1.3, 4.2.3, 13.1, and 13.2).
78. Bockmuehl (1994, 124).

work he came to accomplish moves to the background.[79] In this case, people are more occupied with who Jesus was and what he taught than with what he came to do here on earth. They view him more as the Jewish rabbi or wisdom teacher than as the promised Redeemer (cf. Matt. 1:21, "he will save his people from their sins"). Jesus himself said (regardless of whether the critics accept it as authentic), "[T]he Son of Man came not to be served but to serve, and to give his life as a ransom for many" (Matt. 20:28). And at the institution of the Lord's Supper he said: "[T]his is my blood of the covenant, which is poured out for many for the forgiveness of sins" (26:28).

12.6.2 First Misunderstanding

James Dunn mentioned especially two misunderstandings that characterized the so-called First and Second Quests for the historical Jesus. The first one is the so-called "Easter gulf"[80] that has been created between the pre-Easter historical Jesus and the post-Easter kerygmatic Christ. This gulf is false for the simple reason that the disciples' faith in Jesus did not begin after Easter.[81] Just like, for instance, Raymond E. Brown and Martin Hengel,[82] Dunn emphasized that post-Easter Christology is inconceivable if the essential elements of it had not been accepted by the disciples already before Easter. As Joseph Ratzinger has also said, "Where is post-Easter faith supposed to have come from if Jesus laid no foundation for it before Easter? Scholarship overplays its hand with such reconstructions."[83]

Christianity could originate only through the lasting impression that Jesus had made upon his disciples from the very beginning (cf., e.g., Matt. 7:28–29). This was an impression

---

79. Cf. Van de Beek (2002, 264).
80. See Ouweneel (2007, §3.5.3).
81. Dunn (2005, chapter 1: "The First Faith").
82. Brown (1994); Hengel (1995).
83. Ratzinger (2007, 303).

that gave shape to the Jesus tradition right from the start, so that even long before Easter reliable stories circulated about him. The sayings of Jesus did not begin circulating after Easter, such that they allegedly were modulated to a greater or lesser extent by a church-produced theology (Ger. *Gemeindetheologie*). Rather, they began long before Easter with the disciples, and even with Jesus himself.[84] As an example, Dunn mentioned the present discussion around the so-called "Q material" (the material belonging to the hypothetical Q document), which seems to be strongly Galilean in nature, and which lacks a passion story. According to Dunn the most obvious explanation for this is *not* that the Q material originated after Easter in some "Q community," but rather that it originated in Galilee, and received its ultimate form before Jesus' death.

Ratzinger pointed out that, about twenty years after Jesus' death, we find in the Christ hymn of Philippians 2:6–11 a fully developed Christology; and as an answer to the question how this could have been possible, the notion of some church-designed theology does not help at all:

> How could these unknown groups be so creative? How were they so persuasive and how did they manage to prevail? Isn't it more logical, even historically speaking, to assume that the greatness came at the beginning, and that the figure of Jesus really did explode all existing categories and could only be understood in the light of the mystery of God?[85]

---

84. Dunn discussed (2005, chapter 2: "Behind the Gospels") the enormous significance as well as the trustworthiness, and also the specific character, of the oral tradition between Jesus and the first written sources, a fact that the earlier Questers had strongly neglected because of their "literary mind-set." He argued that the nature of the synoptic Gospel traditions could have been largely determined already during the oral period, and before they were extensively written down in Mark's Gospel and the (supposed) Q source (58; cf. the Appendix).
85. Ratzinger (2007, xxii–xxiii).

And further:

> The anonymous community is credited with an astonishing level of theological genius — who were the great figures responsible for inventing all this? No, the greatness, the dramatic newness, comes directly from Jesus; within the faith and life of the community it is further developed, but not created. In fact, the "community" would not even have emerged and survived at all unless some extraordinary reality had preceded it.[86]

12.6.3 Second Misunderstanding

James Dunn identified in the Quests for the historical Jesus the additional misunderstanding that this figure necessarily had to *differ* from the Christ of faith, the Christ of the *kerygma*. According to Dunn, the historical Jesus is not a kind of objective-scientific Jesus who, as a Kantian thing-in-itself (Ger. *Ding an sich*), can be identified *behind* the Jesus of the Gospels and *behind* the Jesus of Christian faith. There is no objective Jesus who could be severed from the traditions about him, which from the very first were *faith* traditions. We have no other Jesus than the Jesus of faith. Only a view of science that is colored in a positivistic-scientistic way, with its notion of objective facts, can claim that we *therefore* cannot know Jesus as he really was.

The only historical Jesus available to us is the Jesus who, from the beginning, made precisely that overwhelming impression upon people that formed the start of the Jesus tradition. The "fifth Gospel" that was so strongly defended by Martin Kähler, and long after him by the Jesus Seminar — the "scientifically justified gospel" of theologians and historians — is a mirage. Or, to put it a bit differently, it is a "gospel" with a different kind of "believers": present-day rationalists, scientists, anti-supernaturalists, or whatever they may be called. There *is* no (neutral, objective) historical Jesus distinguishable from, or radically different from, the kerygmatic

---

86. Ibid., 324.

Christ. There are basically two kerygmatic Christs, either the One of the first disciples (to whom we feel attracted most because *they* had known the historical Jesus), or the One of present-day positivistic theologians and historians—and many man-made kerygmatic Christs in addition.

Dunn rightly remarked that the fewer elements that the reconstructed "Jesus" took over from the synoptic picture of Jesus, the more this reconstruction expressed the agendas of the individual Questers.[87] To me this means that the further removed the Questers' pictures of Jesus are from the picture of Jesus in the Gospels, thus becoming their own pictures of Jesus, the more easily the respective Questers will be able to inject their own ideas and ideologies into these pictures—and the less such pictures of Jesus have to do with the biblical Christ.

12.7 Biblical-Critical Methodology: Objections

12.7.1 Western Presumption

In addition to a flood of criticism of its details, we can adduce several general and fundamental objections against New (and also Old) Testament criticism.[88] The first objection is the Western arrogance with which Western scholars approach ancient Eastern texts, forgetting the distances both in time and in culture.

With respect to the Old Testament, it is a mockery that modern Western critics, without having contemporaneous Hebrew literature at their disposal to make comparisons, venture to pass judgment about differences in style and vernacular, and about supposed literary forms in writings from a totally different epoch and cultural background. They venture to brush aside phrases and verses, or to arrange them differently, every time their Western ideas of coherence and

---

87. Dunn (2005, 34).
88. See Lewis (1967, especially 153–62); Schaafs (1967, especially 292–305; from the viewpoint of a natural scientist); also see McDowell (1975, 1999); Guthrie (1978; 1979); Tenney (1984); Geisler (1999).

The Modernist View of the New Testament

style are disturbed. They claim to be able to improve the text by replacing rare or unusual words in the Masoretic text — words that they do not understand, or that they expect in the context, or that do not fit their theories — with different words. This is scientism in its most extreme form, if not outright complacency and hubris.

Here is a New Testament example: Ratzinger said with respect to an attempt to attribute a paradox in John 13 to "editorial formation"[89] that "this is too narrow an approach, too closely tied to the thought patterns of our Western logic." And with respect to a similar problem in John 17, he complained about "the kind of academic logic that takes the compositional form of modern scholarly texts as the criterion for something so utterly different in its expression and thought as John's Gospel."[90]

In fact, biblical criticism, which wishes to be *historical* criticism par excellence, makes a rather ahistorical, and therefore unscientific impression by disregarding the different character of those earlier ages and cultures, with their totally different views of style and literature. Moreover, these ancient views are scarcely *known* to us because we lack any Hebrew comparable literary data. From the New Testament era, we have access to very few writings that could be used for a comparative evaluation of the literary character of the Gospels. After these Eastern writings have passed through the filters of the Western critics, they are scarcely recognizable.

12.7.2 No Objective Evidence

A person who is not only a theologian but also a natural scientist and a science philosopher is struck by the absence of any objective documentary evidence within biblical criticism. Even the diehard adherents of the documentary hypotheses, for both Old and New Testaments, must admit that not a shred of evidence exists that the JEDP documents, or anything

---

89. Ratzinger (2011, 62).
90. Ratzinger (2011, 82).

that looked like them, ever existed. Nor does any ancient text exist that looks like the document known as "primitive Mark" (Ger. *Ur-Markus*), or documents such as Q, M, or L, which the critics have postulated.[91] People may argue that such documents were lost, so that finding any of them would have been miraculous. This is perfectly true; but then the critics should admit that their hypotheses are based on pure speculation.

This is even more so for the pericopes that were the supposed products of a church-designed theology but have hardly anything to do with the historical Jesus. The critics dismiss as ahistorical whatever tradition tells us about the origin of the Gospels. But generally speaking, if we no longer have access to the historical Jesus, how can the critics claim to *know* that he differs from the kerygmatic Christ?

An interesting example of this kind of defective scientific thinking is supplied by C. J. den Heyer: "One of the consequences of the study concerning the origin of the Gospels in the nineteenth century was the discovery [!] of the Q source . . . a surprising discovery. . . . Now we know [!] that this Q source is of incalculable significance for the knowledge of early Christianity."[92] The simple truth, of course, is that no Q source was ever discovered, but was merely postulated — and from the viewpoint of scientific accuracy there is an enormous difference between these two. Therefore the most we can know is that the Q *hypothesis* is significant, *not* that a Q *source* existing only in the scholarly imagination would be significant.[93] Moreover, for different reasons the existence of Q is quite unlikely: how could we explain that such well-delineated documents as primitive Mark (Ger. *Ur-Markus*) or Q once existed but later completely disappeared? We possess very old manuscript fragments of the Gospels, some dating from the early second century — so why no fragments of these postulated documents?

---

91. For a survey of all postulated models, see Holladay (2005, 69–74).
92. Den Heyer (2003, 130).
93. Cf. Meier (1991, 44) with references; Stein (1996, 38–40).

The Modernist View of the New Testament

Let me quote here Casper Labuschagne. He claimed that it has *"come to light"*

> how much the human Jesus of the three synoptic Gospels has been pushed to the background in church doctrine and church tradition, and has been supplanted by the divine Christ of the church. In the large stream of studies about the historical Jesus it has been irrefutably demonstrated how one-sided is the picture of Jesus that has become current in the church in comparison with that of the Gospels.[94]

We cannot believe our eyes! "Come to light"? "Irrefutably demonstrated"!? Instead, at most we have only hypotheses that have temporarily acquired great popularity among New Testament scholars. We are dealing here neither with objective evidence nor with any common opinion among New Testament scholars. Even though Labuschagne showed at several places in his study that he had a fair understanding of the nature of science, at other placed he allowed himself to get carried away with his enthusiasm in using such an impermissible expression as "it has been demonstrated" (Dutch, *vast is komen te staan*),[95] and the like.

Joseph Ratzinger rightly argued that

> historical research can at most establish high probability but never final and absolute certainty over every detail. If the certainty of faith were dependent upon scientific-historical verification alone, it would always remain open to revision. . . . [I]f the historicity of the key words and events could be scientifically disproved, then the faith would have lost its foundation. . . . [Faith allows us to] serenely examine exegetical hypotheses that all too often make exaggerated claims to certainty, claims that are already determined by the existence of diametrically opposed positions put forward with an equal claim to scientific ["]certainty["].[96]

---

94. Labuschagne (2000, 45).
95. Ibid., 48.
96. Ratzinger (2011, 104–105).

12.7.3 Ignorance about the Philosophy of Science

Here I will be discussing the widespread denial or ignorance of the ideological biases in biblical criticism. We begin with some Reformed authors. C. Graafland rightly observed how striking it is "that what is presented as the outcome of scholarly Bible research fits in astonishingly well with the already fixed dogmatic (faith) view of the investigator."[97] Fred H. Klooster wrote about the liberal New Testament scholars and Christology specialists that their claim of being objective and without presupposition was itself a myth.[98] Indeed, the entire idea of some neutral, objective, unbiased theology is a disturbing Enlightenment myth.

A. van de Beek said, "Since New Testament research began making a distinction between the historical and the theological, we find [a stalemate] among theologians. The side on which the decision falls depends mainly on theological (or underlying worldview) positions. The *theological* argumentation usually decides the historical debate."[99]

Here are some Roman Catholic authors. New Testament scholar John P. Meier rightly remarked that, whether we call it a bias, a tendency (Ger. *Tendenz*), a worldview, or a faith viewpoint, everyone writing about the historical Jesus writes from an ideological standpoint; no critic is exempt from this.[100] Another New Testament scholar, Klaus Berger, called certain "fundamental 'results'" of liberal exegesis an example of ideological wishful thinking."[101]

It is all the more astonishing that C. J. den Heyer claimed with respect to a traditional approach to the New Testament: "In this case, there cannot be any question of an unbiased exposition of the texts"[102] — as if an "unbiased exposition" *even*

---

97. Graafland (n.d., 28).
98. Klooster (1977, 26).
99. Van de Beek (1998, 139).
100. Meier (1991, 5).
101. Berger (2004, 532–33).
102. Den Heyer (2003, 11).

exists. Den Heyer's own publication, which is saturated with naturalism, is a clear proof that this is not the case. It is quite astonishing that, in our time, such an epistemological ignorance can still be perpetuated.

12.7.4 A Disintegrating Approach

As we have seen, the common approach to interpreting ancient literature is the harmonic one, where apparent discrepancies can be explained from the context as much as possible. In this way, the unity of the text can be maintained as long as it has not been clearly and independently demonstrated that the text consists of compositional patchwork. However, this is not the way that critics have dealt with the Bible. Instead they have treated it as a collection of fragments; this is what Old Testament critics did with the Pentateuch, and New Testament critics with the Gospels. This was done on the basis not of the facts (whatever they are) but of their ideological biases.

Two Jewish scholars, Umberto Cassuto and Moses H. Segal,[103] turned with indignation against this disintegrating treatment of the Tanakh (which we call the Old Testament), especially the Pentateuch, by the critics. They argued that one can find discrepancies in *any* text, if one diligently searches for them, but this is not evidence that the text originated from several different sources. Cassuto, Segal, and others defended primarily and fiercely the unity and harmony of the biblical books.

The New Testament critics, in turn, exhibited little appreciation for the remarkable literary and theological unity of each of the Gospels. Some have claimed, for instance, that the uniform vernacular of John's Gospel excludes the use of sources. But others have claimed, not without reason, that the very same argument can be adduced regarding the synoptic Gospels.[104]

---

103. Cassuto (2006); Segal (1967).

104. See commentaries such as those by Morris (1971); Green (1997); France (2007).

12.7.5 Circular Arguments

The adherents of documentary hypotheses seem to *want* to believe in different sources despite the lack of objective, independent evidence, and despite the literary fragmentation resulting from their approach. Therefore, it is not at all difficult for them to postulate an indefinite number of sources, each with its own characteristics, and then to neatly assign various Bible portions to each. However, the claim that the neat result therefore *demonstrates* the existence of that number of sources is a scientific *non sequitur*, for this conclusion was embedded *a priori* in their presuppositions. Without establishing beforehand, independently and objectively, one's starting points and methods, such a procedure can lead only to a wide divergence of results. This is indeed the very case. And what is presented as a "result" can never be anything more than a (not very scientific) speculation.

The "result" would definitely make a certain impression if indeed it would turn out that all sentences in, for instance, Genesis can be divided more or less seamlessly — of course we must reckon with the work of editors — over 4, or x, sources, each with a good number of well-defined characteristics. The smooth way in which one would manage to do so, as well as the fact that various independent investigators arrive at more or less corresponding results, would of course not be *proofs* but certainly *indications* for the existence of different sources. However, the factual situation is that such a smooth division is not at all possible, so that the critics must resort to a second circular reasoning in order to still arrive at a certain result. All problems that the text yields in view of the splitter's theory are simply brushed aside by accusing the (also postulated) editors and the later copyists of having tampered with the text. Notice what this means: *the very same text material that is trusted to demonstrate the theory, or at least to make it plausible, is rejected each time it conflicts with the theory.*

In the disciplines of the natural sciences, such methods

would simply be inconceivable and unacceptable. It does not help to point out that natural sciences and humanities are very different types of science. I know that from my own personal studies. Nonetheless, they do have a few things in common; for instance, you cannot use certain materials as evidence to support your theory and then dismiss the very same materials when they do not suit your argument.

In New Testament criticism, we encounter similar circular arguments. These are found in (a) the treatment of the New Testament as a whole: on the basis of a few Bible portions, chosen according to subjective criteria, a portrait of the earliest church history is designed and then used to reject New Testament parts as ahistorical on the basis of this same portrait. A similar type of argument is encountered in (b) the treatment of each distinct book: according to equally subjective criteria, certain fragments—which the critics' biases identify as "tradition elements"—are declared to be older, on the basis of which the other passages are identified as representatives of later theological views.

Concerning the study of the Gospels, even the very liberal H. M. Kuitert had to admit that in this investigation we are dealing with mutually contradictory hypotheses, some of which involve circular reasoning.[105]

The warrant for our accusation of circular reasoning is evident from the arbitrariness involved in applying such reasoning, based entirely on the critic's taste and preference. Thus, the Gospels are used to alternately demonstrate or refute one another's trustworthiness. Or Galatians is used to demonstrate the historical *un*reliability of Acts, or vice versa. That such things can happen at all is simply the consequence of the *lack of criteria that are objective and independent of the investigator's biases.*

---

105. Kuitert (1999, 63).

12.8 Other Epistemological Considerations

12.8.1 Speculationism

The most extreme are those (Western) authors who speculate on the sensationalism of the general public, and indulge in the wildest fantasies. Here are a few examples.

(a) *Jesus did not die on the cross.* This Gnostic-Docetic heresy, later adopted by Islam and found in the Koran, has been defended recently by Western authors like Helmut Felzmann and René Frank.

(b) *Jesus died in a remote country*, that is, not in Jerusalem on the cross. In particular India and Tibet have been suggested. In the Western world, this view was defended, for instance, by Erich von Däniken. He had already gathered some renown by his theory that the gods of the nations were in fact astronauts from other worlds.

(c) *Jesus was married to Mary Magdalene, and had children with her*. This speculation goes back to certain Gnostic traditions, too. In our day, it was defended by Henry Lincoln, Michael Baigent, and Richard Leigh, and tremendously popularized by the novel *The Da Vinci Code* by Dan Brown. Jesus and his family were allegedly buried in a tomb in the quarter Talpiot near Jerusalem.

(d) *Jesus is supposedly mentioned in the Dead Sea scrolls*, but this fact is allegedly suppressed by the Vatican because it would be disastrous for the teaching of Christianity, according to John Marco Allegro and Robert Eisenmann. This kind of conspiracy theories can always count on a lot of sensational support, especially if the suggestion is made that the truth is suppressed in order not to hurt certain interest groups.

(e) *Jesus is a fictional Judaized version of Julius Caesar*, according to Francesco Carotta; Jesus himself allegedly never existed, and detail for detail he is supposed to be a copy of the great Roman hero. Christianity is based on a fiction.

Let us quickly leave this field of senseless speculation and return to serious New Testament scholarship. I do this

The Modernist View of the New Testament

through two references, a Protestant and a Catholic one. The first is from C. S. Lewis. He argued that biblical critics must be almost superhuman in order to master the fact that wherever they bump into customs, language, racial traits, a religious background, composition habits and basic assumptions that no science will ever be able to let any living human know just as surely and instinctively as the reviewers can know his (Lewis'), or anyone's, customs, backgrounds, habits, and so on. Lewis asked his readers to consider that, for the same reason, the Bible critics, no matter what reconstruction they may design, can never be directly falsified. Mark is dead (he can no longer be interrogated). And when the critics will meet with Peter (whose memories Mark supposedly wrote down), there will be more urgent matters to discuss, according to Lewis.[106] In other words, many claims by the naturalist Bible critics are just as scientistic, and just as non-falsifiable, as those of the fundamentalists (cf. §§10.4 and 10.5).

My second reference is to Joseph Ratzinger again. He argued that the historical Jesus who is sketched in the most important movement of critical exegesis with its hermeneutical presuppositions is a figure too meager to expect him to have exerted a great influence on history. This Jesus is too much encased in the past; with him no personal relationship is possible. Instead of this, Ratzinger endeavored to look at, and listen to, the Jesus of the Gospels in such a way that it could come to an encounter with him.[107] In other words, the "science" of many critics is not only pseudo-science, but it also hampers the view that Christ really does exist as the One with whom people can enter into a personal relationship.

12.8.2 Methodological Criteria

If we assess all the arguments presented in the previous sections, we must conclude that the methodology of biblical criticism cannot survive scrutiny by the philosophy of sci-

---

106. Lewis (1967, 161).
107. Ratzinger (2011, 11).

ence—that branch of epistemology that studies the nature, presuppositions and methods of science. Let me mention just a few of the criteria that ought to be applied in order to obtain genuinely scientific results.

(a) *Intersubjectivity*. If different investigators independently study the same material, starting from the same scientific criteria, they ought to arrive at comparable results. Within the natural sciences, this is the common procedure. With theories of biblical criticism, however, there are almost as many conflicting opinions and results as there are investigators or schools of thought. This was also the case, for instance, in the first period of special-scientific psychology.[108] This is a sign that a discipline is still in its infancy.

(b) *Non-falsifiability*. In biblical criticism, it is impossible to make risky predictions, predictions that, during further investigation, might not come true, and thus may lead to correction or even rejection of the hypothesis. In other words, theories of biblical criticism are non-falsifiable (cf. §§10.4. and 10.5); with more or less effort, any conceivable datum can be fit into the hypothesis involved. It would be unthinkable to find data in the Pentateuch that would not fit into the JEDP theory, or data in the synoptic Gospels that could not be fit into the primitive Mark/Q/M/L hypothesis. Such theories can prove everything, and therefore they prove nothing. Speaking purely scientifically, they are worthless.

Obviously, if we wished, we could say exactly the same regarding the traditional view of the Bible text; viewed strictly as a theological *theory*, it is just as non-falsifiable as the theories of biblical criticism. However, the traditional view is highly preferable *a priori* because it does justice to the unity and harmony of the text, that is, to the way a Bible book presents itself, and does not apply criteria to the text that are foreign to that book (see [c]).

(c) *Biases alien to the text*. The anti-supernaturalist and sci-

---

108. Cf. Ouweneel (1984, 106–25).

entistic attitude of current biblical criticism makes it *a priori* impossible for the critics to accept the Bible's self-understanding and self-testimony as being the inspired and authoritative Word of God, and thus to accept the Bible *itself*. Therefore, from the outset it is inevitable that the critics will formulate only theories about Scripture that are alien to its spirit.

(d) *Scientific methods appropriate to historical investigation.* Martin Hengel pointed here to the remarkable similarity with fundamentalism. He argued that New Testament exegesis is open to dangers not only of an uncritical, sterile apologetic fundamentalism but also of an equally sterile "[biblical] critical ignorance," which, according to Hengel, had hardly anything in common with sound *historical* critical methods.[109] Elsewhere he argued that earlier orthodox rationalism, which betrayed an ahistorical and fundamentalist desire for certainty, and modern forms of rationalism, which try to domesticate Jesus according to self-centered interests and ideologies, ultimately differ very little at their roots.[110] He also argued that orthodox fundamentalist biblicism finds its counterpart in biblical critical biblicism. Both are naïve and run the risk of violating historical reality, the former by its ahistorical biblical literalism, and the latter by selecting and interpreting according to its modern worldview and theological interests.[111]

12.8.3 Four Approaches

In connection with Hengel's distinctions mentioned in the previous section, I refer to the useful distinction that Raymond E. Brown made between four different approaches.

(a) An "uncritical conservative" (read, fundamentalist) approach, which does not see or acknowledge any difference between Jesus' own Christology (so to speak) and that of his followers. In my words, fundamentalism does not account for the fact that, in the Gospels and epistles, the writers view Je-

---

109. Hengel (1995, 57–58).

110. Ibid., x.

111. Ibid., 71.

sus through their own (different) theological glasses. These glasses may have been given, or at least used, by God—yet, they are glasses. We have *their* portraits of Jesus, and therefore we necessarily have four *different* portraits of Jesus.

(b) An "uncritical liberal" approach, which, on the basis of rationalistic, naturalistic and scientistic biases, unnecessarily creates a deep cleft between the historical Jesus and the kerygmatic Christ (this latter referring to the portrait of Jesus created by his followers). That is, the kerygmatic Christ (the Christ of early Christian preaching) has supernatural, miraculous features that the historical Jesus could not possibly have possessed (according to naturalism and scientism), and *therefore* the two must be essentially different.

(c) A "critical liberal" approach, which accepts a limited continuity between the two (the historical Jesus and the kerygmatic Christ), *or* believes that such a continuity cannot be demonstrated (Bultmann). I add that the former of these two is definitely a partial return to the traditional picture of Jesus; it would even be better if this approach could free itself entirely from its naturalistic and scientistic constraints.

(d) A "critical conservative" approach, which acknowledges widespread continuity between Jesus' own Christology (more accurately, the picture of himself that Jesus provided) and that of his followers, but also leaves room for church-designed theology, that is, the doctrinal shading of this portrait by the earliest Christians, beginning with the New Testament writers.[112] If this approach could remain free of naturalism and scientism, it would deserve our endorsement.

12.9 The Authenticity of the Gospels

12.9.1 Gospel Harmonies

Let us now enter more deeply into the literary and historical problems with regard to the four Gospels against the backdrop of the crucial question of bibliology: How trustworthy is

---

112. Brown (1994, 6–15).

the New Testament? One of the important scholarly questions that have been asked regarding the Gospels is this one: What can we deduce from the Gospels concerning the historical Jesus? What in the Gospels is authentic, that is, what things did Jesus really say and do, and what described events really did occur in space and time, and what part is the product of secondary theological reflection about both Jesus' sayings and the events described?

It has often been noticed, also by more conservative scholars, that the Gospels are not reportorial accounts, not biographies in any sense, not objective historiography in any historical-scientific sense. Each event, each saying of Jesus in the Gospels, stands in a thoroughly theological context; in other words, the Gospels are more theology than history. (I use the word "theological" here in the wider sense of "religious-doctrinal" to adapt to common parlance. Actually, I would prefer limiting the term "theology" to refer to *theoretical-scholarly* reflection on Christian doctrine.[113])

Because of the theological importance of this fourfold character of the Gospels, no modern expositor would think of writing a harmony of the Gospels, as Tatiandid. Later, John Calvin did the same, and wrote a commentary on this "harmony of the Gospels"[114] — in my view, a strange theological mistake because such a procedure ignores the specific character of each of the four Gospels. I could have named Augustine as well,[115] and recently New Testament scholar Kurt Aland.[116]

Today, we understand more clearly that when a specific event is described in all of the synoptic Gospels, or even in all four Gospels, it has a different theological tint, depending on the scope and theological orientation of the Gospel that

---

113. See extensively, Ouweneel (1995; cf. 2007, chapters 13–14; 2015).
114. Calvin (1972).
115. https://en.wikisource.org/wiki/Nicene_and_Post-Nicene_Fathers:_Series_I/Volume_VI/The_Harmony_of_ the_Gospels.
116. Aland (1982).

records it.[117] William Kelly therefore rejected all harmonies of the Gospels because they are mixtures of accounts that were each written with a separate divine aim. The facts have been put together by the Holy Spirit with a clear purpose, such that each Gospel presents both Christ and the ways of God in its own light. To blend all of them is to destroy this goal, and to obscure our insight into the Gospels.[118]

Given these considerations, except in extreme fundamentalist circles, there is less desire to harmonize parallel passages in the Gospels in such a sophisticated way that their historicity is salvaged (see §10.4.4).

12.9.2 An Example of a "Contradiction"

Let us take a well-known example, which also has important Christological implications but which I quote here because of the literary-critical aspects. The Gospel presumed to be the oldest[119] mentions as Peter's answer to Jesus' question, "Who do people say that I am?" only this: "You are the Christ" (Mark 8:28-29). Luke 9:20 gives this as Peter's answer: "The Christ of God." But in Matthew 16:16, the answer is described as follows: "You are the Christ, the Son of the living God," followed by Jesus' important comment: "Blessed are you, Simon Bar-Jonah! For flesh and blood has not revealed this to you, but my Father who is in heaven" (v. 17).

Why this difference between both Mark and Luke in contrast to Matthew? It seems easy to suggest that Mark and Luke, for some reason unknown to us, have omitted the words "the Son of the living God," as well as Jesus' comment. With this explanation, the historicity of these Gospels is salvaged.[120] Or is it conceivable that the additional words in Peter's confes-

---

117. See extensively, Van Bruggen (1998, chapter 2: "Four Gospels—One History?").
118. Kelly (*BT* 5:46).
119. See Brown (1997, ad loc.).
120. This is the way Archer Jr. (1982) resolved many discrepancies in the Gospels.

sion are a theological elaboration from Matthew himself? If so, this would be an elaboration entirely in line with who Jesus really is, and with Peter's actual views about him, as these came to light on various occasions. We do not really know. Perhaps Peter did say it the way Matthew reports it—even if in this case, we do not understand why Mark and Luke did not mention these important words. But this is not the only, or even the required, explanation. I am not averse to suggesting that we have here church-designed theology.

The enormous difference with current New Testament criticism is this. For most critics, the suggestion of church-designed theology involves *essentially changing* the true picture of Jesus (his person, sayings, acts). This alteration involves a cleft between the historical Jesus (now allegedly unknown to us) and the Christ invented by the early church. What *I* propose is church-designed theology that serves as a theological *elaboration* of the real historical facts, *and not some pious projection* without (sufficient) historical ground. What Matthew 16 may have added to Peter's confession was not an invention of the writer, or of the circle to which he belonged, but is entirely in line with the total revelation of the New Testament.

The various interpretations of Matthew 16 clearly display the paradigms of various theologians. We are not amazed, for example, that Rudolf Bultmann and H. Kuitert declare the words "the Son of the living God" plus verses 17–19 to be non-authentic.[121] This is easily done; the underlying reason is that the quoted words do not fit into their ideas about Jesus. I would like to ask such critics: *Why* could the words, despite the differences in their transmission, not basically be authentic? *Why* could Peter not have called Jesus the "Son of God"?

The ease of the critics is identical to the ease with which fundamentalists are disinterested in explaining the differences encountered but simply attribute them to the mysterious ways of divine inspiration. I would ask them: But *why* did

---

121. Bultmann (1952, 45); Kuitert (1999, 62–63).

Matthew, Mark, and Luke need to tell us different—perhaps even contradictory—things? Peter could have said only one thing; does this mean that two of the three writers are telling us falsehoods? Or why did God tell them to write different things? What purpose was served with them? Is not the fundamentalists' smoothing out the differences just as superficial as the critics' elimination of everything displeasing to them?

Please notice here the two meanings of the term (non-)authentic. In my view, the words involved might be non-authentic in the sense that Peter may not have literally used them. However, they would certainly be *true* in the light of the entire New Testament. In the view of theologians like Bultmann and Kuitert, however, non-authentic also means untrue. More than this, because such theologians believe in advance that such words *cannot* be true, or *cannot* have been said, it is *a priori* certain that they will declare them to be non-authentic. If I would presume that the words are non-authentic, this would be due primarily to a *literary* argument, namely, the comparison between the synoptic Gospels. If Bultmann or Kuitert presumes that the words are non-authentic, this would be due primarily to a *philosophical* argument, namely, their naturalistic prejudice: Jesus cannot be the Son of God, at least not in any ontic sense; at best it may be an honorary title. If Christians do claim that Jesus is the Son of God in any ontic sense, this is nothing but pious speculation arising at a (much) later time: the fruit of church-designed theology.

Actually, Ben F. Meyer has argued that the words involved could certainly be genuine words of Peter;[122] they explain better the origin of the other wordings—not only in Mark and Luke but also Peter's formulation "the Holy One of God" in John 6:69 (cf. Luke 1:35)—than the short text of Mark 8:29 does. Oscar Cullman also pleaded for the authenticity of the words, although he believed that they originally belonged to a different setting, namely, the passion story (see, e.g., Luke

---

122. Meyer (1979, 189–191; cf. Tasker (1961, 160–61; Carson (1984, 365–66).

22:31-38).[123] Others have made similar suggestions. Thus, the words can certainly be authentic, either in the sense that Peter literally spoke them on this occasion, or that he said similar words on this or another occasion.

12.9.3 Son of God, Son of Man

In addition to the arguments mentioned in the previous section, I may add that Peter's words do not at all need to involve a full-fledged Christology. Every Jew familiar with the Bible knew that the Messiah (i.e., *Christos*) has, among many other titles, the title "Son of God" (Ps. 2:7; John 1:49; cf. Isa. 9:6; Matt. 14:33; Luke 1:35).[124] Especially John 1:49 is of interest here, not only because of Nathanael's confession of Jesus as "Son of God," but also because of Jesus adding another Messianic title: that of "Son of Man" (v. 51). Hebrews 1:5 quotes Psalm 2:7 to underscore Jesus' title as the "Son of God," and Hebrews 2:5-9 quotes Psalm 8:4-6 to underscore Jesus' title as the "Son of Man."

Here again, the discussion arose as to whether Jesus' self-description as "Son of Man" can be accepted as authentic.[125] In general, the critics accepted as authentic two of Jesus's sayings in Luke's Gospel. One is this: "I tell you, everyone who acknowledges me before men, the Son of Man also will acknowledge before the angels of God" (12:8). The other is this: "For as the lightning flashes and lights up the sky from one side to the other, so will the Son of Man be in his day" (17:24). The reason is that, in these passages, Jesus ostensibly distinguishes himself from the Son of Man. That is, in the minds of the critics Jesus cannot refer to *himself* to the Son of Man. But how then can the passage in Luke 17 continue as follows: "But first he must suffer many things and be rejected by this generation" (v. 25)? Here, Jesus was obviously referring to himself. The same Jesus who accurately announced that he

---

123. Cullmann (1953, 158-70).
124. See Ouweneel (2007, 171-73).
125. See Ratzinger (2007, 378-80).

would be rejected and killed is the One who announced that he would rise on the third day (9:22), would go back to his Father (John 16:18), and would one day return with the clouds of heaven (Luke 21:27; cf. Matt. 24:30; 26:64).

Another counter-argument: how can the parallel of Luke 12:8 in Matthew 10:32 read, "So everyone who acknowledges *me* before men, I also will acknowledge before my Father who is in heaven"? The "Son of Man" in Luke 12 is identical with the "me" (Jesus) in Matthew 10. Moreover, who can seriously doubt that, in Luke 12 and 17, Jesus is referring to himself when using the title "Son of Man"? And what about all the other times when Jesus speaks of the "Son of Man" in Luke's Gospel in clear reference to himself (e.g., 5:24; 7:34; 9:22, 26, 44, 58; 11:30; 12:10, 40; 22:22, 48, 69)? Can all these references be brushed aside that easily?

12.10 Theological Compositions

12.10.1 The Gospels

The Gospels are theological *compositions*, in which the various writers have taken the liberty to put distinct events and sayings of Jesus coherently together, or to arrange them differently, according to the writer's theological design. This phenomenon is well-known and generally accepted also in conservative circles,[126] as long as this does not imply that the Evangelists themselves invented parts of the recorded material. Thus, British scholar Donald Guthrie wrote about Luke's Gospel that nobody denies that Luke's purpose is theological, but this does not mean that Luke *distorted* history in order to conform it to his theology. It would be more correct to say that he brings out the theological significance of Jesus' history.[127]

I emphasize again that the problem is not that in the Gospels we encounter an Evangelist's theology or church-designed theology. Rather, the problem is that certain sayings of Jesus and events around Jesus are judged non-authentic,

---

126. See more extensively, Ouweneel (2007, §6.3).
127. Guthrie (1990, 107).

whereby the critics allege that these *could* not have really happened, but were invented by the earliest Christians. The reason for making such claims is not literary or historical at all, but clearly and exclusively ideological.

Take, for instance, C. J. den Heyer, whom we've mentioned before. From the fact that the Gospels are theological compositions he confidently concludes that much of what they contain is presumably a product of the Evangelists' own imagination.[128] Again, Den Heyer has no literary or historical reason for such a claim, but only his ideological biases. The notion of composition does not mean that the writer *invents* (part of) his materials, but rather that he arranges them in an inventive way.

The moment we make assumptions like those of Den Heyer, the floodgates open wide. This is shown by the enormous discord about which sayings of Jesus and events involving Jesus can still be called authentic. This is no wonder in a discipline where scholars do not start from objective scientific criteria or extra-biblical sources to which one could appeal. Ultimately only the pre-theological paradigm of the theologian prescribes what Jesus is *allowed* to have really said and done. This is how scholars become trapped within a grand circular argument of their own making (cf. §12.7.5): what is authentic in the Gospels determines the scholars' Christology — but their Christology in its turn determines what in the Gospels may be called authentic.[129]

12.10.2 The Early Letters

In my view, the only thesis that possesses a certain measure of objectivity — apart from whether this thesis is also *correct* — is that generally the earliest New Testament writings may be viewed as being closest to the historical Jesus. Conversely, the later a Bible book is dated, the more it may be expected to exhibit the marks of church-designed theology, that is, of

---

128. Den Heyer (2003, 21–24).
129. Regarding this, see Brown (1994, 24).

a higher Christology that exalts Jesus beyond what he really was. In this case, we might even detect a certain development within the New Testament. But is this indeed the case?

Remarkably enough, the situation seems to be the very opposite. Some believe that Galatians was written after the first missionary journey of the apostle Paul;[130] and what a high Christology we encounter here: God revealed his Son in Paul (1:16); God "sent forth his Son, born of woman, born under the law, to redeem those who were under the law, so that we might receive adoption as sons. And because you are sons, God has sent the Spirit of his Son into our hearts, crying, 'Abba! Father!'" (4:4-6).

First and Second Thessalonians were written during the second missionary journey (AD 51/52?, i.e., only about twenty years after Jesus's death and resurrection).[131] Notice what the apostle Paul writes here: "Now may our God and Father himself, and our Lord Jesus, direct our way to you" (1 Thess. 3:11). In the English translation this cannot be seen, but in the Greek original, the verb "may direct" (Gk. *kateuthynai*) is a singular form, which means that Paul places "our God and Father" and "our Lord Jesus" on one level, or views them as One. The same is the case in 2 Thessalonians 2:16-17, "Now may our Lord Jesus Christ himself, and God our Father, . . . comfort [*parakalesai*] your hearts and establish [*stērixai*] them in every good work and word." Again, the verbal forms are in the singular; to Paul, our Lord and our Father are One — not one person but one being.

And as far as the Gospels are concerned, many believe that the Gospels were written later than the letters; Mark's Gospel was perhaps written between AD 60 and 70. However, it is these very Gospels that bring us most near to the historical Je-

---

130. But see Ouweneel (1997a, 13–17), suggesting we must think of the third missionary journey.
131. Regarding 1 Thess., see Brown (1997, 456–66); whether 2 Thess. is to be place in the same period depends on whether it is viewed as authentic (cf. ibid., 594–96); cf. §§6.8.1 and 6.11.2.

sus—and at the same time exhibit such a high Christology.¹³²

12.10.3 Preacher and Preached One

Elsewhere, I have asked the question whether it is true, as has often been alleged,¹³³ that there is a contrast between Jesus the Preacher and Jesus the preached One, between Jesus the believer and Jesus the object of faith.¹³⁴ That is, in the Gospels Jesus is the Preacher of God and his kingdom, but in the early church, people began preaching Jesus *himself* instead of preaching what Jesus had preached. Similarly, in the Gospels Jesus is a Jew who believes in God, but the early church turned Jesus himself into the One in whom people must believe. Some theologians may think this is the case, but it is not hard to see that neither the Gospels nor Acts present this contrast.

First, notice the *similarities* between the two groups of writings. Indeed, the coming of the kingdom of God occupies a central position in Jesus' preaching.¹³⁵ However, this is also the case in the book of Acts (1:3; 8:12; 14:22; 19:8; 20:25; 28:23, 31) and in the letters (Rom. 14:17; 1 Cor. 4:20; 6:9–10; 15:24, 50; Gal. 5:21; Eph. 5:5; Col. 1:13; 4:11; 1 Thess. 2:12; 2 Thess. 1:5; 2 Tim. 4:1, 18; Heb. 12:28; James 2:5; 2 Pet. 1:11), as well as in the book of Revelation (1:6, 9; 5:10; 11:15; 12:10).¹³⁶ Elsewhere, I have dealt with other similarities between the teaching of Jesus and that of the apostles.¹³⁷

Second, if we may take the Gospels historically seriously—and we may—Jesus definitely presented himself as an object of faith.¹³⁸ In the synoptic Gospels, we hear him saying, "Come to me, all who labor and are heavy laden, and I will

---

132. Regarding Mark, see Ouweneel (2007, §1.5.1).
133. See Den Heyer (2003, 9).
134. Ouweneel (2007, chapters 3–4).
135. See extensively, Ouweneel (2007, §§13.3–13.4; 2018j, chapters 3–6).
136. See Ouweneel (2018j, chapter 8).
137. Ouweneel (2007, chapter 13–14).
138. Ouweneel (2007, §14.1).

give you rest" (Matt. 11:28). To (potential) disciples, he says, "Follow me" (Matt. 8:22; 9:9; 19:21; Luke 9:59; John 1:44; 21:19, 22). "Follow me, and I will make you become fishers of men" (Mark 1:17). "If anyone comes to me and does not hate his own father and mother and wife and children and brothers and sisters, yes, and even his own life, he cannot be my disciple. Whoever does not bear his own cross and come after me cannot be my disciple" (Luke 14:26-27).

Especially in John's Gospel, Jesus is very obviously the object of faith (but of course, little of this is authentic in the critics' eyes): "[W]hoever comes to me shall not hunger, and whoever believes in me shall never thirst . . . whoever comes to me I will never cast out" (6:35, 37; cf. 3:15-16; 5:40; 6:47). "Whoever believes in me, as the Scripture has said, 'Out of his heart will flow rivers of living water'" (7:38). "I am the resurrection and the life. Whoever believes in me, though he die, yet shall he live, and everyone who lives and believes in me shall never die" (11:25-26; cf. 12:44, 46; 14:12). "Let not your hearts be troubled. Believe in God; believe also in me. . . . I am the way, and the truth, and the life. No one comes to the Father except through me" (14:1, 6).

12.11 A Tetralogy

12.11.1 One or Four Portraits of Jesus?

Elsewhere, I have extensively written about the pre-existence of Christ, the two natures of Christ, the (one and only) life and death of Christ, and the (one and only) teaching of Christ.[139] Time and again, however, the possibility of using the definite article "the" with each of these has been questioned. We have four canonical Gospels, and this means at least four portraits of Jesus, four different Christological designs.[140] I would venture to draw this parallel: in the case of the Trinity, we can

---

139. Ouweneel (2007, chapters 7–14).
140. Cf. S. C. Barton in Bockmuehl (2001, chapter 11: "Many gospels, one Jesus?"). He spoke of four "portraits," not one (175). Also Burridge and Gould (2004, 53) spoke of "four portraits of Jesus."

look at the one God but also at the three distinct divine hypostases. We can do the same with the person, the life, and the teaching of Christ. We may try to trace the main line in the life of Jesus and the core elements of his teaching. But if we were to limit ourselves to these, we would detract from the different portraits of Jesus in the four Gospels.

Among the Gospels I distinguish first two official Gospels, which present Jesus especially in the dignity of his office:[141] in Matthew Jesus is presented as the *King*, the long promised and expected *Messiah* of Israel, the son of David; and in Mark Jesus is presented as the suffering *Servant* (Isa. 42:1). The other two Gospels present to us Jesus' personal glories because in them the emphasis is upon the person of Jesus: in Luke, where the human origin of Jesus is strongly emphasized, the emphasis falls on the *Son of Man*, who brings God's grace and mercy to sinful people; and in John, the emphasis falls on the incarnate *Son of God*, who descended from heaven to bring eternal life to people.[142]

This distinction must not be taken too strictly, though. For instance, Luke's Gospel also has an official, namely, a *priestly* character. This is not because Jesus is presented in Luke's Gospel as Priest but because of the book's *inclusio*: Luke's Gospel opens with a mute priest in the temple (1:22), and ends with praising worshipers in that same temple (24:53). Between the opening and ending, Jesus is presented in the temple as a baby (2:27; cf. v. 37) and visits the temple as a twelve years old boy (vv. 42, 46). It contains a genuine temple parable in 18:10-14, and what could be called temple teaching in 19:47, 21:37, 22:53, and in chapters 20-21. Thus, we find that the three synoptic Gospels correspond with the three offices of Christ: the kingly, the prophetic, and the priestly offices, respectively.

Perhaps we may add that Matthew addresses his Gospel

---

141. See, e.g., Smith (1987, 1).
142. See Ouweneel (1980).

to the *Jews*, to convince them that Jesus is the promised Messiah. Mark, as the interpreter of Peter at *Rome*, seems to address the Romans, to show them what significance a Jewish prophet from a tiny corner of the Roman Empire could have for them. Luke seems to address the *Greeks*, being a Greek himself. John has the widest scope: the *cosmos*. Each Gospel presents Jesus in terms that suit their respective audiences.

Also notice the person of each of the Evangelists: Matthew, the tax collector who had been betraying the Jewish cause, pleaded the Messiahship of Jesus (Matt. 9:9; 10:3). Mark, who had been an unfaithful servant (Acts 13:13; 15:37–38), presented the true Servant. Luke, the "beloved physician" (Col. 4:14), presented the One who brought God's healing mercy to the people. John, the "disciple whom Jesus loved" (John 13:23; 19:26; 20:2; 21:7, 20), presented God's love to the world (3:16; 14:21, 23; 16:27).

12.11.2 The Canonical Gospels

Let us now look at the four canonical sources for the life and teaching of Jesus: the three synoptic Gospels and John's Gospel. In addition, we will pay some attention to other possible sources about the life of Jesus.

First as far as the synoptic Gospels are concerned, the most important views of their origin are the following:[143]

(1) The *standard view* (or *two-document hypothesis*): Mark's Gospel came about with the use of oral, and possibly written traditions between AD 60 and 70. The other two, Matthew's and Luke's Gospel, were written between 70 and 100 (between 80 and 90?), independently of each other, with the use of Mark and Q, and special traditions that are characteristic for Matthew and Luke, respectively. Today, this seems to be the most current view.[144]

(2) The *Griesbach* hypothesis, named after German scholar

---

143. See Meier (1991, 43–44) and Brown (1997, chapter 6, with references).
144. See, e.g., Head (1997).

Joh. Jakob Griesbach,[145] and more recently defended by David B. Peabody and his colleagues.[146] According to this view, Matthew was first, then Luke (using Matthew), and finally Mark, as a summary of both Matthew and Luke.

(3) The *standard view without Q*: Mark is viewed as having originated first, but the existence of a distinct Q document is considered to be dubious.[147]

(4) Besides these views, there is the theory of the *oral tradition* instead of documents such as *Ur-Markus*, Q, M or L. Thus, James D. G. Dunn again drew our attention to this view.[148] Raymond E. Brown argued that a part of the Gospel material was formed long before the first written Gospel (being Mark), presumably in the sixties.[149]

Here, Luke 1:1-4 is important:

> Inasmuch as many have undertaken to compile a narrative of the things that have been accomplished among us, just as those who from the beginning were eyewitnesses and ministers of the word have delivered them to us, it seemed good to me also, having followed all things closely for some time past, to write an orderly account for you, most excellent Theophilus, that you may have certainty concerning the things you have been taught.

These "ministers of the word" (Gk. *hypēretai tou logou*) possibly had an official function in preserving and transmitting Jesus' words and acts; compare Acts 1:1-2, "In the first book, O Theophilus, I have dealt with all that Jesus began to do and teach, until the day when he was taken up."[150] According to this theory, the synoptic Gospels do not go back to written sources but only to oral tradition, some of which came from the authors themselves. According to church fa-

---

145. Griesbach (1789); cf. Orchard and Longstaff (1978, 74–102).
146. Peabody et al. (2002); see earlier Farmer (1964); Mann (1986).
147. E.g., Goulder (1974).
148. Dunn (2003; 2005).
149. Brown (1994, 108).
150. Guthrie (1990, 1036–37); Bruce (1979, 459).

ther Papias, Matthew personally wrote down the sayings of Jesus in Aramaic, while Mark was the secretary and interpreter of Peter.[151] The church father Irenaeus called Luke's Gospel a representation of Paul's preaching, and attributed John's Gospel to the "disciple whom Jesus loved" (see §12.11.1).[152] Of course, we cannot know for sure whether Papias and Irenaeus were right, but they do form the oldest testimony concerning the authorship of the Gospels: the apostles Matthew and John were ear- and eye-witnesses, while Mark was Peter's secretary, and Luke made personal investigations in the spirit of Paul.[153]

Of course, this does not say it all. For instance, it does not explain why especially John, who was present in the house of Jairus (Luke 8:51), on the mount of transfiguration (9:28), and in Gethsemane (Matt. 26:37), does not describe any of these events. Nor does it explain why Mark and Luke, who presumably were not present at Jesus' ascension, do describe this event (Mark 16:19;[154] Luke 24:50-51; Acts 1:9-10), and Matthew and John, who *were* present, do not describe it. This illustrates that the Evangelists were not *only* ear- and eyewitnesses but produced their Gospels as theologically arranged compositions.[155] But apart from this, if we accept the priority of Mark, we may wonder why Matthew would lean so strongly on Mark, whereas he knew the life and sayings of Jesus far better than Mark did. We do realize, though—and this may be some support for views (1) and (2)—that Matthew and Mark must have known each other in Jerusalem (cf. Acts 1:13; 12:12), and that Luke and Mark must have been together at certain later stages as well (cf. Col. 4:10, 14; 2 Tim. 4:11).

---

151. Eusebius (*Historia Ecclesiastica* III.39).
152. Ibid., V.8.ii–iv.
153. Cf. extensively, Bauckham (2006).
154. Presuming that Mark 16:9–20 is not a later addition (see §8.7.3).
155. See Ouweneel (2007, §6.3).

12.11.3 John and the Holy Spirit

As far as John's Gospel is concerned, there are two views. The older, still defended view is that John knew and used the synoptic Gospels, but did not use elements from them that did not fit with his own project (or that he viewed as sufficiently known among Christians). Perhaps he took for granted that his readers were already familiar with the synoptic Gospels. The newer, majority view is that John's Gospel represents an entirely independent Jesus tradition.[156] If we followed the majority view, we would have three main sources for our knowledge of Jesus: Mark, Q, and John, besides Matthew's and Luke's own material as well as the rest of the New Testament. However, as we saw, in addition to the speculative character of Q, the opinions on this view vary strongly.

Ultimately, the unity and coherence of the four Gospels are guaranteed to us by the work of the Holy Spirit. This is not a flight from reality, not an escape to some refuge of ignorance (Lat. *asylum ignorantiae*), not an attempt to sweep the problems of origin under the rug. Rather, it is a reference to the underlying paradigm from which I wish to consider these problems. It is not correct to call such an appeal to the Holy Spirit an unscientific claim. On the one hand, New Testament scholar John P. Meier argued repeatedly that no science, including that of the New Testament, is neutral and objective;[157] every science always starts from a certain ideological paradigm, which allows or disallows, for example, supernaturalism, and thus the inspiring and preserving work of the Holy Spirit.[158] On the other hand, he argued that quite a few writers about the Gospels acted uncritically by viewing all passages as exact historical descriptions, instead of allowing for the rearrangement as well as the theological elaboration of the material.

---

156. Cf. Brown (1970; 1997, ad loc.); Anderson (2007); Ehrman (2009).
157. Meier (1991).
158. Guthrie (1990, 1041–43).

As I said (§7.11.2), in the Gospels we are dealing not with photographs of reality but rather with paintings, which tell us much, not only about the painted object but, also about the painters.[159] Abraham Kuyper spoke in this connection of impressionism: the Gospels give us impressions of Jesus and his teaching, not precise journalistic accounts. Yet, they do not give us airy fantasies; a portrait must *resemble* its object if it is to be any good.

It is correct to say that serious New Testament scholarship must account for the remarkable (often verbal) similarities between the synoptic Gospels as well as for the many points where the Gospels, internally and with respect to each other, seem to be contradictory.[160] But since, when dealing with ancient literature, we begin to take its self-testimony seriously, there is nothing wrong with beginning with the self-testimony of the New Testament: "All Scripture is breathed out by God" (2 Tim. 3:16), and the Gospels are "Scripture," too (1 Tim. 5:18; see §7.3). Jesus said, "[T]he Helper, the Holy Spirit, whom the Father will send in my name, he will teach you all things and bring to your remembrance all that I have said to you" (John 14:26). Thus, we are confident that, in the Gospels, we find a trustworthy record of Jesus' sayings (cf. 15:26; 16:13-14). The total tradition concerning "all that Jesus began to do and teach" (Acts 1:1) was much more extensive than what was finally included in the Gospels (cf. John 20:30-31; 21:25). It was the Holy Spirit who led the writers in making their selections, without diminishing in any way their personal responsibility and the importance of their own investigations (Luke 1:1-4).

12.12 Four Pillars

12.12.1 The Life of Jesus

Church father Irenaeus called the Evangelists the "four pillars of the world."

---

159. Cf. Macquarrie (1981, 30); Pentecost (1981, 24); Van de Beek (1998, 124); Loonstra (1999, 68).

160. See Ouweneel (2007, §6.3).

The Modernist View of the New Testament

Just like there are four parts of the world in which we live, and four universal winds [East, West, North, South; cf. 1 Chron. 9:24; Ezek. 37:9; Dan. 8:8; 11:4; Zech. 2:6; 6:5], and just like the church is dispersed over all the earth [i.e., to all four quarters], and the gospel is the pillar and foundation of the church [cf. 1 Tim. 3:15] and the breath of life, thus it is natural that it has four pillars [cf. 1 Sam. 2:8; Job 9:6; Ps. 75:3] ... the Word ... has given us the gospel in a fourfold form, but kept together by one Spirit.[161]

These pillars correspond with the four "corners" of the earth (cf. Jer. 49:36; Ezek. 7:2; Rev. 7:1; 20:8), though I do not think Irenaeus would go as far as telling us which Gospel would correspond with what quarter of the earth. (The addressees mentioned in §12.11.1, the Jewish part, the Roman part, the Greek part, and the *cosmos* as a whole, certainly do not correspond with the four quarters of the earth.)

The number four is interesting; I am under the strong impression that the four Gospels correspond with (though here is not the place to explain this):

(a) the four bloody *sacrifices*; in the order of the Gospels: Jesus is presented as the guilt offering, the sin offering, the peace offering, and the burnt offering, respectively (see Lev. 1-7);

(b) the four *colors* in the tabernacle: scarlet, linen white, purple, and blue, respectively (Exod. 25:4; 35:6);

(c) the four *celestial beings*: the lion, the ox, the man, and the eagle, respectively[162] (Ezek. 1:5-10; 10:14, 21; Rev. 4:6-8).

It is my conviction that the four portraits of Jesus supplement each other, that they are not contradictory on any essential point, and that the *four* portraits are necessary to do justice to the multifaceted nature of Jesus' person, life, and teaching. Abraham Kuyper was one of those who emphasized that the

---

161. *Adversus Haereses* III.11.8.
162. My order deviates from the traditional one, which is man, lion, ox, and eagle, respectively.

Holy Spirit intended this:

> When in the four Gospels Jesus, on the same occasion, is made to say words that are different in form of expression, it is impossible that He should have used these four forms at once. The Holy Spirit, however, merely intends to make an impression upon the Church which wholly corresponds to what Jesus said.[163]

Herman Bavinck wrote something similar: "No life of Jesus can be written from the four Gospels, nor can a history of Israel be construed from the OT. That was not what the Holy Spirit had in mind. Inspiration was evidently not a matter of drawing up material with notarial precision."[164]

However, if we cannot reconstruct some "life of Jesus" from the Gospels, then we must allow the four portraits to stand alongside each other. Allow each of them to tell its own story. We may certainly try to sketch one single main line in the life and sufferings of Jesus.[165] And we may also attempt to trace the central line in Jesus' teaching.[166] But we should observe limits in doing this. When it comes to the details, both of Jesus' life and of his teaching, there are four inspired "designs" of Jesus' life, and these must remain distinct. Using a harmony of the Gospels like those of Tatian or Calvin, we may try to make the main life of Jesus' life transparent. However, such a harmony can never yield one single theological picture of Jesus.[167]

12.12.2 The Teaching of Jesus

In fact, it is more complicated with the teaching of Jesus than with his life. This is because we are dealing not with the theology (or Christology) of Jesus himself but with the theologies/

---

163. Kuyper (1898, 550); cf. Bavinck (*RD* 1:444).
164. Bavinck (*RD* 1:444); see Ouweneel (2007, §14.1.3).
165. See my own attempt in Ouweneel (2007, chapters 11–12).
166. Ibid., chapters 13–14.
167. Ibid., §6.1.2.

Christologies of the four Evangelists. These are definitely not the same. Each of them paints a portrait of Jesus that is certainly historical, but is primarily theological. From each of these four theologies/Christologies of the Evangelists, we must try to discover what would have been the theology/Christology of Jesus himself according to each of them. We look through the theological glasses of the four Evangelists at the theology/Christology of Jesus, and what we discover is in fact four theologies/Christologies of Jesus: Jesus the King, Jesus the Servant-Prophet, Jesus the Son of Man, and Jesus the Son of God, each of them painting its own portrait of God himself.

These four theologies have not been designed to make things more complicated for us; rather, their aim is to make things more transparent. If we are look at a diamond from four sides, we will have a better picture than if we could view it from only one angle. We never directly hear the teaching of Jesus; if this had been the intention, the Man Jesus might have written down his teaching himself. We hear four different voices of those who *reflect* upon the teaching and life of Jesus. As John P. Meier put it, each synoptic Evangelist arranged the rosary beads [i.e., the pericopes] on the rosary [i.e., the structure of the Gospel] in a way that served his theological purpose.[168] Here is a metaphor that I am more familiar with: the four voices are joined harmoniously into one wonderfully symphonic choral work.

As we saw, a harmony of the Gospels smooths out the differences, not to mention the (alleged) contradictions, between the Gospels. However, these very differences, these mutual tensions, make the four Gospels often so fascinating.[169] As Bible scholar F. W. Grant put it: since God gave the synoptic Gospels as three, not in one piece, it is evident that the differences are the very matters that will lead us to their significance. Often, what unbelievers consider the most difficult features will have the fullest meaning for any believing inves-

---

168. Meier (1991, 42).
169. See extensively, Ouweneel (1980).

tigation.[170] These differences constitute the marrow, the specialty, of each of the four Gospels. Each constitutes a unique theological treatise.[171] Remove those differences, those blips and bumps, and we could just as well have one Gospel. The wrinkles are no threat for orthodox faith, so that they need to be smoothed out. Rather, they challenge us to trace out the four portraits of Jesus that are presented to us in the four Gospels.

12.12.3 Examples and Closing

Joseph Ratzinger gave us a beautiful example of such interesting discrepancies by pointing to a remarkable difference between the Gospels.[172] He wished to defend the Jews, who throughout the ages have been accused of having killed Jesus, with all the dramatic consequences of pogroms and persecutions. Ratzinger argued that, in John's Gospel, Jesus' opponents are indeed described as "the Jews," but here this term refers to the temple aristocracy. In this Gospel, only (a part of) the spiritual leaders turned against Jesus, not all the people. In Mark it is the crowd (Gk. *ochlos*) that demanded the release of Barabbas; but supposedly these were only the mob, the rabble, *in concreto* the followers of Barabbas, rebels who rose against the Roman rulers. Only in Matthew, says Ratzinger, do we find "[a]n extension of Mark's *ochlos*, with fateful consequences," namely, for the Jewish people. In reference to Matthew 27:25, which speaks of "all the people" calling down Jesus' blood upon themselves, Ratzinger states: "Matthew is certainly not recounting historical fact here: How could the whole people have been present at this moment to clamor for Jesus' death?"[173]

To me, this is a rather far-fetched exegesis of the expression "all the people" (Gk. *pas ho laos*). The expression occurs

---

170. Grant (1897, 22).
171. Kuitert (1999, 59–60).
172. Ratzinger (2011, 184–86).
173. Ibid., 186.

quite often in the Gospels (Luke 7:29; 8:47; 18:43; 20:45; 21:38; 24:19; John 8:2), without the context ever suggesting that literally *all* the nation of Israel in every location (nor in all times) is intended. Thus, Ratzinger might have found the solution in a simpler way. Matthew is almost always referring to the crowd of Jesus' listeners. In Matthew 27:25, too, there is not the slightest ground for the view that, according to Matthew, the *entire* nation of Israel, neither at that time nor in the future, would have invoked the blood of Jesus upon them in judgment. Notice the difference that the apostle Paul makes between "them" (in Jerusalem) and "you" (in Pisidia) (Acts 13:27-29): the former carried responsibility for Jesus' death, whereas the latter did not. However, the problem that does remain is the remarkable difference between the synoptic Evangelists ("the crowd") and John's Gospel ("the Jews").

The crucifixion, which was described by all four, is described differently in important respects. Though questionable at points, the rendering by German monk and author Anselm Grün is nonetheless rather beautiful; he disconnected the cross for a moment from its merely soteriological significance:

> The cross has a different meaning with every Evangelist. For Matthew, it symbolizes the nonviolence of Jesus. Jesus is the merciful prophet who does not go out for power, who lets himself to be nonviolently captivated, and be killed. For Mark, the cross becomes the victory of Jesus over the powers of darkness. With Luke, the cross is an expression of the precarious situations that we, too, must endure on our way to the glory of God. John probably came farthest in the interpretation of the cross. To him, Jesus has demonstrated on the cross his love for us to the end [John 13:1; 15:13]. He has introduced us into the secret of God's love, who granted us his Son in order that we find life in him.[174]

---

174. Grün (2002, 172). For a more extensive discussion of this, see Ouweneel (2007, §6.3).

We need all four Gospels to obtain a full portrait of Jesus, presented from four different angles. In fact, we need all sixty-six books of the Bible to learn the full identity of Jesus: he is the Son of God, Messiah of Israel, and Redeemer of all those who believe in him. A genuinely canonical Bible book is one whose very center is Jesus Christ (see Luther's words quoted in §8.10.2). This pertains not only to the New Testament, not only to the prophetic books of the Old Testament, not only to the historical Old Testament books that present to us wonderful types of Christ, especially Joseph, Moses/Aaron (or Moses/Joshua), and David/Solomon. It pertains as well to, say, the books traditionally attributed to Solomon (Prov., Eccl., Song): Jesus Christ is the Wisdom of Proverbs 8:22-31; he is the mysterious man in Ecclesiastes 4:13 or 7:28 or 9:15; and he is the Bridegroom of the Song of Solomon. He is pre-figured in the Adam of Genesis 1, and he is the "last Adam" presented in the book of Revelation (cf. 1 Cor. 15:45). He is the One who lay down in the dust of death (Ps. 22:15), and the One who is coming on the clouds of heaven (Dan. 7:13; Matt. 24:30; 26:64). This volume, which comes to a close here, was about the good book—but Jesus Christ is the Man who makes it such a good book.

Bibliography

Achtemeier, P. J. 1980. *The Inspiration of Scripture: Problems and Proposals*. Philadelphia, PA: Westminster Press.

Adams, E. and D. G. Horrell, eds. 2004. *Christianity at Corinth*. Louisville, KY: Westminster John Knox Press.

Ahituv, S. and E. Oren, eds. 1998. *The Origin Of Early Israel: Current Debate: Biblical, Historical, and Archaeological Perspectives*. London: University College.

Aland, K. 1962. *The Problem of the New Testament Canon*. London: A. R. Mowbray.

_____. 1982. *Synopsis of the Four Gospels*. New York: United Bible Societies.

Albright, W. F. 1938. "Archaeology Confronts Biblical Criticism." *The American Scholar* 7 (Spring): 176–88.

_____. 1940. *From the Stone Age to Christianity*. Baltimore, MD: Johns Hopkins University Press.

_____. 1942. *Archaeology and the Religion of Israel*. Baltimore, MD: Johns Hopkins University Press.

_____. 1952. "The Bible After Twenty Years of Archaeology." *Religion in Life* 21:537–50.

_____. 1960. *The Archaeology of Palestine*. Baltimore, MD: Johns Hopkins University Press.

_____. 1965. *The Biblical Period From Abraham to Ezra*. New York: Harper and Row.

_____. 1966. *Archaeology, Historical Analogy, and Early Biblical Tradition.* Baton Rouge, LA: Lousiana State University Press.

Allen, D. L. 2010. *Lukan Authorship of Hebrews.* New American Commentary Studies in Bible and Theology. Vol. 8. Nashville, TN: B&H Academic.

Allen, R. B. 1990. *Numbers.* EBC 2. Grand Rapids, MI: Zondervan.

Althaus, P. 1952. *Die christliche Wahrheit: Lehrbuch der Dogmatik.* 3rd ed. Gütersloh: Bertelsmann.

_____. 1967. *Die Prinzipien der deutschen reformierten Dogmatik im Zeitalter der aristotelischen Scholastik.* Darmstadt: Wissenschaftliche Buchgesellschaft.

Anderson, P. N. 2007. *John, Jesus, and History: Critical Appraisals of Critical Views.* Symposium Series 1. Atlanta, GA: Society of Biblical Literature.

Archer, G. L., Jr. 1964. *A Survey of Old Testament Introduction.* Chicago: Moody Press.

_____. 1979. "Alleged Errors and Discrepancies in the Original Manuscripts of the Bible." In *Inerrancy*, edited by N. L. Geisler. Grand Rapids, MI: Zondervan, 1979), 55–82.

_____. 1982. *Encyclopedia of Bible Difficulties.* Grand Rapids, MI: Zondervan.

_____. 1985. *Daniel.* EBC 7. Grand Rapids, MI: Zondervan.

_____. 1994. *A Survey of Old Testament Introduction.* 2nd ed. Chicago: Moody Press.

Armstrong, K. 2008. *De strijd om God: Een geschiedenis van het fundamentalisme.* Amsterdam: De Bezige Bij.

_____. 2009. *De kwestie God: De toekomst van religie.* Amsterdam: De Bezige Bij.

Augustijn, C. 1971. "Politiek relevante ontwikkelingen in de theologie." *Antirevolutionaire Staatkunde* 41:197–209.

Aulén, G. 1960. *The Faith of the Christian Church*. Philadelphia, PA: Muhlenberg Press.

Auwers, J. M. and De Jonge, H. J. eds. 2003. *The Biblical Canons*. Leuven: Peeters.

Bahnsen, G. L. 1979. "The Inerrancy of the Autographa." In *Inerrancy*, edited by N. L. Geisler. Grand Rapids, MI: Zondervan, 1979), 143–93.

Baillie, J. 1956. *The Idea of Revelation in Recent Thought*. New York: Columbia University Press.

Baird, W. 1992. *History of New Testament Research*. Vol. 1: *From Deism to Tübingen*. Minneapolis, MN: Fortress Press.

_____. 2003. *History of New Testament Research*. Vol. 2: *From Jonathan Edwards to Rudolf Bultmann*. Minneapolis, MN: Fortress Press.

Barclay, R. 1827. *An Apology for the True Christian Divinity*. New York: Wood.

Barnett, P. W. 1998. *Historische zoektocht naar Jezus*. Zoetermeer: Boekencentrum.

Barr, J. 1973. *The Bible in the Modern World*. London: SCM Press.

_____. 1980. *The Scope and Authority of the Bible*. London: SCM Press.

_____. 1981. *Fundamentalism*. 2nd ed. London: SCM Press.

_____. 1984. *Beyond Fundamentalism: Biblical Foundations for Evangelical Christianity*. Louisville, KY: Westminster John Knox.

_____. 1990. *The Bible in the Modern World*. Louisville, KY: Westminster John Knox.

Barth, K. 1927. *Die Christliche Dogmatik im Entwurf*. Vol. 6. München: Kaiser.

_____. 1933. *The Epistle to the Romans*. Trans. by E. C. Hoskyns. Oxford: Oxford University Press.

_____. 1948. *Das christliche Verständnis der Offenbarung*. München: Chr. Kaiser.

———. 1956. *Church Dogmatics*. Trans. by T. H. L. Parker et al. Vols. 1/1–4/1. Louisville, KY: Westminster John Knox.

Barton, J. 2007. *The Nature of Biblical Criticism*. Louisville, KY: Westminster John Knox.

Bauckham, R. 2006. *Jesus and the Eyewitnesses: The Gospels as Eyewitness Testimony*. Grand Rapids, MI: Eerdmans.

Bauer, G. L. 1800–1802. *Biblische Theologie des Neuen Testaments*. 4 vols. Leipzig: Bengandschen Buchhandlung.

Baur, F. C. 1831. "Die Christuspartei in der korinthischen Gemeinde, der Gegensatz des petrinischen und paulinischen Christentums in der ältesten Kirche, der Apostel Petrus in Rom." *Tübinger Zeitschrift* 4:61–206.

———. 1847 (repr. 2010). *Kritische Untersuchungen über die kanonischen Evangelien, ihr Verhältnis zu einander, ihren Charakter und Ursprung*. Charleston, SC: Nabu Press.

Bavinck, H. 2002–2008. *Reformed Dogmatics*. Edited by J. Bolt. Translated by J. Vriend. 4 vols. Grand Rapids, MI: Baker Academic.

Beale, G. K. 2003. *1–2 Thessalonians*. IVP NT Series. Leicester: InterVarsity Press.

———. 2008. *The Erosion of Inerrancy in Evangelicalism: Responding to New Challenges to Biblical Authority*. Wheaton, IL: Crossway Books.

Beckwith, R. T. 1985. *The Old Testament of the New Testament Church and Its Background in Early Judaism*. Grand Rapids, MI: Eerdmans.

Beegle, D. M. 1973. *Scripture, Tradition, and Infallibility*. Grand Rapids, MI: Eerdmans.

Beker, E. J. and J. M. Hasselaar. 1978. *Wegen en kruispunten in de dogmatiek*. Vol. 1. Kampen: Kok.

Berger, K. 2004. *Jesus*. München: Pattloch.

Berkhof, H. 1986. *Christian Faith: An Introduction to the Study of the Faith*. Translated by S. Woudstra. Grand Rapids, MI: Eerdmans.

Berkhof, L. 1996. *Systematic Theology*. New edition. Grand Rapids, MI: Eerdmans.

Berkouwer, G. C. [1938]. *Het probleem der Schriftkritiek*. Kampen: Kok.

_____. 1952. *The Providence of God*. Translated by L. B. Smedes. Studies in Dogmatics. Grand Rapids, MI: Eerdmans.

_____. 1955. *General Revelation*. Grand Rapids, MI: Eerdmans.

_____. 1966. *Dogmatische Studiën: De Heilige Schrift*, Vol.1. Kampen: Kok.

_____. 1967. *Dogmatische Studiën: De Heilige Schrift*, Vol.2. Kampen: Kok.

_____. 1975. *Holy Scripture*. Translated and abridged by Jack B. Rogers, from the Dutch edition, *De Heilige Schrift*, I and II. Grand Rapids, MI: Eerdmans. *Note to the reader:* this English volume has been included here only for the sake of completeness; because it contains the English translation of only two-thirds of the original Dutch volumes, careful scholars need to consult those Dutch volumes for accurate access to Berkouwer's thought.

Bette, J. C., G. Van den Brink, and A. W. Zwiep, eds. 2000. *Openbaring van Johannes* Studiebijbel 10. Veenendaal: Centrum voor Bijbelonderzoek.

Bijlsma, R. 1964. *Schriftgezag en schriftgebruik: Een hermeneutiek van de Bijbel*. Nijkerk: Callenbach.

Bird, A. E. 1997. "The Authorship of the Pastoral Epistles: Quantifying Literary Style." *Reformed Theological Review* 56:118–37.

Bleeker, L. H. K. 1948. *Hermeneutiek van het Oude Testament*. Haarlem: Erven F. Bohn.

Blei, K. 1996. *Geloven op gezag: Tussen individualisering en fundamentalisme*. Zoetermeer: Boekencentrum.

Bloch, E. 1954–1959. *Das Prinzip Hoffnung*. 3 vols. Frankfurt: Suhrkamp.

Bloesch, D. G. 1983. "The Primacy of Scripture." In *The Authoritative Word: Essays of the Nature of Scripture*, edited by D. K. McKim. 117–53. Grand Rapids, MI: Eerdmans..

———. 1994. *Holy Scripture: Revelation, Inspiration and Interpretation*. Downers Grove, IL: InterVarsity Press.

Blomberg, C. L. 1986. "The Legitimacy and Limits of Harmonization." In *Hermeneutics, Authority, and Canon*, edited by D. A. Carson and J. D. Woodbridge. 139–74. Grand Rapids, MI: Academie Books.

Blum, E. A. 1979. "The Apostles' View of Scripture." In *Inerrancy*, edited by N. L. Geisler. 39–53. Grand Rapids, MI: Zondervan.

———. 1981. *1,2 Peter, Jude*. EBC 12. Grand Rapids, MI: Zondervan.

Bockmuehl, M. 1994. *This Jesus: Martyr, Lord, Messiah*. Downers Grove, IL: InterVarsity Press.

———, ed. 2001. *The Cambridge Companion to Jesus*. Cambridge: Cambridge University Press.

Bolkestein, M. H. 1949. "Het Woord Gods en de kosmos." *Nederlands Theologisch Tijdschrift* 1949:1–11.

Borg, M. J. 1987. *Jesus: A New Vision: Spirit, Culture and the Life of Discipleship*. San Francisco: Harper.

———. 1994a. *Meeting Jesus Again for the First Time*. San Francisco: HarperCollins.

———. 1994b. *Jesus in Contemporary Scholarship*. Harrisburg, PA: Trinity Press International.

———. 1998. *Conflict, Holiness and Politics in the Teachings of Jesus*. Philadelphia: Trinity Press International.

———, and N. T. Wright. 1999. *The Meaning of Jesus: Two Visions*. New York: HarperCollins.

Bornkamm, H. ed. 1967. *Luthers Vorreden zur Bibel*. Frankfurt: Insel-Verlag.

Bosch, D. J., A. König, and W. D. Nicol, eds. 1982. *Perspektief op die Ope Brief*. Kaapstad: Human and Rousseau.

Bouma, C. 1927. *Het evangelie naar Johannes*. KV. Kampen: Kok.

Bousset, W. 1906. *Die Offenbarung Johannis*. Göttingen: Vandenhoeck and Ruprecht.

_____. 1913. *Kyrios Christos: Geschichte des Christusglaubens von den Anfängen des Christentums bis Irenaeus*. Göttingen: Vandenhoeck and Ruprecht.

Bovell, C. R. 2007. *Inerrancy and the Spiritual Formation of Younger Evangelicals*. Eugene, OR: Wipf and Stock.

Brasher, B. E. 2001. *The Encyclopedia of Fundamentalism*. New York: Routledge.

Bratcher, R. G. and E. A. Nida. 1961. *Translator's Handbook on Mark*. Leiden: Brill.

Briggs, C. A. 1897. *The Higher Criticism of the Hexateuch*. New York: Scribner's.

Bril, K. A. 1986. *Westerse denkstructuren*. Amsterdam: VU Uitgeverij.

Brillenburg Wurth, G. 1951. *Het christelijk leven in de maatschappij*. Kampen: Kok.

Bromiley, G. W. 1978. *Historical Theology: An Introduction*. Grand Rapids, MI: Eerdmans.

Brower, J. E. and K. Guilfoy, eds. 2004. *The Cambridge Companion to Abelard*. Cambridge: Cambridge University Press.

Brown, C. 1969. *Philosophy and the Christian Faith*. Downers Grove, IL: IVF Academic.

_____, ed. 1976. *History, Criticism and Faith: Four Exploratory Studies*. Downers Grove, IL: InterVarsity Press.

_____, ed. 1992 (1976). *The New International Dictionary of New Testament Theology*. 4 vols. Carlisle: Paternoster.

Brown, H. O. J. 1984a. "Romanticism and the Bible" In *Challenges to Inerrancy: A Theological Response*, edited by G. Lewis and B. Demarest. 49–66. Chicago: Moody Press.

———. 1984b. "The Arian Connection: Presuppositions of Errancy." In *Challenges to Inerrancy: A Theological Response*, edited by G. Lewis and B. Demarest. 383–401. Chicago: Moody Press.

Brown, R. E. 1970. *The Gospel According to John*. 2nd ed. Garden City, NY: Anchor.

———. 1994. *An Introduction to New Testament Christology*. New York: Paulist Press.

———. 1997. *An Introduction to the New Testament*. New York: Doubleday.

Brown, R. E., J. A. Fitzmyer, R. E. Murphy, eds. 1999. *The New Jerome Biblical Commentary*. Upper Saddle River, NJ: Prentice Hall.

Brown, W. P. ed. 2007. *Engaging Biblical Authority: Perspectives on the Bible as Scripture*. Louisville, KY: Westminster John Knox Press.

Bruce, A. B. 1979. *The Synoptic Gospels*. EGT 1. Grand Rapids, MI: Eerdmans.

Bruce, F. F. 1945. "The End of the Second Gospel." *The Evangelical Quarterly* 17:169–81.

———. 1976. "Myth and History." In *History, Criticism and Faith: Four Exploratory Studies*, edited by C. Brown. 79–99, Downers Grove, IL: InterVarsity Press.

———. 1984. *The Epistles to the Colossians, to Philemon, and to the Ephesians*. ICNT. Grand Rapids, MI: Eerdmans.

———. 1988a. *The Canon of Scripture*. Glasgow: Chapter House.

———. 1988b. *The Book of the Acts*. NICNT. Grand Rapids, MI: Eerdmans.

Brunner, E. 1937. *The Divine Imperative: A Study in Christian Ethics*. Translated by O. Wyon. New York: Macmillan.

———. 1946. *Revelation and Reason: The Christian Doctrine of Faith and Knowledge.* Translated by O. Wyon. Philadelphia, PA: The Westminster Press.

———. 1949. *The Christian Doctrine of God.* Translated by O. Wyon. Dogmatics. Vol. 1. London: Lutterworth Press.

———. 1964. *Truth as Encounter.* London: SCM Press.

Bryan, C. 2002. *And God Spoke: The Authority of the Bible for the Church Today.* Cambridge, MA: Cowley Publications.

Buber, M. 1954. *Die fünf Bücher der Weisung.* Köln: Jakob Hegner.

———. 2015. *Eclipse of God: Studies in the Relation between Religion and Philosophy.* Princeton, NJ: Princeton University Press.

Buess, E. 1953. *Die Geschichte des mythischen Erkennens: Wider sein Missverständnis in der "Entmythologierung."* München: Chr. Kaiser.

Bullinger, E. W. 1984 (1893). *The Witness of the Stars.* Grand Rapids, MI: Kregel.

Bultmann, R. 1952. *Theology of the New Testament.* Translated by K. Grobel. Vol. 1. London: SCM.

———. 1963. *The History of the Synoptic Tradition.* Translated by J. Marsh. Oxford: Blackwell.

———. 1969. *Faith and Understanding.* Edited by R. W. Funk. Translated by L. P. Smith. New York: Harper and Row Publishers.

Buri, F. 1956. *Dogmatik als Selbstverständnis des christlichen Glaubens.* Vol. 1: *Vernunft und Offenbarung.* Bern: Paul Haupt/Tübingen: Katzmann-Verlag.

Burridge, R. A. and Gould, G. 2004. *Jesus Now and Then.* Grand Rapids, MI: Eerdmans.

Calvin, J. 1972. *A Harmony of the Gospels, Matthew, Mark, and Luke.* 3 vols. Grand Rapids, MI: Eerdmans.

Calvin, J. 1960. *Institutes of the Christian Religion.* Edited by John T. McNeill. Translated by Ford Lewis Battles. 2

vols. Library of Christian Classics 20-21. Philadelphia: Westminster Press.

Caputo, J. D. 2006. *Philosophy and Theology*. Nashville, TN: Abingdon Press.

Carnell, E. 1959. *The Case for Orthodox Theology*. Philadelphia: Westminster Press.

Carpenter, J. A. 1997. *Revive Us Again: The Reawakening of American Fundamentalism*. Oxford: Oxford University Press.

Carson, D. A. 1984. *Matthew*. EBC 8. Grand Rapids, MI: Zondervan.

———. 1986. "Recent Developments in the Doctrine of Scripture." In *Hermeneutics, Authority, and Canon*, edited by D. A. Carson and J. D. Woodbridge. 5-48. Grand Rapids, MI: Academie Books.

———, and J. D. Woodbridge, eds. 1983. *Scripture and Truth*. Grand Rapids, MI: Zondervan.

———, and J. D. Woodbridge, eds. 1986. *Hermeneutics, Authority, and Canon*. Grand Rapids, MI: Academie Books.

———, D. J. Moo, and L. Morris. 1999. *An Introduction to the New Testament*. Downers Grove, IL: InterVarsity Press.

Cassels, W. R. 1874. *Supernatural Religion*. London: Longmans, Green and Co.

Cassuto, U. 1961-64. *A Commentary on the Book of Genesis*. 2 vols. Jerusalem: Magnes Press.

———. 1967. *A Commentary on the Book of Exodus*. Jerusalem: Magnes Press.

———. 1973-75. *Biblical and Oriental Studies*. 2 vols. Jerusalem: Magnes Press.

———. 2006. *The Documentary Hypothesis and the Composition of the Pentateuch*. Jerusalem: Shalem Press.

Chafer, L. S. 1983. *Systematic Theology*. 15th ed. 8 vols. Dallas, TX: Dallas Seminary Press.

Chalmers, A. 1976. *What Is This Thing Called Science?* St. Lucia: University of Queensland Press.

Chambers, O. 1995. *Biblical Psychology*. Grand Rapids, MI: Discovery House Publishers.

_____. 1998. *Biblical Ethics*. Grand Rapids, MI: Discovery House Publishers.

Charles, R. H. 1920. *A Critical and Exegetical Commentary on the Revelation of St. John*. 2 vols. International Critical Commentary. Edinburgh: T. and T. Clark.

Chenu, M. D. 1985. *Une école de la théologie: Le Saulchoir*. Edited by G. Alberigo. Paris: Cerf.

Childs, B. S. 1979. *Introduction to the Old Testament as Scripture*. London: SCM.

Chilton, B. and C. A. Evans, eds. 1994. *Studying the Historical Jesus*. Leiden: Brill.

Clemen, C. 1924. *Religionsgeschichtliche Erklärung des Neuen Testaments: Die Abhängigkeit des* ältesten *Christentums von nichtjüdischen Religionen und philosophischen Systemen*. Giessen: Töpelmann.

Coetzee, J. C. 1984. "Die Skrif en die wetenskap." In *Wetenskap en Woord*, edited by B. Duvenage. Potchefstroom: PU vir CHO.

Cohen, A., ed. 1983. *The Soncino Chumash*. SBB. London: Soncino.

_____, ed. 1985. *The Psalms*. SBB. London: Soncino.

Cole, S .G. 1963. *The History of Fundamentalism*. 2nd ed. Hamden, CT: Archon.

Collingwood, R. G. 1945. *The Idea of Nature*. Oxford: Clarendon Press.

Cone, J. H. 1969. *Black Theology and Black Power*. New York: Orbis Books.

Conzelmann, H. 1993. *Die Mitte der Zeit: Studien zur Theologie des Lukas*. 7th ed. Tübingen: Mohr (Siebeck).

Corduan, W. 1984. "Philosophical Presuppositions Affecting Biblical Hermeneutics" In *Hermeneutics, Inerrancy, and the Bible*, edited by E. D. Radmacher and R. D. Preus. 493–513. Grand Rapids, MI: Zondervan.

Craig, W. L. 1998. "Rediscovering the Historical Jesus: Presuppositions and Pretensions of the Jesus Seminar." *Faith and Mission* 15:3–15.

Craigie, P. C. 1976. *The Book of Deuteronomy*. NICOT. Grand Rapids, MI: Eerdmans.

Cramer, J. A. 1926. *De Heilige Schrift bij Calvijn*. Utrecht: Oosthoek.

Crossan, J. D. 1991. *The Historical Jesus*. San Francisco: HarperSanFrancisco.

———.1995a. *Who Killed Jesus?* New York: HarperCollins.

———.1995b. *Jesus: A Revolutionary Biography*. San Francisco: HarperSanFrancisco.

Cullmann, O. 1953. *Peter: Disciple–Apostle–Martyr*. London: SCM.

———. 1967. *Salvation in History*. London: SCM.

Da Costa, I. 1823. *Bezwaren tegen de geest der eeuw*. Leyden: Herdingh.

Daly, M. 1998. *Quintessence . . . Realizing the Archaic Future: A Radical Elemental Feminist Manifesto*. Boston: Beacon Press.

Danker, F. W. 2000. *A Greek-English Lexicon of the New Testament and Other Early Christian Literature*. 3rd ed., revised and edited by Frederick W. Danker (BDAG). Chicago: University of Chicago Press.

Darby, J. N. n.d. *The Collected Writings of J. N. Darby*. Kingston-on-Thames: Stow Hill Bible and Tract Depot.

Davids, P. H. 1990. *The First Epistle of Peter*. NICNT. Grand Rapids, MI: Eerdmans.

———. 2006. *The Letters of 2 Peter and Jude*. PNTC. Grand Rapids, MI: Eerdmans.

Davies, P. R. 1992. *In Search of "Ancient Israel."* Sheffield: Academic Press.

Davis, J. J. 1984a. *Foundations of Evangelical Theology.* Grand Rapids, MI: Baker Book House.

———. 1984b. "Unity of the Bible." In *Hermeneutics, Inerrancy, and the Bible,* edited by E. D. Radmacher and R. D. Preus. 639–65. Grand Rapids, MI: Zondervan.

Dee, S. P. 1918. *Het geloofsbegrip van Calvijn.* Kampen: Kok.

De Graaff, F. 1987. *Jezus de Verborgene.* Vol. 1: *Een voorbereiding tot inwijding in de mysteriën van het evangelie.* Kampen: Kok.

———. n.d. *Anno Domini 1000, Anno Domini 2000: De duizend jaren bij de gratie van de dode god.* Kampen: Kok.

De Groot, D. J. 1931. *Calvijns opvatting over de inspiratie der Heilige Schrift.* Zutphen: Nauta.

De Jong, J. M. 1958. *Kerygma: Een onderzoek naar de vooronderstellingen van de theologie van Rudolf Bultmann.* Assen: Van Gorcum.

De Klerk, B. J. 1937. *Vorme en karakter van die biblisisme.* Kampen: Kok.

Delitzsch, F. 1955. *Biblical Commentary on the Psalms.* Grand Rapids, MI: Eerdmans.

Demarest, B. 1982. *General Revelation: Historical Views and Contemporary Issues.* Grand Rapids, MI: Zondervan.

Dengerink, J. D. 1986. *De zin van de werkelijkheid.* Amsterdam: VU Uitgeverij.

Den Heyer, C. J. 2003. *Van Jezus naar christendom: De ontwikkeling van tekst tot dogma.* Zoetermeer: Meinema.

Dennison, J. T., Jr., ed. 2008–2014. *Reformed Confessions of the 16th and 17th Centuries in English Translation.* 4 vols. Grand Rapids, MI: Reformation Heritage Books.

Denziger, H. 1954. *Enchiridion symbolorum et definitionum.* 29th ed. Freiburg: Herder.

Derrida, J. 1979. *L'Écriture et la différance*. Paris: Éditions du Seuil.

De Saussure, F. 1916. *Cours de linguistique générale*. Paris: Payot.

De Sopper, A. J. 1948. *Grenzen der openbaring*. Amsterdam: Holland.

Dever, W. G. 2001. *What Did the Biblical Writers Know and When Did They Know It? What Archaeology Can Tell Us about the Reality of Ancient Israel*. Grand Rapids, MI: Eerdmans.

———. 2003. *Who Were the Early Israelites and Where Did They Come from?* Grand Rapids, MI: Eerdmans.

De Vos, H. 1968. *Kant als theoloog*. Baarn: Wereldvenster.

De Wette, W. M. L. 1806–1807 (repr. 1971). *Beiträge zur Einleitung in das Alte Testament*. 2 vols. Hildesheim: Georg Olms.

———. 1826. *Einleitung in das Neue Testament*. Leipzig: Messner and Lüdemann.

Dibelius, M. 1966 (repr.). *Die Formgeschichte des Evangeliums*. Tübingen: Mohr (Siebeck).

Diemer, J.H. 1943. "Natuur en wonder." *Philosophia Reformata* 8:120–25.

Distin, K. 2010. *Cultural Evolution*. Cambridge: Cambridge University Press.

Dodd, C. H. 1946. *The Johannine Epistles*. London: Hodder and Stoughton.

———. 1952. *According to the Scriptures*. London: Nisbet and Co.

———. 1971. *The Founder of Christianity*. London: Collins.

Dods, M. 1979. *The Gospel of John*. EGT 1. Grand Rapids, MI: Eerdmans.

Dooyeweerd, H. 1958. "Philosophie et Théologie." *La Revue Réformée* 35:48–60.

———. 1960. *In the Twilight of Western Thought: Studies in the*

Pretended Autonomy of Philosophical Thought. Philadelphia: Presbyterian and Reformed Publishing Company.

———. 1963. *Vernieuwing en bezinning: Om het reformatorisch grondmotief*. 2nd ed. Zutphen: Van den Brink.

———. 1984 (repr.). *A New Critique of Theoretical Thought*. Vol. 1: *The Necessary Presuppositions of Philosophy* (1953). Vol. 2: *The General Theory of the Modal Spheres* (1955). Vol. 3: *The Structures of Individuality of Temporal Reality* (1957). Jordan Station: Paideia Press.

Douglas, J. D. 1974a. Wellhausen, Julius. In *The New International Dictionary of the Christian Church*, edited by J. D. Douglas. 1033. Grand Rapids, MI: Zondervan.

———, ed. 1974b. *The New International Dictionary of the Christian Church*. Grand Rapids, MI: Zondervan.

Douma, J. 2005. *Genesis: Gaan in het spoor van de Bijbel*. Kampen: Kok.

———. 2009. "Een omstreden dissertatie." *De Reformatie* 84:30.

———. 2017. *Common Grace in Kuyper, Schilder, and Calvin: Exposition, Comparison, and Evaluation*. Translated by A. H. Oosterhoff. Edited by W. Helder. Hamilton, ON: Lucerna CRTS Publications.

Dowey Jr., E. A. 1965. *The Knowledge of God in Calvin's Theology*. New York: Columbia University Press.

Driver, G. R. and J. C. Miles. 2007. *The Babylonian Laws*. Eugene, OR: Wipf and Stock.

Driver, S. R. 1892. *An Introduction to the Literature of the Old Testament*. Edinburgh: T. and T. Clark.

Duffield, G. P. and N. M. Van Cleave. 1996. *Woord en Geest: Hoofdlijnen van de theologie van de Pinksterbeweging*. Kampen: Kok/Rafaël Nederland.

Dulles, A. 1985. *Models for Revelation*. New York: Doubleday.

———. 1992. *The Craft of Theology: From Symbol tot System*. New York: Crossroad.

Dunn, J. D. G. 2003. *Christology in the Making.* Vol. 1: *Jesus Remembered.* 2nd ed. London: SCM.

———. 2005. *A New Perspective on Jesus: What the Quest for the Historical Jesus Missed.* Grand Rapids, MI: Baker Academic.

Du Plessis, J. G. 1988. "Mark's Priority: The Nature and Structure of the Argument from Order." In *Paradigms and Progress in Theology,* edited by J. Moulton et al. 295–308. Pretoria: HSRC.

Dupont-Sommer, A. 1960. *Les Ecrits esséniens découverts près de la mer Morte.* Paris: Payot.

Du Toit, A. B. 1990. "Die toekoms van die Skrifgesag in die moderne eksegese. 'n Hoofsaaklik Nuwe-Testamentiese perspektief." *Ned. Geref. Teologiese Tydskrif* 31:509–19.

Duvekot, W. S. 1998. *Wie is toch deze? Jezus' persoon vanuit de Joodse traditie: een poging.* Zoetermeer: Boekencentrum.

Duvenage, B. 1985. *Christelike wetenskap as Woordgebonde wetenskap.* Potchefstroom: PU vir CHO.

Ebeling, G. 1979. *Dogmatik des christlichen Glaubens.* Vol. 1. Tübingen: Mohr (Siebeck).

Edwards, B. B. 1993. "The Genuineness of the Pastoral Epistles." *Bibliotheca Sacra* 150:598:131–39.

Ehrman, B. D. 2005. *Misquoting Jesus: The Story Behind Who Changed the Bible and Why.* New York: HarperSanFrancisco.

———. 2009. *Jesus, Interrupted.* San Francisco: HarperOne.

———. 2011. *Forged: Why the Bible's Authors Are Not Who We Think They Are.* San Francisco: HarperOne.

Eichhorn, J. G. 1804–1812. *Einleitung in das Neue Testament.* Leipzig: Weidmann.

———. 1820. *Einleitung in das Alte Testament.* Leipzig: Weidmann.

Eissfeldt, O. 1965. *The Old Testament: An Introduction, including the Apocrypha and Pseudepigrapha, and also the works of similar type from Qumran: the history of the formation of the Old Testament.* New York: Harper and Row.

Engnell, I. 1954. *Israel and the Law.* 2nd ed. Uppsala: Wretmans Boktryckeri.

Enns, P. 2005. *Inspiration and Incarnation: Evangelicals and the Problem of the Old Testament.* Grand Rapids, MI: Baker Books.

Erickson, M. J. 1982. "Biblical Inerrancy: The Last Twenty-Five Years." *Journal of the Evangelical Theological Society* 25:387–94.

———. 1998. *Christian Theology.* Vol. 1. Grand Rapids, MI: Baker Book House.

Eskhult, M. 2003. "The Importance of Loanwords for Dating Biblical Hebrew Texts.: In *Biblical Hebrew: Studies in Chronology and Typology,* edited by I. Young. 8–23. London: T. and T. Clark.

Evans, C. A. 1992. *Jesus.* Grand Rapids, MI: Baker.

Fackre, G. J. 1997. *The Doctrine of Revelation: A Narrative Interpretation.* Grand Rapids, MI: Eerdmans.

———, R. H. Nash, and J. Sanders. 1995. *What About Those Who Have Never Heard?: Three Views on the Destiny of the Unevangelized.* Downers Grove, IL: InterVarsity Press.

Farmer, W. R. 1964. *The Synoptic Problem.* New York: Macmillan.

Fee, G. D. 1987. *The First Epistle to the Corinthians.* NICNT. Grand Rapids, MI: Eerdmans.

Feinberg, J. S. 1984. "Truth: Relationship of theories of truth to hermeneutics." In *Hermeneutics, Inerrancy, and the Bible,* edited by E. D. Radmacher and R. D. Preus. 1–50. Grand Rapids, MI: Zondervan.

Feinberg, P. D. 1968. *The Doctrine of God in the Pentateuch.* Dallas: Dallas Seminary Press.

———. 1979. "The Meaning of Inerrancy." In *Inerrancy,*

edited by N. L. Geisler. 267-304. Grand Rapids, MI: Zondervan.

Feyerabend, P. 2008. *Tegen de methode*. Rotterdam: Lemniscaat.

Finkelstein, I., A. Mazar, and B. B. Schmidt, eds. 2007. *The Quest for the Historical Israel: Debating Archaeology and the History of Early Israel*. Atlanta: Society of Biblical Literature.

Flint, P. W. 1997. "The Daniel Tradition at Qumran" In *Eschatology, Messianism, and the Dead Sea Scrolls*, edited by C. A. Evans and P. W. Flint. 41-60. Grand Rapids, MI: Eerdmans.

Flusser, D. 1987. *Jewish Sources in Early Christianity*. Adama Books (Internet Archive).

———. 1988. *Judaism and the Origins of Christianity*. Jerusalem: Magnes Press.

———. 1998. *Jesus*. 2nd ed. Jerusalem: Magnes Press.

———. 2013. *Jesus . . . The Crucified One and the Jews*. Varda Books (e-book only).

Fokkelman, J. and W. Weren, eds. 2003. *De bijbel literair: Opbouw en gedachtegang van de bijbelse geschriften en hun onderlinge relaties*. Zoetermeer: Boekencentrum.

Fowl, S. 1998. *Engaging Scripture: A Model for Theological Interpretation*. Oxford: Blackwell.

Frame, J. M. 1987. *The Doctrine of the Knowledge of God*. Phillipsburg, NJ: Presbyterian and Reformed Publ. Co.

France, R. T. 1976. "The Authenticity of the Sayings of Jesus." In *History, Criticism and Faith: Four Exploratory Studies*, edited by C. Brown. 101-43. Downers Grove, IL: InterVarsity Press.

———. 2007. *The Gospel of Matthew*. NICNT. Grand Rapids, MI: Eerdmans.

Frank, H. T. 1971. *Bible, Archaeology and Faith*. Nashville, Tenn.: Abingdon Press.

Free, J. P. 1950. *Archaeology and Bible History*. Wheaton, Ill.: Van Kampen Press.

———. 1956. "Archaeology and Liberalism." *Bibliotheca Sacra* 113:123–29.

Friedman, R. E. 1987. *Who Wrote the Bible?* New York: HarperOne.

———. 2003. *The Bible with Sources Revealed: A New View into the Five Books of Moses*. New York: HarperOne.

Fuchs, E. 1960. *Zur Frage nach dem historischen Jesus*. Tübingen: Mohr (Siebeck).

———. 1963. *Hermeneutik*. 3rd ed. Bad Canstatt: R. Müllerschön.

———. 1971. *Jesus: Wort und Tat*. Tübingen: Mohr (Siebeck).

Funk, R. W. 1996. *Honest to Jesus: Jesus for a New Millennium*. San Francisco: HarperSanFrancisco.

———. 1998. *The Acts of Jesus: The Search for the Authentic Deeds of Jesus*. San Francisco: HarperCollins.

———. 1999. *The Gospel of Jesus According to the Jesus Seminar*. Santa Rosa, CA: Polebridge Press.

———. 2002. *A Credible Jesus: Fragments of a Vision*. Santa Rosa, CA: Polebridge Press.

———, and R. Hoover. 1993. *The Five Gospels: The Search for the Authentic Words of Jesus*. New York: Macmillan.

Gabler, J. Ph. 1790. *Urgeschichte*. Vol. 1. Altdorf: Monath and Kussler.

Gaebelein, F. E., ed. 1979. *The Expositor's Bible Commentary*. Vol. 1: *Introductory Articles*. Grand Rapids, MI: Zondervan.

Garrett, D. A. 2003. *Rethinking Genesis: The Sources and Authorship of the First Book of the Bible*. New York: Mentor.

Garrett, J. L. 1990. *Systematic Theology: Biblical, Historical, and Evangelical*. Vol. 1. Grand Rapids, MI: Eerdmans.

Gatiss, L. 2008. *Christianity and the Tolerance of Liberalism: J. Gresham Machen and the Presbyterian Controversy of 1922–*

1937. London: Latimer Trust.

Geertsema, H. 2005. "Homo respondens: Het antwoordkarakter van het mens-zijn." In *Homo respondens: Verkenningen rond het mens-zijn*, edited by G. Buijs et al. 25–45. 2nd ed. Amsterdam: Buijten and Schipperheijn.

Geesink, W. 1925. *Van 's Heeren ordinantiën*. Kampen: Kok.

Geisler, N. L. 1979a. "Philosophical Presuppositions of Biblical Errancy." In *Inerrancy*, edited by N. L. Geisler. 305–34. Grand Rapids, MI: Zondervan.

⸻, ed. 1979b. *Inerrancy*. Grand Rapids, MI: Zondervan.

⸻, ed. 1981. *Biblical Errancy: An Analysis of Its Philosophical Roots*. Grand Rapids, MI: Zondervan.

⸻. 1984a. "Response to J. S. Feinberg." In *Hermeneutics, Inerrancy, and the Bible*, edited by E. D. Radmacher and R. D. Preus. 51–56. Grand Rapids, MI: Zondervan.

⸻. 1984b. "Theological Method and Inerrancy: A Reply to Arthur F. Holmes." In *Evangelicals and Inerrancy: Selections from the* Journal of the Evangelical Theological Society, edited by R. F. Youngblood. 137–44. Nashville, TN: Thomas Nelson.

⸻. 1999. "Beware of Philosophy: A Warning to Biblical Scholars." *Journal of the Evangelical Society* 42.1:3–19.

⸻, and T. Howe. 1992. *When Critics Ask: A Popular Handbook on Bible Difficulties*. Grand Rapids, MI: Baker Books.

⸻, and W. E. Nix. 1968. *A General Introduction to the Bible*. Chicago: Moody Press.

⸻, and W. E. Nix. 1974. *From God to Us: How We Got Our Bible*. Chicago: Moody Press.

Generale Synode van de Nederlands Hervormde Kerk. 1966. *Klare wijn: Rekenschap over geschiedenis, geheim en gezag van de Bijbel*. 's-Gravenhage: Boekencentrum.

⸻, Generale Synode van de Gereformeerde Kerken in Nederland, Synode van de Evangelisch-Lutherse Kerk in het Koninkrijk der Nederlanden. 1999. *De bijbel: Taal en teken in de tijd*. Zoetermeer: Boekencentrum.

George, J. F. L. 1835. *Die älteren jüdischen Feste mit einer Kritik der Gesetzgebung des Pentateuchs*. Berlin: E.H. Schroeder.

Gieseler, J. C. L. 1818. *Historisch-kritischer Versuch über die Entstehung und die frühesten Schicksale der schriftlichen Evangelien*. Leipzig: Engelmann.

God met ons. 1981. Rapport over de aard van het Schriftgezag. Leusden: Gereformeerde Kerken in Nederland.

Godet, F. L. 1880-1881. *Commentary on St. Paul's Epistle to the Romans*. Edinburgh: T. & T. Clark.

Goldingay, J. 1994. *Models for Scripture*. Carlisle: Paternoster Press.

Gosse, Ph. H. 2003. *Omphalos: An Attempt to Untie the Geological Knot*. Abingdon/New York: Routlegde.

Goulder, M. D. 1974. *Midrash and Lection in Matthew*. London: SPCK.

Graafland, C. 1981. "De aard van het Schriftgezag, art. V." *De Waarheidsvriend* 2 april.

_____. n.d. *Wie zeggen de mensen dat Ik ben? Over de Persoon van Jezus Christus*. Kampen: Kok.

Graf, K. H. 1866. *Die geschichtlichen Bücher des Alten Testaments: Zwei historisch-kritische Untersuchungen*. Leipzig: Weigel.

Grant, F. W. 1897. *The Numerical Bible: The Gospels*. New York: Loizeaux Brothers.

_____. 1901. *The Numerical Bible: Acts to 2 Corinthians*. New York: Loizeaux Brothers.

Green, G. L. 2002. *The Letters to the Thessalonians*. PNTC. Grand Rapids, MI: Eerdmans.

_____. 2008. *Jude and 2 Peter*. Baker Exegetical Commentary on the New Testament. Grand Rapids, MI: Baker Academic.

Green, J. B. 1997. *The Gospel of Luke*. NICNT. Grand Rapids, MI: Eerdmans.

Greijdanus, S. 1946. *Schriftbeginselen ter Schriftverklaring*. Kampen: Kok.

———. 1955. *Het evangelie naar Lucas*. 2nd ed. Vol. 2. KV. Kampen: Kok.

Gressmann, H. 1913. *Mose und seine Zeit: Ein Kommentar zu den Mosesagen*. Göttingen: Vandenhoeck and Ruprecht.

Griesbach, J. J. 1789. *Commentatio qua Marci evangelium totum e Matthaei et Lucae commentariis decerptum esse monstratur*.

Grillmeyer, A., ed. 1966. *Das zweite Vatikanische Konzil: Dokumente und Kommentare*. Freiburg: Herder.

Groen van Prinsterer, G. 2008 (1847). *Ongeloof en revolutie*. Edited by A. B. Kuiper and R. Kuiper. Barneveld: Nederlands Dagblad.

Grosheide, F. W. 1929. *Hermeneutiek ten dienste van de bestudeering van het Nieuwe Testament*. Amsterdam: H. A. van Bottenburg.

———. 1935. *Algemeene canoniek van het Nieuwe Testament*. Amsterdam: H. A. van Bottenburg.

———. 1948. *De bevooroordeeldheid van de exegese*. Kampen: Kok.

———. 1949. *Het heilig evangelie volgens Johannes*. Vol. 1. Amsterdam: H. A. van Bottenburg.

———. 1955. *De Psalmen*. Vol. 1: *Psalm 1–41*. COT. Kampen: Kok.

Grotius, H. 1646. *Annotationes in Acta Apostolorum et Epistolas Apostolicas*. Paris: Thomas Jolly.

Grün, A. 2002. *Beelden van Jezus*. Tielt: Lannoo/Baarn: Ten Have.

Gunkel, H. 1910. *Genesis*. 3rd ed. Göttingen: Vandenhoeck and Ruprecht.

Gunton, C. 1995. *A Brief Theology of Revelation*. Edinburgh: T. and T. Clark.

Guthrie, D. 1978. "The Historical and Literary Criticism of the New Testament." In *Biblical Criticism: Historical, Literary and Textual*, edited by R. K. Harrison et al. 85–123. Grand Rapids, MI: Zondervan.

———. 1979. The Historical and Literary Criticism of the New Testament. In *The Expositor's Bible Commentary*. Vol. 1: *Introductory Articles*, edited by F. E. Gaebelein. 437–56. Grand Rapids, MI: Zondervan.

———. 1990 (rev. ed.). *New Testament Introduction*. London: InterVarsity Press.

Gutiérrez, G. 1971. *A Theology of Liberation: History, Politics and Salvation*. New York: Orbis Books.

Haenchen, E. 1968. *Der Weg Jesu: Eine Erklärung des Markus-Evangeliums und der kanonischen Parallelen*. 2nd ed. Berlin: Topelmann.

Hagoort, H., ed. 1998. *De Bijbel betrouwbaar*. Kampen: Voorhoeve.

Hahn, H. F. 1966. *Old Testament in Modern Research*. Philadelphia: Muhlenberg Press.

Haitjema, Th. L. 1933. "Het Woord Gods en de bijbel." *Onder eigen vaandel* 8:183–212.

Hall, B. K. and B. Hallgrimsson. 2007. *Strickberger's Evolution*. 4th ed. Sudbury, MA: Jones and Bartlett.

Hamilton, V. P. 1990. *The Book of Genesis Chapters 1–17*. NICOT. Grand Rapids, MI: Eerdmans.

Hannah, J. D., ed. 1984. *Inerrancy and the Church*. Chicago: Moody Press.

Hanson, A. T. and P. C. Hanson. 1990. *Bible without Illusions*. Philadelphia: Trinity Press International.

Harinck, C. 2006. *De Geestesgaven: Een bezinning op de opkomst van de charismatische beweging*. Houten: Den Hertog.

Harinck, G., ed. 2001. *De kwestie-Geelkerken. Een terugblik na 75 jaar*. Barneveld: De Vuurbaak.

Harnack, A. von. 1900. *History of Dogma*. Translated by N. Buchanen. Vol. 7. Boston, MA: Little, Brown and Co.

———. 1958. *History of Dogma*. Translated by N. Buchanen. Vol. 5. New York: Russell and Russell.

Harris, R. L. 1957. *Inspiration and Canonicity of the Bible*. Grand Rapids, MI: Zondervan.

———. 1990. *Leviticus*. EBC 2. Grand Rapids, MI: Zondervan.

———. 1995. *Inspiration and Canonicity of the Scriptures*. Greenville, SC: A Press.

Harrison, R. K. 1969. *Introduction to the Old Testament with a Comprehensive Review of Old Testament Studies and a Special Supplement on the Apocrypha*. Grand Rapids, MI: Eerdmans.

———. 1978. "The Historical and Literary Criticism of the Old Testament." In *Biblical Criticism: Historical, Literary and Textual*, edited by R. K. Harrison et al. 3–44. Grand Rapids, MI: Zondervan.

———. 1979. "Historical and Literary Criticism of the Old Testament." In *The Expositor's Bible Commentary*. Vol. 1: *Introductory Articles*, edited by F. E. Gaebelein. 231–50. Grand Rapids, MI: Zondervan.

———, B. K. Waltke, D. Guthrie, and G. D. Fee, eds. 1978. *Biblical Criticism: Historical, Literary and Textual*. Grand Rapids, MI: Zondervan.

Harrison, V. S. 2007. *Religion and Modern Thought*. London: SCM.

Hart, H. 1968. *The Challenge of Our Age*. Toronto: Association for the Advancement of Christian Studies.

———. 1981. "The Impasse of Rationality Today." In *Wetenschap, wijsheid, filosoferen*, edited by H. Hart et al. 174–200. Assen: Van Gorcum.

———. 1984. *Understanding our world: An integral ontology*. Lanham, MD: University Press of America.

Hauerwas, S. 2001. *With the Grain of the Universe: The Church's Witness and Natural Theology*. Grand Rapids, MI: Brazos Press.

Hayes, C. J. H. 1941. *A Generation of Materialism, 1871–1900*. New York: Harper and Brothers.

Head, P. M. 1997. *Christology and the Synoptic Problem: An Argument for Markan Priority*. Cambridge: Cambridge University Press.

Headlam, A. C. 1934. *Christian Theology*. Oxford: Clarendon Press.

Hegel, G. W. F. 1990. *Lectures on the Philosophy of Religion*. Edited by P. C. Hodgson. Oxford: Oxford University Press.

Heidegger, M. 1962. *Being and Time*. London: SCM Press.

Heim, K. 1931–1952. *Der evangelische Glaube und das Denken der Gegenwart: Grundzüge einer christlichen Weltanschauuung*. 6 vols. Hamburg: Furche-Verlag.

Hempelmann, H. 2000. *Nicht auf der Schrift, sondern unter ihr: Grundsätze und Grundzüge einer Hermeneutik der Demut*. Lahr: Verlag der Liebenzeller Mission.

Hengel, M. 1995. *Studies in Early Christology*. Edinburgh: T. and T. Clark.

Henry, C. F. H. 1976. *God, Revelation and Authority*. Vol. 2: *God Who Speaks and Shows: Fifteen Theses, Part One*. Waco, TX: Word Books.

———. 1979a. *God, Revelation and Authority*. Vol. 3: *God Who Speaks and Shows: Fifteen Theses, Part Two*. Waco, TX: Word Books.

———. 1979b. *God, Revelation and Authority*. Vol. 4: *God Who Speaks and Shows: Fifteen Theses, Part Three*. Waco, TX: Word Books.

———. 1979c. "The Authority and Inspiration of the Bible." In *The Expositor's Bible Commentary*. Vol. 1: *Introductory Articles*, edited by F. E. Gaebelein. 3–35. Grand Rapids,

MI: Zondervan.

Hepp, V. 1936. *Dreigende deformatie*. Vol. 1: *Diagnose*. Kampen: Kok.

Herder, J. G. 2010. *Ideen zur Philosophie der Geschichte der Menschheit*. 2 vols. Charleston, SC: Nabu Press.

Heron, A. I. C. 1980. *A Century of Protestant Theology*. Philadelphia: Westminster Press.

Hess, R. S. 2007. *Israelite Religions: An Archaeological and Biblical Survey*. Grand Rapids, MI: Baker Academic.

Heyns, J. A. 1976. *Brug tussen God en mens: Oor die Bybel*. Pretoria: NG Kerkboekhandel Transvaal.

_____. 1977. "Grondlyne van 'n Algemene Wetenskapsleer, en: Teologie as Wetenskapp." In *Op weg met die teologie*, edited by J. A. Heyns and W. D. Jonker. 13–228. Pretoria: NG Kerkboekhandel.

_____. 1988. *Dogmatiek*. Pretoria: N. G. Kerkboekhandel.

Hick, J. H. 2004. *An Interpretation of Religion: Human Responses to the Transcendent*. 2nd ed. New Haven, CT: Yale University Press.

_____, and P. F. Knitter, eds. 2005. *The Myth of Christian Uniqueness: Toward a Pluralistic Theology of Religions*. Eugene, OR: Wipf and Stock.

Hitzig, F. 2010. *Das Buch Daniel*. Charleston, SC: Nabu Press.

Hobrink, B. 2005. *Moderne wetenschap in de Bijbel*. Hoornaar: Gideon.

Hodge, C. A. 1872. *Systematic Theology*. Vol. 1. New York: Scribner, Armstrong and Co.

Hodgson, P. C. 2005. *Hegel and Christian Theology: A Reading of the Lectures on the Philosophy of Religion*. Oxford: Oxford University Press.

Hoehner, H. 2002. *Ephesians: An Exegetical Commentary*. Grand Rapids, MI: Baker Academic.

Hofmann, J. Chr. K. von. 1869. *Die Heilige Schrift N.T.* Vol. 1. Nördlingen: C. H. Beck.

Hoffmeier, J. K. 2009. *De archeologie van de Bijbel.* Amsterdam: Ark Media.

Holding, J. P. 2009. *Trusting the New Testament: Is the Bible Reliable?* Longwood, FL: Xulon Press.

Holladay, C. R. 2005. *A Critical Introduction to the New Testament.* Nashville, TN: Abingdon Press.

Holland, T. 2009. *De gang naar Canossa.* Amsterdam: Athenaeum – Polak and Van Gennep.

Holmes, A. F. 1977. *All Truth Is God's Truth.* Grand Rapids, MI: Eerdmans.

———. 1984a. "Ordinary Language Analysis and Theological Method." In *Evangelicals and Inerrancy: Selections from the* Journal of the Evangelical Theological Society, edited by R. F. Youngblood. 129–36. Nashville, TN: Thomas Nelson.

———. 1984b. "Reply to Norman L. Geisler." In *Evangelicals and Inerrancy: Selections from the* Journal of the Evangelical Theological Society, edited by R. F. Youngblood. 145–46. Nashville, TN: Thomas Nelson.

Holtzmann, H. J. 1863. *Die synoptischen Evangelien: Ihr Ursprung und geschichtlicher Charakter.* Leipzig: Engelmann.

Holwerda, B. 1971. *Oudtestamentische voordrachten.* Vol. 1: *Historia revelationis veteris testamenti.* Kampen: Van den Berg.

———. 1972. *Oudtestamentische voordrachten.* Vol. 2: *Bijzondere canoniek.* Kampen: Van den Berg.

Honderich, T., ed. 1995. *The Oxford Companion to Philosophy.* Oxford: Oxford University Press.

Hooykaas, R. 1972. *Religion and the Rise of Modern Science.* Edinburgh: Scottish Academic Press.

Hornig, G. 1996. *Johann Salomo Semler. Studien zu Leben und Werk des Hallenser Aufklärungstheologen.* Tübingen: Niemeyer.

Houtman, C. 1980. *Inleiding in de pentateuch*. Kampen: Kok.

Hubbard, D. 1977. "The Current Tensions: Is There a Way Out?" In *Biblical Authority*, edited by J. Rogers. 149-96. Waco, TX: Word.

Hughes, Ph. E. 1983. "The Truth of Scripture and the Problem of Historical Relativity." In *Scripture and Truth*, edited by D. A. Carson and J. D. Woodbridge. 173-94. Grand Rapids, MI: Zondervan.

Hupfeld, H. 1853. *Die Quellen der Genesis und die Art ihrer Zusammensetzung von neuen untersucht*. Berlin: Wiegandt and Grieben.

Huxley, Th. H. 1894. *Collected Essays*. Vol. 4: *Science and Hebrew Tradition*. London: Macmillan.

Jaki, S. L. 1974. *Science and Creation: From Eternal Cycles to an Oscillating Universe*. Edinburgh: Scottisch Adacemic Press.

_____. 1978. *The Road of Science and the Ways to God*. Chicago: University of Chicago Press.

James, W. 1904. *The Varieties of Religious Experience: A Study in Human Nature*. London: Longman and Green.

Jameson, H. G. 1922. *The Origin of the Synoptic Gospels: A Revision of the Synoptic Problem*. Oxford: Blackwell.

Jensen, P. 2002. *The Revelation of God: Contours of Christian Theology*. Downers Grove, IL: Intervarsity Press.

Jeremias, J. 1971. *New Testament Theology: The Proclamation of Jesus*. New York: Scribner.

Joest, W. 1974. *Fundamentaltheologie: Theologische Grundlagen- und Methodenprobleme*. Stuttgart: Kohlhammer.

Johnson, L. T. 1996. *The Real Jesus: The Misguided Quest for the Historical Jesus and the Truth of the Traditional Gospels*. San Francisco: HarperSanFrancisco.

Jones, I. H. 2005. *The Epistles to the Thessalonians*. Peterborough: Epworth Press.

Jongeneel, J. A. B. 1971. *Het redelijke geloof in Jezus Christus: Een studie over de wijsbegeerte van de Verlichting.* Wageningen: Veenman.

Jonker, W. D. n.d. *Die brief aan die Romeine.* Kaapstad/Pretoria: NG Kerk-Uitgewers.

Kaiser, Jr., W. C. 1990. *Exodus.* EBC 2. Grand Rapids, MI: Zondervan.

Kalland, E. S. 1992. *Deuteronomy.* EBC 3. Grand Rapids, MI: Zondervan.

Kalsbeek, L. 1970. *De Wijsbegeerte der Wetsidee.* Amsterdam: Buijten and Schipperheijn.

Kamphuis, J. 1982. *Aantekeningen bij J. A. Heyns' Dogmatiek.* Kampen: Van den Berg.

Kant, I. 1997. *Critique of Practical Reason.* Cambridge: Cambridge University Press.

Karlstadt, A. 1520. *De canonicis scripturis.* Wittenberg: M. Lotter.

Karner, K. 1957. *Einführung in die Theologie.* Berlin: Evangelische Verlagsanstalt.

Käsemann, E. 1954. *Das Problem des historischen Jesus.* Göttingen: Vandenhoeck and Ruprecht.

Keller, W. 1983. *The Bible As History.* New York: Bantam.

Kelly, W., ed. 1856–1920. *Bible Treasury: A Monthly Review of Prophetic and Practical Subjects.* Available at https://bibletruthpublishers.com/bible-treasury/lpvl22465.

Kickel, W. 1967. *Vernunft und Offenbarung bei Theodor Beza.* Neukirchen-Vluyn: Neukirchener Verlag.

Kirkham, R. L. 1992. *Theories of Truth.* Cambridge, MA: MIT Press.

Kitchen, K. A. 1966. *Ancient Orient and the Old Testament.* London: Tyndale Press.

_____. 2003. *On the Reliability of the Old Testament.* Grand Rapids, MI: Eerdmans.

Kittel, G. et al., eds. 1964–1976. *Theological Dictionary of the*

New Testament. Translated by G. W. Bromiley. 10 vols. Grand Rapids, MI: Eerdmans.

Klooster, F. H. 1977. *Quests for the Historical Jesus*. Grand Rapids, MI: Baker.

———. 1984. "Revelation and Scripture in Existentialist Theology." In *Challenges to Inerrancy: A Theological Response*, edited by G. Lewis and B. Demarest. 175-214. Chicago: Moody Press.

Knevel, A. G., W. J. Ouweneel, A. P. De Boer, and W. J. J. Glashouwer, eds. 1981. *De Bijbel in de beklaagdenbank: Antwoord op het rapport "God met ons" van de Gereformeerde Kerken in Nederland over de aard van het Schriftgezag*. Hilversum: Evangelische Omroep.

———, M. J. Paul, and J. Broekhuis, eds. 1987. *Het gezag van de Bijbel: Verkenningen in de hermeneutiek*. Kampen: Kok/Hilversum: Evangelische Omroep.

Knight, D. A. and G. M. Tucker, eds. 1993. *To Each Its Own Meaning: An Introduction to Biblical Criticisms and Their Applications*. Louisville, KY: Westminster John Knox.

Knight, J. 2004. *Jesus: An Historical and Theological Investigation*. London/New York: T. and T. Clark.

Kok, J. H. 1992. *Vollenhoven: His early development*. Sioux Center, Iowa: Dordt College Press.

König, A. 1982. "In gesprek met prof. F. J. M. Potgieter." In *Perspektief op die Ope Brief*, edited by D. J. Bosch et al. 114-22. Kaapstad: Human and Rousseau.

Kooij, A., J. A. M. Snoek, and K. van der Toorn, eds. 1998. *Canonization and Decanonization: Papers Presented to the International Conference of the Leiden Institute for the Study of Religions*. Leiden: Brill Academic.

Krabbendam, H. 1984. "The Functional Theology of G. C. Berkouwer." In *Challenges to Inerrancy: A Theological Response*, edited by G. Lewis and B. Demarest. 285-316. Chicago: Moody Press.

Kraus, H.-J. 1969. *Geschichte der historisch-kritischen Forschung des Alten Testaments*. 2nd ed. Neukirchen-Vluyn: Neukirchener Verlag.

Kreck, W. 1970. *Grundfragen der Dogmatik*. München: Chr. Kaiser.

Krusche, W. 1953. *Das Wirken des Heiligen Geistes nach Calvin*. Unpublished dissertation.

Kuenen, A. 1874. *The Religion of Israel to the Fall of the Jewish State*. Translated by A. H. May. Vol. 1. London: Williams and Norgate.

Kugel, J. L. 2008. *How to Read the Bible: A Guide to Scripture, Then and Now*. New York: Free Press.

Kuhn, T. S. 1996. *The Structure of Scientific Revolutions*. 3rd ed. Chicago: University of Chicago Press.

Kuiper, R. 1996. "Gods hand in de geschiedenis: Overtuiging en verlegenheid van een christen-historicus 1, 2." In *Geloof en geschiedenis*, edited by H. Hagoort, 88–103. Kampen: Kok.

Kuitert, H. M. 1988. *Filosofie van de theologie*. Leiden: Martinus Nijhoff.

⸺. 1993. *I Have My Doubts: How to Become a Christian Without Being a Fundamentalist*. Translated by J. Bowden. London: SCM Press.

⸺. 1999. *Jesus: The Legacy of Christianity*. Translated by J. Bowden. London: SCM Press.

⸺. 2005. *Hetzelfde anders zien: Het christelijk geloof als verbeelding*. Baarn: Ten Have.

Külling, S. R. 1964. *Zur Datierung der "Genesis-P-Stücke" namentlich des Kapitels Genesis XVII*. Kampen: Kok.

Kümmel, W. G. 1972. *The New Testament: The History of the Investigation of Its Problems*. Translated by S. M. Gilmour and H. C. Kee. New York: Abingdon Press.

Küng, H. 1963. *Kirche im Konzil*. Freiburg: Herder.

Kuyper, A. 1898. *Encyclopedia of Sacred Theology: Its Principles*.

Translated by J. H. De Vries. New York: Charles Scribner's Sons.

———. 1908-1909. *Encyclopaedie der heilige godgeleerdheid*, 2nd rev. ed. 3 vols.: vol. 1 (1908): *Inleidend Deel*; vol. 2 (1909): *Algemeen Deel*; vol. 3 (1909): *Bijzonder Deel*. Kampen: J.H. Kok.

———. 2009. *Lectures on Calvinism: Six Lectures from the Stone Foundation: Lectures Delivered at Princeton University*. CreateSpace Independent Publishing Platform.

———. n.d.-1 *Dictaten Dogmatiek*. Vol. 2: *Locus de Sacra Scriptura, Creatione, Creaturis*. Kampen: J.H. Kok.

———. n.d.-2 *Dictaten Dogmatiek*. Vol. 3: *Locus de Providentia, Peccato, Foedere, Christo*. Kampen: J.H. Kok.

Labuschagne, C. J. 2000. *Zin en onzin rond de bijbel: Bijbelgeloof, bijbelwetenschap en bijbelgebruik*. Zoetermeer: Boekencentrum.

Lachmann, K. 1835. "De ordine narrationum in evangeliis synopticis." *Theologische Studien und Kritiken* 8:570-90.

Lackey, D. 1999. "What Are the Modern Classics? The Baruch Poll of Great Philosophy in the Twentieth Century." *Philosophical Forum* 30 (4):329-46.

Ladd, G. E. 1967. *The New Testament and Criticism*. Grand Rapids, MI: Eerdmans.

Lamont, J. R. T. 2004. *Divine Faith*. Aldershot: Ashgate.

Lemche, N. P. 1998. *The Israelites in History and Tradition*. London: SPCK.

———. 2008. *The Old Testament between Theology and History: A Critical Survey*. Louisville, KY: Westminster John Knox Press

Lewens, T. 2015. *Cultural Evolution: Conceptual Challenges*. Oxford: Oxford University Press.

Lewis, C. S. 1967. *Christian Reflections*. Grand Rapids, MI: Eerdmans.

———. 2001. *Miracles*. San Francisco: HarperSanFrancisco.

Lewis, G. and B. Demarest, eds. 1984. *Challenges to Inerrancy: A Theological Response.* Chicago: Moody Press.

_____. 1996. *Integrative Theology: Historical, Biblical, Systematic, Apologetic, Practical.* 3 vols. Grand Rapids, MI: Zondervan.

Liefeld, W. L. 1999. *1 and 2 Timothy, Titus.* NIVAC. Grand Rapids, MI: Zondervan, 1999.

Lightfoot, J. 1865. *Saint Paul's Epistle to the Galatians.* London: Macmillan.

_____. 1889. *Essays on "Supernatural Religion."* London: Macmillan.

_____. 1979. *A Commentary of the New Testament from the Talmud and Hebraica: Matthew–1 Corinthians.* Grand Rapids, MI: Baker Book House.

Lindsell, H. 1976. *The Battle for the Bible.* Grand Rapids, MI: Zondervan.

_____. 1979. *The Bible in the Balance.* Grand Rapids, MI: Zondervan.

Linnemann, E. 1992. *Is There a Synoptic Problem? Rethinking the Literary Dependence of the First Three Gospels.* Grand Rapids, MI: Baker Book House.

_____. 2001. *Historical Criticism of the Bible: Methodology or Ideology? Reflections of a Bultmannian Turned Evangelical.* Grand Rapids, MI: Kregel.

Locher, J. C. S. 1903. *De leer van Luther over Gods woord.* Amsterdam: Scheffer and Co.

Locke, J. and A. W. Wainright. 1988. *A Paraphrase and Notes on the Epistles of St. Paul.* 2 vols. Oxford: Clarendon Press.

Lockton, W. 1922. "The Origin of the Gospels." *Church Quarterly Review* 94:216–39.

Loetscher, L. A. 1954. *The Broadening Church: A Study of Theological Issues in the Presbyterian Church Since 1869.* Philadelphia: University of Pennsylvania Press.

Lohmeyer, E. 1957. *Das Evangelium des Markus*. Göttingen: Vandenhoeck and Ruprecht.

———. 1958. *Das Evangelium des Matthäus*. Göttingen: Vandenhoeck and Ruprecht.

Long, V. P., D. W. Baker, and G. J. Wenham, eds. 2002. *Windows into Old Testament History: Evidence, Argument, and the Crisis of "Biblical Israel."* Grand Rapids, MI: Eerdmans.

Loonstra, B. 1994. *De geloofwaardigheid van de Bijbel*. Zoetermeer: Boekencentrum.

———. 1999. *De Bijbel recht doen: Bezinning op gereformeerde hermeneutiek*. Zoetermeer: Boekencentrum.

Luther, M. 1883–2009. *Luthers Werke*. Weimarer Ausgabe. Weimar: Böhlau Verlag.

Lyotard, J.-F. 1987. *Het postmoderne weten*. Kampen: Kok Agora.

McCain, D. 2002. *Notes on New Testament Introduction*. Bukuru: Africa Christian Textbooks.

McDonald, J. 2006. *God schreef een boek*. Doorn: Het Zoeklicht.

McDonald, L. M. 2007. *The Biblical Canon: Its Origin, Transmission, and Authority*. Peabody, MA: Hendrickson.

———, and J. A. Sanders, eds. 2002. *The Canon Debate*. Peabody, MA: Hendrickson.

McDowell, J. 1975. *More Evidence That Demands a Verdict: Historical Evidences for the Christian Scriptures*. n.p.: Campus Crusade for Christ.

———. 1999. *The New Evidence That Demands A Verdict: Christianity Beyond a Reasonable Doubt*. Nashville, TN: Thomas Nelson.

———. 2006. *Evidence for Christianity*. Nashville, TN: Thomas Nelson.

McGowan, A. T. B. 2007. *The Divine Spiration of Scripture: Challenging Evangelical Perspectives*. Nottingham: Apollos (= *The Divine Authenticity of Scripture: Retrieving an*

Evangelical Heritage. Nottingham: Apollos).

McKim, D. K. ed. 1983. *The Authoritative Word: Essays on the Nature of Scripture*. Grand Rapids, MI: Eerdmans.

Macquarrie, J. 1981. "Truth in Christology." In *God Incarnate: Story and Belief*, edited by A. E. Harvey. 24-33. London: SPCK.

Maier, G. 1974. *Das Ende der historisch-kritischen Methode*. Wuppertal: Rolf Brockhaus.

Malthus T. R. 1926. *An Essay on the Principle of Population*. London: Macmillan.

Mankowski, P. V. 2000. *Akkadian Loanwords in Biblical Hebrew*. Winona Lake, IN: Eisenbrauns.

Mann, C.S. 1986. *Mark*. Anchor Bible Commentaries. Vol. 27. Garden City, NY: Doubleday.

Maoz, B. 2003. *Judaism Is Not Jewish: A Friendly Critique of the Messianic Movement*. Fearn: Mentor.

Marenbon, J. 1997. *The Philosophy of Peter Abelard*. Cambridge: Cambridge University Press.

Maris, J. W. 1998. *Geloof en schriftgezag*. Apeldoornse Studies 36. Apeldoorn: Theologische Universiteit.

Marsden, G. M. 1980. *Fundamentalism and American Culture: The Shaping of Twentieth-Century Evangelicalism, 1870–1925*. New York: Oxford University Press.

Marshall, I. H. 1977. *I Believe in the Historical Jesus*. London: Hodder and Stoughton.

Martineau, J. 1889. *A Study of Religion: Its Sources and Contents*. Oxford: Clarendon Press.

Marxsen, W. 1968. *Introduction to the New Testament: An Approach to Its Problems*. Translated by G. Buswell. Philadelphia: Fortress Press.

———. 1969. *Mark the Evangelist: Studies on the Redaction History of the Gospel*. Translated by J. Boyce et al. Nashville: The Abingdon Press.

Marzano, R. J. 1993/1994. "When Two Worldviews Collide." *Educational Leadership* 51.4 (Dec. 1993/Jan. 1994): 6–11.

Medema, H. P. 1991. *De nieuwe mens: Bijbelstudies bij de Brief van Paulus aan de Efeziërs.* Vaassen: H. Medema.

Meier, J. P. 1991. *A Marginal Jew: Rethinking the Historical Jesus.* Vol. 1: *The Roots of the Problem and the Person.* New York: Doubleday.

Mekkes, J. P. A. 1961. *Scheppingsopenbaring en wijsbegeerte.* Kampen: Kok.

Mendenhall, G. E. 2001. *Ancient Israel's Faith and History: An Introduction to the Bible in Context.* Louisville, KY: Westminster John Knox Press.

Mesoudi, A. 2011. *Cultural Evolution: How Darwinian Theory Can Explain Human Culture and Synthesize the Social Sciences.* Chicago: Chicago University Press.

Metzger, B. M. 1987. *The Canon of the New Testament: Its Origin, Development and Significance.* Oxford: Clarendon Press.

_____. 2005 (rev. ed.). *A Textual Commentary on the Greek New Testament.* Peabody, MA: Hendrickson Publishers.

Meyer, B. F. 1979. *The Aims of Jesus.* London: SCM.

Millard, A. R. and D. J. Wiseman, eds. 1980. *Essays on the Patriarchal Narratives.* Leicester: IVP.

_____, J. K. Hoffmeier, and D. W. Baker, eds. 1994. *Faith, Tradition and History: Old Testament Historiography in Its Near Eastern Context.* Winona Lake, IN: Eisenbrauns.

Miskotte, K. H. 1966. *Sensus Spiritualis.* Nijkerk: Callenbach.

Möller, W. 2010. *Historisch-kritische Bedenken gegen die Graf-Wellhausensche Hypothese von einem früheren Anhänger.* Charleston, SC: Nabu Press.

Moltmann, J. 1967. *Theology of Hope: On the Ground and the Implications of a Christian Eschatology.* New York: Harper and Row.

Montgomery, J. W. ed. 1973. *Crisis in Lutheran Theology.*

Minneapolis, MN: Bethany Fellowship.

Montsma, J. A. 1985. *De exterritoriale openbaring: De Openbaringsopvatting achter de fundamentalistische Schriftbeschouwing.* Amsterdam: Rodopi.

Moo, D. J. 1996a. *The Epistle to the Romans.* NICNT. Grand Rapids, MI: Eerdmans.

———. 1996b. *2 Peter and Jude.* NIVAC. Grand Rapids, MI: Zondervan.

Morris, H. M. 1966. *Studies in the Bible and Science.* Nutley, NJ.: Presbyterian and Reformed Publ. Co.

———. 1968. *The Bible and Modern Science.* Chicago: Moody Press.

———. 1984. *The Biblical Basis for Modern Science.* Grand Rapids, MI: Baker Book House.

Morris, L. 1971. *The Gospel According to John.* NICNT. Grand Rapids, MI: Eerdmans.

Morrison, J. D. 2006. *Has God Said? Scripture, the Word of God, and the Crisis of Theological Authority.* Eugene, OR: Pickwick Publications.

Mounce, W. D. 2000. *Pastoral Epistles.* WBC. Nashville: Thomas Nelson.

Muis, J. 1989. *Openbaring en interpretatie: Het verstaan van de Heilige Schrift volgens K. Barth en K. H. Miskotte.* 's-Gravenhage: Boekencentrum.

Murphy, N. 1996. *Beyond Liberalism and Fundamentalism: How Modern and Postmodern Philosophy Set the Theological Agenda.* Valley Forge, PA: Trinity Press International.

Murray, J. 1968. *The Epistle to the Romans.* NICNT. Grand Rapids, MI: Eerdmans.

Nellen, H. J. M. 2007. *Hugo de Groot: Een leven in strijd om de vrede 1583–1645.* Amsterdam: Balans.

Nestle, E. and E., B. and K. Aland, eds. 1984. *Novum Testamentum Graece.* 27th ed. Stuttgart: Deutsche Bibelgesellschaft.

Nicholl, C. R. 2004. *From Hope to Despair in Thessalonica*. Cambridge: Cambridge University Press.

Nicholson, E. W. 2003. *The Pentateuch in the Twentieth Century: The Legacy of Julius Wellhausen*. Oxford: Oxford University Press.

Nicole, R. 1984a. "The Neo-Orthodox Reduction." In *Challenges to Inerrancy: A Theological Response*, edited by Lewis, G. and B. Demarest. 121-44. Chicago: Moody Press.

———. 1984b. "The Old Testament Quotations in the New Testament with Reference to the Doctrine of Plenary Inspiration." In *Evangelicals and Inerrancy: Selections from the* Journal of the Evangelical Theological Society. 1-12. Nashville, TN: Thomas Nelson.

———, and J. R. Michaels, eds. 1980. *Inerrancy and Common Sense*. Grand Rapids, MI: Baker Book House.

Noordtzij, A. 1924. *Gods Woord en der eeuwen getuigenis*. Kampen: Kok.

Noth, M. 1960. *The History of Israel*. Translated by P. R. Ackroyd. 2nd ed. London: A. and C. Black.

Nullens, P. ed. 1997. *Dicht bij de bijbel: Feestbundel ter gelegenheid van het 75-jarig jubileum van het Bijbelinstituut België 1929-1997*. Heverlee/Leuven: Bijbelinstituut België.

Oberman, H. A. 1992. *Luther: Man Between God and the Devil*. New York: Image.

Ockham, William. 1983. *Predestination, God's Foreknowledge, and Future Contingents*. Translated by M. M. Adams and N. Kretzmann. 2nd ed. Indianapolis, IN: Hackett.

Okholm, D. L. and T. R. Phillips, eds. 1995. *Four Views on Salvation in a Pluralistic World*. Grand Rapids, MI: Zondervan.

Olthuis, J. H. 1976. *The Word of God and Biblical Authority*. Potchefstroom: Pu vir CHO.

Orchard, B. and T. R. W. Longstaff, eds. 1978. *J. J. Griesbach: Synoptic and Text-Critical Studies 1776-1976*. Cambridge: Cambridge University Press.

Orr, J. 1906. *The Problem of the Old Testament: Considered with Reference to Recent Criticism*. New York: Scribner.

Osborne, G. 1999. Higher Criticism and the Evangelical. *Journal of the Evangelical Society* 42.2:193-210.

Ott, H. 1972. *Die Antwort des Glaubens: Systematische Theologie in 50 Artikeln*. Stuttgart: Kreuz Verlag.

Ouweneel, W. J. 1973. *Het Hooglied van Salomo*. Winschoten: Uit het Woord der Waarheid.

———. 1976. *De ark in de branding*. Amsterdam: Buijten and Schipperheijn.

———. 1978. *Jeugd in een stervende eeuw*. 2nd ed. Amsterdam: Buijten and Schipperheijn.

———. 1980. *Die Herrlichkeit des Herrn Jesus in den vier Evangelien*. Neustadt: Ernst Paulus Verlag.

———. 1982. *Wij zien Jezus: Bijbelstudies over de brief aan de Hebreeën*. 2 vols. Vaassen: H. Medema.

———. 1984. *Psychologie: Een christelijke kijk op het mentale leven*. Amsterdam: Buijten and Schipperheijn.

———. 1986. *De leer van de mens: Proeve van een christelijk-wijsgerige antropologie*. Amsterdam: Buijten and Schipperheijn.

———. 1987a. *Woord en wetenschap: Wetenschapsbeoefening aan de Evangelische Hogeschool*. Amsterdam: Buijten and Schipperheijn.

———. 1987b. "Inerrantisme en zijn wijsgerige achtergronden." In *Het gezag van de Bijbel: Verkenningen in de hermeneutiek*, edited by A. G. Knevel et al. 66-74. Kampen: Kok/Hilversum: Evangelische Omroep.

———. 1988/1990. *De Openbaring van Jezus Christus: Bijbelstudies over het Boek Openbaring*. 2 vols. Vaassen: H. Medema.

———. 1994. *Godsverlichting: De evocatie van de verduisterde God: Een weg tot spiritualiteit en gemeenteopbouw*. Amsterdam: Buijten and Schipperheijn.

———. 1995. *Christian Doctrine:* I. *The External Prolegomena*, Amsterdam: Buijten and Schipperheijn.

———. 1997a. *De vrijheid van de Geest: Bijbelstudies bij de Brief van Paulus aan de Galaten*. Vaassen: Medema.

———. 1997b. "Is de Bijbel het Woord van God?" In *Dicht bij de bijbel: Feestbundel ter gelegenheid van het 75-jarig jubileum van het Bijbelinstituut België 1929–1997*, edited by P. Nullens. 13–27. Heverlee/Leuven: Bijbelinstituut België.

———. 1998. *De zevende koningin: Het eeuwig vrouwelijke en de raad van God* (Metahistorische trilogie 2). Heerenveen: Barnabas.

———. 2000a. *De zesde kanteling: Christus en 5000 jaar denkgeschiedenis: Religie en metafysica in het jaar 2000* (Metahistorische trilogie 3). Heerenveen: Barnabas.

———. 2000b. *Het Jobslijden van Israël: Israëls lijden oplichtend uit het boek Job*, Vaassen: Medema.

———. 2004. *Geneest de zieken! Over de bijbelse leer van ziekte, genezing en bevrijding*. 4th ed. Vaassen: Medema.

———. 2007. *De Christus van God: Ontwerp van een christologie*. EDR 2. Vaassen: Medema.

———. 2008. *De schepping van God: Ontwerp van een scheppings-, mens- en zondeleer*. EDR 3. Vaassen: Medema.

———. 2010a. *De kerk van God I: Ontwerp van een elementaire ecclesiologie*. EDR 7. Heerenveen: Medema.

———. 2010b. *De kerk van God II: Ontwerp van een historische en praktische ecclesiologie*. EDR 8. Heerenveen: Medema.

———. 2010c. *Komt er een Grote Opwekking?* Harderwijk: Rock Publ./Bread of Life.

———. 2010d. *Vijf olifanten in een porseleinkast: Vijf brandende onderwerpen waarover christenen verdeeld zijn*. Heerenveen: Medema.

———. 2011a. *Het verbond en het koninkrijk van God: Ontwerp van een foederologie en basileologie.* Heerenveen: Medema.

———. 2011b. *Du bist ungerecht: Hiob.* Lychen: Daniel-Verlag.

———. 2012. *De toekomst van God: Ontwerp van een eschatologie.* EDR 10. Heerenveen: Medema.

———. 2013. *De glorie van God: Ontwerp van een godsleer en van een theologische vakfilosofie.* EDR 12. Heerenveen: Medema.

———. 2014. *Wisdom for Thinkers: An Introduction to Christian Philosophy.* St. Catharines, ON: Paideia Press.

———. 2015. *What Then Is Theology?: An Introduction to Christian Theology.* St. Catharines, ON: Paideia Press.

———. 2016. *Searching the Soul: An Introduction to Christian Psychology.* St. Catharines, ON: Paideia Press.

———. 2017. *The World Is Christ's: A Critique of Two Kingdoms Theology.* Toronto: Ezra Press.

———. 2018a (forthcoming). *An Evangelical Introduction to Reformational Theology. I/2: The Eternal Torah: Living Under God.* Toronto: Ezra Press.

———. 2018b (forthcoming). *An Evangelical Introduction to Reformational Theology. II/1: The Eternal God: God Revealing Himself to Us.* Toronto: Ezra Press.

———. 2018c (forthcoming). *An Evangelical Introduction to Reformational Theology. II/3: The Eternal Spirit: God Living In Us.* Toronto: Ezra Press.

———. 2018d (forthcoming). *An Evangelical Introduction to Reformational Theology. III/I: The Eternal Purpose: Living In Christ.* Toronto: Ezra Press.

———. 2018e (forthcoming). *An Evangelical Introduction to Reformational Theology. III/2: Eternal Righteousness: Living Before God.* Toronto: Ezra Press.

———. 2018f (forthcoming). *An Evangelical Introduction to Reformational Theology. III/3. Eternal Salvation: Christ Dying For Us.* Toronto: Ezra Press.

———. 2018g (forthcoming). *An Evangelical Introduction to Reformational Theology.* III/4: *Eternal Life: Christ Living in Us.* Toronto: Ezra Press.

———. 2018h (forthcoming). *An Evangelical Introduction to Reformational Theology.* IV/1: *The Eternal People: God in Relation To Israel.* Toronto: Ezra Press.

———. 2018i (forthcoming). *An Evangelical Introduction to Reformational Theology.* IV/2: *The Eternal Covenant: Living With God.* Toronto: Ezra Press.

———. 2018j (forthcoming). *An Evangelical Introduction to Reformational Theology.* IV/3: *The Eternal Kingdom: Living Under Christ.* Toronto: Ezra Press.

———. 2018k (forthcoming). *An Evangelical Introduction to Reformational Theology.* V/1: *Eternal Truth: The Prolegomena of Theology.* Toronto: Ezra Press.

———. 2018l (forthcoming). *Adam, Where Are You? – And Why This Matters: A Theological Evaluation of the New Evolutionist Hermeneutics.* Toronto: Ezra Press.

———. 2018m (forthcoming). *The Ninth King: The Last of the Celestial Empires: The Triumph of Christ over the Powers.* Toronto: Ezra Press.

———. n.d. *Het boek Esther.* Alblasserdam: Stg. Boeken bij de Bijbel.

Paas, S. 1998. *Schepping en oordeel: Een onderzoek naar scheppingsvoorstellingen bij enkele profeten uit de achtste eeuw voor Christus.* Heerenveen: Groen.

Pache, R. 1977. *Inspiratie en gezag van de Bijbel.* Amsterdam: Buijten and Schipperheijn.

Packer, J. I. 1958. *"Fundamentalism" and the Word of God.* Grand Rapids, MI: Eerdmans.

———. 1983. "Infallible Scripture and the Role of Hermeneutics." In *Scripture and Truth*, edited by D. A. Carson and J. D. Woodbridge. 325–56. Grand Rapids, MI: Zondervan.

———. 1984. "Exposition on Biblical Hermeneutics." In *Hermeneutics, Inerrancy, and the Bible*, edited by E. D. Radmacher and R. D. Preus. 905-14. Grand Rapids, MI: Zondervan.

Padgett, A. G. and P. R. Keifert, eds. 2006. *But Is It All True? The Bible and the Question of Truth*. Grand Rapids, MI: Eerdmans.

Pannenberg, W. 1968. *Revelation as History*. Translated by D. Granskou. New York: Macmillan.

———. 1970-1971. *Basic Questions in Theology: Collected Essays*. 2 vols. Philadelphia: Fortress Press.

———. 1976. *Theology and the Philosophy of Science*. Translated by F. McDonagh. Philadelphia: The Westminster Press.

———. 1991. *Systematic Theology*. Translated by G. W. Bromiley. Vol. 1. Grand Rapids: Eerdmans.

Parker, T. H. L. 1959. *Calvin's Doctrine of the Knowledge of God*. Grand Rapids, MI: Eerdmans.

Paul, M. J., G. van den Brink, and J. C. Bette, eds. 2004. *Bijbelcommentaar Genesis-Exodus*. SBOT 1. Veenendaal: Centrum voor Bijbelonderzoek.

Payne, J. B. 1979. "Higher Criticism and Biblical Inerrancy." In *Inerrancy*, edited by N. L. Geisler. 85-113. Grand Rapids, MI: Zondervan.

Peabody, D. B., L. Cope, and A. McNicol. 2002. *One Gospel From Two: Mark's Use of Matthew and Luke*. Philadelphia: Trinity Press International.

Pearce, E. K. V. 1974. "Evolution." In *The New International Dictionary of the Christian Church*, edited by J. D. Douglas. 363. Grand Rapids, MI: Zondervan.

Pedersen, J. and G. Cumberlege. 1947. *Israel: Its Life and Culture*. Vol. 1. London: Oxford University Press.

Peelen, G. J. 2016. *Spreken over Boven: H. Kuitert, een biografie*. Amsterdam: Vesuvius.

Pentecost, J. D. 1981. *The Words and Works of Jesus Christ: A*

Study of the Life of Christ. Grand Rapids, MI: Zondervan.

Percy, M. 1996. *Words, Wonders and Power: Understanding Contemporary Christian Fundamentalism and Revivalism.* London: SPCK.

Pererius, B. 1591-1599. *Commentariorum et disputationum in Genesim*, Vol. I-IV. Colonia Agrippina: Antonii Hierati.

Perlitt, L. 1965. *Vatke und Wellhausen.* Berlin: Töpelmann.

Perry, J. 2001. "Dissolving the Inerrancy Debate: How Modern Philosophy Shaped the Evangelical View of Scripture." *Journal for Christian Theological Research* 6.1. Available at: http://digitalcommons.luthersem.edu/jctr/vol6/iss2001/1.

Pesch, O. H. 1987. *Dogmatik im Fragment.* Mainz: Grünewald.

Pinnock, C. H. 1984. *The Scripture Principle.* San Francisco: Harper and Row.

Plantinga, A. 1980. *Does God have a nature?* Milwaukee: Marquette University Press.

Plato. 1986. *Theaetetus.* Translated by Seth Bernardette. Chicago: The University of Chicago Press.

Popper, K. 2002a. *The Logic of Scientific Discovery.* London: Routledge.

_____. 2002b. *Conjectures and Refutations.* London: Routledge and Kegan Paul.

Porter, S. E. 1995. "Pauline Authorship and the Pastoral Epistles: Implications for Canon." *Bulletin for Biblical Research* 5:105-123.

Potgieter, F. J. M. 1982. "Kontinuïteit tussen skepping en herskepping: 'n Reaksie op die Ope Brief." In *Perspektief op die Ope Brief*, edited by D. J. Bosch et al. 106-13. Kaapstad: Human and Rousseau.

_____. Potgieter, P. C. 1990. *Skrif, dogma en verkondiging.* Kaapstad: Lux Verbi.

Preus, R .D. 1984. "A Response to The Unity of the Bible." In *Hermeneutics, Inerrancy, and the Bible,* edited by E. D.

Radmacher and R. D. Preus. 669-90. Grand Rapids, MI: Zondervan.

Puchinger, G. 1970. *Een theologische discussie*. Kampen: Kok.

Puntel, L. B. 1988. "Das Verhältnis von Philosophie und Theologie: Versuch einer grundsätzlichen Klärung." In *Vernunft des Glaubens: Wissenschaftliche Theologie und kirchliche Lehre: Festschrift zum 60. Geburtstag von Wolfhart Pannenberg*, edited by J. Rohls and G. Wenz. 11-41. Göttingen: Vandenhoeck and Ruprecht.

Putnam, H. 1981. *Reason, Truth and History*. Cambridge: Cambridge University Press.

Quispel, G. 1979. *Het geheime boek der Openbaring*. Amerongen: Gaade.

Radmacher, E. D. and R. D. Preus, eds. 1984. *Hermeneutics, Inerrancy, and the Bible*. Grand Rapids, MI: Zondervan.

Rahner, K. 1966. *Theological Investigations*. Translated by K.-H. Kruger. Vol. 5. Baltimore, MD: Helicon Press.

_____. 1978. *Foundations of Christian Faith: An Introduction to the Idea of Christianity*. Translated by W. V. Dych. New York: Seabury Press.

Ramm, B. 1957. *The Pattern of Authority*. Grand Rapids, MI: Eerdmans.

_____. 1971. *Special Revelation and the Word of God*. 3rd ed. Grand Rapids, MI: Eerdmans.

_____. 1983. *After Fundamentalism: The Future of Evangelical Theology*. San Francisco: Harper and Row.

Ratzinger, J. 2007. *Jesus of Nazareth*. Part 1: *From the Baptism in the Jordan to the Transfiguration*. Translated by A. J. Walker. New York: Doubleday.

_____. 2011. *Jesus of Nazareth*. Part 2: *Holy Week. From the Entrance into Jerusalem to the Resurrection*. San Francisco: Ignatius Press.

Die Reformatoriese Sola Scriptura en die Skrifberoep in etiese vrae. 1980. Kaapstad: N.G. Kerk-Uitgewers (namens die

Kommissie van Leer- en Aktuele Sake, Wes-Kaapland).

Reitzenstein, R. 1921. *Die hellenistischen Mysterienreligionen nach ihren Grundgedanken und Wirkungen.* Berlin: Teubner.

Rendsburg, G. A. 1986. *The Redaction of Genesis.* Winona Lake, IN: Eisenbrauns.

Rendtorff, R. 1977. *Das überlieferungsgeschichtliche Problem des Pentateuch.* Berlin: W. de Gruyter.

———. 1993. "The Paradigm Is Changing: Hopes – and Fears." *Biblical Interpretation* 1.1:34–53.

Reuss, E. 1881. *Geschichte der Heiligen Schriften Alten Testaments.* Braunschweig: Schwetschke.

Ridderbos, H. N. 1960. *Aan de Kolossenzen.* CNT. Kampen: Kok.

———. 1967. *De pastorale brieven.* CNT. Kampen: Kok.

———. 1975. *Paul: An Outline of His Theology.* Translated by J. R. DeWitt. Grand Rapids, MI: Eerdmans.

———. 1988. *Redemptive History and the New Testament Scriptures.* Translated by R. B. Gaffin. Phillipsburg, NJ: Presbyterian and Reformed Publishing Company.

Ridderbos, J. 1926. *Gereformeerde Schriftbeschouwing en organische opvatting.* Amsterdam: Vrije Universiteit.

Riehm, E. 1854. *Die Gesetzgebung Moses im Lande Moab: Ein Beitrag Zur Einleitung In's Alte Testament.* Gotha: Perthes.

Ringeling, H. 1968. *Theologie und Sexualität: Das private Verhalten als Thema der Sozialethik.* Gütersloh: Gerd Mohn.

Ritchie, D. G. 2015. *Darwin and Hegel, With Other Philosophical Studies.* n.p.: Palala Press.

Ritschl, O. 1908–1927. *Dogmengeschichte des Protestantismus.* 4 vols. Leipzig: Hinrichs.

Robinson, J. A. T. 1959. *Jesus and His Coming: The Emergence of a Doctrine.* London: SCM Press.

———. 1976. *Redating the New Testament.* London: SCM Press.

Robinson, J. M. 1959. *A New Quest of the Historical Jesus.* London: SCM.

Roessingh, K. H. 1914-1929. *De moderne theologie in Nederland.* Vol. 1 (1914), 2 (1926), 3-4 (1927), 5 (1929). Arnhem: Van Loghum Slaterus.

Rofe, A. 1999. *Introduction to the Composition of the Pentateuch.* Sheffield: Sheffield Academic Press, 1999.

Rogers, Jr., C. and C. Rogers III. 1998. *The New Linguistic and Exegetical Key to the Greek New Testament.* Grand Rapids, MI: Zondervan.

Rogers, J. ed. 1977. *Biblical Authority.* Waco, TX: Word.

_____, and D. McKim. 1979. *The Authority and Inspiration of the Bible: An Historical Approach.* New York: Harper and Row.

Rorty, R. 1989. *Contingency, Irony and Solidarity.* Cambridge: Cambridge University Press.

Rosell, G. M. 2008. *The Surprising Work of God: Harold John Ockenga, Billy Graham, and the Rebirth of Evangelicalism.* Grand Rapids, MI: Baker Academic.

Rosenberg, A. J. 1984. *The Book of Ruth.* The Soncino Books of the Bible. London: Soncino.

Rossouw, H. W. 1963. *Klaarheid en interpretasie.* Amsterdam: Jacob van Kampen.

Rupprecht, E. 1898. *Wissenschaftliches Handbuch der Einleitung in das Alte Testament.* Gütersloh: Bertelsmann.

Ruthven, M. 2005. *Fundamentalism: The Search for Meaning.* Oxford: Oxford University Press.

Ryle, H. E. 1892. *The Canon of the Old Testament.* London: Macmillan.

Sabatier, A. 1916. *Outlines of a Philosophy of Religion.* New York: James Pott.

Saebø, M. ed. 2008. *Hebrew Bible/Old Testament: The History of Its Interpretation.* Vol. 2: *From the Renaissance to the Enlightenment.* Göttingen: Vandenhoeck and Ruprecht.

Sailhamer, J. H. 1990. *Genesis.* EBC 2. Grand Rapids, MI: Zondervan.

Sandeen, E. R. 1970. *The Roots of Fundamentalism: British and American Millenarianism 1800–1930.* Grand Rapids, MI: Baker Book House.

Sankey, H. 2004. "Scientific Realism and the God's Eye Point of View." *Epistemologia* 27(2):211–26.

Saucy, R. 2001. *Scripture: Its Power, Authority, and Relevance.* Nashville, TN: Word Publishing.

Sayce, A. H. 1894. *Higher Criticism and the Verdict of the Monuments.* London: SPCK.

Schaaffs, W. 1967. *Christus und die physikalische Forschung.* Berghausen/Baden: Evangelisationsverlag.

Schaeffer, F. A. 1982. *The Complete Works.* 5 vols. Westchester, IL: Crossway Books.

Schaff, P. and H. Wace, eds. 1976. *A Select Library of Nicene and Post-Nicene Fathers of the Christian Church.* Vol. 1. Grand Rapids, MI: Eerdmans.

Schenker, A. et al. *Biblia Hebraica Quinta.* 2004–2020. Stuttgart: Deutsche Bibelgesellschaft.

Schilder, K. 1936–1949. *Dictaat christelijke religie.* 3 vols. Mimeographed.

Schillebeeckx, E. 1989. "Elke theologie heeft haar eigen filosofie." In *Geloof dat te denken geeft: Opstellen aangeboden aan Prof. dr. H. M. Kuitert,* edited by K. U. Gäbler et al. 221–34. Baarn: Ten Have.

Schirrmacher, T. 2001. *Irrtumslosigkeit der Schrift oder Hermeneutik der Demut? Ein Gespräch unter solchen, die mit Ernst Bibeltreue sein wollen.* Nürnberg: VTR.

Schleiermacher, F. D. E. 1928. *The Christian Faith.* Translated by H. R. Macintosh et al. Edinburgh: T. and T. Clark.

———. 1998. *Hermeneutics and Criticism and Other Writings.* Translated by A. Bowie. Cambridge: Cambridge University Press.

Schmidt, K. L. 1964. *Der Rahmen der Geschichte Jesu: Literaturkritische Untersuchungen zur ältesten Jesusüberlieferung*. Darmstadt: Wissenschaftliche Buchgesellschaft.

Schökel, L. A. 1965. *The Inspired Word: Scripture in the Light of Language and Literature*. New York: Herder and Herder.

Schreiner, Thomas R. 2003. *1, 2 Peter, Jude*. New American Commentary. Nashville, TN: Broadman and Holman.

Schulte, H. 1949. *Der Begriff der Offenbarung im Neuen Testament*. München: Chr. Kaiser.

Schweitzer, A. 1966. *Geschichte der Leben-Jesu-Forschung*. München: Siebenstern.

Searle, J. T. "Literal Meaning." *Erkenntnis* 13:207–24.

Seeberg, R. 1920. *Lehrbuch der Dogmengeschichte*. 2 vols. Leipzig: Deichert.

Segal, M. H. 1967. *The Pentateuch: Its Composition and Authorship and Other Biblical Studies*. Jerusalem: Magnes Press.

Seiss, A. H. 1972. *The Gospel in the Stars*. Grand Rapids, MI: Kregel.

Semler, J. S. 1980. *Abhandlung von freier Untersuchung des Canon*. 2nd ed. 4 vols. Gütersloh: Gerd Mohn.

Shelley, B. L. 1974. "Fundamentalism." In *The New International Dictionary of the Christian Church*, edited by J. D. Douglas. 396–97. Grand Rapids, MI: Zondervan.

Sikkel, J. C. 1906. *De Heilige Schrift en haar verklaring*. Amsterdam: Van Schaik.

Silva, M. 1983. "The New Testament Use of the Old Testament: Text Form and Authority." In *Scripture and Truth*, edited by D. A. Carson and J. D. Woodbridge. 147–65. Grand Rapids, MI: Zondervan.

Slotki, I. W. 1983. *Isaiah*, edited by J. Roseberg. The Soncino Books of the Bible. London: Soncino.

Smit, J. H. 1980. "Skeppingsopenbaring en wetenskap."

Tydskrif vir Christelike Wetenskap 16:174–200.

Smith, H. 1987. *The Gospel of Mark*. Wooler: Central Bible Hammond Trust.

Smith, W. R. 2009. *The Book of Moses, or, The Pentateuch in Its Authorship, Credibility and Civilisation*. Suwanee, GA: General Books LLC.

Snyman, G. 1992. "Kenteoretiese besinning oor teologiebeoefening aan die Teologiese Skool van Potchefstroom die afgelope twintig jaar." *In die Skriflig* 26:247–66.

Sparks, K. L. 2008. *God's Word in Human Words*. Grand Rapids, MI: Baker Books.

Sproul, R. C. 2005. *Scripture Alone: The Evangelical Doctrine*. Phillipsburg, PA: Presbyterian and Reformed Publishing Co.

Spykman, G. J. 1985. *Spectacles: Biblical Perspectives on Christian Scholarship*. Potchefstroom: PU vir CHO.

———. 1988. "Christian Philosophy as Prolegomena to Reformed Dogmatics." In *'n Woord op sy tyd: 'n Teologiese feesbundel aangebied aan Professor Johan Heyns ter herdenking van sy sestigste verjaarsdag*, edited by C. J. Wethman and C. J. A. Vos. 137–55. Pretoria: NG Kerkboekhandel.

———. 1992. *Reformational Theology: A New Paradigm for Doing Dogmatics*. Grand Rapids, MI: Eerdmans.

Stadelmann, H., ed. 2002. *Liebe zum Wort: Das Bekenntnis zur Biblischen Irrtumslosigkeit als Ausdruck eines bibeltreuen Schriftverständnisses*. Nürnberg: VTR.

Stafleu, M. D. 1987. *Theories At Work: On the Structure and Functioning of Theories in Science, in Particular During the Copernican Revolution*. Lanham, MD: University Press of America.

Steen, P. J. 1983. *The Structure of Herman Dooyeweerd's Thought*. Toronto: Wedge Publ. Found.

Stein, R. H. 1996. *Jesus the Messiah: A Survey of the Life of Christ*. Downers Grove, IL: InterVarsity Press.

Stellingwerff, J. 1992. *D. H. Th. Vollenhoven (1892-1978): Reformator der wijsbegeerte*. Baarn: Ten Have.

Stern, D. 1992. *Jewish New Testament Commentary*. Clarksville, MD: Jewish New Testament Publications.

Stoffels, H. 1995. *Als een briesende leeuw: Orthodox-protestanten in de slag met de tijdgeest*. Kampen: Kok.

Strack, H. L. and P. Billerbeck. 1924. *Kommentar zum Neuen Testament aus Talmud und Midrasch*. Vol. 2: *Das Evangelium nach Markus, Lukas und Johannes und Die Apostelgeschichte*. München: C. H. Becksche Verlagsbuchhandlung Oskar Beck.

Strauss, D. F. M. 1971. *Wetenskap en werklikheid: Oriëntering in die algemene wetenskapsleer*. Bloemfontein: Sacum Beperk.

———. 1973. *Begrip en idee*. Assen: Van Gorcum and Co.

———. 1977. "God, wet en kosmos in die Skrifmatige ontologie van B. J. van der Walt." *Tydskrif vir Christelike Wetenskap* 13:31-36.

———. 1978. "Woord en Wet – toegespits op die problematiek van Biblisisme en ontmitologisering." *Tydskrif vir Christelike Wetenskap* 14:95-111.

———. 1979. "Die teoretiese blootlegging van Skeppingsbeginsels." *Tydskrif vir Christelike Wetenskap* 15:254-64.

———. 1983. "The Nature of Philosophy." *Tydskrif vir Christelike Wetenskap* 19:40-55.

———. 1984. "Die gedifferensieerdheid van die Woord van God." *Tydskrif vir Christelike Wetenskap* 20.3/4:115-28.

———. 1988. "Begripsvorming in die sistematiese teologie." *Tydskrif vir Christelike Wetenskap* 24:124-61.

———. 1991. *Man and his World*. Bloemfontein: Tekskor.

———. 2009. *Philosophy: Discipline of the Disciplines*. Grand Rapids, MI: Paideia Press.

———, and P. J. Visagie. 1984. "Die verhouding tussen nie-teologiese wetenskappe en die teologie." *Tydskrif vir Christelike Wetenskap* 20.3/4:51–79.

Strauss, S. A. 1982. *"Alles of niks": K. Schilder oor die verbond.* Pretoria: Patmos.

Strauss, D. F. 1973a. *The Life of Jesus Critically Examined.* Philadelphia, PA: Fortress.

———. 1973b. *Die christliche Glaubenslehre.* 2 vols. Darmstadt: Wissenschaftliche Buchgesellschaft.

———. 1862. *H. S. Reimarus und seine Schutzschrift für die vernünftigen Verehrer Gottes.* Lepizig: Brockhaus.

———. 1872. *Der alte und der neue Glaube: Ein Bekenntnis.* Leipzig: S. Hirzel.

Sungenis, R. A. and R. J. Bennett. 2009. *Galileo Was Wrong: The Church Was Right.* 2 vols. Port Orange, FL: CAI Publishing.

Swinburne, R. 2005. *Faith and Reason.* 2nd ed. Oxford: Clarendon Press.

Tasker, R. V. G. 1961. *The Gospel According to St. Matthew.* Tyndale New Testament Commentary. Grand Rapids, MI: Eerdmans.

Taylor, R. S. 1980. *Biblical Authority and the Christian Faith.* Kansas City: Beacon Hill Press.

Telder, B. 1960. *Sterven . . . en dan?* Kampen: Kok.

Tenney, M. C. 1984. "The Legitimate Limits of Biblical Criticism." In *Evangelicals and Inerrancy: Selections from the Journal of the Evangelical Theological Society*, edited by R. F. Youngblood. 30–34. Nashville, TN: Thomas Nelson.

Theissen, G. and A. Merz. 1998. *The Historical Jesus: A Comprehensive Guide.* Minneapolis, MN: Fortress.

Theron, P. F. 1978. *Die ekklesia as kosmies-eskatologiese teken.* Pretoria: NG Kerkboekhandel.

Thiadens, A. J. H. 1969. "De stamboekmens die niet sterven mag." *Eurosboekje* 1969/1. Amersfoort: Werkgroep 2000.

Thielicke, H. 1977. *The Evangelical Faith.* Translated and edited by G. W. Bromiley. Vol. 2: *The Doctrine of God and of Christ.* Grand Rapids, MI: Eerdmans.

Thiselton, A. C. 2000. *The First Epistle to the Corinthians.* NIGTC. Grand Rapids, MI: Eerdmans.

———. 2008-2009. *Hermeneutics: An Introduction.* Grand Rapids, MI: Eerdmans.

Thompson, T. L. 1992. *Early History of the Israelite People from the Written and Archaeological Sources.* Leiden: Brill.

———. 1999. *The Bible in History: How Writers Create a Past.* London: Cape (= *The Mythic Past.* Mew York: Basic Books).

Tillich, P. 1968. *Systematic Theology.* Digswell Place: Nisbett and Co.

Tol, A. and K. A. Bril, eds. 1992. *Vollenhoven als wijsgeer: Inleidingen en teksten.* Amsterdam: Buijten and Schipperheijn.

Torrey, R. A. et al., eds. 2003. *The Fundamentals: A Testimony to the Truth,* 2 vols. Grand Rapids, MI: Baker Books.

Towner, P. H. 2006. *The Letters to Timothy and Titus.* NICNT. Grand Rapids, MI: Eerdmans.

Trench, R. C. 1976. *Synonyms of the New Testament.* Grand Rapids, MI: Eerdmans.

Trillhaas, W. 1972. *Dogmatik.* 3rd ed. Berlin: W. de Gruyter.

Trimp, C. 1992. "Heilige Geest en Heilige Schrift." In *Hoe staan wij er voor?*, edited by J. Kamphuis et al. Barneveld: Vuurbaak.

———, ed. 2002. *Woord op schrift: Theologische reflecties over het gezag van de Bijbel.* Kampen: Kok.

Troost, A. 1958. *Casuïstiek en situatie-ethiek: Een methodologische verkenning.* Utrecht: Libertas.

———. 1969. "De openbaring Gods en de maatschappelijke orde." *Philosophia Reformata* 34:1-37.

———. 1972. "Christian Alternatives for Traditional Ethics."

Philosophia Reformata 38:167-177.

———. 1976. *Geen aardse macht begeren wij*. Amsterdam: Buijten and Schipperheijn.

———. 1977. "Theologie of filosofie? Een antwoord op "Kritische aantekeningen bij de wijsbegeerte der wetsidee" van Prof. Dr. J. Douma." *Philosophia Reformata* 42 (1977):115-94 (also published as a separate book. Kampen: Kok).

———. 1978. "De relatie tussen scheppingsopenbaring en woordopenbaring." *Philosophia Reformata* 43:101-29.

———. 1983. "Theologische misverstanden inzake een reformatorische wijsbegeerte." *Philosophia Reformata* 47:1-19, 179-92; 48: 19-49.

———. 1985/87. "De vraag naar de zin." *Philosophia Reformata* 50:98-118; 52: 41-65.

———. 1992a. "Normativiteit: Oorsprong en ondergang van het denken over scheppingsordeningen." *Philosophia Reformata* 57:3-38.

———. 1992b. "De tweeërlei aard van de wet." *Philosophia Reformata* 57:117-31.

———. 2004. *Vakfilosofie van de geloofswetenschap: Prolegomena van de theologie*. Budel: Damon.

———. 2005. *Antropocentrische totaliteitswetenschap: Inleiding in de reformatorische wijsbegeerte*. Budel: Damon.

Unger, M. F. 1954. *Archaeology and the Old Testament*. Grand Rapids, MI: Zondervan.

Ursell, M. "Inspiration." In *The Princeton Encyclopedia of Poetry and Poetics*. Fourth ed. Edited by R. Green et al. 709-710. Princeton: Princeton University Press.

Van Buren, P. M. 1963. *The Secular Meaning of the Gospel Based on an Analysis of its Language*. London: SCM Press.

Van Bekkum, K. 2011. *From Conquest to Coexistence: Ideology and Antiquarian Intent in the Historiography of Israel's Settlement in Canaan*. Leiden: Brill.

———, and G. Harinck, eds. 2010. *Botsen over het begin*. Barneveld: Nederlands Dagblad.

———, W. Houtman, R. Van Wiskerke, et al., eds. 2003. *Gods Woord in mensentaal: Denken over het gezag van de Bijbel*. Barneveld: Nederlands Dagblad.

Van Bruggen, J. 1986. *Wie maakte de Bijbel? Over afsluiting en gezag van het Oude en Nieuwe Testament*. Kampen: Kok.

———. 1998. *Christ on Earth: The Gospel Narratives as History*. Translated by N. Forest-Flier. Grand Rapids, MI: Baker Books.

Van de Beek, A. 1998. *Jezus Kurios: De Christologie als hart van de theologie*. Kampen: Kok.

———. 2002. *De kring om de Messias: Israël als volk van de lijdende Heer*. Zoetermeer: Meinema.

———. 2006. *Van Kant tot Kuitert: De belangrijkste theologen uit de 19^e en 20^e eeuw*. Kampen: Kok.

Van den Brink, G. 1999. *Op betrouwbare grond: Over ontstaan en gezag van het Nieuwe Testament*. Heerenveen: Barnabas.

———, H. G. Geertsema, and J. Hoogland, eds. 1997. *Filosofie en theologie: Een gesprek tussen christen-filosofen en theologen*. Amsterdam: Buijten and Schipperheijn.

Van der Kamp, W. 1985. *Houvast aan het hemelruim*. Kampen: Kok.

Vander Stelt, J. C. 1978. *Philosophy and Scripture: A Study in Old Princeton and Westminster Theology*. Marlton, N.J.: Mack Publ. Co.

Van der Toorn, K. 2007. *Scribal Culture and the Making of the Hebrew Bible*. Cambridge, MA: Harvard University Press.

Van Dunné, J. M., P. Boelen, and A. J. Heerma van Voss, eds. 1976. *Acht civilisten in burger*. Zwolle: W. E. J. Tjeenk Willink.

Van Eikema Hommes, H. J. 1982. *Inleiding tot de wijsbegeerte van Herman Dooyeweerd*. 's-Gravenhage: M. Nijhoff.

Van Gemeren, W. A. 1991. *Psalms*. EBC 5. Grand Rapids, MI:

Zondervan.

———, ed. 1996. *The New International Dictionary of Old Testament Theology and Exegesis*. 4 vols. Carlisle: Paternoster.

Van Genderen, J. and W. H. Velema. 2008. *Concise Reformed Dogmatics*. Translated by G. Bilkes and E. M. van der Maas. Phillipsburg, NJ: Presbyterian and Reformed Publishing Company.

Vanhoozer, K. J. 1986. "The Semantics of Biblical Literature." In *Hermeneutics, Authority, and Canon*, edited by D. A. Carson and J. D. Woodbridge. 53–104. Grand Rapids, MI: Academie Books.

———. 1998. *Is There a Meaning in This Text?* Grand Rapids, MI: Zondervan.

———. 2002. *First Theology: God, Scripture and Hermeneutics*. Downers Grove, IL: InterVarsity Press.

Van Houwelingen, P. H. R. 1988. *De tweede trompet! De authenticiteit van de tweede brief van Petrus*. Kampen: Kok.

Van Keulen, D. 2003. *Bijbel en dogmatiek: Schriftbeschouwing en schriftgebruik in het dogmatisch werk van A. Kuyper, H. Bavinck en G. C. Berkouwer*. Kampen: Kok.

Van Kooten, G. H. 2001. *The Pauline Debate on the Cosmos: Graeco-Roman Cosmology and Jewish Eschatology in Paul and the Pseudo-Pauline Letters to the Colossians and the Ephesians*. Leiden: Brill.

———. 2002. *Paulus en de kosmos: Het vroege christendom te midden van de andere Grieks-Romeinse filosofieën*. Zoetermeer: Boekencentrum.

Van Leeuwen, J. A. C. 1928. *Het evangelie naar de beschrijving van Markus*. KV. Kampen: Kok.

Van Niftrik, G. C. 1961. *Kleine dogmatiek*. 5th ed. Nijkerk: Callenbach.

Van Riessen, H. 1980. *Wijsbegeerte*. Kampen: Kok.

Van Segbroeck, F. 2004. *Het Nieuwe Testament leren lezen*. Leuven: Acco.

Van Til, C. 1946. "Nature and Scripture." In *The Infallible Word*, edited by N. B. Stonehouse and P. Woolley. 255-93. Grand Rapids, MI: Eerdmans.

_____. 1955. *The Defense of the Faith*. Philadelphia: Presbyterian and Reformed Publishing Company.

Van Woudenberg, R. 2004. *Gelovend denken: Inleiding tot een christelijke filosofie*. 2nd ed. Amsterdam: Buijten and Schipperheijn.

Van Zyl, H. C. 1991. "Die Nuwe-Testamentiese wetenskap — 'n Perspektief." *Tydskrif vir Christelike Wetenskap* 27(3e kw.):27-49.

Vatke, J. K. W. 1835. *Die biblische Theologie wissenschaftlich dargestellt*. Vol. 1. Berlin: G. Bethge.

Vawter, B. 1972. *Biblical Inspiration*. Philadelphia: Westminster Press.

Velema, J. H. 1997. *Fundament*alist? *Fundament*eel! *Spiegel en stimulans voor de gereformeerde gezindte*. Heerenveen: J. J. Groen and Zoon.

Venter, J. L. 1989. "Die verhouding tussen kateder en kansel: Die implikasies wat dit vir die teologie en die prediking inhou." In *Gees en Woord*, edited by J. C. Coetzee. 163-78. Pretoria: NG Kerkboekhandel.

Verburg, M. E. 1989. *Herman Dooyeweerd: Leven en werk van een Nederlands christen-wijsgeer*. Baarn: Ten Have.

Verkuyl, J. 1992. *De kern van het christelijk geloof*. Kampen: Kok.

Vollenhoven, D. H. Th. 1933. *Het Calvinisme en de reformatie van de wijsbegeerte*. Amsterdam: Paris.

_____. 1950. *Geschiedenis der wijsbegeerte*. Vol. 1: *Inleiding en geschiedenis der Grieksche wijsbegeerte vóór Platoon en Aristoteles*. Franeker: T. Wever.

Volz, P. 1989. *Die biblischen Altertümer*. Wiesbaden: Fourier.

Von Rad, G. 1962-65. *Theology of the Old Testament*. Translated by D. M. G. Stalker. 2 vols. New York: Harper/Harper and Row.

Vroom, H. M. 1979. *De schrift alleen? Een vergelijkend onderzoek naar de toetsing van theologische uitspraken volgens de openbaringstheologische visie van Torrance en de hermeneutisch-theologische opvattingen van Van Buren, Ebeling, Moltmann en Pannenberg.* Kampen: Kok.

Wagner, H. 1981. *Einführung in die Fundamentaltheologie.* Darmstadt: Wissenschaftliche Buchgesellschaft.

Waldenfels, H. 1996. *Einführung in die Theologie der Offenbarung.* Darmstadt: Wissenschaftliche Buchgesellschaft.

―――. 2000. *Kontextuelle Fundamentaltheologie.* Stuttgart: UTB.

Wall, R. W. 1995." Pauline Authorship and the Pastoral Epistles: A Response to S. E. Porter." *Bulletin for Biblical Research* 5:125–28.

Wallace, D. B. 2003. *Ephesians: Introduction, Argument and Outline.* bible.org/seriespage/ephesians-introduction-argument-and-outline.

Waltke, B. K., D. Guthrie, and R. K. Harrison. 1997. *Biblical criticism: Historical, literary, and textual.* Grand Rapids, MI: Zondervan.

Warfield, B. B. 1948. *The Inspiration and Authority of the Bible.* Philadelphia: Presbyterian and Reformed Publ. Co.

―――. 1973. *Selected Shorter Writings of Benjamin B. Warfield.* Edited by J. E. Meeter. Vol. 2. Nutley, NJ: Presbyterian and Reformed Publ. Co.

Weber, O. 1981. *Foundations of Dogmatics.* Translated by D. L. Guder. Vol. 1. Grand Rapids, MI: Eerdmans.

Webster, J. 2003. *Holy Scripture: A Dogmatic Sketch.* Cambridge: Cambridge University Press.

Weiss, J. 1964. *Die Predigt Jesu vom Reiche Gottes.* Göttingen: Vandenhoeck and Ruprecht.

Weisse, C. H. 1838. *Die evangelische Geschichte.* Leipzig: Breitkopf and Härtel.

Wellhausen, J. 1891. *Sketch of the History of Israel and Judah.* 3rd ed. London: Adam and Charles Black.

———. 1963. *Die Composition des Hexateuchs und der historischen Bücher des Alten Testaments.* Berlin: W. de Gruyter.

———. 1987. *Evangelienkommentare.* Berlin: Reimer Berlin: W. de Gruyter.

———. 1994. *Prolegomena to the History of Israel.* Atlanta, GA: Scholars Press.

Wendland, P. 1907. *Die hellenistisch-römische Kultur in ihren Beziehungen zu Judentum und Christentum.* Tübingen: Mohr (Siebeck).

Wenham, G. J. 1976. "History and the Old Testament." In *History, Criticism and Faith: Four Exploratory Studies*, edited by C. Brown. 13–75. Downers Grove, IL: InterVarsity Press.

———. 1987, 1994. *Genesis 1–15, 16–40.* WBC. Waco, TX: Word.

———. 2003. *Exploring the Old Testament.* Vol. 1: *A Guide to the Pentateuch.* Downers Grove, IL: InterVarsity Press.

Wenham, J. 1979. "Christ's View of Scripture." In *Inerrancy*, edited by N. L. Geisler. 3–36 Grand Rapids, MI: Zondervan.

Wentsel, B. 1981. *Het Woord, de Zoon en de dienst. Dogmatiek.* Vol. 1. Kampen: Kok.

———. 1982. *De openbaring, het verbond en de a priori's. Dogmatiek.* Vol. 2. Kampen: Kok.

Westcott, B. F. 1902. *Introduction to the Study of the Gospels.* New York: Macmillan.

Westermann, C. 1982. *Elements of Old Testament Theology.* Atlanta, GA: John Knox Press.1978.

Wettstein, J. J. 1962. *Novum Testamentun Graecum.* Graz: Akademische Druck- u. Verlagsanstalt.

White, J. R. 2004. *Scripture Alone: Exploring the Bible's Accuracy, Authority, and Authenticity.* Minneapolis, MN: Bethany House.

Whitelam, K. W. 1996. *The Invention of Ancient Israel*. London: Routledge.

Whybray, R. N. 1987. *The Making of the Pentateuch: A Methodological Study*. Sheffield: Sheffield Academic Press.

Wielenga, B. 1960. *De Bijbel als boek van schoonheid*. 6th ed. Kampen: Kok.

Wieman, H. N. 1963. *Man's Ultimate Commitment*. 2nd ed. Carbondale, IL: Southern Illinois University Press.

Wight, F. H. 1955. *Highlights of Archaeology in Bible Lands*. Chicago: Moody Press.

Wildeboer, G. 1900. *Het ontstaan van den kanon des Ouden Verbonds: Historisch-kritisch onderzoek*. 3rd ed. Groningen: J. B. Wolters.

Wilder, T. L. 2004. *Pseudonymity, the New Testament and Deception: An Inquiry into Intention and Reception*. Lanham, MD: University Press of America.

Wilkins, J. and P. Moreland, eds. 1995. *Jesus Under Fire*. Grand Rapids, MI: Zondervan.

Wilson, C. 1977. *Ebla Tablets: Secrets of a Forgotten City*. San Diego: Creation-Life Publ.

Windisch, H. 1914. "Die göttliche Weisheit der Juden und die paulinische Christologie." In *Neutestamentliche Studien: Georg Heinrici zu seinem 70. Geburtstag dargebracht*, edited by P. Krüger. Untersuchungen zum Neuen Testament. Vol. 6. 220–34. Leipzig: J. C. Hinrichs.

Wiseman, P. J. 1960. *Ontdekkingen over Genesis: Het eerste Bijbelboek in het licht van archeologisch onderzoek*. Groningen: Jan Haan.

Witherington, III, B. 1997. *The Jesus Quest: The Third Search for the Jew of Nazareth*. 2nd ed. Downers Grove, IL: InterVarsity.

———. 2006. *1 and 2 Thessalonians: A Socio-Rhetorical Commentary*. Grand Rapids, MI: Eerdmans.

Witter, H. B. 1711. *Jura Israelitarum in Palæstinam terram Chananæam*. Hildesiæ : Sumptibus Ludolphi Schröderi.

Wolstenholme, G., ed. 1963. *Man and His Future*. London: Churchill.

Wolterstorff, N. 1969a. "On God Speaking." *The Reformed Journal* July/Aug. 1969:7-10.

———. 1969b. "How God Speaks." *The Reformed Journal* Sept. 1969:16-20.

———. 1969c. Canon and Criterion. *The Reformed Journal* Oct. 1969:10-15.

———. 1969d. "When Did We See Thee?" *The Reformed Journal* Nov. 1969:2-3.

———. 1981. "Once again: creator/creature." *Philosophia Reformata* 46:60-67.

———. 1995. *Divine Discourse: Philosophical Reflections on the Claim that God Speaks*. New York: Cambridge University Press.

Woodbridge, J. D. 1982. *Biblical Authority: A Critique of the Rogers/McKim Proposal*. Grand Rapids, MI: Zondervan.

Wrede, W. 1971. *The Messianic Secret*. Cambridge: J. Clarke.

Wright, G. E. 1947. "The Present State of Biblical Archaeology" In *The Study of the Bible Today and Tomorrow*, edited by H. R. Willoughby. 74-97. Chicago: University of Chicago Press.

Wright, N. T. 1996. *Jesus and the Victory of God*. Minneapolis, MN: Augsburg Fortress.

———. 2005. *The Last Word: Scripture and the Authority of God – Getting Beyond the Bible Wars*. New York: HarperSanFrancisco.

Yahuda, A. S. 1935. *The Accuracy of the Bible*. Boston: E. P. Dutton.

Yaron, R. 1969. *The Laws of Eshnunna*. Jerusalem: Magnes Press.

Young, E. J. 1957. *Thy Word Is Truth: Some Thoughts on the Biblical Doctrine of Inspiration.* Grand Rapids, MI: Eerdmans.

———. 1969. *An Introduction to the Old Testament.* Grand Rapids, MI: Eerdmans.

Young, I., Rezetko, R. and M. Ehrensvärd. 2008. *Linguistic Dating of Biblical Texts: An Introduction to Approaches and Problems.* 2 vols. London: Equinox Publishing.

Youngblood, R. F. 1971. *The Heart of the Old Testament.* Grand Rapids, MI: Baker Book House.

———, ed. 1984. *Evangelicals and Inerrancy: Selections from the Journal of the Evangelical Theological Society.* Nashville, TN: Thomas Nelson.

Zagzebski, L. ed. 1993. *Rational Faith: Catholic Responses to Reformed Epistemology.* Notre Dame, IN: University of Notre Dame Press.

Zimmermann, J. ed. 2017. *Re-Envisioning Christian Humanism: Education and the Restoration of Humanity.* Oxford: Oxford University Press.

Zirkle, C. 1959. *Evolution, Marxian Biology, and the Social Science.* Philadelphia: University of Pennsylvania Press.

Zuck, R. B. 1995. *Teaching As Jesus Taught.* Grand Rapids, MI: Baker Books.

Zuidema, S. U. 1953. "Theologie en wijsbegeerte in de 'Kirchliche Dogmatik' van Karl Barth." *Philosophia Reformata* 18:77–138.

———. 1955. "De openbaringsideeën van Karl Barth en Martin Heidegger: De vergelijkbaarheid van beider denkstructuur." *Philosophia Reformata* 20:162–75.

———. [1956]. "Heidegger." In *Denkers van deze tijd.* Vol. 2. Franeker: T. Wever.

Scripture Index

OLD TESTAMENT

Genesis

1	607	3:15	85	10:21-31	645
1-2	78, 528	3:16	358, 470	11:1-9	645
1-3	630	3:17	645	11:7	455
1-11	645	3:20	238	11:10	643
1:1	80, 537	4:1-6	645	11:10-11	645
1:1-6:8	644	4:25-26	645	11:10-26	644
1:1-2:3	644	5:1-6:8	644	11:26	645
1:1-19	550	5:3-8	645	11:27	643
1:2	645	5:29-32	645	11:27-22:24	645
1:14-18	84	6:1-4	645	11:27-25:11	644
1:26	455	6:4	80	12	79
1:26-27	451	6:5	188	12-50	646
1:26-28	171, 208	6:9	643	12:6	637
1:27	386	6:9-9:29	644	12:7	14
1:28	77, 207, 236	6:9-11:26	644	14	619
2	79	6-8	551	14:3	637
2:1	211, 446	6-9	70	14:14	619
2:4	643	8:2	645	14:18-20	71
2:4-4:26	644	8:21	188	15:1	14, 283, 645
2:15	207	9	34, 79	15:1-16:16	645
2:16-17	77	9:1-17	84	15:19	71
2:19-20	236, 238	9:6	451	16:10-11	14
2:20-24	241	9:21	645	17:1-18:15	645
2:24	386, 467	9:22	645	17:26	80
3	79	9:23	645	18:25	638
3:6	645	9:25	645	19	79
3:9	645	9:26-27	645	19:1	15
		10:1	643	20:7	15
		10:1-11:9	644	22:15-18	15

22:18	473	11:10	124, 152	**Leviticus**	
23:1-25:18	645	12:2	87	9:23	14
24:12-15	15	12:12	116, 638	11:6	567
25:12	643	13:4	87	11:7	492
25:12-18	644	15	622	11:44	129
25:19	643	15:1-21	282, 622	11:45	129
25:19-30:24	645	15:11	638	17:7	16
25:19-35:29	644	15:14-16	98	17:15	391, 621
25:26	471	15:18	219	19:2	129
26:5	208	16:10	14	19:9	637
28:12-17	14	17:14	330	19:18	165, 170, 238, 301
28:18	637	18	71		
30:6	619	18:10	71	19:31	16
30:25-436	45	18:11	638	20:6	16
31:17	637	19:6	638	20:7-8	129
34:7	619	19:18	639	23:5	87
35:19	474	19:21	25	23:39	391, 621
35:23-36:43	645	20:1	128, 175	26	455
36:1	643	20:2	129	26:11-12	472
36:1-8	644	20:4-6	82		
36:9	643	20:25	637	**Numbers**	
36:9-37:1	644	22:29	638	7:89	14, 25, 67, 246, 280
36:31-39	619	23:15	87		
37:2	643	23:16	88	9:17-23	545
37:2-50:26	644, 645	24:3-4	175	11:11-15	455
40:14	619	24:4	177, 461	11:12	176
41:8	284	24:5	638	11:25-26	15
44:1-34	645	24:7	177	12:6	16
45:1-28	645	25:4	727	12:6-8	246
47:31	411	25:8	472	12:8	14, 25, 67, 280
49:26	209	28:1	638, 639	14:10	14
		32	638	15:22-31	242
Exodus		33:9-11	246	15:31	175
1:7	619	33:11	25, 280	16:19	14
2:10	471	33:20	25, 82, 558	16:42	14
3:1	455	34:1	175	19:31	15
3:4	454	34:6	499, 639	20:3	80
3:6	384, 471	34:11-26	638	20:6	14, 15
3:15-16	471	34:18	87	20:10-12	398
4:5	471	34:22	88	21:8-9	638
4:22	473, 642	34:27	457	21:14	330
6:2	30	34:27-28	175	21:29	116, 220, 638
7:3	124, 152	34:28	128, 174, 546	22:24	432
7:17-21	578	35:4	175	22:28	432
9:3	131	35:6	727	23:21	220

Scripture Index

23:22	579	18:10-11	15	10:13	319, 330
23-24	72	18:15	344	13:22	432
27:14	175	18:16	620	14:6	344, 391
27:21	175	18:18	344, 461	18:8	345
28:9	386	18:21-22	15	22:5	454
35:15-25	242	19:18-19	257	22:22	220
		24:1	620	23:6	318
Deuteronomy		25:4	314, 462	24:25	345
1:26	175	25:5	620	24:26	318, 461
1:31	473	27:9	639		
1:43	175	27:12	639	**Judges**	
2:15	131	28:14	175	3:20-21	280
4:2	175	28:58	175	4:11	71
4:10	175	28-29	455	4:17	71
4:11	639	29:21	318	5	282, 622
4:13	128, 174	29:29	1, 175	6:17	15
5:5	175	30:14-20	162	6:22-23	558
5:22	175	30:6	165	7:14	98
5:23	639	30:10	318	8:14	661
5:26	298, 558	30:14	181	9:7-15	458
6:5	165, 238, 301	31:9	133	11:23-27	221
6:6	175, 181	31:12	175	11:24	116, 638
8:3	31, 148, 162, 176, 343, 385	31:19	457	13:22	25, 558
		31:24	175	18	619
8:5	473	31:26	318		
9:10	175	32:8	219	**Ruth**	
9:23	175	32:17	16	4:16	176
10:2	175	32:21	454		
10:4	128, 174	32:46-47	175	**1 Samuel**	
10:17	220	32:47	162	1:3	640
11:1	165	33:1	344, 391	2:8	727
11:13	165	33:5	220	2:27	391
11:18	181	33:15	209	3:1-14	246
12	635	33:27	301	3:4-9	25, 280
12:28	175	34:10	25, 280, 344	3:4-10	14, 67
13:1-5	15			3:9-10	335
13:3	165	**Joshua**		3:20-21	344
14:1	473	1:7-8	318, 454	3:21	258
14:21	391, 621	3:11	638	4:6-8	98
15:11	359	3:13	638	9:6-10	345, 391
16:1	87	4:24	131	9:9-11	14
16:13	391, 621	8:31	318	9-10	15
16:16	88	8:31-32	454	10:6	394
17:14	220	8:34	318	10:25	330, 345
17:14-20	319	10:12-13	559	21:6	386

23:9-11	15	**2 Kings**		32:32	330
26:19	638	1:9-13	391	33:19	331
28:6	15	5	71	34:13-33	635
28:7	16	8:26	588	34:14-15	318
28:8	34	10:1	176	35:25	331
30:29	71	10:5	176	36:23	328
		10:15	71		
2 Samuel		10:31	182	**Ezra**	
1:18	319, 330	14:6	318	1:1-4	72
4:4	176	14:9	458	2:63	15
6:6	602	18:4	264, 638	3:2	344
7:14	472	22:8	318	4:7-22	248
8:4	587	22:11	318	4:8-6:18	283
10:18	587			4:11-22	455
11	398	**1 Chronicles**		5:6-17	455
23:1-3	345	1:1	328	6:2-12	455
23:2	394, 397, 461	2:55	71	7:12-26	283
24:9	587	9:24	727	9:4	264
		18:4	587		
1 Kings		19:18	587	**Nehemiah**	
2:3	454	21:5	587	2:1	312
3:9	177	23:14	344	2:8	284
3:11-12	177	25	640	8:1	318
4:29-34	345	25:1	345	8:3	318
5	71	27:24	330	8:15	454
5:7	71	29:29	330, 345	8:18	318
7:23	577			9:3	318
7:26	587	**2 Chronicles**		9:14	346
8:4	639	4:5	588	9:17	499
11:41	330	9:29	330	9:29-30	346
12	638	11:15	16	9:31	499
13:1-31	391	12:15	330	13:14	455
13:2	627	13:22	330	13:22	455
13:11	432	16:11	330	13:29	455
13:21-22	432	17:9	318		
14	15	20:34	330	**Esther**	
14:19	330	22:2	588	2:7	176
14:29	330	24:21-22	327	3:12	284
17:18	391	24:27	330		
17:24	391	25:4	454	**Job**	
19:6-8	546	26:22	330	1:6	80
20:23	220, 638	27:7	330	1:7-11	455
20:28	220, 391, 638	30:9	499	1:21	71
22	487	30:12	131	2:1	80
22:21	33	30:16	344	2:2-5	455

2:11	71	38:34	97, 121, 124,	37:4	299	
3:8	358, 489		163	37:31	182	
4:12-21	487	39:1-33	124	40:7	319	
4:15-17	34	42:7	358	40:8	179	
5:9	124, 152	42:7-8	487	42	345	
5:13	358, 488			45:1	397, 461	
8:3	71	**Psalms**		45:2	410	
8:5	71	1:2	126	47:8	219	
9:6	580, 727	2:7	467, 715	50:1	220	
9:10	124, 152	8	171, 195	51:6	182	
11:7	71	8:4-6	715	53:1	464	
12:9	131	8:6	176	53:6	471	
12:13	219	10:11	26	55:1	26	
15:25	71	11:2-3	503	56:10	264	
20:3	34	12:6	301	73	345	
22:3	71	14:1	464	75:3	580, 727	
22:17	71	14:7	471	78:10	133	
22:21-26	164	15:2-5	92	82:1	116	
22:22	181	16:10	467	82:5	550	
22:23-26	71	19	65, 113, 126,	86:15	499	
22:25	301		195	88	345, 455	
22:26	299	19:1	77, 125	88:13-14	26	
26:11	580	19:1-2	63, 64	89	133, 345	
26:13	489	19:1-3	66	89:1-2	165	
27:10	299	19:1-4	163	89:1-5	130	
28:28	177	19:1-7	130	89:2-3	122, 156, 164	
29:18	578	19:3-4	65, 162	89:5	122, 165	
29-30	455	19:4	474	89:8	165	
32:2	71	19:7	302, 569	89:14	165	
32:8	71, 388	19:7-8	64, 162, 165,	89:24	165	
33:4	388		299	89:28-29	130	
34:19	176	19:10	164, 299, 301	89:33	165	
36:2	283	20:9	397	89:35-37	164	
37-38	130	22:15	732	89:36-37	130	
37:2-14	124	27:9	26	89:37	122, 165	
37:5	121	28:5	176	89:49	165	
37:14	124	29	195	90	345	
37:14-16	152, 153	29:3	64	90:1	344	
37:16	124	29:3-9	124	90:12	182	
38:7	80	30:7	26	91:13	579	
38:11-12	97	33:6	31, 96, 121,	93	195	
38:12	163		299, 388	94:12	126	
38:22-38	124	33:9	96, 121	96:10	219	
38:31-33	124	34:8	299	99:1	98	
38:33	121	36:9	100	102:25	176	

103:8	499	119:106	164, 301	6:23	177, 207
104	130, 195	119:113	301	7:2	177
104:4	550	119:117	299	8	176
104:6-7	121	119:119	301	8:22-31	732
104:7	97, 121, 124, 163	119:127	301	8:25	209
		119:128	164	8:30-31	175
104:10	124	119:130	162	9:6	207
104:10-11	124	119:137	164	10:8	177
104:13	124	119:138	165, 301	14:33	182
104:14	124	119:140	301	15:24	207
104:16	124	119:142	165, 301	16:17	207
104:19-23	124	119:143	163, 299	21:1	131, 219
104:27-30	124	119:144	164, 301	30:5	247
104:30	97, 446	119:159	301		
106:37	16	119:160	165, 301	**Ecclesiastes**	
110:1	455	119:163	301	2:24	131
110:4	71	119:164	165, 301	4:13	732
111:4	499	119:167	301	5:2	16
112:4	499	119:172	165	5:6	16
118:22-23	386	119:174	163, 299	7:28	732
119	126	127	345	9:1	131
119:11	181	136:2	220	9:15	732
119:14	163	139:13-14	152	12:10	462
119:16	162, 299	139:14	124		
119:24	163, 299	139:14-17	153	**Isaiah**	
119:28	298	145:8	499	1:1	280
119:34	182	147	130	1:10	126
119:35	163	147:15	121, 128	1:11-17	639
119:39	301	147:15-19	127	1:15	26
119:47	163, 299	147:18	121	1:20	162, 176
119:47-48	301	147:18-19	128	1:24	639
119:62	164, 301	148:6	121	2:1	280
119:68	301	148:8	121	2:2-4	126
119:70	163, 299			2:3	126
119:72	164	**Proverbs**		5:2	469
119:75	164, 301	2:1-2	177	5:9	639
119:77	163, 299	2:10	182	5:24	126, 641
119:89	121, 128, 261	3:1	127, 177	5:29	639
119:89-94	164	3:19-20	127	6	280, 348
119:89-96	126	3:19-27	164	6:1-8	454
119:90	165	4:2	177	6:8	246, 455
119:91	121	4:4	181	8:14	386
119:92	163, 299	4:4-5	177	8:19	15, 16
119:97	301	6:14	188	9:6	715
119:105	162, 298	6:20	177	10:5	422

Scripture Index

10:15	422	49:3	473	18:19-23	455
11:1	319, 470	49:8	474	19:5	638
11:6-8	170	49:23	176	20	287
12:3	320, 470	51:4	126	20:7-12	455
19:3	16	51:4-9	126	20:9	348
22:14	258	51:5	165	20:14-15	452
26:19	88, 320	51:7	126, 182	20:14-18	357, 455
27:9	472	52-53	473	21:8	207
28:16	386	52:11	320, 472	23	487
28:26	239	54:8	26	23:9	189
28:26-29	239	55:8-9	163, 300	23:29	162, 280, 298, 359
29:8	16	55:10-11	298		
30:9	641	55:11	31, 164, 299, 300, 343, 350	23:39	349
33:14-15	92			25:11-12	281, 310, 454
33:24	170	55:13	170	26:2	461
34:8	639	56:1	17	28	358, 487
34:14	579	58:11	470	29:10	281, 310, 454
34:16	162, 176	58:14	162, 176, 299	30:2	457
35:4	639	59:2	26	31:1	320
40-66	626, 651	59:17	639	31:5	474
40:5	162, 176	59:20	472	31:22	136
40:8	208, 261	59:20-21	472	31:31-34	182
40:11	301	59:21	472	31:33	181
40:13	403	60:1	320	31:35	121
41:20	131	60:12	320	32:27	219
42:1	721	61:1	394, 398	32:38	472
42:3-7	126	63:4	639	33:20	122, 130, 133, 156
42:4	126, 165	64:4	320		
42:21	126	64:7	26	33:25	84, 121, 122, 130, 133, 156
43:6	472	65:1	454, 467		
43:10	456	65:6	319	35	71
43:12	456	65:25	170	36:2	457, 461
43:14	627	66:3	639	36:4	461
44:8	456			36:18	461
44:28	328, 626, 651	**Jeremiah**		36:27	461
45:1	626, 651	1	348	36:32	461
45:7	136	1:5	354, 454	38:7-12	71
45:12	121	1:7	394	45:1	461
45:15	26	1:9	461	49:36	727
45:23	31, 299	7:22-23	639	50:15	639
46:1	116	10:10	5	51:44	116
47:1	627	10:11	283	51:60	461
48:14	627	15:16	298		
48:16	398	17:9	188	**Ezekiel**	
48:20	627	18:18	346	1	348

1:3	639	9:11-12	461	**Jonah**	
1:5-10	727	9:13	454	4:2	499
2:2	394	9:27	628		
2:8-3:1	298	11	628	**Micah**	
3:17	31, 299	11:4	727	1:1	280
7:2	727	11:21-35	628	3:8	398
10:14	727	11:33	391	4:4	162, 176
10:21	727	11:35	391	5:2	405
11:5	398	11:36	220	6:4	639, 640, 642
16:20	638	12:2	88	6:6-8	639
20:31	638	12:3	391	6:8	288, 391
20:34	472	12:8	394	7:15	639
25:12-17	639	12:10	391		
33:7	31, 299			**Nahum**	
37:9	727	**Hosea**		1:2	639
40:3	317	1:10	320, 473, 474		
44:7-16	639	2:23	474	**Habakkuk**	
		3:4	638	1:4	165
Daniel		4:6	641	3:6	209
1:5	284	4:12	33		
2	628	5:4	191	**Zechariah**	
2:4-7:28	283	8:1	133, 641	1:1	328
2:21	219	9:7	394	2:6	727
2:22	63	11:1	473, 639, 642	6:5	727
2:47	72, 220	12:10	639	7:12	346
3:19	567	12:13	642		
3:28-29	72	12:14	639	**Malachi**	
4:1-37	455			1:6-14	639
4:34-35	72	**Joel**		1:8	83
5:21-23	81	2:28	16, 394	2:8	133
5:23	81, 124, 219			4:5	15
5:31	72	**Amos**		4:5-6	329
6:26-27	72	1:1	280		
6:26-28	455	2:4	641	**NEW TESTAMENT**	
7	628	2:10	639, 642	**Matthew**	
7:13	732	3:7	1	1:5	308
8	628	3:13	472	1:18	261
8:8	727	3:14	638	1:21	695
8:9-14	628	4:4	638	2:2	694
8:23-25	628	4:13	136, 472	2:4	694
8:27	394	5:5-6	638	2:5	319
9	628	5:21-26	639	2:15	474
9:2	310, 346, 454	9:7	219, 639, 642	2:17-18	474
9:6	346			2:23	319, 470
9:11	346			3:3	626

Scripture Index

3:15-17	498	12:5	385, 386	23:34	346
4:2	546	12:17-21	626	23:35	308, 327, 456
4:3	455	12:36	257	24:14	345
4:4	31, 148, 298, 299, 385, 483	13:11	19	24:15	386, 628
		13:17	395	24:27	27
4:6	455	13:43	454	24:30	27, 716, 732
4:6-7	483	13:58	582	24:37	27
4:7	385	14:33	264, 715	24:39	27
4:9	455	15:6	68	25:31	27
4:10	385, 483	15:18-19	188	26:24	385, 483
5:17	175, 179	16:1-4	357	26:28	695
5:17-18	346, 385	16:16	712	26:31	385, 483
5:17-20	463, 500	16:17	17, 22, 129, 447, 712	26:34	583
5:18	283, 290, 410, 463			26:37	724
		16:27-28	27	26:53	284
5:21-22	500	17:12	329	26:54	483
5:22	283	17:29	355	26:56	483
5:27-28	500	18:1-4	495	26:64	483, 716, 732
5:26	283	19:3-8	241	27:8	283
5:31-34	500	19:4-5	385, 386	27:25	730, 731
5:38-39	500	19:5	467	27:35	345, 487
5:41	284	19:7-8	620	27:46	283
5:43-44	500	19:8	643	27:48	469
5:45	163, 167	19:17	582	27:52	88
7:14	207	19:21	720	27:64	27
7:28-29	695	20:20	264	27:65-66	284
8:2	264	20:28	695	28:9	264
8:4	643	21:9	282	28:17	264
8:17	626	21:13	385	28:18	200, 349
8:22	720	21:16	385	28:19	612
9:8	349	21:23-27	357		
9:9	452, 720, 722	21:40-41	583	**Mark**	
9:13	315	21:42	385, 386	1:17	720
9:15	308	22:24	620	1:27	356
9:18	264	22:29	273	1:34	677
10:1	349	22:29-32	379, 383	1:44	677
10:3	347, 722	22:31	385, 386	2:17	315
10:10	314, 382	22:34-40	180	3:12	677
10:29	283	22:36-40	170	3:16	343
10:32	716	22:37-40	238	4:31	579
11:14	329	22:40	346	5:6	264
11:25	17, 351	22:43	398, 454, 468	5:41	283
11:27	17, 22, 447	22:43-45	467	5:43	677
11:28	720	23:2	643	6:5	582
12:3	385, 386	23:23-24	412	7:10	643

7:13	247, 409	2:11	694	11:25-26	720
7:34	283	2:15	18	11:30	716
7:36	677	2:22	125	11:35	423
8:26	677	2:27	721	11:49	348
8:28-29	712	2:32	17	11:51	327
8:29	714	2:37	459, 578, 721	11:52	497
8:30	677	3:8	396	12	716
9:9	677	3:15-16	720	12:8	715, 716
9:12	483	4:14	418	12:10	716
10:18	582	4:17	626	12:40	716
10:46-52	406	4:21	388	14:26-27	720
11:28-29	349	4:22	453	15:20	453
11:33	349	5:24	716	16:9-13	283
12:10	388	5:39	465	16:16	346
12:24	273, 561	5:40	720	16:27-31	352
12:26	384, 643	6:13-15	346	16:29	346, 643
12:36	343, 454, 468	6:35	720	16:29-31	484
13:31	208	6:36	453	16:31	346, 357, 643
14:61-62	694	6:37	720	17:24	715
14:30	583	6:47	720	18:10-14	721
15:28	388	7:8	349	18:19	582
15:39	283	7:13	453	18:43	731
15:44-45	283	7:29	731	19:20	284
16:9-20	478, 479, 480	7:34	716	19:47	721
16:12	17	7:38	720	20:15-16	583
16:14	17	8:11	298	20:37	471
16:19	724	8:15	181	20:45	731
		8:42	459, 578	21:27	716
Luke		8:47	731	21:37	721
1:1-4	396, 399, 417, 431, 457, 458, 723, 726	8:51	724	21:38	731
		9:14	349, 459	22:22	716
		9:20	712	22:31-38	715
1:14	288	9:22	716	22:34	583
1:15	283	9:26	716	22:37	483
1:17	329	9:28	459, 578, 724	22:41	459
1:22	721	9:44	716	22:48	716
1:35	261, 265, 714, 715	9:58	716	22:53	721
		9:59	720	22:54-62	398
1:50	453	10:7	314, 382, 462	22:59	459
1:54	453	10:19	349	22:69	716
1:56	459	10:21-22	17	23:33-34	405
1:58	453	10:24	394	23:44	459
1:72	453	10:25	496	23:45	579
1:78	453	10:33	453	23:45-46	581
1:70	343	10:37	453	24:19	731

24:22	311	3:5	90	9:5	179
24:25-27	497	3:8	448	9:38	264
24:27	346, 643	3:14	643	9:39	75
24:31-32	404	3:15-16	720	9:41	406
24:39-43	27	3:16	166, 179, 722	10:4	356
24:44	303, 346, 483, 497, 643	3:18	179	10:27	356
		3:19	75	10:30	495
24:45	404	3:19-20	75	10:34	409
24:50-51	724	3:21	17	10:34-35	247, 409
24:53	721	4:1-30	115	10:35	68, 313, 383, 388, 409
		4:22	694		
John		4:48	357	11:9	359
1:1	537	5:18	263	11:11	88
1:1-2	98	5:19	498	11:25-26	720
1:1-3	96, 160, 171, 174, 176, 202, 267	5:38-40	611	11:27	74
		5:39	256, 386, 468, 496, 497	11:51	432
				12:8	359
1:1-4	179	5:40	720	12:24	88, 579
1:1-13	203	5:45-46	643	12:32	90
1:1-14	74, 202	5:45	257	12:34	409
1:2	202	5:46	454, 620	12:38	454
1:3	173, 201, 205	5:47	319	12:44	720
1:4	33, 298	6:14	74	12:46	720
1:4-9	179	6:19	459	12:46-47	74
1:5	72	6:31	385	12:48	257
1:9	73, 75, 76	6:32	643	12:49	263
1:9-10	72	6:33	179	12:49-50	174
1:13	33, 343	6:35	720	13	699
1:14	24, 179, 202, 203	6:37	720	13:1	731
		6:45	385	13:4	284
1:14	171, 174, 179, 205, 259, 559	6:47	720	13:7	395
		6:51	179	13:18	483
1:18	205, 290, 453	6:63	33, 90	13:23	453, 722
1:21	329	6:69	714	13:34	170, 180
1:23	454, 626	7:19	643	13:48	218
1:25	329	7:22-23	643	14:1	720
1:31	17	7:38	320, 388, 470, 581, 720	14:6	71, 393, 551, 589, 720
1:44	720				
1:45	620	7:42	388	14:9	27
1:46	454	8:2	731	14:12	720
1:49	715	8:12	179	14:15	125, 180
2:11	17, 129, 248	8:12-19	456	14:16	353
2:15	284	8:17	385	14:21	125, 174, 180, 722
2:23-25	357	8:32	89, 405		
3:1-21	115	9:3	17	14:21-22	18

14:23	722	**Acts**		13:27-29	731
14:23-24	125, 174	1:1	288, 726	13:29-30	483
14:26	406, 458, 726	1:1-2	723	13:35	467
14:28	495	1:3	719	14	93
15:10	180	1:8	418	14:15-17	185, 190
15:12	170	1:9-10	724	14:16-17	219
15:13	731	1:13	724	14:8-19	115
15:15	18	1:16	343, 454, 468,	14:17	65, 80, 167
15:17	170		483, 487	14:22	719
15:25	409	2:2	397	15:6	97
15:26	726	2:28	18	15:20-29	492
15:26-27	456	2:29-30	345	15:32	250, 462
16:13	406	2:30	487	15:37-38	722
16:13-14	726	2:45	545	15:37-39	453
16:13-15	393	3:14-17	405	16:1-17	347
16:14	29	3:18	343, 454	16:7	393
16:18	716	3:21	343	16:12	284
16:27	722	4:12	90	17	93
16:28	74	4:25	343, 454	17:3	690
17	699	4:32	545	17:11	361, 561
17:3	295	7:22	455, 587	17:16-34	115
17:6	17	8:4	266	17:23	83
17:17	115	8:9-24	275	17:24-28	81
17:20-21	300	8:12	719	17:25	80, 124
17:24	29, 87	8:19	349	17:26	80, 219
17:26	18	8:21	97	17:26-27	16
18:37	456	8:28	626	17:26-28	185, 186, 190
19:11	349	8:30	626	17:27	89, 196
19:20	284	8:32	388	17:28	80, 196, 205, 309
19:26	453, 722	8:35	388		
19:28	483	9:7	489	18:5	690
19:37	388	9:22	690	18:28	690
20:2	453, 722	9:26	581	19:7	459
20:7	453	10:25	264	19:8	719
20:16	283	11:19	266	19:9	390
20:28	264	11:27	462	19:12	284
20:30-31	726	11:27-28	250	19:23	390
21:1	17	11:28	251	20:5-21:18	347
21:7	722	12:12	724	20:7-12	458
21:11	459	12:25	453	20:25	719
21:14	17	13:1	462, 482	20:35	315
21:19	720	13:5	453	21:9-11	250
21:20	453, 722	13:11	250	21:10	462
21:22	720	13:13	453, 722	21:10-11	251
21:25	27, 726	13:15	346	21:38	284

22:3	405, 455	1:23	82	9:1	54
22:4	390	1:24-32	83	9:5	263
22:9	489	1:32	66, 82	9:6	247, 409
22:17-21	348	2	107	9:17	263, 468
22:21	354	2:1	66	9:21	432
23:9	33	2:5-16	76	9:22-23	18
23:26-30	455	2:6-11	90	9:23	218
24:2	390	2:12-16	90	9:25	474
24:14	346, 390	2:14-15	66, 82, 92, 111	9:26	474
25:8	409	2:14-16	190	9:29	283
26:16-18	348	2:15	182, 192	10:4	173, 175, 180
26:18	349	2:27	463	10:6	626
26:20	90	2:29	463	10:8	181
26:22	346	3:2	247, 288, 321, 411, 462, 694	10:19-20	454
26:22-23	483			10:20	626
27:1-28:16	347	3:4	483	11:5	218
27:14	284	3:6	499	11:8-10	483
27:27	579	3:10-18	483	11:25	19
27:37	459	3:10-19	125, 409	11:26	387, 483
28:17	690	3:21	17, 346	11:26-27	471
28:23	346, 719	3:21-22	129	11:32	218
28:25	343, 454	3:23-24	218	12:6	250, 462
28:25-27	454, 483	4:16-18	275	13:1-7	546
28:31	719	4:17	96, 97, 211	13:8-10	180, 182
		5-8	465	13:10	165, 170
Romans		5:1	275	13:14	182
1	107, 113, 190, 191	5:5	57, 181, 182	14:12	257
		5:14	498	14:17	719
1:1	348	5:18	90, 218	15:4	387
1-2	79, 93, 111	6:18	465	15:8	690
1:3	690	6:22	465	15:8-9	694
1:5	346	7:6	60, 90, 463	15:12	96
1:18	70, 89, 116, 196	7:7-13	491	15:13	418
		7:12	166	15:18-19	398
1:19	17, 66, 69	7:14-26	465	15:19	418
1:19-20	119, 129	7:22	299	15:33	301
1:19-21	76	7:24	466	16:16	546
1:20	4, 26, 65, 66, 75, 82, 116, 131, 163, 166, 173, 192, 194, 613	8:1-17	105, 465	16:17	423
		8:2	465	16:20	301
		8:9	393	16:22	344, 420, 457
		8:11	448	16:25	17, 19, 29, 30
		8:16	54, 446, 603	16:25-26	303, 314, 376
1:20-21	189, 190, 199	8:29	129, 179, 204, 205	16:26	17, 18, 19, 30, 388, 462
1:21	78, 83, 116, 191, 196				
		8:29-30	218	17:27	196

17:28	196	7	241, 484	14:37	180, 355
		7:1	457	15	623
1 Corinthians		7:6	357, 484	15:1	18
1:1	348	7:10	357	15:3-4	483
1:11	18	7:12	357, 484	15:6	88
1:14-16	458	7:19	180	15:17	684
1:16	458	7:25	484	15:18	88
1:18	129, 266	8:6	399	15:20	88
1:20-24	691	9:1	348	15:24	719
1:24	173, 180	9:9	314	15:27	18
1:27-28	218	9:9-10	498	15:28	218
1:30	180	9:10	387	15:32	164, 301
2:1	19	9:16	348	15:33	309
2:1-5	458	9:21	175, 180	15:35-36	448
2:4	418	10:1-11	498	15:36	88, 579
2:6	177	10:4	309, 470	15:45	109, 159, 732
2:6-7	20	10:6	387	15:50	719
2:6-10	30	10:11	387	15:51	19
2:7	19	10:25	284	16:21	344
2:9	319, 320, 321, 581	10:31	35, 154	16:22	283
		11:2	344		
2:9-10	671	11:2-16	465	**2 Corinthians**	
2:9-16	379, 400	11:3-15	492	2:9	457
2:10	17, 401	11:7	451	2:14	18, 295
2:10-13	129	12:1-2	416	3	182
2:10-14	20	12:3	18	3:3	18
2:12	402	12:7	17	3:6	60, 398, 463, 490
2:12-14	29	12:7-11	124		
2:12-13	245	12:10	251	3:8	398
2:13	287, 353, 409, 462	12:28	251, 462, 482	3:14	323
		12:28-29	348	4:2	17
2:14	20, 188	13:2	19	4:4	70, 181
2:14-3:3	20	14:2	19	4:6	295
3:1-2	458	14:3	15, 248, 286, 359	4:7	162
3:1-3	495			4:13	275, 398
3:2	298	14:6	17	4:18	423
3:9	33	14:7	433	5:14	482
3:13	17, 18	14:21	409	5:20	482
3:19	358, 488	14:26	17	6:2	474
4:1	19	14:29	462	6:16-18	472
4:5	18, 499	14:30	17	6:17-18	320, 581
4:20	719	14:32	417	8:1	18
5:3	348	14:34	470	9:14	162
5:13	499	14:34-35	242	10:1-6	348
6:9-10	719	14:36	266	10:5	295

10:8	349	5:16-24	452	5:5	719
10:13	317	5:16-26	105	5:14	88, 320, 321
10:16	317	5:21	719	5:22-33	241
11:4	484	6:1	423	5:32	19
11:13	344	6:2	125, 170, 175, 180	6:2	129
11:14	309			6:5-9	547
12:1	17	6:11	344	6:17	68, 247, 491, 541
12:2	309, 458				
12:7	17, 162	**Ephesians**		6:19	18
12:12-13	458	1:3-5	218		
13:10	349	1:4	29	**Philippians**	
13:13	498	1:9	18	1:19	275, 393
		1:9-10	19	1:22	458
Galatians		1:10	215	1:29	275
1	348, 355	1:11	218	2:6	264
1:1	344	1:17	249, 295, 447	2:6-11	696
1:8	484	1:17-18	27, 34, 406	3:15	17
1:8-9	344	1:18	89, 196	3:17	423
1:11	18	2:5	90	3:20-21	27
1:11-12	344	2:15	182	4:6	18
1:11-24	458	2:20	251, 348, 462	4:7	162
1:12	17, 355	3:1-10	314	4:9	301
1:14	455	3:3	17, 18, 19, 462	4:12	18
1:15	454	3:4	19		
1:15-16	348	3:4-6	30	**Colossians**	
1:15-18	582	3:4-12	103	1:8	18
1:16	17, 447	3:5	17, 18, 129, 348, 462	1:10	295
1:17	455			1:13	719
1:19	347	3:9-11	19	1:13-16	205
2:2	250, 251	3:10	18	1:15	82, 181, 204, 205
3:1-5	455	3:16	418		
3:8	388, 468	3:17	182	1:15-16	613
3:10	483	3:19	162	1:16	176, 201
3:11	18	4:8	78	1:16-17	97, 123, 160, 171, 199, 201, 204, 215
3:13	166, 483	4:10	218		
3:16	473	4:11	348, 462, 482		
3:22	388	4:11-13	251	1:17	129
4:4	246, 259, 690	4:17	188	1:18	204
4:6	393	4:17-18	89	1:20	215
4:9	295	4:17-19	83	1:24-28	314
4:12-20	455	4:18	79, 91	1:26	18, 19
4:21-31	498	4:21	551	1:27	18, 19
5:12	455	4:22-6:9	209	2:2	19
5:13-14	170, 180	4:23-24	213	2:2-3	180
5:14	165	4:24	182	2:9	27

2:13	90	**1 Timothy**			448, 726
3:3	27	1:10	491	3:16-17	286, 379, 391,
3:9-11	182	1:13	405		395, 540, 574,
3:9-4:1	209	1:15	129, 302		604
3:10	182, 213	1:17	82, 613	4:1	18, 499, 719
3:12	218	1:18	462	4:2	266
3:15	34	2:3-4	90	4:3	491
3:15-16	181	2:5	90	4:8	18
3:17	35, 154	2:5-6	218	4:11	347, 453, 724
3:18-21	241	2:7	346	4:13	284, 457, 466,
3:22-4:1	547	2:11-12	242		486
4:3	19	3:9	19	4:18	719
4:4	18, 129	3:15	482, 727		
4:10	453, 724	3:16	18, 19, 24, 27,	**Titus**	
4:10-14	366		129	1:2	29
4:11	719	4:5	247	1:3	18
4:14	453, 722, 724	4:9	302	1:9	302, 491
4:17	366	4:14	462	1:12-13	309
4:18	344	5:10	546	1:16	191
		5:14	492	2:1	491
1 Thessalonians		5:17	266, 482	2:1-10	209
1:4	218	5:18	314, 382, 388,	2:3-5	241
1:5	418		726	2:5-6	218
1:5-6	398	6:3	491	2:9	547
1:6	334	6:11	391	2:11	18, 90, 218
1:8	266	6:14	18, 180	2:13	18, 264
2:12	719	6:15	220	3:1	546
2:13	129, 266, 334,	6:16	25, 82, 558	3:4	18
	344, 361, 403			3:5	90
4:15	458	**2 Timothy**		3:8	302
5:20	462	1:9	29		
5:23	301	1:9-10	18, 129	**Philemon**	
		1:10	18	19	344
2 Thessalonians		1:11	346	24	347
1:5	719	1:13	491	2	366
1:8	191	2:8	690	8-10	457
2:2	344, 366	2:11	302	22	466
2:7	19	2:17	358	24	453
2:8	18	3:10-11	392		
2:13	218	3:15	319, 359	**Hebrews**	
2:16-17	718	3:15-17	379	1	467
3:16	301	3:16	129, 261, 299,	1:1	343, 401, 432
3:17	344		359, 382, 387,	1:1-2	30, 160
			390, 391, 392,	1:2	201, 205
			397, 398, 419,	1:2-3	123

Scripture Index

1:3	4, 77, 97, 128, 135, 163, 181, 205, 300	13:8	261	**2 Peter**	
		13:20	301	1	395, 399
				1:2	295
1:5	467, 715	**James**		1:3	173
1:6	179, 204	1:18	33	1:11	719
1:8-12	264	1:21	129	1:14	18
1:12	489	1:25	180	1:16	18
2:3-4	367	2:5	218, 719	1:16-18	458
2:14	24	2:8	165, 170, 180	1:17-19	484
3:7	468, 487	2:8-12	180	1:19-21	395, 574
3:7-11	454	3:9	451	1:20	388
4:7	454	4:5	320	1:20-21	129, 343, 397, 438, 494
4:12	68, 162, 164, 208, 247, 298, 300, 359, 409, 603	5:4	283	1:21	3, 261, 264, 267, 346, 382, 389, 410, 418, 419, 432, 448
		1 Peter			
		1:10	343		
4:12-13	257	1:10-11	379, 393, 397		
5:1	643	1:10-12	30, 343, 437	2	673
5:6	71	1:11	18, 398, 405, 430, 431, 484	3:2	180
5:10	71			3:9	90, 218
5:11-14	495	1:12	17	3:15	314
5:12-13	298	1:16	129, 319	3:16	314, 382, 388, 462
5:14	177	1:19-21	382		
6:5	247	1:20	18, 29, 129		
6:20	71	1:21	299	**1 John**	
7:1-10	498	1:23	33, 68, 162, 208, 247, 261, 290, 298, 359	1:1	300
7:1-22	71			1:1-2	98, 174
8:10	181			1:1-4	402
9:8	18, 468	1:24	290	1:2	18
9:14	498	1:25	247, 290	1:3	300
9:26	18, 129	2:2	298, 359	1:4-6	295
10:15-17	454	2:3	299	1:5	181
10:16	181	2:9	218	1:9	90
10:20	207	2:10	474	1:18	260
11:6	79	2:13-14	546	1:20-21	343
11:17-19	473	2:13-3:9	209	2:3	180
11:21	411	2:18	547	2:5	181
11:27	82, 613	3:1-7	241	2:7-8	180
11:32	308	3:20-21	498	2:7-11	170
11:35	308	4:1-6	105	2:14	68, 247
11:37	308	4:3-4	83	2:15	181
12:27	18	4:5	257	2:18-19	344
12:28	719	5:12	457	2:26	457
13:4	499	5:13	347, 453	3:5	18, 129
13:7	266	11:11	267	3:8	18, 129

3:11	170	1:7	27	19:9	68, 457
3:17	181	1:8	580	20:4	456
3:22	180	1:9	456, 719	20:6	349
3:23	170	1:10	398	20:8	727
3:24	180	1:11	457	21:5	457
4:1-3	344	1:19	457	22:16	96
4:1-6	105	1:20	19	22:18-19	462
4:2-3	24, 453	2:1-3:14	457	22:19	462
4:7	165	2-3	455		
4:7-8	181	2:13	456		
4:8	86, 180, 181	3:14	145, 204, 205		
4:9	18, 179, 205	4:2	398		
4:11-12	165	4:6-8	727		
4:12	181	4:11	121, 163		
4:16	86, 180, 181	5:5	96		
4:19	154	5:10	719		
4:20-21	165	6:6	283		
5:2-3	180	6:9	456		
5:3	165, 166, 181	7:1	727		
5:7-8	477, 478	7:2	298		
5:20	174, 180, 264	9:19	349		
		10:4	248, 401		
2 John		10:4-7	20		
1:1	288	10:7	19		
1:5	170, 180	10:9	298		
1:6	180	11:1-13	329		
1:7	24, 261	11:3	456		
		11:15	719		
3 John		11:17	580		
1:1	288	12:10	719		
		12:11	456		
Jude		12:17	456		
3	457	13:12	349		
4	499	14:7	499		
9	309	14:13	457		
12	546	15:3	219		
14	309	15:4	18		
25	349	16:5	580		
		17:5	19		
Revelation		17:6	456		
1:1	17	17:7	19		
1:3	386, 462	17:12-13	349		
1:4	580	17:17	68		
1:5	204	18:20	348		
1:6	719	19:1	264, 282		

Subject Index

A
Aaron 639, 640, 642, 732
Abandon 152, 167, 263, 553
Abel 327, 645
Abolished 111, 175, 187, 385, 500
Abraham 30, 208, 274, 383, 384, 468, 471, 473, 637, 645, 665
Abrahamic 116
Adam 67, 78, 98, 109, 158, 159, 160, 208, 212, 238, 274, 309, 328, 449, 498, 644, 645, 732
Afraid 356, 449, 595, 691
Aspect 12, 21, 22, 30, 34, 45, 99, 100, 132, 141, 142, 159, 182, 186, 203, 262, 281, 282, 285, 286, 296, 297, 299, 322, 422, 423, 436, 446, 457, 524, 553, 684
Athanasius, St. 318, 362
Atheism 40, 80, 535
Athenagoras 426, 433
Atonement 76, 505, 640, 654
Augustine, St. 153, 249, 413, 414, 540, 541, 711
Authority 9, 11, 42, 51, 54, 60, 61, 240, 241, 249, 253, 254, 255, 256, 257, 268, 290, 303, 304, 306, 307, 311, 312, 318, 332, 333, 334, 335, 336, 338, 339, 348, 349, 350, 353, 354, 355, 356, 357, 358, 359, 361, 371, 372, 373, 380, 381, 390, 392, 398, 399, 412, 438, 439, 440, 480, 481, 482, 483, 484, 485, 486, 488, 490, 491, 492, 493, 496,

500, 505, 511, 513, 516, 521, 540, 541, 546, 552, 556, 557, 562, 567, 593, 601, 653, 663

B

Baptism i, 356, 493, 678
Baptist 60, 329, 356, 505
Beautiful 177, 181, 247, 248, 264, 458, 497, 622, 730, 731
Believers ii, iii, 19, 34, 54, 57, 58, 89, 115, 129, 181, 182, 209, 249, 250, 251, 264, 265, 286, 304, 332, 338, 344, 351, 355, 359, 360, 361, 362, 363, 374, 418, 465, 482, 488, 489, 495, 496, 520, 526, 538, 572, 574, 596, 597, 598, 684, 694, 697
Binding 34, 439

Bishop 94, 389
Body 27, 34, 157, 213, 216, 309, 375, 422, 458, 471, 519, 606, 609, 630
Booths 88, 326, 391, 621
Born 7, 94, 209, 305, 387, 405, 448, 452, 465, 506, 619, 643, 646, 689, 690, 694, 718
Builder 176
Building 176, 250, 285, 348, 351, 501, 544, 663
Built 164, 249, 348, 664
Burden 93

C

Caiaphas 432
Cain 645
Cake 542
Capitalism 553
Captive 587, 690
Ceremonies 83
Christ i, ii, iii, 4, 5, 6, 17, 18, 19, 22, 24, 27, 34, 38, 45, 49, 60, 68, 71, 74, 75, 76, 90, 96, 97, 98, 99, 102, 103, 104, 107, 109, 110, 111, 112, 113, 114, 120, 123, 125, 129, 131, 133, 136, 137, 142, 147, 153, 159, 160, 162, 171, 173, 174, 175, 176, 178, 179, 180, 181, 182, 183, 186, 195, 199, 200, 201, 203, 204, 205, 206, 207, 209, 210, 214, 215, 216, 217, 218, 222, 225, 227, 232, 235, 238, 258, 259, 260, 261, 262, 264, 265, 266, 267, 268, 288, 291, 300, 309, 314, 320, 323, 329, 343, 346, 351, 355, 359, 376, 379, 393, 394, 399, 400, 404, 406, 407, 408, 412, 413, 414,

Subject Index

415, 418,
423, 424,
428, 437,
445, 447,
450, 453,
458, 473,
474, 476,
481, 482,
483, 484,
490, 496,
497, 498,
505, 512,
516, 517,
520, 521,
523, 549,
551, 559,
572, 589,
592, 595,
602, 604,
605, 606,
607, 608,
642, 671,
677, 679,
680, 681,
684, 685,
688, 689,
691, 692,
693, 694,
696, 697,
698, 700,
701, 707,
710, 712,
713, 718,
720, 721,
732

Circumcision
347
City 87, 94, 319, 619
Civil 92
Commandments
77, 92,
121, 125,
127, 128,
135, 156,
161, 162,
164, 174,
175, 177,
180, 181,
182, 208,
210, 213,
238, 301,
408, 431,
485, 486,
488, 491,
500, 621,
640

Congregation
178, 676,
678, 680,
687

Contrast 72, 101,
151, 174,
186, 207,
233, 264,
279, 291,
318, 357,
360, 462,
531, 551,
563, 565,
587, 600,
630, 642,
712, 719

Covenant i, 16, 34,
84, 120,
121, 132,
133, 134,
156, 178,
181, 182,
196, 201,
213, 238,
323, 435,
471, 472,
498, 593,
604, 641,
664, 695

Curse 166, 645
Customs 83, 664, 707

D
Daughter 283, 459, 578
David 71, 96,
133, 330,
345, 386,
396, 398,
454, 467,
468, 587,
660, 661,
665, 690,
721, 732

Dead Sea Scrolls
219, 312,
321, 476,
575, 587,
692, 706

Death 6, 25, 87,
88, 242,
265, 352,
361, 450,
465, 493,
495, 507,
583, 620,
627, 628,
658, 677,
681, 683,
685, 696,
718, 720,
730, 731,
732

Deed 35, 154
Deity 11, 80, 81,
82, 83, 89,
146, 201,
205, 505

Deuterocanonical
3, 304,
305, 311,
316, 323,
331, 339,
341, 373

Dispensations
30, 217
Distinction v, 12, 16,

29, 32, 35,
37, 42, 47,
63, 66, 67,
68, 69, 76,
77, 78, 94,
97, 100,
101, 102,
104, 109,
110, 124,
134, 137,
139, 140,
141, 149,
151, 152,
155, 167,
168, 169,
181, 187,
195, 197,
204, 206,
209, 210,
211, 216,
227, 228,
232, 240,
241, 242,
259, 267,
270, 289,
291, 294,
325, 337,
373, 382,
407, 409,
417, 419,
424, 443,
484, 485,
486, 534,
555, 557,
558, 572,
577, 592,
594, 605,
614, 616,
625, 630,
633, 649,
702, 709,
721

Dooyeweerd, Herman
21, 35,
104, 105,

136, 137,
138, 145,
155, 157,
158, 159,
161, 166,
172, 180,
189, 197,
209, 240,
261, 486,
497, 537,
604

Dualism 6, 23, 49,
57, 63, 64,
69, 79, 93,
94, 95,
104, 105,
106, 108,
109, 110,
114, 115,
121, 149,
150, 151,
152, 157,
158, 167,
186, 188,
189, 201,
204, 206,
213, 214,
215, 216,
228, 232,
259, 273,
291, 296,
306, 381,
409, 415,
417, 421,
422, 423,
440, 441,
442, 449,
461, 503,
517, 518,
519, 520,
522, 523,
538, 554,
556, 567,
595, 600,
605, 606,

Duty

E
Earth

Ecclesiastical

Effect

Egypt

649, 684
12, 83, 216,
406

7, 27, 30,
65, 80,
116, 120,
121, 127,
128, 133,
136, 157,
163, 175,
176, 185,
199, 208,
215, 218,
219, 226,
236, 248,
251, 298,
300, 328,
356, 385,
444, 460,
473, 474,
478, 481,
484, 527,
528, 538,
549, 550,
559, 579,
580, 586,
594, 638,
644, 695,
727

9, 382,
493, 518,
535, 688

97, 350,
353, 390,
402, 426,
491, 518,
557, 559,
591, 598,
652, 659

84, 129,
219, 287,
316, 473,

Subject Index

	578, 642, 663		196, 225, 257, 265,		288, 295, 298, 306,
Elders	242, 356		268, 323,		307, 314,
Elements	5, 38, 40, 41, 49, 70, 73, 115, 116, 275, 293, 306, 324, 400, 421, 422, 534, 544, 632, 633, 640, 645, 653, 672, 679, 681, 682, 684, 695, 698, 705, 721, 725	Ezekiel F Faith	326, 386, 404, 406, 411, 423, 443, 444, 655, 701, 720 316, 345 iii, 4, 6, 7, 11, 12, 13, 33, 35, 37, 42, 43, 44, 45, 46, 47, 49, 51, 52, 54, 56, 58, 59, 60, 63, 64, 72, 77,		317, 318, 322, 332, 333, 335, 336, 338, 339, 341, 342, 343, 351, 352, 359, 361, 363, 364, 370, 374, 379, 383, 392, 397, 407, 423, 430, 445, 450, 456, 460, 466, 468, 497, 503, 506,
Elijah	321, 328, 329, 546				
Empire	626, 722		89, 91, 95,		507, 508,
Epoch	698		96, 97, 98,		511, 512,
Essence	1, 40, 151, 179, 180, 210, 224, 294, 425, 442, 520, 521, 550, 608, 616, 657, 679, 682, 684		99, 102, 105, 106, 110, 113, 114, 121, 144, 146, 149, 171, 173, 182, 183, 187, 188, 190,		515, 516, 517, 518, 519, 521, 523, 524, 525, 526, 527, 529, 530, 533, 534, 538, 539, 543,
Erroneous	78, 107, 132, 149, 186, 189, 211, 411, 440, 441, 478, 533, 566, 567, 568, 580, 581		191, 195, 196, 209, 213, 214, 216, 228, 230, 231, 232, 233, 250, 251, 258, 271, 273, 274,		544, 549, 550, 551, 552, 554, 559, 560, 562, 563, 566, 567, 568, 569, 572, 573, 574, 585,
Eyes	26, 27, 34, 66, 78, 82, 89, 92, 100, 153,		275, 276, 279, 282, 284, 285, 286, 287,		586, 587, 589, 590, 591, 593, 595, 596,

817

	597, 598,		706	Function	20, 21, 40,
	601, 602,	Feast	88, 326,		51, 52,
	603, 604,		391, 621		122, 138,
	607, 608,	Festivals	87, 88		141, 147,
	613, 616,	Figurative	88, 170,		155, 188,
	622, 636,		280		191, 202,
	646, 649,	Food	64, 185,		213, 216,
	653, 677,		219, 284,		221, 269,
	679, 680,		489, 491,		277, 279,
	683, 684,		572		289, 292,
	685, 686,	Foundation	2, 29, 39,		335, 336,
	690, 691,		51, 87,		342, 359,
	692, 694,		91, 92, 93,		399, 418,
	695, 697,		94, 107,		421, 422,
	701, 702,		177, 178,		433, 464,
	719, 720,		207, 249,		488, 503,
	730		251, 278,		519, 521,
Father	7, 22, 27,		348, 374,		522, 540,
	35, 42, 71,		376, 435,		604, 606,
	87, 98,		506, 507,		656, 658,
	127, 154,		537, 539,		723
	176, 179,		540, 543,	Future	18, 27, 81,
	257, 260,		552, 573,		207, 355,
	266, 283,		631, 633,		627, 630,
	300, 320,		654, 695,		731
	323, 353,		701, 727		
	355, 372,	Framework	49, 51, 52,	**G**	
	375, 386,		108, 131,	Garden	470, 542
	396, 399,		183, 196,	Garment	261, 454
	401, 406,		211, 351,	Gentile	7, 19, 34,
	413, 414,		480, 481,		70, 71, 72,
	447, 452,		488, 503,		82, 92, 111,
	453, 471,		519, 525,		346, 354,
	472, 478,		595, 607,		468, 474,
	483, 490,		609, 633,		489, 630,
	495, 498,		635, 636,		631, 675,
	596, 619,		637, 656,		694
	625, 643,		657	Gift	31, 187,
	657, 712,	Freedom	132, 204,		250, 424,
	716, 718,		213, 228,		516, 595
	720, 724,		518, 605,	Giver	31, 83, 89,
	726		649, 684		126, 145,
Family	214, 229,	Fulfilled	15, 303,		146, 170,
	281, 515,		319, 483,		173, 195,
	639, 640,		497		523

THE ETERNAL WORD: GOD SPEAKING TO US

818

Subject Index

Godly	15, 321, 322, 323, 332, 356, 385, 391, 398, 399		208, 213, 214, 218, 248, 270, 275, 305, 315, 324,		422, 423, 428, 432, 456, 462, 476, 477, 478, 523,
Good	6, 39, 42, 48, 64, 90, 91, 143, 164, 167, 168, 177, 178, 185, 207, 217, 219, 221, 231, 253, 285, 288, 289, 291, 299, 301, 313, 332, 356, 369, 379, 390, 391, 392, 412, 437, 465, 466, 473, 491, 492, 499, 507, 519, 524, 536, 555, 558, 561, 582, 584, 585, 591, 592, 602, 604, 627, 639, 643, 704, 718, 723, 726, 732		347, 355, 361, 364, 370, 371, 385, 417, 431, 452, 453, 458, 468, 478, 479, 480, 484, 505, 609, 639, 674, 675, 677, 682, 684, 685, 687, 696, 697, 699, 703, 710, 711, 712, 715, 716, 718, 720, 721, 722, 723, 724, 725, 727, 729, 730, 731	Guard Guidance Guilt **H** Hair Harvest Heart	573, 575, 580, 598, 599, 679, 690, 718, 722, 727 284, 429, 463 106, 114, 246, 337, 392, 404, 457, 482, 494, 543, 545 76, 77, 111, 406, 472, 547, 727 32 88 1, 2, 7, 8, 26, 27, 34, 35, 36, 39, 40, 43, 44, 45, 46, 52, 53, 56, 57, 58, 76, 78, 80, 92, 96, 102, 106, 109, 110, 136, 142, 148, 151, 157, 158, 159, 160, 164, 167, 171, 172, 173, 178, 188, 190, 191, 194, 196, 209,
Gospel	ii, 19, 44, 61, 74, 76, 85, 89, 92, 104, 105, 110, 111, 113, 114, 115, 116, 120, 129, 167, 207,	Greek	17, 18, 19, 20, 26, 70, 74, 75, 90, 96, 97, 117, 146, 173, 213, 266, 281, 282, 283, 284, 292, 309, 311, 314, 317, 318, 319, 326, 340, 347, 349, 356, 387, 388, 389, 418,		

819

219, 225,
233, 234,
257, 258,
265, 269,
273, 274,
275, 276,
285, 289,
291, 295,
299, 320,
332, 334,
335, 354,
357, 397,
400, 401,
404, 406,
424, 429,
430, 448,
449, 450,
452, 470,
497, 500,
503, 519,
520, 521,
522, 560,
562, 565,
597, 603,
606, 617,
671, 720

Heaven 7, 17, 64,
80, 90, 120,
125, 133,
152, 176,
185, 199,
208, 215,
219, 239,
309, 328,
383, 385,
437, 458,
478, 481,
484, 580,
644, 712,
716, 721,
732

Hebrew 17, 97, 126,
174, 205,
220, 282,
283, 311,

312, 313,
317, 319,
320, 321,
326, 327,
328, 331,
394, 411,
416, 463,
466, 470,
473, 495,
573, 579,
580, 614,
622, 643,
645, 660,
664, 665,
698, 699

Heidelberg 275
Heirs 123
History ii, 4, 5, 10,
16, 27, 29,
30, 43, 67,
69, 79, 81,
95, 97, 101,
107, 112,
113, 114,
116, 119,
120, 123,
130, 131,
136, 145,
186, 206,
207, 210,
216, 217,
218, 219,
220, 221,
222, 223,
224, 225,
242, 262,
266, 282,
286, 288,
310, 330,
337, 338,
364, 368,
371, 416,
428, 434,
440, 449,
453, 466,

489, 498,
499, 501,
504, 506,
517, 535,
545, 547,
548, 550,
551, 552,
553, 559,
562, 563,
564, 567,
592, 594,
607, 613,
616, 617,
618, 625,
627, 629,
630, 631,
632, 634,
635, 636,
641, 642,
643, 645,
649, 654,
655, 656,
657, 658,
660, 663,
665, 666,
667, 676,
678, 680,
681, 682,
687, 705,
707, 711,
716, 728

Humanity 1, 14, 16,
22, 24, 45,
67, 68, 69,
78, 80, 84,
91, 98, 99,
101, 111,
129, 134,
135, 144,
146, 155,
156, 167,
169, 170,
171, 177,
179, 190,
191, 193,

Subject Index

Husband
205, 206, 207, 210, 219, 224, 236, 238, 240, 258, 262, 263, 265, 269, 274, 276, 287, 294, 299, 352, 415, 416, 430, 431, 439, 443, 447, 453, 459, 467, 468, 516, 518, 520, 521, 542, 547, 551, 569, 571, 593, 594, 598, 602, 677, 679
209, 241, 291, 470, 485

I
Idol 168
Idolatry 191, 193, 638
Ignorant 314, 405
Immorality 14, 90, 192
Irenaeus 67, 258, 315, 325, 361, 369, 413, 724, 726, 727
Iron 154, 622, 666, 667
Irrelevant 95, 286, 337, 408, 428, 500, 551, 596, 608, 653,

Israel
656, 678, 680
i, 14, 15, 16, 19, 30, 67, 71, 72, 80, 83, 88, 98, 127, 128, 177, 178, 181, 191, 195, 218, 219, 220, 221, 230, 238, 264, 282, 287, 288, 303, 304, 312, 328, 330, 340, 356, 360, 361, 387, 411, 462, 469, 470, 471, 472, 473, 474, 543, 546, 587, 619, 620, 633, 635, 636, 638, 639, 641, 642, 648, 655, 660, 663, 664, 667, 669, 694, 721, 728, 731

J
Jacob 69, 77, 127, 128, 383, 384, 431, 471, 472, 619, 620, 644, 645, 665

Jew
90, 305, 347, 385, 390, 391, 630, 672, 689, 690, 693, 715, 719
Joachim 686
Joy 86, 470
Judaism 116, 305, 342, 390, 425, 463, 636, 647, 648, 655, 673, 681, 689, 693, 694
Judge 81, 83, 89, 116, 219, 220, 221, 257, 334, 336, 569, 591, 638
Judgment 13, 76, 81, 187, 224, 242, 249, 257, 264, 357, 363, 364, 480, 485, 499, 501, 507, 551, 570, 603, 617, 698, 731
Juridical 91, 141, 146, 147, 159, 161, 164, 177, 178, 204, 234, 236, 239, 281, 284, 288, 289, 301, 343, 363, 545, 546

821

Justice	92, 132, 137, 143, 147, 165, 192, 203, 217, 226, 228, 231, 273, 288, 289, 301, 306, 363, 391, 412, 432, 469, 481, 482, 493, 515, 584, 623, 639, 688, 708, 727		219, 220, 222, 264, 280, 289, 312, 328, 330, 339, 345, 394, 405, 410, 422, 452, 546, 575, 588, 619, 620, 626, 627, 628, 635, 651, 664, 668, 690, 694, 721, 729	Language	329, 474, 579, 619, 620, 635, 642, 661, 663 4, 24, 31, 35, 42, 65, 97, 112, 149, 170, 239, 240, 251, 253, 261, 270, 280, 282, 283, 284, 286, 287, 288, 290, 293, 306, 325, 331, 352, 416, 454, 460, 473, 481, 497, 516, 517, 518, 528, 530, 535, 563, 613, 622, 707
K Keeper Kerygma Ketubim Kinds King	10, 11 428, 461, 464, 595, 658, 679, 684, 685, 686, 697 310, 311, 313, 326, 327, 331, 333, 345, 346 46, 64, 67, 68, 69, 78, 79, 81, 139, 144, 188, 189, 223, 380, 391, 423, 424, 428, 457, 486, 504, 535, 564, 567, 594, 595, 597, 601, 645, 658 71, 72, 81, 92, 124,	Kingdom Kiss Kuyperian Kyrios **L** Lamb Lament Land	19, 35, 84, 87, 94, 169, 180, 181, 201, 205, 206, 207, 210, 213, 219, 223, 225, 328, 376, 394, 399, 400, 423, 424, 477, 481, 498, 523, 557, 598, 602, 604, 628, 634, 639, 719 546 251, 252, 253, 411, 506 679 170, 220 469 129, 162, 219, 255, 286, 328,	Law-Word Liberty Life	138, 140, 142, 160, 162, 163, 165, 268 180, 413, 716 3, 4, 20, 21, 30, 33, 42, 66, 78, 80, 81, 83, 87, 88, 90, 91, 104, 105, 106, 110, 124, 125, 126, 127, 141, 159, 160, 162, 168, 169,

Subject Index

Living
170, 174, 175, 177, 178, 179, 198, 207, 209, 214, 215, 225, 228, 235, 236, 240, 259, 266, 269, 273, 277, 286, 298, 299, 300, 308, 309, 312, 318, 352, 359, 363, 376, 386, 390, 392, 393, 408, 413, 451, 465, 483, 496, 497, 515, 517, 525, 532, 533, 546, 547, 555, 557, 562, 596, 597, 608, 611, 637, 643, 646, 656, 672, 676, 678, 679, 680, 681, 682, 683, 685, 687, 693, 695, 697, 720, 721, 722, 724, 726, 727, 728, 729, 731

Logos 8, 19, 60, 112, 141, 162, 164, 182, 185, 207, 238, 239, 257, 298, 306, 317, 318, 320, 350, 362, 383, 429, 465, 470, 471, 474, 495, 515, 603, 707, 712, 713, 720

Lord 27, 75, 82, 96, 97, 104, 146, 160, 171, 173, 174, 175, 178, 179, 181, 183, 199, 202, 205, 225, 247, 260, 266, 414, 462, 559

i, iii, 1, 5, 14, 15, 16, 17, 26, 35, 63, 64, 67, 71, 80, 83, 90, 92, 96, 98, 113, 114, 123, 127, 128, 129, 136, 154, 156, 162, 164, 176, 191, 196, 219, 220, 221, 247, 252, 274, 280, 281, 283, 288, 299, 301, 309, 328, 330, 335, 354, 355, 357, 390, 391, 394, 396, 400, 403, 406, 447, 455, 456, 461, 467, 471, 472, 473, 485, 487, 568, 569, 620, 638, 640, 641, 642, 663, 679, 694, 718

Luther 24, 54, 65, 104, 105, 106, 110, 188, 192, 193, 342, 373, 374, 388, 416, 463, 496, 540, 604, 618

Lutheran 9, 53, 59, 105, 106, 133, 213, 251, 270, 342, 373, 411, 530, 544

M
Mankind 81, 124, 185, 218, 219

Manifestation 17, 27, 96, 126, 128, 162, 163, 165, 171, 218, 229,

	266, 268, 401, 453		296, 299, 540, 543		322, 339, 341, 353,
Marriage	108, 214, 229, 241, 291, 380, 383, 435, 436, 515, 546	Money Moses	92 25, 71, 125, 178, 215, 242, 246, 257, 264, 274, 282,		354, 426, 468, 473, 479, 504, 505, 584, 620, 633, 634, 640,
Master	7, 60, 97, 175, 176, 355, 370, 707		303, 308, 309, 311, 315, 318, 326, 327,	Negative	656, 661, 668, 706 19, 46, 55, 72, 241,
Messiah	17, 131, 328, 405, 452, 470, 471, 473, 497, 628, 677, 680, 690, 694, 715, 721, 722, 732		344, 345, 346, 384, 398, 454, 455, 461, 467, 471, 483, 484, 497, 500, 546, 587, 618, 619,	Neighbor Noah	248, 286, 294, 360, 362, 367, 407, 422, 465, 507, 591, 603 92, 180 30, 34, 67, 70, 85, 524,
Millennialism	317, 505		620, 621, 622, 624,	Noahic	644, 645 76, 84
Ministry	251, 376, 458, 631		634, 636, 638, 639,	Notion	1, 4, 8, 10, 12, 13, 14,
Miracle	67, 150, 322, 356, 380, 406, 407, 428, 435, 436, 442, 587, 682, 683	Murder Muslim	642, 648, 661, 662, 663, 664, 669, 732 242 7, 72, 87, 91, 264,		16, 19, 20, 21, 22, 37, 52, 64, 68, 74, 81, 97, 103, 104, 108, 110, 111, 120,
Miriam	642		304		121, 125,
Mirror	402	Muzzle	314		138, 145,
Mishnah	621, 622				146, 149,
Missionary	92, 324, 343, 396, 718	N Nations	16, 19, 30, 67, 76, 81, 87, 91, 116,		157, 167, 186, 188, 189, 190, 194, 195,
Modalities	21, 22, 26, 122, 155, 160, 163, 169, 188, 277, 279, 286, 288,		126, 136, 185, 196, 218, 219, 220, 221, 222, 254, 303, 314,		197, 198, 204, 211, 212, 223, 224, 233, 234, 246, 249, 271,

Subject Index

	303, 304, 318, 322, 338, 342, 350, 351, 354, 372, 373, 381, 383, 418, 426, 430, 434, 435, 442, 444, 463, 476, 490, 496, 503, 515, 519, 520, 521, 525, 527, 532, 555, 568, 574, 577, 579, 585, 592, 593, 594, 595, 599, 608, 637, 673, 676, 678, 696, 697, 717
Numbering	128, 530

O

Oasis	545
Obedience	7, 121, 168, 214, 218, 224, 227, 314, 431, 471, 497, 555
Object	2, 11, 22, 38, 45, 56, 59, 60, 134, 147, 171, 178, 189, 238, 255, 276, 277, 278, 322, 434, 476, 613, 623, 684, 719, 720, 726
Offerings	264, 471, 640
Omen	176
Omissions	500, 668
Opposite	8, 26, 85, 100, 143, 144, 148, 161, 224, 306, 307, 429, 465, 466, 478, 533, 545, 551, 553, 556, 557, 588, 592, 624, 656, 687, 689, 692, 718
Opposition	8, 9, 10, 56, 57, 64, 104, 111, 137, 141, 151, 259, 291, 347, 413, 417, 426, 520, 522, 526, 528, 537, 538, 540, 542, 553, 559, 560, 562, 563, 564, 589, 612, 615, 623, 627
Ordinances	104, 106, 108, 110, 121, 122, 124, 133, 140, 158, 159, 160, 161, 166, 167, 174, 186, 189, 210, 223, 224, 225, 226, 227, 228, 229, 234, 238, 240, 546, 555
Orthodox	13, 41, 43, 46, 47, 49, 50, 52, 203, 209, 252, 254, 256, 271, 273, 340, 341, 362, 392, 408, 475, 478, 497, 501, 505, 506, 535, 553, 562, 576, 601, 603, 622, 625, 649, 681, 689, 690, 693, 709, 730
Outward	28, 83, 547, 689
Ox	170, 314, 727

P

Parallel	28, 74, 99, 133, 146, 165, 173, 174, 177, 179, 188, 233, 245,

260, 261,
262, 263,
265, 269,
298, 343,
435, 558,
564, 577,
581, 582,
588, 595,
599, 631,
656, 712,
716, 720

Patriarchs
67, 546,
646, 648,
661, 662,
665, 669,
690, 694

Paul, the apostle
19, 20, 34,
35, 66, 80,
81, 89, 92,
93, 111,
115, 182,
205, 209,
219, 249,
250, 266,
274, 309,
314, 315,
317, 321,
322, 323,
324, 329,
333, 342,
343, 344,
346, 347,
348, 355,
357, 358,
361, 365,
366, 367,
370, 371,
373, 375,
376, 382,
387, 391,
392, 393,
396, 398,
401, 403,

406, 414,
416, 418,
433, 435,
447, 455,
456, 457,
458, 460,
462, 463,
465, 466,
469, 470,
471, 472,
473, 474,
475, 484,
485, 486,
488, 495,
574, 581,
623, 625,
631, 674,
675, 679,
681, 685,
690, 694,
718, 724,
731

Peace
90, 162,
164, 204,
228, 301,
363, 395,
727

Perfect
28, 47, 52,
63, 135,
152, 153,
162, 164,
165, 181,
207, 218,
262, 299,
301, 413,
422, 428,
476, 494,
497, 548,
566, 567,
568, 569,
570, 571,
573, 575,
578, 596,
599

Period
281, 318,

329, 342,
345, 366,
370, 371,
439, 636,
637, 638,
639, 648,
665, 667,
685, 687,
696, 708,
718

Pesachim
326, 678

Pharisee
313, 333,
412, 465,
482, 500

Physical
2, 21, 24,
25, 27, 29,
99, 132,
146, 155,
159, 169,
215, 216,
234, 240,
265, 277,
278, 279,
280, 284,
304, 342,
359, 363,
417, 435,
495, 505,
528, 549,
594, 608

Picture
11, 79, 85,
122, 176,
198, 219,
254, 296,
412, 532,
639, 641,
642, 662,
664, 676,
681, 698,
701, 710,
713, 728,
729

Subject Index

Pious	10, 85, 371, 464, 671, 677, 680, 686, 713, 714		593, 598, 603, 638, 682, 685, 731	Prophecy	249, 250, 309, 310, 312, 329, 330, 354, 395, 396, 437, 438, 458, 462, 501, 650
Plague	41, 527	Practice	71, 92, 191, 204, 280, 343, 352, 353, 365, 370, 421, 466, 481, 541, 546, 593, 616, 624		
Power	4, 27, 28, 29, 36, 40, 44, 56, 59, 60, 65, 66, 77, 81, 89, 97, 106, 109, 113, 114, 119, 121, 123, 131, 135, 151, 156, 162, 163, 166, 167, 173, 178, 181, 189, 190, 192, 194, 195, 198, 200, 202, 205, 207, 212, 220, 236, 268, 273, 275, 298, 300, 339, 349, 350, 357, 359, 360, 363, 371, 379, 383, 384, 397, 399, 409, 411, 418, 432, 435, 443, 451, 455, 456, 465, 468, 477, 481, 488, 516, 525, 561, 565,			Prophets	1, 3, 4, 15, 18, 246, 248, 249, 250, 251, 267, 303, 309, 310, 311, 312, 313, 314, 315, 319, 326, 327, 329, 343, 345, 346, 348, 349, 355, 358, 385, 388, 393, 394, 395, 396, 400, 401, 402, 405, 416, 417, 425, 426, 432, 433, 437, 462, 470, 482, 484, 486, 487, 497, 500, 524, 619, 632, 638, 639, 641
		Praise	152, 264, 386, 566		
		Priest	15, 146, 346, 353, 360, 391, 432, 634, 721		
		Principle	6, 71, 86, 89, 90, 91, 100, 117, 148, 157, 168, 181, 197, 206, 207, 211, 232, 235, 238, 240, 241, 242, 243, 255, 258, 266, 329, 337, 344, 356, 369, 370, 404, 422, 443, 501, 512, 517, 534, 545, 546, 585, 608, 616		
				Psychology	45, 189, 236, 542, 543, 708
		Promises	10, 156, 201, 436, 473, 567, 690, 694	**Q**	
				Quakers	75

Quantitative 292

R
Rabbi 643, 693, 695
Reconciliation
    77, 84, 498
Reconstruction
    632, 652, 676, 698, 707
Redemption
    25, 84, 85, 104, 110, 120, 121, 187, 207, 208, 211, 212, 214, 217, 218, 222, 352, 395, 450, 490, 498, 602, 603, 604, 605, 639, 679
Redemptive
    26, 68, 84, 101, 109, 110, 111, 120, 126, 129, 131, 134, 186, 199, 206, 207, 208, 210, 214, 217, 218, 223, 233, 235, 266, 267, 310, 348, 418, 423, 489, 499, 551, 559, 602, 607, 694
Relationship
    2, 3, 5, 8, 10, 16, 19, 23, 34, 39, 49, 57, 59, 68, 89, 92, 101, 104, 106, 107, 110, 111, 114, 119, 120, 131, 134, 136, 143, 145, 151, 156, 157, 158, 165, 171, 172, 175, 186, 199, 202, 208, 213, 218, 226, 245, 269, 270, 273, 274, 275, 281, 289, 295, 296, 297, 345, 349, 379, 427, 430, 431, 438, 441, 442, 443, 444, 449, 464, 499, 522, 523, 528, 547, 553, 554, 558, 593, 599, 609, 707
Religion
    34, 73, 83, 104, 112, 116, 151, 192, 194, 197, 198, 221, 339, 390, 518, 523, 537, 625, 629, 630, 636, 637, 640, 641, 642, 648, 654, 655, 656, 657, 660, 677, 678, 683
Renewal
    90, 110, 120, 209, 217, 275, 359
Restoration
    84, 110, 121, 211, 212, 214, 228
Resurrection
    6, 87, 88, 187, 383, 394, 404, 448, 450, 495, 505, 523, 524, 623, 630, 677, 682, 686, 688, 718, 720
Rich 191, 206, 284, 682
Righteousness
    81, 82, 83, 90, 92, 165, 217, 288, 301, 359, 363, 379, 387, 390, 391
Risk 10, 216, 256, 336, 389, 407,

Subject Index

Ritual	423, 709, 638		166, 212, 213, 214, 309		235, 514, 525, 636, 664
Rock	162, 280, 309, 470	Sea	185, 219, 312, 321,	Sociological	515
Royal	180, 218		474, 476,	Sophia	173, 179
Rule	55, 84, 88, 94, 107, 108, 110, 134, 200, 214, 317, 318, 329, 363, 446, 465, 470, 494, 495, 497, 593, 632	Season Sect Secular	575, 577, 587, 605, 692, 706 64, 80, 84, 87, 185, 219, 583 333 53, 94, 105, 106, 110, 210, 213, 214, 227, 231, 248, 255, 306, 350, 440, 524, 536, 547, 600	Soul Sound	7, 10, 26, 27, 45, 63, 162, 164, 213, 257, 298, 299, 406, 519, 520, 521, 543, 569, 606 65, 194, 257, 292, 293, 416, 448, 511, 562, 573, 613, 646, 709
S					
Sabbath	386				
Sacrifice	83, 89, 90, 471				
Sacrificial	640				
Sadducees	333, 383, 384	Sick	83, 169, 170, 543	Supernaturalism	v, 94, 252, 415, 523, 625, 633, 637, 688, 690, 692, 725
Salt	605	Similarities			
Salvation	3, 42, 66, 89, 90, 91, 114, 156, 196, 203, 205, 273, 274, 351, 352, 354, 359, 379, 391, 393, 395, 408, 437, 470, 471, 474, 512, 542, 549, 559, 593, 594, 598, 602, 606, 607, 694	Sinai Snare Society	v, 92, 539, 552, 557, 673, 675, 719, 726 30, 34, 80, 127, 128, 174, 177, 208, 209, 546, 639, 642, 648, 664 12, 13, 93, 216, 225, 286, 294, 463, 535, 562 64, 105, 106, 110, 116, 167,	Supper, Lord's Synagogue System **T** Tabernacle	678, 695 425 55, 56, 92, 105, 121, 122, 175, 521, 544, 568, 660 640, 663, 664, 727
Satan	64, 105, 109, 110,		210, 212,	Talmud	3, 39, 128,

Tanakh	179, 305, 312, 475, 619, 621 304, 305, 310, 311, 313, 322, 323, 326, 385, 388, 497, 703		95, 111, 112, 113, 114, 163, 190, 195, 215, 256, 263, 268, 290, 299, 339, 360, 371, 375, 382, 386, 402, 429, 430, 444, 446, 456, 464, 484, 536, 540, 569, 599, 603, 630, 674, 692, 709, 724, 726		298, 299, 304, 306, 307, 325, 332, 353, 354, 374, 390, 393, 395, 396, 406, 412, 430, 431, 442, 464, 511, 521, 523, 578, 615, 623, 624, 701, 709
Teaching	ii, 7, 9, 48, 90, 126, 127, 144, 174, 266, 270, 355, 356, 359, 361, 370, 379, 383, 387, 390, 392, 393, 395, 408, 412, 462, 482, 488, 496, 504, 543, 547, 557, 594, 602, 672, 674, 687, 694, 706, 719, 720, 721, 722, 726, 727, 728, 729			Urgent	33, 242, 243, 253, 707
				V	
		Textual	411, 438, 475, 476, 477, 478, 479, 488, 529, 573, 575, 611, 614, 641, 663	Value	47, 72, 274, 277, 281, 301, 344, 363, 374, 377, 380, 407, 409, 435, 463, 469, 484, 488, 493, 552, 577, 594, 657, 677, 682
		Theophany	681		
		Theophilus	288, 426, 723	Venerable	440, 590
Temple	284, 328, 386, 471, 577, 635, 640, 663, 721, 730	Thunder	130	Vengeance	89
		U		Victory	731
		Understanding	20, 24, 35, 40, 41, 45, 47, 48, 75, 78, 89, 91, 120, 127, 162, 165, 166, 209, 260, 265,	Viewpoint	77, 99, 143, 188, 195, 204, 217, 232, 233, 286, 288, 358, 364,
Testify	54, 57, 359, 382, 394				
Testimony	i, 2, 3, 40, 52, 53, 54, 55, 56, 57, 58, 63, 75,				

Subject Index

	430, 449, 485, 536, 549, 550, 551, 553, 559, 563, 586, 594, 602, 605, 607, 608, 637, 648, 698, 700, 702		66, 120, 127, 135, 173, 175, 176, 177, 178, 180, 181, 182, 183, 202, 245, 249, 287, 311, 334, 340, 400, 402, 406, 454, 470, 522, 587, 617, 683, 690, 695, 732
Vile	92, 191		
W			
Walk	127, 133, 153, 161, 185, 207, 219, 256, 263, 288, 317, 362, 391, 400, 472, 497, 567	**Y** Yahweh Yard Young	80 532 170, 330, 477, 492, 638, 645
Washing	35, 546, 577	**Z**	
Water	91, 153, 219, 309, 320, 404, 424, 470, 478, 578, 598, 605, 720	Zeal Zion Zodiac	456 280, 471, 472 83, 84, 85
Weak	49, 115, 146, 421, 424, 440, 452, 454, 605		
Weakness	56, 142, 421, 454, 459, 563		
Welcome	320, 472, 520		
Wisdom	19, 20, 34,